JOHN RIGG was born and raised in Leeds, Yorkshire. He graduated from the University of Cambridge with a First Class degree in Economics, later completing a Ph.D. He worked as an economic consultant in London and in the Senior Civil Service in Scotland.

John has been researching his family history for nearly 40 years and has published several articles for the *Cleveland Family History Society Journal*. His non-family history articles include those on economics and statistics for the *Scottish Economic Bulletin* and *Scottish Economic Statistics*.

John has written extensively on watching sport. *An Ordinary Spectator: 50 Years of Watching Sport* was published by SilverWood Books in 2012 and *Still An Ordinary Spectator: Five More Years of Watching Sport* in 2017. The third book in the series – *An Ordinary Spectator Returns: Watching Sport Again* – was published in 2023. He has also written sport-related articles for the magazines *Backpass* (football), *Backspin* and *The Nightwatchman* (cricket), the *Rugby League Journal* and *Forty-20* (rugby league) and (co-authored with Richard Lewney) the *International Review of the Sociology of Sport*.

John's fiction is written under the name of JR Alexander. The novels – *Shouting at the Window* (2020) and *On the Carousel* (2021) – are published by High Ridge Publishing and available on Kindle and other online platforms. *Long Forgotten Events* will be published in 2025.

He is married with two children and lives in Scotland.

Find out more about John and his writing at www.anordinaryspectator.com and www.jralexanderauthor.com.

Also by John Rigg

An Ordinary Spectator: 50 Years of Watching Sport
Still An Ordinary Spectator: Five More Years of Watching Sport
An Ordinary Spectator Returns: Watching Sport Again

THE LINE OF SIXTEEN

Searching for my children's
great, great grandparents

John Rigg

SilverWood

Published in 2025 by SilverWood Books

SilverWood Books Ltd
14 Small Street, Bristol, BS1 1DE, United Kingdom
www.silverwoodbooks.co.uk

Copyright © John Rigg 2025

The right of John Rigg to be identified as the author of this work has been asserted in accordance with the Copyright, Designs and Patents Act 1988 Sections 77 and 78.

All rights reserved. No part of this publication may be reproduced, stored in a retrieval system, or transmitted in any form or by any means, electronic, mechanical, photocopying, recording or otherwise, without prior permission of the copyright holder.

ISBN 9781800422940 (paperback)
Also available as an ebook

British Library Cataloguing in Publication Data
A CIP catalogue record for this book is available from the British Library

Page design and typesetting by SilverWood Books

To our ancestors, on whose shoulders we stand

CONTENTS

	Preface	xi
	PART ONE Great, great grandparents: the Line of Sixteen	
1	North Yorkshire	5
2	Scotland and Lancashire	47
3	Gloucestershire and Germany	93
4	London	141
5	Tyneside	174
6	Malta	209
7	County Mayo	230
	PART TWO Great grandparents: the Line of Eight	
8	Rigg/McBride	258
9	Niblett/Wilson	281
10	English/Stapleton	296
11	Murray/McManamon	312
	PART THREE Grandparents and Parents	
12	Rigg/Niblett	325
13	English/Murray	334
14	Rigg/English	341
	PART FOUR Reflections and Chronology	
15	Reflections	345
16	Chronology	351
	ANNEXES	
A1.	The Riggs in North America	366
A2.	The 1911 Census of England and Wales: Transcription Errors	377
A3.	"Here I Stand"	379
A4.	Roll of Honour	383
A5.	Sources	385
A6.	Bibliography	394
A7.	Glossary	402
A8.	Acknowledgements	404
A9.	Index of Surnames	409
A10.	Index of Locations	411

BRANCHES OF THE FAMILY TREE

Table 1.1   The parents and siblings of Henry Rigg
Table 1.2   The parents and siblings of Jane Boynton
Table 1.3   The family of Henry and Jane Rigg

Table 2.1   The parents, siblings and step-siblings of Peter McBride
Table 2.2   The parents and siblings of Agnes Charlotte Runcorn
Table 2.3   The family of Peter and Agnes Charlotte McBride

Table 3.1   The parents, siblings and step-siblings of Charles James Niblett
Table 3.2   The parents, siblings and step-siblings of Anna Karoline Borstelmann
Table 3.3   The family of Charles James and Anna Karoline Niblett

Table 4.1   The parents, siblings and step-sibling of Charles Herbert Wilson
Table 4.2   The parents and siblings of Rosa Mary Whines
Table 4.3   The family of Charles Herbert and Rosa Mary Wilson

Table 5.1   The parents and siblings of Arthur English
Table 5.2   The parents and siblings of Helen Kelly
Table 5.3   The family of Arthur and Helen English

Table 6.1   The parents and family of Joseph and Guiseppa/Josephine Stapleton

Table 7.1   The family of John and Margaret Murray
Table 7.2   The family of Francis and Honor McManamon

Table 8.1   The family of John and Catherine Kerr Rigg

Table 9.1   The family of Alfred Edgar and Marie Rosa Niblett

Table 10.1 The family of Arthur Joseph and Mary Stella English

Table 11.1 The family of John and Honoria (Annie) Murray

Table 12.1 The family of William Alexander and Enid Peggie Rigg

Table 13.1 The family of Denis Arthur Stapleton and Anne Catherine English

Table 14.1 The family of John Alexander and Angela Mary Rigg

THE RIGG/ENGLISH FAMILY TREE
Table 15.1 The family tree of the Line of 16

CHRONOLOGY
Table 16.1 A chronology of events

LIST OF PHOTOGRAPHS
(between pages 208-209)

Harriet Boynton (c1823-1905, née Stirk), the earliest-born family member in the direct line for whom there is a photograph.

Gravestone of William Boynton (c1820-1895) at All Saints Church, Great Thirkleby, North Yorkshire.

The Baptism Register of St. Bartholomäus Kirche, Kirchwalsede, Niedersachsen. The entry for Anna Margreta Marquardt on 30th October 1772 is the third from bottom.

St. Bartholomäus Kirche. Photograph taken in 2018.

Gravestone of John Pipe (1713-1797) at St Mary's Church, Horham, Suffolk. The year of birth is the earliest found to date of any member of the direct family line. Photograph taken in 2022.

Charles Tyler Wilson (c1838-1888) when aged about 20.

Patrick Kelly (1830-1893), Frances Kelly (1830-1902, née Davis) and their family. Helen English (1869-1949, née Kelly) is standing directly behind Jane. Photograph taken in around 1891.

An extract from the Army records of Joseph Stapleton (c1859-1933), which lists his wife Josephine (Guiseppa) Stapleton (1863-1954, née Brincau) and their children (to 1898). Josephine's maiden name is given in a handwritten correction.

The household record of John Murray (c1839-?) and Margaret Murray (c1846-?, née Mullowney) in the 1901 Census of Ireland. The return illustrates the generational differences in those able to read and write and those able to speak Irish as well as English.

John Murray (1873-1952) and Honoria (Annie) Murray (1878-1967, née McManaman)

St Johannis Kirche, Visselhövede, Niedersachsen. The location of the baptism of Johann Friedrich Borstelmann (1811-1854). His great (x2) grandfather (Johann Bostelmann) was buried there in 1716. Photograph taken in 2018.

Die Peter und Paul Kirche, Elze, Hannover. The location of the marriage of Charles James Niblett (1851-1927) and Anna Karoline Borstelmann (1853-1938) in 1872. Photograph taken in 2018.

St John the Baptist Church, Peterborough. Location of the marriage of Daniel Whines (1827-1906) and Mary Whines (1831-1916, née Wadsworth) in 1851. Photograph taken in 2022.

John Rigg (1887-1959) in his First World War uniform of the Royal Garrison Artillery.

John Rigg (born 1954, the author) and William (Bill) Rigg (1921-2004) at the grave of Robert Rigg (1885-1918) in Montigny-sur-Hallue, France. Photograph taken in 1990.

Catherine Kerr Rigg (1893-1969, née McBride)

Marie Rosa Niblett (1890-1968, née Wilson) with John Rigg (born 1954, the author)

Alfred Edgar Niblett (1888-1973)

First World War Ruhleben camp magazine

Arthur Joseph English (1892-1970)

Mary Stella English (1899-1978, née Stapleton)

Certificate of Competency as Steamship Master in the Merchant Service of Arthur Joseph English (1892-1970)

Ph.D. dissertation of Alfred Edgar Niblett (1888-1973)

Denis Arthur Stapleton English (1921-2009) and Anne Catherine English (1919-1994, née Murray)

Bill Rigg (1921-2004) and Peggie Rigg (1922-2000, née Niblett). Ruby wedding photograph taken in 1989.

PREFACE

On Sunday 27th June 2010 – in the Free State Stadium, Bloemfontein, South Africa – the England football team was beaten 4-1 by Germany in a last 16 knock-out match of the World Cup. Not just beaten, it has to be said, but overwhelmed and humiliated.

The following morning, I – a disappointed, but not hugely surprised, England football supporter, born and raised in Leeds – entered a room to chair the weekly meeting of my team leaders. I was the member of the Senior Civil Service responsible for advising Ministers on the use of the European Structural Funds made available from the European Union. The regular get-together was so that my colleagues and I could review the progress on the disbursal of funds and discuss any immediate issues that were likely to arise in the week ahead.

The slight difficulty I faced was that the meeting was in Glasgow. I was the Head of the European Structural Funds Division in the Scottish Executive and the officials seated around the table – 7 or 8 in number – were, with one exception (a lady born in Northern Ireland), Scottish.

I'm not sure if there is a word in either Scots or Scottish Gaelic for *schadenfreude*. However, as I took my seat to call the meeting to order, I sensed that my colleagues, having not been wholly supportive of England's (fairly dismal) efforts during the World Cup campaign – and with Scotland somehow having failed to qualify – were taking a friendly enjoyment from my potential discomfort.

I sat down on my chair, pulling it underneath me and placing my papers on the table in front of me. I looked quickly around the room at the attentive faces of my colleagues, who generally seemed to be attempting to hide their smirks behind some benign smiles. I addressed the group:

> *"It's on mornings such as these that I am really grateful to have had a German great grandmother".*

****

The origins of this book date back to an evening in August 1987. I was with my fiancée (now my wife) Angela and my parents in the bar of the Travellers' Rest in Harewood on the Harrogate Road to the north of Leeds. For some reason, the conversation got on to ancestors and family trees and my Dad mentioned that one of his father's brothers had been killed in France in the latter stages of the First World War.

I knew that my grandfather had been called John Rigg and that he had died when I was very young. Dad said that, in addition to his ill-fated brother, whose name was Robert Rigg, John had had another brother called Thompson Rigg and three sisters – Margaret, Mary and Jane, the last of whom was usually known as Ginny. Their father's name was Henry. The family had lived in the village of Pickhill in North Yorkshire.

It was during the course of the conversation that I had my "eureka" moment. I knew there and then that I wanted to find out more about the Rigg family history.

That was nearly forty years ago. Since then, family history has been a keen interest of mine – albeit intermittently pursued – in common with hundreds of thousands, if not millions, of like-minded researchers throughout Britain and overseas. However, whilst family history obviously involves looking back into the past, time itself does not stand still. In the period since the conversation in the Travellers' Rest – and after getting married in 1988 – Angela and I have raised two children who are themselves now adults: Thomas Alexander Rigg (Tom) and Katherine Anne Bazley, née Rigg (Katie).

This book seeks to help Tom and Katie in understanding where they came from. Its starting point is the generation of their great, great grandparents – one of whom was Henry Rigg, of course – whom I label for shorthand as the "Line of Sixteen" or, more commonly, the "Line of 16".

I should perhaps state at the outset that, whilst, as the title suggests, the structure of *The Line of Sixteen: Searching for my children's great, great grandparents* is based around the cohort of direct ancestors who were 4 steps back in the generational lines that led directly to Tom and Katie, the book's presentation of some of the lines within the family story goes back much further in time. In other words, I have not restricted my research to the period from the middle years of the 19th Century onwards. Rather, it will be seen that the narrative also identifies ancestors in earlier periods, including 16th Century Yorkshire and Hannover and 17th Century Suffolk.

At the same time, it is also important to emphasise that the exercise has not simply been one of finding as many pieces as possible of the (never-ending) jigsaw puzzle. I have also been keen to reflect on the circumstances of the lives being led by the various members of the cast-list: the work they did, the challenges they faced, the journeys they undertook, the languages they spoke…

At first sight, Tom and Katie's heritage appears to be unequivocally English. Both their parents (Angela and I) were born in England. So were three of their four grandparents, the fourth – Angela's father, Denis – having been born overseas, where the call of Empire had taken his father. The direct Rigg line catalogues a series of Yorkshire births dating back to the early years of the 19th Century.

However, when we look at the places of birth of the Line of 16, things change a little. Not only is there a range of English regions and localities (for example, Merseyside, Gloucestershire and London as well as Yorkshire), but the non-English representation increases as well (including Scotland, Ireland and Malta as well as Germany). In other words, by going back only four generations, Tom and Katie's gene pool contains much more of a geographical mix than might be immediately apparent.

It was this variation in Tom and Katie's ancestors' places of origin that interested me. What were the circumstances – economic, social, cultural, political – that the Line of 16 and their successors had to endure and overcome? What were the major events that shaped their lives? What overlaps were there in their respective experiences? How were the points of difference eroded over time so that the genealogical paths c

onverged on the same end points?

For Tom and Katie's generation – who have inherited the task of making sense of the world and shaping it for the better – the challenges to be faced are formidable. However, the essential prerequisite to addressing today's difficult issues is through attempting to gain a full understanding of them. This itself is far from easy, of course. In the age of instant communication and vacuous celebrity, it is a daunting exercise to work out what is or is not important: what should rightly demand attention and what is simply dross.

In this, the historian – including the family historian – can make a modest contribution: we can aid an appreciation of the contemporary world by examining the past. I hope that, in Tom and Katie's case, the pathways followed by the Line of 16 and their descendants do help them to gain a clearer understanding of their own places in that world and of the opportunities that lie ahead.

*****

Chronicles of family history often have only a relatively limited interest as, by definition, they tend to be personal or familial in scope and restricted in their attraction for outsiders. I hope that, in the case of this book, things might be different and that there will be a more general readership, particularly amongst other family historians.

The reason for this is that I have been as keen to describe the research journey I have undertaken as much as the findings that have resulted. As noted, this journey began in the mid-1980s – pre-Internet, of course – when a combination of library-based enquiry and enthusiastic naivety constituted the principal components of my research methodology. Since then, the widening access to the various electronic databases has obviously played a significant role, often with results that are bewildering in their comprehensiveness and speed of delivery. However, there are also well-known pitfalls and frustrations associated with Internet-based research and, where relevant, I have set out my experiences of these.

I am aware, of course, that, in starting the presentation of the findings with the Line of 16 and working forwards to the present day, I am travelling in the reverse direction to that undertaken on the research journey itself. In common with the overwhelming majority of family historians, I began by asking questions of my parents and then, armed with a few names and approximate dates, tentatively worked my way backwards (and sideways) through the years and the generations. The family tree took root in the present day and gained its expanding number of branches as I went back in time. However, as noted – and with the huge benefit of hindsight as to where those branches were located – my particular interest is in the strict chronological progression. Who exactly was to be found on the tree's branches four generations ago and, as we descend the tree, what have been the various circumstances that have brought about the convergence in the family line?

A standard difficulty with most descriptions of family history is that of complexity. For the reader, it is not easy to remember who is who, particularly when – as is usually the case – there is a repetition of given names from one generation to the next. I have sought to alleviate this problem with the presentation of the relevant branches of the family tree within each chapter.

It will be seen that the branches are usually comprised of the parents and children. My preference would have been to adopt the convention of the members of each generation being presented horizontally with the names of the father and mother sitting on a line above those of the children. However, in some cases, the number of children is large – 14 in one family and 11 in three others, for example – which, whilst not being a problem in a family tree presented with unlimited spacing online – would have necessitated an unwanted reduction in the size of the print on the page. I have therefore adopted a tabular approach in which we move horizontally between the generations by reading from left to right. Although even this carries some of the branches across more than one page, it does retain the required clarity of presentation for the individual entries. I have maintained this approach even when the size of the branch is relatively small. In each table, the direct family line is presented in bold type.

I have provided some supplementary information (on spouses) within each of the tables to complement the usual dates and places of birth and death. However, it will also be seen that, within the tables as presented, some of the dates of death, in particular, are missing. Where this has happened, I have given the date of the last reference I have found to that person within the official (or family) records. This is perhaps another way of stating that the information provided in this book is incomplete, but I make no apologies for this; family history research is never fully concluded. Indeed, I hope that any responses to the book will include new details that might be incorporated in future editions. (On a technical note, the presentation of double dates – e.g. 1863/64 – usually occurs when the date of birth is known to have been in one of the years shown, though not which one).

It should also be noted that there are occasional inconsistencies in the presentation of the names of places of birth and/or death. This is due to the variations in the geographical or administrative units on which the sources are based – parishes, local authority districts, townships and so on – which may differ for a given individual as well as between countries or in separate time periods.

One final introductory point should perhaps be made. It is to confirm that I am not a professional historian or genealogist and – as a result, no doubt – some of the research methodologies that I have employed might be viewed with amusement (if not disdain) by those that are. For example, on occasion, I have taken an irrelevant detour – or, more accurately, gone down a blind alley – in my approach to uncovering the Line of 16 and their successors and the circumstances in which they lived.

Again, I make no apologies for this. In common with most family historians, I have found that the satisfaction is derived not only from the formal identification of people, places and dates, but from the research efforts themselves that led to those results. Accordingly, in the narrative that follows, it will be seen that we will be side-tracked by brief discussions on: Puritan iconoclasm in Suffolk churches in the 1640s; conditions in the Gloucestershire weaving industry of the 1840s; the East-Westphalian Saxon dialect of the Osnabrück region of Germany; the development of Britain's submarine capability in the First World War; and the key manning issues facing the merchant marine industry in the early 1960s – to name but a few of the fairly esoteric subjects, amongst several, that I would not otherwise have had occasion to learn about.

Likewise with individuals. Whilst the narrative obviously focuses on the extensive family networks of Tom and Katie's ancestors, it has inevitably also been the case that there are other – non-family – members of the cast list, in whom we find ourselves interested. Hence it is that – amongst others – we learn what became of a Catholic priest in 1799 (hanged in Newport, County Mayo), a sea captain in 1845 (drowned in the Moray Firth), a convicted murderer in 1921 (resident in a mental hospital in Sunderland) and a carpenter's mate in 1943 (killed in an explosion on the Firth of Forth). We can only note their names and fates in passing, whilst recognising that they will each have had family networks of their own.

There is an important supplementary aspect to this, however. Whilst the research methodology might have been that of an enthusiastic amateur – the status of most family historians, after all – this would have been no excuse for permitting short-cuts or guesswork. On the contrary: it will be seen that I have been diligent in the checking of sources and the identification of possible non-sequiturs in the compilation of the family history. Where reasonable assumptions have been considered, I have been at pains to say so, usually to the exclusion of content that it would have been tempting to include in the family tree. There was no alternative, of course: once the family historian plays fast and loose with the information available, it becomes a complete waste of time.

****

In the literal sense, the research journey began the day after our family drink in the Travellers' Rest. The following day, my parents, Angela and I drove up from Leeds to North Yorkshire.

Pickhill is just off the A1, near Thirsk. As we drove into the village, my father instantly recognised a row of three cottages as including one – Pegmau Cottage – in which he had stayed as a young boy when visiting his grandmother. He remembered sleeping in an upstairs bedroom. (In 1987, this would have been nearly 60 years earlier).

We continued past the two public houses and turned right up a small hill to park near the All Saints Church, which had been hidden by the trees. Near the entrance to the churchyard, on the left, is a dignified British Legion war memorial. The dead are listed in order of rank and Sergeant Robert Rigg is the third name down; I saw it immediately.

Around the back of the church, in a quiet, shaded corner of the graveyard, was the grave of Henry Rigg, my great grandfather. It was on his headstone that the first new information on my research journey was provided:

IN
LOVING MEMORY
OF
HENRY RIGG
WHO DIED JULY 16TH 1920
AGED 72 YEARS
ALSO
SERGT ROBERT RIGG
SON OF THE ABOVE
KILLED IN FRANCE AUGUST 7TH 1918
AGED 33 YEARS

> BLESSED ARE THE DEPARTED
> ALSO OF JANE, WIFE OF
> HENRY RIGG
> WHO DIED OCT 2ND 1939
> AGED 80 YEARS

My father – born in 1921 – never met his grandfather, although his grandmother had lived until he was 18. She had died shortly after the outbreak of the Second World War, having lost one of her sons in the First. Robert, dad's uncle, had died just three months before Armistice Day.

In the narrative that follows, it will be seen that Robert Rigg is the first of several references to members of the extended family tree to have died whilst in the Armed Forces during the two World Wars. These are listed in the Roll of Honour presented in Annex A4 below.

****

We walked down to one of the pubs – the Nag's Head – for lunch. Afterwards, my father struck up a conversation with an elderly man, who was in an allotment on the other side of a wall by the side of the road. The man had white hair at the sides and soft blue eyes. He wore a brown string vest with a hole under one arm. The man said that he had come back to Pickhill after the Second World War in 1946 and had remained as he preferred the country way of life to the towns. It was quiet and peaceful. He said that the bus to Thirsk passed through the village only a couple of times each week; the fare was £1. He also said that he had just returned from a holiday in Jersey, which he had really enjoyed because the people had been so friendly. He had lost his wife a couple of years earlier.

Dad referred to the Wesleyan Chapel, built in 1864, on the other side of the road – a small, square building in a state of some disrepair with boarded windows and peeling paint. He said that, when he was young, it had seemed very spacious inside. The man agreed that, at one time, it had been a very busy place of worship and village activity. He looked down the street and pointed to where the blacksmith's and the cobbler's had once been.

My father mentioned to the man that we were looking up our family history and that he had stayed in the village as a boy. He referred to the plum trees at the back of the cottage; the man remembered those, but said they were no longer there. Then, dad told the man his surname: Rigg.

The man gave a warm smile before responding.

"Ginny Rigg".

PART ONE

Great, Great Grandparents:
THE LINE OF SIXTEEN

The first thing I must do is list the Line of 16: Tom and Katie's great, great grandparents. In the order that they will be introduced in the following chapters, they are:

		Dates	Place of birth
*	Henry Rigg	1847-1920	Baldersby, North Yorkshire
*	Jane Boynton	1859-1939	Thirkleby, North Yorkshire
*	Peter McBride	1861-1949	Rutherglen, Scotland
*	Agnes Charlotte Runcorn	1862-1942	Warrington, Lancashire
*	Charles James Niblett	1851-1927	Cheltenham, Gloucestershire
*	Anna Karoline Borstelmann	1853-1938	Elze, Hannover
*	Charles Herbert Wilson	1862-1946	Cambridge
*	Rosa Mary Whines	1863-1937	Westminster or Pimlico, London
*	Arthur English	1869-1936	Clonallon, County Down, Ireland
*	Helen (or Ellan or Hellen) Kelly	1869-1949	North Shields, Northumberland
*	Joseph Stapleton	c1859-1933	Liverpool or Ireland
*	Guiseppa Lucarda (or Josepha) Brincau	1863-1954	Vittoriosa, Malta
*	John Murray	c1839-?	County Mayo, Ireland
*	Margaret Mullown(e)y	c1846-?	County Mayo, Ireland
*	Francis McManamon	1836-1882	Newport, County Mayo, Ireland
*	Honor McManamon	1838-1917	County Mayo, Ireland

It can be seen that I do not know some of the exact names and the dates of birth and/or death. There might be several reasons for these gaps in knowledge, including inconsistency in the data in the official sources. We will return to this.

It is also evident that there are considerable ranges in the years of birth and the years of death. In the case of the former, the range is from 1836 to 1869; for the latter, it is from 1882 to 1954. In other words, by going back (only) four generations, these bands are stretched to over 30 years and over 70 years, respectively.

CHAPTER ONE

NORTH YORKSHIRE

THE LINE OF 16: 1. HENRY RIGG (1847-1920)

The initial steps

The day after our trip to North Yorkshire, my father and I visited Dad's older brother, Jack, who also lived in north Leeds. He was actually another John Rigg – John Kerr Rigg (1916-1999) to be exact – but Jack was what he was invariably called by the members of our family. (His wife, Audrey, always referred to him as John).

Jack clearly knew a considerable amount about the Rigg family of North Yorkshire and, although some of the information he provided turned out to be not fully accurate, tapping into his knowledge was a vital part of my early family researches.

The information flowed out from Jack. **HENRY RIGG (1847-1920)** – the first of my Line of 16 – was a Wesleyan lay preacher. His son Robert had been in the West Riding Police Force in Normanton. Another son Thompson was buried at the Methodist church in College Road, Harrogate. Of John (my grandfather) and Robert's sisters, Margaret had married a man called Driver from Huddersfield, Anne had married Bob Easton and had lived in the railway houses in Goathland near Whitby and Mary had been a housekeeper and had had an illegitimate son called Douglas. Ginny was the youngest sister. According to Jack, she had taught herself music and had played the organ in chapel. An early bout of pneumonia had stunted her growth and she had later died in hospital in York. She and Mary were buried, without a headstone, in the cemetery at Pickhill.

Two thoughts occurred to me. The first was the determination to scribble down as many of Jack's remembered details as I possibly could. I was aware, even at that stage, that – however incomplete or confusing it might initially be – the information provided by the current, living generations is often the essential foundation for any later, more formal, research. (How many family researchers have said in retrospective frustration: "I wished I'd asked him/her that". Nearly all of us, I suspect). Second, I could understand why the elderly man in the allotment in Pickhill had remembered Ginny Rigg.

In addition to the anecdote and hearsay, Jack produced some documentary evidence in the form of an old photograph album. This included my grandfather John Rigg's Certificate of Good Conduct in the Police Service, on which was written:

Leeds City Police
This is to certify that P.C. 162 John Rigg
joined the LEEDS CITY POLICY FORCE as a Constable on the
eighteenth day of June 1909 and
was pensioned on completion of service
on the seventeenth day of June 1935.
During the above period his conduct was exemplary.

PERSONAL DESCRIPTION		Given under my hand and seal
Date of birth	1887, May 30th	
Where born	Topcliffe, Ripon	
Height	5 feet 11 ins	
Complexion	Fair	PRO REGE ET LEGE
Colour of Hair	Dark Brown	R.L. Matthews
Colour of Eyes	Blue	Chief Constable
Religion	Wesleyan	Chief Constable's Office, Leeds 1
		22nd day of July 1935

I shall return to my uncle Jack's photograph album at a later stage. For the present, however, I shall note that, by confirming John Rigg's date and place of birth, his police certificate gave me a couple of fixed points of reference around which to establish a database of the family of Henry Rigg.

In the months that followed the visit to Jack, I sought information on the family into which Henry Rigg had been born through three different methods. The first was to consult the Census returns.

Censuses have been held in England and Wales at ten-year intervals (except for 1941) since 1801, although the 1841 Census was the first to contain names. At the time of my initial researches (in 1987), the Censuses (to 1881) were open to the public on microfilm in the Public Record Office in London and in local record offices. I found the first reference to Henry in the 1851 return for Baldersby, North Yorkshire, in the public record office in Harrogate.

Name and surname of each person who abode in the house	Relation to head of family	Condition	Age	Rank, profession or occupation	Where born
George Rigg	Head	Married	48	Agr Lab	York, Baldersby
Jane	Wife	Married	41	"	York, Helperby
William	Son	Unmarried	22	"	York, Baldersby
Elizabeth	Daughter	Unmarried	14	"	"
Edward	Son		11	Scholar	"
Robert	Son		8	"	"
Jane	Daughter		6	"	"
Henry	Son		3		

I followed this up by going back 10 years to the 1841 Census. The relevant records were in the Northallerton public library and covered "the whole of the township of Baldersby in the Parish of Topcliffe, which lies on the east side of the Turnpike Road leading from Boro'bridge to Catterick". The village had 296 people in 57 inhabited dwellings and the occupations of at least half the inhabitants – including Henry's father, George Rigg – were given as agricultural labourer, with the others reflecting either the rural economy or the basic trades of village life: carpenter, blacksmith, shoemaker, and so on.

George Rigg	35
Jane Rigg	30
Mary Rigg	75
William Rigg	12
George Rigg	9
Mary Rigg	5
Elizabeth Rigg	3
Edward Rigg	1

The inconsistency between the Censuses in the ages of George and his wife Jane (a problem with which family historians will be familiar) is legitimately explained in this case by the fact that the 1841 ages of adults were rounded down to the nearest 5 years.

The additional family member in 1841 was the older Mary Rigg. On the Census form, the age was not easy to read, but I was reasonably confident that it was 75 rather than 15 (as there was also a 5 year-old Mary in the household) and, less confidently, that she was George's mother.

The second general source was provided by the indexes of the Registrations of Births, Marriages and Deaths (BMD), which, at that time, were held at what used to be called St Catherine's House in Kingsway, London. These were great heavy volumes – one each for births, marriages and deaths in each quarter-year – in which the records for the whole of England and Wales were listed alphabetically by surname.

As the location was only a few minutes walk from where I was working at the time, I was able, over the course of many visits, to build up a database of all the BMD registered with the Rigg surname in the Ripon, Thirsk and Northallerton districts of North Yorkshire between 1837 (when the records start) and 1920 (the year of Henry's death): 142 in total, comprising 74 births, 26 marriages and 42 deaths. Of course, the list did not include the marriages that had taken place outside the district, nor the deaths of females who had married and adopted their husbands' names.

The age at death is given after 1865 and the records solemnly confirm the high incidence of infant mortality – death before the age of one year – over the whole period. Three names were followed by the sad figure 0 in the death registers between 1865 and 1920 and another six infants died within the first year between 1837 and 1865. In England and Wales as a whole, infant mortality was still as high as 130 per 1,000 live births in 1911; the 2021 rate – 3.7 per 1,000 – illustrates the vast improvement in living standards which the 20th Century brought.[1] At the same time, the North Yorkshire database also included some impressive examples of longevity: an Ann Rigg died aged 90 in 1869, another George Rigg aged 86 in 1871 and yet another George aged 87 in 1891.

During this part of my researches, I was effectively looking at the list of the BMD in England and Wales over this period of everyone with the surname of Rigg. Although I only made a note of those in the parts of North Yorkshire in which I was interested, I could not help but notice the more unusually named Riggs born elsewhere. I wonder what became of Braithwaite Rigg (born in Cockermouth in December 1848), Ephraim Rigg (born in Bradford in March 1867) and Hephzibah Rigg (born in Dewsbury in December 1865).

It was also noticeable that, even towards the end of the 19th Century, there were relatively few Rigg births in the south of England. In the 1880s and 1890s, there were usually between 12 and 20 Rigg births each quarter, but the clear majority were in west and north Yorkshire, the Lake District, the North East and, especially, Rochdale. At this early stage, I started to prepare myself for the possibility that I might have been descended from a Lancastrian.

The third source was given by the individual BMD certificates. Once a reference number had been found from the register, the certificate could be obtained for a fee of £5. I began with the birth certificate for Henry Rigg, which had 10 numbered columns.

---

[1] *Infant Mortality and Health Inequalities*, Elizabeth Rough and Carl Baker, House of Commons Library Research Briefing No. 9904, November 2023. The 2014 rate is the lowest to have been recorded in England Wales: 3.6 per 1,000.

1. When and where born	Third December 1847
	Baldersby Parish of Topcliffe
2. Name, if any	Henry
3. Sex	Boy
4. Name and surname of father	George Rigg
5. Name, surname and maiden name of mother	Jane Rigg formerly Wells
6. Occupation of father	Labourer
7. Signature, description and residence of informant	X The mark of George Rigg
	Father Baldersby
8. When registered	Eighteenth December 1847
9. Signature of registrar	Anthony Gayll Registrar
10. Name entered after registration	

Two details jumped off the certificate. First, I now knew the maiden name of Henry's mother (Jane Wells). Second, in the response to question 7, the registrar had written "the mark of George Rigg" next to a small cross in the corner of the box. George Rigg – Henry's father – could not write.[2]

The mysterious Mary Rigg of Baldersby

I then purchased the death certificate of Mary Rigg, who died in Baldersby in February 1845 at the age of 81. (Her given age of 75 in the 1841 Census was again attributable to rounding). She had been born, therefore, in either 1763 or 1764. George registered the death with his mark. The cause of death was "decay of nature" and Mary's occupation – remember, this was a woman in her 80s – was clearly given as "labourer".

The 1841 Census had revealed that, like the other members of George Rigg's household, Mary Rigg had been born in Yorkshire. However, her birth had obviously been well before the period covered by the Registration of BMD (from 1837) and, therefore, to seek more information on her I knew that it would be necessary to consult the parish registers. To find out more about these, I joined the Society of Genealogists in London, where I looked at Cecil Humphrey-Smith's book *The Phillimore Atlas and Index of Parish Registers* (1984). This listed the parish registers of England and Wales and gave details of their availability. The relevant references for me were as shown overleaf:

---

[2] I learned later – from the *North Yorkshire, Church of England Births and Baptisms 1813-1921* database available on Ancestry – that Henry Rigg was baptised in Baldersby on Christmas Day 1847.

	Deposited original registers	International Genealogical Index	Copies of registers at Society of Genealogists
Pickhill	1571-1880	1567-1848	1567-1812
Thirsk	1556-1956	1556-1864	1556-1721
Topcliffe	1570-1887	1714-1856	

The original registers were held locally, in this case at the North Yorkshire County Record Office (NYCRO) in Northallerton. The International Genealogical Index (IGI) is compiled by the Genealogical Society of the Church of the Latter Day Saints (the Mormons) and, at that time, was available on microfiche at the Society of Genealogists.

In the years since the initial researches into Mary Rigg, she has remained a mysterious and captivating figure. A visit to the NYCRO in 1989 revealed that George Rigg had been born in Baldersby on November 29th 1802 and had been baptised the following day. He was the first son of "Mary Rigg of Baldersby" and an "unknown father". Given Mary's age at death, I searched for a record of her birth in the Topcliffe parish returns (which would have included the village of Baldersby) between 1760 and 1779, the Thirsk returns between 1761 and 1765 and the records for Pickhill when I returned to the Society of Genealogists in London. It was not to be found.

I spent some considerable time exploring two possibilities for Mary Rigg. First, the IGI list of births in North Yorkshire, as copied from the parish returns, had an entry for Mary Rigge as the daughter born to Fletcher and Susannah Rigge of Northallerton in 1784. I was not put off by the variant in the spelling of the surname, as the transcripts of the birth registers in the NYCRO had given this spelling at later dates for the births of some of Henry Rigg's older siblings. Mary Rigge's year of birth would also have been consistent with giving birth to the illegitimate George as an 18 year-old in 1802. However, the entry did not sit with George's mother's appearance as a 75 year-old in the 1841 Census or with her death in 1845 at the age of 81. (I later learned that Mary Rigge of Northallerton married Francis Philip Bedingfield in 1831 and that she died in 1851).[3]

---

3   Details of the Rigge family, based on papers from 1581-1880, are available in the Cumbrian Archive Service Catalogue (CASCAT). The family originated from Keenground, Hawkshead, in Westmorland (present-day Cumbria), where they were resident in 1568. It had estates in Westmorland and Yorkshire.

The Fletcher Rigge noted here lived from 1743 to 1829 and married Susannah Gray of Ealing, Middlesex, in 1782. They lived in Northallerton, where he was a Barrister at Law, and they are buried in Northallerton parish church. A copy of Fletcher's will is in The National Archives in Kew.

Fletcher and Susannah Rigge's only son – Gray Rigge, 1783-1857 – was a magistrate in Lancashire and Westmorland. He married his cousin Sarah Moore from Stockwell in Surrey. Their eldest son, (Henry Fletcher Rigge) became High Sheriff of the county Palatine of Lancaster and the second son (Charles Gray Rigge) was a captain in the Royal Navy.

The second candidate was the Mary Rigg born in the parish of Great Ayton in North Yorkshire in 1763, the daughter of Thomas Rigg junior, a wright. She would have been 78 in 1841 and, therefore, not far in age from that of George Rigg's mother, Mary. (Great Ayton is about 25 miles from Baldersby as the crow flies). However, a 78 year-old Mary Rigg was also listed in the 1841 Census record for Great Ayton in the household of the 71 year-old Thomas Rigg and, whilst I cannot be certain that this was the person born in the same parish in 1763 – i.e. Thomas's sister rather than his wife – I had to conclude that this was not the Mary Rigg I was seeking. This was confirmed when I came across the death record for the 82 year-old Mary Rigg in Great Ayton in 1846.

It was to be many years later, in 2003, when I hit upon the idea of tracking down the bastardy papers for Topcliffe covering the period when George Rigg was born in Baldersby. I had found that, in the general introductory books on family history, the references to bastardy papers tended to be relegated to a footnote – if they appeared at all – though Don Steel did cover the subject in his *Discovering Your Family History* (1986):

> "When an unmarried girl gave birth to a bastard, she was examined to ascertain the identity of the father. When, as was often the case, she was reticent, considerable pressure was exerted. Once identified the father was usually compelled to make weekly payments towards the maintenance of the child. So too was the mother if she were working".

My letter to the NYCRO followed. The reply from the Acting County Archivist was prompt, but disappointing:

> "We do hold some bastardy papers for Topcliffe, which would include Baldersby at this time, but I am very sorry to say that there are no papers for the period 1801 to 1805. I am sorry that we cannot help you".

It remains an intriguing question as to whether the Mary Rigg listed in George Rigg's household in the 1841 Census was his mother or grandmother. If the former – which I continue to assume (albeit with some reservation) – it implies that she gave birth to an illegitimate (and first) son at the age of 38 or 39. Alternatively, there is a missing – much younger – Mary, who was her daughter and George's mother. I have searched in vain in the available parish records for a Mary Rigg who might have given birth to George in 1802 and then died in North Yorkshire

---

A contributor to the public pages of the Ancestry website – Judith Wilde – has reported on the male Rigge line stretching back from Fletcher Rigge to William Rigge in the first half of the 17th Century. I have not found any connection between the Rigge family and the direct line going through George Rigg and his mother, Mary Rigg of Baldersby.

in the period before the Census of 1841.[4] In any event, it is here that I lose track of the paternal Rigg line.

By contrast, the North Yorkshire parish records were useful in explaining some of the entries that were unknown to me in the database that I had compiled of BMD in Thirsk, Ripon and Northallerton between 1837 and 1920. The Topcliffe marriage register also confirmed that Henry Rigg's parents – George Rigg and Jane Wells – had married on 22nd December 1828. However, within the same register, the very next record revealed a complication typical of those faced by the family historian: it was of the marriage of another George Rigg (from Thirsk) to Mary Hornby (from Topcliffe) on 1st January 1829.

In due course, I started to compile a family tree for this second George Rigg, who was born in Thirlby in 1804, the illegitimate son of the 16 year-old Elizabeth Rigg, whose father was John Rigg of Thirlby. (We have already noted that he lived to the age of 87, dying in the Thirsk district in 1891). George's father could have been Thomas Yarker, whom Elizabeth married in 1806.

The marriage of George Rigg to Mary Hornby produced 10 children between 1830 and 1849, 4 of whom died in infancy. The family lived in Sandhutton, which is only about 4 miles from Baldersby as the crow flies. In effect, therefore, this was a parallel family to that of "my" George Rigg, living relatively close by, and – needless to say – a general and regular source of some confusion, as I sought to piece together the family of George and Jane Rigg.

The Georges would not have been brothers, of course. Nor can I find any evidence that they were cousins or in any other way related: a contribution on the Ancestry public page refers only to Elizabeth Rigg having two brothers (John and William), but no sister called Mary.

Libraries and databases

I suspect that, in the early years of my research, my general trawl of possible – and unlikely – sources of information was not dissimiliar to the optimistic and naive approach adopted by many family historians. An obvious starting point was the Rigg surname itself, about which I initially consulted two standard (and scholarly) reference books by PH Reaney: *A Dictionary of British Surnames (1968)* and *The Origin of English Surnames* (1967). The latter did not have an entry under Rigg, but the dictionary noted that the earliest references were to William de Rigge in a 12th Century Shropshire pipe roll (a collection of financial records maintained by the Exchequer/Treasury) and, 130 years later, John del Rigg in a subsidy roll

---

[4] I did wonder about the Mary Rigg who died in Coley, York, in 1840 at the age of 55. This implies a year of birth around 1785, which would have meant her being a 17 year-old at the time of George Rigg's birth in 1802. However, this Mary Rigg was born in Halifax, West Yorkshire, and so does not fit the Topcliffe parish register's description of "Mary Rigg of Baldersby".

(a taxation record) in Cumberland. Although the names William and John are Norman in origin and would have been introduced from 1066, Reaney noted that "hryggr" was the Old Norse for ridge and dated from 400-600AD. I have settled for "dweller by a ridge" as the origin of the name, which implies that it could have been applied in many different localities.[5]

My broadbrush approach to examining possible data sources received a boost when I joined the Society of Genealogists in 1988. On my early visits to its (then) location in the Charterhouse Buildings in Goswell Road, London, I found the library to be somewhat overwhelming, due to the huge range of material on its shelves. However, it was still very enjoyable to make a random inspection of what was available, particularly anything with a North Yorkshire connection that would give me a sense of the life and times of the early 19th Century. Hence, Pigot and Co's *Royal National and Commercial Directory and Topography for Yorkshire* in 1841 noted that travel from Topcliffe to London is "on the Wellington coach from Newcastle which calls at the Golden Fleece every afternoon at 2.30pm". An earlier document dramatically entitled "To escape the monster's clutches" was subtitled "Notes and documents illustrating the preparations in North Yorkshire to repel the invasion threatened by the French from 1793". Three schedules (or questionnaires) were despatched to parish constables in October 1801; the returns for townships in the wapentake of Langbaurgh East included, in Skelton, Richard Rigg and John Rigg, both listed as "farmer sons". A later John Rigg was described as "25 years of age, 5 foot 11 inches high, dark brown hair, brown eyes, dark complexion, a native of Yorkshire". He was listed in a book by Jim Melton – *Ships' Deserters 1852-1900* (1986) – as having deserted from HMS *Clio* in Sydney in 1873, most probably to try his luck in the Australian goldfields.

The NYCRO in Northallerton had a similarly enticing set of books and papers. During a visit there to examine the Bishops Transcripts of the Topcliffe parish records in 1989, I stumbled across *North Riding Naval Recruits, 1795-97: The Quota Acts and the Quota Men* and *The Transportation of Felons to North America, 1717-75*. There were no Riggs in either volume.

Of more direct relevance in the Society of Genealogists library was the (as in 1993) 34 volume set of Yorkshire Monumental Inscriptions (YMI) compiled in the 1980s by the Cleveland Family History Society (CFHS). These listed the inscriptions on many of the gravestones in the area, as compiled by volunteers in the society, including (in Volume 27) that of Henry and Jane Rigg in Pickhill. (By the time of a later visit to the library in 2004, the collection had expanded to 48 volumes of YMI and two volumes of Yorkshire Memorial Inscriptions). It was clear that I had to join the CFHS, which I duly did.

---

5 A later analysis by George Redmonds in *A Dictionary of Yorkshire Surnames* (2015) reported that there were 2517 entries of the Rigg surname in the 1881 Censuses, of which 40 per cent were in Lancashire and a further 38 per cent in Yorkshire, Cumberland or Westmorland.

The short paragraph summarising my family history interests in the January 1994 edition of the *Cleveland Family History Society Journal* – focusing on the birth of George Rigg in 1802 to Mary Rigg of Baldersby – drew immediate responses from correspondents in Stockton-on-Tees, Darlington and Australia. Although none were able to add any new information about Mary, it was clear from all the replies – particularly the one from Rosemary Allen of Eltham, Victoria – that there had been an extensive community with the Rigg surname in the very north of Yorkshire (or present-day Cleveland) in the 17th and 18th Centuries.

This prompted me to look again at *The Phillimore Atlas and Index of Parish Registers* to note the names of all the parishes to the north and east of Topcliffe as far as the coast – I listed 75 in total – and to see which of their parish records were held in hard copy at the Society of Genealogists. There, I found 11 in total (this was still in 1994), of which 7 had references to the Rigg name, including Danby (31 references between 1635-1749), Great Ayton (33 references between 1614-1811), Kirkleatham (30 references between 1637-1797), Lythe and Stokesley. Whilst I remain unclear about the origins of Mary Rigg of Baldersby, I think that it reasonable to speculate that, at some time during the late 17th or early 18th Centuries, one or more members of the Rigg community in the very north of Yorkshire – to the west and north of the Cleveland Hills – made the journey south to the Topcliffe/Thirsk locality.

In recent years, the type of general search that could previously only be made along library shelves has been possible through the online databases available on the Internet. For the family historian, this can provide hours of (often fruitless) fun, tinged with the promise of a significant discovery, even when a direct link to the family line cannot be proved. Hence, for example, the early 19th Century trade directories that are accessible by members of the CFHS confirm that the Rigg surname was not uncommon across North Yorkshire and South Durham at this time. John Rigg was a shopkeeper in Malton in 1822-23 and then a "groceries and sundries dealer" in 1833-34; William Rigg was a "victualler" at the "Queen Catherine" in Osmotherley in 1822-23, when the Reverend Hugh Rigg was a curate in Patrick Brompton; another John Rigg was a tailor in Middleton on Teeside in 1827-28.

Similarly, as the Ancestry records to which I have had access include *England & Wales Criminal Records 1791-1892*,[6] I looked up possible misdemeanours by those named Rigg in North Yorkshire. None were found. The most promising case was that of Geo Rigge (sic) who, with two others, was charged at York in January 1813 with "an attack on Mr Cartwright Mills as aforesaid and damaging

---

6   This database is the first of many to which I shall refer in the narrative that follows as having been accessed via www.ancestry.co.uk. The full list of the Ancestry databases on which I have drawn is given in Annex A5 below. Where possible, I have also noted the original sources in the Annex.

machinery". There was no prosecution. So close to having a genuine Luddite in the family.

The same source revealed that a much more serious crime had resulted in the trial of William Rigg at Durham in February 1889. He was convicted of "common assault and wilful murder" and sentenced "to be hanged". However, I noted that the death registers did not include an entry for a William Rigg in Durham in 1889 or 1890. Nor was there anyone of this name on a (non-Ancestry) website listing most criminal executions in England and Wales between 1100 and 1964.[7]

I followed up this story, therefore, in the March 1889 editions of the *York Herald*. William Rigg was a 27 year-old forge roller and the victim of the murder was his wife, Jane. The edition of the 1st of the month reported that, after "his lordship passed sentence in the usual way", William Rigg pointed to a Detective Atkinson and claimed "That is the man who did it". Two weeks later, in a macabre report entitled "In the Condemned Cell at Durham", it was noted that "all hopes have been abandoned" by the condemned man and that he was "preparing himself for the approaching doom", the execution date having been set for four days hence. "His disposition is calm… [and although] his sleep is at times somewhat disturbed and fitful, he is stated to take his food well and regularly".

There was a twist in the tale, which was clearly not regarded at all favourably by the editor of the Durham-based *North Eastern Daily Gazette*. The 20th March edition stated that:

> "It is impossible to evade the strong impression of disapproval expressed in all circles of the city of Durham at the decision of the Home Office in reprieving… Rigg. The feeling is freely expressed that there has been a miscarriage of justice and, furthermore, it is generally a feeling of disregard for the consequences which follow the act of murder… The letter [from the Home Office] in regard to Rigg finishes by stating that he is respited "with a view to the sentence being commuted to one of penal servitude for life"".

The 39 year-old William Rigg – recorded as born in Sunderland and a widower (not surprisingly) – was listed as a convict in Parkhurst Prison in the 1901 Census, where his occupation was again given as "forge roller". He was released on licence in 1909 after serving 20 years in prison.[8] His entry in the 1911 Census suggested some form of return to the life of an everyday citizen, as he was recorded as a 49 year-old blacksmith in an ironworks living alone in Hardwicke Street, Sunderland.

---

7   www.britishexecutions.co.uk

8   See Judith Knelman, "Why Can't a Woman be More like a Man? Attitudes to Husband-Murder, 1889-1989" in Judith Rowbotham and Kim Stevenson, eds, *Behaving Badly: Social Panic and Moral Outrage – Victorian and Modern Parallels*, Routledge, 2017. The reference contains graphic details of the murder of Jane Rigg.

However, by the time of the following Census in 1921, William Rigg had again been institutionalised: an inmate in the Sunderland Mental Hospital in Ryhope. He died in Sunderland in 1939 at the age of 76, fifty years after his reprieve from the gallows.

For completeness, I should record that neither Geo Rigge nor William Rigg have (yet) been shown to be part of the extended family tree. The same comment applies to the 8 entries under the Rigg surname who appear in the *New South Wales and Tasmania: Settlers and Convicts, 1787-1859* database available on www.Findmypast.co.uk, which includes Harriet Rigg (convicted at the Preston Quarter Sessions in Lancaster in 1846 and sentenced to 7 years transportation) and my namesake John Rigg (convicted at the Norwich City Quarter Sessions in 1842 and sentenced to 15 years). All these cases of crime and punishment are examples (amongst several in this volume) of how the family historian can be side-tracked into some interesting areas, the research into which is difficult to resist.

The migration of two of Henry Rigg's nephews to the USA – specifically, Stephen and Henry Rigg to Vermont in the 1890s – is noted in footnote 16 below and described in detail in Annex A1. More generally in America, Riggs (with an 's') is a much more common surname than Rigg.[9] Extensive research on the latter has been done by David L Rigg, who has traced his line back to the mid 18th Century and suggests that a Riggs from Hampshire was the original immigrant. (This is consistent with the findings presented by George Redmonds in *A Dictionary of Yorkshire Surnames* that, whereas the origins and early incidence of Rigg were in the northern counties of England, the "home" of Riggs was along the south coast).

In a September 2000 entry on the Cyndilist bulletin board (found within www.rootsweb.com), David L Rigg referred to documents concerning the Rigg family in Charles County, Maryland, going back to at least 1676. He also stated that a Charles Rigg, born in 1756, served in the Revolutionary War between 1777 and 1780. I contacted Mr Rigg via his website without reply. There is no connection, as far as I can see, to the families of Henry Rigg(s) and Stephen Rigg(s) in Vermont.

Other research, noted separately on the Cyndilist bulletin board in February 2000 and September 2000 by Elaine Fillmore and Charlotte Nugent, respectively, referred to Rigg families in pre-revolutionary Maryland later migrating west and

---

9   The respective incidences of the Riggs and Rigg surnames in the USA are illustrated on the Vietnam War Memorial in Washington DC, on which all the 58,000 American casualties of that conflict are listed. There are 11 entries for Riggs and one for Rigg, the latter being William C Rigg of Los Angeles, California, who was aged 19 when he was killed in February 1966. The evidence from various Federal Censuses shows that William's great (x2) grandparents were James and Sarah Riggs (with the 's') and that James – a farmer – had been born in England. However, James and Sarah were resident in Washington, Iowa, as 30 year-olds in 1860, which was over 30 years before Stephen and Henry Rigg migrated from North Yorkshire to Vermont and it is reasonable to conclude, therefore, that there was no connection between them.

south to Illinois, West Virginia, Virginia, Kentucky, North Carolina, Alabama and Georgia.

Graveyards and the Tudors

On the day that my parents, Angela and I made our first visit to North Yorkshire in August 1987, after we had left Pickhill, we called at the church of St James the Great in the next village, Baldersby St James. It is a more modern structure than the church in Pickhill, having been consecrated in September 1857. The graveyard extended on three sides of the church and included some recent plots. Many of the gravestones were frustratingly illegible – victims of the weather – but we found three of relevance: Kate, daughter of George and Mary Ann Rigg, who died in February 1939 aged 58; Elizabeth, wife of George Rigg, who died in September 1882 aged 50; and Mary Jane Rigg (1871-1943) and her husband George (1865-1948) and son William (1902-1945).

I suspected that all these people were members of Henry Rigg's extended family, of course, but I had no idea who they were. I knew that it would be a fascinating detective exercise to find out.[10]

In common with many in the vast ranks of family historians, I have spent innumerable hours traipsing around various graveyards in search of enlightenment from a revealing headstone. It is not perhaps the most efficient use of one's time – but it is good fun, with the occasional surprise or discovery thrown in. In June 1989, my father and I spent an interesting – and wholly unproductive – day looking for relevant headstones in various North Yorkshire churchyards and cemeteries: Dishforth (where there are several Second World War graves commemorating lost RAF and Canadian Air Force personnel), Sowerby (where we aroused the curiosity of the gardener), Thirsk, Northallerton, North Otterington, South Otterington (where we missed the gravestone of the 8 year-old Eleanor Annie Rigg, who died in 1918) and Kirby Wise. It is amazing what is retained in the memory: I can recall listening to Luciano Pavarotti singing "Nessum Dorma" on the car radio and then, tuning into *Test Match Special*, learning that Steve Waugh had scored a century for Australia against England at Headingley.

The family into which Henry Rigg was born is summarised in Table 1.1.[11] He had 7 siblings, of whom 5 – William, George, Elizabeth, Edward and Robert – married and had children of their own. The other two – Mary Ann Rigg and Jane Rigg – died of "congestion of the brain" and "phthisis pulmonalis" (or tuberculosis)

---

10 In due course, I was able to place all these names within the Rigg family tree in North Yorkshire. All family historians will recognise the sense of satisfaction when the jigsaw pieces fit into place.

11 As noted in the Preface, the branches of the family tree shown in the numbered tables read horizontally from left to right – rather than vertically, as is more conventional – due to the sizes of some of the families.

at the ages of 20 and 19, respectively, in 1856 and 1864. (I purchased both these death certificates, the latter again witnessed by George Rigg with a cross). The third sister, Elizabeth, also died of phthisis – at the age of 25 in 1863 – having already lost a first husband and married a second time. Hence, none of Henry's three sisters lived beyond the age of 25; by contrast, all four of his brothers lived into at least their 60s.

Henry Rigg's father, George, remained in Baldersby all his life, as did his brothers William and George, with Henry himself moving only to nearby Pickhill. Not surprisingly, their wives were found in nearby North Yorkshire: Henry's mother, Jane Wells, was born in Helperby and the wives of these three of her sons came from Thirsk, Upsal and Thirkleby, respectively.

Table 1.1. The parents and siblings of Henry Rigg	
George Rigg 1802-1865 **(born in Baldersby)** **(son or grandson of Mary Rigg 1763/4 (tbc) -1845 and an unknown father)** **(died in Baldersby aged 81)**	
married	
Jane Wells 1807-1886 **(born in Helperby)** **(daughter of Edward Wells 1767-1808 and Sarah Croft 1774-?)** **(died in Baldersby aged 79)**	William Rigg 1829-1905 (born in Baldersby) (died in Ripon district aged 76) *married* 1. Anne Jefferson 1829-1880 (born in Thirsk) (died aged 50) 2. Ann Hullah 1829-1904 (born in West Tanfield, nr Thirsk) (died aged 75)
	George Rigg 1832-1893 (born in Baldersby) (died in Ripon district aged 61) *married* Elizabeth Harland 1831/2-1882 (born in Upsal) (died in Ripon district aged 50)

	Mary Ann Rigg 1835-1856 (born in Baldersby) (died in Dishforth aged 20)
	Elizabeth Rigg 1837-1863 (born in Baldersby) (died in Baldersby aged 25) *married* 1. George Umpleby (or Humpleby) 1832/3-1860 (born in Ripon district) (died in Ripon district aged 27) 2. Francis Foxton 1830-1900 (born in Ripon district) (died in Ripon district aged 70)
	Edward Rigg 1840-1913 (born in Baldersby) (died in Middlesbrough aged 72) *married* Jane Jackson 1839/40-1924 (born in Berrier or Greystoke, Cumberland) (died in Middlesbrough aged 83)
	Robert Rigg 1843-1923 (born in Baldersby) (died in Stokesley aged 80) *married* Margaret Thompson 1843-1892 (born in Kirkleavington, nr York) (died in Stokesley aged 48)
	Jane Rigg 1845-1864 (born in Baldersby) (died in Ripon district aged 19)
	Henry Rigg 1847-1920 **(born in Baldersby)** **(died in Pickhill aged 72)** *married* **Jane Boynton 1859-1939** **(born in Thirkleby)** **(died in Pickhill aged 80)**
All places in North Yorkshire	

I examined the Helperby records in the 1841 Census to see if there were any clues about the family of George Rigg's wife, Jane Wells (1807-1886). In the Ancestry database, the only person with that surname in the village was the 79 year-old Ann Wells, who was living alone. However, I noted that Sarah Walls (sic) was a 67 year-old agricultural labourer in a household with Thomas Watson aged 21. I did not think any more about this until I came across a contribution on the Ancestry public pages from Roselyn Kirton, who reported that Jane was the third of the four children of Edward Wells (1767-1808) and Sarah Croft (born 1774) and that, in turn, Edward's parents were Edward Wells (1727-1777) and Mary Bilton (born 1732).

Ms Kirton did not give a date of death for Sarah Wells (née Croft), but clearly the age of 67 given for Sarah Walls/Wells in the 1841 Census would fit the year of birth of Sarah Croft. Frustratingly, there is no record of the death of Sarah Wells in the Ripon or Thirsk districts until someone of that name in Ripon in June 1859;[12] nor could I find an entry in a thorough search of the 1851 Census in Helperby.

After these initial enquiries into the background of Jane Wells, I parked my research into this branch of the family for some considerable time. Then, in July 2020, I was astounded to note that another contributor to the public pages of Ancestry, David Pratt, had traced a direct line going back from Edward Wells (1727-1777) – the grandfather of Jane Wells – through a further six generations to Robert Welles[13], who was born in Galphay, near Ripon, in about 1516. This research had included the examination of wills, land records and other sources (including at the Borthwick Institute in York and the Archives Department of Leeds City Council). These had revealed – for example – that Robert Welles bequeathed to his grandson Ffrancis "a cowe and one quye" [a heifer under three years of age].

For even the most experienced researcher into family history, it is these types of result that make the head spin. I contacted David Pratt to congratulate him on his work and to note that, as Jane Wells is seven generations back from my son and daughter – Tom and Katie – this means that Robert Welles goes back to the 13th generation. In the estimated year of his birth (1516), Henry the Eighth was on the throne of England. Interestingly, the land leased for 45 years by Robert Welles in June 1538 was from "Abbot Marmaduke and the Convent of Fonteyn" i.e. Fountains Abbey.[14]

---

12   The death certificate showed that this was Sarah Wells, a 38 year-old domestic servant, who died in Dishforth on 1st May 1859. The cause of death was "disease of liver some years, congestion of brain 7 days, bronchitis 10 days, certified".

13   The second "e" in Welles appears to have been dropped after one or two generations.

14   This was immediately prior to the buildings, estates and assets of Fountains Abbey being seized by the Crown during the Dissolution of the Monasteries. The Abbey and its grounds were purchased by Sir Richard Gresham MP in 1540.

David Pratt's research shows that the Wells family remained in Galphay through several generations. Robert's son – Thomas Wells (1539-1597) – was born and died there. In turn, his grandson – Christopher Wells – died there in 1657 and Christopher's grandson – William Wells (1680-1728) – was born and died in Azerley, which is nearby. William Wells was the father of Edward Wells, Jane's grandfather.

The place of burial for Robert, Thomas and Christopher (and probably others) is reported to have been St Andrew's Church in Kirkby Malzead. Accordingly, I consulted the www.billiongraves.com database and found that there were four gravestones listed for the Wells surname in the church grounds. None were in the direct family line, although that for Edward Wells (1718-1742) is of a second cousin to Jane Wells's grandfather, Edward.

The extended Rigg family: key features

In the more than three decades that have passed since the first visit to North Yorkshire, I have filled in most of the details of George and Jane Rigg's family through the subsequent generations. Not surprisingly, given this is my family name, this is the line of the tree to which I have devoted the most attention. The 8 children of George and Jane Rigg had a total of 8 spouses (though not one each!) and 29 children (who were George and Jane's grandchildren, of course). To date – and this exercise will always be prefaced "to date" – I have placed a total of 111 great grandchildren and 178 great, great grandchildren on George and Jane's family tree.

Of course, it is one thing to identify the family members and to place them on a family tree. It is another to interpret the results of the 10 yearly Censuses – including those for 1891, 1901, 1911 and 1921 when they became available – and the details from BMD certificates to find out what sorts of lives they led. I think there are half a dozen key features, which I note here in the context of George and Jane Rigg and their descendants, but which – as we will see – also apply in the different family lines elsewhere across the Line of 16.

*   There were some large families, starting with George and Jane, who had 8 children, of whom 6 were to marry and raise families of their own. One of George's grandchildren – George Pattison Rigg (1855-1919) and his wife Mary Ann (1854-1936) – had 14 children. Another of George's grandchildren, a later Jane Rigg (1878-1931) and her husband William Merryweather also had 12 children, of whom at least 6 died before the age of one. And, of course, Henry

Rigg and his wife Jane Boynton had 8 children, one of whom was my grandfather, John Rigg (1887-1959).

*   As a result of the large family sizes, the syncronicity of the generations became distorted. The children of George Rigg (1802-65) were born between 1829 (William) and 1847 (Henry). William's first son (George Pattison Rigg) was born in 1855, whilst Henry's last-born son (Thompson) was born in 1895. Hence, although George Pattison Rigg and Thompson Rigg were first cousins, there was a 40 year difference in the dates of birth. Indeed, George Pattison Rigg's grandson (Henry) was born in 1898, only three years after Thompson.

*   For the most part, the members of the family worked in hard, manual occupations. As noted in more detail below, the occupation of "agricultural labourer" or "farm labourer" is found consistently in the Censuses between 1841 and 1911 for both male and female members of the family.

Over time, the agricultural-based occupations became more differentiated (cowkeeper, milk carrier, gamekeeper, etc). From about 1870 onwards, the range of male occupations within the family widened to include various non-agricultural jobs on the railways, heavy industry and construction (railway platelayer, signalman). For the females, the dominant occupations by far were in domestic service as general servants, housemaids or cooks. A broader range of service sector occupations began to appear in the 1901 and 1911 Censuses for both males and females, particularly in retailing (butcher, draper's assistant, outfitter), but the role of unskilled manual work remained important (general labourer, railway labourer, general carter).

A specific point to make here is to confirm the significance of the railway industry as a source of employment for males within the extended Rigg family from the 1870s onwards. Within the families and descendants (including spouses) of Henry and his siblings, I have identified 23 individuals as having railway-related occupations – platemen, signalmen, porters, etc – in the period up to and including the 1939 England and Wales Register.[15]

*   There was a gradual dispersal of the family away from Baldersby. As noted, George and Jane Rigg remained in Baldersby all their married lives and all 8 of their children were born there. However, during the

---

15   The *1939 England and Wales Register* (henceforth referred to here as the 1939 Register) was a mini-census – announced by the Government in December 1938 – which was undertaken in anticipation of the requirements of the domestic war effort, for example in the issue of identity cards and ration books. It is an important source for

19th Century, there was a general migration of the family, particularly to the far north of Yorkshire and south Durham, no doubt determined by the availability of better job prospects in the railway and steel industries. We see the first signs of movement away from the village in the cases of two of George's sons: Edward was a railway platelayer in Thornaby by 1881, later settling in Middlesbrough, whilst Robert worked as a tanner and cowkeeper in Yarm and died in Stokesley. By 1911, the dispersal had widened to several other parts of North Yorkshire, West Yorkshire (including John Rigg – my grandfather – as a 23 year-old police constable in Leeds) and outside Yorkshire altogether.[16]

Not everyone moved, however. An address in either Baldersby or Pickhill remained in the 1911 Census for several branches of the extended Rigg family, including my great grandparents, Henry and Jane Rigg. Following Henry's death in 1920, Jane was duly recorded as the head of the household in Pickhill in the 1921 Census of England and Wales, living with her unmarried daughter Jane (or Ginny). Indeed, the matriarch Jane Rigg remained to be listed as a resident of Pickhill in the 1939 Register – the year of her death[17] – in a household with Ginny and another

---

family historians, given that the 1931 Census records were destroyed in the Second World War and no census was undertaken in 1941.

16 Two of the sons of William Rigg – Henry Rigg's oldest brother – emigrated to Vermont, USA, in the 1890s, where they lived eventful lives and raised large families. I described my researches into Stephen Rigg (later Riggs, 1868-1951) and his descendants in two articles for the *Cleveland Family History Society Journal* in January 2015 and April 2015. These have been complemented by an article on Henry Rigg (later Riggs, 1863-1924) in the same journal in April 2020. The articles are reproduced in Annex A1 below.

Prior to their emigration, Stephen and Henry Rigg had been employed by the North Eastern Railway Company. The *Daily Gazette for Middlesbrough* of 5th January 1891 reported that, on the previous 13th December, they had both been assaulted by one John Allen, a cartman, whilst working at the West Stockton Ironworks crossing. They had remonstrated with Allen, who had "so managed his horse and cart as to cause an inconvenience to the shunting traffic". Allen had "first struck Stephen Rigg in the mouth and a little later, on returning, assaulted Henry Rigg in the same manner". The Bench "pronounced it a serious case" and Allen was fined a total of £2 plus £2 15s in costs. How much this incident persuaded Stephen and Henry that there might be better employment opportunities available in the US is not known.

Between them, Stephen and Henry had 14 children (including one adopted), of whom 10 survived into adulthood. The growths of their family trees have been such that I have placed over 500 people in them (including spouses) over another four generations. Not surprisingly, many of their descendants are to be found in Vermont. However, the mobility and fluidity of inter-generational life in the USA has meant that many others have migrated to other parts of the country. I estimate that, based on the BMDs of the direct family line or their spouses or resulting from their current places of residence, there are descendants to be found in at least 19 other States: California, Colorado, Connecticut, Florida, Idaho, Illinois, Maryland, Massachusetts, Michigan, New Hampshire, New Jersey, New Mexico, New York, Ohio, Rhode Island, North Carolina, South Carolina, Tennessee and Virginia.

17 In fact, the week of her death. The 1939 Register was conducted on 29th September. Jane Rigg's headstone in the graveyard of All Saints Church in Pickhill (noted in the Preface above) records her death as being on 2nd October.

unmarried daughter, Mary. Other members of the family also continued to live locally in Melmerby and Rainton.

* There was significant longevity within the family. I have recorded the birth and death dates of 133 members of George and Jane Rigg's family and their descendants (including spouses) who were born between 1829 (the year of birth of George and Jane's first son, William) and 1900 <u>and</u> who lived in North Yorkshire and/or South Durham. No fewer than 67 of these (50 per cent) lived to the age of 70 or over and 30 (23 per cent) reached the age of at least 80.[18] Within this group, I have not discovered any centurions so far: of the direct descendants of George and Jane Rigg, the longest-lived was Edward Rigg, born in Baldersby in 1891, who died at the age of 91 in 1982.[19] [20]

At the same time, as again noted, there were several instances of infant mortality and deaths in early adulthood. Five family members (including one spouse) were killed in action in the First World War. John Rigg's brother, Robert – my great uncle – was one of these (see Chapter 8).

* There were many examples of long marriages. As divorce was far less common in the period up to the 1930s – and I have neither seriously looked for nor discovered any examples of it – the only reason for a marriage formally coming to an end would have been the death of one of the spouses. Therefore, because of the longevity of the individuals concerned, it is not surprising to see that many marriages were of long duration. Of those marriages that took place before the First World War, I have found 9 examples of 40 years or over, the longest being the 54 years of George Rigg (1865-1948) and

---

[18] I am aware that there is a possibility of statistical bias in these calculations to the extent that the births and deaths of some infants between Censuses might have been missed during the researches. However, as noted at several points in the narrative that follows, the General Register Office has (since 2016) released the maiden names of mothers for the whole period from September 1837. This has greatly assisted in ensuring that such omissions have not occurred.

[19] Edward Rigg is almost certainly the "E Rigg" who appears in the Baldersby vs Melmerby scorecard of the cricket match played in Baldersby in July 1907 and reported in the *Ripon Chronicle*. Baldersby totalled only 51, but this proved more than sufficient as their opponents were dismissed for 15, the first five batsmen all failing to score. Edward, who would have been 16 at the time, batted at number 11 in the Baldersby innings and was run out for nought.

[20] Including spouses, the greatest age reached by a member of the extended Rigg family has been that of Harriet Elizabeth Wheatley Riggs, who was born in Rutland and died in Richmond (both in Vermont, USA). Aged 104 when she died in 2024, she was the wife of Heath Kenyon Riggs (1918-2011), a great (x2) grandson of George and Jane Rigg.

his wife Mary Jane (née Thorpe, 1871-1943), who married in 1889. This was later surpassed by the 68 year marriage of Douglas Rigg (1905-95) and his wife Winifred Mary (née Hayward, 1908-2005), who married in 1927.

Against this background, I am quite clear about my main feeling about this family. It is that I admire them greatly. They worked in tough, hard jobs, which were, in the main, poorly paid. There were examples of considerable impoverishment. They moved in search of better paid employment opportunities, though the jobs would still have been grim and dirty. They raised their families. Their marriages endured. They went to war, some not to return.

The family's experience reflected the economic and social changes that carried the Victorian and Edwardian working classes forward. The patriarch of the family, George Rigg (1802-65) could not write his name. But, slowly, the family progressed. Amongst George's grandchildren were a stationary engine driver, a family butcher, an outfitter and shopkeeper and two police constables. By the time of the 1911 Census, the dozen or so members of the extended family aged 7-13 would have been in full-time schooling.

Above all, they kept going – from one generation to the next and to the next again. That, in itself, was some feat.

THE LINE OF 16: 2. JANE BOYNTON (1859-1939)

Wharfedale to Swaledale

The second name in my Line of 16 is **JANE BOYNTON** (1859-1939), whom Henry Rigg married in 1880.[21] This was my Dad's grandmother, whom he had remembered visiting in Pickhill when he was a small boy. I purchased Henry and Jane's marriage certificate.

The "marriage [was] solemnized at St James's Church in the Parish of St James Baldersby in the County of York... according to the Rites and Ceremonies of the Established Church". The certificate provided some basic information.

When married	Dec 4th 1880	
Name and surname	Henry Rigg	Jane Boynton
Age	32	22
Condition	Bachelor	Spinster

---

21 In his *A Dictionary of Yorkshire Surnames*, George Redmonds notes that the Boynton surname is derived from the village of the same name near Bridlington on the county's east coast. The modern spelling of the name dates from the 15th Century: records show a Thomas Boynton in York in 1408 and another Thomas Boynton in Acklam in 1461.

Rank or profession	Labourer	
Residence at the time of marriage	Baldersby	Pickhill
Father's name and surname	George Rigg	William Boynton
Rank or profession of father	Labourer	Labourer

The first information that I obtained on Jane Boynton's family was from my father and his brother, Jack. In the Travellers' Rest conversation, dad said that Jane had had an older sister who had married a man called Burrell and either inherited or taken control of their parents' farm, which henceforth became known as Burrell's Farm. I was able to follow this up the following day, when we visited Pickhill. In the hallway of the Nag's Head, in which we had had lunch, there was a detailed Ordnance Survey map. I wrote down the names of the surrounding farms, seven in total, though none was now called Burrell's Farm. (I also noted that the proprietors of the pub were Edward and Raymond Boynton). On the subsequent visit to Uncle Jack, he reported that Burrell's Farm had been one of the largest and wealthiest in the area and that it used to hire out its own machinery to other farms. He had visited the farm when he was about 12. My dad and Jack's testimony struck me as being both precise and obscure, as if there were some unspoken agenda.

At first, Jane Boynton was difficult to find in the 1861 and 1871 Censuses, as the actual records give the surname as Bointon and, in the transcription made available on Ancestry, it was given as "Bornton".[22]

1861: Thirkleby Mill, Thirkleby

					Occupation	Where born
William Bointon	Head	Married	M	38	Agricultural labourer	Yorkshire, Thirkleby
Harriet	Wife	Married	F	36	" wife	Yorkshire, Kilburn
Harriet	Daughter		F	12		Yorkshire, Thirkleby
Mary	Daughter		F	4		"
Jane	Daughter		F	1		"
William	Son		M	1		"

1871: Thirkleby

					Occupation	Where born
William Bointon	Head	Married	M	50	Agricultural labourer	Yorkshire, Thirkleby
Harriet	Wife	Married	F	47	" wife	Yorkshire, Kilburn
Jane	Daughter		F	11	Scholar	Yorkshire, Thirkleby
Elizabeth	Daughter		F	6	Scholar	"

---

22   There was also inconsistent information on the year of Jane Boynton's birth. The Census records for 1861 and 1871 imply 1859 or 1860, whereas the marriage certificate implies 1858 and the International Genealogical Index (IGI) records her christening in April 1860. She was actually born in Thirkleby in the fourth quarter of 1859.

Table 1.2 summarises the family into which Jane Boynton was born. Her parents – William and Harriet – were married in Thirsk in the fourth quarter of 1845 and appeared in the 1851 Census (before Jane was born) already living in Thirkleby (and recorded as Boyinton). (In the various official records, Harriet is spelt with either one or two "t"s; I shall use Harriet throughout).

I could not find William Boynton in the 1841 Census, when he would have been about 18 (but recorded down to the nearest 5 as 15). The Ancestry database lists eight people of that name born in Yorkshire between 1823-27, but none are obvious candidates. However, from at least 1851 (and probably considerably before), William and Harriet lived in Thirkleby for the rest of their lives – William was still employed as an agricultural labourer in the village at the age of 70 in 1891 – in Harriet's case until her death over 50 years later in 1905.

Table 1.2. The parents and siblings of Jane Boynton	
William Boynton 1822-1895 (born in Thirkleby) (son of John Boynton c1801-1878 and Jane Holmes 1798-1860) (died in Thirsk district aged 73)	
married	
Harriet Stirk 1823-1905 (born in Kilburn) (daughter of William Stirk 1796-1878 and Harriet Bentley 1798-1870) (died in Thirsk district aged 82)	Ann Boynton 1846-1924 (tbc) (born in Thirkleby) (died in Middlesbrough aged 78) (tbc) *married* James Bell 1847-1907 (tbc) (born in Thornton-le-Moor) (died in Middlesbrough aged 60) (tbc)
	Harriet Boynton 1849-1919 (born in Thirkleby) (died in Thirsk district aged 70) *married* Philip Rogers 1843-1891 (born in Longford, Ireland) (died in Thirsk district aged 47)

	William Boynton 1852-1937 (born in Thirkleby) (died in Thirsk district aged 84) *married* Emma Bosomworth 1853-1931 (born in Bagby) (died in Thirsk district aged 77)
	Mary Boynton 1856-1890 (born in Thirkleby) (died in Knaresborough aged 34) *married* Edward Yates 1858-1944 (tbc) (born in Harrogate) (died in Bolton, Lancashire, aged 86) (tbc)
	Jane Boynton 1859-1939 **(born in Thirkleby)** **(died in Pickhill aged 80)** *married* **Henry Rigg 1847-1920** **(born in Baldersby)** **(died in Pickhill aged 72)**
	Elizabeth Boynton 1864-1917 (tbc) (born in Thirkleby) (died in Thirsk district aged 54) (tbc) *married* Joseph Briggs 1846-1918 (born in Armthorpe) (died in Thirsk district aged 72)
All places in Yorkshire unless stated	

William Boynton died in 1895 at the age of 73 and was buried in the churchyard of All Saints Church, Great Thirkleby. I visited his grave on a bright, sunny day in March 2022. It is in an isolated spot in a corner of the graveyard, the immediate area covered in bramble, though with the nearby trees and bushes offering from some protection from the elements.

Rather mysteriously, the gravestone is much more substantial that would normally have been expected for an agricultural labourer especially as, at the time of her death 10 years later at the age of about 82, Harriet Boynton was living on her own and "in receipt of parochial relief". The inscription reads:

IN AFFECTIONATE REMEMBRANCE
WILLIAM BOYNTON
OF HIGH THIRKLEBY
WHO DIED MARCH 22ND 1895
AGED 75 YEARS
"THY WILL BE DONE"

A contributor to the public pages of Ancestry, Edward Thornton, has made the plausible suggestion that William Boynton might have been employed by the Frankland family at Thirkleby Hall and that they – with their reputed interest in the welfare of village families – could have funded the memorial.[23] I had an interesting e-mail exchange with Mr Thornton, who informed me that, although Harriet's name does not appear on the gravestone in the space left for it, she was interred in the same grave. The grave itself is noted as being of special interest in the Church burial record notes due to the edged stone pattern chiselled into the stone facing.[24]

I obtained the names and dates of birth of William Boynton's parents from Virginia Burrell, another contributor to the public pages of the Ancestry website. They were John Boy(i)nton (c1801-1878) and Jane Holmes (1798-1860). John was born in Snape, North Yorkshire, and the couple lived in Thirkleby in 1841 with four of their children (though not William). John was still in Thirkleby in 1861, though as a 60 year-old widower and agricultural labourer, Jane having died the previous year at the age of 62. His entry in *England and Wales, National Probate Calendar (Index of Wills and Administrations), 1858-1966* recorded that he left effects of "under £100" on his death in 1878 at the age of 76. I will return to the family of John Boynton in Chapter 8 below.

A separate contribution on Ancestry by Janet McNeilly takes this particular family line in Yorkshire back through Jane Holmes another two generations. Her parents were Thomas Holmes (1776-1842) and Elizabeth Fairweather (1774-1855) and her grandparents William Holmes and Mary Paul (both born in around 1755) and Richard Fairweather (c1730-1816) and Elizabeth Hardwick (1746-1831). The latter couple both died in Hawnby, North Yorkshire, where Thomas and Elizabeth

---

23 Thirkleby Hall was built in 1790 and demolished in 1927. Edward Thornton informed me that Lady Frankland financed the construction of the new church in the 1850s in memory of her deceased husband, Sir Robert Frankland-Russell. By the time of William Boynton's death in 1895, the estate had passed to their daughter Emily, who married Sir William Payne-Gallwey.

24 I learned the significance of the exact location given on William Boynton's gravestone in an article by Carol McLee – "Know Your Parish – Thirkleby" – in the April 2024 edition of the *Cleveland Family History Society Journal*.
   "Thirkleby consists of two villages: Great (High) Thirkleby which was an 'estate village', while Little (Low) Thirkleby consisted of several farms let to tenants. There is no road between the two, but they are connected by a pleasant bridle path crossing the beck by a narrow footbridge".

Fairweather had been recorded as 65 year-olds (to the nearest 5 years) in the 1841 Census.

The details of Harriet Boynton's ancestry, as derived again from the information in the parish registers, has been made available on the Ancestry public pages by yet another contributor, Ron Smith. Her maiden name was Stirk and she was the third of the 11 children of William Stirk (1796-1878), a master shoemaker in Kilburn, and Harriet Bentley (1798-1870). William's parents were Christopher Stirk (1762-1814) and Dinah Sharrow (1769-1855). His grandfather, John Stirk (1731-1792), was born in Ilkley and married Alice Raistrick (1733-1775) in 1752. (After Alice's death at the age of 42, he went on to marry Elizabeth Drake with whom he had 5 more children). Alice had been born in Otley, as had her father and mother and both her grandfathers, Jonas Raistrick (1664-1719) and Christopher Dade (1685-1707).[25]

Not for the first time, we are seeing the strength of a locality in retaining several generations of a family: the Dade/Raistrick/Stirk connections in Otley lasted for at least a century to the birth of William Stirk's father, Christopher, in 1762. It was at this juncture that the break was made, however, as Christopher's wife, Dinah Sharrow, was a native of Thirsk and this was where William was born in 1796. The family locus remained in Yorkshire, but shifted from Wharfedale to Swaledale. As the crow flies, the distance between Otley and Thirsk is about 27 miles, so this would have been a significant relocation by 18th Century standards.

Edward Thornton has included a wonderful photograph of Harriet Boynton (née Stirk) in old age on his Ancestry public page. (It is reproduced in this volume). I would guess that it was taken some time at the end of the 19th/beginning of the 20th Century; as noted, she was about 82 years of age when she died in Thirkleby in 1905. Dressed in a full billowing dress and wearing decorative headgear, Harriet is looking straight at the camera with the hint of a wry smile.[26]

In May 2016, I purchased a CD from the Wharfedale Family History Group of the Memorial Inscriptions in the churchyard and inside the church of All Saints Parish Church in Otley. None of the Dade/Raistrick/Stirk family

---

25   In *A Dictionary of Yorkshire Surnames*, George Redmonds states that the Stirk surname originated in Skipton and established itself initially in Kildwick (both of which are only a few miles from Ilkley). It is likely to have derived from the Yorkshire word "stirk" – a young heifer or bullock – along with similar by-names such as Kidd and Lamb. One Rainery Styrke appears in the records for 1305. Redmonds notes that the surname ramified only modestly and was not common by 1881, when there were 563 entrants in the Censuses, a sizeable proportion of the name-bearers (28 per cent) living close to the point of origin in Skipton, Bradford and Keighley.

26   The image of Harriet Boynton represents that of the earliest-born person – in about 1823 in her case – for whom there is a known photograph of one of the ancestors of the Line of 16. In correspondence, Mr Thornton informed me that the photograph might have belonged to his great grandfather – Edward Yates – who was born in Harrogate in 1857 and a son-in-law of Harriet Boynton.

As noted in Chapter 3, there is a rival claim from Charlotte Browning, who was born in Gloucestershire in 1801 and whose photograph appears on several Ancestry public pages. However, whilst this Charlotte Browning is definitely part of a direct line within the family tree, there is firm evidence that the photograph is of a namesake (born in about 1812) with no family connection.

members identified by Ron Smith were listed, although one Thomas Dade – a contemporary of Jane Boynton's great (x4) grandfather, Christopher Dade (1685-1707) – was given as the church's vicar between 1701 and 1708.[27]

The sisters of Jane Boynton

There were several Boynton/Bointon births in the Thirsk district in the 1840s, 50s and 60s, implying that there was more than one branch of the family resident in the area. From the Census and BMD records, I could discern that Jane had at least 4 sisters and 1 brother – all of whom were born, like her, in Thirkleby.

In the usual way, it is possible to uncover at least some of the dramas of family life. Jane's oldest sister, Ann, married James Bell in 1872 and they had 12 children, of whom one died in infancy. In 1891, the whole family lived together in Thornton-le-Moor – about half-way between Northallerton and Thirsk – where James was employed as a foreman platelayer on the railway. However, 10 years later, James, although in the same occupation, was a boarder in a house in Stockton-on-Tees, his wife remaining with five of their children (including a married daughter) in Thornton-le-Moor. At this time, the status of both Ann and James was given as "married", though it is not clear whether this implied a separation without divorce or whether James was simply working away from home. James died before the next Census in 1911 – probably in Middlesbrough in 1907 – as Ann was a widow living with a son and grandson (also in Middlesbrough) when that record was taken.

Another of Jane's older sisters, Mary, was a single 24 year-old domestic servant at the time of the 1881 Census. She died in Knaresborough in June 1890 shortly after giving birth to her daughter, Florence Yates, who died at 3 days. Mary's age at death was given as 32, although she was actually born in 1856. Her husband was Edward Yates, who was born in Pannel in 1858 and whose occupations were given in successive Censuses as coach builder and maltster.

Some caution was required in tracking Mary's marriage and death. Two girls were born with the name Mary Boynton in 1856 – one in Ripon and one in Thirsk – and 3 marriages took place in Knaresborough and Ripon involving women of that name in the 1870s and 1880s. One of the marriages was in 1877, however, and I know that Mary still had her maiden name in 1881. The other marriage was of a Mary Boynton to Charles Wesley Greaves in 1886. I could

---

27   In the way that will be familiar to many family historians researching a relatively uncommon surname, I took myself on another detour in August 2017, after reading an article in the *Yorkshire Post* entitled "Trench hero remembered a century on". This recounted the exploits of William Boynton Butler who, a hundred years earlier, had been awarded the Victoria Cross for his "most conspicuous bravery" in using his own body as a shield when disposing of a shell in a trench near Lempire in northern France. Mr Butler survived the ordeal and died in 1972 at the age of 77; he is buried in Hunslet Cemetery. I traced his lineage back from his birth in Armley, Leeds, in 1894 through his father and grandfather to his great grandfather, Henry Boynton (1806-1881), all of whom were born in Armley. There did not appear to be a connection to the Boynton families in North Yorkshire.

eliminate her from my enquiries through examination of the 1891 Census, in which the 28 year-old Mary Greaves was stated as having been born in Rievaulx, Yorkshire.

The sad fate of Mary Yates (née Boynton, 1856-1890) in Knaresborough represents the first of the several examples of maternal mortality within the extended family tree that we will come across in this narrative.[28] In England and Wales, the data collected by the Registrar General reveal that the maternal mortality ratio (MMR) had a generally level trend in the period 1850-1900, albeit with considerable irregularity, as the annual figures ranged between 40-65 maternal deaths per 1,000 live births.[29]

For another of Jane's older sisters – Harriet Rogers – it is clear that everyday life could be one of difficulty, if not violence, as evident from a report in the *Richmond and Ripon Chronicle* of 28th August 1869:

> LOCAL POLICE REPORTS: THIRSK MONDAY
>
> Harriet Rogers, wife of Philip Rogers, a labourer, living in Sowerby, was charged with having assaulted and beat Mr Henry Elgie, bailiff, of the County Court of Yorkshire holden at Thirsk on the 18th inst. at Sowerby, he being then and there in the execution of his duty. Mr Rhodes, Thirsk, appeared for Mr Elgie. In conjunction with the assault the complainant stated that the defendant had followed him about the house with a fire poker and an axe and would have struck him with them had not PC Norman of Sowerby prevented her from doing so. Fined 5s and costs. The bench allowed the defendant one week to pay or to be imprisoned in the Northallerton House of Correction for seven days.

At the time of the assault, Harriet Rogers was aged 20 with two children. She had married Philip Rogers, an agricultural labourer from Longford in Ireland, 4 years earlier. Given that the state of the household finances had resulted in the action of a bailiff, it is difficult to see how Harriet would have avoided the term of imprisonment following a failure to pay the 5 shillings fine and costs, unless she was assisted by one of her parents or siblings.

---

28 The other examples – reported in the chapters that follow – are Mary McBride (née King, 1830-1859) in Rutherglen, Miriam Lydia Roberts (née Niblett, 1842-1867) in Swindon, Mary Julia Niblett (née Walton, 1853-1888) in Gloucestershire, Minna Karoline Katharina Fuellekrug (née Borstelmann, 1846-1874) in Hannover, Germany and Frances Whines (née Wye, 1821-1854) and Louisa Mary Whines (née Durrant, 1893-1915), both in London.

29 See Geoffrey Chamberlain, "British maternal mortality in the 19th and early 20th centuries", *Journal of Royal Society of Medicine*, Vol. 99, No. 11, November 2006, pp 559-563.

In January 2024, the National Perinatal Epidemiology Unit at the University of Oxford reported that the UK MMR was 13.4 deaths per 100,000 maternities in the 2020-22 triennium. Excluding those who died due to complications resulting from Covid-19, the rate was 11.5. The latter figure lies between 0.19%-0.26% of those noted by Chamberlain in the second half of the 19th Century.

I do not know whether Harriet Rogers had a subsequent history of chronically violent behaviour, but a subsequent incident – though not involving the wielding of an axe – was reported in the Leeds Mercury of 18th November 1902:

> ASSAULTED THE SCHOOLMASTER
> Harriet Rogers of Sowerby was at Thirsk yesterday summoned by Alfred Busfield, headmaster of the National School for Sowerby, for assault.
> It appeared that the defendant's son had attended the complainant's school and in October she considered that the defendant [*sic, should be complainant*] had unduly punished him for bad behaviour. On the 4th inst. the defendant met the complainant in the village of Sowerby and after making use of bad language took the complainant by the coat collar.
> The Chairman said a technical assault had been committed and the defendant was ordered to pay the costs and be bound over.

Philip and Harriet Rogers had 9 children. However, Albert – the defendant's son in this case – was born in June 1893, some 18 months after Philip had died at the age of 47. He would have been aged 9 when the assault charge was made against Harriet.

Albert Rogers was a Rifleman in the 1st Battalion of the Rifle Brigade when he died of his wounds in France in April 1917 at the age of 23. His name appears as Rodgers in the Army records, but the Harriet and Sowerby references there confirm that it is him. (He is listed correctly, along with 58 other residents of the village who were killed in the First World War and 18 in the Second World War, on the Sowerby war memorial). Harriet Rogers died in 1919 at the age of 70.

Burrell's Farm: a minor mystery solved

It was through researching another of my great grandmother Jane Boynton's siblings – her brother William Boynton (1852-1937) – that I was able to take a slight detour and examine the family story flagged up by my father and uncle Jack, noted earlier, of a Boynton-owned farm that had been re-named Burrell's Farm. Most family historians will recognise the task that I set myself here: the desire to tie up a nagging – if not trivial – loose end.

The connection of names was straightforward. I was able to make the Burrell connection through William's wife – the gloriously named Emma Bosomworth (1853-1931) – a native of Bagby in Yorkshire. It was one of their daughters, Emma Boynton (1895-1963), who married Guy Burrell (1895-1974) in the Thirsk district in 1930.

The younger Emma Boynton was Jane Boynton's niece, therefore, not her sister (as my father had stated in the Traveller's Rest conversation). The question was: how had the farm come into her possession? In the Censuses from 1881, William Boynton's occupation had been, successively, road labourer, agricultural labourer (twice) and grazier – i.e. with no indication of farm ownership in the pre-First World War period.

I decided to look into the family background of Emma Bosomworth, who was recorded as a 7 year-old living in Bagby in the 1861 Census. At that time, she was in the household of her 67 year-old grandfather, the widowed Richard Bosomworth, along with his unmarried son and daughter (John and Ann), another granddaughter (Jane, aged 2) and two servants. The residence was named as Split Farthing Hall and Richard Bosomworth's occupation was "farmer of 70 acres employing 1 man".

Richard Bosomworth died in the Thirsk district in 1864 at the age of 71. In the 1871 Census, John Bosomworth (aged 35) was the head of the household and a farmer, still living at Split Farthing Hall with his sister Ann listed as a 44 year-old housekeeper and Emma given as his 17 year-old niece. This implied that Emma was the illegitimate daughter of Ann, something that I duly confirmed in the online *England, Select Births and Christenings*, 1538-1975 index. Later the same year, Ann married Thomas Metcalf(e) and they later appeared in the 1881 Census as a "cordwainer" and "cordwainer's wife", aged 71 and 52 respectively, together with Ann's 7 year-old grandson (another Richard Bosomworth). Thomas and Ann's residence in Thirkleby was in the cottage next to that occupied by William and Harriet Boynton and one of their daughters, the ill-fated Mary. Nearby lived the younger William Boynton and his wife Emma (née Bosomworth).

The only minor detail I have about John Bosomworth is that, according to the *Richmond and Ripon Chronicle* of 23rd November 1867, he and another man were each fined 2s 6d at the Thirsk Petty Sessions "being suspected of having been on land in search of game" and "being in possession of a hare at Kirkby Knowle". His occupation was given as farmer. I am fairly sure that John Bosomworth died in the Easingwold district in 1878 at the age of 42 and that he did not have a family.

The most likely scenario is that, at that point, the farm passed across to his sister Ann although, as noted, neither her occupation nor that of her husband Thomas Metcalfe indicated this in the 1881 Census. In the 1891 Census, Thomas's occupation was given as "retired shoemaker", although he was also described as a "yeoman" (with effects left in his will of £70 18s 3d in his 1894 entry in the *National Probate Calendar (Index of Wills and Administrations) for England and Wales, 1858-1966*). Less likely, though possible, is that John Bosomworth bequeathed the farm directly to his niece, Emma (the wife of William Boynton), who would have been in her mid-20s at that time.

In the former scenario, the line of inheritance for the farm would appear to have been to Emma Bosomworth (by then Emma Boynton) on the death of her mother, Ann, in the Thirsk district in 1917 at the age of 90. (The effects left in her will were £99 19s 4d, with "Emma Boynton (wife of William Boynton)" being named as the administrator. As noted, Thomas Metcalfe had died in 1894 at the age of 84). The difficulty with this scenario is that William Boynton is already being described as a "farmer" by the time of Ann Metcalfe's death, notably in 1914 and again in 1916 in the respective marriage records of his sons, William Edward Boynton and Christopher Boynton. He is then similarly listed at Norman Castle, Pickhill, in the 1921 Census of England and Wales.

The farm would been inherited in the next generation by the younger Emma Boynton on the death of either her mother Emma in 1931 or – more likely – her father William in 1937. By that stage, she would have been Emma Burrell, having married Guy Burrell in 1930.

The full explanation of this particular family story remains elusive, therefore, not least in terms of the stewardship of the farm after the death of John Bosomworth in 1878. Nonetheless, at least some of the steps of the pathway – from Bosomworth (possibly to Metcalfe) to Boynton to Burrell – can be identified. There had indeed been a Boynton-owned farm that – presumably at a later stage – was re-named (or, at least, commonly known as) Burrell's Farm. (The 1939 Register records that Guy Burrell was the farmer of Town Farm).

One intriguing question that does remain, however, is why William and/ or Emma Boynton should have bequeathed the farm to Emma Burrell, who had been the youngest of their 9 children. Assuming that Emma did inherit the farm on her father's death in 1937 (when she would have been aged 42), she would have had two older brothers still alive at that stage (two others having died). The answer is almost certainly that Guy Burrell was well established as a farmer: it had been the occupation given in his marriage record (in 1930). By contrast, both Emma Burrell's two older brothers – the 49 year-old James Boynton and the 47 year-old William Edward Boynton – had moved away from Thirkleby. In the 1939 Register, they are recorded in Jarrow and Sedgefield, respectively, and might not have wished for the significant changes in location and lifestyle that taking on the farm would have represented.[30]

Finally – as if there are not enough queries about the Boynton family and Burrell's Farm – there is a separate issue to consider. This concerns the additional figure of Richard Bosomworth, the 7 year-old grandson living with Ann Metcalfe and her husband Thomas in 1881. He was the illegitimate son of Emma

---

30 William Edward Boynton lived to the age of 99 and died in the Durham West district in 1990. This is the greatest age of any member of the extended Boynton family of North Yorkshire presented in this narrative. He was a first cousin of my grandfather, John Rigg. Christopher Boynton – another of the sons of William and Emma Boynton (and, likewise, also a first cousin of John Rigg) – was killed in France in 1918 at the age of 24. He was a Private in the 1st/6th Battalion of the Northumberland Fusiliers and is commemorated on the Pozieres Memorial in Picardie, France.

Bosomworth, born in 1873 when Emma was about 20. The entry for his birth in the Thirkleby parish register notes that Emma was a "singlewoman", late of Bagby.

Richard Bosomworth appeared in each of the following Censuses up to and including 1921. In 1911, he was a 37 year-old farm labourer, still living with his grandmother, the 83 year-old Ann. Ten years later, after the death of Ann in 1917, he was resident in the Thirkleby household of William and Emma Boynton – together with their daughter, Emma – when his status was given as a single man, aged 47, who was employed by William as a "cowman" at the Norman Castle in Pickhill.

There is a disconcerting aspect to Richard Bosomworth's entry in the 1921 Census, which would have been completed by William Boynton as the head of the household. Richard's relationship to William was given as "servant". This overlooked the fact that William's wife, Emma Boynton (née Bosomworth), was Richard's mother and, accordingly, that William was his stepfather. One suspects that, in this single entry, there are family tensions which will now never be explored.[31] I have been unable to find any death record for Richard Bosomworth.

It is the familiar story. A minor mystery is (partly) resolved through the examination of the official records, only for other tantalising questions to be raised.

Working life in North Yorkshire

By far the most common occupation of many members of both the Rigg and Boynton families in the Censuses from 1841 onwards and into the second half of the 19th Century was "agricultural labourer". This definition covered a wide variety of jobs – shepherd, hedger, cowman, ditcher, and so on – many of which were highly seasonal and it is likely that the agricultural employment was supplemented by work in cottage industries. Unlike farm servants, who tended to have fixed-term contracts, agricultural labourers were employed on an annual basis and basic education was not considered necessary.[32]

Indeed, for George and Jane Rigg (and also Mary Rigg) this must also have been their line of work earlier in the century – prior to the 1841 Census – in George's case from being a young boy at the time of Waterloo in 1815. Accordingly, both families would inevitably have been buffeted by the wide sweep of changes affecting the agricultural sector during the first three quarters of the 19th Century – the completion of the enclosure movement in the period to 1815, the rapid rise in wheat prices during the Napoleonic War, the post-war slump in prices, the

---

31 I have not uncovered the father of Richard Bosomworth. One possibility is obviously William Boynton, whom Emma Bosomworth married in 1877, four years after Richard's birth. The 1921 Census – when they are all in the same household – would have been an opportunity to record this, had it been the case, but this did not happen.

32 See Ian Waller, *My Ancestor was an Agricultural Labourer,* Society of Genealogists, 2020.

introduction (1815) and repeal (1846) of the Corn Laws, the rising prosperity of the sector from the 1850s, and so on.[33]

Of course, given that they were agricultural labourers – i.e. part of the rural proletariat working for wages – rather than farmers or landlords, the living standards of the Rigg and Boynton families would have been dependent on how those wages changed relative to changes in the price level, especially the price of food. Here, it is relevant to note that economic historians have contrasted the relative "stickiness" of money wage rates for workers in the industrial sectors in the first half of the 19th Century (with changes in the demand for labour being reflected in employment levels) with the greater flexibility of money wages in agriculture. For example, according to Peter Matthias:

> "The real wage index of London artisans thus becomes virtually a mirror image, the inverted curve, of the cost-of-living index… [whereas] the sharp declines in agricultural wage rates in bad times underline the conclusion that agriculture was the great reservoir of marginal producers, having much less resistance to adverse movements in the labour market than wages in the expanding industrial areas".[34]

FC Harrison has noted that, in mid 19th Century Yorkshire, several types of agricultural organisation existed. In parts of the North Riding, something of the tradition of an independent peasantry probably survived to this time:

> "… but the custom of annual hirings in Stokesley, Thirsk, Pickering, York and the larger villages of the North Riding is alone sufficient evidence of the extent to which a large class of landless agricultural labourers existed in the district".[35]

Harrison is unsentimental about the life of an agricultural labourer in the early years of Victorian Britain. "A tied cottage was often only a damp hovel", whilst the traditional diet was "stodgy, monotonous and nutritionally deficient… for almost everyone in rural England the basic diet was bread, potatoes and tea, with bacon two or three times a week".[36]

---

33 The agricultural sector remained the largest source of male employment in Britain in 1851: over 20 per cent of the population aged 10 and over were employed as farmers, graziers, labourers or servants. 11 per cent of females aged over 10 were in domestic service (excluding farm service). (Peter Matthias, *The First Industrial Nation: An Economic History of Britain, 1700-1914*, 1969, Table V, p260).

34 ibid, pp 220-221.

35 *Early Victorian Britain, 1832-51*, 1979, Fontana, page 61.

36 ibid, pp 62, 63, 90-91.

As previously noted, the range of working-class occupations in North Yorkshire widened during the course of the 19th Century as the structure of the economy continued its move away from being tied to the land. Hence, at the end of the century – in the family folklore supplied by my father – Henry Rigg had worked on the railway and "been responsible for the track between Northallerton and Thirsk", leading a team of gangers. This prompted me to pay some attention as to what his exact occupation had been.

The early purchase of Henry's marriage certificate – on which his age was incorrectly given as 32, rather than 33, as he had become the day before – showed that Henry's occupation in December 1880 was "labourer", just like his father and father-in-law. Later, on his youngest daughter Jane's birth certificate – in 1893 when he was 46 – he was still a "railway labourer". In the Censuses of 1891, 1901 and 1911 (the last of these at the age of 63), he was, respectively, "a railway platelayer's labourer", a "ganger railway platelayer" and a "ganger platelayer". In 1906, at the time of the marriage of his daughter, Margaret, in the parish church at Pickhill to the 25 year-old Daniel Reuben Driver, an "electrical car conductor", Henry's occupation was simply "platelayer". Finally, in 1911, he was again recorded as a "platelayer" in the Northallerton 2 branch of the National Union of Railwaymen.[37]

It is evident that Henry's job advancement on the railways was in line with what my father had understood, as his occupation of "ganger" – as recorded in the 1901 and 1911 Censuses – was the term given to the foreman of a group of labourers. To follow up the general context, I consulted *Was Your Grandfather a Railwayman?* by Tom Richards – published by the Federation of Family History Societies and purchased in 1994 – which is a directory of railway archive sources for family historians.

Henry would have worked on the North Eastern Railway (NER), which was formed in 1863 when the Leeds Northern Railway (LNR) merged with three other railways. (The LNR had begun as the Leeds and Thirsk Railway in 1849). The NER later became part of the London and North Eastern Railway (LNER) on the latter's formation in 1923. Richards directed me to the (then) Public Record Office in Kew, where I looked at three sets of records: the Darlington District staff histories for 1856-1954, NER employees listed by grade and rates of pay for 1857-1931 and the NER pensions records for 1884-1924. I could not find Henry Rigg in any of the volumes.

However, there is a reference to Henry in a report in the *York Herald* of 6th October 1877 of the "Petty Sessions for the Division of Hallikeld", which had been held in Wath:

---

37 The *Britain, Trade Union Membership Registers* database was accessed via Findmypast. It mainly covers railway workers and carpenters and joiners.

"Joseph Marwood of Melmerby, labourer, and George Fairbairn of Melmerby, labourer, were charged with having on the 13th August last trespassed on the North Eastern Railway. The defendants admitted the offence and Marwood was further charged with an assault on Henry Rigg, a servant in the employ of the company, and Fairbairn was further charged with aiding and abetting Marwood. Mr Campbell, chief superintendent of police, appeared in support of the information. Witnesses were called in support of the information. The defendants denied the assault.

Marwood was fined 10s for trespassing on the railway and 10s costs, in default 14 days; and for the assault he was sent to the House of Correction for one month with hard labour. Fairbairn was fined 10s for trespassing on the railway and 11s 6d costs, and 10s for aiding and abetting and 10s 6d costs, in default one month".

It is clear that employment on the North Eastern Railways was not without its risks, not least from assault by members of the public. There is a clear parallel between the incident concerning Henry Rigg in 1877 and that involving his nephews Stephen and Henry Rigg thirteen years later (see footnote 16 above). However, there was a notable difference in the respective penalties imposed on Joseph Marwood and John Allen: a fine plus a month's hard labour, compared with only a fine.

As with Henry Rigg's detailed employment records, I have not been successful (to date) in finding out more about his activities as a Methodist lay breacher, about which both my father and uncle Jack had been so confident in our earliest family history conversations. In November 2022, I spent a long day at the North Yorkshire County Record Office in Northallerton examining the late 19th Century and early 20th Century Circuit records. These included monthly editions of the Wesleyan Methodist Church Record (between 1905-1913) for Thirsk, the "horse hire account book" (1872-1916) for Northallerton and the Centenary Celebrations Committee minute book (1894-95) for Ripon as well as the local preachers' meeting minute books for each of the three Circuits for various years between 1863 and 1914.

Although there were no entries for Henry, I did find some for George Rigg of Baldersby. His name is to be found on the Wesleyan Methodist Historic Roll (1899-1901), which presented the results of an initiative at the Methodist Conference of 1898 to raise £1 million by inviting members to contribute one guinea or more to church funds. The Roll lists over 1,000 such local members of the Thirsk circuit. Separately, Mr G Rigg is also listed in the Thirsk Circuit Church Record for July 1905 as a subscriber to the presentation fund to Mrs W Bibby (which paid for a Queen Anne Silver Teapot) in recognition of her role as "a worker in the Sinderby church district... [where she] had accorded cheerful and impartial hospitality to ministers and local preachers for nearly 40 years; she knew the joy of serving God and his servant". Finally, Mr Rigg of the Catton and Baldersby district is recorded as having subscribed one shilling in the Harvest Festival Accounts reported in the Church Records of December 1905 and June 1908.

I cannot be certain to which George Rigg these references apply as there are two possibilities, both of whom were Henry's nephews: his brother George's son (George Rigg 1865-1948) or his brother William's oldest son (George Pattison Rigg, 1855-1919). If pushed, I would speculate that it was the former.

Vignettes of life in Durham and North Yorkshire

The online databases provide some fascinating indicators of the changing social conditions in Durham and North Yorkshire during the second half of the 19th Century. One example is that of the *National School Admission Registers and Log-Books, 1870-1914*, which I accessed via Findmypast (FMP).

The 1870 Education Act, introduced by WE Forster, was the first piece of legislation to deal specifically with the provision of education in Britain. It established a system of "school boards" – locally elected bodies which drew their funding from the local rates – to build and manage schools in areas where they were needed. This had followed the campaign of the National Education League for free, compulsory and non-religious education for all children. A further Education Act in 1880 finally made school attendance compulsory between the ages of 5 and 10.

The FMP database is not complete, but it does give some interesting examples of the legislation in effect. Hence, on the roll of the South Bank Wesleyan School in Middlesbrough in 1899 were William, Alfred and Stephen, grandsons of William Rigg, Henry's oldest brother. The records show that Alfred left school in 1902 (aged 14) to go to work, whilst the 11 year-old Stephen left in 1903 because of "continued illness". Alfred is also recorded in the school's register in September 1901 as being "…away with scarlet fever. This is the second case". (Alfred duly survived this bout of potentially serious illness, though he died in 1936 at the age of 48, whilst the apparently chronically ill Stephen lived to the age of 71, dying in 1964. However, William – John William Rigg – had a much shorter life, as reported in Chapter 8 below).

Likewise, three of William's granddaughters – cousins of the three boys – appear on the roll of the Tilery Road (Girls) School in Stockton in 1893: Margaret Ann (aged 11), Nellie (Mary Ellen aged 9) and Emily (aged 6). One of their younger sisters, Jessie, was on the same school's roll as a 7 year-old in 1898; she was aged 14 when she left school in 1905.

It was the education (or temporary lack of it) of another young boy – Harold Rigg, the youngest son of George Pattison Rigg and another grandson of William – that featured in a newspaper report in the *Ripon Chronicle* in October 1912. Robert Stubbs, a farmer, pleaded guilty to employing Harold on his farm during the school term.

> "James Crisp, school attendance officer, stated that the boy Rigg was 10 years of age and should have been attending school on 16th September. On that day, witness visited Baldersby school and found that the boy was absent. He proceeded to Baldersby and found that the boy was employed by Mr Stubbs and was driving a horse attached to a cart laden with grain".

It is clear from the report that Stubbs, who pleaded guilty, had had previous warnings and, moreover, that he was unrepentant about his actions. The Bench imposed a fine of 1s and costs of 9s 6d. For me, the most striking aspect of this report is that 10 year-old Harold was sufficiently skilled as to be given responsibility for driving the laden horse and cart. Harold Rigg later became a signalman on the London and North East Railway (as recorded in the 1939 Register) and died in Durham in 1961 at the age of 60.

The local newspapers thus also provide some nice vignettes of life in the North Yorkshire of the late 19th and early 20th Centuries. Another example is given in the *York Herald* of 1st August 1893, which carried the report of the recently held Wath (North Riding) Petty Sessions:

> "George Rigg of Baldersby, labourer, was ordered to pay costs £5 for allowing a pony to stray on the highway at Baldersby on July 13th".

There are two minor mysteries associated with this story. The first – as with the entries for George Rigg of Baldersby in the Methodist records – is the issue of which George it is referring to; the same candidates as noted above are in the frame. The second is what the finding of the Petty Sessions actually was. The report of the same meeting in the *Ripon Chronicle* on 3rd August states that the case against George Rigg of Baldersby was dismissed.

The name of George Rigg also appeared in the same newspaper on 28th August 1899:

> "James W Holborn of Baldersby is being sued by Baldersby Tanning Company for leaving the firm without notice. George Rigg, foreman to the firm, stated that it had always been usual for men to have one week's notice before leaving and notice was also expected from the men. The Bench ordered the defendant to pay £1 including costs".

Henry's aforementioned nephew, George, had been a tanner's labourer in the 1891 Census, although he was an agricultural labourer in 1901. However, it is more likely that the foreman was the 44 year-old George Pattison Rigg, who was a "labourer in a tanyard" in 1897 (on his son's marriage certificate), although he too was listed as only a labourer in 1901. This is because the report of this case in the *Ripon Chronicle* refers to the alleged use of some unfortunate language by the foreman's son and we know from the Census records that William – George Pattison Rigg's oldest son – was also a tannery worker in 1891 and 1901.

During my visit to the NYCRO in November 2022, I discovered that "George Rigg of the township of Baldersby, labourer" had fallen foul of the law 10 years earlier. The Quarter Sessions records for 1883 report his summary conviction

> "… in contravention of the Local Authority Regulation of the North Riding of the County of York in relation to the 'England and Wales Movement into District (Foot and Mouth Disease) Order of 1883'.
>   …[and] unlawfully removing certain animals to wit four pigs from the district of the Local Authority of the West Riding of the County of York into the said North Riding of the County of York, he being the said George Rigg, he being the owner of the said animals, contrary to the statute in such cases made and provided".

The fine was one pound with a further 8 shillings and 6 pence to be paid to the informant, Joseph Ellerby. The terms for immediate non-payment were potentially severe:

> "And it is ordered that the said sums to be paid forthwith.
>   And if default is made in payment according to this adjudication and order, it is ordered that the sum due thereunder be devised by distress and sale of the defendant's goods.
>   And in default of insufficient distress, it is adjudged that the defendant be imprisoned in Her Majesty's prison in Northallerton for the space of one calendar month unless the said sums and all costs and charges of the said distress of his commitment and conveyance to said prison be sooner paid".

The respective ages of the older George Rigg (Henry's brother), the younger George Rigg (George's son) and George Pattison Rigg (Henry's nephew) in 1883 – the year of the conviction at the Quarter Sessions – were 51, 18 and 28 and, as all three had been resident in Baldersby at the time of the 1881 Census, it is again not clear to whom the summary conviction applied. (The record also does not show whether the fine was paid or whether "distress" and/or imprisonment incurred). It is perhaps relevant, however, that although (as we have seen above) the occupation of George Pattison Rigg had been tanner's labourer in 1891, he had been a farm labourer in 1881, just two years before the conviction.

On a happier note, there was a reference to Henry Rigg himself in the *Darlington and Stockton Times, Ripon and Richmond Chronicle* of 20th May 1911 in connection with one of his village's major events of the pre-First World War years. An article entitled "Festival Difficulties in Pickhill Parish" reported that:

> "Most of the villages of the Thirsk district are now busy with their arrangements for celebrating the Coronation [of George V]. The proceedings are on the whole characterised by a great deal of sameness, but those of the Pickhill parish have been enlivened by some friction as to the selection of the place for holding the proposed festivities".

It would appear that after the village of Sinderby had initially been selected at the focal point for the celebration, on the basis of its general convenience as a central location within the Pickhill district, there had been a meeting in Pickhill village itself at which this arrangement had been voted down; it was argued that the schools in Pickhill would be available in the event of inclement weather. Meanwhile, another village – Ainderby Quernhow – had already decided on its own separate festivities.

It was also reported that the Pickhill programme would comprise "tea, sports and a dance" and that Mr JW Greenist JP had been appointed chairman of the Men's Committee, which contained 20 other named people, including "H Rigg". In addition, a Women's Committee of 25 would be under the "chairmanship" [the quotes are the newspaper's] of Mrs Greenist.

The coronation of the new king was obviously regarded as an occasion to be accorded the fullest festival treatment. It would require almost 50 committee members to ensure that things were organised properly.

The family of Henry and Jane Rigg

The family of Henry and Jane Rigg is summarised in Table 1.3. As before, the principal sources were the successive Censuses of England and Wales and the Registrations of Births, Marriages and Deaths in England and Wales.[38]

Henry and Jane had eight children between 1882 and 1895. One of these – Annie Rigg – died at the age of one month in 1890 from "weakness from premature birth"; the daughter born the following year was also christened Annie

---

38 I suspect that, for many family historians, the excitement at being able to access the 1911 Census of England and Wales was tempered by the frustration caused by the prevalence of transcription errors. I set out my views in a letter to the *Cleveland Family History Society Journal*, which was published in January 2010. It is reproduced in Annex A2 below.

(Elizabeth). My grandfather, John Rigg, was the fourth oldest, the ill-fated Robert Rigg was the third and Jane (or Ginny) Rigg, remembered by the old man in Pickhill, was the seventh. All the children were born in Baldersby, although only Annie was to die there.

I was able to put some faces to the names thanks to the photograph album shown to me by my uncle Jack. Many of the photographs were in excellent condition. Perhaps the most interesting was the group photograph taken at the wedding of Annie Elizabeth Rigg to Robert Edwin (Bob) Easton. To Annie's left is the diminutive Ginny and to her left is seated Henry, resplendent in a smart three-piece suit, holding a bowler hat in his lap and with a white carnation in his button hole. He has penetrative eyes, white hair and a short, white beard. Behind him, with her left hand on his shoulder, is his wife Jane, wearing a dark hat, rimless glasses and a frilly collar to a dark blouse, on which there is a large brooch. Next to Jane is a younger woman, who looks very handsome in her lighter coloured clothes and large dark hat: could this have been the other sister, Mary? On the far left of the group stands the young Thompson Rigg, also in a three-piece suit and with a carnation in his breast pocket. Initially, I thought that, because of Thompson's age and the absence of John and Robert from the photograph, the wedding might have taken place in the First World War years; I later found out that it had been in the summer of 1914.

I shall return in a later chapter to the other photographs of John Rigg and his brother, Robert. In the meantime, I will note that, although few in number, the photographs were a treasure trove. I could see what my great grandfather and his family looked like, albeit on a special occasion, thanks to my dad and Jack's knowledge of the family's composition and some sensible guesswork. The photographs were unlabelled, however, and I realised that, on this occasion, I had been fortunate to avoid the common frustration amongst family historians of being confronted by valuable photographic evidence that could not be fully interpreted.

Table 1.3. The family of Henry and Jane Rigg		
Henry Rigg 1847-1920 (born in Baldersby) (died in Pickhill aged 72)		
married		

Jane Boynton 1859-1939 **(born in Thirkleby)** **(died in Pickhill aged 80)**	Margaret Rigg 1882-1950 (born in Baldersby) (died in Leeds aged 69) *married* Daniel Rueben Driver 1880-1971 (born in Melbourne, Leicestershire) (died in Carluke, Scotland, aged 90)
	Mary Rigg 1883-1964 (born in Baldersby) (died in Sowerby aged 80)
	Robert Rigg 1885-1918 (born in Baldersby) (killed in France aged 33)
	John Rigg 1887-1959 **(born in Baldersby)** **(died in Leeds aged 72)** *married* **Catherine Kerr McBride 1893-1969** **(born in Glasgow)** **(died in Leeds aged 76)**
	Annie Rigg 1890-1890 (born in Baldersby) (died in Baldersby aged 1 month)
	Annie Elizabeth Rigg 1891-1974 (born in Baldersby) (died in Whitby aged 82) *married* Robert Edwin Easton 1885-1955 (born in Grosmont) (died in Whitby aged 70)
	Jane (Ginny) Rigg 1893-1963 (born in Baldersby) (died in York aged 69)

	Thompson Rigg 1895-1975 (born in Baldersby) (died in Claro district aged 79) *married* Violet Emily Adamson 1899-1947 (born in Stokesley) (died in Claro district aged 48)
All places in Yorkshire unless stated	

CHAPTER TWO

SCOTLAND AND LANCASHIRE

THE LINE OF 16: 3. PETER McBRIDE (1861-1949)

The starting point: Catherine Kerr McBride in Glasgow and Leeds

My researches into the McBride family began in earnest in 2007 with the purchase of credits – initially at £6 for 30 credits – on the official www.scotlandspeople.gov.uk website. The starting point was Catherine Kerr McBride – my Dad's mother – whom I knew was born in 1893. In the 1901 Census of Scotland, she is found in her father's household at 185 Butterbiggins Road in the parish of Govan (and the burgh of Gorbals) in Glasgow.

The building was a tenement: five other families are listed on the same page. The McBride home had two rooms with windows. Within the dwelling, the other heads of household were a draper and clothier's traveller, potato salesman, butcher and shopkeeper, railway clerk and commercial clerk: all respectable, working class occupations. (Later, when I accessed the Valuation Rolls for 1895, I noted that the annual rent had been £14 for each of the households, bar one, in the property).

In 1901, the McBride household comprised:

Peter McBride	Head	Married	39	Engineer's Patternmaker (Foreman)
Agnes	Wife	Married	39	
Ethel J	Daughter		9	Scholar
Catherine K	Daughter		8	Scholar
William A	Son		2	
Lily R	Daughter		1	

PETER McBRIDE (1861-1949) – the father of Catherine Kerr McBride – is the third name in my Line of 16. He was born in Rutherglen, Lanarkshire, his wife Agnes in England and all their children (up to the 1901 Census) in Glasgow. Some of the names were familiar. I can remember meeting my "aunties" Ethel and Lily – they were actually my great aunts, of course – when I was young. In particular,

I can recall visiting Ethel and her husband John Bain in Blackpool with my father in the mid-1960s.

At the time of the previous Census, in 1891, Peter and Agnes McBride were living at 3 Cathcart Road in Govanhill.[1] The dwelling had two rooms with windows. At least five other families shared the same building as they had the same address on this page of the Census return.

This was a period of significant change within the burgh. In *Old Govanhill*, published in 1994, Eric Eunson reported that the population of Govanhill had increased from 9,636 in 1881 to 14,339 in 1891. This growth had significant political and administrative implications:

> "Glasgow was surrounded by the expanding burghs and resented the independence of so many ratepayers who lay outwith the jurisdiction and coffers of George Square. Many bitter and protracted battles were fought with the Corporation, who claimed to have improved parks, gas and water facilities in the suburbs. Finally, in 1891, Govanhill and Crosshill were annexed by the city, along with the burghs of Maryhill, Springburn, Hillhead, Mount Florida and East Pollokshields".

Eunson is also revealing about the living conditions in Govanhill during this period:

> "When the sandstone tenements in Glasgow were erected, between 1870 and 1910, they were probably the best contemporary working class housing anywhere in Britain… Sadly, although the regulations governing building were stringent, rules about maintenance were not. Absentee landlords and their factors took a short-term view of their property and were only concerned with profit from rent".

I was able to track Peter McBride's ancestry back through the generations through a combination of Census of Scotland records, the centralised records of BMDs in Scotland (which date from 1855) and the details of births/baptisms and banns/marriages available from the parish records. First of all, however, I will jump forward ten years to report the results from the 1911 Census for England and Wales. By then, his family was living at 24 Oakley Grove, Hunslet, Leeds.[2]

---

1 Two streets with the name of Cathcart Road feature in the narrative of Peter McBride. The other is the one in Rutherglen, where he was born in 1861.

2 Oakley Grove still stands as a row of Victorian brick terraced houses running into the main Dewsbury Road in Hunslet. I took a stroll down the street in August 2019. Number 24 was bounded by a sturdy wooden fence, which carried a prominent warning to "beware of the dog".

Peter McBride	Head	Married	49	Engineers pattern maker
Agnes C	Wife	Married	49	
Catherine K	Daughter	Single	18	Confectionery
William A	Son	Single	12	School
Lily R	Daughter	Single	11	School
John S	Son	Single	8	School
Mary B	Daughter	Single	7	School
Dorothy L	Daughter	Single	4	
Charles O	Son	Single	2	

Peter and Agnes McBride's family is summarised in Table 2.3 (below). The 1911 Census records and the places of birth of their children inform us about their migration pattern: as we have seen, Peter and Agnes were resident in Cathcart Road in Govanhill in the 1891 Census of Scotland, after which the family moved to the nearby Butterbiggins Road until sometime between the births of John Savage McBride in 1902 and Mary Bennett McBride in 1904. Thereafter, they moved to Prestwich in Manchester until 1908 and then to Leeds.

The original 1911 Census record is intriguing. It also had an entry for Ethel J McBride, aged 19 and single, which was crossed out. I assume that this was because Peter – as the head of household completing the return – realised that she was not living in the household at the time. Alternatively, the Census enumerator made the correction afterwards.

In addition to Ethel, entries for 3 other children were made and crossed out. These were for Joseph aged 1, Agnes R aged 1½ and Osborne aged 1. All were born in "Lanarkshire, Glasgow". I assumed that these children had died at these ages in Scotland as the Census page included numbers for "children born alive" (11), "children all living" (8) and "children who have died" (3).

Again, my initial reaction was that Peter McBride had inadvertently filled in the Census form incorrectly. However, on reflection, I was not so sure. For one thing, Peter was a 49 year-old engineer's pattern-maker, who had had a Scottish education (in Rutherglen). He would have been able to read and understand a form. Of course, we can all make mistakes in dealing with paperwork, but Peter's background does cast some doubt on whether this was a genuine slip-up.

My suspicion is that, when (incorrectly) filling out the 1911 Census return in Leeds, Peter McBride made a deliberate error. He did not wish his deceased infant children to be forgotten, even though the first of their deaths had occurred over 20 years earlier. This was a way of registering – if only for himself – that their short lives had taken place. Moreover, it transpired that Peter listed them on the Census return in their exact places within the order of births of the 11 children in the family. It was if, a hundred years on, he was telling me where to find them. My response to my great grandfather was: Peter, thank you, I have found them, and they are not forgotten.³

Later, I purchased copies of the death certificates. Joseph Runcorn McBride died at the age of "5 minutes" at 10.35am on 21ˢᵗ July 1890 of "debility from birth"; he was a "premature birth, stillborn". Agnes Runcorn McBride died aged 2 years on 21ˢᵗ February 1897 of "diphtheria, 1½ days". Osborne McBride died aged 4 months on 2ⁿᵈ December 1901, the cause of death being given as "convulsion, 24 hours".⁴ Joseph died at 3 Cathcart Road and Agnes and Osborne both died at 185 Butterbiggins Road.

By the time of the 1921 Census, Peter and Agnes McBride were living at 54 Moor Crescent in south Leeds with six of their adult and teenage children, the only absentee from those present in the household 10 years earlier being Catherine Kerr McBride, who had married and left home. This Census was the first to give the names and addresses of employers and Peter is duly recorded as being a patternmaker with J Buckton & Sons, machine tool makers, of Meadow Lane, Leeds.⁵ Of his sons, whilst the 23 year-old William Alexander McBride was employed at the same firm in "engineering erecting", this was not the occupation of the 19 year-old John Savage McBride. The latter was working as a pawnbroker for Mr FW Rushforth in Whitehall Road, Leeds.

Peter and Agnes's three daughters were also in employment: the 21 year-old Lily as a shop assistant and the teenagers, Mary and Dorothy, in tailoring. The individual wages would not have been high, but this was nonetheless a household in which 6 of the 8 members were making formal contributions to the family budget. (Agnes McBride herself was on "house duties" and the 13 year-old Charles Osborne McBride was still at school). Unlike in 1911, when completing the Census form, Peter McBride did not refer to the previously deceased children.

The family into which Peter McBride was born in 1861 is shown in Table 2.1. His father was also Peter McBride, a joiner (journeyman), and his mother was Catherine McBride, whose maiden name was Kerr. Peter McBride was present at the birth of his son and seems to have signed the register himself, unlike for the

---

3   I described my interpretation of this entry in the 1911 Census in an article for the *Cleveland Family History Society Journal* in April 2016: "The 1911 Census – and a Century-old Message?"

4   In *A Century of Change: Trends in UK Statistics Since 1900* (House of Commons Research Paper 99/111, December 1999), Joe Hicks and Grahame Allen note that, whilst often given as the cause of death, "convulsions" were a symptom of some other cause, probably meningitis, encephalitis or brain tumour.

5   In the first three decades of the 20ᵗʰ Century, Joshua Buckton and Company Limited was a prominent firm at the heart of manufacturing in south Leeds, having been established in 1842. The website of the Science Museum Group (www.sciencemuseumgroup.org.uk) records that: "By 1914 they had 500 employees with specialities in heavy ordnance and turbine lathes, armour plate and turbine planning machines, universal testing machines of largest capacity and the Buckton testing machine". The machine tool business transferred to Reddish on Merseyside in 1928.

two other births on the page, for which the respective fathers' marks were given by crosses. The registrar was Archibald Gilchrist.

On Peter and Catherine's marriage certificate, the bridegroom was given as a 30 year-old joiner and a widower. (I learned later that his first wife, Mary King, had died at the age of 28, nine days after giving birth to their second child, Mary King McBride, in 1859). Peter and Catherine McBride's marriage was also short-lived as she died at the age of 36 in October 1868 at the family home in Chapel Street, Rutherglen. The cause of death on the death certificate is hard to read – it might be cancer – though it was 3 years certified. Peter's third marriage – to Janet Park in 1871 – lasted for the quarter-century to his death in Rutherglen at the age of 65 in 1896.

There are many examples in all family stories of the fragility of the circumstances that have accompanied the growth of the family tree. This is one such example. The place of Peter McBride in the Line of 16 was dependent on his birth during the relatively short period – no more than five years – in which his parents were married and had their children before the illness and death of his mother (Catherine McBride, née Kerr). She was commemorated in the name of his second daughter (my grandmother) Catherine Kerr McBride, who was born in 1893, and my uncle John Kerr Rigg, born in 1916. Earlier, the name had also been passed on to Peter and Catherine McBride's second son – Alexander Kerr McBride – who was born in Rutherglen in 1864.[6]

Table 2.1. The parents, siblings and step-siblings of Peter McBride	
Peter McBride 1829-1896 (born in Glasgow) (son of Peter McBride 1797-1864 and Williamina Walker 1800/01-1885) (died in Rutherglen, Scotland aged 66)	

---

6   I have been unable to locate Alexander Kerr McBride in the official records after 1881, when he was a listed as a 16 year-old house joiner in Rutherglen. This is a considerable frustration as, if he did later have children of his own, they would have been first cousins of my grandmother, Catherine Kerr McBride.
   I did wonder about the Alexander McBride, who died in Leeds in 1899 at the age of 34, given that he was of the same age and, also, that his brother, Peter McBride, had later migrated to that city. His death certificate recorded that he had been a market porter who had died of phthisis. However, the informant of the death was Alexander's sister – M McBride – who was resident at 23 Paradis, Greengate, Salford. In the 1901 Census, the 29 year-old Margaret McBride, who had been born in Salford, was living in that street (at number 1) with an older brother and sister, Alfred and Agnes, the latter being the head of the household. This was clearly a different family to that in which Peter and Alexander McBride had been born in Rutherglen. The search for Alexander Kerr McBride continues.

	married	
	1. Mary King 1830-1859 (born in Glasgow) (daughter of John King and Mary Halliday) (died in Rutherglen aged 28)	William Walker McBride 1857-1929 (born in Rutherglen) (died in West Derby, Liverpool, aged 72) married Marina McDonald 1859-1919 (born in Seaforth, Lancashire) (died in West Derby aged 60)
		Mary King McBride 1859-1926 (born in Rutherglen) (died in Rutherglen aged 67) married Alan Watt 1856-1921 (born in East Kilbride) (died in Rutherglen aged 65)
	married	
	2. Catherine Kerr 1831-1868 (born in Largybeg, Arran) (daughter of Alexander Kerr 1801-1862 and Janet Shaw 1810-1899) (died in Rutherglen aged 36)	Peter McBride 1861-1949 (born in Rutherglen) (died in Leeds aged 87) married Agnes Charlotte Runcorn 1862-1942 (born in Warrington) (died in Leeds aged 80)
		Alexander Kerr McBride 1864-? (born in Rutherglen)
	married	
	3. Janet Park 1835-1909 (born in Rutherglen) (daughter of John Park and Christian Wallace) (died in Rutherglen aged 74)	

Port Glasgow

Between 2007 and 2011, I spent many hours tracking back the ancestry of Peter McBride from the Line of 16 through the earlier generations by following the lines of descent to his parents Peter McBride and Catherine Kerr. The main sources were the Old Parochial Registers available either on www.scotlandspeople.gov.uk or in hard copy in the Mitchell Library in Glasgow, supplemented by material in the International Genealogical Index (IGI). It made for a fascinating story.

Peter's McBride's parents were yet another Peter McBride and Williamina Walker, who married in Port Glasgow in 1820. This Peter was born in Port Glasgow in 1797, later becoming a joiner and carpenter in the Gorbals before dying of "debility" in 1864, reportedly at the age of 65.[7] Williamina also died of "debility from age": in her case in 1885 at the age of 84. In turn, Peter's father was Neil McBride, born in Port Glasgow in 1771, whose occupation was given as a "King's Searcher (Customs)" or a "Weigher (Customs)" and who married Janet Lindsay in 1797. Janet had been born in Port Glasgow in 1770, her parents being William Lindsay, a cooper, and Elizabeth Crum (or Crumb). The IGI database reveals that Peter had at least five siblings, born between 1799 and 1813.

The available records also allowed me to go back another generation from Neil McBride to Peter McBride and his wife, Jane Tarbet, who married in 1764. However, it is at this point that the evidence presents some ambiguities and uncertainties. I purchased a copy of Neil's birth record in the Old Parochial Register of Port Glasgow for 18th November 1770. It comprised one line and read: "Peter McBride, weaver in Port Glasgow, and Janet Tarbet, a son, b[or]n 18th b[aptise]d 6 Dec, Neil". (This was new information on Peter McBride's occupation as well as the names of Neil's parents, of course). However, the microfilm version of the parish records in the Mitchell Library gave two entries – 18th November 1770 and 18th August 1771 – on both occasions with the parents named as Peter McBride and Janet Tarbet and with identical reference numbers. This duplication was confirmed in the IGI records.

I did wonder whether the first date was for the birth and the second for a christening, but the record is clearly of births and the gap between the two events would have been far longer than the norm between birth and christening, which was usually only a few days. An alternative explanation is that the first child died in infancy and that the subsequent record represents a second boy called Neil. The dates are exactly nine months apart, however, so this also looks rather doubtful.

On the other hand, there do appear to be examples of other names being repeated amongst the children of Peter McBride and Janet Tarbet in Port Glasgow. The Old Parochial Register records the births of William in October 1769 and Christian in June 1773, whilst the IGI's index lists Susanna (November 1765), Christian (April 1775), Mary (April 1777), Susannah (May 1779) and Agnes (July 1781). This suggests that for three of the names – including Neil – there might have been second children named after earlier children who had died.

---

7   The repetition of Peter as the given McBride name throughout the family tree is no accident, of course. It followed the Scottish tradition of allocating Christian names, in which, amongst other things, the first-born son was given the name of the father. I also benefited from the excellence of the Scottish parish records and the information that they held that was not provided in the corresponding records in England: for example, on death certificates the names of the deceased's parents (including the maiden name of the mother) and the occupation of the deceased's father.

In general, therefore, for the McBride line, I was able to track a direct link in Port Glasgow back at least as far as the mid-18th Century with some confidence. These family researches were complicated, however, by the influx of McBrides from Ireland into the west of Scotland in the first half of the 19th Century – sometimes with variations in spelling such as McBryde and McBreid – especially following the Irish Famine of the 1840s. I liked the occupation given to Mary McBryde, a 78 year-old born in Ireland and living in Port Glasgow at the time of the 1851 Census, as a "ropemaker's mother".

The reference to Neil McBride (assumed to have been born in 1771) as a "King's Searcher (Customs)" comes from the death certificate of his son Peter McBride in 1865. A "searcher" was a customsman or "rummager" who searched for contraband and the King (from 1760 until 1820, when Neil would have been 50) was George III. These were turbulent times. Britain was at war with Revolutionary and then Napoleonic France at various times between 1793 and 1815, and there were threats of invasion, particularly in 1798 and 1803. There were Royal Navy mutinies in 1797 and the Irish Rebellion took place in 1798. (The historian Tom Devine has reported that 13 of the 20 British regiments that put down the Rebellion were comprised of Scottish troops and that "several were known to have carried out their orders with uninhibited ferocity").[8]

In February 2007, I spent an anticlimactic 3 hours in West Register House in Edinburgh attempting to follow this up. I knew from the IGI that Neil McBride had raised a family in Port Glasgow between at least 1797 and 1813. However, a search of the files of the salaries of "Officers of His Majesty's Customs in North Britain" between 1783 and 1822 produced no mention of him in Port Glasgow, Glasgow or Greenock. I concluded that there might be several possible explanations for this: Neil McBride was not a searcher and his occupation had been made up on Peter's death certificate (unlikely); he only became a searcher after 1823, when the Scottish customs office was merged into that for the UK as a whole (unlikely, as he would have been aged 52); he was in another department, perhaps Excise (possible, though there are virtually no pre-19th Century records for Excise Officers at the National Archives of Scotland, as these were lost in a fire). Such are the dead-ends of family history research, although I did learn that, in Port Glasgow, a searcher's annual salary was £15 in both October 1791 and October 1809.[9]

It is a common theme within this overall narrative that, in examining the various branches of the extended family tree, I have been naturally drawn to look more closely at the places they inhabited.

---

8   T.M. Devine, *The Scottish Nation, 1700-2000*, Allen Lane, The Penguin Press, 1999, page 210.

9   One of the searchers earning £15 per annum in 1791 was a William Lindsay, which was the name of the father of Neil McBride's wife, Janet. This might have been the same person although, as noted earlier, Janet Lindsay's father had been a cooper at the time of her birth in 1770.

Hence, having bought and read the excellent *Old Port Glasgow* (2003) by Joy Montieth, I went there one Sunday afternoon in early 2007 to get a sense of the town: Fore Street (the original frontage), the municipal buildings (1815, now a library), Newark Castle, the reconstruction in Shore Street of the *Comet* (the world's first commercially viable steamship, built in 1812), Coronation Park (set out in the 1930s), Customshouse Lane and the West Quay, where the customs house was built in 1754 (and where Neil McBride would have been based) and demolished in 1965. On the Port Glasgow war memorial, I noticed that Private Thos R McL McBride was listed as one of the 31 First World War casualties from the Highland Light Infantry and I made a mental note to investigate whether there was a family connection (see footnote 13 below).

I later consulted a much older source about Port Glasgow. The period of Neil McBride's early adulthood in the town – the 1790s, when he was in his 20s – is contemporaneous with the great *Statistical Account of Scotland*, which was undertaken under the direction of Sir John Sinclair and published as 21 volumes between 1791 and 1799. The entry for "New Port-Glasgow" was compiled by the Reverend Mr John Forrest, who provided a vivid description of the parish: its history, topography, climate, wildlife, population, industry, trade, schools, church and governance. Although Port Glasgow had been adversely affected by the decline in trade during the American War of Independence (1776-83), there had been some recovery in the long distance trade with the Baltic, Americas and West Indies, as well as in the coastal trade bringing grain and other provisions from Dumfriesshire and Ireland. (The longer-term prospects for Port Glasgow as a port were less favourable as, by the 1840s, the Clyde had been developed to make it navigable for ocean-going vehicles into the centre of the city. Port Glasgow's economic base shifted to shipbuilding and related industries).

Reverend Forrest had a generally upbeat perspective on his parish; noting, for example, that there were 14 days more rain in the year than in the city of Glasgow, he stated that:

> "New Port Glasgow is a very healthy place.... and it has frequently been remarked that, the wetter the weather is, the healthier the inhabitants are".

Reflecting his calling, he was also complimentary about the character of his parishioners as "the better sort of people here are sober, industrious and charitable" although he did also note that:

> "[I]t is almost incredible what quantities of spiritous liquors, and especially the worst species of whisky, are consumed in this town, and it is painful to add, but truth requires it, that not a little of it is consumed by women".

A month after my visit to Port Glasgow, the *Herald* of 8 March 2007 contained a feature article on the town, following the news that the last remaining commercial shipyard on the Lower Clyde – Ferguson – had announced that 99 of its remaining 126 workers would shortly be made redundant.[10] The report summarised the town's history as a trading port and then as a shipbuilding centre:

> "Port Glasgow ....was the portal through which the wealth of the New World would flow into Glasgow.... Two million pounds of sugar [for example] were imported in 1715; by 1771, that had soared to 47 million.... This was once a boom town, responsible for about one-quarter of the total tonnage of ships launched on the Clyde".

The *Herald*'s article made dismal reading:

> "....a community blighted by drugs, gang violence, some of the worst poverty in Scotland and dire health"

Govan and Rutherglen

The migration of the McBride family through the generations is a recurrent theme in this branch of the family history. After Neil McBride (born in Port Glasgow in 1771) and Peter McBride (born in Port Glasgow in 1797), it is the dates of birth of the children of Peter McBride and Williamina Walker that inform us when the family migrated from Port Glasgow to Glasgow. Janet McBride – an older sister of Peter McBride (my grandmother's grandfather) – was born in the former in September 1820. The next birth of which I have a record – of Mary McBride in 1825 or 1826 – was in the Gorbals. This change in location reflected the powerful economic forces drawing population into Glasgow at this time, as well as the relative decline of Port Glasgow as a port. With these dates in mind, I was interested in a description of the establishment of the Southern Necropolis in the *Southern Necropolis Newsletter* of December 1988, which I came across in the Mitchell Library. It gave a graphic account of the "village" into which Peter McBride and his family had moved.

> "The Southern Necropolis was established for two main reasons. First, the old burial ground, first established in 1770 to meet the needs of the one-time village of Gorbals, was, by the late 1830s, in an appalling state; the unfortunates "on the Parish" were buried in long trenches, left barely

---

10   The Ferguson shipyard was founded as a partnership by the four Ferguson brothers in 1903. The company underwent many changes in ownership over the years. The Scottish Government took over ownership of the yards – renamed Ferguson Marine (Port Glasgow) Ltd – in December 2019.

boarded over until the trenches were full; it had been used for mass pit burials in the cholera outbreak of 1832; the bought lairs were full, and not much space was left.

Secondly, the city had its great Necropolis by the cathedral, and the new Sighthill cemeteries – both places of great dignity. Gorbals, now joined by Laurieston and Hutchestown, and full of merchants and professional people, and prospering mill owners and engineers, aspired to similar dignity. But with a difference. The dignity was to be shared by all.

Public meetings were held in November 1839 and February 1840; the burial records date from July 1840".[11]

Five days after Christmas of 1857, one of Neil McBride's sons, William, died in the Govan Poor House at the age of 54. He was single and the cause of death, certified by the surgeon HA Liddell, was "paralysed, 2 years". The informant of the death was Williamina McBride, his sister-in-law, who marked her name with a cross. William was buried in the Gorbals Burying Centre.

The purpose of tracking William's death had been to get another clue on the occupation of his father, Neil. On William's death certificate, this is given as "weigher (customs)", which is not the same as – and sounds less important than – the "King's Searcher" that is given on Peter McBride's death certificate in 1864 (on which Peter's son is the informant). An additional possible explanation for Neil's absence from the Port Glasgow customs house staff records, therefore, is that he was not a permanent member of the staff, but a casual employee. I was somewhat distracted from all this, however, by the consideration of William's desperate circumstances, dying alone and infirm in the Poor House.

Prior to entering the Govan Poor House, the unfortunate William McBride had lived at 43 Dale Street in Govan. This was the same street in which Peter and Williamina McBride had lived with their children in 1841 and 1851 (at number 42) and where they had both died (at number 52, in 1864 and 1885, respectively). A nephew of Peter and Williamina (and William) – Thomas Chalmers McBride – had lived with his first wife, Marion, and their children at number 51 in 1871.

The upper part of the road is now called Tradeston Street and runs away from the River Clyde on the south side of the new Tradeston Bridge. (The current Dale Street in Bridgeton has no connection with the McBride family as far as I know). In 1894-95, according to the old street map of Glasgow in the Mitchell Library, this area was just to the west of Bridge Street station, which was then a significant terminus for railway lines from the south of the city.

---

11 The full version of the Newsletter's article is available on the website of the South Glasgow Heritage Educational Trust (SGHET).

I took a walk down Tradeston Street on a cold, bright morning in December 2012. As far as I could see, nothing remained from the 19th Century and the street contained mainly car parking or routine (or decrepit) warehousing. There were one or two fine brick buildings in the nearby streets, though my guess was that these dated from the turn of the 20th Century, as they appeared similar in style to the front of the nearby Ibrox Stadium, which is dated 1902. Still, it was good to inhabit the same space – if not the actual street – as that populated by several members of the McBride family between the 1840s and 1880s.

Peter McBride (born in Glasgow in 1829) settled with his family in Rutherglen, where Peter McBride (of the Line of 16) was born in 1861. I have already noted that (this last) Peter McBride's mother, Catherine, died in her home in Chapel Street, Rutherglen, in 1868 at the age of 36. That was at number 15, which remained the residence of his father – also Peter – and his four children in 1871. (In 1861, Peter and Catherine had lived with their two young children – William and Mary – at 29 Glasgow Road, sharing the address with four other families). The older Peter and his third wife, Janet McBride (née Park), lived at number 31 in 1881 and at number 23 in 1891, where the widow Janet remained in 1901, living with two of her nieces.

A book of old photographs of Rutherglen – *Old Rutherglen* by Rhona Wilson, published in 1996 – contains a distant view to a house in Chapel Street, the caption noting plaintively that "much of the old Rutherglen disappeared… to accommodate the new dual carriageway". However, I noted from an 1894-95 map of Glasgow and its surrounding area in the Mitchell Library that the shape of Chapel Street looked to have been very similar to that part of the road that remains today, with a junction to Glasgow Road.

I visited Rutherglen in June 2016. A short walk from the railway station took me past the front of Rutherglen Town Hall (constructed in 1862, two years after Peter and Catherine had married in the town) and the much older Rutherglen Old Parish Church. A plaque near the two stone shelters by the latter's entrance stated that they dated from 1761 and were where the church's elders had collected the offerings from the congregation; Rhona Wilson states that the gates were "either for protecting elders from rain or to house guards keeping a watch for body-snatchers, depending on whom you read".

Chapel Street was in the shape of an arc – its ends indeed truncated by bigger urban roads – on the inner corner of which stood a convenience store and a couple of other small shops. On the downslope was a collection of squat four-storey council house blocks culminating in a low-level public house, the walls of which were sprayed in anti-royalist graffiti.

Around the corner, on the top side of the arc and opposite a grassy open space, stood the Rutherglen West and Wardlaw Hill Parish Church with its recently refurbished stone entrance and an immaculately maintained garden in front of what I took to be the rectory. The church itself was closed, but one of the adjacent halls was open and I wandered in just as a community meeting of about a dozen elderly folk was breaking up. One of the ladies told me that the original church dated from 1849 and, sure enough, the Wikipedia entry states that: "[T]he Munro Church opened in 1850 and that is the church that stands today (undergoing six different name changes)".

In the McBride family records, the earliest references to Rutherglen are the birth of Mary King McBride and the death of her mother Mary McBride in Glasgow Road in 1859 followed by the birth of Peter McBride in Cathcart Road in 1861. Thereafter, as noted, the references are to the nearby Chapel Street, dating from the death of Catherine McBride in 1868 through to the residence of Janet McBride – the widow of Peter – in 1901. The church on the upper side of Chapel Street would have been very familiar to the family.

Later, in the Mitchell Library in Glasgow, I came across a booklet listing the Monumental Inscriptions for the "list of gravestones in Chapel Street Graveyard which were removed during levelling operations commenced on 17th April 1963 and stored at New Monkland Cemetery". It was something of a relief that no McBrides were listed.

In the usual way, the compilation of the family tree throws light on all manner of personal dramas and sadness. For example, the birth of Mary King McBride was registered by her father, Peter, on 22nd February 1859, the day after her mother, Mary McBride (née King) had died. The mother was marked as deceased on the birth certificate. It is difficult to imagine what emotions Peter must have been feeling on that day.

Migration to England

As noted, the Line of 16's Peter McBride migrated to England with his wife and family sometime between 1904 and 1908. By then, Peter would have been in his early 40s. However, the road from Scotland to England had been taken much earlier by his half-brother – William Walker McBride, the son of Peter McBride and Mary King, born in 1857 – who married Marina McDonald in the Presbyterian Church, West Derby, Liverpool in 1883 when he was 26. By 1891, William and Marina were living in Canterbury Street, Everton, with their children Peter and Mary Grace.

Like his father, William was a joiner and this was also the trade taken up by his son, Peter, who was a joiner's apprentice in 1901 and a joiner in 1911. William and Marina stayed on Merseyside, all four of their surviving children (out of seven to 1911) being born in West Derby. (One of the deceased children was the first daughter to be named Mary Grace McBride, who died before her first birthday in 1888). Peter McBride, having married Agnes Lloyd (1892-1941) in West Derby in 1919, later moved to South Yorkshire; in the 1939 Register, he is recorded as a 54-year-old joiner/carpenter in Bentley-with-Arksey, near Doncaster.

William McBride died in West Derby in 1929 at the age of 72 and his wife Marina in 1919 officially aged 60 (though I think she was 62, as she had been 4 years old in the 1871 Census). Their youngest son – also William Walker McBride – was a 16 year-old office boy in 1911 and lived to the age of 80, dying in Liverpool in 1975 one day after his wife of nearly 42 years, Lucilla Bower McBride (née Malley).[12] In turn, their son – the next William Walker McBride, born in 1930 – inherited the full name of his great (x3) grandfather, William Walker, whose daughter Williamina Walker had married Peter McBride in 1820.

The passing on of names within this branch of the McBride family was clearly of some significance. William and Marina McBride's youngest daughter was Marina McDonald McBride who was a 19 year-old dressmaker in 1911, later marrying Allen Watt in 1919. She lived to a fine old age, dying in Corby, Northamptonshire, in 1983 at the age of 92. Her older sister – the second child to be called Mary Grace McBride – was named after Marina McBride's mother, Grace Myers, who had been the head of the household in Seaforth at the time of the 1871 Census and mother of the 4 year-old Marina McDonald (sic); John McDonald was listed as a lodger. Mary Grace McBride was recorded as a 21 year-old blouse machinist in Liverpool in 1911; she died in the same city in 1936 at the age of 45.

Other entries on the extended McBride family tree required some detective work to resolve some minor mysteries. For example, an apparently routine entry in the 1911 Census of Scotland for the family of Thomas Chalmers McBride – an uncle of the Line of 16's Peter McBride – and his wife Marion revealed names of their children resident in the household that were consistent with the corresponding entries that I had recorded in each Census since 1871. However, the return stated that the marriage had produced 8 children, of whom 7 were still living; my calculation was 11. Moreover, it was stated that Thomas and Marion had been married for 33 years; I thought this should have been 45 or 46.

The answer – obvious in retrospect – was that there had been two Marions. Thomas McBride had had 3 children with his first wife, Marion Norton, who had died of tuberculosis in 1876 at the age of 28. He had married his second

---

12 The *British Army World War I Service Records, 1914-1920* – made available by The National Archives (TNA) and also accessible on Ancestry – provide some poignant details of the experiences of this generation. In the case of William Walker McBride, he joined the Army Service Corps as a motor driver in September 1915 and served in France until his demobilisation in August 1919. He was disciplined twice – "Absent from 7.15am parade. Found asleep in bed at 7.18am" (December 1916) and "neglect of duty i.e. did not see that the radiator on his lorry was properly emptied thereby causing it to be damaged by frost" (March 1917) – for which he was fined 4 days and 21 days pay.

The descriptive details enable the family history researcher to derive a mental picture of their subject. William Walker McBride was 5' 5" and 115 lbs and had a scar below his right eye. We will return to the First World War records at other places in this narrative.

wife, Marion McLellan, two years later and they had indeed had 8 children. It took a while before the penny dropped but, when it did, there was a sense of quiet satisfaction. Most family historians will recognise the feeling engendered by such modest triumphs.[13]

The fact that Thomas McBride had 11 children during the course of his two marriages means, of course, that he produced this considerable number of first half-cousins to the Line of 16's Peter McBride and that there was a correspondingly large cohort of half- second cousins to my grandmother, Catherine McBride.[14] (This is in contrast to the Rigg side of the family, as the Line of 16's Henry Rigg's father – George Rigg – was an only child). It is clear that there is a rich swathe in the history of this part of the extended family to explore here, though I will touch on it only briefly.

Hence, for example, there is the intriguing story of Ann Fraser McBride – Thomas's first child through his first marriage (to Marion Norton) – who migrated from London to Brisbane, Australia, on the *Perthshire* in 1910, when she and her husband (Robert Mackie, 1863-1926) were in their 40s and their 11 children were aged between 2 and 19. At least two of their sons – Thomas and Peter – enlisted for service abroad in the Australian Imperial Force during the First World War. Ann Mackie died in Brisbane in 1964 at the age of 97.

Likewise, Thomas McBride's first child with his second wife (Marion McLellan) was Peter McLellan McBride who married Rachel Margaret Ferguson and migrated to Wellington in New Zealand. He died at the age of 78 and is buried in the Karori Cemetery in that city. Peter and Rachel's only son – Thomas Chalmers Glen McBride RNZNVR – died in the Far East on *HMS Indefatigable* on 10th August 1945 i.e. just five days before VJ Day.

If I were to summarise the detailed family history of the McBrides, I would inevitably draw one inescapable conclusion. They kept going – notwithstanding the formidable challenges that they faced with early deaths and/or the harshness of their living conditions. They learned their trades and raised their families and moved to where the jobs were available. The occupations of the male members

---

13 The maiden name of Thomas McBride's second wife – McLellan – did cause me to wonder if there was any connection with the name that I had seen on the war memorial in Port Glasgow: Thos R McL McBride. I realised that this was a long shot – Thomas's family was centred on Govan in Glasgow – and this was duly confirmed. The war memorial commemorates Thomas Rennie McLeod McBride, who was the son of Peter McBride (born in Ayrshire in 1862) and Mary Park Rennie (born in Greenock in 1870). He was 19 years old when he was killed on 15th July 1916 i.e. two weeks after the start of the Battle of the Somme. In addition to the war memorial in Port Glasgow, he is commemorated on the huge Thiepval Memorial to the Missing of the Somme in Picardy, France.

14 One of my grandmother's second cousins was – after his father and grandfather – also called Thomas Chalmers McBride. He was killed in action at the age of 19 in March 1918, having been a Lance Bombardier in the Royal Garrison Artillery, and is buried in the Huts Cemetery near Ypres in western Flanders. At first, I could not find his entry in the Commonwealth War Graves Commission database of war dead, as it is filed under MacBride. The database lists his parents as Thomas Chalmers MacBride and Margaret Bigg MacBride. (It should be Begg). His grandfather died in Govan in 1919 and, therefore, would still have been alive at the time of the death of the youngest Thomas Chalmers McBride.

within the family tree included joiner, turner, engineer and carpenter, whilst the women found work as domestic servants and in the cotton factories. As with the various generations of the Rigg family as agricultural labourers in North Yorkshire, there is something admirable about the determination and fortitude that they – and tens of thousands like them – displayed, as Glasgow developed through the 19th Century and into modern times.

The Arran connection

The parents of Catherine Kerr – the mother of Peter McBride (of the Line of 16) – were Alexander Kerr and Janet Kerr (née Shaw), who married in the parish of Kilbride on the island of Arran in 1831.[15] In the 1841 Census of Scotland, Catherine, at 9 years of age, was the oldest of 4 daughters, the family living in South Kiscadale in the same parish. Alex's (sic) occupation was given as "fisher". This was also his occupation 10 years later, by which time there were also two boys – Finlay and John – although Catherine had left the Kerr household. Catherine's youngest sister – Mary – was born in 1855, which meant that Alexander and Janet had seven children over a period of 21 years.

The Kerr surname was (and is) extremely common on Arran. For example, the 1841 Census shows that, in the village of Newton Lochranza at the north of the island, there were literally dozens of people with this name. The name also features heavily in the Monumental Inscription records, as given in *Pre-1855 Gravestone Inscriptions in Bute and Arran*, edited by Alison Mitchell and published by the Scottish Genealogical Society (SGS) in 1987, that I consulted in the Mitchell Library in Glasgow. In the graveyard at Lochranza, in the Kilmory parish, there are references to Kerr (or a spelling variation such as Ker or Kear) in no fewer than 48 of the 144 plots. In the cemetery at Sannox in the north east – where Alexander Kerr was born – the name occurs 9 times in the 60 graves that are recorded.

The males in Alexander Kerr's family made their living at sea. Alexander was also variously described as a "fisherman" (on his death certificate in 1862), a "late merchant seaman" (on Catherine's death certificate in 1868) and as a "herring fisherman" (on his widow Janet's death certificate in 1899). Both Alexander's father and his older son – both called Finlay – have "sailor" as their stated occupation in official records.

Alexander Kerr's death certificate records that he died at Whiting Bay in the parish of Kilbride in December 1862 at the age of 61. The cause of death column was left empty, which initially prompted the thought that he might have drowned. On reflection, however, I realised that the Whiting Bay reference was to

---

15   At this time, Arran was divided into two parishes on a near north-south basis. In the west, the Kilmory parish dated from 1701, having incorporated Lochranza in 1732. In the east was the parish of Kilbride. The village of South Kiscadale is located at Whiting Bay on the lower part of the eastern shore.

the general area containing the village of South Kiscadale, where the family lived, rather than simply to the bay itself. (As an illustration of the valuable additional information provided on the death certificates in Scotland, it was this document that confirmed that Alexander's parents were given as Finlay Kerr and Grace Kerr – maiden name McKillop – both Christian names later being passed on to Alexander and Janet's children).

I have not yet been able to close up the loose end of Alexander Kerr's death. In May 2011, I wrote to the Isle of Arran Heritage Museum to ask if the museum held any local newspaper records for that time, which might give an obituary or – pursuing the drowning thought – a description of an accident in Whiting Bay. I also mentioned that the only female McKillop with a first name beginning with "G" born in Bute between 1750 and 1785 seemed to have been Grizel McKillop in October 1766.

A prompt response came from the museum's Grace Small, who reported that there did not seem to have been anything about a possible accident to Alexander in the local paper. However, she did mention – with some pride, I detected – that the Gaelic name for Grace is Grizel. I was confident, therefore, that Grizel McKillop, born in the Kilmory, Shiskine and Lochranza parish to John McKillop and Mary Brown, was indeed the mother of Alexander Kerr.[16] This was later confirmed when I purchased the birth record of Alexander Ker (sic), which comprised one line in the Old Parochial Register of the same parish on 30th July 1801.[17] As noted, he was born in the village of South Sannox on the north-east coast of the island.[18]

As discussed below, my wife Angela and I have made two visits to Arran – in 2019 and 2024 – and it was following the second of these that I obtained some fascinating insights into the languages spoken on the island from Charles Currie of the Arran Heritage Museum. He informed me that, at the beginning of the 19th Century, most Arran people spoke exclusively Gaelic, especially those of Alexander's social level. It was about this time that English began to be taught in schools and, as the century progressed and Brodick, Lamlash and Whiting Bay grew as tourist destinations, the locals would speak more English. (Whiting

---

16 The Findmypast records reveal that John McKillop and Mary Brown were married in Kilbride parish in September 1761. The www.scotlandspeople.gov.uk database of Old Parish Registers does not include any other children in the period to 1780.

17 The importance to family historians of the inclusion of the names of the deceased's parents on death certificates in Scotland cannot be overestimated. In the case of Alexander Kerr, this enabled me to distinguish him from the two other births recorded for the same name on the same page in the Old Parochial Register of Kilmory, Shiskine and Lochranza which covered the period from December 1800 to September 1801.

18 The McKillop surname occurs 11 times in the 60 graves for which the Monumental Inscriptions have been recorded in the cemetery at Sannox. However, there is no reference to either John McKillop or Mary Brown. Similarly, although the Shaw surname is also not uncommon in the Monumental Inscriptions recorded in the SGS's *Pre-1855 Gravestone Inscriptions in Bute and Arran*, I could not find any references to the specific members of the family noted here: John, Lillias (or Lily, née Kennedy), Archibald or Catherine (née McBride).

Bay did not get a proper pier until 1898 so their tourists would come ashore in small boats).

This discussion of the languages spoken in Alexander Kerr's family is particularly relevant because of the migration of Alexander's daughter, Catherine Kerr, from Arran to the Scottish mainland as a teenager in the 1840s in order to improve her employment prospects. I cannot be absolutely certain of her location in 1851, but the most likely place is Stewarton in Ayrshire, where the 19 year-old of that name (born in Buteshire) was a house servant in the household of John Nairn and his mother. (By the time of her marriage to the older Peter McBride in 1860, Catherine had moved a further 16 miles inland to Rutherglen).

I did wonder if Catherine's Gaelic would have been any use to her in Ayrshire or whether, in addition to having to leave the comfort and familiarity of her home, she would have had the additional challenge of doing so whilst also having to become familiar with Lowland Scots. Charles Currie informed me that Catherine would have learned English in its purest sense before going to Ayrshire, but would have had to pick up Lallans (Lowlands) English to survive in Ayrshire. Lallans Scots was very like English by then, but was based on the Scots that Robert Burns spoke in the 18th century. (Catherine would have had little chance of using Gaelic in Ayrshire as few people spoke it. Galloway had a Gaelic tradition, but not Ayrshire).

The parents of Alexander Kerr's wife – Janet Shaw – were Archibald Shaw, a farmer, and Catherine Shaw (née McBride), who had married in the Kilbride parish in July 1809. Janet was the oldest of the seven children born between 1810 and 1824, one of whom died in infancy.

Archibald Shaw was born in Kilbride in about 1782 and one of the two sons of John Shaw and Lillias Kennedy, who married in the same location in 1779. The other son was Neil Shaw (c1786-1876), who married Catherine Ferguson (c1800-1869) in Kilbride parish in December 1824. They had six children, of whom the first two died in infancy.

The information in www.scotlandspeople.gov.uk reveals that both Archibald and Catherine Shaw lived to good ages: Archibald died in 1865 at the age of 84 and Catherine in 1862 at the age of 79. The latter record gives Catherine's mother's maiden name as Hunter. I will have to purchase Catherine's death certificate to get further details about her parents, however, as there were four McBride/Hunter marriages in the Kilbride parish between 1760 and Catherine's birth in 1782.

It was to be many years after I first made contact with Grace Small at the Arran Heritage Museum – in August 2019 – that Angela and I visited Arran for the first time. It was a very enjoyable and productive visit. Margaret Wright, a genealogist at the Museum, drew my attention to the Monumental Inscription of a gravestone in the Kilbride Cemetery in Lamlash.

ERECTED
BY
FINLAY KERR
MARINER
IN MEMORY OF HIS
FATHER ALEXANDER KERR
WHO DIED 2ND DEC 1862
AGED 61 YEARS
AND HIS SISTER
MARY KERR
WHO DIED 6TH FEBY 1884 AGED
29 YEARS
ALSO HIS BROTHER JOHN KERR
WHO DIED 25TH AUGT 1886
AGED 38 YEARS

IN MEMORY OF
CHARLES FINLAY
DIED 21ST JULY 1937

Angela and I visited the graveyard, which is at a pleasant location on a hill overlooking Whiting Bay. The family story that my father had relayed to me – that there is a McBride buried at Whiting Bay – turned out to be not quite accurate, but not far from the truth: there is a Kerr buried in Lamlash. In fact there are several Kerrs commemorated, because the references on the gravestone are to not only Alexander (who died in 1862), but also to two of his children: Mary (who died in 1884) and John (who died in 1886).

Later, Angela and I walked up the hill behind the excellent Coffee Pot café at Whiting Bay through the small settlement of South Kiscadale. This was where Alexander and Janet Kerr are recorded as living with their family in the Censuses of 1841 and 1851 and where Janet lived until her death in 1899 at the age of 88. One or two of the cottages were recognisable as having the same basic shape as perhaps they had had in the 19th Century. Margaret Wright said that the collections – or *clachan* – of crofts remained in place in the southern part of Arran until the First World War. (The fate of crofting in the north was a different story: see below).

Given that Alexander Kerr was a herring fisherman, I was particularly interested in one of the display boards at the Heritage Museum:

"Following land enclosures in the early 19th Century, when many Arran tenants lost their land, fishing became a major industry on Arran. By 1847 there was a fleet of 98 boats manned by 380 men, netting both white fish and herring. As the century wore on herring became the dominant harvest…

The main fleet were Loch Fyne skiffs up to 30 feet long at the keel, although some bigger boats with bunks, a stove and a covered-in forecastle were also used. The Loch Fyne boats fished in pairs and the money earned would be divided into shares, six shares per skiff. The crew was normally four men and a boy cook. The men would each get a share, the boy half a share and the skipper one and a half shares for the upkeep of the boat and the equipment.

Glasgow fish buyers would be on hand with little steam launches to buy the first catches landed and sail to the Kingston Docks in Glasgow to sell them. Some catches were taken to the mainland (usually Fairlie) by steamer and then loaded on to a waiting train. However, a lot of catches were taken ashore at Lochranza and Old Neil Clarke's gutting and curing team would get to work packing barrels with a layer of fish and a layer of salt. These barrels were sent as far afield as the Baltic… Ungutted fresh fish were packed in canvas-topped barrels for the Dublin market".

A significant name on Alexander Kerr's gravestone is that of the person responsible for its erection: his son, the "mariner" Finlay Kerr. Given the size of the stone, he was obviously reasonably well-off. A search for the name in *UK and Ireland, Masters and Mates Certificates, 1850-1927* on Ancestry revealed that Finlay Kerr of Arran had qualified as a First Mate in September 1869.

However, I don't think that this story ends happily. Another Ancestry database – *UK Registers of Birth, Marriages and Deaths at Sea, 1844-1890* – includes a reference to a 43 year-old Finlay Kerr of Arran, 1st Mate, being lost with (I assume) all 27 hands (including the Master) when the cargo ship the *Barremman* went down at the Seven Stones Rock off The Lizard, Cornwall, on 7th July 1887 on its way from North Shields to San Francisco. (The ship was a 3-masted iron sailing vessel built in Port Glasgow in 1884 by Robert Duncan & Co for Thom & Cameron Ltd. It had twice sailed from Glasgow to Sydney, Australia, in 1885 and 1886). I cannot be certain that this is the same Finlay Kerr, but the date of his death falls after the latest date given on the Lamlash gravestone and his implied age on the database is only one year out from his known year of birth of 1845.[19]

---

19 A complicating factor here is that there is another Finlay Kerr from Arran listed as becoming a Second Mate in 1868, a First Mate in 1884 and a Master in 1889. However, in each case, his birthplace is given as Lochranza (not South Kiscadale, as for the Finlay Kerr we are interested in) and the implied year of birth ranges from 1848 to 1851. In addition, the 1881 Census record refers to a sister called Flora. It is the acquisition of Master status in 1889 that definitively rules out this Finlay Kerr as being the direct family member, however, as the *Barremman* went down in 1887.

In a later visit to the Mitchell Library, I looked up *The Scotsman* of 6th and 8th September 1887. These editions included reports about the Board of Trade Inquiry into the loss of the *Barremman* held at the County Buildings in Glasgow with Sheriff Muir presiding. The conclusion of the Court was damning:

> "Though the Court was unable to pronounce on the actual and immediate cause of the loss of the vessel, the late master could not be considered free from blame for navigating his vessel in such dangerous waters when he had ample sea room in every direction. The Court was further of opinion that culpable negligence, if not inhumanity, was shown by the mate in charge and crew of the Seven Stones lightvessel [a type of floating lighthouse] in not sending a boat or making any attempt to rescue the crew of the *Barremman* after they had made her out to be in the Seven Stones. The Court also expressed an opinion that the mate had failed to carry out the regulation of the Trinity House as to firing a gun when the vessel was seen to be getting into danger".[20]

Margaret Wright informed me that Alexander Kerr had two siblings: Mary (born in 1805) and Finlay (born in 1808). Later, I was able to confirm this in the Old Parish Records held on www.scotlandspeople.gov.uk, where I also found another brother, John, born in 1803. I wonder if there was also an earlier – and deceased – child called Finlay, as Finlay Kerr/Ker was the name of Alexander's father and, following tradition, this would have been the name given to Finlay and Grace Kerr's first-born son.

Ms Wright's researches also revealed that the Charles Finlay commemorated on the gravestone in the Kilbride cemetery was Charles Finlay Cook, who was the son of Janet Kerr (1840-1918, one of Alexander and Janet's daughters and a sister of Catherine Kerr) and Charles Cook, a farmer. Charles Finlay Cook is recorded as an 11 year-old in the 1871 Census living with his grandmother Janet Kerr (the widow of Archibald Kerr) in Whiting Bay. (Also in the household was Janet's daughter, Mary, then aged 15. She is also commemorated on the Kilbride Cemetery gravestone). At the time of the Censuses of 1881 to 1901, Charles Finlay Cook was working as a house joiner/carpenter in Blantyre and then Glasgow, although it was also he who registered the death of Janet Kerr in South Kiscadale in January 1899 at the age of 88. His own death was in South Kiscadale in 1937 at the age of 77.

In addition, the research commissioned from the Arran Heritage Museum provided some information about those of the siblings and cousins of Janet Shaw

---

20 For clarity, the Court is referring to the mate on the Seven Stones lightship, not the mate of the *Barremman*, Finlay Kerr.

(Alexander Kerr's wife) who married and had families (the latter being the children of Neil and Catherine Shaw).

This led to the identification of another First World War casualty within the extended family. One of Janet Kerr's cousins – another Neil Shaw (1835-1922) – married Helen Miller (1844-1927) and they had a son, also called Neil, who was born in 1886. He was killed in action in France in April 1917 at the age of 31. (The stretching of the generations meant that he was a second cousin of Catherine Kerr, who had died in Rutherglen almost 50 years earlier).

The Commonwealth War Graves website at www.cwgc.org confirms that Private Neil Shaw of the 1st/6th Battalion of the Black Watch (Royal Highlanders) – Service No. 268259 – is buried at the Maroeuil British Cemetery in Pas de Calais. The *UK Army Registers of Soldiers' Effects, 1901-1929* on Ancestry reveals that Neil Shaw (the father) received £3 4s 9d in July 1917 and a further £3 in December 1919.

The Clearances

In the branch of the family tree emanating from Arran, the McKillop surname also generates an area of historically resonant research, as it features prominently in the list of those who were "cleared" from the north part of the island in 1829. Much of the historical attention on this event focuses on the emigration of some of those cleared to Canada. However, other families were displaced to the south of the island or to the Scottish mainland and it is in this regard that there is a family connection with this significant occurrence in the history of Arran (and Scotland).

Let us begin with the emigration to Canada. The information provided on the display boards at the Arran Heritage Museum gives the general background:

> "All the people from the north end of the island – North, Mid and South Sannox, Laggantuine, Laggan, Cuithe and the Cock – were evicted in 1829 and replaced by a single large sheep farm at Mid Sannox and a smaller enclosed farm at the Cock.
>
> The emigration of these people was organised by the estate and half the fare to Canada, £8 for an adult or three children under 15, was paid by the tenth Duke of Hamilton. The first to leave, twelve families, numbering 86 people, boarded the sailing vessel *Caledonia* at Lochranza on 25th April 1829.
>
> The *Caledonia* was at sea for two months and arrived in Quebec on 25th June. There had been one dreadful storm off the coast of Ireland and a stowaway Paisley weaver was found on board, for whom the passengers held a ceilidh to pay his fare, but otherwise the voyage was unremarkable".

In *Arran to Canada – One Way* (2012), James Henderson sets out further details on the background context to the emigration and the subsequent experience of the emigrants in Canada:

> "Improved agricultural efficiency meant that fewer workers were needed, and the surplus unemployed hands were turning into a social problem the landowners did not want to deal with. Against an economic background in which a minority earned reliable money, there were far too many with no means of making a living.
>
> The cause of this imbalance was not acknowledged, though it was obvious. In Sannox, 27 families had been evicted to create one large sheep farm extending to over 100 acres. Not surprisingly, discontent among the have-nots was rising...
>
> The Rev. Alexander McBride noted in his *New Statistical Account of Kilmory* that as early as 1821, 500 persons were sent away from the Sannox district. His phrasing makes it clear that these people were not merely deprived of their traditional land but actually cleared from the islands. Some of the ejected families emigrated to North America, but by far the greater number removed to Ayrshire towns. Following this, the pressure to get rid of surplus ex-agricultural workers was stepped up. The 10th duke, Alexander Hamilton (1767-1852) offered 100 acres of land to every able-bodied man over the age of 21 who was willing to go to Canada, and said that he would pay 50% of the cost of the passage...
>
> The brig *Caledonia* [was] captained by Donald Miller who... was a native of Arran... Archibald McKillop from Lochranza, who had been a schoolmaster and had collected taxes for the Duke, took charge. He had been educated at Edinburgh University and was evidently a man of authority".

In *Les Ecossais: The Pioneer Scots of Lower Canada, 1763-1855* (2006), Lucille H Campey provides the "List of 26 tenants from the Duke of Hamilton's estate in Arran who are to emigrate, 1829". In the event, 12 families departed on the *Caledonia*, the details of whom were recorded in *Annals of Megantic County, Quebec*, which was written and published by Dugald McKenzie McKillop of Lynn, Massachusetts, in 1902. This group included 4 sets of McKillops, totalling 33 people – 38 per cent of the overall number of 86 from Arran in the ship's full complement of 180 passengers, the vessel having initially sailed from Greenock.

The details of the families listed by Dugald McKenzie McKillop do not include the occupations of the heads of household or the locations on Arran in which they had lived. However, the information can be matched with that obtained from a document now held at The National Archives in a file entitled "War and Colonial Department and Colonial Office: Emigration, Original Correspondence, 1817-1857 and 1872-1896", which is included in the Ancestry database *Canada, Immigration and Settlement Correspondence and Lists, 1817-1896*. This is dated 28th February 1829 and, also containing 12 families, is headed "This List of Persons intending to go, this Spring, from Arran to Upper Canada".

The two lists do not match exactly. 4 of the families "intending to go" in February 1829 were not on the *Caledonia* in April (although one of these travelled shortly afterwards on the *Albion*). However, the 4 McKillop families were in both lists, two of the heads of household being the namesakes Archibald McKillop, who were farmers and fishermen from Lochranza.

The other two families came from North Sannox: Donald McKillop, a 54 year-old farmer, with this wife Catherine (née Kelso) and their 6 children aged between 8 and 24 years; and Neil McKillop, a 61 year-old farmer, with his wife Mary (née McKelvie) and their 6 children aged 17-30 years.

Given that Grizel McKillop – the mother of Alexander Kerr and grandmother of Catherine Kerr – was born in South Sannox in 1766, these are the families in which I am most interested. Whilst I have not yet directly linked Grizel or her father, John McKillop, to the Arran emigrants to Canada, it is highly likely – I would say, almost certain – that there is a family connection (perhaps via cousins or nephews/nieces), given Grizel's places of birth and residence and the fact that the north of Arran was subjected to wholesale Clearances.

In addition to the frequent McKillop names, I think that two features of "This List of Persons…" jump off the page. First, there is the confirmation that these were large families: 9 "souls" in one case. Second, even though the very elderly within the households would have been left behind, some of the heads of household (and their spouses) were themselves approaching what would have been old age at that time: as noted, Neil McKillop was aged 61 (and his wife Mary was 57). Given this background, it is notable that no-one in the Arran group died on the *Caledonia*'s crossing.

Once in Canada, following a reconnaissance by Archibald McKillop and five others (including the local land agent), the group decided not to remain in the proposed area of McNab township, Renfrew County, but to settle some distance away in Megantic County, Lower Canada. Henderson reports that the agent reneged on the Duke of Hamilton's promise of 100 acres per able-bodied man and changed this to 100 acres per family group (though Archibald McKillop received 200 acres).

Over time, the first immigrants were joined by another small groups from Arran, including Mrs J McKillop and her family of 9 on the *Albion* in 1829 and another group of McKillops on the *George Canning* in 1831. Thorbjorn Campbell's excellent *Arran: A History* (2007) includes a reference to the figures given in WM Mackenzie's *The Book of Arran Vol ii: History and Folklore* (1914) on the size of the expatriate Arran colony in 1833, when it comprised 222 people, of whom 51 had the surname McKillop. There were also 13 Kerrs, though no Shaws.

The published research on the Arran emigrants to Canada consistently emphasises the heroic efforts in establishing their community in the Inverness township of Megantic County and the subsequent developments. Henderson notes that they were aided in the first years by the native Abenaki tribes, who showed them how to use tree barks in making canoes and tents. Archibald McKillop's son – also Archibald McKillop (1824-1905) – lost his sight in an accident, but became a noted poet and public speaker: the Blind Bard.

For my purposes, Thorbjorn Campbell's book also provides a highly relevant passage on the Clearances' effect on internal migration within Arran:

> "The Duke of Hamilton took thought for those of the community who remained. The alternative of resettlement on small southern farming/fishing units was open to families who were left in Arran after the "thinning-out" process had been carried out. This kind of land distribution, of small coastal plots for people displaced from inland holdings by sheep-walks, is to be found right across the periphery of Scotland…
>
> Many people settled down quite well to coastal occupations such as fishing… [C]oastal plots of land [were] allocated with relative success: the Hamilton estate made available sites – "acres" – for homes and smallholdings at the heads of coastal bays and inlets: Brodick, Lamlash, Whiting Bay and right round the south and south-west coasts, in addition to Lochranza in the north-west. These were specifically for fishermen and other maritime workers such as kelp-gathers".

This description fits very neatly with the migration of Alexander Kerr – who was born in South Sannox in the north-east of Arran – with his wife Janet Shaw and their family to the small settlement of South Kiscadale at Whiting Bay in the south east, where they were resident in the 1841 Census. Indeed, the evidence suggests that they had lived in the south east for some time before the Census, as their oldest daughter – Catherine Kerr – was born in Largybeg in 1831.

This is consistent with the timing of the Clearances from the north of the island – and the sailings to Canada, beginning with that the *Caledonia* – in 1829. In addition, the chronology fits with the migration of Alexander's sister, Mary, who – as Mary Hamilton, the wife of William Hamilton (1805-1898), a farmer – was resident in Largybeg in 1841. (William and Mary were married in 1827 and had 9 children between 1828 and 1849; she died in 1850 at the age of about 45). It is reasonable to assume that Alexander and Mary's parents – Finlay Kerr and Grizel McKillop – would have made the same journey (if they had still been alive at that point), though I have not found any record of either of them in that year's Census.

The return visit that Angela and I made to Arran in 2024 gave us the opportunity to visit the north of the island. The present-day South Sannox comprises a relatively short strip of houses on the coastal road. The northern side of the Sannox-to-Lochranza road would once have been the stamping ground of the four McKillop households who sailed to Canada on the *Caledonia* in 1829, especially the two McKillop families from North Sannox. Amongst the bracken on the steep-sided hills, the occasional remnants of stone walls can just be made out, but very little remains of any of the crofts of the pre-Clearance era.

One dwelling that does remain, however, is the church in Sannox, which has been skilfully refurbished and is now the site of the Sannox Christian Centre. The church was built in 1822 by Gaelic evangelists as a place of worship, contemplation and prayer. Alexander Kerr would have been resident in South Sannox at this time, an unmarried 20 year-old, prior to the Clearance of the local community, in his case to South Kiscadale. As I stood in the entrance to the church, I wondered – not for the only time in the course of conducting these various strands of family history researches – whether I was effectively occupying the same space as that of an ancestor several generations in the past.

THE LINE OF 16: 4. AGNES CHARLOTTE RUNCORN (1862-1942)

Warrington[21]

Peter McBride married **AGNES CHARLOTTE RUNCORN** (1862-1942) – the next in the Line of 16 – in West Derby (Merseyside) in 1890. Agnes was born in Warrington in 1862, the daughter of Joseph Runcorn (1823-1874) and Jane Twaddle (1830-1893), as shown in Table 2.2.[22]

Table 2.2. The parents and siblings of Agnes Charlotte Runcorn		

---

21 Historically within Lancashire, Warrington was incorporated as a municipal borough in 1847. In 1974, it was made a borough within Cheshire County Council. It became an independent unitary authority in 1998. Given the period of interest for the Runcorn family history reported here, it is appropriate to include Lancashire in the chapter heading.

22 In the *1939 England and Wales Register*, which records that Peter and Agnes McBride were living at 11 Ashfield Road in Leeds, her entry is as Charlotte A McBride. However, her gravestone in Hunslet Cemetery in south Leeds contains her baptised name of Agnes Charlotte and my father recalled to me that his grandmother had been known as Agnes, so that is the name I shall use in this narrative. In the 1939 Register, Peter McBride's occupation is given as "model maker engineering, retired".

Joseph Runcorn 1823-1874 (born in Runcorn, Cheshire) (son of Thomas Runcorn 1779-1860 and Catharine Seed 1785-1837) (died in Warrington aged 51)	
married	
1. Jane Sherlock 1831-1852 (born in Whitby, Cheshire) (daughter of John Sherlock c1803-1877 and Mary Sherlock 1805-1883) (died in Warrington aged 21)	
married	
2. Jane Twaddle 1830-1893 (born in Liverpool) (daughter of Robert Twaddle 1806-1895 and Elizabeth Irwin 1811-1865) (died in Warrington aged 62)	Thomas Runcorn 1856-1878 (born in Warrington) (died in Warrington aged 22)
	William Runcorn 1858-1940 (born in Warrington) (died in Southport, Lancashire, aged 82) *married* Eliza Ainsworth 1858-1941 (born in Warrington) (died in Southport aged 82)
	Edith Runcorn 1859-1922 (born in Warrington) (died in Warrington aged 62) *married* John Savage 1860-1929 (born in Hatton, Cheshire) (died in Warrington aged 68)
	Agnes Charlotte Runcorn 1862-1942 **(born in Warrington)** **(died in Leeds aged 80)** *married* **Peter McBride 1861-1949** **(born in Rutherglen, Scotland)** **(died in Leeds aged 87)**

	Charles Lewis Runcorn 1864-1937 (born in Warrington) (died in Crosby aged 73) *married* Mary Ellen Hindley 1866-1935 (born in Aston, Cheshire) (died in Crosby aged 69)
	Robert James Runcorn 1866-1867 (born in Warrington) (died in Warrington aged 1)
	Francis Runcorn 1868-1868 (born in Warrington) (died in Warrington aged 0)
	Catherine Ann Runcorn 1869-1909 (born in Warrington) (died in Lanarkshire aged 40) *married* Robert Smith 1872-after 1901 (born in Bonnyrigg, Edinburgh) (1901: aged 39 in Glasgow)
	Elizabeth Jane Runcorn 1872-1935 (born in Warrington) (died in Liverpool aged 62) *married* Roger Curtis Trim 1882-1926 (born in Hinton Martel, Dorset) (died in Liverpool aged 44)
	Jessie Runcorn 1874-after 1939 (born in Warrington) (1939: aged 65 in Chesterfield, Derbyshire) *married* 1. James Salthouse 1868-1913 (born in Blackpool) (died in Blackpool aged 45) 2. Alfred Jones 1886-before 1939 (born in Widnes, Cheshire) (1921: aged 35 in West Derby, Liverpool)

A contributor to the information on the Runcorn family on the public pages of the Ancestry website – Mariner Tonge – has consulted the parish records to report on the ancestors of Joseph Runcorn. The strong ties with Warrington – and Cheshire more widely – are confirmed. Joseph's paternal grandparents, William Runcorn (1745-1812) and Catherine Gorstage (born in 1745), were married in Warrington in 1768. In turn, William's paternal grandfather, John Runcorn, was born in the locality of Runcorn in 1680. (I return to Jane Twaddle's background below).

In 1871, the 9 year-old Agnes lived with her family in Bridge Street, Warrington, in a dwelling called the Hart's Building, which housed no fewer than 79 people in 7 households. The Runcorn household also had two lodgers: William Fisher, a 29 year-old musician, and his wife.

					Occupation	Where born
Joseph Runcorn	Head	Married	M	48	Joiner	Runcorn
Jane	Wife	Married	F	40	Joiner's wife	Liverpool
Thomas	Son		M	14	Joiner's asst	Warrington
William	Son		M	13	Scholar	"
Edith	Daughter		F	11	"	"
Agnes	Daughter		F	9	"	"
Charles	Son		M	7	"	"
Catherine	Daughter		F	1		"

The living conditions endured by the Runcorn family reflected the rapid growth of Warrington in the mid and late 19th Century. The population rose from about 10,500 in 1801 to 26,000 in 1861 and nearly 65,000 by 1901. The market town was transformed into a major industrial centre, particularly in textiles, iron and metalworking and the manufacture of wires, files and pins.

The unsanitary conditions of the first half of the century – which led to 169 people dying in a cholera epidemic in 1832 – were eased by the improvement in civil amenities such as the introduction of piped water from 1846, the construction of sewers in the 1860s and 1870s and the opening of Warrington Infirmary in 1877. However, it can be seen from the Runcorns' dwelling in Hart's Building that overcrowding remained prevalent in 1871.[23]

I took a walk along Bridge Street – the location of the residence of Joseph and Jane Runcorn's family in 1871, and (as we shall see) Joseph's death in 1874 and Jane's death in 1893 – in April 2019. It carried the traffic at the lower end of a pedestrianised shopping precinct, its array of shops comprising the usual inner-city constituents: a small newsagents, a bookmakers, several fast-food outlets, and

---

23 These two paragraphs draw on *A Brief History of Warrington, Cheshire, England* by Tim Lambert at www.localhistories.org/warrington.html.

so on. Intriguingly, above the narrow entrance from Bridge Street to a dimly lit courtyard – closed off by a sturdy locked wooden gate – the name "Hart's Place" was set in stone next to a bearded warrior-like face. On one side of the entrance, the face also appeared above the windows on the top floor of the solid three-storey dwelling and so I concluded that this had once been Hart's Building. A little way down the road, an old sign attached to the iron railings that closed off the entrance to another courtyard indicated that that building had once been the Lion Hotel. It had been the names of the occupants of this dwelling who had immediately preceded those of Hart's Building in the 1871 Census records.[24]

Family tragedies

Joseph Runcorn had followed his father into the family trade; in the 1841 Census, Thomas Runcorn was listed a 60 year-old joiner living in Heath Side, Warrington, with his 25 year-old daughter Catherine and the 15 year-old (actually aged 18) Joseph. Thomas Runcorn's wife, the former Catharine Seed, had died in Warrington in 1837 at the age of 52.

Joseph Runcorn remained in Warrington for the whole of his adult life. In the 1851 Census, he was living with his father (now the widowed 70 year-old Thomas Runcorn) and his wife Jane at 84 Foundry Street. Ten years later, Thomas Runcorn having died in 1860, Joseph and Jane (and 3 children) were living at 8 Cook's Buildings, Bewsey Fields. An apparent anomaly in the Census records was that Jane, who had been 19 years old in 1851 and born in Whitby, Cheshire, had become a 30 year-old in 1861 born in Liverpool. My experience with the two Marion McBrides suggested that these might be different Janes and, indeed, that turned out to be the case. The first Jane Runcorn, née Sherlock, died of consumption in Warrington in 1852 at the age of 21. Joseph then married Jane Twaddle in 1855.

The family tragedies certainly did not end there. I noted that Joseph Runcorn did not appear in the 1881 Census and, sure enough, the BMD records showed that he died in Warrington in 1874 at the age of 51. I did not think too much more about that until 2013, when I consulted the contributions on the Runcorn family that had been posted on the public pages of the Ancestry website.

One of these contributions was from Judy Hitchcock, who had drawn on the contemporary inquest and newspaper reports provided to her by Sue Stenning, a descendent of Joseph Runcorn living in Australia. This led me to the *Warrington*

---

24   There is much less to see of Foundry Street, Joseph and Jane Runcorn's residence (with Joseph's father, Thomas) in 1851. Its former route runs through an open-air car park close to Warrington Central railway station. Similarly, Bewsey Fields (the location of the Runcorn family in 1861) and Gas Street (where the widowed Jane committed her theft in 1879 and she and her four children lived in 1881) do not appear on present-day maps.

Examiner of 21st November 1874 and 28th November 1874 (which I was able to access in the British Newspaper Archive via Findmypast):

> FATAL FALL DOWN STAIRS IN BRIDGE STREET
>
> A man named Joseph Runcorn, a joiner, residing at Hart's Court, Bridge Street, met a sad death on Thursday morning. He returned home on Wednesday evening in a state of intoxication and went to bed. At one o'clock (mid-night) he wife spoke to him and at half-past four he was found at the bottom of the stairs by his brother, a soldier on furlough, who had been sleeping on a sofa below. The deceased was lying on his back, with his feet on the stairs, and bleeding from the head. Mr TS Smith, surgeon, was at once sent for, but the poor fellow's skull was fractured, and medical aid was of no avail. The inquest will be held this (Saturday) evening.
>
> A CHAPTER OF ACCIDENTS
>
> The inquest on the body of Joseph Runcorn, 51 years of age, who met his death by falling down stairs on Thursday morning, was held on Saturday last at the Public Hall Hotel, Rylands-street. The evidence showed that the deceased and his brother-in-law (James Twaddle) returned home drunk on Wednesday evening. Next morning Runcorn was found at the bottom of the stairs. A verdict of "Accidental Death" was returned. The deceased has left a wife and eight children behind him.

Drawing on the inquest report, Ms Hitchcock notes that:

> Both [Joseph Runcorn and James Twaddle] had returned home "the worse for drink". It was further reported that "he [James] had been drinking the previous day and for some time past"… Jane Runcorn stated that, having returned home, the pair continued to drink another quart of ale between them and Joseph was then helped to bed by his daughter, whilst Jane's brother slept on the sofa.
>
> At about one in the morning Jane told her husband to move his arm from off the baby, who must therefore have been in the same bed with them. Jane then went back to sleep and heard no more until she was awakened at about half past four by her brother shouting Jane "Come here Jane, Joe is dead". She got up and found her husband lying at the bottom of the stairs bleeding profusely from the back of the head. Dr Starkey Smith was sent for and pronounced Joe dead".

The daughter who helped the drunken Joseph Runcorn to bed would have been either the 12 year-old Agnes or her older sister, Edith, who was aged 15. (The latter is the more likely, as Judy Hitchcock reports that she gave evidence at the inquest). The baby in the bed was almost certainly the two-month old Jessie Runcorn.

As noted in the second of the *Warrington Examiner* reports, Joseph Runcorn's death in 1874 from his drink-induced fall made a widow of Jane (at the age of 43) with 8 children. (Two other children – Robert James Runcorn and Francis Runcorn – had died in infancy in Warrington). She appeared in the Censuses of 1881 (at 25 Gas Street, Warrington, as the widowed head of household with 4 of her children) and 1891 (at 164 Knutsford Road, Latchford, Cheshire, living with the family of her daughter Edith, who had married John Savage in Warrington ten years earlier). When she died in Warrington in 1893 at the age of 62, Jane Runcorn bequeathed £163 3s 4d, according to the *England and Wales, National Probate Calendar (Index of Wills and Administrations), 1858-1966*. Interestingly, Latchford was also where the 20 year-old Agnes Charlotte Runcorn had been employed as a general domestic servant (in the household of Charles S Burgess, a wholesale grocer, at 336 Knutsford Road) in 1881.

However, these returns from the official sources do not tell the full story of the life of Jane Runcorn after her husband's death. A much fuller – and sadder – picture is evident from other local newspaper reports of the subsequent period. Perhaps the most startling is from the account in the *Warrington Evening Post* of 1st December 1879 of a case heard at Warrington Borough Court:

A MOTHER ROBBING HER OWN SON

Jane Runcorn was charged with stealing from the dwelling-house of her son, William Runcorn, 25, Gas-street, on Wednesday last, a suit of boy's clothes, the property of Warrington Blue Coat School, value £1 18s. It appeared that on Tuesday night last Wm Runcorn had occasion to leave the town giving his mother (the prisoner), who lived with him, 2s. On his return he found that a suit of clothes lent to his younger brother on certain conditions were missing, a box having been broken open to get them out. He then gave information to the police. Another pair of trousers and 1s had also been taken out of the box. The whole of the clothing had been pawned at Mr Morton's, Latchford. Sergeant Spinks apprehended the prisoner in the Rose and Crown vaults and, on charging her with stealing the clothes, she replied: "You can't call it theft; I took them out of my own house". Prisoner, who had only been out of gaol about three weeks, pleaded guilty to the charge, and was sentenced to six months with hard labour.

One or two questions arise from this account. First, it is not clear whether William Runcorn alerted the police to the theft before or after it was clear that his mother was the perpetrator. One probably has to assume that he suspected Jane, given that she had been absent from the scene. (Her guilt would have been duly confirmed by the pawnbroker, of course). However, despite this, there does appear to have been some subsequent family reconciliation. It is notable that two years later, in the 1881 Census, Jane and William (who was 21 in 1879, not 25) were still living in the same house at 25 Gas Street, along with three of Jane's other children: Charles Lewis Runcorn and Elizabeth and Jessie Runcorn. (As we have seen, Agnes Runcorn was living as a servant with a family in Latchford).

Second, there is the severity of Jane Runcorn's sentence: six months with hard labour. The reason for this is probably to be found in the events described in a succession of articles in either the *Warrington Examiner* or the *Warrington Evening Post* during the 1870s. The first of these refers to a breach of the Lodging Houses Act in July 1875 – a year after Joseph's death – when she was fined 1s and costs for "keeping lodgers without registering". However, thereafter, Jane has a series of convictions in Warrington Borough Court for drunkenness, including one in July 1877 (when the *Warrington Evening Post* already referred to her as "a very old offender") and two in February 1879 when, on the 13th, the newspaper reported as follows:

DRUNK AND DISORDERLY

Jane Runcorn, an elderly woman, who was before the court a few days ago for being drunk and disorderly, was charged with a similar offence in Buttermarket-street last night. Mr Hunt (Chief Constable) stated that on the previous occasion the prisoner was ordered to pay the costs only, and some time was allowed to get the money. She had not, however, paid the costs, and now she was again found drinking and creating a disturbance in the streets. The prisoner was to pay a fine of 20s and costs, or go to gaol for a month.

One suspect that the fine of this size, plus costs, might have been too much for Jane and that the gaol time might needed to have been served. In any event, worse was to follow, as described in the *Warrington Evening Post* report of the proceedings at Warrington Police Court on 19th May 1879.

THEFT OF MONEY

Jane Runcorn, widow, was charged with stealing 5s 9d from the dwelling-house of Miss Elizabeth Coward, dressmaker, Friars-gate. On Sunday morning, the prisoner, who resides in Gas-street, went to Miss Coward's house and asked to go inside to drink a bottle of botanic beer. Miss Coward gave her permission and lent her as glass to drink the beer. The prisoner went near to the fire-place and appeared as if she was warming her feet. She left the house very abruptly, and shortly after she went out Miss Coward discovered that 5s 9d in silver and copper coin had been taken from the mantelpiece. Information was given to Police-Constable Crickett who, on Sunday night, found the prisoner drunk in a public house. He took her into custody and charged her with the theft of the money. She denied that she had taken 5s 9d, but admitted taking 2s 9d. The prisoner, who had nothing to say in defence, was committed to prison for three months.

It is clear, therefore, that by the time of her guilty plea for the theft of the school coat in December 1879, Jane Runcorn would have been well known to the magistrates as a serial offender for both drunkenness and theft. Reflecting the penal thinking of the times, the increase in her tariff was inevitable. It was probably her third gaol sentence of the year.

The local newspaper reports of Jane's charges and convictions for drunkenness continued in the 1880s. Her last entry was in the *Warrington Examiner* of 7th January 1893 in a summary paragraph (with 7 others) of recent deaths in Warrington: "Jan 3rd,1893, 7 Bridge-street Buildings, Jane Runcorn, 63".

In researching the siblings of Agnes Charlotte Runcorn, shown in Table 2.2, I found that, in addition to the information provided by the Census and BMD records, there were again some useful clues in the contemporary newspaper records. In one of these, Agnes's older sister – "a little girl named Edith Runcorn" – featured in "Theft from a Public House" reported in the *Warrington Examiner* of 23rd March 1872. It was reported that, after Edith had paid for "a pint of porter" in the Public Hall Hotel with a 2s piece, the change of 1s 9d was laid on the counter by the proprietor's wife and prompted stolen by one Daniel Connor. The report states that "after a long consultation, the Bench decided to send the prisoner [Connor] to gaol for 21 days". The interesting thing from our perspective is that Edith was aged 12 at the time.

As noted, Edith Runcorn married John Savage in Warrington in 1881. In the 1911 Census, it was recorded that they had had 5 children, of whom only 2 were still living. The circumstances of one of the deaths were described in the *Warrington Examiner* on 1st September 1888, which reported on the Coroner's Inquest.

DROWNED IN THE MERSEY

Mr HC Yates, coroner, held an enquiry at the Norton Arms Hotel, on Monday, into the circumstances attending the death of Robert Savage, seven years of age, the son of John Savage, a carter, who lives at 164 Knutsford-road. The boy was drowned on Saturday afternoon. His mother was shopping in the town and during her absence he went to play near the river and fell into the water. The occurrence was seen by a little girl named Annie Hatton, who informed her father. That person at once secured grappling hooks and recovered the body of the deceased after a lapse of about a quarter of an hour. The jury, after hearing evidence, found that the deceased had been accidently drowned.

Another of Agnes's sisters – Elizabeth Jane Runcorn – lost her husband in his 40s. Roger Curtis Trim was aged 44 when he died in 1926, leaving effects of £485 17s. In the 1911 Census, Roger's occupation was described fully as a "clerk in engineer's department in steamship company" – a job description that had expanded further to "Chief Clerk in the Engineering Department [of] The Bootle Steamship Co Ltd" ten years later. In both entries, the location was Liverpool: some distance from his birthplace in Hinton Martel, Dorsetshire (sic). Elizabeth was older than her husband by ten years, though this had been reduced to six by the time of the 1911 Census and then to three by 1921; she died in Liverpool in 1935 at the age of 62.

Of Agnes Runcorn's siblings, the one I had the most difficulty tracking was Catherine Ann Runcorn, who was born in 1869, after her appearance in the 1891 Census as a 22 year-old servant in Lymm, Cheshire. However, an Ancestry connection linked her by marriage in 1894 to Robert Smith, who was born in Bonnyrigg, Edinburghshire (sic again) in 1872. He was a foreman patternmaker in Dennistoun, Glasgow, in 1901. An entry on the www.scotlandspeople.gov.uk website records that Catherine Ann Smith died in the Johnstone and Elderslie district of Renfrewshire in 1909 at the age of 60.

This leaves Agnes Runcorn's youngest sister – Jessie – who was born in September 1874 and, as we have seen, only two months old when her father, Joseph, died. She was aged 4 when her mother, Jane, began the first of her three gaol sentences in the first half of 1879. However, notwithstanding these distinctly unpropitious circumstances, hers is a much more positive story, beginning at school – the same Warrington Blue Coat School,[25] the uniform of which Jane had been found guilty of stealing and pawning in December 1879 – where she was a consistent prize-winner (as reported, for example, in the *Warrington Examiner* twice in 1887 and again in 1889).

Jessie Runcorn married James Salthouse in the Fylde district in 1900. At the time of the 1911 Census, he was a restaurant keeper in Blackpool with Jessie "assisting in the business" and the couple had had 5 children, all of whom were still living. However, two years later, James was dead. The *England and Wales, National Probate Calendar (Index of Wills and Administrations), 1858-1966*,

---

25 According to *Slater's Warrington Directory, 1895*, Blue Coat School, Winwick Road, was founded in the year 1665 by Mr. John Allen, a native of Warrington, whose object was to apprentice annually "five poore boys to some handicraft trades". The building attended by Jessie Runcorn was opened in 1782 "under the name of the Blue Coat Hospital, 30 legitimate children of poor parishioners being admitted & boarded, lodged, clothed & educated". The number of foundation scholars in 1894 was 57. The premises were later taken over by the Warrington Co-operative Society, with the school moving to the Oaklands, Preston Brook, until its closure in 1949.

shows that when he died in 1913 (aged 45) he left effects of £6,863 7s in his will. This tidy sum would have passed on to his widow, the 39 year-old Jessie.

As an aside, we might note that James Salthouse seems to have had a lucky escape when a young boy. The *Blackpool Gazette and Herald* carried the following report on 10th August 1877:

ACCIDENT

On Sunday evening last, a boy named James Salthouse of Bank Hey-street narrowly escaped being killed. It appears he was playing, along with some other boys, under the North Pier, and took it in his head to climb on one of the supports from which he fell onto the stones below. He was picked up insensible and taken home, where he was seen by Dr Richardson, who paid every attention to him and, we understand, he is getting on very nicely.

James Salthouse was aged 9 at this time. Such are the quirks of life and death and – in Jessie Runcorn's case – the later opportunity to make a good and prosperous marriage with this particular man.

Jessie Salthouse (née Runcorn)'s second husband was the Widnes-born Alfred Jones, whom she married at St Clement's Church, Toxteth Park, in April 1919. He was a 33 year-old widowed engineer. It took me some time to confirm the Jones/Salthouse match as relevant for these researches as, according to the record given in the *Liverpool, England, Church of England Marriages and Banns, 1754-1932* database, Jessie was also 33 (she was actually 45) and her late father's name was Thomas (rather than Joseph). I know that this is the same person, however, as the widowed Jessie Jones in the 1939 *England and Wales Register* (when she was correctly listed as having been born in 1874) was living with her daughter Dora Holgate and son-in-law Archibald in Chesterfield, Derbyshire. (Dora Salthouse had been born in the Fylde district in 1903 and had married Archibald Holgate in 1932).

In the 1921 Census, Alfred and Jessie Jones – aged 35 and 46, respectively – were recorded as resident in the Grapes Hotel, West Derby, Liverpool. Alfred's occupation was "licensed victualler" and the place of work was "at home", which was consistent with his occupation in the 1911 Census (if not the one given at the time of his 1919 marriage), when he had been a 25 year-old barman in Liverpool. Jessie was a "licensed victualler's assistant". Also in the household were Jessie and Alfred's children by their previous marriages: the 15 year-old James Salthouse and the 14 year-old William Faulder Jones.

It is interesting that, of the 8 sons and daughters of Joseph Runcorn and Jane Twaddle who survived into adulthood – all of whom were born in Warrington – 6 of the families moved away from the town for a significant part of their working lives, although all the destinations were in northern Britain: Southport, Leeds,

Wakefield, Glasgow, Liverpool and Blackpool. The skilled manual trades of William Runcorn and Charles Lewis Runcorn (monumental mason and "wire galvaniser", respectively) were complemented by those of their sisters' spouses (engineer's patternmaker), though it was James Salthouse's role as the restaurant keeper that seems to have been the most lucrative.

Merseyside

The combination of the 1841 and 1851 Censuses allowed me to investigate the background of Jane Runcorn, née Twaddle. Her parents were Robert and Elizabeth Twaddle, who, in the latter record, were revealed to have been born in Scotland and Ireland, respectively. Robert was a baker, the later occupation also of his son, James, Jane's younger brother (as a 28 year-old in Warrington in the 1861 Census). Elizabeth Twaddle was my great (x3) grandmother and the first direct ancestor in any of the branches of my family tree whom I have discovered to have been born in Ireland.

The *Lancashire Church of England Marriage and Banns, 1813-1921* database shows that Robert Twaddle married Elizabeth Irwin in St Philip's Church, Liverpool, in 1829.[26]

I was obviously interested in finding out about Elizabeth Irwin's background and, although the available evidence is not complete, it does permit some tentative conclusions to be drawn. I began by considering whether the original parish register might give more information about Robert and Elizabeth's respective families than was available in the Banns (or the Bishop's Transcripts). My enquiries on this were answered swiftly by the Liverpool Record Office, which provided a scan of the relevant microfilm. This confirmed that the witnesses to the marriage had been Samuel Irwin and Alice English (as reported in the Bishop's Transcript), but the names of the fathers of the bride and groom were not given.

The *Liverpool Church of England Baptisms, 1813-1919* database shows that Robert and Elizabeth Twaddle's daughter Jane was born in 1830 and sons James, William and Dilworth in 1834, 1836 and 1839, respectively.[27] However, William and Dilworth were not listed in the 1841 Census, which gave Elizabeth at age 25 (she was actually 30), Jane aged 11 and James aged 7. (Robert was also absent from the household).

The FreeBMD database shows that Dilworth Twaddle died in the same quarter that he was born: the second quarter of 1839. The same source also reveals that a William Twaddle was listed in the death records for Liverpool in the fourth

---

26 One interesting point is that both Robert and Elizabeth appear to have signed the registers themselves, as there are no crosses next to their names.

27 This source has been made available on Ancestry by Lancashire Archives.

quarter of 1837. However, the *England and Scotland Select Cemeteries Register, 1800-2016* states that this William Twaddle – who had died at the age of 7½ months prior to being buried in the St James Cemetery, Liverpool, in October of that year – was actually the son of a different couple, Peter and Mary Twaddle. From this, I conclude that Robert and Elizabeth Twaddle's son, William, died sometime between his baptism in May 1836 and the introduction of the national registration of births, marriages and deaths from the third quarter of 1837. The deaths of William and Dilworth imply that Jane Twaddle had lost two younger siblings before she had reached the age of 10.

The database available from the Irish Family History Foundation on www.rootsireland.ie records that the name Elizabeth Irwin applied to 9 births in Ireland between 1807 and 1813, though none had Samuel as the name of the father. I wondered, therefore, if Elizabeth's marriage in Liverpool had been witnessed by a brother. There were 5 such names registered between 1794 and 1814, of which 3 were in County Armagh (where an Elizabeth Irwin had been born in 1809) and one in County Down (where there had been corresponding births in 1808 and 1812). As the latter was in 1814 (implying that Samuel would have been only 15 at the time of Elizabeth's wedding in 1829, I have (tentatively) concluded that the birth of Elizabeth Irwin in Loughcall, County Armagh in January 1809 – the daughter of Edward and Elinor Irwin – is likely to have been the most relevant for my purposes.[28]

Elizabeth Twaddle died of "chronic rheumatism" and "effusion on brain" in September 1865. On the death certificate, her age was given as 52, though 56 would have been consistent with the possible 1809 birth noted earlier. The informant was her husband Robert, a baker journeyman, resident at 31 Salisbury Street, Everton.[29]

With a little detective work, I was able to locate where Elizabeth Twaddle was buried. The Find A Grave website (www.findagrave.com) records that she was buried on 3rd October 1865 in what is now the Anfield Cemetery and Crematorium in Liverpool. After confirming the plot reference on the database of Monumental Inscriptions for the cemetery given on www.rootsweb.com, I contacted the Friends of Anfield Cemetery (FAC), whose details are available on their excellent website (www.friendsofanfield.com).

Tom Bradburn and Ray Beeton – two trustees of FAC – were quickly able to confirm that Elizabeth shares a public grave (previously known as a pauper's grave) with nine other people (aged from 6 weeks to 58 years) who were buried in

---

28 The religious denomination given for the 1809 birth of Elizabeth Irwin was Church of Ireland. This is consistent with two of the Samuel Irwin birth records in County Armagh (in 1803 and 1811) and with Elizabeth's wedding in St Philip's Church – which was Church of England – in Liverpool.

29 The site of this house is now the small carpark of the Salisbury Amateur Boxing Club. On the other side of the road is the imposing St Francis Xavier RC church, which opened in December 1848.

the same plot between 20th September and 19th October 1865. Although the grave is in a section where there are a lot of public graves, without headstones or markers, the trustees provided detailed information on its position, based on the locations of other graves for which there are headstones. I was impressed by the thoughtful presentation of their detailed research, which included a photograph of the site with flowers placed on the exact spot.

Robert married again – at the age of 64 in 1872 – his second wife being the 47 year-old widow Ann Goldsmith and the ceremony taking place in St George's parish church, Everton. She died in the West Derby district of Liverpool in 1879 at the age of 56 and is also buried in Anfield Cemetery. (On both Robert's marriage certificates and Ann's death certificate, his occupation was given as "provision dealer"). Robert lived to the age of 88, dying in West Derby in 1895; his bequest, as given in the *England and Wales, National Probate Calendar (Index of Wills and Administrations), 1858-1966*, was £602 5s 8d, one of the executors being William Runcorn (Robert's grandson and the older brother of Agnes, whom we met in connection with Jane Runcorn's theft of the school uniform).

I was initially uncertain as to the parents of Robert Twaddle (Agnes Charlotte Runcorn's maternal grandfather). His ages in the various public records make his year of birth difficult to pin down and three possible births in Scotland were considered: to James Twaddle and Janet Stuart in Lesmahagow, Lanarkshire, in January 1806; to William and Ann Twaddle in Edinburgh in January 1807; and to Robert Twaddle and Marion Cooper (variously Cowper or Couper in the public records posted on Ancestry) in Carmichael, Lanarkshire, in September 1808.

For dramatic licence, the last of these – Robert and Marion – seemed the most attractive, as this couple later emigrated to Canada (both dying in the 1850s); however, the year of the emigration was 1821 and it is unlikely that they would have taken the rest of the family (as they did) and left the young Robert Twaddle behind. Other things equal, I would have gone for the first option – James and Janet – as James was the name given to Robert and Elizabeth Twaddle's first son (with the ill-fated William being the second son). However, Robert's second marriage certificate gives his father as William Twaddle, a clerk. It is therefore the Edinburgh-based William and Ann Twaddle who are the grandparents of Jane Twaddle and the great grandparents of Agnes Charlotte Runcorn (later McBride).

Before leaving Robert Twaddle, I can report a little quirk of the type that occasionally pops up in family history research. In 1871, before Robert married for the second time and when he was living in Everton with his 16 year-old son (also Robert), the servant in the household was the 14 year-old Marina McDonald, whom we met earlier as marrying William Walker McBride in 1883. It was, of course, Robert Twaddle's granddaughter (Agnes Runcorn, born in 1862) who would marry William's half-brother (Peter McBride) in 1890.

The family of Peter and Agnes McBride

One question that I have not yet addressed is how the two members of the Line of 16 – Peter McBride and Agnes Charlotte Runcorn – might initially have met. The Census records tell us that, in 1881, Peter was a 20 year-old house joiner in Rutherglen, Scotland, whilst Agnes was a 19 year-old domestic servant in Knutsford, Cheshire. How did their paths cross such as to lead to their marriage in West Derby (Merseyside) in 1890?

I think a key figure might have been Peter's half-brother – William Walker McBride – who, as we have seen, migrated to England and married Marina McDonald in West Derby in 1883. His full name does not appear in the Census records for either Scotland or England in 1881, though there is a 22 year-old William McBride (born in Scotland and a joiner) registered as a boarder in Wallasey, Cheshire. (Wallasey is in the Wirral, just across the Mersey from Liverpool (and West Derby)). It is a reasonable assumption that Peter McBride followed William's lead in migrating to England sometime after the 1881 Census, if not to Wallasey then to somewhere else on Merseyside or in Cheshire.[30]

The family of Peter and Agnes McBride is shown in Table 2.3. As noted, they had 11 children, of whom three died in infancy. My grandmother – Catherine Kerr McBride – was the third child, born in 1893. Peter McBride died in Leeds in 1949 at the age of 87; the probate records show that he left effects of £393 11s 10d. (One of his sons, William Alexander McBride, had died two months earlier at the age of 50, having lived at the same address of 11 Ashfield Road). Agnes was 80 when she died in Leeds in 1942.

Peter and Agnes McBride were buried in the Hunslet Cemetery, south Leeds, the plot also containing William McBride and another of their children – Mary Bennett McBride – who died in Leeds in 1930 at the age of 26.[31] I visited the grave in October 2016 following the help received from Shelbie Foster of the Bereavement Services Department of the Leeds City Council, who had previously not only supplied me with a map of the site, but had taken the trouble to attend the grave herself and send me a photograph: assistance that was much appreciated.

---

30 It is interesting that Agnes Runcorn's wedding took place in West Derby, rather than Warrington (where she had grown up) or Latchford (where, in 1891, her widowed mother Jane Runcorn lived with the family of one of Agnes's sisters, Edith Savage).

31 There is a poignant entry in the Notices section of the *Yorkshire Evening Post* on 10th June 1948:
   McBRIDE. In loving memory of MARY, who passed away June 19th 1930. Jock.
This was 18 years after Mary McBride's death. "Jock" could have been a friend or fiancé or, possibly, John Savage McBride (1902-1980), one of Mary's older brothers.

Table 2.3. The family of Peter and Agnes Charlotte McBride	
Peter McBride 1861-1949 (born in Rutherglen, Scotland) (died in Leeds aged 87)	
married	
Agnes Charlotte Runcorn 1862-1942 (born in Warrington) (died in Leeds aged 80)	Joseph Runcorn McBride 1890-1890 (born in Glasgow) (died aged "5 minutes")
	Ethel Jane McBride 1892-1976 (born in Glasgow) (died in Blackpool aged 84) *married* John Bain 1890-1970 (died in Blackpool aged 79)
	Catherine Kerr McBride 1893-1969 **(born in Glasgow)** **(died in Leeds aged 76)** *married* **John Rigg 1887-1959** **(born in Baldersby, Yorkshire)** **(died in Leeds aged 72)**
	Agnes Runcorn McBride 1894-1897 (born in Glasgow) (died in Glasgow aged 2)
	William Alexander McBride 1898-1949 (born in Glasgow) (died in Leeds aged 50)
	Lilian (Lily) Runcorn McBride 1900-1979 (born in Glasgow) (died in Blackpool aged 79) *married* Simon Rosenberg 1901-1984 (changed name to Samuel Goodman) (born in Leeds) (died in Blackpool aged 82)

	Osborne McBride 1901-1901 (born in Glasgow) (died in Glasgow aged 4 months)
	John Savage McBride 1902-1980 (born in Glasgow) (died in Bradford, Yorkshire, aged 78) *married* Elsie Hakney 1914-1999 (born in Halifax, Yorkshire) (died in Bradford aged 84)
	Mary Bennett McBride 1904-1930 (born in Manchester) (died in Leeds aged 26)
	Dorothy Lucy McBride 1907-1989 (born in Manchester) (died in Leeds aged 82) *married* Harry Gomersall 1900-1978 (born in Leeds) (died in Leeds aged 78)
	Charles Osborne McBride 1908-1954 (born in Manchester) (died in Leeds aged 45) *married* Eileen Alice Walton 1914-2012 (born in Wharfedale district, Yorkshire) (died in Yorkshire aged 97)

Agnes Charlotte McBride's maiden name of Runcorn was carried forward in one of her daughters: my "auntie" Lily – Lilian Runcorn McBride – who was born in Glasgow in 1900. In Table 2.3, it is seen that her husband was Simon Rosenberg, who was born in Leeds a year later, and here lies a fascinating story relating to the history of that city at that time.

Simon's given name was actually Samuel and he was the third child of Goodman and Annie Rosenberg, both of whom had been born in Warsaw in Poland. An Ancestry contributor, Patricia Goodman, has posted a copy of Goodman Rosenberg's "Certificate of Naturalization to an Alien", which contains his Oath of Allegiance on becoming a British subject in July 1903. He was a 31 year-old tailor with, at that time, four children; there were to be nine in total, one of whom died in infancy. The Certificate was issued by Aretas Akers-Douglas – later 1st Viscount Chilston (1851-1926) – who was the Home Secretary in the Conservative Government of Arthur Balfour between 1902 and 1905. For his part, Goodman Rosenberg, who could not write his name, signed the Oath with a cross. It is a poignant record.

By 1908, Goodman's family business was listed at his home address of 5 Brunswick Terrace in that year's *Kelly's Business Directory of Leeds*. Its progress seems to have been based on a combination of lawful and underhand methods, as evident in a *Yorkshire Evening Post* report on 28th June 1920:

> "At Leeds today, Simon Rosenberg (19) of Waggett's Court, Newton, was remanded until Thursday on a charge of warehouse breaking and stealing 49½ yards of blue serge cloth, the property of Messrs Kauffmann clothiers, Ashley Road".

The business became a limited liability company in 1930, as recorded in the *Leeds Mercury* on 3rd March:

A NEW LEEDS COMPANY

R Goodman and Sons Limited (246,025) registered February 24 1930, 68 North Street, Leeds, to take over the business of a trimming and wholesale warehouseman carried on at Leeds as R Goodman and Sons. Nominal capital: £3,000 in £1 shares. Directors: Goodman Rosenberg, Harehills Avenue Leeds (managing director); Mrs A Rosenberg, Harehills Avenue, Leeds; Abraham Rosenberg, Copgrove Road, Harehills, Leeds; Simon Rosenberg, Apsley Street, Hyde Park Road. Qualification of directors: 1 share. (Two first-named are permanent).

Goodman Rosenberg died in 1936 at the age of 64 and is buried in the United Hebrew Congregation Cemetery in Gildersome, West Yorkshire. In addition to being used in the business, his name was passed down to the later generation, as most of his children adopted Goodman as their surname sometime in the 1930s. (Amongst the other sons, Yewdall Rosenberg died aged 38 in 1933, but Abraham Goodman is again mentioned in his father's probate record three years later). Simon and Lily Rosenberg became Samuel (Sammy) and Lilian (Lily) Goodman.

When I first began my researches into the immediate McBride family in 1987, my initial sources of information were not extensive: in essence, my father's reminiscences and uncle Jack's photograph album. However, Dad's recollections were not inaccurate. He said that Peter McBride had worked as a patternmaker/draughtsman for Buckton's in Leeds and, as we recorded above, this has been most recently confirmed with the release of the 1921 Census. My father also stated that

Peter had been an excellent swimmer and water polo player in Scotland and in Leeds formed a swimming club called the Springgarden Rovers, of which he was president. His son Charles Osborne McBride – my Dad's uncle Charlie – swam for the Hunslet Dolphins club.[32]

I report in Chapters 8 and 12 below the long (taped) conversations that I had with my father in December 2000 about growing up in south Leeds in the 1920s and 1930s. In these, the occasional references to his McBride uncles provided a tantalising glimpse of their background and lifestyles:

> "Willy McBride joined the Black Watch in the First World War. Went and marched all through Germany and never saw a bit of action, because it was the end of the war. Came back and got demobbed. He was a staunch Hunslet [rugby league club] supporter, with my grandad…
>
> Charlie McBride started a band. There were about six in the band and they called them Mac's Melody Makers. They went round the local clubs…
>
> Sammy Goodman had bags of cash and a big tailor's shop. He used to do trimmings for suits. He was well known in Leeds…"

In Jack's album, the photographs of Peter McBride show a man with a rather strict face, strong nose and full moustache. In one, he is sitting in a deckchair on a beach, dressed in casual trousers and shoes (and jacket and tie). He looks at his strictest in the wedding photograph of his daughter Lucy, in which he is sitting on the extreme left with his arms folded and a stern expression on his face.

In a revealing photograph of Agnes McBride, she looks quite a strong lady, with her soiled apron providing clear evidence of hard work. Dad said that it had been taken in the garden of the sports and social club of the Stewart and Lloyd's engineering firm in Coatdyke, near Airdrie in Scotland, where John Bain – the husband of one of Peter and Agnes's daughters, Ethel – had been a manager.[33] Dad had visited his aunt and uncle there when he had been much younger.

A few years later, in 1993, after my family and I had moved to Scotland, I took my father to Coatdyke. In the telephone directory, Stewart and Lloyds was listed under "British Steel Corporation, Tubes Division, Imperial Works". My

---

32 See footnote 23 in Chapter 8 below.

33 It was in seeking to find out more about John Bain that I was taken down another of those research detours with which all family historians are familiar. In the *British Army World War I Service Records, 1914-20*, there are a couple of dozen entries under that name, one of which was for a soldier who deserted in 1919, later admitting to the offence in 1940 (when no further action was taken). This man's mother's name was Barbara with a contact address in Glasgow.

The only clue I had to work on for Ethel McBride's husband (from his death record in 1970) was that he was born on 4th May 1890. The use of some of my credits of www.scotlandspeople.co.uk enabled me to identify the relevant birth (out of 12 for John Bain in Scotland in 1890) as being that of the son born to John and Janet Bain in the town of Mid Calder, Midlothian. Ethel's husband – they married in 1920 – had therefore not been a deserter from the Army. However, at the end of this detour, his First World War service record remained elusive.

father described the sports club as having been on the right-hand side of Coatdyke station on the train journey towards Glasgow. The ground was precisely where dad had said, though it was derelict apart from the lawn used by the Barrowfield Bowling Club. The tennis courts and football pitches were overgrown and in disrepair and, rising up the hill on one side of the ground, was a housing estate with its new cars and satellite dishes. A tall flagpole remained, however, along with the detached house in which John and Ethel had lived.

Another photograph of Peter and Agnes McBride – when they were in their mid-70s – has been made available on the public pages of Ancestry. This was taken at the wedding of their son Charles Osborne McBride to Eileen Alice Walton in Leeds in 1936. Both are looking intently at the camera although, whilst Peter has an air of inquisitiveness, Agnes appears to be weary and uncomfortable, perhaps not used to having her picture taken. Unfortunately, the photographer seems to have focused on Eileen's side of the family, as her maid-of-honour and another adult with a small child are shown with her parents; on the McBrides' side, the shot is cut off after showing Peter and Agnes and we do not see any of Charles's siblings, who on this occasion might well have included one of his sisters, Catherine Kerr Rigg, my grandmother.

I end this chapter where I began – in Butterbiggins Road in Govan – where Peter and Agnes McBride and their family were recorded in the 1895 Valuation Rolls and the 1901 Census, the latter's records including the 8 year-old Catherine.

I took a walk down this street, which is about a mile and a half south of Glasgow Central Station, one sunny morning in May 2011. Not surprisingly, it had changed a great deal. A large portion of the odd-numbered side of the street was the outer wall of a large bus depot. On the other side of the road, entering from Victoria Road, a scruffy piece of wasteland was followed by a depot for the Scottish Ambulance Service (SAS) and then a rather gaudily signed health centre. Further down the road, some dwellings looked as if they might have been the rebuilt or renovated versions of their earlier counterparts, though the odd numbers ended at 171. The location of the McBride household at 185 was another open space, which, although with much litter, was tidier than at the Victoria Road end; there were some trees and concrete benches. Later, in the Mitchell Library, the 1894-95 street map of Glasgow showed that the Victoria Baths had stood where the SAS depot currently is and, at 185's end of the street, there had been a Wesleyan Methodist church.

As an aside, I should note that it was at about this time that I read Ralph Glasser's *Growing up in the Gorbals*, the first part of his Gorbals trilogy. It is a fascinating and evocative description of Glasser's life and environment during his childhood and youth in the 1920s and 1930s, prior to his departure on a scholarship to Oxford. The descriptions of some of the social conditions are not for those with a weak stomach.

But Peter and Agnes McBride did not stay in Butterbiggins Road. As we have seen, by the time of the 1911 Census, the family had moved to Leeds, where Peter and Agnes were to remain until their deaths in 1949 and 1942, respectively. Given their respective hinterlands of Rutherglen (and, for the earlier generations, Port Glasgow and Arran) and Warrington, the McBride/Runcorn story within the Line of 16 therefore incorporates a notable element of mobility. This contrasts with the corresponding Rigg/Boynton narrative of Chapter 1, in which the strong North Yorkshire connection – which (certainly on the Boynton side) had previously been evident for several generations – remained in place.

CHAPTER THREE

GLOUCESTERSHIRE AND GERMANY

THE LINE OF 16: 5. CHARLES JAMES NIBLETT (1851-1927)

Deep roots

The next person in the Line of 16 is my mother's grandfather: **CHARLES JAMES NIBLETT** (1851-1927).

A substantial amount is known about the Niblett family. A researcher in Canada – Mike Niblett – has done extensive work on the family's deep Gloucestershire roots.[1] He has reported that there were several variations of the Niblett name in the county from the 16th Century onwards – Nyblat, Nyblet, Niblat *et al* – with it being likely that the name Nyblett first arose in the Berkeley area of the city.

One possibility for the name's origin relates to it being a derivative of Isabelle or Isobel (with *let* or *lette* being an old French word for small or little), given the common feature in the dialect of parts of Gloucestershire to add consonants – in this case "n" – at the beginning of words. Another explanation connects the name to the Battle of Nibley Green in 1470: the last pitched battle in England between the private armies of feudal magnates.[2] Yet another possible derivation of the name makes a connection to the Saxon word *knibb* meaning a beak or nose. Mike Niblett has examined the case for each of these without coming to a firm conclusion. For my purposes, the relatively uncommon occurrence of the surname, compared with some of the others across the Line of 16, aids the process of family history research.

Mike Niblett has also noted that, between the mid-17th and mid-19th Centuries, the highest numbers with the family name were to be found in Stroud,

---

1   I was in touch with Mike Niblett in 2011 and contributed to the "Famous Nibletts" series on his excellent and detailed website. Since then, the website appears to have been closed.

2   Wikipedia reports that the armies of Thomas Talbot, 2nd Viscount Lisle, and William Berkeley, 2nd Baron Berkeley, numbered about 300 and 1,000, respectively. The dispute was over the inheritance of Berkeley Castle and other Berkeley lands. Berkeley's forces won decisively and Lisle was killed. Wikipedia draws on *Gloucestershire's Forgotten Battle: Nibley Green, 1470* by Peter Fleming and Michael Wood (2003).

which was the centre of a flourishing cloth trade. According to him, Charles James Niblett's father (Charles Niblett, 1817-1881) was born in Painswick, which is a couple of miles to the north of the town, and his grandparents (Daniel Niblett and Susannah Buckingham) were married in Rodborough (a parish on the south side of Stroud) in 1805.[3] Both Daniel and Susannah were "of this parish". In correspondence, Mike Niblett also informed me that Daniel Niblett operated a haulage business between Rodborough and Bristol.[4]

It was a considerable time later – and after spending many hours speculating on the lineage of Daniel Niblett the haulier – that I came to the conclusion that he and his wife Susannah were not the parents of the Charles Niblett born in Painswick in 1817.[5]

---

3 The name also appears as Susana and Susanna in the official records.

4 Mike Niblett's reference to the haulage business of Daniel Niblett prompted my interest in the will of an earlier Daniel Niblett (who died in Rodborough in 1749), which is available in The National Archives. This man was also a "carrier" – and an extremely successful one, given the portfolio of property that he bequeathed to his "now" wife, Elizabeth, and the sums of £200 that he placed in trust for his grandsons, John and Jeremiah Niblett. (These were the sons of another Daniel Niblett – who had already died by the time that the will was drawn up in 1748 – and his wife, Sarah). The carrier Daniel Niblett's married daughters, Sarah Ballard and Elizabeth Stiff, received £10 each, another grandson John Pates – who might have been a son of Sarah from an earlier marriage – received £20, a granddaughter Sarah Stiff received £50 and his widowed daughter-in-law Sarah (who might have re-married) received one shilling. The will of Elizabeth Niblett, drawn up in 1749, passed on most of the bequest she had received from Daniel for John and Jeremiah eventually to inherit. I have not found a direct family connection between the earlier Daniel Niblett and his namesake, the father of Charles Niblett.

5 The false trail took me deep into the woods. Mike Niblett had suggested that Daniel Niblett (the haulier) was possibly born in Painswick in 1785, the third of the seven children of Thomas Niblett of Misenden and Mary Cook, who were married there in 1778. In turn, Thomas Niblett, born in Misenden in 1750, was the first-born of the five children of Thomas Niblett and Elizabeth Dowell, who were married in the same parish in 1749.

A 65 year-old Daniel Niblet (sic) – a paper-maker born in "Penswick, Gloucestershire" – appears in the 1851 Census (thus having been born in about 1786) living in Sundridge, Kent with his wife Margaret and a 19 year-old niece, Sarah Vans. He died in Sevenoaks in 1864. Various contributors to the public pages of Ancestry state that that this particular Daniel married Margaret Vanns in Hadlow, Kent, in 1809 and Mike Niblett has suggested that he also married Mary Boon in Plumstead, also in Kent, in 1806. Accordingly, whilst this particular Daniel Niblett could have been the son of Thomas Niblett and Mary Cook, he could not have been the parent (with Susannah Buckingham) of Charles Niblett in Painswick in 1817.

The *All Gloucestershire, England, Church of England Burials, 1813-1988* database, available on Ancestry, records that a Daniel Niblett died in Painswick in 1817 at the age of 60. The same source also includes an entry for the death of Susannah Niblett, a widow, in Rodborough in 1819 at the age of 56. The ages at death would imply their respective years of birth as about 1757 and 1763, respectively. These years are broadly consistent with the birth of Daniel Niblett to Samuel and Alice Niblett in Stroud in 1758 and the birth of Susannah Buckingham to John and Mary Buckingham in Haresford, Gloucestershire, in 1762, as recorded in *All Gloucestershire, England, Church of England Baptisms, Marriages and Burials, 1538-1813*.

There were other possible leads. The birth of a Daniel Niblett was recorded to Richard and Elizabeth Niblett in Randwick (which is near Stroud) in 1773. To further complicate matters, there is a marriage between John Niblett and Betty Buckingham in the Thornbury parish in 1769 (given in *Gloucestershire, England, Marriages and Banns, 1754-1938*). Buckingham was, of course, the maiden name of Daniel Niblett's wife when they married in Rodborough in 1805 and Mike Niblett has suggested that this might have been a marriage between cousins.

I mention this detour into the list of persons named Daniel Niblett in late 18th Century Gloucestershire to illustrate how precarious the journey is when speculating on the possible linkages between one generation and the next. It is certainly the case that various contributors to the public pages of Ancestry have listed Daniel and

As it happens, I believe that, amongst the huge amount of research that Mike Niblett presented on his website, he did identify the correct connection. In a file on the branches of the family resident in Painswick, he noted the marriage of Daniel Niblett to Maria Wood in that parish on Christmas Day 1813 and listed the names of their 8 children, the first-born of whom (also in about 1815) was Charles. I return to this family below, after noting that the vital clue on Charles Niblett's parentage is revealed some time later – in the Census record for 1851.[6]

Occupational changes

When Charles James Niblett was born in 1851 – he was three weeks old on the date of that year's Census – the occupation of Charles Niblett was "ginger beer manufacturer". The latter's family circumstances were somewhat complex, however. Charles was recorded in the Census as a 34 year-old lodger living at 4 Hungerford Arcade, Charing Cross, London, with the family of William S Cove. I assume that he was there on business, as the rest of the family, headed by Selina Niblett (née Hunt, 1826-1890) and including Charles James Niblett, was resident in Cheltenham.

1851: 4 Hungerford Arcade, Charing Cross, St Martin in the Fields

					Occupation	Where born
William S Cove	Head	Married	M	33	Tailor (master)	Devon, Modbury
Regia	Wife	Married	F	33		Devon, Dodbrook
William J	Son		M	2		Middlesex, St John's Wood
Emma Whitall	S-in-law	Single	F	16		Devon, Dodbrook
Charles Niblett	Lodger	Married	M	34	Ginger beer manufacturer	Gloucestershire, Painswick

1851: Attached home to "Prince of Wales", Albion Street, Cheltenham

					Occupation	Where born
Selina Niblett	Head	Married	F	30	Bread & flour dealer	Gloucestershire, Stroud
Sarah	S-in-law	Single	F	30	Nurse	Gloucestershire, Painswick
Miriam	Daughter		F	9	Scholar	Gloucestershire, Cheltenham
James	Son		M	3 weeks		"

Susannah Niblett as the parents of the Charles Niblett born in Painswick in about 1817 (who is definitely a member of my direct family tree) when it can be shown that this is not the case (see below).

6   I have not been able to find a database that confirms the year of birth of Charles Niblett as 1815, rather than 1817, as implied by the subsequent marriage and Census records. I have used the latter.

There are one or two details that look odd in the 1851 Census. One is Selina Niblett's age, which is clearly given as 30. It should have been 24, given that she was 14 in the 1841 Census and, from later Censuses, 33 in 1861, 44 in 1871 and 54 in 1881. I am assuming this to have been an error by the enumerator, as the next line also gives an age of 30 for Selina's sister-in-law, Sarah.

As an aside, I note again the critical role that Biblical names have in several of the extended families that have been researched for this volume. Selina Niblett's father was Absalom Hunt, who was a 45 year-old agricultural labourer in Stroud, Gloucestershire, in 1841 and a 58 year-old labourer in the same town in 1851. Absalom married Charlotte Browning (1801-1876) from Stonehouse, Gloucestershire, on Christmas Day 1819; he died in Stroud in 1860.[7]

However, it is the second oddity that provides the key clue on Charles Niblett's ancestry: the presence of the 9 year-old Miriam Niblett in Selina Niblett's household. Her relationship to the head of the household is given as "daughter", but we know that Charles Niblett and Selina Hunt were only married in 1849. I thought that the most likely explanation, given that Charles's status is given as "widower" on the marriage certificate, was that Miriam was his daughter from an earlier marriage and this proved to be the case.

Charles Niblett had married Sarah Ann Swain in the Old Meeting House in Stroud "according to the Rites and Ceremonies of the Congregationalists" in November of 1839. The marriage certificate records that Charles was "of full age" and Sarah, who signed it with a cross, was a "minor" i.e. under 21. They were resident in Bisley, Gloucestershire. The certificate also states that their respective fathers – Daniel Niblett and Joseph Swain – were both weavers, as was Charles himself. (In other words, Charles's father was not a haulier).

In the 1841 Census, Daniel Niblett was a 50 year-old weaver living in Bisley with his wife Maria, also aged 50, and two of the children, Sarah aged 20 and Benjamin aged 14. From this and other Census records, it is evident that Daniel and Maria were born in 1789 or 1790 in Bristol and Painswick, respectively. Whilst I cannot be absolutely certain about who were their two sets of parents, I judge – from the *Gloucestershire, England, Church of England Births Marriages and Burials, 1538-1813* database – that it is highly likely that they were Samuel and Mary Niblett (and that Daniel was baptised in St James's Church, Bristol, in November 1789) and Thomas and Sarah Wood (with Maria baptised in Painswick

---

7   Absalom (or Avshalom) was the third son of David, King of Israel, and Maacah, daughter of Talmai, King of Geshur (1 Chronicles 3:2 and 2 Samuel 3:3). 2 Samuel 14:25 describes him as the most handsome man in the kingdom: "from the sole of his foot even to the crown of his head, there was no blemish in him". Absalom eventually rebelled against his father and was killed during the Battle of Ephraim Wood (2 Samuel 18:15). In the various Niblett records noted here, there are variations in the spelling.

in October 1790). The latter record is consistent with the marriage of Thomas Wood and Sarah Luck in Painswick in February 1790.⁸

In the same (1841) Census, Charles and Sarah Niblett are listed as 20 year-olds living in Cheltenham – the former, a gardener – with their 1 year-old son Alfred (who died later that year).⁹ Their daughter, Miriam – to whom I shall return later – was born in the same town the following year.¹⁰ Also in the household was the 15 year-old Eli Niblett.

1841: 8 Nelson Street, Cheltenham

James Townley	40	Baker	Born in county
Harriet	28		Not born in county
Charles Niblett	20	Gardener	Born in county
Sarah	20		"
Alfred	1		"
Eli	15		"

Sarah Niblett died in Cheltenham in 1848 at the age of 29. The following June, at the age of 32, the widowed Charles married the 24 year-old Selina Hunt at the Bridge Street Chapel in Bristol "according to the Rites and Ceremonies of the Independents".¹¹

Interestingly, the occupations given on this second marriage certificate for both the bride and groom's fathers – Absalom Hunt and Daniel Niblett – and for Charles himself are "labourer". The weaving trade, which had provided employment for Daniel and Charles ten years earlier, no longer did so.¹²

---

8   Alternatively, it is possible that Thomas Wood and Sarah Luck were the parents of the 32 year-old Maria Wood, who died in Painswick in November 1822 at the age of 32. However, I think it more likely that her maiden name was Maria Leech and that she was the wife of Samuel Wood, whom she married in June 1810 (when she would have been aged 19).

9   The *Gloucestershire, England, Church of England Burials, 1813-1988* database includes an entry for the two-year old Alfred Niblett in Cheltenham in November 1841.

10   I was able to confirm this with the release by the General Register Office in 2016 of the online database of births in which the maiden name of the mother was given back to 1837 (rather than 1911, as previously).

11   The comprehensive Places of Worship Database at https://churchdb.gukutils.org.uk records that the local Nonconformist congregation moved to a building in Bridge Street, Bristol, in 1786. In 1837, the location was certified as a place of religious worship under the previous year's Marriage Act. The chapel was closed in 1868 when a new chapel was built on Clifton Down.

The footprint of the old chapel can be discerned within its present day (2023) ruins, as the stone walls – now covered in graffiti – some steps and an archway are identifiable amongst the weeds and surrounding foliage.

12   A fascinating insight into the conditions in the local weaving industry at the beginning of this period is provided by the Gloucestershire Section of the *Royal Commission of Inquiry into the Condition of the Hand-Loom Weavers in England and Wales (1837-41)*, which was undertaken by William Augustus Miles. He spent 10 months in Stroud during 1838 before providing a hugely detailed report, which appeared in the House of Lords papers for 1840. In his conclusion, Miles focused on the impact of mechanisation and other structural changes on the wages of those working in the industry:

Two years later, in the 1851 Census, Daniel Niblett was a 61 year-old gardener (the occupation Charles had had as a 20 year-old in 1841) residing in Commercial Street, Cheltenham, and he was still in this occupation in 1861. Indeed, even in the Census of 1871, at the age of 81, Daniel's occupation was "unemployed gardener". By that time, he had been widowed, his wife Maria having died in Cheltenham in 1867 at the age of 77. Daniel Niblett lived to the age of 87, dying in the same town in 1876.

I confirmed that the 15 year-old Eli Niblett listed in the same household as Charles and his (first) wife Sarah in Cheltenham in 1841 was a brother of Charles because, in the 1851 Census, he is recorded as a 25 year-old umbrella maker living with his parents – the 61 year-old Daniel and Maria – in Cheltenham along with the 24 year-old Benjamin.[13][14] He died in Cheltenham in 1876 at the age of 50.[15]

"…The evidence I have collected leads me to conclude that the wages of weaving have been materially injured by the introduction of female and juvenile labour to the loom under the name of "colts" or "half-taught" weavers; that the system of making cloth upon commission for the London houses forced the contracting manufacturers of this county to seek a profit from the only source from which a profit under that system *could* be procured, namely, wages of labour; that, in consequence of the many persons who, in better times, were brought up to the loom, the labour market became overstocked, and consequently the commission houses obtained labour at the cheapest rate, as the weavers were the first to undersell each other; that wages thus had a tendency to reduction, and other better paying manufacturers were compelled to have recourse to the lowest rate of wages, in order to meet the goods of the commission houses in the market.

The distress exists amongst the out-door weavers and their journeymen, in consequence of the scarcity of work among them since the establishment of the shop-loom factories, where the weaving is performed upon the premises.

It is evident that the distressed condition of the out-door weavers is in a great measure attributable to the fact of a surplus number of hands, who are glad to receive work at any price and on any conditions, rather than leave their precarious trade, or seek for other labour, whereby they drag their fellow-workmen to their own level by constantly underselling them in wages…"

WA Miles subsequently emigrated to Australia, where he was Commissioner of Police in Sydney between 1841-48. He died in Sydney in 1851 at the age of 53.

13 As noted, this family – including Charles Niblett – was recorded by the Canadian researcher Mike Niblett in his catalogue of the branches of the Niblett family resident in Painswick. Sarah, Eli and Benjamin Niblett are listed amongst Charles's 7 siblings.

14 In Mike Niblett's list of "Famous Nibletts", William Roy Niblett (1906-2005) – a distinguished educationalist, who held professional chairs at the Universities of Durham, Leeds and London – is listed as a great grandson of Eli Niblett and his wife Ann Ridler. Unfortunately, this is not the case. William Roy Niblett was the son of William Niblett (born in 1858) and the grandson of John Niblett, who was born in about 1808. Eli Niblett was born in 1825.

15 Eli Niblett's branch of the extended Niblett family includes one of the people in this narrative closest to reaching 100 years of age. The wife of one of Eli's grandsons, Rowland James Niblett (1875-1963), was Amelia Ellen Eliza Pool, who was born in Newport, Wales, in 1874 and died in Barnstable, Devon in 1973 at the age of 99. As Eli was one of the brothers of the Line of 16's Charles James Niblett, Amelia's husband was a second cousin of my grandfather, Alfred Edgar Niblett. (We noted in Chapter 1 that William Edward Boynton – a first cousin of my grandfather, John Rigg – died in the Durham West district in 1990 also aged 99).

Soda water and ginger beer

By 1861, Charles and Selina Niblett had been married for nearly 12 years and the family was living together again – excluding Miriam – having just moved down the road in Albion Street, Cheltenham. Charles J Niblett was a 10 year-old scholar. At first sight, it looks as if the family was reasonably well-off; one Mary Higgins was resident in the household as "nurse", possibly to Selina's mother, the 63 year-old Charlotte Hunt.

1861: Princes Cottage, Albion Street, Cheltenham

Charles Niblett	Head	Married	M	44	Confectioner	Gloucestershire, Painswick
Selina	Wife	Married	F	33		Gloucestershire, Stroud
Charles J	Son		M	10	Scholar	Gloucestershire, Cheltenham
Alfred	Son		M	6	Scholar	"
Catherine	Daughter		F	5		"
George	Son		M	1		"
Samuel	Son		M	3 days		"
Charlotte Hunt	M-in-law, Widow		F	63	Housekeeper	Gloucestershire, Stroud
Mary Higgins	Nurse		F	43	Monthly nurse	Gloucestershire, Dursley

According to Mike Niblett, "Niblett & Co soda water and ginger ale manufacturers of Stroud and Cheltenham" was a well-known name in that part of the country in the 19th Century. In the Census records, it can be seen that the occupation of Charles Niblett evolved from ginger beer manufacturer in 1851 to confectioner in 1861, soda water manufacturer in 1871 and "soda water maker, employing 6 men", in 1881.

Charles and Selina Niblett had moved out of the centre of Cheltenham by the time of the 1871 Census; the family was resident a few miles away in Sandford Road in Charlton Kings. (The road runs alongside the playing fields of Cheltenham College, which was founded in 1841. The Cheltenham Cricket Festival has been played at this location for over 140 years). Charlotte Hunt remained in the household – registered as a 72 year-old lodger, though she was actually aged 70. She died in Cheltenham in 1876 at the age of 77.

Charles and Selina had returned to Cheltenham by 1881: indeed, not only to the town but to their old haunts of the "Prince of Wales" in Albion Street.[16] Charles died in the same year at the age of 64.

---

16 The website www.closedpubs.co.uk records that the Prince of Wales public house was actually located at 6 Portland Street (which runs into Albion Street) before relocating to 11 Portland Street in the 1920s. The pub closed in 2014 and 11 Portland Street is now a multiple occupancy, though the Prince of Wales feathers are carved in the archway above the main entrance. 6 Portland Street is now a pizzeria. The building at the junction of Portland Street and Albion Street is the Cheltenham Masonic Hall, which was built between 1820 and 1823.

All family historians will be familiar with the methodology – employed here – of tracking an individual family over the course of several Censuses in order to chart the growth or decline in the household numbers, the changes in occupation and status, and the variations in location. When combined with the information from BMD registers, this is a rich source of information on the family dynamic. In addition, however – as also described here – one is also able to draw on other sources to derive a more detailed picture.

In the case of the Niblett family of Cheltenham, it is the local newspaper records that fulfil this role. For example, the *Cheltenham Chronicle* of 15th July 1852 in its "alphabetical list of the names of persons who voted in the recent Election for a Member to represent this borough in Parliament" recorded that "Niblett, Charles, ginger beer manufacturer, Albion Street" voted for the Hon Craven F Berkeley, who defeated Sir W Jones Bart by 999 votes to 869.[17]

This suggests that, as early as the 1850s, Charles Niblett was a typical member of the aspiring bourgeoisie who had been enfranchised by the 1832 Reform Act. However, his business was to run into periodic difficulties. Under the heading "Cheltenham Insolvents at Warwick", the *Cheltenham Examiner* of 18th September 1861 reported that "Charles Niblett, ginger beer manufacturer of Albion Street" intended to petition the Insolvency Court "to be released from [his] difficulties". In the following decade, the "Liquidations" column of the *Gloucester Journal* of 11th October 1873 listed "Charles Niblett, Cheltenham, aerated water manufacturer and fruitier, trading as Charles Niblett and Son".

The local newspapers also provide a separate set of indirect clues as to the precarious trading position that Charles Niblett's businesses endured. There are several reports of Charles bringing charges for relatively minor thefts from his business or property to be prosecuted in the courts. Hence, the 12-year old James Parker was charged with "stealing from a tent in Montpelier Gardens five bottles containing ginger beer, value 1s" and was "committed for a fortnight" (*Cheltenham Chronicle*, 9th July 1861), whilst Charles Ramnell was committed to the House of Correction for seven days for stealing two bottles of ginger beer (*Cheltenham Chronicle*, 27th November 1866). Similarly, two 16 year-olds – Alfred Spreadbury and Tom Baugham – were "charged with stealing six fowls and two ducks, value £2" from Charles's property in Charlton Kings (*Cheltenham Examiner*, 18th December 1872) and William Smith was charged "with having stolen a quantity of peas from his plot of ground" for which the penalty was a fine of £1 plus 12s 9d expenses or one month's imprisonment with hard labour (*Cheltenham Chronicle*, 15th August 1876).

These cases suggest to me that Charles's businesses might often have been run as fairly hand-to-mouth affairs with recourse to the courts being taken not

---

17 The secret ballot for UK Parliamentary Elections was not introduced until the Ballot Act of 1872.

only to punish these transgressions but also to send a clear signal – given the nature of the sentences handed down – to other potential thieves.

In a reversal of roles, Charles himself was the one prosecuted in a case heard in Cheltenham Crown Court (*Cheltenham Mercury*, 16th December 1865). One Mary Ann Blanton brought "an action to recover £5 for the rent of a piece of ground on the Tewkesbury Regatta Ground in July last".

And yet. I think that the newspaper archives also provide an insight into some compassion within the Niblett household. An example was presented by an entry in the *Cheltenham Chronicle* of 24th April 1855:

CHELTENHAM POLICE

Passing Bad Coin. Mary Williams, at present residing in Ashchurch, but who recently kept a beer shop in the High Street, as well as a home of questionable fame, was placed at the bar on a charge of passing a spurious half-crown and some shilling pieces.

Mr W Winterbotham appeared for the prisoner.

Mrs Selina Niblett, wife of Mr Niblett, ginger beer manufacturer, proved that on Thursday last the prisoner called at her husband's shop and asked to be served with a bottle of ginger beer, for which she tendered one shilling in payment.

Witness looked at the coin and thought it was a bad one. She did not however tax her with it, because knowing that she had been in business in Cheltenham, she imagined that she would not be knowingly guilty of passing spurious coin. Witness consequently gave her 11d in change. The prisoner then left the shop and witness then kept the shilling until Monday, when she gave it to PC Stephen Day. The shilling is the same as the one now produced and is a bad one...

...The prisoner was remanded until Monday in order to afford time to ascertain whether the Mint would prosecute.

Mr W Winterbotham made an application for bail, which the Bench refused.

The article is of interest in a number of respects. First, it is one of several reporting the passing of "spurious coin" in Gloucestershire in the 1850s: a significant problem in the county at that time. In addition, there is something impressive about how the newspaper referred to a separate issue of some delicacy – Mary Williams's "house of questionable fame". For my purposes, however, I am struck by what it says about the character of Selina Niblett: in particular, that she was willing to give Mary Williams the benefit of the doubt, notwithstanding the financial cost – effectively one shilling – that the family's ginger beer business would incur.[18]

As noted, the financial highs and lows of the Gloucestershire Nibletts' business(es) do not appear to have been straightforward. Mike Niblett has reported that, when Charles Niblett's company went into bankruptcy in 1873, it was acquired by another branch of the family. However, as we have also seen, Charles Niblett was employing six men in the manufacture of soda water in 1881. Moreover, although Charles himself died in that year, the location in Albion Street, Cheltenham, was still listed as the address of Niblett & Sons at the end of the decade; it was one of the county's 26 "Soda Water, Ginger Beer, Lemonade and Mineral Water Manufacturers" in *Kelly's Directory of Gloucestershire, 1889*. The same listing also included Niblett & Co. in Union Street, Stroud.

Academic connections

Charles and Selina Niblett's son – Charles James Niblett – was absent from the 1871 Census, when he would have been aged 20. This was almost certainly because he was by then resident in Germany, where he had moved to teach English and, as will be seen below, he married Anna Karoline Borstelmann in Elze, Hannover, in 1873. The absence of him and his family – including his son (and my grandfather) Alfred Edgar Niblett – from the Censuses in England is repeated for the remainder of the century.

An intriguing insight into the activities of Charles James Niblett in Germany is provided by an advertisement in the 26th April 1884 edition of the *Army & Navy Gazette*:

> EDUCATION IN GERMANY.
> Preparation for Sandhurst. The increased importance of modern languages under the new regulations[19] has induced the Directors of the International College of Osnabrück to open a special course for Young Gentlemen Preparing for Sandhurst. Thorough tuition in English subjects, Latin, German, French, Mathematics, Drawing, etc. Particular attention given to backward youths. Board in the house of the undersigned Master of the

---

18 Although a number of other local retailers and traders also gave evidence that Mary Williams – "the prisoner" – had passed spurious coin, the authorities of the Mint declined to prosecute the case.

19 From 1868, the Secretary of State for War in the Liberal Government, Edward Cardwell, introduced a series of reforms to the British Army. These included the abolition of the purchase of commissions, with most officers henceforth to obtain their commissions after attending the Royal Military Academy, Sandhurst. Officers were still largely drawn from the upper classes, but they had to pass competitive examinations before entering the Academy and to attain minimum standards of education and military training before receiving their commissions. Charles James Niblett clearly saw the business opportunity in assisting the "backward youths" of the upper classes to reach these standards.

English Department – Particulars and list of references on application to Mr CHARLES NIBLETT, Osnabrück, Hanover.

It was a downturn in the family business fortunes that might have accounted for the change of occupation of one of Charles James Niblett's brothers – Alfred Niblett (1854-1931) – who was a foreman at his father's soda water manufacturers in 1881 and a school tutor in classics and mathematics (though still in Cheltenham) in 1891. Similarly, in the latter year, another brother – Harry Edward Niblett – was a school tutor in natural sciences. This suggests an academic strain to the family, which – as discussed in a later chapter – was inherited by my grandfather.[20]

Alfred and Harry both remained in this profession in 1901, though Harry died the following year in King's Norton, Staffordshire, at the age of 35. This must have been a devastating loss for the family – including for my grandfather, Alfred Edgar Niblett, who would have been 14 at the time of his uncle's death – as Harry had had a formidable academic record. The *Cheltenham Examiner* of 27th September 1882 reported:

> SCHOLARSHIP IN NATURAL SCIENCE
>
> We have pleasure in recording the success of Harry E Niblett… who has just gained an open scholarship at the Royal College of Science, Dublin of a value of £50 a year for three years with free education. A scholarship was awarded by the Science and Art Department on the result of the last May examination of science schools.

Harry Edward Niblett was aged 16 when he was awarded the scholarship. After studying in Dublin, he moved on to the University of Oxford. *England, Oxford Men and Their Colleges, 1880-1892* by Joseph Foster (published in 1893 and available on Ancestry) records that he matriculated at [i.e. entered] Trinity College in October 1886 at the age of 20. He completed his BA Honours in 1890 with a First Class degree in Chemistry.[21] [22]

---

20 The scholarly background of the Niblett family goes back at least one further generation. Thomas Niblett (1819-1891) – a brother of Charles Niblett – was recorded in the 1851 Census as the Curator of the Literary and Philosophical Institution in Cheltenham (at the age of 32) and he remained in this post ten years later. He was later a librarian in the city. Another brother – Benjamin Niblett – was recorded as a bookseller in Cheltenham in 1864; he died five years later at the age of 39.

21 The *Leominster News* of 4th November 1892 reported that "Mr H Niblett of Trinity College, Oxford, who took first class honours in chemistry" had given a lecture in the town's Free Library.
> "The subject was 'The meaning and uses of chemistry' and the lecturer, in an interesting way, dwelt on the objects of chemistry, its importance in agriculture, its use in arts and manufacture, and the changes caused by heat on matter, introducing simple but striking experiments to illustrate his subject".

22 Seven years after his graduation from Oxford, the *Gloucestershire Echo* report on the Annual Dinner of the Highbury Old Boys Union on 21st January 1897 referred to "…Harry Niblett, who had passed through Oxford University and was now one of the University Extension lecturers…"

Harry Edward Niblett died of "ataxic paraplegia exhaustion", the medical dictionary definition of which is: "Severe or complete loss of motor function in the lower extremities and lower portions of the trunk. The condition is most often associated with spinal cord diseases, although brain diseases, peripheral nervous system diseases, neuromuscular diseases and muscular diseases may also cause bilateral leg weakness". On the death certificate, Harry's occupation was given as "of independent means". The informant was "M Niblett, sister-in-law" – this was either Marion (or Mary Ann), the first wife of Alfred Niblett, or Margaret, the wife of another of the brothers, George Edward Niblett, who managed a public house in Birmingham.

Alfred Niblett remained in teaching for the rest of his career. The *Birmingham Daily Gazette* noted on 23rd June 1931 that "many old boys paid their tribute at a memorial service at Oxford Road Baptist Church to the late Mr Alfred Niblett, for many years principal of the Greenhill Preparatory School, Moseley".

Alfred's (second) wife was also a headteacher. The same newspaper carried an advertisement on 31st July 1930 for the Moseley Modern School for Girls:

> "The principal is Mrs Alfred Niblett... The School provides a general education for girls between six and sixteen years of age. The objects of the school are to impart useful instruction and to draw out and develop the children's natural powers and set before them a high standard of conduct and morals".

This was Annette Niblett (née Poulton), whom Alfred had married in 1912, six years after the death of his first wife, Marion/Mary Ann. Annette Niblett lived to the age of 75, dying in Birmingham in 1941, and left the tidy sum of £3,786 8s 6d as her effects.

I later discovered that the academic strain within the Niblett family had another interesting strand: none other than Charles James Niblett himself. The online *List of Nineteenth Century University of London Examinees* includes a record for him in June 1873.

This obviously poses something of a mystery as Charles certainly married Anna Karoline Borstelmann in Germany in December of the same year. However, the University of London's records confirm that he was aged 22 with a home address of Sandford, Cheltenham. I am not in any doubt that this is the same person, as there was no-one else with this name born in England in or around 1851. Moreover, the general nature of the address, whilst close to that of his parents (in Charlton Kings, Gloucestershire, in December 1872) suggests that Charles might not actually have been resident there at the time.

Charles James Niblett's name is also included in *Part I of the University of London General Register*, which includes those who were undergraduates up to

31st March 1883 but had not passed an examination before 31st December 1890. It has the designation "Pr. St." – private study – which appears to have been an early form of distance learning. (The University's Archivist has suggested that it probably meant that Charles had no attachment to a particular college). Charles does not appear in the *University of London Historical Record, 1836-1926* as one of the University's graduates in the period up to December 1926.[23]

Other siblings: detailed research

We have seen how, in the usual way, information from the 19th Century Censuses and from the later BMD and National Probate records has enabled me to compile some information on the family into which Charles James Niblett was born, as shown in Table 3.1. Charles Niblett and Selina Hunt had 9 children between 1851 and 1866, of whom three died in infancy.

Table 3.1. The parents, siblings and step-siblings of Charles James Niblett		
Charles Niblett 1817-1881 (born in Painswick, Gloucestershire) (son of Daniel Niblett 1789-1876 and Maria Wood 1790-1867) (died in Cheltenham aged 64)		
married		
1. Sarah Ann Swain 1819-1848 (died in Cheltenham aged 29)		Miriam Lydia Niblett 1842-1867 (born in Cheltenham) (died in Swindon aged 25) *married* James Roberts 1834/5-? (born in Pontypool, Monmouth) (1875: aged 43 in Swindon)
		Alfred Niblett 1840-1841 (born in Stroud) (died in Cheltenham aged 1)
married		

---

23 The excellent database of University of London records is available online from the Senate House Library (www.senatehouselibrary.ac.uk). My helpful contacts in June 2018 were Richard Temple (Archivist) and Charles Harrowell (Special Collections Administrator).

2. Selina Hunt 1826-1890 (born in Stroud, Gloucestershire) (daughter of Absalom Hunt c1792-1860 and Charlotte Browning 1801-1876) (died in Cheltenham aged 64)	Charles James Niblett 1851-1927 (born in Cheltenham) (died in Wallington/Croydon, London, aged 76) *married* Anna Karoline Borstelmann 1853-1938 (born in Elze, Hannover) (died in Osnabrück aged 84)
	Alfred Niblett 1852-1852 (born in Cheltenham) (died in Cheltenham aged 0)
	Alfred Niblett 1854-1931 (born in Cheltenham) (died in Birmingham aged 76) *married* 1. Marion/Mary Dutton 1851-1906 (born in Billingsley, Shropshire) (died in Birmingham aged 54) 2. Annette Poulton 1866-1941 (born in Aston, Birmingham) (died in Birmingham aged 75)
	Catharine/Katharine Maria Niblett 1856-1937 (born in Cheltenham) (died in Cheltenham aged 80) *married* Henry Belcher 1847-1919 (born in North Cerney, Gloucestershire) (died in Bristol aged 72)
	Alice Louisa Niblett 1857-1858 (born in Cheltenham) (died in Cheltenham aged 1)

	George Edward Niblett 1859-1929 (born in Cheltenham) (died in Birmingham aged 69) *married* 1. Mary Julia Walton 1854-1888 (born in Cheltenham) (died in Gloucester aged 33) 2. Margaret Mary Menzies Oliver 1865-1951 (born in Argentina) (died in Birmingham aged 86)
	Albert Samuel (Samuel Albert) Wood Niblett 1861-1941 (born in Cheltenham) (died in Knaresborough, Yorkshire, aged 79) *married* Anna Marie Borstelmann 1852-1919 (born in Hannover) (died in Aston aged 67)
	Harry Morton Niblett 1864-1865 (born in Cheltenham) (died in Cheltenham aged 1)
	Harry Edward Niblett 1866-1902 (born in Cheltenham) (died in King's Norton, Staffordshire, aged 35)

Also typically, however, the exercise of compiling the details of Charles and Selina's family is a good illustration of how some details can be confidently filled in, whilst others can only assume the status of probability or tentative speculation. The family historian will recognise the familiar cocktail of repeated Christian names,[24] incomplete databases and missing persons which can make the drawing of firm conclusions an easy exercise in self-deception.

For example, I realised that, initially, I knew very little for certain about Miriam Lydia Niblett – Charles James Niblett's oldest (half) sibling – other than

---

24 For example, the repeated use of the Christian name Alfred is noticeable. This was the name of the son of Charles and Sarah Niblett (née Swain), who died in Cheltenham in 1841 at the age of 2. It was also the name of Charles and Selina Niblett's second son, who was born and died in Cheltenham in the fourth quarter of 1852. The next son, born in 1854, was given the same name; he lived to the age of 76, dying in Birmingham in 1931. Likewise, following the death of Harry Morton Niblett at the age of 1 in 1865, the next (and youngest) son was christened Harry Edward. (I had wondered if the Morton name was in reference to Henry Morton Stanley, the journalist and explorer, who famously tracked down David Livingstone in Africa; alas, their meeting did not occur until 1871).

that she was born in 1842 and appeared as a 9 year-old in Cheltenham in the 1851 Census. The following Census, in 1861, presents a hugely misleading record of her circumstances, as she is recorded as an 18 year-old confectionary worker living in Stroud with a 5 year-old daughter, Catherine. In fact, Catherine is her step-sister – a daughter of Charles and Selina Niblett – who must have been visiting Miriam on this particular day, but who is also listed in Charles and Selina's household in Cheltenham. (The latter includes the 3 day-old Samuel, so it can be safely assumed that Catherine was spending time with Miriam in order to reduce the domestic pressures in the Niblett household).

Miriam Niblett married James Roberts in Cheltenham in June 1866, the wedding taking place at the Congregational Chapel in Winchcomb Street. As reported on the marriage certificate, her husband was a 31 year-old iron-worker, the son of the deceased Daniel Roberts, a "valuer of building works". Miriam's father was confirmed as Charles Niblett, ginger beer manufacturer, and her home address as Albion Street, Cheltenham.

Sadly, Miriam's story does not have a happy ending. She died in the family home at 18 Bridge Street, New Swindon (in the Highworth district of Wiltshire) the following April at the age of 25. The cause of death was "puerperal fever, certified", which the dictionary defines as "a serious, formerly widespread, form of blood poisoning caused by infection contracted during childbirth". Her husband, James, was present at her death. Her occupation had been "hooker, factory iron works".

The BMD records show that a Miriam Roberts was born in the Highworth district in the second quarter of 1867; this would have been in early April, prior to her mother Miriam's death on the 11th of that month. The infant died in Highworth at the age of 3 in the third quarter of 1870.

In the 1871 Census, there is a 39 year-old James Roberts lodging in a household in Stratton St Margaret, Wiltshire. The age is not quite consistent with that given on James and Miriam's marriage certificate, but I would be reasonably confident that this is the same person, given his location (Stratton St Margaret is now part of Swindon), marital status (widower) and occupation (iron-worker). He had been born in Pontypool, Monmouth.[25]

The fate of another of Charles James Niblett's sisters also proved slightly tricky to find out about. Catherine Niblett was a 15 year-old dressmaker living with her parents in Cheltenham at the time of the 1871 Census. It took me some time to realise that she was the Katharine Maria Niblett who married Henry

---

25 There is an interesting postscript to this part of the narrative in the form of a short item in the *Devizes Advertiser* of 6th May 1875:
  COMMITTED TO THE COUNTY JAIL, DEVIZES
  Mary O'Harra, 14 days, for stealing one petticoat, the property of Charles Niblett, and further
  21 days for stealing one vest, the property of James Roberts of Swindon.
This suggests that James Roberts was still in contact with the Niblett family some 8 years after the death of his wife Miriam Roberts (née Niblett).

Belcher in the same town in 1875. Thereafter, through the next three Censuses, they appeared to have formed a conventional lower middle class household raising 5 children. (The oldest child – Miriam Elizabeth Belcher – was born in 1878 and obviously named after Katharine's deceased older half-sister). Henry Belcher – who was born in North Cerney, Gloucestershire, in 1847 to Job and Percille Belcher – was an insurance agent and, by 1901, an "insurance and commission agent".

It was in 1901 that Miriam Elizabeth Belcher got married – in India. The *Cheltenham Chronicle* of 2nd March carried the following announcement:

> "Williams-Belcher-January 31st at Balaghat CP India by H Halifax Esq Deputy Commissioner assisted by the Rev J Lampard, Thomas Williams, youngest son of the late Thomas Williams of Ashperton, Herefordshire, to Miriam Elizabeth Belcher, eldest daughter of Henry and Catherine Belcher of Cheltenham, both of the Balaghat Mission".[26]

By the time of the 1911 Census, matters had gone badly awry. At the age of 54, Katharine Belcher was a "sick nurse" resident in the household of the 75 year-old Albert Ricketh and his wife in Westbury-on-Trym, Bristol. Henry Belcher was a 63 year-old lodger in a municipal lodging house in Wade Street, Bristol, sharing the accommodation with a total of 97 other adult males. His occupation was "musician (street)". In both – separate – records, Katharine and Henry's status was given as married and there were references to them having had 5 children, all of whom were still alive.

According to the *London, England, Workhouse Admission and Discharging Records, 1764-1930* database on Ancestry, a Henry Belcher is recorded as having been discharged from the Mint Street Workhouse at South East London on 23rd August 1910. I cannot be certain that this was the same Henry Belcher, but there can be no doubt that the 1911 Census record does refer to the same man, as his place of birth was again given as North Cerney.

Katharine Belcher died in Cheltenham in 1937 at the age of 80. Her husband predeceased her, having died in Bristol in 1919 at the age of 72. It will be difficult for me to find out about the causes of their changed circumstances

---

26 According to the *Imperial Gazetteer of India, 1908*, published by The Clarendon Press, Oxford: "Balaghat District is in the Nagpur Division of the Central Provinces... Christians number 219, including 191 natives, most of whom belong to the Balaghat Mission. This institution is unsectarian and its effects are principally directed to the conversion of the Gonds and Baigas. It was founded by the Rev. J Lampard, who still directs it and it has four stations – at Balaghat, Baihar, Nikum and Khurslpar – with schools at each station, an orphanage and an industrial farm".
It was seen above that it had been the Rev Lampard who had conducted the wedding service between Thomas Williams and Miriam Elizabeth Niblett in 1901.

between 1901 and 1910: the loss of employment, perhaps, or a more personal set of incidents within the household. It all makes for a fairly sad story, I think.

On a much broader geographical front, a noticeable feature of Table 3.1 (and also Table 3.3 below) is the impressive range of international connections made by some of Charles James Niblett's other siblings and, later, by some of his children.

An example was George Edward Niblett (1859-1929), who, after the 1871 Census (when he was aged 11), did not appear in the Census records again until 1911. At that point, he was a 51 year-old "manager of a fully licensed public house": the Railway Inn in Winson Green, Birmingham.[27] From later articles in the *Birmingham Daily Gazette*, it can be seen that George Edward Niblett rose to a prominent place within his profession. Reports of the weddings of two of his children – Alfred Oliver Niblett and Nora Beatrice Niblett – in March 1927 and October 1928, respectively, record that he was Vice Chairman of the Birmingham Licensed Victuallers Association.

The Christian names of George Edward Niblett's wife were given in the 1911 Census as Margaret Mary Menzies. She had been born in Argentina (in about 1865), as were the 5 (out of 6) children still resident in the household in that year. Initially, I wondered if her maiden name might have been used in the given name of one of her sons – William Morrison Niblett – who was born in 1896). Earlier, in the *Argentina, National Census, 1895*, available on Ancestry, Margarita De Niblet was recorded as a 29 year-old resident of Partido Chascomus in Buenos Aires, with Margarita M Niblet and Alfredo Niblet, who were aged 2 and 1, respectively; all three had been born in Buenos Aires.

As it turned out, it was Alfredo – the Alfred Oliver Niblett noted earlier – to whom Margaret's maiden name had been passed on. I learned from a detailed contribution from Hazel Hill on the family to the Ancestry public pages that Margaret was the daughter of William Morrison Oliver (1828-1897) and Elizabeth Buchanan (1840-1892) and had been baptised in the St Andrew's Presbyterian Church in Buenos Aires.

I searched the records to see if George and Margaret had married in England. Nothing was found but, intriguingly, I discovered that a 20 year-old George Edward Niblett had married Mary Julia Walton in Cheltenham in the fourth quarter of 1879. The marriage certificate confirmed that the ceremony had taken place in the Highbury Congregational Chapel in Winchcomb Street – as had also that of George's half-sister, Miriam, 13 years earlier – on 8th November

---

27 The www.winsongreentobrookfields.co.uk website is an informative source of information on the history of this part of Birmingham. The Railway Inn was built in 1900. It closed in 1983 and was demolished in 2005, the site – at the junction of Wellington Street and Vittoria Road – now occupied by a motor car scrapyard.

1879.[28] George was resident at 2 Selkirk Place, Cheltenham, a clerk, his father Charles being an "aeriated water manufacturer".

At 25, his wife Mary Julia Walton was five years older (placing her year of birth at either 1853 or 1854), her father William Walton being a master cabinet-maker.[29]

I learned from the register of deaths that Mary Julia Niblett died in the second quarter of 1888. The Bishop's Transcript of the burial record given in *Gloucestershire, England, Church of England Burials, 1813-1988* reports that she was aged 33 and the wife of George Edward Niblett, "clerk". The full circumstances became clear when I consulted the *Cheltenham Chronicle* of 14th April 1888, which, in the same edition, had relevant entries in both the births and deaths sections of the personal announcements:

BIRTHS
Niblett. March 26 at Fir Tree Cottage, Churchdown, near Gloucester, the wife of Mr George Niblett of a son, Hubert Walton.

DEATHS
Niblett. April 10 at Fir Tree Cottage, Churchdown, near Gloucester, Maria Julia, the wife of Mr George Niblett, aged 33 years.

The timing of the first marriage of George Edward Niblett – from 1879 to 1888 – was consistent with the 1911 Census record, which reported that he and Margaret had been married for 19 years (i.e. from 1892). George died in Birmingham in 1929 at the age of 69, leaving effects in his will totalling £486 4s 2d. Margaret died in the same city in 1951 at the age of 86; her effects were £1,327 7s 6d.

I noticed that, in the Census records of Charles and Selina Niblett's family, Samuel Niblett was a 3 day-old boy in 1861 and Albert Niblett was aged 10 years in 1871 and I wondered if these were the same person. They were indeed. Albert Samuel Wood Niblett was 51 years old in 1911, when he was a "foreign correspondent" for a firm of metal rollers in Birmingham. (As his birth record refers to Samuel Albert Wood Niblett, this is the version I shall use here). His wife Marie was born in Germany, though a British subject. I had more or less given up finding out her maiden name, until I consulted the Ancestry link to the *Belgian Antwerp Police Immigration Index 1840-1930* where, next to Samuel Albert Wood

---

28   The Places of Worship Database records that the Highbury Congregational Chapel was built in 1852 and closed in 1932. The building was demolished to make way for the Gaumont Cinema, later to become the Odeon Cinema, itself later closed.

29   I could not find a record for the birth of Mary Julia Walton in 1853 or 1854, though her status as spinster on the marriage certificate indicates that this was her maiden name. However, the birth of a Julia Mary Walton was registered in Cheltenham in the fourth quarter of 1853.

Niblett's name in a summary of the records from 1916 to 1930, was that of Marie Borstelman. Even though this surname was spelled with only one "n", I thought it highly likely that Marie must be from the same family – possibly even a sister – as that of the wife of Charles James Niblett, Anna Karoline Borstelmann. I return to this later.

The Tudors (again)

I have focused so far in this chapter on the family of Charles Niblett and Selina Hunt, into which the Line of 16's Charles James Niblett was born in 1851. However, it is also relevant to report that the line through Selina Hunt has been taken back through several generations, beginning with her parents Absalom Hunt (c1792-1860) and Charlotte Browning (1801-1876), as noted in Table 3.1. The detailed research on the background of Charlotte Browning, which effectively complements the extensive work that Mike Niblett has undertaken on the Niblett side of the family tree, has been presented on the public pages of Ancestry.[30] As usual with these pages, it is difficult to tell which family history researcher had accessed the parish records first and which others have simply replicated the information (including any faults or risky assumptions that might have been made). However, the overall picture is fascinating.

Charlotte Browning's parents were Samuel Browning (1764-1825) and Elizabeth Cordy (1774-1852). On the Ancestry public pages, the Browning line goes back a further seven generations to Thomas Browning, who was born in Berkeley in 1550 and died in 1604 at the age of 54 in Woodchester (both in Gloucestershire). Each Browning in the direct line from Thomas down to Samuel was born in Berkeley. A similar story has been found with respect to Elizabeth Cordy, albeit not stretching back quite so far. Her father, grandfather and great grandfather were all associated with the village of Cam, near Dursley in Gloucestershire, the last of these being Charles Cordy (1695-1774).

There are references to Charles Cordy – and to his wife Bridget Cordy (c1693-1779), their son William Cordy (1719-1779) and daughter-in-law Ann Cordy (née Cox, 1722-1781) – in the database of Gloucestershire Monumental Inscriptions held on Findmypast.[31] In their case, it was for headstones in the

---

30 There is no doubt that the Charlotte Browning born in Stonehouse, Gloucestershire, in 1801 is in a direct line of the family tree. However, it is much less clear that the photograph presented of her on several Ancestry public pages is valid. Other Ancestry contributors state that this is actually of another Charlotte Browning (1812-1878) with one specifically noting that the photograph was carefully preserved in an envelope with her identification. Accordingly, I will hold to the view (recorded in Chapter 1 above) that Harriet Boynton (née Stirk), who was born in Kilburn in North Yorkshire in around 1823, remains the earliest-born person amongst the Line of 16 of whom there is a known photograph.

31 These were originally published by Ralph Bigland between 1786 and 1794. The FMP database draws on the extended 4-volume edition of Bigland's work published by the Bristol and Gloucestershire Archaeological Society between 1989 and 1995.

graveyard of St George's Church in Cam. The same database includes an entry for the headstone of William Browning (1725-1786) – Charlotte Browning's paternal grandfather – in the graveyard of St Mary's Church in Berkeley. Unfortunately, in both cases, many of the graveyards' headstones are now absent and none of the Cordy or Browning references are included in the separate and detailed listing of MIs in churchyards and cemeteries of the west and south-west of England compiled between 2002 and 2004 and published on www.places.wisful-thinking.org.uk.

THE LINE OF 16: 6. ANNA KAROLINE BORSTELMANN (1853-1938)

Visselhoevede and Kirchwalsede

In the early 1990s – pre-Internet – a genealogical researcher called John S Eckersley of New Hudson, Michigan, USA, reported to my aunt, Joy Gardiner, on some impressive work he had undertaken for her on the European connections of the Niblett family. The results, which were copied across to me in a couple of summary sheets, included a reference to the marriage of Charles James Niblett to **ANNA KAROLINE BORTSELMANN** (1853-1938). According to Mr Eckersley, Anna Borstelmann was born in Glockensee, Hannover, Germany, the daughter of Johann Friedrich Borstelmann (1811-1854) and Anna Perlasky (1827-1899). In turn, Anna Perlasky was the daughter of Christoph Perlasky and Marie Angelika Herwig.

Over 20 years later (in October 2014), I registered with a Hannover-based genealogical network – hannover-l@genealogy.net – and sent out a general request for information on these names. A respondent, Heinz Promann, referred me to a website labelled www.genpluswin-database.de/nofb. (The English language versions of network and website were discontinued in 2021).

The website provided a wealth of information on significant components of a family tree stretching back from Johann Friedrich Borstelmann. Its database was based on the extensive Lutheran records of births, baptisms, deaths and burials and linked the generations together. The only (slight) doubt I had was that Johann's surname was given as Bostelmann. However, his Christian names and year of birth were the same and, significantly, I could make a link to his parents – Peter Christoph Borstelmann (1773-?) and Anna Margreta Marquardt (1772-?) through one of the separate German databases held on Ancestry. Peter Christoph Borstelmann was a *Häusling* or farmer.

On the Bo(r)stelmann side of the family, the main locality is Visselhövede, which is about 25 miles east of Bremen and 40 miles north of Hannover. Peter Christoph Borstelmann's parents were Jurgen Bo(r)stelmann (c1719-?) and Ann Trin Apps (dates unknown), who married in Visselhövede in 1759. (It was his second marriage). The previous generation on this side of the family comprised

Johann Hinrich Bo(r)stelmann (1683-?)/Margareth von Wielding (or von Wiehen) and Johann Hinrich Arps (c1698-1768)/Margaretha Catharina Gevers (or Gefers, c1708-1784). One generation further back, Johann Bostelmann (c1641-1716) – a *Halbhofer* or small farmer in Hessen – was buried in Visselhoevede.

These were not the earliest dates to which the records took us. Johann Friedrich Borstelmann's mother – Anna Margreta Marquardt – was born and baptised in nearby Kirchwalsede and this is the locality that consistently features throughout the earlier generations on her side of the family. There are 2 separate paths going back another 5 generations: to Lutke Dieckhoff (or Dieckhof) and to Lutke Lange, who were born in about 1605 and about 1600, respectively. Both died and were buried in Kirchwalsede, where the former was also born and baptised.

Further researches on the same website had the startling effect of taking a separate – but still direct – family line back a further generation to the birth of Harm Hencke in about 1582. He was a *Halbhofner* in Kirchwalsede, who also died and was buried in Kirchwalsede. His wife's surname was Koopmann. She was born (and baptised) in Kirchwalsede in about 1585 and she also died and was buried there.

The direct line from this couple thus extends down through the last 430 years via Lutke Henke/Hencke (c1611-?), Casten Henke/Hencke (c1640-1691), Johann Henke/Hencke (c1673-1746), Gert Henke/Hencke (1708-1749), Anne Henke/Hencke (1736-1786), Anna Margreta Marquardt (1772-?) and Johann Friedrich Borstelmann (1811-1854) to Anna Karoline Borstelmann (1853-1938) and Alfred Edgar Niblett (1888-1973), the last of whom was my grandfather.[32]

As already implied, the Lutheran records gave some occupations. From a combination of my *Collins English-German Dictionary* and some useful websites on old German occupations,[33] I translated references to *Hauswirt* (landlord), *Schafer* (shepherd), *Kotner* (cottager with small house, garden and a little land for animals), *Häusling* (farmer), *Hofbesitzer* (farm owner) *Halbhofner* (small farmer), *Kirchenjuraten* (church juryman) and *Hausmann* (housekeeper).

Another website[34] gives the geographical distribution of surnames throughout present-day Germany, based on the collation of entries in telephone directories. Perhaps not surprisingly, the Borstelmann name is predominantly in the north west of the country, centred on the Bremen/Hamburg/Hannover triangle.

---

32 In February 2018, I contacted the *Touristverband Landreis* in Rotenburg to make a general enquiry about Visselhövede and Kirchwalsede. The reply came from Verena Henke, whom I contacted again to mention my interest in her surname. It turned out that her husband's family was from Kirchwalsede. A little later, Christian Henke e-mailed me to say that all the Henke family in the line from Harm Henke (born c1582) and Lutke Henke (born c1611) through to Ann Henken (born 1736) were born on the farm "Koopmans Nr. 17". Koopmans has been the name for the farm since the 16th Century and is still in use today; the number 17 was the old house number, which was used until the 1990s. He also gave me the current address of the house.

33 www.rootsweb.ancestry.com, www.jewishgen.org and www.european-roots.com/german.

34 www.kartezumnamen.eu.

The obvious next step was to find out some more about the localities in which several generations of the families had lived their lives. A Wikipedia search for Kirchwalsede generated the following entry. The form of words is virtually identical for Visselhövede, which lies just to the south east. The 2020 populations were 1,118 and 9,579, respectively.

> "Kirchwalsede is a municipality in the district of Rotenburg in Lower Saxony, Germany.
>
> Kirchwalsede belonged to the Prince-Bishopric of Verden, established in 1180. In 1648 the Prince-Bishopric was transformed into the Principality of Verden, which was first ruled in personal union by the Swedish Crown – interrupted by a Danish occupation (1712–1715) – and from 1715 on by the Hanoverian Crown. In 1807 the ephemeric Kingdom of Westphalia annexed the Principality, before France annexed it in 1810. In 1813 the Principality was restored to the Electorate of Hanover, which – after its upgrade to the Kingdom of Hanover in 1814 – incorporated the Principality in a real union and the Princely territory, including Kirchwalsede, became part of the new Stade Region established in 1823".

A much more detailed history of Visselhövede is *Visselhövede: Chronik einer Stadt [Visselhövede: Chronicle of a City]*, edited by Klaus Heinze, which was published in 1999. The chapter on "Visselhövede im Spätmittelalter und in der frühen Neuzeit" ["Visselhövede in the late Middle Ages and early modern times"] by Dieter Brosius includes the long period in which the Borstelmann family was resident in the area: from at least Johann Bo(r)stelmann, who was born in 1641 and buried in Visselhövede to Johann Friedrich Borstelmann, who was baptised there in 1811.

Brosius reports on the implications of the religious turmoil of the Thirty Years War (1618-1648). The parish had undergone its Lutheran Reformation in the 1570s only for the Catholics to regain control in 1629. However, the Jesuit priest Father Arnoldi was murdered by a peasant mob in November 1631 and the Protestants regained control of the parish the following year. According to Brosius:

> "… the contributions and maintenance payments that the various alternating troops squeezed out of the country indicated an economic decline and extensive impoverishment, the consequences of which were felt for a long time".

It was a similar story in the following century, when northern Germany became one of the battlegrounds of the Seven Years War (1756-1763). After one battle of 1758 between the Hanoverians and the French, "… the district looked like a complete devastation and the subjects were totally ruined for many years".

Brosius provides some interesting figures on the growth of the village, reporting that the number of citizens and residents in Visselhövede rose from 291 in 1740 to 464 in 1811 and 513 in 1823.³⁵ (I found a curious echo here with the 1841 Census number – 296 – reported for Baldersby in North Yorkshire in Chapter 1 above).

I have to say that I found – and still find – both the timescales and the locational histories of this component of the Line of 16 quite difficult to get to grips with. Harm Hencke and his wife were the great (x10) grandparents of my children, Tom and Katie. His birth in about 1582 was six years before Philip II of Spain launched his great Armada against the England of Elizabeth I. (In a slightly mischievous e-mail, I suggested to a Welsh friend of mine that Harm Hencke's year of birth even pre-dated the last Welsh rugby win over the New Zealand All Blacks).

Similarly, even the brief Wikipedia description noted above – let alone the detailed history given in *Visselhövede: Chronik einer Stadt* – catalogues how that the part of Germany, in which several generations of the extended Borstelmann family lived, belonged to (or was occupied by) the Swedes, Danes, Hanoverians, French (under Napoleon) and Hanoverians again, even before the creation of the modern state. It is clear that there must have been a (literal) procession of invading armies and new rulers and migrant refugees. But the family remained – durable and obstinate – living their lives, working as shepherds or farmers or housekeepers and raising the next generation. There is something deeply heroic about all this.

Other Borstelmann and Perlasky marriages

I had more mixed – though still interesting – results in researching the connections of Anna Perlasky, the mother of Anna Karoline Borstelmann. I found two sets of references to her in a general search of the name in the German records on Ancestry. One of these connected her (and her husband Johann Friedrich Borstelmann) with the births of Anna Marie Borstelmann in 1852 and Anna Karoline Borstelmann in 1853, as shown in Table 3.2.

---

35 Not everyone could become a citizen, as citizenship was tied to the possession of a house. Strangers who married into Visselhövede had to acquire citizenship; in 1800, the fee was 10 Reichstaler.

Table 3.2. The parents, siblings and step-siblings of Anna Karoline Borstelmann	
Johann Friedrich Borstelmann 1811-1854 (born in Visselhovede, Germany) (son of Peter Christoph Borstelmann 1773-? and Anna Margreta Marquardt 1772-?) (died in Hannover, Germany aged 42)	
married	
1. Friederike Christiane Dorothee Grimm (or Gramme) 1815-1851 (born in Hamburg, Germany) (died aged 36)	Minna Karoline Katharina Borstelmann 1846-1874 (died in Hannover aged 27) *married* Heinrich Friedrich Conrad Füllekrug 1837-? (born in Hannover)
married	
2. Anna Perlasky 1827-1899 (born in Bad Münder am Diester, Germany) (daughter of Christoph Perlasky and Marie Angelika Herwig) (died in Osnabrück, Germany aged 72)	Anna Marie Borstelmann 1852-1919 (born in Hannover) (died in Aston, Birmingham aged 67) *married* 1. George Christian Kracke 1838-? (born in Prussia) 2. Albert Samuel (Samuel Albert) Wood Niblett 1861-1941 (born in Cheltenham) (died in Knaresborough, Yorkshire, aged 79)
	Anna Karoline Borstelmann 1853-1938 (born in Elze, Hannover) (died in Osnabrück aged 84) *married* **Charles James Niblett 1851-1927 (born in Cheltenham) (died in Wallington/Croydon, London aged 76)**
Anna Perlasky 1827-1899 later married August Heinrich Gottleib Wöbbekind 1828-? (born in Hannover)	Karl Julius Ludwig Wöbbekind 1860-1903 (born in Hannover) (died in Barrackpore, Bengal, India aged 43) *married* Marion Mendies

It was at this point that the tantalising prospect arose that the older sister might have been the wife of one of Charles James Niblett's older brothers – Samuel Albert Wood Niblett – given that, as noted above from the index of Antwerp Police immigration records, her maiden name was Marie Borstelman (without the second "n"). It appeared that the evidence did not quite fit, however. In the 1901 Census of England and Wales, Marie Niblett's age was given as 44 (and ten years later it was 53), which would imply that her year of birth was 1857. This was consistent with her age at death (in Birmingham in 1919), which was given as 62. On the other hand, I knew that it was possible that she was being economical with the truth with regard to her age – a far from uncommon occurrence throughout this narrative – but, if taken at face value, these implied dates meant that Samuel Niblett's wife was not the sister of Anna Karoline Borstelmann, as the latter's father (Johann Friedrich Borstelmann) died in 1854. More on Anna Marie Borstelmann was to follow, however.

A potentially different outcome that occurred to me was that Anna Marie Borstelmann might have died in infancy in 1852, given that the Christian name is repeated with Anna Karoline Borstelmann the following year. To check this out, in June 2016, I sent a general enquiry to the membership of the Hannover genealogical network to ask whether the repeated given name implied that the first child had indeed died before the second child was born. I received a very helpful reply from Uschi Boes, who stated that that would not necessarily have been the case.

Uschi Boes also informed me – much to my surprise, needless to say – that Joseph Friedrich Borstelmann had had a previous marriage: to Friederike Christiane Dorothea Grimm (1813-1851), who had died of tuberculosis at the age of 38. They had married in Hannover in 1844 and had had a daughter, Minna Karoline Katharina Borstelmann, in 1846.

Uschi Boes reported that Joseph Friedrich Borstelmann had been a *fourier* (quartermaster) and that he had been a sergeant in the *Leibregiment* in 1851. In 1854, he had been a *Pensionaer* (i.e. retired, probably because he was very sick) and he died in that year at the age of 42 because of *Auszehrung*, which (she said) was an old name, perhaps indicating tuberculosis or cancer. She also stated that Anna Perlasky had been born in Münder and her father, Christoph, had been a musician. (The www.familysearch.org site of the Mormon church reports that Christof (sic) Perlasky was born in Muender am Deister, Springe, Hannover, in 1800).

I looked up some of the details of Minna Borstelmann – Joseph's daughter by his first marriage – on Ancestry. It was a sad tale. She married Heinrich Friedrich Conrad Füllekrug (who was born in Hannover in 1837) and, according to *Germany, Select Births and Baptisms 1558-1898*, they had 5 children in the six years from 1868. The last of these – Marie Theresa Füllekrug – was baptised on 18th July 1874 and (from *Germany, Select Deaths and Burials 1582-1958)* died ten days later. As Minna Füllekrug herself had died on 16th July at the age of 27, I must assume that her death was related to this birth. The second youngest child – Anna Theresa Jeanette Füllekrug – died the following month at the age of one year. All these births and deaths were registered in Hannover.

The second reference in the German records held on Ancestry connected Anna Perlasky with the birth of Carl Julius Ludwig Wöbbekind, the father being August Heinrich Gottlieb Wöbbekind. No date was given, but I noted that a 14 year-old Carl Wöbbekind was listed as a passenger on a Hamburg-New York ship in 1874, suggesting that his year of birth was about 1860. (This was later confirmed as 30th April 1860 by Uschi Boes). A separate Ancestry database – *India Marriages, 1792-1948* – recorded that Carl Julius Louis Wöbbekind married Marion Mendies in Calcutta, Bengal, India, in 1884, the respective fathers being "Henry" Wöbbekind and John Mendies. Further contributions to the public pages of Ancestry have reported that Carl Wöbbekind died in Barrackpore, Bengal, in 1903. (As is often the case, the submissions on Ancestry were near-identical and it was not clear which contributor had undertaken the original research).[36]

It was clear, therefore, that Anna Perlasky married August Heinrich Gottlieb Wobbekind at some point after the death of her first husband, Johann Friedrich Borstelmann, in 1854. Uschi Boes informed me that this was in 1858 (see footnote) and that August Heinrich Gottlieb Woebbekind was a *Kanonier* (artilleryman). He was born in Elze in 1828, the son of Heinrich Woebbekind, a shoemaker, and Charlotte Abelmann. Interestingly, as both of Anna Perlasky's husbands were soldiers in Hannover, the marriages were held in the city's

---

36 A couple of contributions to the public pages of Ancestry also link Anna Perlasky to the birth of August C Wöbbekind in Germany in 1856. However, Uschi Boes did not mention him in her response to me and I noted from her that the Wöbbekind/Perlasky marriage did not take place until December 1858. I was able to confirm this later by consulting the *Bremen, Germany, and Hannover, Prussia, Germany, Lutheran Baptisms, Marriages and Burials, 1574-1945* database on Ancestry.

August C Wöbbekind also migrated to the US, where he appeared in several official US databases. He became a naturalised US citizen in 1878 in New York, when he was a bartender at 58 Market Street. He was also in *US, City Directories 1822-1995* for 1884 (amongst other years), which listed his occupation as "beer" with a home address of 68 Henry Street, New York City. According to *New York Marriages, 1686-1980*, he married Bertha Steinbeck in New York in 1893; they subsequently raised a family. August C Wöbbekind was also recorded in several US Censuses, including as a 74 year-old in New York in 1930, and he died in the Bronx in 1934 at the age of 78. Crucially, the record of his marriage refers to his mother's name as being Wilhelmina Harmon.

Until I discovered the name of August C Wöbbekind's mother (who was also given as Wilhelmina in the *New York, New York City Municipal Deaths, 1795-1949* record of his death in 1934), I had been wondering whether he was part of the extended Borstelmann/Perlasky family. However, whilst this clarification of his mother's name confirmed that this was not the case, it did not help in throwing light on a minor mystery arising from the research on the Niblett family that John Eckersley had passed on to my aunt Joy. His summary reported that Anna Perlasky had died in Osnabrück in 1899 at the age of 72. However, the copy of one of the death certificates of Anna Karoline Niblett (née Borstelmann), who did die in Osnabrück in 1938, states that her parents, including "Anna, geborene Perlasky… beide verstoben in Amerika" ("both died in America"). It was not until I commissioned research from a genealogist in Germany in 2019 (see below), that I was able to confirm that Anna Wöbbekind – formerly Borstelmann and née Perlasky – did indeed die in Osnabrück in 1899.

Garnisonskirche (garrison church).[37] The Ancestry records show that the baptisms of Joseph Borstelmann and Anna Perlasky's daughters – Anna Marie and Anna Karoline – both took place in the *Garnisongemeinde* (garrison parish).

I was able to confirm Anna Perlasky's second marriage by examining the database of *Bremen, Germany, and Hannover, Prussia, Germany, Lutheran Baptisms, Marriages and Burials, 1574-1945* on Ancestry. This source also revealed that Anna Perlasky had a younger brother – Johann Wilhelm Adolph Parlasca (sic) – who was born in 1829 and who married Friederike Charlotte Barteldes (1826-1870) in Buch, Hannover, in April 1854. In this database, the references to the seven children of the marriage are given under the name of Parlaska.

A separate database – *Hannover, Germany, Lutheran Baptisms, Marriages and Burials, 1643-1887* – includes an entry for the death of Marie Engel Parlaska in Hannover in November 1857 at the age of 78. I did wonder if this was Anna Perlasky's mother – Marie Angelika Perlasky (née Herwig) – but the implied year of birth (around 1779) was some 20 years before that which I had previously understood from the pre-Internet researches of John Eckersley (and also considerably pre-dated the year of birth – 1800 – of Christoph Perlasky, Anna's father).

Of course, she could have been Christoph's mother and, whilst this is only speculation, it is interesting to note that the name of Marie Engel Parlaska's husband was given in the database as Johann Christoph Parlaska.

The search for other Perlasky references on the Ancestry databases produces only a few leads. Of Anna Perlasky's near contemporaries, *Bremen, Germany, and Hannover, Prussia, Germany, Lutheran Baptisms, Marriages and Burials, 1574-1945* includes an entry for Luise Perlasky (1834-1862) who died in Hannover and, further afield, for Simon Perlasky, who was born in Poland in about 1823, but appears in the *California, US, State Census, 1852*. I have not been able to link either of these to the family of Anna Perlasky.[38]

---

37 This was the older of the two garrison churches in Hannover. It was initially called the Holy Spirit Church – and later the Old Garrison Church – and dated from the 13th Century. The church was situated at the junction of Knochenhauerstrasse and Schmiedestrasse in the old city and was demolished in 1875. The new garrison church in Goetheplatz was commissioned in 1896 and demolished in 1960. I visited the site of the original church on my visit to Hannover in September 2018 (see below); it is now an unremarkable parade of shops.

38 The more general Google search on the Perlasky name also does not generate many leads. There is a link to a website of Argentinean Jews and this prompted me to search the database of Holocaust victims compiled by the World Holocaust Remembrance Center in Jerusalem – www.yadvashem.org – the reference to which I had noted on a visit to Berlin in September 2014. There are no references to the Perlasky surname (or to Borstelmann). Similarly, the *Judisches Familienbuch* database on www.genpluswin-database.de/nofb does not give any references to Perlasky, Perlaska, Perlasca, Borstelmann or Herwig.

The Perlasky surname is also not recognised on the www.kartezumnamen.eu. website giving the current distribution of surnames in Germany. However, the website does give a few entries for both Parlasca and Parlaska, notably in the southern part of Niedersachsen. Moreover, these variants on the Perlasky surname also generate some Google references, including in the USA. By contrast, there are a sizeable number of entries for the Herwig surname, especially in Niedersachsen and the adjoining *Land* of Hessen.

There is one further aspect to the research on the Perlasky name. A couple of the original sources – including that of the marriage of Anna Perlasky to Johan Friedrich Borstelmann in *Bremen, Germany, and Hannover, Prussia, Germany, Lutheran Baptisms, Marriages and Burials, 1574-1945* – include a diaeresis diacritical mark above the final letter i.e. Perlaskÿ. Wikipedia states that this is a Latin script character that is now found in a few French proper nouns and a few Hungarian surnames. How much farther this takes us, I'm not sure: we now have Perlasky references in Germany, France, Poland and Hungary. And the itinerant profession – musician – of Anna Perlasky's father, Christop, means that any of these could be of relevance.

Visits to Niedersachsen: 80 years apart

I have copies of two death certificates of Anna Karoline Niblett. The first is the German version (*die Sterbeurkunde*), which recorded that she died at her home at Ludwigstrasse 15, Osnabrück, on 4th August 1938. Her birthplace was noted as Elze, Hannover, and her religion as Lutheran. In addition to giving the names of her parents – Sergeant Johann Friedrich Borstelmann and Anna, geborene Perlasky – the certificate stated that she had been married "*mit dem Handelsschullehrer* [commercial school teacher] *Charles James Niblett, verstorben in England*". (Charles had died in London in 1927). The stamp of the registry office (*das Standesamt*) comprised the Nazi eagle and swastika.

The English version of the certificate was issued by the British Consulate in Bremen and refers to the anglicised version of her name: Anne Caroline Niblett. The Consulate had been informed by letter by her son – my grandfather, Alfred Niblett – who had enclosed a copy of the German certificate.

By the time of his mother's death in Osnabrück, Alfred Niblett was living in England. However, he certainly visited her on at least two occasions before she died, as his 1935-40 passport has stamps from *die Ortspolizeibehorde* in the summers of 1935 and 1937. There are also two designs of the eagle and swastika, each clearly and chillingly jumping off the page as if they had been stamped yesterday. The visas page of the passport carries details of two withdrawals of 50 Reichsmarken from one of the Osnabrück branches of Deutsche Bank und Disconto-Gesellschaft.[39]

There was an obvious line of enquiry to investigate whether anything relating to Anna Karoline Niblett (née Borstelmann) or Anna Borstelmann (née Perlasky) had survived in modern-day Osnabrück. In April 2013, I e-mailed the city's cemetery administration (*das Friedhofsverwaltung*) with their details. No reply was received. However, a repeat enquiry in June 2016 did produce a

---

39 For a fascinating discussion of the experiences of the various types of foreign visitor to Nazi Germany – diplomats, tourists, businessmen, students et al – see Julia Boyd's *Travellers in the Third Reich: The Rise of Fascism Through the Eyes of Everyday People* (2017).

prompt response from the department, which appeared to draw a blank: there were no data about either ancestor in the cemetery administration's records and a "Ludwigstrasse" did not now exist in Osnabrück. It was a disappointing outcome, but I felt that I had pursued this line as fully as I could and, with that, there was a feeling of closure.

It turned out that that feeling was somewhat premature. In September 2018, my sister Rosie and I spent a week in the Niedersachsen *Land* visiting some of the places associated with the German side of the family history. In a local bookshop, I came across a map of the Osnabrück tram system of 1906 on which the location of Ludwigstrasse was marked at the end of one of the lines.[40] On transposing this on to a modern map of the city, it was evident that the road is now called Ludwig Baete Strasse (after a 20th Century writer and historian). It is a pleasant tree-lined street of post-Second World War housing; number 15 is a sizeable and sturdy red-brick building with a characteristically sharp-angled roof.[41]

In addition to Osnabrück, our September 2018 visit incorporated Elze, Visselhövede, Kirchwalsede, Bad Münder am Deister and Hannover. It was an unforgettable trip and, undoubtedly, one of the highlights of my long years of family history research. The short article about it – "Here I Stand", reproduced in Annex A3 below – that was published in the April 2019 edition of the *Cleveland Family History Society Journal* includes a reference to seeing the 1772 baptism record of Anna Margreta Marquardt (my great x3 grandmother) in the original church records of Kirchwalsede: "I felt the lump in my throat as I saw her name on the page: I just about held it together".

A detour: Waldermar Kracke

I am now going to take what appeared at the time to be something of a detour, partly because I think it is interesting and partly because, in its story, it highlights the fascinating tangents that are available to family historians on the margins of their central research interests. As it happens, it also proved highly relevant to the Borstelmann narrative.

In the 1901 Census of England, one Waldemar Kracke appeared as a 24 year-old stepson living in the household of Samuel AW Niblett – one of Charles James Niblett's younger brothers – and his wife Marie in Birmingham. (This is

---

40 *Die Osnabrücker Strassenbahn* [The Tramway of Osnabrück] in *Die Geschichte der elektrischen Strassenbahn, deren Voraenger und Nachfolger* [The History of Electric Tramway and its Predecessor and Successor] by Alfred Spuhr and Claude Jeanmarie, Verlag Eisenbahn, Switzerland, 1980.

41 In the excellent tourist information office in Osnabrück, Rosie and I came across (and purchased) the second of two wonderful books of photographs of the city taken in the first three decades of the 20th Century by Rudolf Lichtenberg Sr and Rudolf Lichtenberg Jr. *Lichtenberg – Bilder einer Stadt II: Fotografische Ansichten Osnabrück, 1900-1930 [Scenes of a City II: Photographic sights of Osnabrück, 1900-1930]* was compiled by Rolf Spilker and Birte Tost and published in 2007.

the Marie Borstelman who appeared with Samuel Niblett in the index of Antwerp Police immigration records). I assumed, given the surname, that he was the son of Marie from an earlier marriage. His place of birth was given as America.

A trawl through the Ancestry sources produced details of a much-travelled life. Waldemar Kracke was: a 34 year-old photographer living as a boarder in Mountpleasant Parade, Dublin (from the 1911 Census of Ireland); a 39 year-old (born on 30th December 1876 in New York, New York) travelling on SS *Philadelphia* from Liverpool to New York in August 1916 with a destination address of 332 Beckmann Avenue, Bronx, New York; a photographer living in Trenton, New Jersey, according to his US World War 1 Draft Registration Card with a nearest relative of Mrs Albert S Niblett of Sparkhill, Birmingham; a 43 year-old studio photographer lodging in Peoria, Illinois, with both parents reported as having been born in Germany with German as their mother tongue (1920 US Census); resident in Sacramento, California, in 1924 and 1925 (from the *US City Directories*); a 52 year-old photographer living in Eugene, Oregon, having been married to his 36 year-old wife Olga (a music teacher) for 7 years (1930 US Census); a 63 year-old owner of a photography studio, with the 45 year-old Olga a piano teacher, still in Eugene (1940 US Census); in the *US Social Security Applications and Claims Index* (in October 1944). Waldemar Kracke died in Oregon in January 1951 at the age of 74 (*Oregon Death Index, 1898-2008*).

The story does not quite end there. I did not find out Olga Kracke's maiden name, but the US Census records that she was born in Northern Germany. In January 1960, nine years after the death of Waldemar and at the age of 65/66, she married Edgar Addison Dugan (1898-1984). She also died in 1984 at the age of 89/90; Edgar and Olga are buried together in the Marcola Cemetery, Marcola, Lane County, Oregon (*Oregon, Find a Grave Index*).

The Ancestry records also led me to an article on page 4 of *The Washington Post* of Sunday May 30th 1915:

AMERICAN MUST GIVE BAIL
BONDED AND FORCED TO REGISTER IN IRELAND AS ALIEN

Dublin, May 29. Waldemar Kracke, who was charged with being a German and neglecting to register as an alien enemy, has proved his American citizenship in the magistrate's court… The magistrate held, however, that although Kracke was an American, he was bound to register as an alien. Kracke was ordered to find bail to the sum of $50 and to come up before the magistrate for judgment if such action was required of him… Hitherto most Americans in Ireland have not considered registry obligatory on them.

I was able to find the family into which Waldemar Kracke was born in December 1876 by consulting the *New York Marriages, 1686-1980* database available on the Church of the Latter Day Saints's Family Search website. This included an entry for the marriage of George Christian Kracke to Mary Ann (sic) Borstelmann in Manhattan, New York, on 10th July 1871. George's parents were named as George Kracke and Caroline Heldje, whilst those of Mary Ann were Frederick Borstelmann and Ann Palaska (sic again). A separate entry in the same source reported that George Kracke was born in Prussia (though Google Maps does not locate the specific place mentioned, Nuva Holdelaker). The *United States Marriages* database on Findmypast reveals that George Kracke was aged 33 and Mary Borstelmann aged 19 at the time of the marriage. There was no reference to the family of George and Marie/Mary Ann Kracke in the *1875 New York State Census*.

It is the listing of Mary Ann's parents that is the significant finding here. It confirms that the Anna Marie Borstelmann (born in Hannover in 1852) and the Anna Karoline Borstelmann (born in Elze, Hannover in 1854) were indeed sisters, who married the brothers Samuel Albert Wood Niblett and Charles James Niblett, respectively.

George Kracke and Mary Borstelmann had other children. The *California Death Index, 1940-1997* includes an entry for Anna Walter, who died in Sacramento in 1956 at the age of 81. Her parents' names in this entry are given as Krocke (sic) and Boestelmann (sic again) on the transcription on Ancestry, but she had been born Anna Kracke in New York in June 1875, when her father's occupation was listed as "merchant". She married Eduard Edwin Walther (the "h" later being dropped) in Sacramento in 1909. He was a music teacher, who pre-deceased Anna by six years at the age of 74.

A contributor to the public pages of Ancestry – Heather Shepard – has researched the Kracke family of New York in some depth. She has listed another child, Erma Kracke (though no dates are given) and also uncovered evidence that there might have been 2 stillborn children and one other case of infant mortality prior to Anna's birth in 1875. In addition, Ms Shepard has posted an intriguing excerpt from the *New York Herald* of 7th April 1878:

> "George Kracke and Mrs MA Kracke, dealers in fluting machines, at 106 Chambers Street have left, it is said, for parts unknown, leaving their creditors in the lurch. The business was carried on by George Kracke in his wife's name. They owe four firms in this city and Newark about $1,500 and it is thought the entire indebtedness is about $3,000. Numerous creditors have called at the store, but have failed to discover their whereabouts. A creditor

said yesterday that he had learned that Mrs Kracke had sailed for Europe, but her husband had not accompanied her. There are no assets".[42] [43]

In the 1911 Census of England and Wales, Samuel AW Niblett and his wife Marie were stated as having been married for 30 years. At first, I thought that this must have implied that George Kracke died sometime between 1876 (given that Waldemar was born in December of that year) and 1881. However, in the light of the newspaper extract undercovered by Ms Shepard, it would appear that the more likely explanation is either that the Kracke/Borstelmann marriage was dissolved in or sometime after 1878 or that Marie/Mary Borstelmann's marriage to Samuel Niblett was bigamous.

There is no record of a death for George Kracke's death in the *New York, New York Death Index 1862-1948*. This would not be surprising, if he had either fled New York after defaulting on his sizeable debts and/or changed his name.[44] [45] Nor any there any references to Marie/Mary Borstelmann/Kracke and her young family in either the US Federal Census of 1880 or the UK Census of 1881. Again, this is to be expected, if – as the newspaper report suggested – she had travelled to Europe, as a likely destination would have been Germany (and possibly her sister Anna Karoline Niblett's home in Osnabrück). Indeed, it is almost certainly through the connection to Anna Karoline's husband – Charles James Niblett – that Marie/Mary became attached to his brother, Albert Samuel.

As I have not been able to find a marriage record for Albert Samuel Niblett and Marie Borstelmann/ Kracke in England, I assume that this ceremony must have taken place in Germany in 1881. However, if this did occur, the couple must have moved to England quite quickly as, in the 1891 Census, all 6 of their own children had been born in Cheltenham. At this stage, Albert Samuel Niblett was a "mineral water manufacturer" and the family was living in Charlton Kings in Gloucestershire (where Samuel's parents had lived with their family 20 years earlier) with one servant. Albert and Marie's household does not contain any of the Kracke children.

---

[42] The *Chambers Twentieth Century Dictionary* definition of a fluting machine is: "a machine for corrugating sheet metal; also a wood-turning machine for forming twisted, spiral and fluted ballisters".

[43] $3,000 in 1878 would have been the equivalent of approximately $85,000 in 2022.

[44] For the purposes of this narrative, the fate of George Kracke is a detour of a detour. In other words, an unexpected – and usually, as in the case, welcome – occupational hazard for the family history researcher.

[45] Although (as yet) he is not part of the extended Niblett family, I could not help but notice the reference to another George Kracke in the *British Army Service Records* held by Findmypast. He was born in Friedland, Hannover, and joined the 1st Regiment of Hussars, First German Legion as a 19 year-old Private in 1804, remaining in the regiment for over 10 years. At the time of his discharge, he was about 5 ft 10 ins, with brown hair, blue eyes and fair complexion. The discharge was due to the severe wounds he received during a battle in the Peninsula War, specifically "in consequence of having been wounded through his right arm in an Action at Tolosa on 11th April 1814, in consequence of which he lost the whole use of the right arm".

There is one other set of records available on Ancestry that relates to Marie Niblett (née Borstelmann). Her name appears in the *UK, The Midwives Roll, 1904-59* for the years 1910 and 1926, in both cases with a Date of Enrolment in November 1908 and a qualification of the CMB Examination.[46] There is no doubt that this is the same person, as the home address in Sparkhill, Birmingham, given in the Roll is the same as that in the 1911 Census. (Interestingly, the latter document has a blank entry in the "occupation" column). Given what I know about Marie's year of birth, this implies that she enrolled as a midwife as the age of 56.

I was to discover later that the wedding announcement of Charles James Niblett and Anna Karoline Borstelmann had provided additional evidence that Anna Marie Borstelmann and Anna Karoline Borstelmann had been sisters. The *Cheltenham Mercury* of 7th February 1874 carried the following:

> MARRIAGES
>
> Dec 30 1873 at the Christus Kirche, Elze, by the Rev Pastor Sievers of Elze and the Rev Pastor Rabens of Hanover, Charles James Niblett, eldest son of Mr Chas Niblett of this town to Anna Carolina, youngest daughter of the late Major Borstelmann of Hanover.[47]

I rather suspect that the rank attained by Anna Karoline's father had been slightly exaggerated. However, in addition, it is noticeable that the announcement refers to his youngest daughter. This implies that there were at least three altogether; as noted, I have also identified Anna Marie Borstelmann as well as Johann Friedrich's Borstelmann's daughter by his first marriage, Minna Karoline Katharine Borstelmann.

The family of Charles James Niblett and Anna Karoline Borstelmann

The family of Charles James Niblett and Anna Karoline Borstelmann is shown in Table 3.3. My grandfather – Alfred Edgar Niblett – was the ninth of eleven children born in Osnabrück between 1874 and 1893. Charles is listed in an 1898 directory – *Handels- und Gewerke- Adressbuch der Provinz Hannover* [Trade and Trades Address Book for the Province of Hannover] – as resident at Martinistrasse

---

46 The website of the Royal College of Obstetricians and Gynaecologists and the Royal College of Midwives (www.rcog.org.uk) states that an important feature of the first Midwives Act of 1902 was the establishment of the Central Midwives Board (CMB) for England and Wales. The CMB was responsible for the regulation of the certification and examination of midwives, admission to the Roll of Midwives and the annual publication of the Roll. From April 1905, no person could assume the title of midwife unless she held a certificate issued by the CMB. From April 1910, no person could habitually and for gain attend women in childbirth, except under the direction of a doctor, unless she was certified under the Act.

47 The announcement was repeated in the *Cheltenham Chronicle* three days later.

39. I have not found Charles in any of the pre-First World War census records for England and Wales and I assume that he was resident in Germany throughout this period.

Some of the table's detail on Alfred's siblings has been derived from the notes that John Eckersley provided to my aunt Joy and from the research published on the internet by Mike Niblett. This has been significantly supplemented by research that I commissioned from a German genealogist – Monika Mohring – in 2019. It was her examination of the State Archives of Osnabrück that confirmed that Anna Wobbekind (formerly Borstelmann, née Perlasky) had died in the city (at the same Martinistrasse 39 address noted above) in 1899 at the age of 72. (This does beg the question as to where the confusion generated by the "both died in America" reference to the places of death of her parents on Anna Karoline Niblett's own death certificate in 1938 came from).

It was also Ms Mohring who produced the information on the short life of Albert George Niblett (1881-1887) and noted the registered names at the baptisms in Osnabrück of Charles (Carl Julius Heinrich), Annetta (Selina Anna Catharine), Lola (Elisabeth Miriam) and George (Georg).

Table 3.3. The family of Charles James and Anna Karoline Niblett		
Charles James Niblett 1851-1927 (born in Cheltenham) (died in Wallington/Croydon aged 76)		
married		
Anna Karoline Borstelmann 1853-1938 (born in Elze, Hannover) (died in Osnabrück, Germany, aged 84)		Charles Julius Henry Niblett 1874-1967 (born in Osnabrück) (died in Lisbon, Portugal, aged 92) *married* Maria Angelina Pinto da Rocha 1883-1965 (born in Porto, Portugal) (died in Lisbon aged 82)

	Selina Anna Catharine (Annetta) Niblett 1875-1959 (born in Osnabrück) (died in Osnabrück aged 83) *married* Christian Eduard Henning Frömbling 1873-before 1935 (born in Friedeburg, Niedersachsen, Germany)
	Adolf Alfred (Alphonso) Niblett 1877-1966 (born in Osnabrück) (died in Southampton, aged 89) *married* Charlotte Mary Patterson 1876-1960 (born in Omagh, County Tyrone) (died in Chilworth, Hampshire, aged 83)
	Elizabeth Miriam (Lola) Niblett 1878-1964 (born in Osnabrück) (died in Leeds aged 86)
	Harry Niblett 1879-1959 (born in Osnabrück) (died in Lewisham aged 80) *married* Christine Charlotte Emily Sturm (or Sturn) 1873-1958 (died in Greenwich district aged 84)
	Albert George Niblett 1881-1887 (born in Osnabrück) (died in Osnabrück aged 6)
	Therese Marie Niblett 1883-1965 (born in Osnabrück) (died in Osnabrück aged 82) *married* Georg Ernst Wilhelm Fremdling 1879-before 1934 (born in Gottingen, Germany)

	George Niblett 1887-1948 (born in Osnabrück) (died in Greenwich district aged 61) *married* Regina Lillian Boocock (or Beauchamp) 1900-1993 (born in Edmonton, London) (died in Bromley, Kent, aged 93)
	Alfred Edgar Niblett 1888-1973 **(born in Osnabrück)** **(died in Leeds aged 84)** *married* **Marie Rosa Wilson 1890-1968** **(born in Wood Green, London)** **(died in Leeds aged 78)**
	Marion Niblett 1890-1958 (born in Osnabrück) (died in Osnabrück aged 68)
	Elfriede Auguste Niblett 1893-1961 (born in Osnabrück) (died in Wehnen, Ammerland, Germany aged 68) *married* Bernhard Hamschmidt 1893-1965 (born in Rietberg, Germany) (died in Oldenburg, Germany aged 72)

The sisters of Alfred Niblett

The only personal recollection I have of any of my grandfather's siblings is from the early 1960s, when my "Aunt Lola" occasionally stayed with my grandfather and his wife at their home in north Leeds. She was actually my grandad's spinster sister, Elisabeth Miriam Niblett (1878-1964). I remember her as an elderly white-haired lady, who seemed to be always dressed in black and who spoke very little English. However, the release of the 1921 Census of England and Wales in January 2022 has caused me to revise the last of these details (see below).

Some fascinating information on the life of the other unmarried sister – Marion Niblett (1890-1958) – was uncovered by Monika Mohring, who found that she had naturalised as a German in 1914 and was a teacher by profession. Her denazification report of 1946-47 stated that she had not been a member of the

National Socialist Party and that she had been in the German Democratic Party in 1932 and 1933.[48]

I was able to find more information on Marion from the databases published online at www.compgen.de by Compgen, a German genealogical association. These included two directory entries for Maria/Marion Niblett as a teacher living at 50 (and then 5) Hauptstrasse in the Bentheim district of Nordhorn (which is close to the Dutch border) in 1937 and 1951 – i.e. both pre- and post-War. (We return to this location later).

Monika Mohring confirmed the surnames (Frömbling and Fremdling, respectively) of the husbands of Annetta Niblett (1875-1959) and Theresa Marie Niblett (1883-1965) that I had previously come across from the pre-Internet research undertaken by John Eckersley for my aunt Joy. Mr Eckersley had also reported that the husband of the other sister – Elfriede Augusta Niblett (1893-1961) – was Bernhard Hamschmidt. Separate correspondence with Uschi Boes had revealed that this marriage had been in 1919; an online directory of the *Osnabrücker Zeitung* stated that this had also been the year of their engagement.

This focus on the sisters of Alfred Niblett prompted me to consider a significant issue: namely, the citizenship of the wife and children of Charles James Niblett, especially his 5 daughters.

To enquire about this, in August 2021, I contacted Andreas Fahrmeir – Professor of Modern History at the Johann Wolfgang Goethe University in Frankfurt-am-Main – one of whose specialisms is 19th Century citizenship in the states and countries of Europe. I struck lucky, as Professor Fahrmeir was kind enough to provide an immediate and detailed response.

Professor Fahrmeir reported that it was a longstanding tradition in most countries of Europe that women automatically acquired their husbands' citizenship. This applied in the individual states of Germany prior to unification and to the German Empire from 1871. (Charles James Niblett and Anna Karoline Borstelmann were married in Elze in 1873).

Professor Fahrmeir referred me to the *Gesetz über die Erwerbung und den Verlust der Bundesund Staatsangehörigkei*t of 1st June 1870 [*The law on the acquisition and loss of citizenship in the states and the Federation*], which applied until 1913 for the "North German Federation" (for which read the "German Empire"). Rule 5 stated that *"Die Verheirathung mit einem Norddeutschen begründet für die Ehefrau die Staatsangehörigkeit des Mannes"* [*"The marriage to a North German transfers the citizenship of the man to the woman"*] and Rule 13

---

48 The DDP (*Deutsche Demokratische Partei*) was a social liberal party formed in 1918. Its Wikipedia entry reports that it obtained 18 per cent of the vote in the federal election of 1919, but that this proportion fell to 5 per cent in 1928 and 1 per cent in 1932. Together with the Social Democratic Party (*Sozialdemokratische Partei Deutschlands*), it was banned in June 1933 during the process of *Gleichschaltung* (coordination) by means of which the Nazis established totalitarian control over German society.

that *"Die Staatsangehörigkeit geht fortan nur verloren... bei einer Norddeutschen durch Verheirathung mit dem Angehörigen eines anderen Bundesstaates oder mit einem Ausländer". ["Citizenship is... lost... in the case of a North German woman through marriage to a citizen of another federal state or to a foreigner"].*

Accordingly, Anna Karoline Niblett would have been considered British by the German authorities, as – initially – would her daughters, as they automatically acquired the citizenship of the husband/parents. However, the daughters who married German men automatically acquired their husbands' citizenship. This applied until 1969, although from 1957 it only covered marriages that took place in Germany, if the wife expressed the desire to acquire German citizenship. (The marriages of Annette, Theresa and Elfriede Niblett took place in 1899, 1913 and 1919, respectively). Finally, Professor Fahrmeir confirmed that the Niblett daughters could have applied for naturalization whilst single; as we have seen, this was what Marion Niblett did in 1914.

The family historian Mike Niblett noted that a post-First World War reference to the family business of Niblett Limited lists the directors of the company as my grandfather's brothers – CJH Niblett, AA Niblett, H Niblett and G Niblett – with Dr AE Niblett himself as the company secretary. Evidently, none of my grandfather's 5 sisters had a directorial role and I did wonder how many of them were resident in England.[49]

At first, I thought that none of them were. As noted, Marion Niblett was naturalised as a German in 1914, certainly lived in Germany in 1932-33 and was the subject of a (positive) denazification report in 1946-47, whilst three of the other sisters – Annetta (or Annette), Theresa and Elfriede – all married German men.

This left the unmarried Elisabeth Miriam (Lola) Niblett, my memory of whom – from when I had met her in Leeds as a young boy – had been that she had spoken very little English. However, I have had to revise this in the light of the 1921 Census, which records that Charles James Niblett was the head of an extended household in Beckenham, Kent (see below) and also a "general export and import merchant" at the head of Niblett Limited of 21 Mincing Lane, London EC3. His son Harry Niblett lived with his young family at the same address and was an employer with the same company. In addition, crucially, the Census reveals that Elisabeth Miriam Niblett was employed with Niblett Limited as a "private secretary". It is difficult to see how she could have fulfilled this role without having a working command of English.

I do not know how long Elisabeth Miriam Niblett remained in England after 1921, although she is recorded in the 1939 Register as a "foreign correspondent" living in the household of Harry and Emily Niblett in Battersea and she was to die in Leeds in 1964 at the age of 86. The *England and Wales, National Probate*

---

49 The Niblett Limited company is discussed further in Chapter 9.

Calendar (Index of Wills and Administrations), 1858-1966, lists my grandfather, Alfred Niblett, as the "legal executive" administering her estate of £392. I am not sure that he would have had this role if her permanent residency had been in Germany.

Let us return to Alfred Niblett's three married sisters. There were a whole host of questions, of course, relating to the experiences of the sisters and their families in the Second World War and the likely current-day presence of the grandchildren of those sisters: an additional cohort of my second cousins. Initially, the combination of Monika Mohling's researches and the (limited) coverage of the German databases held on Ancestry enabled me to piece together some further information on the Fremdling and Frömbling connections.

Theresa Niblett married George Ernst Wilheim Fremdling in Osnabrück in March 1913; she died in the same city's *Stadtkrankenhaus* in 1965 at the age of 82. Under her married name, there is a series of entries for Therese at Lotterstrasse 88A (which is not far from her mother's last address at Ludwigstrasse 15) between 1934-37 and in 1950-51 and 1954-55, as given in *Adressbucher der Stadt und des Landkreises Osnabrück [Osnabrück and Surrounding Areas Address Books, 1815-1974]*. In the first of these, her occupation is given by the abbreviation "Wwe" – i.e. she was a *Witwe* or widow by 1934.

The same sources reveal that Annette Frömbling, who had married Eduard Christian Henning Frömbling in 1899, was resident at Ludwigstrasse 15 in 1950-51 and 1954-55. Hugo Frömbling – a *Kaufmann* (businessman or shopkeeper) – lived at the same address, whilst ECH Frömbling & Co was the name of a *Lotterieineinnahme und Reiseburo* business (lottery sales and travel agents) at Grosse Strasse 4 near the centre of the city. The business's telephone number was the same as that of Henning Frömbling, another *Kaufmann* resident at Augustenstrasse 84. Although there are no direct references in these two directories to Annette's husband, the initials of the business are clearly his.

The reference to the name of the Frömbling business prompted further searches for it in other address books for German cities held on Ancestry. The earliest I could find was in the *Hamburger Adressbuch* 1925 at Papenhuiderstrasse 12 in Hamburg, where its interests were in *Ole und Fette* (oils and greases). 10 years later, the business address had moved to Ludwigstrasse 15 in Osnabrück, where Ed Frömbling (sic) – *Handelsvertreter* (sales representative) – was also resident. Significantly, it was Anna Niblett's maiden name that was given in the 1935 directory when, like her sister Theresa the year before, she was also described as a widow. In that year, Hugo Frömbling was a *Kapitan dHM* (captain in the *Handelsmarine* or merchant marine) resident at Grosse Strasse 87. (At this stage, I could only speculate that Hugo, Henning and Ed Frömbling were sons of Annette and her husband).

As the access to German 20th Century BMD data is restricted to close family members, I was obviously constrained in terms of following up these branches of the Niblett family into modern times. I judged that the only recourse – and one to be taken with consideration caution – was to examine whether the current version of the internet telephone directory for Osnabrück (the White Pages of *Das Telefonbuch*) yielded any possible avenues to follow for either the Frömbling or Fremdling surnames. (The latest references I had for the Hamschmidt surname were not in Osnabrück).

The directory – dated 2022 – had 10 Osnabrück addresses for Frömbling (and none for Fremdling) with the nearest entry to the old Ludwigstrasse address appearing to be for one Peter Frömbling. I was somewhat puzzled by this, as I had separately come across an obituary notice (dated 2018) for someone of this name (although I realised it might have been a different person). The notice listed two married daughters of Herr Frömbling, one of whom – Dr Simone Frömbling-Fulbier – I decided to contact in February 2022.

My letter was – I hope – properly respectful of the circumstances in which an unsolicited communication of this kind would be received. I set out the background of my family history research and the Frömbling-Niblett connection and explained that I was wondering whether there might be a branch of the family tree in Germany. I also apologised in advance if my enquiry was inappropriate.

The response was more generous than I could have expected. Simone Frömbling-Fülbier and her husband sent an acknowledgement the following month and then, in July 2002, provided me with a detailed listing of several generations of the family going back to Caspar Frömbling (1620-1685), a *Förster* (ranger) in Bösinghausen, near Göttingen. As with several other examples in this overall narrative, the family remained in the same general locality (in this case, the environs of Göttingen) from one generation to the next until Johann Friedrich Wilhelm Frömbling (1813-1893) took up a post of *Oberförster* (head ranger) in Rulle, near Osnabrück.

Simone Frömbling-Fülbier's great-grandfather was one of the three brothers of Eduard Christian Henning Frömbling (the husband of Annetta Niblett), who had been a *Kaufmann* (merchant) in Osnabrück.

Eduard and Annetta's three children were indeed the Eduard, Hugo and Henning Frömbling, whom I had previously (and tentatively) identified from the Osnabrück address books: my mother's first cousins. Specifically, they were: Wilhelm Charles Friedrich Eduard Frömbling (1900-1935), a merchant in Hamburg; Henning Ferdinand Harry Frömbling (1901-c1965), a merchant in Osnabrück; and Hugo Karl Bernhard Philipp Frömbling (1906-c1978/80), a ship's officer in Hamburg and later a jewellery wholesaler in Osnabrück.

Finally, Simone Frömbling-Fülbier also provided the names of family members in the next two generations, who are my second cousins and the third cousins of Tom and Katie.

As we have seen, the information that the name of Elfriede Augusta Niblett's husband was Bernhard Hamschmidt was initially provided by John Eckersley in his pre-Internet research for my aunt Joy. (A later – unsourced – contribution to the public pages of Ancestry has given his dates as 1893-1965 and reported that he had been born and died in Rietberg and Oldenberg in Germany, respectively).

The name Bernhard Hamschmidt appears in *Germany and Surrounding Areas, Address Books, 1815-1974* as a *Reichsbahnoberinspekteur* (Reichsbahn Chief Inspector) in the north Niedersachsen town of Emden in 1937. It is also given in the Compgen.de databases in the *Adressbuch Kreis Grafschaft Bentheim* [Address Book for the Bentheim district] for 1927 as a *Gueterinspecktor* (goods inspector) living at Bahnhofstrasse 37 and in *Adressbuch Oldenburg* for both 1940 and 1955 living at Ziegelhofstrasse 92. In themselves, these references are not firm evidence that this is the same Bernhard Hamschmidt who had married Elfriede Niblett. However, the Bentheim district of Nordhorn is the same as that recorded above for his sister-in-law Marion Niblett in 1937 and 1951 and, I would argue, this is too much of a coincidence to be ignored.

The Compgen.de database had one other reference to Berhard Hamschmidt which, at first, was slightly puzzling. He was included on an extensive *Verlustlisten 1 Weltkreig* [Loss List for the First World War], having been a member of the *Reserve-Infanterie-Regiment 218*, with a date given of 9th October 1915. Clearly his recorded death in that year would have made my findings on his subsequent marriage and railway career totally redundant.

The answer was provided by a closer inspection of the (fairly difficult to read) Gothic script used for the Loss List. The casualities ranged across those who were the *gefallen* (the fallen) through to those who had been *leicht verwundet* (slightly wounded). Berhard Hamschmidt was in the latter category.

We will see in Chapter 9 that Alfred Edgar Niblett, my grandfather, was interned as a British civilian in the Ruhleben camp near Berlin during the First World War, having been arrested by the German authorities whilst working as a teacher in Osnabrück after the war had started. The *Verlustlisten* shows that, the following year, the husband on one of his sisters – herself born in Germany and with German nationality through her marriage – was injured whilst in action with the *Reserve-Infanterie-Regiment 218*. A century later – standing back and attempting to consider these circumstances – it is difficult to imagine how the internal tensions in the Niblett family might have been reconciled, if indeed they ever were.

The brothers of Alfred Niblett

Table 3.3 shows that the first-born of the children of Charles James Niblett and Anna Karoline Borstelmann – and, therefore, the eldest of the siblings of my grandfather, Alfred Edgar Niblett – was Charles Julius Henry Niblett (1874-1967), who married the Portuguese-born Maria Angelina Pinto da Rocha (1883-1965) in Porto in 1905. They both lived to an old age and died in Lisbon.

Their family provides a good example – amongst several – of the international connections of the Niblett family through the succeeding generations, as amongst their children and grandchildren are to be found later residents of Australia, the USA and Brazil. One of these was George William Niblett – the youngest son of Charles and Maria, born in 1912 – who was a plant manager for Shell Mex Brazil Ltd in Rio de Janeiro; his wife Ena Clair Niblett (née Weniger, born in 1916) has immigration records for Brazil, Argentina, Venezuela and the USA from the late 1940s through to the early 1960s. (The rich source of this information is the international migration database of the Church of the Latter Day Saints).

Another Portuguese reference is to be found in the *Staats Archiv Bremen* record of the passenger list of the ship *Aachen*, which sailed from Bremen to Leixos (Porto) – where Charles lived – in November 1908. The list included his sister, Therese Niblett, who was aged about 24 at this time; as we have noted, she married George Fremdling in Osnabrück in 1913.

The international reach of the Niblett family business had been maintained in the post-First World War years. The *UK Outward Passenger Lists, 1890-1960* includes a reference to five members of the family departing from Liverpool for Leixos in October 1919 on the *Darro*, a ship of the Royal Mail Steam Packet Co, which was onward bound for Brazil and Argentina. They were Charles James Niblett and his wife Anne (i.e. Anna Karoline) aged 68 and 64 respectively, Charles Julius Henry Niblett and his wife Mary (i.e. Maria Angelina) aged 43 and 36 respectively, and Alfred E Niblett (my grandfather) aged 30. The occupation of all three men was given as "merchant".[50]

For Charles Julius and Mary Niblett, the "country of permanent residence" as stated on the *Darro*'s 1919 Passenger List was Portugal. They had had five children between 1905 and 1913, all born in Porto, and, as noted, both Charles Julius and Mary were to live until the 1960s and die in Lisbon.[51] Some members of the succeeding generation did marry in Porto – and at least one died there – but

---

50 For Alfred E Niblett, the country of permanent residence given in the Passenger List of the *Darro* was England – not surprisingly, as he was to marry my grandmother, Marie Rosa Wilson, in Edmonton, London, two months later.

51 Charles Julius Henry Niblett and his wife Marie are listed in the *London Electoral Registers of 1923-25* in the household of Alfred Edgar Niblett in Palmers Green and then in Enfield. However, their "abode" is given as 116 Castelo do Aneyo, Foz do Douro, Oporto.

the inherent mobility of this branch of the family saw subsequent movement to Australia and the USA as well as to Britain. I made contact with a grandson of Charles Julius and Mary Niblett, resident in Portugal, in 2019.

For Charles Joseph Niblett – another son of Charles Julius and Mary Niblett – the foray into international business dealing appears to have been markedly less successful. His experience was set out as the background context to a petty crime reported by various newspapers on 23rd May 1936, including the *South West Suffolk Echo*.

LOST £30,000 IN SPECULATION
IMPRISONMENT FOR STEALING BICYCLE

Said to have speculated and lost £30,000 on the cotton exchange in the United States of America, Charles Joseph Campbell Niblett (29), described as a linguist of 9 St George's Square, London, was sentenced to one month's hard labour by the Norwich Magistrates of Monday on a charge of stealing, while bailee, a bicycle belonging to Mrs May Clarke of 12 Lady Lane, Norwich, on November 26th 1934.

The evidence was that the bicycle was lent to Niblett, who had been a lodger at Mrs Clarke's house, to go to the bank to cash a cheque. He did not return. Later, in December 1934, the bicycle was recovered by a police officer at the M&GN Railway Station – a label attached showing that it had been despatched from Summertown, London.

Accused pleaded guilty and said he had no excuse to offer for doing a thing like this,

Inspector HW Ball said Niblett was born in Portugal of British parents and came to England when he was 10 years of age. He went to 2 preparatory schools and when he was 17 years old he went to King's College, Cambridge, which he left in 1928 after taking his Degree in Literature. He then commenced to travel the world. He speculated on the cotton exchange (USA) and lost all his money, which he (Niblett) said was about £30,000. He returned to England and secured a job as a clerk at £1 a week. He had since had various other places of employment. There was nothing previously known to his detriment. Niblett owed Mrs Clarke £12 10s for rooms whilst he was lodging at her house.

Replying to a question from the Bench, Niblett said that he had been employed as a guide to tourists visiting the Continent and he should have gone to France that day with a party.

This is an astonishing story and my immediate reaction on reading it was to wonder how much validity it had. The sum of £30,000 in 1936 would be worth approximately £2.67 million in 2023, so the scale of such losses would obviously have been huge. Or was Charles Joseph Niblett simply prone to exaggeration and fantasy? (Separately, I was also struck by the severity of the punishment meted out for stealing a bicycle – one month's hard labour – to someone with no previous criminal record. This was in 1936, not the 19th Century). We return to this story in Chapter 9 below, where I suggest that there might have been an alternative explanation of events.

As in the case of my grandfather, Alfred Edgar Niblett, the country of permanent residence given in the *Darro*'s 1919 Passenger List for Charles James Niblett and his wife Anna Karoline (née Borstelmann) was also England. Hence, notwithstanding the four years of conflict between the nations of their respective births, the marriage survived as the couple lived in England after the First World War.

The 1921 Census records that Charles James and Anna Karoline Niblett were resident in Hayne Road, Beckenham, Kent, with their daughter – the 43 year-old Elisabeth Miriam Niblett – and one of their sons and his family (Harry and his wife Emily and their children Harry George and Alfred Edgar).[52] Later in the decade, the *Surrey, England, Electoral Roll, 1832-1962* database records that the same extended family group (possibly without Elisabeth) shared a house in Stanley Park Road, Mitcham, in each year between 1924 and 1927.

Charles James Niblett died in 1927 at the age of 76. The Electoral Roll shows that Anna Karoline, Harry and Emily remained in the Stanley Park Road property until 1929 (and Harry and Emily for a year after that before moving to Bermondsey) and I assume that it was at that point that Anna Karoline returned to her native Germany. The *Osnabrück and Surrounding Areas Address Books, 1815-1974* database shows that she was living in Osnabrück at Ludwigstrasse 15 in the residence year 1935-36. As noted, another of her sons, Alfred Edgar Niblett (my grandfather), visited her twice in Osnabrück before her death at this address in 1938 (see also Chapter 9 below).

The burial place of Charles, Anna Karoline, Harry and Emily Niblett is the Bandon Hill Cemetery in Sutton. I came across the location of Charles's grave in the database at www.deceasedonline.com and followed this up with correspondence with Kathy Scott, a Cemetery Assistant at idverde (the company that maintains the cemetery). Ms Scott was very helpful in providing information on the contents and directions to the Niblett plot, even to the extent of sending me some photographs of the location. I visited the grave in September 2018.

Kathy Scott's list of the Niblett family members buried in the Bandon Hill Cemetery generated an immediate query, given its inclusion of Anna Karoline

---

52 Harry and Emily Niblett's son, Alfred Edgar Niblett (1916-2002), should not be confused with my grandfather, who was his namesake. A solicitor's clerk, he married Grace Emily Richards (1912-1978) in 1940. He died in Bournemouth at the age of 85.

Niblett, who had died in Osnabrück. Had her remains been transported back to Sutton? The answer was yes. A closer inspection of the www.deceasedonline.com database revealed that her cremation urn was buried (to a depth of three feet) on 6th September 1938, just over one month after her death at Ludwigstrasse 15.

The combination of Census and BMD records has enabled me to track the families of those of my grandfather's brothers who came to Britain. Thus, for example, Adolf Alfred Niblett, who was born in Osnabrück in 1877, married an Irish girl – Charlotte Mary Patterson (1878/9-1960) from Omagh, County Tyrone – in Grangegorman, Dublin in 1902.[53] He was a "foreign correspondent for a cotton broker" in Liverpool in 1911, a "merchant/employer" in Crosby in 1921 and a "retired cotton broker" in Taunton in 1939; later known as Alphonso Niblett, he lived to the age of 90, dying in Southampton in 1966.

Likewise, Harry Niblett (1879-1959) married Christine Charlotte Emilie Sturm (or Sturn) in Italy in 1910. As we have seen, they were living with Harry's parents in Beckenham in 1921, when, like his father, he was a general export and import merchant with Niblett Limited in the City of London; in the *1939 England and Wales Register*, he was recorded as a 60 year-old "hide merchant importer" living in Battersea. (The National Archives has a record of a British passport issued to Harry Niblett – a clerk resident in Genoa – in October 1907).

George Niblett (1887-1948) was born two days after the death of the infant Albert George and obviously named in his memory. He married Regina Lillian Boocock (1900-1993) in London in 1920. There is an intriguing entry for him in the *UK Incoming Passenger Lists, 1878-1960* database, in which he is listed as a passenger on the *Atlantis* between Hamburg and Southampton in November 1946. I wondered what his business had been in post-war Germany, given that he was aged 59 at the time. The answer was provided in the "profession, occupation or calling" column, which stated "CCG" and prompted a Wikipedia search:

> "After the defeat of Germany in 1945, a Control Commission was set up to support the Military Government which was in place at that time. The Military Government was gradually phased out and the Control Commission took over the role of "Local Government". It was responsible for public safety, health, transport, housing and Intelligence. The forward HQ was in Cumberland House, Berlin. Recruits had to be over 21 and were recruited from the Civil Service, the Foreign Office and demobbed military personnel".

George Niblett – born in Osnabrück like all his siblings and, certainly, a fluent

---

53 The notice of the marriage of Adolf Niblett and Charlotte Patterson in the *Newry Reporter* of 9th October 1902 referred to Adolf's father as "Professor" Charles Niblett of Osnabrück, Hanover, Germany.

Germany speaker – would have been an obvious candidate for this type of work. Although his story is ultimately a sad one – he was to die in Greenwich only two years later[54] – it is also fascinating, as it is illustrative of how the family historian can use the online databases to explore a facet of British history that might not have been familiar and place a member of the family firmly at its centre.

The extended Niblett family suffered its losses in the Second World War. The oldest son (and third child) of Charles Julius and Maria Niblett – whose catastrophic speculative losses on the US Cotton Exchange were reported above – was Charles Joseph Niblett, who was killed in France at the age of 37 on 3rd June 1944. He was an air gunner with the rank of Flying Officer in the RAF Volunteer Reserve. This was three days before D Day, of course, when the RAF would have been preparing the ground for the Normandy invasion both in Normandy itself and by suggesting other possible locations for landing to deceive the enemy. Charles Joseph Niblett is buried in the St Desir War Cemetery near Calvados in France. (His wife Vera Walsh Niblett (née Dank) lived to the age of 82, dying on the Isle of Wight in April 1994; she was a widow for just two months under 50 years). I cannot but wonder what sort of adventurous life this fascinating character – Cambridge-educated, linguistically talented, risk-taking – might have had if he had survived into the post-War period.

A similarly sad story is to be found in the case of Eric Harry Niblett (1907-1941), who was the son of Adolf and Charlotte Niblett (née Patterson) and therefore a first cousin of Charles Joseph Niblett. He was a Second Lieutenant in the Royal Army Service Corps, Mentioned in Despatches, when he was lost at sea at the age of 34. His body was not recovered and he is commemorated at the large Pharleson War Cemetery in Athens. His wife Rose Niblett (née Dyson) died in Solihull in 1997 at the age of 93; her widowhood lasted 56 years.

It is clear that a striking feature in this discussion of the siblings of my grandfather, Alfred Edgar Niblett, is the distinct geographical division in the countries of residence. The oldest brother (Charles Julius Henry Niblett) settled in Portugal, whilst the other three brothers surviving into adulthood all became resident in Britain, as did Alfred himself.[55] By contrast, at least 4 of the 5 sisters stayed permanently in Germany with the fifth (Elisabeth Miriam Niblett) probably spending time in both countries.

---

54 George Niblett was also buried in the Bandon Hill Cemetery, Sutton. His wife – Regina Lillian Niblett (née Boocock) – lived to the age of 93 and died in Bromley in 1993.

55 The tracking of the descendents of Adolf/Alophonso, Harry and George Niblett provides me – through their grandchildren – with another tranche of second cousins (with surnames of Clegg, Foster and Niblett) born in Liverpool, Greenwich, Lambeth, Colchester and Taunton.

Two important themes

The presence of Charles James Niblett and Anna Karoline Borstelmann in the Line of 16 represents two important – and apparently contradictory – themes within the overall family history. The first – which we have already seen in the context of the Rigg family in North Yorkshire and which we will come across again in the next chapter on another branch of the extended family tree in Suffolk – is the remarkable longevity of the attachment to particular local areas: in these cases Gloucestershire and northern Germany, respectively. Of course, there were significant restrictions on movement brought about by circumstance or income or regulation, but the limitations of the families' geographical horizons – physical and cultural – is something with which present-day generations are generally unfamiliar.

The second theme concerns the radical way in which this geographical parochialism was usurped from the middle of the 19th Century onwards. The key figure is Charles Niblett – the father of Charles James Niblett – whose entrepreneurial drive in developing the family's ginger beer/confectionery/soda water business was no doubt instrumental in the absence from the 1871 Census of England and Wales of his son – Charles James Niblett – who was establishing his own business in Germany. From there, in the lives of those included within Tables 3.1 to 3.3, the international linkages expanded to cover Portugal and Argentina (business) and India and the USA (migration).

Mike Niblett has described the family business as "general merchants and importers and exporters" with offices in London, Liverpool, Spain and Portugal. As an aside, it might be noted that, for much of the period in which the family is known to have conducted its foreign trade affairs, the overall trading environment was difficult. The consensus amongst economic historians is that, whilst there was a significant increase in the value of British foreign trade between about 1850 and 1875, for much of the remainder of the late 19th Century exports ran into difficulty. There was a stagnation of export values in the 20 years to 1895 before another substantial increase in activity in the years leading up to the First World War.[56] Of course, the prosperity of individual export sectors would have varied considerably depending on the growth of overseas incomes, the ability to maintain (or increase) prices in foreign markets and the incidence of tariffs on British products by importing countries.

---

56 See, for example, Peter Matthias, *The First Industrial Nation: An Economic History of Britain 1700-1914*, 1969, Table VII, page 305. The annual average of total exports of UK products was £239m between 1871-1875, £217m between 1876-1885 and £232m between 1886-1895 before rising to £275m between 1896-1905 and £432m between 1906-1913.

CHAPTER FOUR

LONDON

THE LINE OF 16: 7. CHARLES HERBERT WILSON (1862-1946)
The Master and Matron of the workhouse

As we have seen, several members of the Line of 16 have surnames that are relatively uncommon: Rigg, Boynton, Niblett *et al*. For the next one – **CHARLES HERBERT WILSON** (1862-1946) – this is not the case, thereby presenting a new set of challenges.[1]

My search for the records on Charles Herbert Wilson in the Census records began, in the familiar way, by working back from the first appearance of my grandmother, Marie Rosa Wilson, as a 1 year-old in the 1891 Census of England and Wales. Charles and his wife – Rosa Mary Wilson (née Whines) – were staying in the household of Rosa Mary's father, Daniel Whines, in Chelsea.

1891: 39 Smith Street, Chelsea

					Occupation	Where born
Daniel Whines	Head	Married	M	63	Joiner	Northamptonshire, Peterborough
Mary	Wife	Married	F	57		"
Flora	Daughter	Single	F	19	Warehouse asst	London, Chelsea
Charles H Wilson	Visitor	Married	M	28	Cashier	Cambridge
Rosa M	"	Married	F	27		Westminster
Marie R	"		F	1		Wood Green

By 1901, Charles, Rosa and Marie Wilson had moved to 2 Park Terrace, Wood Green, Middlesex and later, by 1911, to Reservoir Road, Southgate. For my purposes, the latter record was significant because also within that household was

---

1   In his *A Dictionary of Yorkshire Surnames* (2015), George Redmonds records Wilson as the 7th most common surname in Britain in the Censuses of 1881 with 137,640 entries.

Charles's (apparently) widowed older brother, George Wilson. This gave me a fix on the presence of Charles Herbert Wilson in earlier Censuses, beginning in 1871 at 15 Cambridge Terrace, Islington.[2]

1911: "Coniston", Reservoir Road, Southgate

					Occupation	Where born
Charles Wilson	Head	Married	M	48	Company secretary Furniture manufacturer	Cambridge
Rosa	Wife	Married	F	47		Pimlico
Marie	Daughter	Single	F	21	Shorthand typist	Wood Green Commercial college
George Wilson	Brother	Widowed	M	47	Accountant (bankers)	Cambridge

1871: 15 Cambridge Terrace, Islington

					Occupation	Where born
Charles T Wilson	Head	Married	M	33	Warehouseman	Leicestershire, Overseal
Emma	Wife	Married	F	32		Norfolk, Norwich
Alice M	Daughter		F	9		Cambridge
Charles H	Son		M	8		Cambridge
George H	Son		M	7		Cambridge
Leonard K	Son		M	1		Middlesex, Islington
Mahala Goodchild	Visitor	Widow	F	69	Former matron of Union	Suffolk, Laxfield
Sarah Esther Sharpe	Lodger	Widow	F	44	Milliner	Middlesex, London

The head of Charles Herbert Wilson's household in 1871 was Charles Tyler Wilson, who was born in Overseal (then in Leicestershire, now Derbyshire) in about 1838 and who was employed as a warehouseman. In the normal way, I thought that I would be able to track this family in successive Censuses. To start with, this was indeed the case; after a while, however, things became a little more complicated.

I tracked the family of Charles Tyler Wilson's parents through the 1841, 1851 and 1861 Censuses. (I am reasonably confident that it was the same family, even though the age of the father – Joseph, an agricultural labourer – increased rather dramatically and the surname was spelt differently – Willson – in 1861). In the first of these records, Joseph Wilson's place of birth was given as "not born in county" with a tick in the box for "born in Scotland, Ireland or foreign parts". His wife, Catherine Tyler, was born in 1795 in Desford, Leicestershire. As I was later

---

2   Park Terrace and Cambridge Terrace do not appear in the 2015 edition of the *London A-Z*. When I visited Reservoir Road in October 2019, there did not appear to be any dwellings remaining from the pre-First World War period.

to learn from an Ancestry contributor – Caroline Webber (see below) – Catherine was the 7th of the eight children of Thomas Tyler and his wife Ann, née Plant, born between 1783 and 1797.

Moving on to the 1871 Census record (noted above) for the household of Charles Tyler Wilson – Joseph Wilson's son – there was a "visitor": Mahala Goodchild, a 69 year-old widow, born in Laxfield, Suffolk, whose occupation was given as "formerly matron of union". In fact, she was more than just a visitor: Mahala Goodchild (née Holmes, 1802-1883) was the mother of Charles Tyler Wilson's wife, Emma Goodchild and the grandmother of the Line of 16's Charles Herbert Wilson.

Mahala's husband – James Goodchild – had been born in Horham, Suffolk, and they had married in the parish of St John Timberhill, Norwich, in 1827. James had died in 1857 at the age of 56. In 1851, he had been the "master of union house" in Horsham St Faith, Norfolk, when she had been the matron.

The workhouse of the St. Faith's Union, comprising 30 parishes, was built at Horsham St. Faith in 1805 for the elderly, infirm and their children.[3] The mid-19th Century workhouse regimes were tough. As a master – or governor – James Goodchild's responsibilities would have required him to uphold the strict disciplines of these institutions. Three examples from the local press – respectively, the *Norfolk News* of 10th February 1852 and the *Norfolk Chronicle* of 13th March 1852 and 21st April 1855 – illustrate his roles is liaising with the county magistrates and coroners:

COUNTY POLICE

Mary Ann Britcher, an inmate of St Faith's Union Workhouse, was brought up charged with having, on 14th January, at the workhouse, refused to work. Mr Goodchild, the master, had repeatedly warned her against such unwillingness, but she persisted in it and he was necessarily obliged to bring her before the Magistrates. She not only refused to work but her language and behaviour to the nurse was most disgraceful. The Magistrates were determined to make an example of her and committed her to Wymondham bridewell for 21 days, with hard labour.

---

3   Wikipedia reports that *White's History, Gazetteer, and Directory of Norfolk, 1845* stated that the St Faith's Union "had room for 330 inmates, but seldom so many as 200" and that, whilst the average annual expenditure of the Union had been £10,525 between 1832-35, this had fallen to £6,054 in 1842. *William White's History, Gazetteer and Directory of Norfolk, 1883* stated that, although there was room for 450, there had been only 84 pauper inmates in 1881. The workhouse building was badly damaged by a fire in 1922 and not repaired; a crematorium was later built on the site.

A DISORDERLY PAUPER

A lad who had been an inmate of St Faith's Union was charged with having run away from the house and taken away a quantity of clothes, the property of the Guardians. Mr J Goodchild, the master of the house, said the prisoner had run away on Feb 26th with the clothes and returned on the 27th. He had been confined to the refractory ward; and he was now sent to prison for 21 days.

INQUEST

On Wednesday, Mr Wilde held an inquest at the Catherine Wheel, St Augustine's, on the body of James Holmes aged 82 years. Mr James Goodchild deposed that he was Governor of St Faith's Union; deceased was an inmate of that house and had been so for the last eight years. He had leave to come to Norwich; he had been quite well then, and had been so all the time he had been in the house. Charles Gibson stated that he was passing near that house on Wednesday, at about a quarter past nine o'clock, and he saw deceased lying in the road opposite. He appeared to have just fallen down. He was alive then. Witness assisted him into the house and sent for a surgeon. Mr Payne attended and said that life was extinct. Verdict: Died by the Visitation of God.

Let us return to Emma Goodchild, the mother of Charles Herbert Wilson. In the 1841 Census, she was a 3 year-old living in Norwich. The head of the household was her mother, Mahala, then aged 38, and there were six other children, including the 2 year-old William.[4] Emma's father – the 40 year-old James Goodchild – was not present in the household on this evening; his Census record places him as a "turnkey"[5] at the County Gaol in Norwich Castle. Ten years later, when Emma was 13, the head of the household was her oldest brother – the 22 year-old George Pipe Goodchild[6] – and there were 4 other siblings in the household aged between 11 and 21.[7]

---

4   The *Norfolk Chronicle* carried a notice of William's death in its edition of 5th November 1853:
    DIED
    On the [28th October], in St Julian, in the 14th year of his age, after a few days of his illness, William, fourth son of Mr James Goodchild of Horsham St Faith's in this county, deeply regretted by his family and friends, and much respected and esteemed by his schoolfellows, with whom he was a great favourite.

5   A keeper of the keys, especially in a prison; a warden or jailer.

6   Pipe was the surname of James Goodchild's mother – and George Pipe Goodchild's and Emma Goodchild's paternal grandmother – Esther Pipe (1776-1845). It will be seen below that the name has a very long pedigree in the direct family line, arguably extending back to the 14th Century.

7   Two other siblings – both named Rebecca – had died in infancy: 1841-42 and 1843-43.

Hence, by 1851, the family was located on two sites in Norwich as Emma's parents were resident in Horsham St Faith – which is approximately 4 miles from the centre of the city – as master and matron of St Faith's Union House with two of their other children (Esther aged 15 and Arthur aged 6) in the household. *Melville and Co's Directory and Gazetteer, 1856*, which covered Norfolk and the surrounding area, listed James and Mahala Goodchild as remaining in those roles in that year, though now with Esther as assistant matron.

The evidence suggests, therefore, that for part of her childhood – certainly at the ages of 3 and 13 – Emma was not living with one or both her parents. By 1861, Emma was married to Charles Tyler Wilson – a 23 year-old "bookseller traveller" – and living at 2 James Street, Cambridge.[8] Her mother, Mahala Goodchild, by then widowed, was also in the household.[9]

It was in the strange way of reporting Charles Tyler Wilson's family in the 1881 Census that the puzzles started to emerge. Three of the returns were relevant: Emma Wilson (née Goodchild) was living in Leicester; Charles himself was living with his wife Charlotte (sic) in a shared house in Poplar, East London; and his son Charles Herbert Wilson (of the Line of 16) was living with his aunt and uncle (more Goodchilds) in Cheetham, Lancashire.

1881	30 Waring Street, Leicester						
						Occupation	Where born
William Yiend	Head	Single	M		21	Railway clerk	Gloucestershire
Emma Wilson	Mother	Married	F		41	Housekeeper	Norfolk, Norwich
Alice	Daughter	Single	F		19	Milliner	Cambridge
Geo[rge]	Son	Single	M		17	Yarn agent's clerk	Cambridge
Leo[nard]	Son		M		11	Scholar	Middlesex, Islington
Ed Haughton (or Haughter)	Nephew	Single	M		23	Soliciting shorthand clerk	Norfolk, Hellesdon

1881	246 Manchester Road, Poplar						
						Occupation	Where born
Charles T Wilson	Head	Married	M		43	Medical assistant	Leicestershire, Overseal
Charlotte A	Wife	Married	F		40		Suffolk

---

8   Charles Tyler Wilson married Emma Goodchild in Norwich in July 1860. The marriage register gives his occupation as "traveller" and that of his father, Joseph Wilson, as "steward".

9   Mahala Goodchild died in 1883 at the age of 81. She is buried in the Rosary Cemetery, Norwich, in the same plot as her husband, James, and young son, William, both of whom had pre-deceased her by over 25 years.

1881		19 Bedford Street, Cheetham, Lancashire				
					Occupation	Where born
Arthur P Goodchild	Head	Married	M	35	Commission agent	Norfolk, Old Catton
Lily	Wife	Married	F	35		Hants, Southsea
Charles Wilson	Nephew	Single	M	18	Clerk to Commission agent	Cambridge

The Census form for the Leicester household was filled in incorrectly. William Yiend was (correctly) given as the head of household, but Emma Wilson was not William's mother, as stated. Similarly, Alice, George and Leonard were obviously the children of Emma, not William. This is not the source of the puzzle, however. Rather, this relates to the status of Emma Wilson in the 1881 Census return. It is not easy to read, but close inspection does seem to reveal "married" rather than "widow".

Two other questions then raised themselves. First, I noted that when Charles Herbert Wilson (a 25 year-old bachelor and clerk) married the 24 year-old Rosa Mary Whines at the church of St Ann, Tottenham, Middlesex, in March 1888,[10] it stated on the marriage certificate that the groom's father was "Charles Wilson (deceased), a chemist". So far so good, except that the death of Charles Tyler Wilson was recorded in the second quarter of 1888, which was obviously after the wedding date. I could only put this down to a slight delay (from end March to early April) in the registration of his death, which would have had the effect of pushing the date on by one quarter.

The second question related to Charles Tyler Wilson's occupation: how was it that the 33 year-old warehouseman of the 1871 Census had become the medical assistant in 1881 and the chemist of 1888?

Two cases of bigamy

It was at this point – in February 2013 – that I entered into a very productive e-mail correspondence with Caroline Webber. She confirmed what I had now strongly suspected – that Charles Tyler Wilson was a bigamist – by reporting his second marriage to Charlotte Amelia Hambling in 1880. I was able to check this by accessing the online record of *London, England, Church of England Marriages and Banns, 1754-1921*, in which his status was given as "widower" in November of that year. (Charlotte then became the "wife" in the 1881 Census). In addition, Ms Webber reported that Charles Tyler Wilson had been made bankrupt as a

---

10   Rosa Mary Whines's brother – Frank Daniel Whines (1865-1954) – married Annabella Attwell (1863-1920) in the same church four months later.

chemist in 1866.[11] Thus, I concluded, his transition was not from warehouseman to chemist, but the other way round: bankrupt chemist to warehouseman.

The turbulent family into which Charles Herbert Wilson was born in 1862 is summarised in Table 4.1. The online database of births (with mothers' maiden names) released by the GRO in 2016 revealed that two of his siblings – Minnie Margaret Wilson and William Arthur Wilson – had died in infancy, the latter in the St Ives Union in Huntingdonshire in 1867. (This date and location are consistent with Charles Tyler Wilson's bankruptcy a year earlier).

Table 4.1. The parents, siblings and step-sibling of Charles Herbert Wilson	
Charles Tyler Wilson c1838-1888 (born in Overseal, Leicestershire) (son of Joseph Wilson 1790-1864 (tbc) and Catherine Tyler 1795-1868) (died in London aged 50)	
married	
1. Emma Goodchild 1838-1912 (born in Norwich) (daughter of James Goodchild 1801-1857 and Mahala Holmes 1802-1883) (died in Chelsea, London, aged 73)	Alice Maude Wilson 1861-1941 (born in Cambridge) (died in Edinburgh aged 80) *married* William Yiend 1861-1939 (born in Winchcombe, Gloucestershire) (died in Cheltenham aged 77)
	Charles Herbert Wilson 1862-1946 (born in Cambridge) (died in Leeds aged 84) *married* Rosa Mary Whines 1863-1937 (born in Westminster/Pimlico, London) (died in Leeds aged 74)

---

11   I later confirmed this by looking at the *London Daily News* for 1st December 1866, in which the list in the "bankrupts" column included "Charles Tyler Wilson, Cambridge, chemist". The *Cambridge Independent Press* of 8th December listed him as a "druggist" and then as a "chemist and druggist" on 9th February 1867, when reporting on the County Court's "Order of Discharge to the said Bankrupt".

		George Herbert Wilson 1864-1940 (born in Cambridge) (died in Cheltenham aged 76) *married* 1. Retti Betsy Maud Maxon Skinner 1867-1961 (born in Bow, London) (died in Matsqui, British Columbia, Canada, aged 94) 2. Euphemia McBean 1881-1953 (born in Inverawe, Argyllshire) (died in Cheltenham aged 72)
		Minnie Margaret Wilson 1866-1867 (born in Cambridge) (died in St Ives, Huntingdonshire, aged 1)
		Leonard Kebbel Wilson 1869-1946 (born in Islington, Middlesex) (died in San Francisco, California, aged 76) *married* Rose Mary Easby-Smith 1876-1953 (born in Alabama) (died in San Bernadino, California, aged 77)
		William Arthur Wilson 1871-1874 (born in Islington) (died in Poplar, London, aged 2)
	married (bigamous)	
	2. Charlotte Amelia Hambling 1839-1907 (born in Rendham, Suffolk) (daughter of Cotton Hambling 1790-1858 and Amelia Fenton Garrod 1796-1872) (died in Poplar aged 67)	Charlotte Isabel Amelia Wilson 1882-1897 (born in Poplar) (died in West Ham district, London, aged 14)

The Census and BMD records allow us to follow the lives of Charles Tyler Wilson's two wives – Emma Wilson (née Goodchild) and the bigamous Charlotte Amelia Wilson (née Hambling) – after his death in 1888.

By 1891, Emma Wilson was living in a three-room house at 3 Margaretta Terrace, Chelsea; there was one visitor, 23 year-old Elizabeth Wilkes. Emma's status was as a 52 year-old widow and her occupation, intriguingly, was "missionary" after which there was added the word "preach" on the Census form. Ten years later, in 1901, the 62 year-old Emma was living at 7 Phene Street, Chelsea, in the household of her supposedly widowed son, George Wilson, the 37 year-old chartered accountant, and his two children. In the 1911 Census, Emma was recorded as living in the household headed by her brother George Pipe Goodchild, an 82 year-old "retired law clerk with private means", at 1 West Parade, Norwich. (Remarkably, as noted earlier from the 1851 Census, George had also been the head of the household in which Emma had been living 60 years earlier).[12] Emma's occupation – she was by now 73 years old – was "Bible woman".[13]

The development of Chelsea in the latter part of the 19th Century is discussed in detail in *A History of the County of Middlesex: Volume 12, Chelsea*, edited by Patricia EC Croot and published in 2004. In summarising the social character of Chelsea in about the year 1890, she states:

> "As elsewhere in London in this period, the rich and poor lived in close proximity: the rich occupied the houses lining the main streets and squares, while the smaller streets and mews behind were filled with a range of tradesmen and working class residents… South of King's Road between Smith and Flood streets [which is very close to where the separate households of Daniel Whines and George Wilson were at this time], there was very little poverty; the fairly well-to-do majority included artisans in regular work, policemen and clerks. Houses were generally in fairly good repair".[14]

Emma Wilson died in Chelsea in 1911 at the age of 73. An entry in *England and Wales, National Probate Calendar (Index of Wills and Administrations) 1858-1966* records that she had lived at 10 Bramerton Street. Probate was awarded to "Charles Herbert Wilson, cashier, and Alice Maud Yiend (wife of William Yiend)". The effects left in the will totalled £355 5s.

I am bound to reflect on the sadness of certain aspects of the life of Emma Goodchild/Wilson. Her parents' occupations as master and matron of the union house in Horsham St Faith seemed to have required the family – in which there

---

12 George Pipe Goodchild died in January 1915 at the age of 85. He is buried in the same plot in the Rosary Cemetery, Norwich, as his wife Mary Ann Goodchild (née Myers, 1833-1919), their son George Harry Goodchild (1860-1917) and daughter-in-law Wilhelmina Goodchild (née Whitmore, 1857-1938).

13 Wikipedia reports that the title "Bible woman" was first used in London in connection with the evangelical work of Ellen Henrietta Ranyard (1810-1879), who attempted to reach sick and poor women in the poorest area in the mid-19th Century. She and her followers would read from and distribute the Bible. By the time of her death, there were about 170 Bible women employed in what became the London Bible and Domestic Female Mission.

14 In December 2013, I happened to be in Chelsea one evening – for the triennial reunion of our 1970s college rugby team – and I took the opportunity to wander round some of the addresses mentioned here. 3 Margaretta Terrace is a solid brick townhouse, three storeys high with a balustrade; 7 Phene Street is another three-storey building opposite the busy Phene public house; 39 Smith Street (where Charles Herbert Wilson and his wife Rosa and daughter Marie Rosa had lived with Rosa's parents in 1891) is a four-storey townhouse just off the King's Road. Today, all these properties are highly desirable: sizeable, well-maintained and in a fashionable part of London.

were at least 8 children – to have been split between two locations during her childhood. Having had 6 children of her own with Charles Tyler Wilson, two of whom died in infancy, she was deserted by him at the age of 41 when he bigamously married Charlotte Hambling. Thereafter, she resided either by herself (1891) or in the households of one of her children (1881, 1901) or brothers (1911) in several different places (Leicester, Chelsea, Norwich). I hope that she found some consolation in her occupation of "missionary" or "Bible woman".

I reported earlier that Charlotte Amelia Wilson (née Hambling) was given as 40 years old in the 1881 Census – the age is unmistakeable – when she was living with Charles Tyler Wilson in Poplar. (She was actually 41, having been born in Rendham, Suffolk, in June 1839). In the subsequent Censuses – following Charles's death in 1888 – her age increased rather slowly. In 1891, Charlotte A Wilson was a 45 year-old lodger (and widow) in a single room at 53 Upper North Street, Poplar. The other occupants of the house were Thomas Clitherow, aged 45, with his wife and 6 children, and it is interesting that Thomas's occupation was "chemist's assistant". (This was the same address at which Charles Tyler Wilson had been registered on the Electoral Rolls of 1885, 1887 and 1888, as confirmed in the *London, England, Electoral Rolls, 1832-1965* database).

Charlotte A Wilson was still at 53 Upper North Street in the 1901 Census. She was the head of the household, with two boarders, and now a widow of 51 (sic). Her occupation was given as "store/shopkeeper, own account". The BMD database states that Charlotte Amelia Wilson died in Poplar in 1907 at the age of 56; in fact, she was 11 years older than this. The effects left in her will totalled £83 10s 3d.

Charles Tyler Wilson and Charlotte Amelia Hambling had a daughter in their bigamous marriage: Charlotte Isabel Amelia Hambling was born in Poplar in the third quarter of 1882. (The register of baptisms at the All Saints Church records that Charles's profession had reverted back to "chemist"). It is another sad story. In the 1891 Census, she is recorded as a resident in the Infant Orphan Asylum in Wanstead, Essex, along with just under 600 other children. (Her father had died by that time though, as noted, her mother was still alive and living in Poplar). The younger Charlotte died in the West Ham district in 1897 at the age of 14.

The marital status of George Herbert Wilson – a younger brother of the Line of 16's Charles Herbert Wilson – was also complicated. As noted, he was recorded as a widower and an accountant in the 1911 Census, living in the household of Charles Herbert Wilson in Southgate. He had also been a widower in 1901 – occupation "independent chartered" – living at 7 Phene Street, Chelsea, with his mother Emma, daughter Dora (aged 14) and son Harold (aged 11). Ten years earlier, the 27 year-old George Herbert Wilson had been an accountant clerk with a young family – his wife Maud aged 24, Winifred D (who became Dora presumably) aged 4 and Harold aged 1 – resident in Rochester, Kent. All this fitted nicely with the marriage to Retti Betsy Maud Maxon Skinner recorded in Kennington, London, in 1886. The problem I faced was that there was no reference to the death of a Retti Wilson or Maud Wilson of the right age – she had been born in Bow in 1867 – between 1891 and 1901.

The solution was provided in the correspondence with Caroline Webber, who reported that Retti Betsy Maud Maxon Skinner (also using the surname of Goodchild) had died in Matsqui, British Columbia, Canada, in 1961. Sure enough, this is confirmed in the *British Colombia Death Index 1872-1990*, which also lists the death in the same location of Henry William Goodchild (1865-1956). Their respective ages at death were 94 and 91 years. The final resting place of the couple is listed in the *Canada, Find a Grave Index* as being in Hazelwood Cemetery, Abbotsford, British Columbia.

From there, it was a question of working backwards, beginning with the British Columbia records in the 1931 *Census of Canada*. By that time, the 66 year-old Henry William Goodchild had retired to Burnaby, near Vancouver, whilst Maud Maxon (sic) Goodchild was a 63 year-old "homemaker". They rented a 4-room detached home constructed of wood for $15 per month and had access to a radio. The religion of both was given as Roman Catholic.

Ten years earlier, the couple had been resident in Ottowa, Ontario, where Henry had been an "agent" and Maud's middle name had been recorded as Mason. This entry is consistent with those of Henry W Goodchild, a 54 year-old insurance agent sailing from Quebec to Liverpool on the *Empress of France* in July 1920. The return journey in September was on the *Minnedosa*, the reason for the visit having been "visiting parents" in Ipswich.[15]

According to both Censuses, the couple had migrated to Canada in 1912 (when they would have been in their mid-40s). This suggested that they might have still been in England at the time of the 1911 Census and, indeed, in that record, Henry William Goodchild – a "traveller, cigars and tobacco" – and his wife Maud Goodchild were living with their 19 year-old son, Frederick Henry Goodchild, in Clacton-on-Sea. In the 1901 Census, the family had been living in West Ham, where Henry was a commercial traveller.

In the 1911 Census, it was stated that Henry and Maud Goodchild had been married for 20 years. However, I cannot find any record of Henry William Goodchild marrying anyone called Retti/Maud Skinner/Wilson in or around 1891 and I am not sure if this couple actually did marry. If they did, then – in the absence of a divorce from George Herbert Wilson (and there is no record of such for George and/or Maud Wilson in *England and Wales Civil Divorce Records*,

---

15 The respective sources for the transatlantic crossings were *UK and Ireland, Incoming Passenger Lists, 1878-1960* and *Canada, Ocean Arrivals (Form 30A), 1919-1924*, both on Ancestry.

1858-1916)[16] – Retti/Maud was a bigamist. If they did not, they gave false records to the Census enumerators of both England and Canada. In either event, George Herbert Wilson was certainly not a widower in 1901 or 1911.

The obituary of HW Goodchild in British Colombia's *The Province* of 7th November 1956 stated that Henry and Maud "celebrated their 71st wedding anniversary last September". This would have placed the marriage in September 1885, which is different again from the year of 1891 implied by the 1911 Census return let alone the 1886 record of the actual marriage of George Herbert Wilson to Retti Betsy Maud Maxon Skinner. Of greater accuracy would have been the obituary's reference to Henry William Goodchild's employment as a life assurance salesman for Metropolitan Life in Ottawa prior to his retirement to British Columbia.

At first, I also had difficulty in finding a birth record for Frederick Henry Goodchild. However, a secondary source – *US World War I Draft Registration Cards, 1917-18* – records that he had been born in Liverpool on 8th March 1892. This led me to the birth of Henry Frederick Wilson (with the mother's maiden name of Skinner) in West Derby, Liverpool.[17] This was just under a year after his mother, Maud Wilson, had been recorded in the household of George Herbert Wilson in Rochester.

Most family historians will recognise this detour into the family circumstances of George Herbert Wilson as illustrative of the difficulties that arise when apparently reputable official sources are known to be not fully accurate due to absent records or misleading entries or changes of name. In the absence, also, of family stories passed down through the generations, we are left to speculate on what the actual truth of those circumstances might have been. In this case, my best guess is that Maud Wilson (née Skinner) had begun her relationship with Henry William Goodchild by 1891 and that their subsequent entries (with Frederick Henry Goodchild) in the 1901 and 1911 Censuses, a number of passenger/immigration lists and the official Canadian records reflect their status as common law husband and wife. For George Herbert Wilson – assuming that his wife Maud simply did not mysteriously disappear so that the presumption of death could reasonably have been made – the status of widower would have constituted a presentable (albeit false) entry in the official records after her departure from his household.

---

16   This database has been made available by The National Archives and is on Ancestry.

17   Frederick Henry Goodchild had been an apprentice journalist at the time of the 1911 Census, living in Clacton-on-Sea. His inclusion on this American database from the First World War is attributable to his residence in 1917 at 230 West 101 Street in New York through his employment with the *Montreal Gazette*. Goodchild was applying for an exemption from the US draft due to his status as an "alien". He died in Murrayville, British Colombia, on Christmas Day 1955 at the age of 63.

Of course, in this particular case, there is a further mystery, given the entrance of the Goodchild name into this part of the Wilson story, as this, of course, had been the maiden name of George Herbert Wilson's mother. However, whilst there are common Suffolk origins, I have not been able to find a connection. Henry William Goodchild was born in Saxmundham in 1865, his father Francis Goodchild was born in Rushmere in 1841/42, his grandfather George Goodchild was born in Badingham in about 1795 and his great grandfather Thomas Goodchild was born in 1763. There is no obvious link to the father of Emma Goodchild (James Goodchild, born in Horham in about 1801) or to her grandfather (also James Goodchild, born in Horham in 1776).

George Herbert Wilson also married again – in Islington in 1920 to Euphemia McBean, who had been born in Inverawe, Argyllshire, in 1881. By then he was aged 56 and she was 39: "widower" and spinster, respectively, according to the marriage register. A year later, when George and Euphemia were living in Islington with George's daughter Dora, he was a self-employed accountant working from home. By the time of the *1939 England and Wales Register*, George and Euphemia Wilson were living at "Homestead" in Gretton Road, Winchcombe, near Cheltenham, where he was an "accountant (retired)". It is interesting that, when George died in Cheltenham the following year at the age of 76, the names given in the *England and Wales, National Probate Calendar (Index of Wills and Administrations) 1858-1966* are Alice Yiend (his widowed sister) and Charles Herbert Yiend (his nephew) – and not Euphemia Wilson, who outlived him by 13 years and died in Cheltenham at the age of 73.[18] The effects left in his will totalled £295 14s 7d.

Emigration

It is an interesting feature of the specific Line of 16 generation that emigration from the UK appears regularly in the family histories. We have already seen that this was the case with the Line of 16's Charles James Niblett (to Germany) and his brother George Edward Niblett (to Argentina). We will also learn in later chapters of the emigration of the Line of 16's Joseph Stapleton (to Malta) and that of Sarah McManamon – a sister of the Line of 16's Honoria McManamon – to the USA. To this list, we can add Leonard Kebbel Wilson (1869-1946), another younger brother of Charles Herbert Wilson.

By the time Leonard was born – on the 4th of July, as it happily turned out – Charles Tyler Wilson's family had moved to Islington in Middlesex. Leonard

---

18 Euphemia Wilson's residence at Homestead was noted in the *Gloucestershire Echo* on 28th September 1940, in which it was reported that she had been fined 10 shillings for "for allowing lights to be displayed from inside a roofed building". This was at the height of the Battle of Britain, of course, which raged between July and October of that year.

emigrated to the USA in 1894 and married Rose Mary Easby-Smith (1876-1953) in Washington DC in October 1899. He died in San Francisco, California, at the age of 76, his occupation in successive US Federal Censuses having been given as "editor: historical" (1920) and "author: heraldic reference books" (1930). He was also stated to have been a "publisher" in a Liverpool-to-New York Passenger List of 1921. The office card in the *California, San Francisco Area Funeral Home Records 1895-1985* includes a reference to Emma Goodchild as his mother.[19] Rose Mary Easby-Smith was born in Alabama and lived to the age of 77; her death in San Bernadino is recorded in the *California Death Index 1940-1997*.

Leonard and Rose Wilson had at least 8 children between 1900 and 1911 during their periods of residence in Maryland, the District of Columbia, New Jersey and Ohio. In the normal course of events, therefore, one would have expected that I would have had a substantial number of third cousins.

However, this turns out not to have been the case. At least 4 of Leonard and Rose's children pursued careers in the Catholic church: Dorothy and Winifred taught in Catholic schools, the latter also spending some time in West Africa; Margaret became a nun, Sister Mary Margaret; and William became a teacher in the Loyola University in Los Angeles. From the evidence that I have been able to accrue from the Ancestry records (including the public pages of members' contributions), it appears that none of these – the 4 youngest – were to marry and have families.

Leonard and Rose's oldest child did have a family. Rosemary Mildred Wilson (1900-1963) married Sandor Halvax (1897-1981) in 1926 and they had a daughter the following year. Sandor Halvax, who had been born in Nagykamizsa, Hungary, was listed as a "professor of languages" resident in Los Angeles in the US Census of 1930. 10 years later, he was a "social worker – teachers" earning $1,500 per annum, when his wife was working as a librarian earning $1,570. Rosemary Mildred Halvax (née Wilson) died in Los Angeles at the age of 62.

An incorrect route and an unexpected bonus

It is evident from the above discussion that researching the extended family of Charles Herbert Wilson presented some interesting challenges and fascinating results. All family researchers will be familiar – I am sure – with the approach taken here: examining the sources, following up hunches, seeking confirmatory

---

19 On her public page on Ancestry, Caroline Webber has posted a copy of a page from the *San Jose News* of 13th February 1929. Under the heading "Exhibition of Heraldry is Interesting", there is an interview with Leonard Wilson "who is the first British expert in heraldry to offer an exhibit of this kind in San Jose". The article referred to Leonard's annual visits back to Britain to undertake research in Somerset House. In the newspaper's next column – "Lindy Engaged" – there was a report of the recently announced engagement of Colonel Charles A Lindbergh.

evidence and attempting to solve nagging puzzles. Equally, they will certainly recognise the frustrations that arose when I realised that, at one stage, I had taken a completely false trail. For some time, I thought that the genealogical path back from Charles Herbert Wilson led to Edward West Wilson (1831-1921), a bank manager. I discovered my error some time after I had visited the grave which Edward West Wilson shares with his wife, Elizabeth Martha Wilson, in the quiet churchyard of St Mary's Church, Nun Monkton, near York. My initial annoyance at wasting time on an incorrect route within the family researches was fully mitigated by the realisation that I would not otherwise have had any reason to visit a delightful church, the entrance to which is framed by some beautiful trees.

Still on the positive side, my correspondence with Caroline Webber generated an unexpected bonus. She drew my attention to William Yiend, who – as shown earlier in one of the records taken from the 1881 Census – appeared in the same household in Leicester as Emma Wilson and her daughter (with Charles Tyler Wilson) Alice. Not only had William Yiend subsequently married Alice Wilson (as reported in Emma Wilson's probate record, noted above) – and thus become a brother-in-law of the Line of 16's Charles Herbert Wilson – but he had had an extensive rugby career and played several times for England.

The Wikipedia entry for William "Pusher" Yiend (1861-1939) reports that he played 6 times for England between 1889-93 and was on the winning side on 5 occasions, including the Triple Crown winning side of 1892. His club sides were Peterborough, Keighley (pre rugby league), Hartlepool Rovers, Gloucester and the Barbarians.[20] Wikipedia gives Yiend's height as 5 ft 11 in and his weight as 14 st 8 oz [possibly 8 lb], a considerable size for a rugby player in those days.[21]

THE LINE OF 16: 8. ROSA MARY WHINES (1863-1937)

The Peterborough background

As previously noted, Charles Herbert Wilson married **ROSA MARY WHINES** (1863-1937) – the next in the Line of 16 – in 1888. She was the daughter of Daniel Whines (1827-1906) and Mary Wadsworth (1832-1916) and the family into which she was born in shown in Table 4.2.

---

20 William Yiend was one of the original 50 members when the Barbarian Football Club was established in October 1890. In *Barbarian Football Club*, edited by A Wemyss and published in 1955, he is listed as having played in the club's first fixture, when he captained the opposition Hartlepool Rovers in Hartlepool on 27th December 1890. Two days later, he played for the Barbarians in their drawn match at Bradford.

21 Yiend was also a notable cricketer. The *Hartlepool Northern Daily Mail* of 12th April 1890 noted that he had headed the Seaton Carew CC 1st XI batting averages in 1889 and had been re-appointed captain for the forthcoming season. The same newspaper reported that he had also represented the Durham county XI in 1890.

Table 4.2. The parents and siblings of Rosa Marie Whines		
Daniel Whines 1827-1906 (born in Peterborough) (son of John Whines 1794-1866 and Rebecca Rycraft 1795-1849) (died in London aged 79)		
married		
Mary Wadsworth 1832-1916 (born in Peterborough) (daughter of William Wadsworth 1797-1851 and Lucy Dear 1795-1862) (died in Peterborough aged 83)		John Charles Whines 1852-1854 (born in St Pancras district, London) (died in St George Hanover Square district, London, aged 1)
		Charles William Whines 1856-58 (born in St Square Hanover Square district) (died in Westminster district aged 1)
		Catherine Lucy Charlotte Whines 1860-1861 (born in Alnwick, Northumberland) (died in Oundle district aged 1)
		Rosa Mary Whines 1863-1937 (born in Westminster/Pimlico, London) (died in Leeds aged 74) *married* **Charles Herbert Wilson 1862-1946 (born in Cambridge) (died in Leeds aged 84)**
		Frank Daniel Whines 1864-1954 (born in Camberwell, Surrey) (died in Enfield, London, aged 89) *married* Annabella Attwell 1863-1920 (born in Bow, London) (died in Edmonton, London, aged 57)
		Charlotte Whines 1867-1867 (born in Uckfield, Sussex) (died in Uckfield aged 0)

	Flora Lizzie Whines 1871-1942 (born in Chelsea, London) (died in Peterborough aged 71) *married* John Henry Mann 1873-1945 (born in Peterborough) (died in Peterborough aged 72)

Daniel and Mary Whines were both born in Peterborough, but they had moved to London by the time they married in 1851, initially to 7 Liverpool Street, St Pancras (where they were visitors in the home of Daniel's brother, John Whines, and his family) and later to Chelsea, as Daniel followed the work available to a journeyman carpenter and then joiner. They also had a spell in Northumberland, as they were sharing a dwelling at Spring Gardens House, Alnwick, at the time of the 1861 Census and their daughter – Catherine Lucy Charlotte Whines – was born in the town the previous year.

For the earlier generations of the Whines family, the Peterborough connection had been strong, as Daniel's father (John Whines, 1794-1866), grandfather (Thomas Whines, born in about 1765) and great grandfather (Thomas Whines or Wines, born in about 1735) were all born in the city.[22] John Whines married Rebecca Rycraft in the church of St John the Baptist in Peterborough in 1817 and the baptism of at least three of their children (including Daniel in 1827) also took place there. Indeed, a generation later, after Daniel and Mary Whines's first child – John Charles Whines – was born in St Pancras in 1852, he was taken to Peterborough to be baptised at the same church. (*Northamptonshire Baptisms, 1813-1912*, available on Ancestry, gives the names of both parents). Sadly, the infant died in 1854 at the age of 20 months; he is recorded in the burial register of St Giles-in-the-Fields, Camden.[23][24] (I return to the church of St John the Baptist below).

---

22 The information on the place of birth of John Whines and Thomas Whines was drawn from the contribution of Terry Wilkins to the public forum on Ancestry. I e-mailed Mr Wilkins to suggest that Daniel Whines married Mary Wadsworth, not Mary Yates (see below).

23 Wikipedia states that, as the population of the St Giles-in-the-Fields parish grew in the 18th and 19th centuries, so did their dead and eventually there was no room left in the graveyard. It is likely that the infant John Charles Whines was one of the first to be buried at the St Pancras and Islington Cemetery in East Finchley, which was established in 1854 as the first municipally-owned cemetery in London. This followed legislation – including the Metropolitan Burial Act of 1852 and the Extramural Internment Act of 1854 – which sought to alleviate the health and other problems brought about by the overcrowding of the existing burial grounds. I visited the church of St Giles-in-the-Fields in November 2016; the inscriptions on the few remaining headstones in the graveyard, which is now mainly concrete and grass, have been badly eroded by the elements.

24 The death of the infant John Charles Whines provides a textbook example of the perils of drawing on the public pages of Ancestry. In March 2021, his name was to be found on 33 family trees on these pages, of which 16 gave a year of death and all these stated that it was 1876 (at the age of 24). However, a basic search of the FreeBMD

Daniel Whines was easy to find in the 1841 Census, living with his family in the parish of St John the Baptist. (His father, John Whines, lived to the age of about 75 and died in Doncaster in 1866. Rebecca Whines (née Rycraft) was aged about 58 when she died in Islington in 1849).

		Occupation	Where born
John Whines	47	Labourer	Born in county
Rebecca	50		"
John	20	Carpenter	"
Sarah	18		"
Daniel	14		"

To find out the maiden name of Daniel's wife, Mary, I initially looked at the FreeBMD records for marriages in Peterborough. For the first quarter of 1851, on the same page as Daniel, there are two Marys: Mary Wadsworth and Mary Yates. There are two other bridegrooms – John Cornwell and John Southwell – so I looked both of these up in the 1851 Census records for Peterborough. Sure enough, John Southwell and his wife, Mary, were living with his in-laws: the Yates. This cleared the way for Daniel Whines to have married Mary Wadsworth.

It was some time later that I came across the more definitive source: the *Northamptonshire, England, Church of England Marriages, 1754-1912* site on Ancestry, which includes the marriage of Daniel Whines to Mary Wadsworth in March 1851 in the parish of St John the Baptist in Peterborough. (The respective fathers were John Whines, labourer, and William Wadsworth, tailor). This database also includes an entry for the banns of the marriage of John Whines's father – Thomas Whines – to Sarah Smith in the same parish in November 1790. Neither Thomas nor Sarah could write; they denoted their names with crosses.

This gave me the lead into Mary Wadsworth's family. In the 1841 Census, William Wadsworth and his wife, Lucy, were both aged 40 (rounded down to the nearest 5 years) living in Peterborough with two of their children. Mary Wadsworth, then aged 9, was resident elsewhere in Peterborough on the Census evening: in the household of Richard Bailey, a 45 year-old tailor, and his wife, Mary. By 1851, William Wadsworth was aged 54 (and still a tailor) and Lucy was 56. They died in June 1851 and March 1862, respectively, at the ages of 54 and 67; both were buried at St John's.

The *Northamptonshire, England, Church of England Marriages, 1754-1912* site also revealed that William Wadsworth (a widower) had married Lucy Dear at

---

database reveals that John Charles Whines was aged 1 when he died in the St George Hanover Square district of London in 1854 and that the (different) John Whines who died in 1876 was aged 55. There is no doubt that the public pages of Ancestry can be a useful source of information – or, at least, of research ideas – but the family historian must always guard against following the herd instinct of lazy plagiarism.

St John the Baptist, Peterborough, in January 1827.[25] I looked in *Northamptonshire, England, Church of England Burials, 1813-1912* to see if there was an obvious entry for the death of William's first wife, given that he had been born in about 1797 and therefore might have married from about 1814 onwards. There were four other marriages between 1814 and 1827 in which the bridegroom was named William Wadsworth, but I could not find a corresponding death record under the name of any of the brides. (I did discover the name of William Wadsworth's first wife later – see footnote 31 below).

The *Northamptonshire, England, Church of England Baptisms, Marriages and Burials, 1754-1912* site includes a record for the birth of William Wadsworth to Jane Wadsworth in 1799, again in the parish of St John the Baptist in Peterborough; no father is listed. A check of the voluminous Names Index compiled and made available online by the Peterborough and District Family History Society also gave a reference to this birth (in 1797) and linked it to bastardy and settlement papers of 1804. I can explore this further (at www.peterborofhs.org.uk/resources/Names), though I am not certain that I would be able to confirm that this was the same William.

Changes of location

It is clear from the places of birth of Daniel and Mary Whines's children given in the Census records that the early years of the marriage involved frequent changes of location. After John's birth in St Pancras in 1852 and Catherine's in Alnwick in 1860, there followed the births of Rosa (in Pimlico in 1863), Frank (in Camberwell, Surrey, in 1865) and Flora (in Chelsea in 1871).

For a long time, the presence of Daniel and Mary Whines in Alnwick in 1860 and 1861 was somewhat puzzling to me. As the crow flies, the town is about 280 miles from central London. I judged that Daniel's occupation – a joiner in the 1861 and 1871 Censuses – was not so specialised that he operated in a national labour market. Nor could I find any relatives of Daniel in that part of the world; his is the only Whines family in Northumberland in the 1861 Census and there are no families with the Wadsworth surname.

I decided to draw on some local expertise in order to examine this point and I met with some success. Mary George, a member of the Alnwick Branch of the Northumberland and Durham Family History Society, informed me that, between 1851 and 1869, the Duke and Duchess of Northumberland arranged for the replacement of the previous alterations to Alnwick Castle with a "modernisation" in the gothic style. There was also some substantial re-building elsewhere in the

---

25 The herd instinct of the public page entries on Ancestry suggests that William's wife was Lucy Gunn, who was born in Woodford, Northamptonshire in 1795. However, the 1851 Census records not only that William was still a tailor, but that his wife Lucy had been born in Peterborough.

town throughout this period. She wondered whether my ancestor could have been one of the many craftsmen involved with this work and I formed the view that that had been distinctly possible.

The complete picture was revealed when Angela and I visited the church of St John the Baptist in Peterborough in July 2022. At the entrance, we happened to be met by June Bull, the church archivist. After I had mentioned my interest in the church, Mrs Bull explained that Daniel Whines would have been employed by John Thompson jnr (1824-1898), whose firm of building contractors – John Thompson & Sons – was one of the largest in the country and did indeed operate at a national level.

John Thompson jnr had taken over the running of the firm on the death of his father – John Thompson snr – in 1853. As a skilled stonemason and master-builder, he was engaged with the reconstruction of part of Peterborough Cathedral as well as repair and restoration schemes at the cathedrals in Hereford, Chester, Lichfield, Ripon and Winchester. June Bull informed me that the firm's commissions included work at Westminster Hall and the royal residence at Sandringham, amongst others. It is easy to see how the rebuilding work at Alnwick Castle would have been part of this list of prestigious commissions.

In the 1871 Census, John Thompson is recorded as a "builder and brickmaker employing about 550 men" living with his wife and family in Peterborough. It is clear, therefore, that he oversaw a substantial business operation, of which Daniel Whines was a key member as part of the core team that travelled around the country to work on the major projects. From the family history perspective, the particularly interesting feature is that Daniel's wife and young family travelled with him.

In 1871, Daniel and Mary Whines were living in with their family in Chelsea, where they were one of the three households resident at 32 Oakley Crescent. Ten years later, they were at number 33, when their daughter Rosa was a 17 year-old draper's assistant. As we noted earlier, the family was still in Chelsea in 1891, at 39 Smith Street.[26][27]

Daniel Whines's changes of location were to continue, however. In 1898, his place of residence was given as Wenhaston in east Suffolk in the announcement of 21st January in the *Stamford Mercury* of the marriage in Peterborough of his daughter Flora Lizzie Whines to John Henry Mann. However, three years later, in the 1901 Census, the 73 year-old Daniel Whines was recorded as being retired and

---

26 Oakley Crescent does not exist now, but there is an Oakley Gardens, which is a half-circular shape and into which Phene Street runs (see above). Number 33 has a square frontage on which there is a blue plaque: "George Gissing 1857-1903 novelist lived here 1882-84".

27 We have seen that several members of the Wilson family were also resident in Chelsea. However, this was at a later date. In 1881, Rosa Mary's future husband – Charles Herbert Wilson – was living in Lancashire and his (separated) parents were in Leicester and Poplar.

living with the family of his and Mary's son, Frank Daniel Whines, at 41 Russell Street, Tottenham. Meanwhile, Mary was living with their married daughter, Flora Mann, and her family back in Peterborough at 41 New Road. The Census records her as "Mary W Lines" (which is how it is transcribed in the Ancestry version) and as a widow. In the 1911 Census, Mary Whines (correctly spelt and, by that time, genuinely widowed) was living with the same family at the same address. Her son-in-law, John Henry Mann, was a 38 year-old butcher.[28]

What to make of the 1901 records? One possibility is that, in the absence of a formal divorce, Daniel and Mary Whines had gone their separate ways, albeit to stay with different members of their family. A more likely explanation, I think, is that their children – Frank and Flora, respectively – were sharing the burden of looking after their elderly parents, who were then aged 73 and 68. The fact that the Census enumerator made such a hash of Mary's surname suggests that he might also have been careless about her marital status and just assumed that she was a widow when, in fact, her husband was still alive.

The actual death of Daniel Whines is recorded in the *National Probate Calendar (Index of Wills and Administrations) for England and Wales, 1858-1966*. He died in June 1906 at 49 Russell Road, South Tottenham and left his widow, Mary Whines, his effects of £197 5s. The bequest does not suggest estrangement between the couple.[29]

For some time, I did also wonder if there were other children in the family who also died young – in particular, who were born and died in the period between 1852 (the birth of John) and 1860 (the birth of Catherine) and therefore not picked up in the Census records. The FreeBMD records include those for Susannah Whines (1854-1854) and Alice Whines (1855-1857) in the St George Hanover Square district (where the death of John Charles Whines was recorded). Initially, however, I could not conclude that these were members of the same family, as, within the district, there were other Whines births (but not deaths) of children who did not appear in Daniel and Mary's household in the 1861 Census.

The purchase of the death certificates of Susannah Whines and Alice Whines showed that this caution had been vindicated. They were both daughters of John Whines, described as a carpenter (and then carpenter/builder's foreman) living at 29 Jackbrook Street, Pimlico. (This was Daniel's brother, of course). Their respective causes of death were "convulsions, certified" and "bronchitis (12 days),

---

28   John Henry Mann died in Peterborough on Christmas Day 1945. His obituary in the *Peterborough Standard* on 28th December recorded that he was Secretary of the Peterborough Meat Traders Association for 33 years "being most assiduous in the duties, especially during the trying conditions set up by the coming of rationing and other wartime controls". His wide-ranging interests included being a Vicar's Warden at St Mary's Church, judging the homing pigeon shows of the Peterborough Association and breeding whippets.

29   The same source reveals that the effects of John Thompson jnr totalled £80,296 9s 10d when he died in 1898. This was the equivalent of approximately £12.1 million in 2023 prices.

measles, certified". The informant was Caroline Whines (John's second wife), who was present at the deaths.[30]

I was able to address this general question in November 2016, when the General Registry Office released an online version of the births database from 1837 which included the mothers' maiden names for the whole period. This included the birth of Charles William Whines into the family of Daniel and Mary Whines in the St George Hanover Square district in the third quarter of 1856. He died in the Westminster district at the age of 1 at the beginning of 1858 and, according to the *England and Wales Nonconformist and Non-parochial Registers, 1567-1970*, he was buried in the Victoria Park Cemetery in Hackney.

Daniel and Mary Whines's third child also died at the age of 1. The tragic details were reported in the *Peterborough Advertiser* on 14th September 1861:

> ELTON
>
> SINGULAR DEATH OF A CHILD. An inquest was held at Elton on Thursday by Wm Lawrence Esq. on the body of Catherine Lucy Charlotte Whines, an infant twelve months old, the daughter of Mr Daniel Whines, the foreman of an extensive works now near completion at the residence of the Right Honorable the Earl of Carysfort, who came to her death in the following distressing manner. Mr and Mrs Whines and their daughter, and Mr Whines's sister Mrs Wadsworth (schoolmistress at Weedon) with her two children, were taking tea on Wednesday evening, when the deceased, who was being nursed on the father's knee, either had incautiously given to it, or helped itself to the half of a shrimp, and endeavoured to swallow it, but it went, as is commonly said "the wrong way" and got into the windpipe. The child died after three-quarters of an hour's suffering, and more than an hour before medical attendance could be obtained. Mr Pearce, surgeon, Peterborough, made a post-mortem examination of the throat and chest of the deceased. He carefully opened the windpipe until he arrived at the point where it divides to enter each lung, and at the division found the head and shoulders of a considerably sized shrimp with the shell on. He considered that that was sufficient to cause almost instantaneous death, and that the child died from suffocation. The jury found a verdict accordingly. It was a very interesting healthy child and the loss was most severely felt by its parents, it being the third child they have lost in infancy under painfully sudden circumstances.[31]

---

30 John Whines's first wife was Frances Wye (1821-1854), who died at the time of the birth of their daughter, Susannah.

31 The newspaper report generated one of those minor – but captivating – queries that family history researchers often find hard to resist: specifically, who was "Mr Whines's sister Mrs Wadsworth (schoolmistress at Weedon)"? From the various Census records, it was straightforward to find out that the expected relationship of sister or

Yet another infant death was that of Charlotte Whines in the first quarter of 1867 – the quarter of her birth – in Uckfield, Sussex. Although this town is some distance from the usual locations in and around London in which Daniel Whines and his family were usually to be found, I am confident that she should also be included on this branch of the family tree. The maiden name recorded for Charlotte's mother was Wadsworth and the marriage between Daniel Whines and Mary Wadsworth appears to have been the only one in England and Wales involving that combination of surnames in the period between September 1837 and the ill-fated Charlotte's birth/death in 1867.

The intra-Census information provided by the births and deaths of the infants Charles William and Charlotte in the mid-19th Century provides further evidence that Daniel Whines was extremely mobile in his search for work. When combined with the Census data noted above, it can be seen that, in the 20 years to 1871, the family was resident in at least four different parts of London/Middlesex/Surrey as well as Northumberland and Sussex.

From this distance, we don't know if this was through the "pull" of seeking occupational progress or the "push" to avoid the consequences of joblessness. My interpretation/guess is a simple and positive one: Daniel was driven by the worthy ambition to provide for his family and, accordingly, took full advantage of the available employment opportunities, not least those provided by John Thompson & Sons. In this respect, I see a clear parallel with another member of the Line of 16 – Peter McBride – whose search for better employment prospects, described in Chapter 2 above, took him and his young family from Glasgow to Manchester and then Leeds in the early years of the 20th Century.

The death of the infant Charlotte Whines in 1867 meant that 4 of the 7 children of Daniel and Mary Whines died before their second birthday, including the first three to be born. The other three – including the future Rosa Mary Wilson – lived into old age.

One of these was Daniel and Mary's daughter, Flora Lizzie, who maintained the family links with Peterborough after her marriage to John Henry Mann in 1898. Their three children were born in the city in the 15 years prior to the First World War and I have discovered that at least one grandchild – my mother's second cousin – was born there in the 1930s. Both John Henry Mann and Flora Lizzie

---

sister-in-law did not apply. Daniel Whines had one sister, Sarah, who married a man named William Cole. In addition, neither of the sons of William and Lucy Wadsworth – Charles and William, Mary's brothers – married a schoolmistress.

I eventually discovered that the person concerned was Francis Wadsworth – a 37 year-old schoolmistress in Great Weldon (sic) in Northamptonshire – whose husband, Benjamin Wadsworth, was a schoolmaster. Benjamin was born in Stamford, Lincolnshire – which is about 8 miles from Peterborough – his parents being William Wadsworth and Sarah Woodward, who had married in the town in 1820. Thus, I was able not only to conclude that "Mrs Wadsworth" was not Daniel Whines's sister – rather, the wife of Daniel's wife's stepbrother – but also to find out the name of William Wadsworth's first wife.

Mann (née Whines) were in their 70s when they died in Peterborough in 1945 and 1942, respectively. However, there was a movement away from the city in the next generation – my third cousins – as three Mann births are registered in Surrey.

The other of Daniel and Mary's children to survive into adulthood was Frank Daniel Whines (1864-1954), who married Annabella Attwell (1863-1920) in 1888. They had 7 children, all of whom were born in north London and all of whom did survive into adulthood. Frank was a teenage solicitor's clerk in Chelsea and later a journeyman butcher before settling into the carpenter/joiner trade. He died in Enfield at the age of 89, his wife having pre-deceased him by over 30 years.

Frank and Annabella Whines's first-born child was Frank Cyril Whines, who was a civil servant in Her Majesty's Stationary Office in Bristol at the time of the 1939 Register. He died in Worthing in Sussex (in 1955 at the age of 65), where there appears to have been a long-standing family conclave: the town was also the place of death of Frank Cyril Whines's sister Mary Winifred (aged 75 in 1967), brothers Edward George (aged 72 in 1973) and Herbert Daniel Nollage (aged 77 in 1971) as well as Herbert's widow Ada Florence Whines (née King, aged 84 in 1983) and Frank's daughter Dorothy Mary Whines (aged 90 in 2005).[32]

The entry in the 1939 Register for another of Frank Cyril Whines's siblings – Norman Thomas Wadsworth Whines (1897-1979) – brings us firmly into the mid 20th Century, as his occupation in Upper Edmonton was "designing air raid shelters". He became a surveyor and – judging by the effects of over £31,000 that he left in his will – quite a successful one.

Norman Whines's middle name of Wadsworth takes us back to Mary Whines (née Wadsworth) – his grandmother – who died in Peterborough on 1st July 1916 at the age of 83.[33] (In another land, not far away, this was the first day of the Battle of the Somme). I looked for a record of her death in the Peterborough and District FHS Names Index and found one entry, which simply said "Broadway Cemetery" (with no dates). The website of the Crematorium Department of the Peterborough City Council reported that the Department had responsibility for the cemetery though the location was no longer used for burials.

---

32 Dorothy Mary Whines's mother – Louisa Whines (née Durrant, 1893-1915) – died a few days after giving birth. She was aged 22. Frank Cyril Whines later married Elsie Annie Kebbell (1888-1972).

33 The 8th July 1916 notice of the funeral in the *Peterborough and Hunts Standard* used a curious form of words. To have died "somewhat suddenly" at the age of 84 was surely not unusual, even if the deceased had previously been in robust health.
"The funeral of Mrs Mary Whines… who died somewhat suddenly at her residence, Hadley Villa, Eastfield Road, on Saturday, took place on Wednesday". The list of mourners included Mr and Mrs Wilson, son-in-law and daughter and Miss Marie Wilson, one of her grandchildren.
The "Miss Marie Wilson" listed in the mourners was my maternal grandmother, then aged 16.

I followed this up in October 2016 – just over 100 years after her death, as it happened – with a tentative enquiry[34] about whether the Mary Whines buried in Broadway Cemetery might be the one in which I was interested. I received a reply – within minutes – from Teena Wright confirming that it was indeed and attaching a plan of the cemetery with the grave marked. This was another very impressive response, akin to those which I received from Leeds City Council following my enquiry about the McBride grave in Hunslet Cemetery and from the idverde company in reply to my query about the Niblett grave at the Bandon Hill Cemetery in Sutton.

Notwithstanding Teena Wright's swift response to my enquiry, it took me nearly another six years – until July 2022 – before I visited the cemetery and located the grave of Mary Whines. It comprised a three-step pyramid on which a Calvary Cross had originally been elevated, though the cross itself had been toppled and was lying on the grass. One of the sides of the bottom step was engraved with Mary Whines's name whilst, on an adjacent side, the lower two steps read:

ALSO
DANIEL
THE BELOVED HUSBAND
OF
MARY WHINES

The family of Charles Herbert Wilson and Rosa Mary Whines

The family of Charles Herbert Wilson and Rosa Mary Whines is shown in Table 4.3. For many years, I assumed that my grandmother – Marie Rosa Wilson (1890-1968) – was their only child, born in Wood Green, London. It was a considerable shock, therefore, when I saw in the 1911 Census that not only had Charles and Rosa been married for 23 years, but they had had three children, of whom only one was still living.

Marie Rosa Wilson was, therefore, the surviving child in a solid lower middle-class family. The occupation of her father evolved from "cashier" (aged 28 in Chelsea) in 1891 to "commercial cashier" (aged 37 in Wood Green) in 1901. By 1911, he was a company secretary at a furniture manufacturers and, at the time of Marie Rosa's wedding (to Alfred Edgar Niblett) in 1919, he was a merchant.

---

34 To crematorium@peterborough.gov.uk.

Table 4.3. The family of Charles Herbert and Rosa Mary Wilson	
Charles Herbert Wilson 1862-1946 (born in Cambridge) (died in Leeds aged 84)	
married	
Rosa Mary Whines 1863-1937 (born in Westminster/Pimlico, London) (died in Leeds aged 74)	Marie Rosa Wilson 1890-1968 (born in Wood Green, London) (died in Leeds aged 78) *married* Alfred Edgar Niblett 1888-1973 (born in Osnabrück, Germany) (died in Leeds aged 84)
	Winifred Flora Wilson 1895-1895 (born in Edmonton district, London) (died in Wood Green aged 10 days)
	Gladys Emma Wilson 1897-1898 (born in Edmonton district) (died in Wood Green aged 9 months)

By the time of the 1921 Census, Charles Herbert and Rosa Mary Wilson were living at 36 St George's Road, Palmers Green. (They had each lost a couple of years to be recorded as aged 56 and 55, respectively). Charles was an accountant with White Cross Insurance Ass. Ltd at 5 Moorgate Street, London EC1. In addition to a servant – the 21 year-old Annie Griffiths – they had a visitor in John William Mann, their 22 year-old nephew, who was an insurance clerk with the same company. Charles and Rosa Wilson are duly to be found in the *London Electoral Registers 1832-1965* for the Wood Green district in each year from 1919 to 1935, at which point they moved to Leeds, where Rosa died two years later. At the time of leaving London, they were aged 72 or 73, so I must assume that the move was so that they could be close to their daughter and her husband. (See Chapter 9 below).

For a long time (that is, until the end of 2016), in seeking to research the names of Marie Rosa's deceased siblings, I faced the same difficulty as that incurred with some other branches of the family tree in that the available databases of births in England and Wales gave the maiden name of the mother only from the third quarter of 1911 onwards. In this case, there was the additional complication brought about by the relatively common surname. My grandmother was born in the district of Edmonton, London, so I looked for the deaths of Wilsons aged 0-23 in that district between March 1888 and June 1911. There were no fewer than 143, of whom 81 died before their first birthday; even over the shorter period from March 1888 to March 1901, there were 76, of whom 49 died before the age of 1.

There were some entries in the databases with possible family names – Charles and Leonard included – so I decided that some selective (or inspired) purchases of birth certificates (of those who had also died before 1911) might be worthwhile, albeit with fairly long odds on striking anything relevant. To start with, therefore, I purchased the birth certificates of Sarah Mahale Wilson (1891-1907) and Charles Wilson (1898-1898); in neither case were the parents given as Charles and Rosa Mary Wilson. The search of a more specific database – *All London Church of England Births and Baptisms, 1813-1906* – did not reveal any Wilson births to parents with the names Charles and Rosa.

A separate line of enquiry – a long shot – was the gravestone (if any) of Charles Herbert Wilson and/or Rosa Mary Wilson. The parish registers tell me that both were buried in the St Matthew's graveyard in the Chapel Allerton district of Leeds. Rosa died at the age of 74 in 1937 and Charles at the age of 84 in 1946. In both cases, the last recorded residence was 38 Nunroyd Road: the home of my grandparents (Alfred and Marie Niblett) with which I was so familiar.

I made two visits to the graveyard in 2016. At the time of the first, in May, it was a sorry sight. A few headstones remained legible, mainly from the 19th Century, but the grass was heavily overgrown and the identifiable markers could only have represented a small proportion of the total numbers interred there.

When I visited the graveyard for the second time, in August, I was relieved to see that the grass had been cut and a general tidying up had taken place. Beforehand, I consulted various documents relating to the cemetery at the West Yorkshire Archive Service (WYAS) in Morley. These included the burial books for the Old Church Site (in which Charles and Rosa Wilson were listed in plot number 37) and the New Burial Ground, the *Plan of the Chapel Yard of Chapel Allerton and the piece of ground to be added to it: 1834* and the *Plot Plan of Chapel Allerton Graveyard, dated 17-11-[19]72*. The last of these was in two parts – "A" and "B" – and had been drawn up in preparation for some major tidying up of the cemetery under the auspices of the "Ripon Diocesan Advisory Committee for the care of churches" in 1972.

It took me a while to work out what "old" and "new" meant in this context. The New Burial Ground dated from a meeting of the ratepayers of the township on 20th September 1868, when it was agreed that the original burial ground should be extended. Its burial book listed the subscribers to the Chapel Allerton Burial Ground Extension Fund; they raised £1,149 4s 4d and every penny was accounted for in the itemised expenditures.

After the present St Matthew's Church was completed (at a cost of £20,500) in 1898 and consecrated in 1900 – in Wood Lane, about a quarter of a mile away

– the old chapel fell into disrepair and it was demolished in 1935. However, the lower part of some its walls can still be seen through the undergrowth and this enabled me to identity the location of the Old Church Site, which effectively represented a post-1935 extension to the cemetery.

The graves in this part of the cemetery were shown (in Plan B) to have been in a rectangular grid – 14 by 9: 126 graves in total – with vaults down two sides. On the plan, prepared for the repair works of 1972, there had been a "list of headstones to be re-sited" (22 in total). The graves were also individually marked with those having headstones to be re-sited marked in blue and those with headstones to be left on site marked in red. Plot number 37 was in neither list which probably meant – as I realised when I was at the location – that the Wilsons had not had a headstone but a horizontal flagstone. It was clear that, whilst I could work out roughly where plot number 37 was, the long shot of discovering the names of Marie Rosa Wilson's deceased young siblings by this route would come to nought.

It required another visit to the WYAS in Morley (in July 2018) for me to locate plot number 37 exactly. I made a careful record of the location of the remaining headstones in Plan B, particularly for plot numbers 31 (Leonard Jefferson), 34 (Mary Hannah Dowgill) and 51 (Norman Howard). On returning to the graveyard, I was able to use these as markers to conclude that plot number 37 was covered with some straggly grass and weeds and partly under the corner of a large bush. I had brought a small gardening fork to see if the grass might have rested on top of a flagstone and been relatively easy to lift off, but this was not the case. Better, I thought, to leave the site undisturbed. I had succeeded, at least, in determining its precise location.

In the adjacent Chapel Allerton library, there was a small – but informative – local history section. I consulted *Chapel Allerton: from village to suburb* by R Faulkner (Chapel Allerton Residents Association, 1986) and *The Church in Chapel Allerton, Leeds* by George E Kirk (Yorkshire Archaeological Society, 1949).

It is a fascinating story. The first chapel in Chapel Allerton was built by the Cistercian monks of Kirkstall Abbey. When the sexton's cottage (which had been marked on the 1834 Plan) was demolished in 1880, a Roman altar was unearthed in its foundations, suggesting that the monks had used an earlier pagan site. Kirk noted that, by the mid-1890s, the old chapel was "damp, unhealthy, ugly and not arranged for reverent worship in a manner most for the honour and glory of God. The only satisfactory solution seemed to be the erection of a new church". Hence, the commissioning of the present-day St Matthew's: a fine building, which I remember with some affection from my visits each Sunday when I attended the local primary school (long demolished and replaced by housing) in the nearby Woodland Lane.

As with the puzzle of the names of Rosa Mary Whines's deceased siblings (see above), I was able to resolve the analogous query about her daughter Marie

Rosa Wilson's deceased siblings in 2016, when the GRO released its online database of births from 1837 with the maiden name of the mother included from this date. Interrogation of the database has to be done in a somewhat piecemeal manner – for males and females separately over two-year periods – but it was no real difficulty to find out that the infants in question had been Winifred Flora Wilson (1895-1895) and Gladys Emma Wilson (1897-1898), both of whom, like Marie Rosa Wilson, had been born in the district of Edmonton. I was glad to have found them. The feeling was similar to that experienced when I first came across the 1911 Census record that Peter McBride had completed, in which he had included the names of his 3 long-deceased children.[35] The record is somehow complete with their inclusion and they are not forgotten.

I purchased the death certificates. Winifred Flora Wilson died at the age of 10 days of "congestion of the lungs, 5 days", the informant being L Powell, who was present at the death. Gladys Emma Wilson lived to the age of 9 months, her cause of death being "congenital cystic kidney ascites, 1 month"; Rosa Mary Wilson, who was present at the death, was the informant. In both certificates, Charles Herbert Wilson's occupation was stated to have been a cashier and the family's address was Palace Gates Road in Wood Green.

I visited Palace Gates Road in October 2019.[36] The road climbs up a hill away from a routine shopping parade towards Alexandra Park Road and consists of solid 2 or 3-storey terraced dwellings with several different styles in their refurbished facades. One had the date of its construction – 1895 – prominently displayed: Charles and Rosa Wilson must have been newly ensconced in their recently built property (with the 5 year-old Marie Rosa) at the time of the death of the infant Winifred Flora Wilson.

East Anglia

I have given this chapter the title of "London" because that is where Charles Herbert Wilson and Rosa Mary Whines spent most of their lives and where my grandmother, Marie Rosa Niblett, was born. However, as we have seen, if we go back to earlier generations, other localities take on a greater prominence: for example, Peterborough in the case of the Whines family.

This is emphatically the case for (some of) the ancestors of Charles Herbert Wilson's mother: Emma Goodchild. A trawl through the contributions to the public pages of Ancestry – including from Caroline Webber – takes us deep

---

35 See Chapter 2 above.

36 The "palace" is, of course, the Alexandra Palace which was built (and re-built) in the 1870s as a private centre of recreation, education and entertainment. It was designated as a charitable trust in 1900; the current trustee is the London Borough of Haringay. It was the home of the BBC's first public television service in 1936.

into the centuries of life in East Anglia. Indeed, working back through Emma Goodchild's father (James Goodchild, 1801-1857) and her grandmother (Esther Pipe, 1776-1845), there were no fewer than another 8 generations of the family – dating back to William Dowsing (or Dowsinge) and William Pipe (who were born in Laxfield, Suffolk, in about 1527 and 1530, respectively) – who lived in a network of villages covered by an area of only a few square miles to the south-east of present-day Diss.

In addition to Laxfield, these locations included Brundish, for which the www.findagrave.com website lists 5 generations of the direct line of the Pipe family and their spouses who were buried in the St Lawrence churchyard: from William Pipe (c1485-1517) through to Rebecca Pipe (née Rebacker, 1590-1615).[37] It is a remarkable continuity. At the extreme, Hoxne in Suffolk is identified as a location in the family tree in about 1457 (the birth of John Pipe, who died in the same village in 1484 and is buried in the graveyard of St Mary's Church) and 1852 (the death of Emma Goodchild's grandfather, also James Goodchild): a span of almost 400 years.

As noted in earlier chapters on the replicated contributions on Ancestry's public pages covering the parish records in Yorkshire and Gloucestershire, there was no way of telling which family history researcher had got there first. However, the Webber and other contributions present an extraordinary catalogue of work on the extended Wilson/Goodchild family.

As I have not attempted to check all this information from the primary sources, I must take these presentations on trust, noting that there are some variations in detail between the various contributors. There are one or two common errors: I think that the village named as Sexlead should be Saxtead and that Fressington should be Fressingfield. It is also obvious that at least two (and probably three) generations have been missed out between the two earliest generations given in the family tree: Jeremiah Pipe (born in 1372) and Robert Pipe (1450-1482).

But the basic story is clear. Up to two generations before the Line of 16 is reached (in the person of Charles Herbert Wilson), one of the family lines had an unbroken attachment to a small area in Suffolk that lasted for almost four centuries. I cannot but note that, in terms of longevity, this dwarfs the proven (male) part of the proud Yorkshire line that extended from George Rigg (born in 1802) down to me.[38]

---

37 The burials in the St Lawrence churchyard in Brundish include the wonderfully named Mildred Thymblethorpe (born in 1530), who became the wife of William Pipe (also born in 1530). Mildred's parents – Robert and Agnes Thymblethorpe – were born in Worsted and Knapton, respectively, in the northern part of Norfolk.

38 The direct Yorkshire line extending down to me is longer, of course – over 430 years – when it is taken back through Jane Wells (1806-1887) – the wife of George Rigg (1802-1865) – to Robert Welles, who was born

To repeat, Jeremiah Pipe was born in 1372. This is very difficult to get one's head round. In 1372, the King of England was Edward III and the royal court spoke French.

My wife Angela and I followed up the Suffolk connection with a mini-tour of some of the county's churches and graveyards in July 2022. It was a delightful trip. Each of the churches – at Laxfield, Dennington, Hoxne, Horham and Brundish – was open for the casual visitor to explore their rich histories, the information on which was readily available in the respective church guides.

We realised very quickly, of course, that, although an ancestor might have a reference on the www.findagrave.com website, this does not necessarily mean that the grave can actually be found. It is clear that some of the references on the site, whilst recording a burial in the location, are not accompanied by a headstone; moreover, even if the headstone were to exist, the passage of time has meant that in many cases any inscriptions on it were now illegible. It was noticeable that, of all the Pipe references in which I was interested on the website, only one was accompanied by a photograph.

But one photograph was sufficient. In the graveyard of St Mary's Church in Horham, we found the grave of John Pipe (1713-1797). We were not able to read the inscription on the lower part of the gravestone, but the upper half was clearly legible:

In Memoriam
JOHN PIPE
who departed this life 24th day of March 1797
at the 83rd year of his Age

It was clear that this grave was part of a family plot. Nearby, a smaller headstone was leaning back and resting against another Pipe marker. The former simply read:

J-P
1793

It is almost certain that this was the gravestone of another John Pipe (1736-1793), who was the son of the first John Pipe, but pre-deceased him.[39]

---

in Galphay, near Ripon, in about 1516 (see the separate contribution to the public pages of Ancestry by David Pratt reported in Chapter 1). It is interesting that the year of Robert Welles's birth falls in the same era as those of William Dowsing(e) and William Pipe (1527 and 1530, respectively) reported by Caroline Webber.

39 The photograph on the www.findagrave.com website lists the headstone as that of John Pipe (the son), who died in 1793. As noted, it is actually that of John Pipe (the father), who died in 1797. The error is immaterial, however. It was the photograph that drew me to the location.

The discovery of the two gravestones marked a significant development in the family history researches. The larger of the two marks the earliest year of birth (1713) of anyone within the family tree for whom a gravestone has been found. The smaller marks the earliest year of death (1793).[40] The route to the older John Pipe from my grandmother Marie Rosa Niblett (née Wilson, 1890-1968) goes back through the Line of 16's Charles Herbert Wilson (1862-1946), Emma Wilson (née Goodchild, 1838-1911), James Goodchild (1801-1857), Esther Goodchild (née Pipe, 1776-1845), John Pipe (1736-1793) and John Pipe (1713-1797).

These records were tantalisingly close to being broken by William Dowsing (1526-1614), who was a great (x4) grandfather of the older John Pipe. He was born in Laxfield, where he died at the age of 88. There are slightly different accounts as to exactly whereabouts in the village's All Saints Church William was buried. The church's guide states that his was one of a number of burials in the nave of the church and it is implied that this was in the area near the entrance, which is now covered by a protective green carpet. (Visitors are requested not to move the carpet, as there are no brasses).

A different location for the final resting place of William Dowsing has been reported by Michael Otterson, who – like me – is a great (x12) grandson and whose family history website (www.otterson.org) reports his extensive and detailed research. Mr Otterson agrees that William – a "gentleman of Laxfield" – was buried in the nave of the church, but that this was close to the chancel. He states that the tomb was for centuries identified by a contemporary brass plate bolted to the floor but, in order to prevent its further deterioration, church officers removed the brass in 2019 with the intention of mounting it on one of the church walls. The plate's inscription reads:

> "Here lyeth the body of Willm Dowsing who had issue by Elizabeth his wife 4 sones and 1 daughter being of about ye age of 88 yeares deceased the second day of November Anno Dni 1614"

It is not clear if William Dowsing's brass plate has indeed been mounted on a church wall. Angela and I did not see it on our visit to All Saints Church, Laxfield, in July 2022. A loose end to be tidied up, perhaps.

However, there is a further twist to the tale. A grandson of William Dowsing – and his namesake – was the notorious "Smasher" Dowsing (1596-1668), who was also born in Laxfield. He was not in the direct Pipe line with which I am

---

40 For historical reference, the two Treaties of Utrecht in 1713 marked the end of the War of Spanish Succession between Great Britain and France/Spain. In 1793, Louis XVI and Marie Antoinette were guillotined in Paris.

concerned, but was a second cousin to the William Pype (born in Brundish in 1586) who was.[41]

In December 1643, William Dowsing was appointed "Commissioner for the destruction of monuments of idolatry and superstition" in the Puritan regime. Such monuments were defined in a Parliamentary Ordinance of the previous August as "fixed rails, altar rails, chancel steps, crucifixes, crosses, images and pictures of any one of the persons of the Trinity and of the Virgin Mary and pictures of saints or superstitious inscriptions".

Dowsing's Wikipedia entry records that he carried out his work in 1643 and 1644 by visiting over 250 churches in Cambridgeshire and Suffolk, including several of the college chapels in the University of Cambridge, removing or defacing items that he thought fitted the requirements outlined in the Ordinance. The specific details of Dowsing's iconoclasm were recorded in his "Journal" of the period.[42] His destructive activities ceased in 1644 when his patron – Edward Montagu, 2nd Earl of Manchester – fell out with Oliver Cromwell. Dowsing subsequently returned to obscurity in Laxfield, where he died in 1668 at the age of 72.

---

41 "Smasher" Dowsing's father (Wolfran Dowsing, 1558-1607) was a sibling of William Pype's mother (Margaret Dowsing, 1562-1630).

42 The 1885 version of the Journal, published in Ipswich, includes the "Pedigree: Dowsing of Laxfield, Suffolk" in an Annex. This confirms the family connection between the older William Dowsing (in the direct family line) and William "Smasher" Dowsing.

CHAPTER FIVE

TYNESIDE

THE LINE OF 16: 9. ARTHUR ENGLISH (1869-1936)

County Down

We have now reached the Continental Divide in the Line of 16. Having covered my 8 great grandparents, we turn to those of my wife, Angela English.

There is a very strong Irish connection, beginning with **ARTHUR ENGLISH** (1869-1936), who was born in County Down. This itself represents a good starting point as, for Arthur's first two appearances in the Census of England and Wales – as a 2 year-old in 1871[1] and as a 12 year-old in 1881 – he is stated as living in Jarrow, Durham, and born in Ireland. However, in the next Census – in 1891, when he is a 23 year-old engine fitter living in North Shields, Northumberland – Arthur's place of birth is given as Jarrow; likewise in 1901, when he was aged 34 and a mechanical engineer resident in North Shields.

1871: 29 Walter Street, Jarrow

					Occupation	Where born
John English	Head	Married	M	34	Labourer	Ireland
Catherine	Wife	Married	F	28		"
Mary	Daughter		F	8		Durham, Jarrow
James	Son		M	4		"
Arthur	Son		M	2		Ireland
Felix Woods	Friend	Widower	M	45	Labourer	Ireland
Mary Woods			F	13		Durham, Jarrow

---

[1] In the household headed by John English in 1871, there were also 3 lodgers, all of whom were single male labourers. The surnames of two of them are hard to read, but the third was clearly Patrick Magee, aged 32.

1891: 8 Wellington Street West, North Shields

					Occupation	Where born
Arthur English	Head	Married	M	23	Engine fitter	Durham, Jarrow
Helen	Wife	Married	F	22		Northumberland, North Shields
Helen Mary	Daughter		F	10 mths		"

There is no doubt that Arthur English was born in Ireland. The *Ireland, Catholic Parish Register, 1655-1915* – compiled by the National Library of Ireland in Dublin and made available on Ancestry – includes a record for his baptism in the parish of Clonallon (in the diocese of Dromore) in County Down in January 1869. Similarly, the *Ireland, Civil Registrations of Births Index, 1864-1958* includes an entry for him in Newry, County Down, on 27 January 1869. The names of his parents – John English (1836/7-1885) and Catherine English (née Woods, 1842-1911) – are given in the corresponding entry in *Ireland, Selected Births and Baptisms, 1620-1911*,[2] as they are also for the birth of Arthur's brother, Peter English, in nearby Warrenpoint in 1874.

I am bound to wonder if this was a simple (albeit repeated) mistake in the 1891 and 1901 Censuses or whether, for some reason, Arthur felt obliged to play down his Irish birthplace in these later records. The latter might well be the more likely explanation, given the prejudices that existed against the Irish-born in many communities in England at that time.[3]

Although I know from Census of England and Wales records that John English was born in Ireland in about 1836, the available parish records in the Public Record Office of Northern Ireland (PRONI) do not enable me to identify his parents or his place of birth. There were four baptisms under this name in County Down or County Armagh between 1831-36, but all were in Presbyterian or Church of Ireland, rather than Roman Catholic, families. Nor were there any relevant entries for neighbouring parishes now in the Republic of Ireland: Carlingford (1835-38), Louth (1835-38) and Cooley (1835-37).

In the absence of extensive Census material for Ireland in the mid 19th Century, the family historian is drawn to the Primary Valuation of Ireland, better known as Griffith's Valuation after the Commissoner of Valuation, Sir Richard

---

2   This database has been compiled by the Church of the Latter Day Saints and is available on Ancestry.

3   Another interesting question is how a Roman Catholic family with the surname of English came to be resident in County Down. In *Surnames of Ireland: Origins, Numbers and Distribution of Selected Irish Surnames* (2002), Edward Neafsay notes that the name has two origins: in the south, it was Anglo-Norman and probably served to distinguish its families from settlers of French or Welsh origin; in the north, it was a mistranslation of the Irish surname Mac an Galloglaigh, son of the gallowglass (a soldier). In the dated but authoritative *More Irish Families* (1960), Edward MacLysaght states that the former explanation in Counties Tipperary and Limerick goes back to the 12th Century, later being found in variants such as L'Englys, L'Angleys and Lenglais. As well as English and Inglis, the mistranslations of Mac an Galloglaigh include MacGallogly, Gallogly, Ingoldsby and Golightly.

Griffith. This huge undertaking is the earliest listing of the value of privately owned property in Ireland and was carried out between 1848 and 1864.[4] County Down was one of the last areas to be completed (in July 1864). A search on Griffith's Valuation (on Ancestry) for the English surname in Clonallon produced one record: for Thomas English, who leased 9 acres 2 roods and 35 perches[5] from JW Dickenson, the rateable value of the land being £7 and that of the buildings 10 shillings.

In 2019, I commissioned the Ulster Historical Foundation (UHF), based in Belfast, to examine other possible contemporary sources for any references to John English. These included the tithe applotment books,[6] freeholder registers and lists of flax-growers.[7] None were found. This suggests that John English migrated from outside the South Down area. It is not possible to draw any conclusions on whether the Thomas English named in Griffith's Valuation was the father or brother of John English (or no relation at all).

As noted, Catherine English's maiden name was Woods. I was able to take this family back a further generation by consulting the database (www.ancestryireland.com) made available by the UHF during an excellent family history course that Angela and I attended in Belfast in June 2017. Catherine Woods was baptised in the Clonallon parish in December 1841, her parents being Peter and Mary Woods. The database showed that she had five older siblings born in Clonallon between 1827 and 1838.[8]

Interestingly, the Griffith's Valuation of 1864 shows that, in addition to being the landlord of Thomas English, JW Dickenson was also the immediate lessor of two properties in Clonallon to Peter Woods. These were more sizeable – houses, offices, flax mill and land totalling 34 acres 3 roods and 10 perches with a combined rateable value of £35 15 shillings – than the property of Thomas English. In addition, Dickenson leased two other small properties – totalling just over 6 acres and with a combined rateable value of £5 – to one Felix Woods.

There is an entry for Peter Woods for Milltown in Clonallon in the tithe applotment book of 1834. Although it is not certain that this is the same person,

---

4   The 1848-1864 Valuation gave a complete list of occupiers of land, tenements and houses. It provided information on: the name of the townland, the name of the householder or leaseholder, the name of the person from whom the property was leased, a description of the property, the property's acreage and the valuation of the land and buildings.

5   There are 4 roods in an acre and 40 perches in a rood.

6   The tithe records are an early 19th Century census of farmers resulting from the 1823 Composition Act, which stipulated that all tithes due to the Established Church (the Church of Ireland) were to be paid in money rather than kind as they previously could have been. This necessitated a complete valuation of all titheable land in Ireland.

7   At www.rootsireland.ie, PRONI and www.ancestryireland.com, respectively.

8   There might also have been other (older) siblings. The Clonallon baptisms given in the UHF database date from 1826.

I suspect that it is. Whilst Woods is a far more common surname than English in Clonallan and the surrounding parishes – the UHF researchers found no fewer than 33 examples in this source – this is the only entry with Peter as the given name in Clonallon itself.

What became of the Woods family is unclear. The UHF database does not include death or burial records for Clonallon – assuming that they survived infancy and adolescence, Catherine's siblings would have been aged between 9 and 20 at the height of the Great Famine in 1847 – and there are no obvious candidates in the subsequent 19th Century Census records of England and Wales.[9] However, it is clear that the English and Woods families were near-neighbours in and around Clonallon in County Down at the time of John and Catherine's marriage in 1861. I return to some possible Woods connections below.

Given that, through Arthur English and his parents, there is a component of the Line of 16 that had its origins in the southern part of County Down, I turned to a description of the locality that was near-contemporaneous with the birth of Catherine Woods in 1841: the *Ordnance Survey Memoirs of Ireland* written by J Hill Williams in 1836.[10]

Hill Williams provided a detailed picture of Warrenpoint: its natural features, topography, industries, religions and social economy. He noted that, in the Census of Ireland taken in 1831, the population was given as 1400 – rather than the 1000 actual residents of the town:

> "... the increased number arising from the census having been taken in the summer when the town is filled with strangers who come there for the bathing season".[11]

---

9   I also tried a long shot by examining the online records provided by the National Archives of Ireland of the applications for the new non-contributory state pension for those aged 70 and over (with incomes below a certain threshold) which was implemented from January 1909. As the civil registration of births, marriages and deaths in Ireland did not commence until 1864, Irish applicants for the pension were obliged to provide proof of their dates of birth by referring back to the Censuses of 1841 and 1851. The vast bulk of these Census records were lost when the Four Courts building in Dublin was destroyed during the Easter Rising of 1916, but the pension applications still exist and transcripts are available on www.censussearchforms.nationalarchives.ie. Had they been alive at the time the pension was introduced, Catherine Woods's siblings would have been aged between 71 and 82. Unfortunately, there are no applications in the database from anyone who had parents called Peter and Mary Woods.

10   The 40-volume *Ordnance Survey Memoirs of Ireland*, edited by Angelique Day and Patrick McWilliams, was published by the Institute of Irish Studies in 2003. The description of Warrenpoint is to be found in *Volume 3, Parishes of County Down (1), 1834-36: South Down*, pp115-124.

11   The point made by Hill Williams had an interesting echo in the 1921 Census of England and Wales. This had originally been scheduled for April of that year but, due to the threat of widespread industrial action, was actually conducted in June. This meant that seaside towns such as Blackpool and Southend recorded larger populations than would otherwise have been the case – and *vice versa* for those localities that had supplied their holiday-making visitors.

Hill Williams's attention to detail extended to the names of the two inns in the dock square: The Crown ("a 2-storey house with billiard room... established about 1795") and The King's Arms ("a 3-storey house with billiard room... established in 1806"). He also noted the numbers, ages and religions of the 294 pupils – 157 males and 137 females – in the three schools. Interestingly, all the schools contained pupils with Protestant, Presbyterian and Roman Catholic backgrounds.

A different source provided information on the Roman Catholic Church in the locality during the 19th Century. *The Diocese of Dromore: Past and Present. Parish of St. Peter's, Clonallon, Warrenpoint* by Fr Andrew McMahon was published by the Dromore Diocesan Historical Society in 2004.[12]

In the 1860s, when John English married Catherine Woods and Arthur English was born, there was a single parish of Clonallon served by three churches: St. Peter's in Warrenpoint (opened in 1841), St Mary's in Burren (1833) and St Patrick's in Mayobridge (1862). I was fairly sure that the first of these was the one of primary interest as "Clonallon (Warrenpoint)" was the label on the front of the *Ireland, Catholic Parish Register, 1655-1915* that I had previously consulted.[13]

Fr McMahon's book provides a detailed history of the Church within the parish and, whilst the focus of the publication is on religious and administrative developments, the underlying politics are inevitably not far from the surface. For example, between 1847 and 1868, the Administrator of Clonallon was Fr John Brennan.

> "Fr Brennan was... associated prominently with the campaign for the 'Repeal of the Union'. He worked hard for the relief of the poor of Warrenpoint during his pastorate and also continued his political affiliations. The leading Young Irelander, William Smith O'Brien, visited Fr Brennan in Warrenpoint on his release from prison in 1854".[14]

Fr McMahon's also reports on collaboration across the religious divide. One such heartwarming episode concerned the dedication and opening of St Peter's in August 1841, which drew a crowd estimated by the *Newry Telegraph* to be in the region of twenty thousand.

---

12 www.lisburn.com/books/dromore-diocese/.

13 The former parish of Clonallon was sub-divided in January 1984 to enable the emergence of independent parishes centred around Burren and Mayobridge as well as St. Peter's.

14 William Smith O'Brien (1803-1864) was an Irish Nationalist MP and leader of the Young Ireland movement. After being convicted of sedition in 1848, his death sentence was commuted to transportation to Van Diemen's Land. He was released in 1854 and pardoned in 1856. A statue of him stands in O'Connell Street in Dublin.

> "Several members of the local Protestant community were present at the ceremony and were thanked for their generous support in the building of the new church. Fr Murphy thanked them with these words: 'May I be permitted in the name of religion to return to you my most grateful thanks, not only for your liberal support and many services on the present occasion, but also for your former assistance and cooperation in the same meritorious object… I hope that you, gentlemen of the Press, will let it go forth to the world that were it not for the support I received from my dissenting brethren this house could not have been built. When I went to solicit their assistance I did not meet a refusal and I thank them from the bottom of my heart for their kindness'".

This is a poignant description, given what we know about much more recent events in County Down, especially in Newry and Warrenpoint. It was also made in the pre-Famine period, of course. Fr McMahon notes that, notwithstanding Warrenpoint's economic development during this period due to its attraction as a seaside resort and its growth as a shipping port:

> "The Warrenpoint docks bade farewell to many emigrants from the Clonallon and wider South Down area who did not share in the rising fortunes enjoyed by some… The years of the Great Famine and its aftermath were particularly harsh in this regard".

Tuberculosis in South Shields

John English and Catherine Woods married in Clonallon in December 1861. The witnesses were Michael McAlinden and Alice Smith and both bride and groom were stated to have been of "full age" i.e. 21 or over. (In fact Catherine had just turned 20). The registration fee was £1.

There is evidence that John and Catherine's family – into which Arthur English was born in 1869 – moved back and forth between Ireland and Tyneside at regular intervals, as shown in Table 5.1. When John and Catherine made their first Census of England and Wales appearance in 1871, Arthur's older siblings (Mary Ann and James) were both reported as having been born in Jarrow. The order of the places of birth of Arthur's younger siblings (Alice, Peter and Septimus John) were Jarrow, Warrenpoint (as noted) and Jarrow again, respectively.

Table 5.1.
The parents and siblings of Arthur English

John English 1836/7-1885 (born in Ireland) (died in Jarrow, County Durham, aged c48)	
married	
Catherine Woods 1842-1911 (born in County Down, Ireland) (daughter of Peter and Mary Woods) (died in Sunderland, County Durham, aged 69)	Mary Ann English 1863-1877 (born in Jarrow) (died in Jarrow aged 14)
	James English 1866-1883 (born in Jarrow) (died in Jarrow aged 16)
	Arthur English 1869-1936 (born in Clonallan, County Down) (died in Whitley Bay, Northumberland, aged 67) *married* **Helen (Ellan/Hellen/Nellie) Kelly 1869-1949** (born in North Shields) (died in Whitley Bay aged 80)
	Alice English 1872-1947 (born in Jarrow) (died in South Shields aged 75) *married* John Curran 1878/9-1919 (born in County Galway, Ireland) (died in Jarrow aged c40)
	Peter English 1874-1890 (born in Warrenpoint, County Down) (died in Jarrow aged 15)
	Joseph English 1876-1877 (born in South Shields) (died in South Shields aged 0)

	Septimus (John) English 1878-1895 (born in Jarrow) (died in Jarrow aged 17)
Catherine Woods 1842-1911 later married Edward Campbell 1841/2-1915 (tbc)	

The information on most of the family of John and Catherine English was provided through a combination of successive Censuses of England and Wales, parish records in County Down and the registers of BMD. However, having examined these sources, I realised that I had been missing someone. The name Septimus John implied (very strongly) that he was their 7th child, not the 6th as I had hitherto estimated. I began to search for the birth and death between Censuses of another member of the family.

Initially, I knew that it would be a difficult task. For the period March 1860 to March 1878, there were no fewer than 67 births with the surname of English in the South Shields district; of these (from March 1866, when the age at death is given) almost exactly half – 33 – died before the age of four. The obvious first choice was Catherine English, who was born in South Shields in August 1865 and died in the same district in the fourth quarter of 1866. However, her birth certificate showed that she was the daughter of Michael English and his wife Ann (née McLaughlan).

As noted in the reporting of other branches in this narrative – for example, those of Runcorn, Niblett, Wilson and Whines – the solution to this difficulty was provided in 2016 when the GRO released an online database of births which included the mothers' maiden names for the whole period back to 1837. This revealed that Joseph English had been born in the Tynemouth district (to a mother with the maiden name of Woods) in the second quarter of 1876. The child died shortly before reaching his first birthday.

Like tens of thousands of his compatriots, John English came to England to better himself and his family, in his case by finding work as a labourer. This was his occupation in Jarrow in both 1871 and 1881 (the latter as "iron labourer") prior to his death in 1885 at his home of 95 Monkton Road, Jarrow, at the age of 48; the occupation given on his death certificate was "engine works labourer". The cause of death was "pulmonary phthisis" i.e. tuberculosis of the lung; Arthur English, then aged 16, was the informant.

It is a sad and rather bizarre fact that, whilst 6 of John and Catherine English's 7 children all survived infancy and childhood to the age of at least 14, only Arthur and his younger sister (Alice English 1872-1947, who married John Curran in 1901) lived beyond the age of 17. I purchased the death certificates for these siblings of Arthur: Mary Ann English died in 1877 aged 14 of "tuberculosis, 3 months"; James English died in 1883 aged 16 of "phthisis pulmonalis, 12 months"; Peter English died in 1890 aged 15 of "apoplexy"; and Septimus John English died in 1895 aged 17 of "tuberculosis". Arthur's father, John English, was the informant for the first two of these deaths, the certificates carrying his mark (rather than a signature). In all 4 cases, the certification of death was provided by MM Bradley MD.

The poignancy of these teenage deaths seems to be emphasised by the single-line entries in the "deaths" column of the *Jarrow Express*:

> At 27 North Street, on the 25th inst, Peter English, 15 years
> (28th February 1890)

> At 27 North Street, 13th, Septimus John English, aged 17 years
> (25th February 1895)

By 1891, Catherine had married again – to Edward Campbell, an Irish-born labourer in an engine works – their joint family (including Alice and Septimus John) continuing to live in Jarrow. As noted, at the time of the deaths of Peter and Septimus John, this was at 27 North Street. As with Catherine's first husband, Edward Campbell could not write his name; he provided a mark as the informant on Peter's death certificate, his status being given as stepfather.

For Catherine English (later Campbell), therefore, there was the despair of losing a husband and four teenage children, mainly to tuberculosis, between the years 1877 and 1895. Arthur English must also have suffered a similar desperate distress; his father and four of his siblings had died whilst he had been aged 8 to 26.[15]

For Arthur English's sister, Alice, these losses occurred between the ages of 5 and 23. However, she did survive into adulthood, her marriage to John Curran producing four children, of whom one died in infancy. Their oldest child was Catherine Curran (1901-1973), who married George Shippen in 1924 and had 8 children in the period to 1940. It is in the household of another daughter

---

15 The first medical officer of health in Newcastle-upon-Tyne (between 1873-1913) was Dr HE Armstrong, who kept detailed records of the incidence of tuberculosis in the city. (The requirement for formal notification of all types of tuberculosis was not introduced until January 1913). His findings have been summarised in "Decline and fall of the tubercle bacillus: the Newcastle story, 1882-1988" by FJW Miller and Mary D Thompson in *Archives of Disease in Childhood*, 1992, Vol. 67, pp 251-255. In 1885 – the year of John English's death – there were 506 deaths from tuberculosis in Newcastle (a death rate of 3.13% of the total population), of which 368 were from pulmonary tuberculosis. In 1895 – the year of Septimus John's death – the respective numbers were 624 (or 3.15%) and 406.

More generally, I noted from an online review of *Spitting Blood: The History of Tuberculosis* by Helen Bynum (Oxford University Press, 2012) that it has been estimated that 4 million people died from tuberculosis in England and Wales between 1851 and 1910.

The tubercle bacillus was identified as the agent that causes tuberculosis by the German physicist, Robert Koch, in 1882. He was awarded the Nobel Prize for Physiology or Medicine in 1905.

– Margaret Stannard (1905-1970) – in Jarrow that the widowed Alice is to be found in the 1939 Register. She died in 1947 at the age of 75.

The great grandchildren of Alice Curran (née English) are the third cousins of my wife, Angela, of course. Their birth records have been found in the 1950s and 1960s in Bedfordshire, Durham and South Australia.

Family networks

The mid 19th Century migration from Ireland to England in search of work was also evident in one of the other entries in the 1871 Census household record of John English and his family, shown above. This was for Felix Woods, a widowed 45 year-old labourer born in Ireland. (I assume that the 13 year-old Mary Woods was his daughter). Initially, I did wonder if Felix and Catherine could have been siblings. However, the 1871 Census record contains the unusual description of Felix Woods as "friend" (to John English), rather than "brother-in-law", in the "relation to head of household" column.

I could not find any record of either Felix or Mary Woods in the Census records for either 1861 or 1881, though a 70 year-old Felix Woods – a widowed general labourer – was recorded in the household of Peter and Maria Woods in Jarrow in 1891 and a 63 year-old with the same name died in South Shields in February 1892 and was buried in Jarrow. The 1871 Census record implies that Felix Woods was born in 1825 or 1826, whilst that for 1891 implies a birth year of 1820 or 1821.[16]

In the usual way for the family historian, this new reference provided another line of enquiry. I was interested in the names Peter and Maria Woods as they were similar to those (Peter and Mary) of Catherine Woods's parents. In the 1891 Census, their respective ages were 33 and 32, so they were at least two generations further on. However, the 1911 Census stated that the place of birth for both was Clonallon, whilst the *Ireland, Catholic Parish Register, 1655-1915* gives an entry for the birth of Peter Woods – with parents Felix Woods and Margaret McGoverah – in that parish in 1856.[17] From the Census information, we can deduce that Peter and Maria had married in 1880 or 1881 and, given the places

---

16 The Irish parish records include at least two baptism entries in County Down in the 1820s under this name: in the Newry, Down and Armagh parish in November 1821 and in Kilbroney in May 1824. In addition, there is a record in *Ireland, Catholic Parish Register, 1655-1915* of a marriage between Felix Woods and Margaret McCavera in Clonallon in January 1853. Whether any or all of these Irish parish records refer to the same Felix Woods who was resident in Jarrow in 1871 and 1891 is not clear, however.

17 The McGoverah surname given here is obviously close to that of McCavera noted in the previous footnote. Both are best estimates of entries in the Register which are difficult to read. A third possibility is the more common McGovern.

of birth of their children, that they had emigrated to England between 1886 and 1891.[18][19]

I think that it is reasonable to assume that Peter Woods was related to Catherine. The former could have been the son of one of her brothers – Patrick (born 1827), Peter (born 1829) or Michael (born 1832). Alternatively, Catherine and Peter could have been first cousins with their respective fathers (Peter and Felix) being brothers.[20]

I was not able to determine the fates of Catherine Woods and her second husband Edward Campbell with absolute certainty. However, there was some evidence to support a rather sad tale. A clue comes in the "Local and District News" section of the *Jarrow Express* of 6th May 1904, in which, under the heading "Poor Law Arrears", it was reported that:

> "At the Police Court yesterday an order was made for £3 16s 6d and costs against Arthur English, at the instance of the poor law authorities, in respect of his mother, who was chargeable to the union".

Seven years later, the 1911 Census of England and Wales included a record for a 69 year-old Catherine Campbell as an inmate in the Sunderland Borough Asylum; her name and age corresponded with what was already known as did her marital status "married" and place of birth "County Down". The only detail that looked (distinctly) odd was her previous occupation: "owner of farm". In the BMD records, the 69 year-old Catherine Campbell died in Sunderland in the third quarter of 1911.

---

18   Peter Woods signed his name as Petter (sic) in the 1911 Census, when he was a 54 year-old labourer in a colliery. Interestingly, the remainder of the household's entry is without any spelling errors. He died in South Shields in 1921 at the age of 64.

19   In 1901, Peter and Maria Woods were resident in the same dwelling in Ferry Street, Jarrow, as the household of a 30 year-old James Magee and his wife, Alice, and their four children. In 1911, Bernard Magee, a 56 year-old labourer, was present as a boarder in the Woods household, also in Jarrow. We have already seen that, in 1871, a 32 year-old Patrick Magee was resident with Felix Woods in the household of John and Catherine English in Jarrow.

The Magee connection can be traced back to Clonallon in County Down. The Griffith's Valuation records of 1864 include references to the prolific JW Dickenson being the immediate lessor of separate small properties to Patrick Magee, Thomas Magee and Bernard Magee. It is reasonable to assume that it is their descendants – one or two generations on – who are the residents of Jarrow from the 1870s onwards.

From this, I am minded to conclude that, in addition to the established English/Woods family connection, there is a formal link to the Magee family. Indeed, I believe that Maria Woods's maiden name was Magee. As noted, the 1911 Census reports that Peter and Maria Woods had been married for 30 years, whilst the UHF's *Irish Marriage Records – Co. Antrim and Co. Down c1660-1930* database records a marriage between Peter Woods and Maria Magee in County Down in 1881.

20   If this is the case – and I realise that it is a big "if" – this would imply that the descendants of Peter and Maria Woods provide a set of distant relatives to successive generations of the English family that now extends down to 5th or 6th cousins.

Supportive evidence that I was on the right track was provided by the same Census's entry for Edward Campbell: a 68 year-old engineering labourer in the shipbuilding industry boarding in the household of James Magee – a 59 year-old bricklayer's labourer – and his family in Hebburn-on-Tyne (which is only a few miles from Jarrow). Edward's status was also given as "married", though there were no other members of his family with him, and his place of birth was "Down, Newry". Although the later age did not match exactly, I think that he died in South Shields in the second quarter of 1915 aged 70.

Not surprisingly, the various places of residence of John and Catherine English and their family in Jarrow have been lost to the passage of time. For example, whilst Walter Street (the family's location in the 1871 Census) and North Street (in which their sons Peter and Septimus John died in the 1890s) still exist, they now comprise neat modern housing, in the former case supplemented by a couple of functional tower blocks. Charles Street (where the deaths of Mary Ann English and James English were recorded) and Monkton Road (the location of the death of the head of the household, John English, in 1885) are no longer to be found on the modern street map, the latter now constituting the unmarked road leading into the carpark of a superstore. (We will return to the ex-Monkton Road later).

However, one building that does remain from the period of John and Catherine English's residence in the area is St Bede's Roman Catholic Church at the bottom of what used to be Monkton Road, the first service in which was held in December 1861. The church was the principal outcome of the "Jarrow Mission" of the Catholic community in South Shields to build a place of worship in their expanding neighbouring town.

Maritime career

The details of Arthur English's maritime career in the Eagle Oil Transport Co Ltd fleet staff were set out in a note that Angela's father – Arthur's grandson, Denis English – passed down to her. This seems to have been a transcript of a written tribute – possibly published in a company magazine – made at the time of his retirement from the company at the age of 60 in 1929.

According to the article, Arthur joined the Eagle fleet in January 1914, when he was already in possession of a 1st Class (Steam) Certificate of Competency, which he had obtained at North Shields in April 1894 (when he would have been aged 26). After being appointed as 2nd Engineer to SS *San Lorenzo* at a rate of pay of £15 per month, he was promoted to Chief Engineer of the same ship in

July 1914 and served until May 1915.[21] As with the other vessels listed in the note of Arthur's career, there is a full description, which does suggest that the original document was aimed at a readership with some technical expertise.

> "SS *San Lorenzo* was a new ship built by Wallsend Slipway and Engineering Co Ltd of 12097 gross, 9003 nett register tonnage. Machinery – quadruple expansion, direct acting, vertical cylinder – boilers 4. Cylindrical multi-tubular steel 220 lbs to sq. inch. Designed speed 11 ¼ knots. Ship 527' 4" overall, breadth 66' 6"".

There are three particular features of Arthur English's career report that stand out. The first is the short-term nature of the postings: Arthur was the Chief Engineer on 11 different ships between July 1914 and February 1929. Whilst he had the benefit of the continuity of employment with the Eagle Oil Transport Co., he also had to deal with the usual issue facing the merchant seaman of having regularly to adjust to a new working environment and a different set of circumstances. Second, the report does not hold back from listing Arthur's periods of sickness, either ashore (August to October 1918) or "abroad" (October to December 1926).

However, the most noticeable characteristic of the report is its utterly dispassionate nature. Only the last sentence gives a clue as to anything about Arthur's individual personality traits: "He is remembered by a number of the older members of the Eagle shore staff, and his almost copper-plate handwriting is vividly recalled". It is for the reader to draw his or her conclusions about some of the desperate circumstances that Arthur faced during this period of his maritime career: "Whilst serving in this ship as Chief Engineer, he was torpedoed on the 26th September 1917 off the south coast of Ireland. SS *San Zeferino* was eventually brought into port and repaired. Mr English was awarded half a month's pay in consideration of salvage services". Likewise: "Left *San Gerardo* 5th April 1922, after an accident which partially disabled him".

For further information on the latter incident, I consulted the *Shields Daily News* of 6th April 1922:

> FELL DOWN HOLD
> ENGINEER LANDED AND TAKEN TO TYNEMOUTH INFIRMARY
> The chief engineer of the oil-tanker steamer *San Gerardo,* Arthur English, 53, was admitted to the Tynemouth Infirmary yesterday suffering from a fractured pelvis. The injured man accidentally fell down a hold in the

---

21 In fact, the chronology of Arthur English's promotion was slightly different. *The Crew Lists of the British Merchant Navy – 1915 –* available online from the National Maritime Museum at www.1915crewlists.rmg.co.uk – record that he was the 1st Engineer on the *SS San Lorenzo* from November 1914 to February 1915 and then the Chief Engineer until May 1915.

steamer, while the vehicle was proceeding to sea. The man was landed on to the New Quay and conveyed by the police ambulance to the infirmary.

THE LINE OF 16: 10. HELEN KELLY (1869-1949)

"The Kelly Centenary"

Arthur English married **HELEN KELLY** (1869-1949) in North Shields in 1888 and she becomes the next in the Line of 16.

It is here that I benefit from one of those fortuitous set of circumstances that sometimes befalls a family history researcher as, through one of her aunts, my wife had passed down to her a valuable portfolio of written documentation on this particular branch of the family. This included a set of detailed family trees showing the descendants of Helen Kelly and her many siblings (though without any dates of death), as compiled by Adrian McMullen, Joseph Scarr and Kathleen Johnson in the early 1980s. In addition, there was a separate note headed "The Kelly Centenary" written by one of Helen's brothers – Henry Joseph Kelly (1867-1948) – to commemorate the hundred years of the family being resident in North Shields, the anniversary also being celebrated at an event held on 29 August 1947 in the Roslyn Hall, North Shields.[22][23]

I should note that Helen Kelly shares a characteristic with several members of the family tree on my wife's side that is not particularly helpful to the family researcher. Her given name changes over time, in this case being variously Ellan, Hellen and Nellie – as well as Helen – even in official documentation. It is known, however, that she was the 11th of the 14 children of Patrick Kelly (1830-1893) and Frances (or Fanny) Kelly (née Davis, 1831-1902), as shown in Table 5.2.

Table 5.2. The parents and siblings of Helen Kelly		
Patrick Kelly 1830-1893 (born in Strokeston, Roscommon, Ireland) (son of James and Jane Kelly) (died in Tynemouth, Northumberland, aged 63)		
married		

---

22 The Roslyn Hall remained standing in 2023, a derelict building at 114 Stephenson Street.

23 One of the notes in the Kelly family documentation refers to another "gathering of the clan" in August 1972 to mark the 125th anniversary of Patrick Kelly's arrival in England.

Frances (Fanny) Davis 1831-1902 (born in North Shields) (daughter of John Davis ?-1845 and Lucy Purvis c1806-1882) (died in North Shields, Northumberland, aged 71)	James Kelly 1851-after 1920 (born in North Shields) (1921: aged 70 in Lemington, Newcastle) *married* Ellen Thompson Esdale 1852-1925 (born in North Shields) (died in South Shields, Durham, aged 73)
	Lucy Kelly 1853-1931 (born in New York, USA) (died in South Shields aged 78) *married* James Short 1852/3-1915 (born in Paisley, Scotland) (died in Jarrow aged c63)
	Thomas Kelly 1854-1891 (born in New York) (died in Tynemouth aged 37)
	Mary Jane Kelly 1956-1937 (born in North Shields) (died in Sunderland aged 81) *married* William Cunningham 1854-1921 (born in Newcastle-upon-Tyne) (died in Sunderland aged 66)
	Frances Anne Kelly 1858-1936 (Sister M Catherine) (born in North Shields) (died in Sheffield, Yorkshire, aged 78)
	John Michael (Jack) Kelly 1859-1935 (born in North Shields) (died in Tynemouth aged 75)
	Margaret (Maggie) Kelly 1861-1927 (born in North Shields) (died in Newcastle-upon-Tyne aged 66) *married* John Scarr 1855-1910 (born in Felling, County Durham) (died in Newcastle-upon-Tyne aged 55)

	Sarah Agnes (Sally) Kelly 1863-1939 (born in North Shields) (died in Durham district aged 75) *married* Michael Brennan 1860-1938 (born in Tiernakill, Galway, Ireland) (died in Jarrow aged 78)
	Alice Kelly 1865-1919 (born in North Shields) (died in Newcastle-upon-Tyne aged 54) *married* James Daley 1863-1927 (tbc) (born in Newcastle-upon-Tyne) (died in South Shields aged 63)
	Henry Joseph (Harry) Kelly 1867-1948 (born in North Shields) (died in North Shields aged 80) *married* Helen Gilmore 1864-1941 (born in Glasgow) (died in North Shields aged 77)
	Helen (Ellan/Hellen/Nellie) Kelly 1869-1949 **(born in North Shields)** **(died in Whitley Bay, Northumberland, aged 80)** *married* **Arthur English 1869-1936** **(born in Clonallan, County Down)** **(died in Whitley Bay aged 67)**
	Elizabeth Teresa Kelly 1872-1951 (born in South Shields) (died in Birkenhead, Cheshire, aged 79) *married* Daniel Finch Tuohey 1873-1933 (born in Tynemouth) (died in Birkenhead aged 60)

	Paul Vincent Kelly 1875-1943
	(born in North Shields)
	(died in Barrow-in-Furness, Lancashire, aged 68)
	married
	Elizabeth Inglis Johnstone 1882-1967
	(born in Annan, Dumfries, Scotland)
	(died in Barrow in Furness aged 85)
	Winifred Kelly 1876-1963
	(born in North Shields)
	(died in Whitley Bay aged 87)
	married
	James Thomas McMullen 1872-1914
	(born in Jarrow)
	(died in South Shields aged 42)

According to Henry Kelly, his father Patrick was born in Stokeston (actually Strokeston), Roscommon, Ireland, the eldest of 5 children. As a youth, he lived in the presbytery, where he received his education and assisted the parish priest when he visited parishioners in the outlying districts. His responsibilities included serving Mass at the homes of the parishioners and attending to household duties at the priest's house.[24]

Henry Kelly reported that, at the height of the Great Famine in 1847, Patrick Kelly "tramped" with his father, James, to Belfast, where they got a passage on a "hooker" or small sailing vessel which took three days to reach Glasgow. (He would then have been about 17 years old). From there, they walked to North Shields – via Preston! – where they stayed for a while with James's brother.[25] James's wife (Jane) and 4 other family members arrived soon afterwards.

---

24 The UHF researchers reported that, according to the Valuation Office Books of 1824-54, the Rev. Michael Kelly was resident at 10 Bawn Street, Strokeston, in April 1840. There are 3 other Kelly references in this source, including Bernard Kelly, a surgeon living at 9 Bawn Street. It is possible that either or both were paternal uncles (or other relations) of Patrick Kelly.

25 It is almost certain that the brother was Lachlan Kelly, though this given name was spelled as Laachlan in the 1851 Census of England and Wales, when he was aged 50, Lockland in 1861 (aged 67) and Lackland in 1871, when his age was given 78. Not only was Lachlan also born in Roscommon but, throughout this period, he was a lodging house keeper in North Shields, so he obviously would have had access to the provision of accommodation for James and Patrick Kelly on their arrival from Ireland. In 1851, his household also comprised his wife, Catherine (aged 48 born in Cork, Ireland) and 6 children, the four youngest of whom had been born in Tynemouth. There were 18 lodgers, all of whom were single men occupied as bricklayer's labourers (which was also the occupation of James Kelly in 1851).

In the 1861 and 1871 Censuses, Lachlan's wife was successively named as Jane (aged 56) and Isabella (aged 35), both born in Scotland. I have been unsuccessful in finding either the death records for Catherine Kelly or Jane Kelly or the marriage records for Lachlan Kelly to Jane or Isabella.

Henry Kelly covered the journey of James and Patrick Kelly to England in only a few lines of "The Kelly Centenary". However, it cannot be overstated how traumatic the background circumstances to this migration must have been. To get something of a sense for this, I drew on the passionate *The Leaving of Loughrea* (2013) by Stephen Lally, which describes the effects of the Famine on the Lally family of County Galway. From the beginning of 1847:

> "Previous fears of the unknown abroad were cast aside because nothing could be worse than staying in the face of certain death. There began a great mobilisation of stick men, women and children. From the west of Galway, there was a stampede to the east… with the intention to get out across the Irish Sea to England or, better still, to America via Liverpool or Cork… The canal boats were full, but most travellers could not have afforded them at any price so most looked forward to a journey of at least a week on foot.
>
> The Irish poor set sail for every port, small and large, in England, Scotland, Wales… How did they afford the fare? Many pawned everything they owned. [However], the most common means of acquiring the fare was for a pauper family to be given it by their Poor Law Union. To get rid of a poor family for ten shillings was better than looking after them for five shillings a week".[26]

For James and Patrick Kelly, the destination of Glasgow might have been fortuitous, given the main alternative used in the migration.

> "Liverpool… was by far the greatest recipient of this human cargo… In the five months between January and May 1847, 300,000 Irish landed in the port… [The city] which had proudly been at the forefront of building and sanitary improvements, was facing ruin beneath a tidal wave of destitute Irish living packed together in cellars, attics, sheds and underbridges without any belongings or sanitation".

Notwithstanding these variations, there is little doubt that I have identified the same person throughout as James Kelly's brother. The consistency in the names and ages of Lachlan Kelly's children in the 1851 and 1861 Censuses provides evidence for this, as does the same address being given for his lodging house in these two records.

There is no obvious entry in the death register for Lachlan Kelly, though that of a 68 year-old Lochran Kelly was reported in Tynemouth in the fourth quarter of 1874 (when, to be consistent with the previous Census, his actual age would have been 81).

26 Chapter 11 below includes a discussion of the patterns in the secondary migration (i.e. within Britain) of the Irish during the second half of the 19th Century. It is seen that significant proportions of the first and second generation migrants in Newcastle and elsewhere in Northumberland were from Ulster and Connacht. It is clear, therefore, that the migrants within both the English and Kelly branches of the family tree took advantage of established local connections when determining the places in which to settle.

By the time of the 1851 Census, James Kelly was a 48 year-old bricklayer's labourer in North Shields. As Henry Kelly reported, the rest of his family arrived from Ireland soon after he had settled in the town, as also in the household at this date were his 45 year-old wife, Jane, and their children Margaret Garvey (aged 23 with her 7-month old daughter Mary), Mary Kelly aged 13 and Bridget Kelly aged 11. Ten years later, James Kelly was a 57 year-old "scavenger"[27] in North Shields with Jane (who, at 53, had lost two years in age over the course of the decade) and their daughter Mary (aged 23) and granddaughter Mary Garvey (aged 10) still in the household. He died in the Tynemouth district in 1865.[28]

I am not exactly certain about the fate of Jane Kelly. The most likely outcome is that she also died in the Tynemouth district (in December 1861) – and this is the one that has been posted by several contributors to the public pages of Ancestry. However, for some time, I did wonder if she had been the 60 year-old widowed washerwoman in North Shields in the 1871 Census (having thus managed to lose another three years in age) and/or the 69 year-old charwoman who was an inmate of the Tynemouth Union Workhouse in 1881 and who died in the Tynemouth district in 1882. The washerwoman of 1871 lived in Causeway Bank, which was the next street to both the 42 year-old Margaret O'Neil (Margaret Garvey having married Lawrence O'Neal/O'Neil in 1861) and the 33 year-old Mary Johnson (Mary Kelly having married Charles Johnson, a mariner born in Norway, also in 1861), who were resident in the same house at 6 Church Stairs.

In turn, this led me to speculate on whether Jane Kelly's children would have been content with their mother being placed in a workhouse, if this is what actually happened. Of course, the family circumstances might have meant there had not been much choice. In 1881, Patrick Kelly and his wife Frances were living with 9 children in North Shields and, by that time, Mary Johnson had died (aged 40 in Tyneside in 1878), leaving her son, Charles, as a 12 year-old in the Certified Poor Law School in Tudhoe, Durham. (Charles and Mary Johnson's other son – Thomas – had died as a 7 year-old in Tyneside in 1872). I also think that James and Jane Kelly's first grandchild – the 7 month-old Mary Kelly of 1851 – died at the age of 19 in Newcastle in 1870.

The family historian's researches are never complete and, for the present, I am content to leave these questions about Jane Kelly for resolution at a later date. For my purposes, the more important issue concerns the migration of the Kelly family from Roscommon to Tyneside – initially by James and Patrick and later

---

27 In their *Dictionary of Old Occupations*, Jane Hewitt and Paul Jack Hewitt state "sometimes called a scaffie, a scavenger was a dustman or street cleaner". The term was also used in the textile industry for a child employed in the highly dangerous job of darting under moving industrial machinery to snatch up waste material.

28 The information in the 1851 and 1861 Censuses implies that James Kelly was born in about 1803 and his wife Jane in about 1805/08. Unfortunately, the Catholic Church records for Strokeston only survive from 1830 and therefore do not shed light on the earlier generations of the Kelly family.

supported by Jane and the rest of the family. James was an unskilled worker, who took on the most menial of jobs, and he and Jane raised their four children in what were clearly impoverished circumstances, in which the family dwellings were cramped and overcrowded. But – notwithstanding these difficulties – James and Jane Kelly established a foothold for their branch of the family in the midst of the sizeable Irish community of the north-east of England.

To New York – and back

According to "The Kelly Centenary", Patrick Kelly's first job in England was on a collier brig, which took six weeks on the return journey to London, and for which he received no pay, as he refused to re-join the ship. This persuaded Patrick that he did not have a future as a seaman – "He had had sufficient of the sea" – though it transpired that he was still to make some long sea voyages. Patrick married Frances Davis in the Catholic Chapel, North Shields, in August 1850.

Shortly after the birth of his and Frances's first son (James) in 1851, Patrick went to New York to see if it was worthwhile settling there. He subsequently returned to the USA with his wife and child and the family lived in New York between 1852 and 1855. Two of their children (Lucy and Frances) were born in the city and baptised in St Patrick's Cathedral. The *1855 New York State Census* records that the family was resident in the 8th District of the 11th Ward of New York City and that Patrick was a 25 year-old shoemaker; Patrick and Frances had been resident for three years. However, Henry stated that "the climatic conditions were more than mother could endure" and so the family returned to Tyneside, where Patrick and Frances remained for the rest of their lives.[29]

Following his return from the USA, Patrick Kelly's occupation, as given in successive Censuses, was shoemaker/boot manufacturer/boot maker until his

---

29 As an aside, it is instructive to note that the Kelly family documentation provides another nice illustration of how a family story or myth often hides the actual truth, even though the initial examination of it suggests falsehood. (We came across a similar example – the Boynton claim to Burrell's Farm in North Yorkshire – in Chapter 1).

The Kelly family documentation includes a reference to Patrick and Frances's eldest son James (Jim) later settling in the USA. As he was also the father of 14 children, "there is supposed to be a strong contingent of Kellys there". For a while, this presented something of a mystery. James Kelly and his wife Ellen Thompson Eskdale certainly had a large family. But, of the 11 children I traced, four were born in North Shields between 1874 and 1879 and seven in Consett, Durham, between 1881 and 1892 (when James would have been 52).

James is recorded in each Census of England and Wales between 1871 (as a 19 year-old draper's assistant) and 1921 (as a 70 year-old "billiard marker" in the local social club in Lemington, Newcastle). It is instructive – if also somewhat disconcerting – that, of the 86 references to him in the public pages of Ancestry, no fewer than 44 record his death in 1918 and another 3 in 1906.

It was later that I discovered that it was one of Patrick and Frances's grandsons – James C Kelly (1873-1953) – who had lived in America. He migrated at the age of 52 in 1925 with his wife Mary (née Tansey) following with four of their children in 1926. In 1930, James and his family were living in Philadelphia, where he was a stationary engineer in a cold storage depot. In the next US Census, in 1940, he was a clerk in a business office in Washington DC. James had returned to the UK by the time of his death in Newcastle-upon-Tyne in 1953 at the age of 80.

death in 1893 at the age of 63. According to Henry Kelly, Patrick opened a boot and shoe shop in Bell Street, North Shields, making, repairing and "translating" boots and shoes. (Translating was the fixing of new soles and heels on to the uppers which, being hand-made, lasted for a long time). Henry reported that his father also specialised in the making of sea boots and deck boots and had such a demand for these that he employed 10 men. Patrick opened other premises, including one in Whitley Bay which, Henry reports, didn't last long "for want of efficient management". (Henry's brother, Tom, was in charge). However, Patrick gave up his businesses in 1881 "as a consequence of the coal trade's bad state" and, although he made another fairly successful attempt with a business in Clive Street a little later, he retired in 1887, doing a few repairs for his old customers until his death six years later.[30]

Patrick Kelly is listed as a shoemaker – resident at 40 Nelson Street, North Shields – in both *Kelly's Directory of Newcastle and Suburbs, 2nd edition, 1887* and *Kelly's Directory of Durham and Northumberland, 1890*. As this had been his address – with his wife Frances and their 9 children – in both the 1871 and 1881 Censuses, it is clear that Patrick maintained separate domestic and business dwellings and chose not to live "above the shop". (40 Nelson Street remained the address of the widowed Frances Kelly until her death in January 1902).

Nelson Street – which is now an unmarked private road leading to a small trading estate – was a short road in the centre of the town. By contrast, Bell Street and Clive Street were prime sites for shops specialising in sea boots and deck boots. Bell Street ran behind the Western Quay on the north bank of the Tyne; its continuation ran through Liddell Street into Clive Street and the floating landing stage at New Quay.

Henry Kelly acknowledged his mother's central roles in both the business and the family. She "used to assist in the shop at certain times and even attended to a stall in South Shields market, where she sold some of the translated boots and shoes". Poignantly, Henry added: "She also had to share in the business worries and bring up a large family. They were, indeed, exemplary parents". In an interesting detail in his note, Henry stated that "I have heard Mother speak about going to Newcastle to see her [his great grandmother, Frances Howe, see below] and Aunt Ann. It took almost a whole day to make the passage up the river in the steam boat which sometimes ran on to the sandbanks".

---

30 A plaque on the excellent North Shields Heritage Trail records that Clive Street constituted part of the warren of streets and alleyways in the "Low Town" about which the *Shields Daily News* enquired in 1855: "Who can estimate the amount of immoral conversation that passes, the unlawful schemes plotted, or the low, filthy literature read in common lodging houses and the intemperance that prevails in this nest of vice?"

Deaths at sea

Frances Kelly's maiden name was Davis and she was born in North Shields in 1831, the eldest of the 6 children of her mother, Lucy Davis. It is her family that provides the earliest evidence of the maritime connection that, as we have seen, distinguishes the English (surname) branch of the family tree. According to Henry Kelly, Frances's father – John Davis – was a mariner employed chiefly on the colliers plying a trade between the Tyne and the Thames, although he also fished for herring off the coast of Eyemouth, went whaling in the Davis Straits (between Canada and Greenland) and spent a winter in the Arctic.

According to Henry:

> "John Davis made his last voyage in a Shields brig from Liverpool to the Tyne. The ship foundered in the Moray Firth and all on board were drowned. Their bodies were washed ashore and buried in Rosehearty Churchyard, where the local inhabitants erected a memorial".

Henry did not give a date for John Davis's death; for this, I drew initially on an annotation to the extensive set of Kelly family trees compiled by Adrian McMullen and others: "drowned Moray Firth 1836". In any event, this was a sad case of family history repeating itself as, again according to Henry, John Davis's father (and Frances Davis's grandfather) – also John Davis, a lieutenant in the Royal Navy – had met his death by drowning in Cork harbour.

Lucy Davis appeared as a widow in the Censuses from 1851 through to 1881, her occupation changing over time – logically enough – from "washerwoman" to "formerly washerwoman". She mainly remained in North Shields, being resident in Bell Street in 1841 and then at various addresses in Church Road and Churchway. The details of her place of birth did change – Brighton, Lewes and Ringmer in successive censuses – though the Sussex background was consistent (notwithstanding the 1861 Census enumerator placing Brighton in Gloucestershire). Lucy died in the Tynemouth district in 1882.

I wondered about how to check the details of the death of John Davis in 1836, as this not did appear to have affected the growth of Lucy's family. Three of her children were born between 1840 and 1845 and, as neither Lucy's surname nor her marital status changed in the subsequent censuses, this would imply that these births were illegitimate. (As noted, Frances Davis had been born during her father's lifetime).

Rosehearty is a settlement on the north coast of Aberdeenshire, about four miles to the west of Fraserburgh, with a population of about 1250. It is one of the oldest seaports in Scotland, at one time having had a fishing fleet supporting over 600 people, but is now a quiet place with about 20 boats regularly using the harbour for recreation and part-time fishing. The old cemetery is in Peathill, which is about ¾ mile up Castle Street past the ruins of Pitsligo Castle. The original Pitsligo Parish Kirk dates from 1634 and its replacement, the New Parish Kirk, from 1890; the latter was closed for worship in 1977.

I walked around the cemetery for a couple of hours on a bright afternoon in September 2016. The new part was still in use, as revealed by a couple of other visitors and the work being done at one spot by a monumental mason, who told me he was based in Aberdeen. The whole cemetery was well maintained, including the older part, although many of the inscriptions in the latter had been worn away by time. There were also several vacant spaces from which, I supposed, the worn or broken memorials might have been removed.

In the older part of the cemetery I did come across some headstones with venerable dates – 1668, 1678, 1723, 1755 – but apparently none to mark the loss of John Davis and his fellow seamen in 1836. The nearest equivalent was a worn headstone, only some of the inscription on which I could just make out: "Alexander Howe… Shipowner and… on the 20th October 1845… and perished… all of whom lie here". At this point, I suspected that the people of 19th Century Rosehearty might not have been strangers to the bodies of drowned sailors washing up on their shore and, even though this particular monument did not appear to have been the one that I had been seeking, I could fully believe that John Davis and the other members of his crew had been buried in this cemetery and that a similar memorial had been placed for them.

The following morning, I took a short walk along those parts of the harbour walls that had not been closed off to the casual pedestrian. I had wondered if there might have been any plaques or other memorials placed there, but there were none; the walls are for functionality rather than memorial. The wind freshened off the Moray Firth and a combination of spray and drizzle filled the air along with the pervasive smells of fish and salt. I looked out on to the grey waters stretching into the far distance and made a mental note of where John Davis had perished.

On returning home, I searched for online references to "Alexander Howe 1845". I came across a reference to *Peathill: The Auld Kirk and Kirkyard* by Janet McLeman, published in 2012, which included the following extract.

> "The grave of Alexander Howe has apparently empty space around it. The gravestone reads: 'Alexander Howe, shipowner and captain from North Shields, shipwrecked on this coast 20 October 1845 and perished with his whole crew, all of whom lie interred around him'. Howe's ship was almost certainly the vessel mentioned in the following Lloyd's Shipping List entry: 'Fraserburgh October 21st. The *John Williams*, Howe, from Liverpool to Berwick, was totally wrecked on the coast yesterday during a tremendous gale from the North West. Crew drowned'".

Not for the first time in this family narrative, the penny dropped. John Davis was a member of Alexander Howe's crew on the ill-fated *John Williams*. The year of his drowning was 1845, not 1836. This was consistent with the presence of the Howe monument in the Peathill cemetery, the contents of the inscription on the headstone – that the ship had been based in North Shields and travelling between Liverpool and the Tyne/Berwick (as reported by Henry Kelly) – and, crucially, the birth of the three children to John and Lucy Davis between 1840 and 1845.[31]

A second (slighter) puzzle was posed in the 1851 Census. Lucy Davis and her four children were living in North Shields and the place of birth of the youngest (the 6 year-old Sarah) was given as Scotland. I wondered how this could have been, given Lucy's apparently firm commitment to the town. The answer was provided in the next Census (1861), when the place of birth of the now 16 year-old Sarah was given as Eyemouth, Berwickshire.

Eyemouth is a few miles on the Scottish side of the border just to the north of Berwick-on-Tweed. I recalled that not only had Henry Kelly reported that his grandfather (John Davis) regularly fished for herring off the Eyemouth coast, but that his mother (Frances Kelly, née Davis) "had had relatives there". Later consultation on Ancestry of *Scotland, Select Marriages, 1561-1910* revealed that John Davis and Lucy Purvis had married in Eyemouth in 1830.

It is noticeable that John Davis's fate did not appear to have affected the choice – or, perhaps, the availability – of occupation of at least one of his sons: Thomas Davis was a 21 year-old "boatman" in 1861 and remained in this occupation ten years later.

I also followed up Henry Kelly's reference to the drowning of the elder John Davis in Cork harbour. I did not have a date for this; some time at the beginning of the 19th Century was the best guess. A promising lead was the online *Royal Navy Officers Service Records 1756-1931*, which is available from The National Archives. However, although this included servicemen with the rank of lieutenant, it did not have a John Davis listed from the relevant period. Nonetheless, a note on the website suggested that this was not necessarily the last word.

> "Service records were not kept for all officers. It was only from the 1840s that service records of Royal Navy officers began to be systematically kept. Before

---

31 The details given of the lost vessel and its master were similar, though slightly different, in the paragraph headed "Shipwreck and Loss of Life" in the "Shipping Intelligence" section of the *Aberdeen Press and Journal* of 29th October 1845.
"Fraserburgh, October 22. On Monday [20th October], we were visited by a terrific storm, which continued its ravages on sea and land until next morning... Sad to state, a schooner, *John and William* of Newcastle, about half-past nine pm, was totally wrecked near Rosehearty and the whole crew perished. From the ship's papers, which have come ashore, we learn that the crew consisted of four (James Hewitt, master and owner inclusive) and that the vessel had sailed from Liverpool on the 7th for Berwick, guano laden. Several articles have been picked up, but none of the bodies".

this, there were records only of officers still alive at this time, and a small number of records created for specific purposes".

Some general trawling on Google yielded some conflicting results. I came across an online copy of something called – to give it its full title – *The Gentleman's Magazine and Historical Magazine for the Year MDCCCIII, Volume LXXIII, Part the Second* by Sylvanus Urban, Gent. The wonders of the internet.[32] This was a detailed chronicle of the year 1803, which – under "Country News" – included the following in the entry for 25 December:

> "His Majesty's sloop of war *La Suffisante*, of 16 guns, Capt Heathcote, was lost in the entrance of Cork harbour. Seven of the crew were unfortunately drowned and 3 killed by the fall of a mast. *La Suffisante* sailed from Cove on the preceding day, with a number of volunteer seaman and soldiers on board for England; and, in attempting to return for shelter, she struck upon Spike Island and, in a very short time, went to pieces. No other material accident happened in that direction during the late tremendous gale, though the harbour of Cork was crowded with West Indiamen waiting for convoy".

Another online record was from *The naval gazetteer, biographer and chronologist*, which was "compiled and arranged" by JW Norie in 1827 and contained "a history of the latest wars from their commencement in 1793 to their final conclusion in 1815; and continued, as to the biographical part, to the present time". This stated that *La Suffisante* was lost on 15 December 1803 and that the crew was saved.

It is known that *La Suffisante* was originally a French corvette, launched in 1793, which was captured by the Royal Navy in 1795 and used by the British thereafter. Capt Heathcote was court-martialled and blamed for its loss, though he was not punished. I cannot confirm that the incident reported in Cork harbour was the one in which John Davis was drowned. It is a strong possibility, however, and I am content with that.

Religious and political convictions

One theme that comes across very powerfully in the Kelly (and Davis) family documentation is the strong influence of the Roman Catholic Church. Patrick Kelly's role as a "priest's boy" has already been noted. Henry Kelly reported that

---

[32] In *Enlightenment: Britain and the Creation of the Modern World* (2001), Roy Porter includes a fascinating discussion of the development of the print media in the 18th Century. He reports that the *Gentleman's Magazine* was founded in 1731 by a Midlander, Edward Cave, who passed himself off as "Sylvanus Urban, Gent". The magazine boasted that it contained "more in Quantity, and greater Variety, than any Book of the Kind and Price" (which was sixpence).

when his great grandmother – Frances McGuire, the widow of Lt John Davis RN and by then married to Walter Howe – arrived in North Shields, "she attended Fr Worswick when he came to say Sunday Mass before St Cuthbert's was built" and that she "acted as Sacristan and looked after the little room at the corner of West Percy Street and Bedford Street where Mass was said". The extensive family trees prepared by Adrian McMullen and others show several members who became ordained priests or nuns. Amongst the latter were a sister of Helen and Henry Kelly – Frances Anne, who became Sister Catherine – and all four daughters of another of their sisters, Alice. In his "The Kelly Centenary", Henry stated that "my earliest recollection of them [his parents] was their daily attendance at Mass".

The family's commitment to Roman Catholicism is also evident from local newspaper reports. For example, Henry and Helen Kelly's oldest brother – James – was one of the founders of the Catholic Benefit Society in North Shields in 1873 which, according to the *Shields Daily News* of 20th February 1923, was "still in a flourishing condition" fifty years later. However, the key figure was James Short (1852/3-1915), the husband of Lucy Kelly (Helen's sister), as illustrated in a sample of reports from the *Jarrow Express*:

11th **March 1881**
ST BEDE'S CATHOLIC MUTUAL IMPROVEMENT SOCIETY
On Friday evening the weekly meeting of the above society was held in the school room Chapel Road. There was a good attendance of members present. Mr James Short presided. The principal business of the event was an essay on William Pitt...

2nd **October 1885**
THE REV FATHER KIPPERSCLUIS
The residence of this Catholic priest in this town terminated a few days since, when he moved to Bishop Auckland... A meeting was held on Sunday morning to take into consideration the question of raising a suitable testimonial for presentation to him... It was decided to elect Mr James Short chairman of the presentation committee...

3rd **September 1909**
SECULAR EDUCATION: CATHOLIC TRADE UNIONIST PROTEST
A meeting of Catholic trade unionists was held in Jarrow on Tuesday night... On a motion of Councillor A Callighan, seconded by Mr James Short, a resolution was unanimously agreed to protesting against a resolution in favour of secular education being included in the programme of the Labour Party...

For James Short, the strength of his religious commitment clearly overlapped with his social and political convictions. His perspective would no doubt have been affected by the death of his father – also James Short – shortly before Christmas 1884:

> 24th December 1884
> FATAL ACCIDENT AT PALMER'S YARD
> On Monday night, a terrible accident, which resulted in death shortly afterwards, befell a labourer named James Short aged 58 years, employed at Palmer's Yard. The deceased was carrying some wood up a gangway into a vessel lying in the quay, when he fell between the quay and the ship. His head and face were shockingly cut and bruised. He was at once carried to the Memorial Hospital, but died shortly after his admittance. Mr Coroner Graham held an inquest over the remains at the Station Hotel this afternoon. The inquiry was proceeding at the time we went to press.

> 2nd January 1885
> INQUEST
> The Jury, at the inquiry held before Mr Coroner Graham on Wednesday afternoon, touching the death of James Short (58), who fell from a gangway in Palmer's Yard and was killed, returned a verdict of "accidental death".

It is also evident that, within the clusters of migrants in the North East of England, the very strong sense of Irishness prevailed. James Short (the younger) was also active in this respect, as well as in his trade union capacity as a stoker in the gasworks:

> 19th May 1882
> The first meeting of the Irish Literary Institute was held in the institute, Monkton Road, on Sunday evening. Mr James Short, vice-president, was in the chair…[33]

> 3rd December 1886
> THE NATIONAL LEAGUE
> There still exists a Jarrow branch of the Irish National League and what's more the members have commenced the winter series of lectures etc… Amongst those who will either lecture or give papers are Mr James Short and Mr Gourley. Both these members will be well worth hearing. Mr Short is well-known…

---

33 The clustering of the families of the Irish migrants – and the locations of their social activities – in Jarrow in the last quarter of the 19th Century is evident. We noted earlier that John English – the father-in-law of James Short – died at his home of 95 Monkton Road in 1895.

12th September 1890
 THREATENED LABOURERS' STRIKE AT PALMER'S YARD
 On Sunday last, a mass meeting of labourers was held in the circus, the Pit Heap, Jarrow, under the auspices of the National Labour Union. The chair was occupied by Mr James Short...

In the years before the First World War, Home Rule for Ireland was one of the central issues in British politics. In the North East, James Short was at the centre of events, as shown by his unequivocal contribution at a meeting to hear a speech by Mr W Redmond MP (the brother of the Irish Parliamentary leader, John E Redmond):

3rd May 1901
 DEMONSTRATION OF IRISHMEN AT JARROW
 A great demonstration of Irishmen took place in the Mechanics Institute on Monday evening, when the hall was crowded in every part... Mr James Short said the Irishmen of Jarrow would support the United Irish Party, both financially and morally. Some people could not understand why the Irish people stuck so tenuously to things; it was because of the moral purity of the Irish and they stuck to the Irish Parliamentary Party because of the moral purity of Irish politics. That was going to be England's downfall – that she had only one object and that was to get wealth at any cost.

I am fairly confident that there was one other member of the Kelly family who took a keen interest in Irish affairs – Henry Kelly himself.

In an article entitled "United Irish League in Great Britain", the *Shields Daily News* of 30th November 1909 reported a "largely attended" political meeting of the John Mandeville Branch in Coach Lane, North Shields. The main address by a Councillor from Gateshead, Patrick Bennett, emphasised that "the principal question for Irishmen to keep before them in the approaching contest [i.e. next UK General Election, which was held in January 1910] was Home Rule". This was followed by a vote of confidence: "That we, the Irishmen of North Shields and districts, wish to express our unabated confidence in the Irish Party so ably led by John E Redmond, also to thank them for the splendid work achieved in the House of Commons on Ireland's behalf, as to assure them of our continued support in the future".

It was also reported that "Mr Henry Kelly seconded the vote, which was carried unanimously". In addition, Henry Kelly was elected vice-president for the ensuing year.

I have not definitively confirmed whether this Henry Kelly is the same man who was to write "The Kelly Centenary" in 1947 – i.e. the son of James Kelly, brother of Helen and Lucy Kelly and brother-in-law of James Short (and Arthur English). However, in 1909, he would have been aged 42 and, in 1911, he was the only person of that name aged between 30-80 resident in North Shields (although there were three others elsewhere in Northumberland, including Tyneside).

A family photograph

One of the items in the Kelly family documentation passed down to my wife was a description – effectively a seating plan – of a photograph of Patrick and Frances Kelly with most of their children and their spouses. At first, this was something of a frustration as there was no actual photograph to accompany it. However, it turned out that this was contained in a separate album of family photographs that my wife had gathered together some years earlier.

The photograph enabled me to put some faces to the names that had only previously appeared in Census records or BMD certificates or in the family correspondence. Patrick and Frances are seated in the centre of the photograph. He has neatly parted grey hair and a full white beard; his mouth is slightly open, as if he is in mid-breath. Frances is a plumpish lady with a round face, full lips and grey hair. Helen English (Nellie in the seating plan) stands behind them, the shortest of the figures in the row, though all the others are males, either brothers or brothers-in-law. Her husband Arthur English is not present; the note to the photograph states that he was probably at sea.

A total of nine of Helen's siblings are present, the absentees being Thomas (or Tom), John Michael (or Jack, a sailor probably at sea), Frances Anne (Sister Catherine) and Elizabeth Teresa.[34][35] The note to the photograph states that Tom had died by the time it was taken. The dress is formal: the men wear jackets and waistcoats with starched collars and ties; the women wear long full dresses.

At first, I thought that the photograph could be easily dated, as another of Helen's sisters, Sarah (also known as Sally) Brennan, is holding a baby named in the note as her first son, Michael Ignatius Brennan. Her husband – also Michael

---

34 Both John Michael Kelly and his brother-in-law, Arthur English, are listed as recipients of the Mercantile Marine Medal in The National Archives' online *Registry of Shipping and Seaman: Index of First World War Mercantile Marine Medals and the British War Medal*. The Index also includes Arthur's son, Arthur Joseph English (see Chapter 10 below).

35 In Table 5.2, John Michael Kelly is recorded as dying in the Tynemouth district in 1935 at the age of 75. This is in contrast with a number of entries on the public pages of Ancestry, which give his death as being in the same district in 1896 at the age of 37. I discounted these entries on reading the death notice in the *Newcastle Evening Chronicle* of 28th May 1896, which refers to a sister called Mrs Thomas Connolly. None of the Kelly sisters married anyone called Connolly. In addition, of course, a death in 1896 is difficult to reconcile with the First World War decoration.

Brennan – stands behind her. This would have meant that the photograph was taken in 1888.

However, I now think that this is not the case. I believe that this might be a photograph taken at the wedding of Alice Kelly – another daughter of Patrick and Frances and a sister of Helen – to James Daley, even though the couple are not in centre stage. Alice is wearing white, as is Lucy Kelly's daughter, Fanny. This would date the photograph as being in the second quarter of 1891. The supporting evidence for this is three-fold: two of Helen's other siblings – Paul Vincent Kelly and Winifred Kelly were born in 1875 and 1876, respectively, and they appear to be of the relevant ages; Tom Kelly died at the age of 37 in the first quarter of 1891; and the baby being held by Sarah Brennan would have been her daughter, Cecelia, born in 1890.

It is a captivating photograph, about which two other thoughts occur. First, the image of Patrick represents that of the earliest-born person – in 1830 in his case – for whom there is a known photograph amongst the ancestors on my wife Angela's side of the family tree. (As noted in Chapter 1, in the discussion of the Rigg family history, there is a wonderful photograph of Harriet Stirk – the mother of the Line of 16's Jane Boynton – who was born in about 1823).

Second, there is my feeling of gratitude towards the unknown person who, at some stage, took the trouble to list those who were present in the photograph. As also noted in Chapter 1, it is a common frustration for the family history researcher to come across an old photograph of people and places, the names of which can only be guessed at, albeit sometimes intelligently. To hold a piece of evidence, the details of which are known with certainty, is a much rarer occurrence.

I spent some time examining the Census and BMD records in the attempt to discover the fates of Helen Kelly's 13 siblings. The years of death of all but one of them (James) are shown in Table 5.2.

I have noted that one of the brothers – Thomas – died in the Tynemouth district at the age of 37. Further information about this was reported in the *Shields Daily News* of May 25th 1891:

THE WHITE MARE POOL MYSTERY

An inquest on the body of the man found on the road at White Mare Pool on Friday night was held on Saturday afternoon at the house of Mr Duncan before Mr Graham the coroner. James Short identified the body as that of Thomas Kelly who, he said, was a native of Ireland and had been only four days in this country. The witness further stated that the first intimation he had received of the man's death was from the description published in the papers. The jury returned a verdict to the effect that the death was due to failure of the heart's action.

The name Thomas Kelly was far from uncommon in the North East of England at this time; the 1891 Census records 50 such entries of those aged 21 or over in Northumberland and Durham. However, I am confident that the newspaper's reference does refer to the brother of Helen Kelly. Quite apart from the year of death, the article notes the deceased's body as having being identified by one James Short, which as we have seen, is the name of the husband of Helen's sister, Lucy. Thomas Kelly being a native of Ireland is consistent with his absence from the Census of England and Wales in both 1881 and 1891 following his entry as a 17 year-old bootmaker in the Census of 1871.

Excluding Thomas, Helen's other siblings (and Helen herself) lived to old age, averaging 78 years at death. They also had large families; between them (and again including Helen), the 10 siblings who married had had a total of 73 children (of whom 8 were deceased) by the time of the 1911 Census.

Including Helen, 10 of the 12 surviving children of Patrick and Frances Kelly remained in the north-east of England in 1911 with the places of residence being North Shields, Jarrow, Sunderland and Newcastle-on-Tyne. For 8 of them, their subsequent deaths – from Alice Daley (née Kelly) in 1919 to Winifred McMullen (née Kelly) in 1963 – were in the same region.

One of the exceptions was Frances Anne Kelly (Sister Catherine), who was a 51 year-old teacher in Sheffield living as a boarder at Abbeyfield House on Burngreave Road. The 1911 Census record noted that she "suffers from nervous debility". (Interestingly, in the 1871 Census forty years earlier, when living in the family home in North Shields, the 13 year-old Frances A Kelly had been given the occupation of "pupil teacher").

A contributor to the Catholic Family History website[36] has suggested that, in the civil records (i.e. Census, death and municipal burial registers), it is the given name (normally the birth name) of the nun that is used; by contrast, on a gravestone, the religious name is used, though sometimes the given name is also recorded. This seems to have applied in the civil records of Frances Anne Kelly, whose given name was used in the Censuses of 1881 (when she was a 23 year-old schoolmistress in Sacriston, near Chester-le-Street) and 1901 (when she was a 43 year-old "high class of governess" in the Brightside borough of Sheffield) as well as 1911. (I could not find a record for 1891). In 1901, she was one of 10 single women (plus 2 servants and a young child) aged between 21-67 years living at 152 Burngreave Road. 10 years later, Abbeyfield House on the same street housed 17 single women aged 17-51 years plus an elderly widow.

The "boarders" and "domestics" in the Convent of Mercy, Sheffield, are again recorded at 152 Burngreave Road in the 1921 Census, when the 63 year-old Frances Kelly was one of the latter, her occupation being "household duties" (rather

---

36 www.catholicfhs.wordpress.com

than teacher). It is noticeable that there were several other members of the convent, whose birthplaces had been in the north-east of England, particularly Jarrow.[37] Amongst these were three of Frances's nieces: Winifred McMullen, Honora Daley and Frances Daley, respectively aged 19, 25 and 16. Frances Anne Kelly died in Sheffield in 1936 at the age of 79.

In the case of the other of Helen Kelly's siblings who migrated from the north-east by 1911 – Paul Vincent Kelly (and his wife Elizabeth Inglis Kelly, née Johnstone) – the place of residence was Barrow-in-Furness: another significant shipbuilding town.[38] A similar (later) move by Daniel Finch Tuohey and his wife Elizabeth Tuohey (née Kelly) took them to Birkenhead.

The subtle gradations of the social milieu in which the Kelly family was located are evident from the Census information on occupations and the records from the *National Probate Calendar (Index of Wills and Administrations) for England and Wales, 1858-1966*. For example, James Thomas McMullan – the husband of Winifred Kelly (1876-1963) – who died in South Shields in 1914 at the age of 42, was a "roller in steel works" in 1911 and left effects of £141 8s 8d.[39] Similarly, Paul Vincent Kelly – a former blacksmith and fitter – left £377 10s on his death in Barrow-in-Furness in 1943 at the age of 63. By contrast, William George Cunningham – a fruit merchant and commercial trader – left effects of £689 11s 2d to his widow Mary Jane Cunningham (née Kelly) on his death in Sunderland in 1921 at the age of 66. Henry Joseph Kelly, who died in North Shields a year after writing his "The Kelly Centenary" note in 1947 – at various times a metal planer, fitter and turner – left effects of £1,594 5s 11d. The latter were tidy sums for their time, though (as noted below) not to the extent of the effects left by Arthur English.

The family of Arthur English and Helen Kelly

The family of Arthur English and Helen Kelly is shown in Table 5.3. It is firmly placed in the north east of England, notwithstanding Arthur's maritime career as the chief engineer on various ships of the Eagle Oil Transport Company. Both Arthur and Helen were to die in Whitley Bay – at the ages of 67 (in 1936) and

---

37 The dwelling at 152 Burngreave Road is now a residential care home. The St Catherine of Alexandria RC Church retains a prominent position a short distance away.

38 The *Barrow Herald and Furnace Advertiser* of 7th March 1914 reported on the recent lecture entitled "Walney Chapel and its Registers" given by Mr Paul V Kelly to the Barrow Naturalists Field Club:
AN INTERESTING PAPER
The material… forms a notable addition to the history of Walney of considerable interest and value… A hearty vote of thanks was accorded the lecturer.

39 Winifred McMullen outlived her husband by almost 50 years. Her effects were £2,607 6s when she died in 1963.

80 (in 1949), respectively. All three of their children – Helen Mary (or Nellie), Gertrude Amy and Arthur Joseph English – were born in North Shields and Gertrude died in the Tynemouth district in 1969 at the age of 73.

Table 5.3. The family of Arthur and Helen English	
Arthur English 1869-1936 (born in Clonallan, County Down) (died in Whitley Bay, Northumberland, aged 67)	
married	
Helen (Ellan/Hellen/Nellie) Kelly 1869-1949 (born in North Shields, Northumberland) (died in Whitley Bay aged 80)	Helen Mary (Nellie) English 1890-1969 (born in North Shields) (died in Hampstead, London, aged 78) *married* Patrick Joseph Cooney 1888/9-1971 (died in Hampstead aged c82)
	Arthur Joseph English 1892-1970 (born in North Shields) (died in Richmond-on-Thames district, London, aged 78) *married* **Mary Stella Stapleton 1899-1978** (born in Sliema, Malta) (died in Wandsworth district, London, aged 79)
	Gertrude Amy English 1896-1969 (born in North Shields) (died in Tynemouth aged 73)

The first appearance of Arthur and Helen English's family in the Census records was in 1891, when the household (including the 10 month-old Helen Mary) had two rooms at 8 Wellington Street West, North Shields. Ten years later, they were at 53 West Percy Street, North Shields, and Arthur's occupation had changed from "engine fitter" to "mechanical engineer". As noted at the beginning of this chapter, his place of birth in both these records was clearly stated as Jarrow, even though it was actually Clonallon in County Down. (It was also noted above that West Percy Street had been the location of "the little room... where Mass was said", when Helen English's grandmother – Frances Howe (formerly Davis, née McGuire)

– had acted as Sacristan half a century earlier). Arthur English was absent from the 1911 Census, as he would have been at sea; Helen was then resident at 14 Spence Terrace, North Shields, with two of their three children (Helen Mary and Gertrude Amy).

Arthur and Helen English are recorded together in the 1921 Census, when they were resident – with 25 other boarders and 9 staff – at the Clarendon Hotel in Gravesend, Kent. Arthur's occupation was a "marine engineer" with Eagle Oil Co and, interestingly, his work location was recorded as "no fixed place". His place of birth was given as Jarrow-upon-Tyne.

Given that the Census was conducted in June (rather than April, as originally planned), this could have represented a holiday for Arthur and Helen by the coast. However, I am minded to think that their presence in Kent was work-related. In addition to Arthur, there were two mariners staying at the hotel whose employer was also Eagle Oil Co and the other boarders included three US Naval Officers and a Trinity House pilot. Under "place of work", Helen English's entry – duly crossed out – was given as 4 Beaumont Street in North Shields; I think it almost certain that this erroneous entry inadvertently provides her usual place of residence.

When my wife Angela and I visited North Shields in April 2023, we were able to get a sense of the progress that Arthur and Helen English – Angela's great grandparents – had been able to make up the local property ladder. There no longer exists their early residence in Wellington Street West (as given in the 1891 Census, three years after they were married), but their 1901 dwelling remains in place: the upper level of a two-storey brick terrace in West Percy Street, its boarded-up windows in a state of some disrepair, that now stands above a Turkish barber's. In the 1911 Census, with Arthur away at sea, Helen is again recorded as being on upper floor in a row of terraced houses, this time with her daughters Helen Mary and Gertrude Amy in the much more solid-looking Spence Terrace. The Beaumont Terrace address noted from 1921 is another terraced dwelling, but much more substantial, albeit with a whitewashed façade covering the original brickwork and a row of rather unsightly attic windows inserted into the sloping roof.

One of the notes in the Kelly family documentation that has been passed down to Angela refers to an item in a North Shields local newspaper in September 1913: "At St Cuthbert's North Shields, 9th Sept 1888, by the Rev Canon Stark, Arthur English of Jarrow to Helen English of North Shields – Silver Wedding 1913".[40]

---

40 St Cuthbert's RC church was built in Bedford Street in 1820-21. It was replaced by the present-day church of the same name in nearby Albion Road, which opened in 1975. The original location was therefore in the proximity of "the corner of West Percy Street and Bedford Street where Mass was said" to which Henry Kelly referred in "The Kelly Centenary" as the location in which Lucy Davis – Arthur English's great grandmother –

The marriage of Arthur English and Helen Kelly was eventually to last 48 years, ending with Arthur's death in 1936 at the age of 67. The *National Probate Calendar (Index of Wills and Administrations) for England and Wales, 1858-1966* records that the effects left in his will totalled £5,378 2s 4d. Helen remained in Whitley Bay – in the *1939 England and Wales Register*, she was resident at 5 Chollerford Avenue with her married daughter, Helen Cooney – and she died in the town in 1949 at the age of 80.

Helen English had married Patrick Joseph Cooney (1888/89-1971) in the Tynemouth district in 1915. They had two sons, whose children – born in London between 1946 and 1957 – are Angela's second cousins.

---

had acted as Sacristan prior to the church being built. On the four corners of the junction there are now (2023) a charity shop, bank, building society and vacant retail premises.

(Above) Harriet Boynton (c1823-1905, née Stirk), the earliest-born family member in the direct line for whom there is a photograph.

(Below) Gravestone of William Boynton (c1820-1895) at All Saints Church, Great Thirkleby, North Yorkshire.

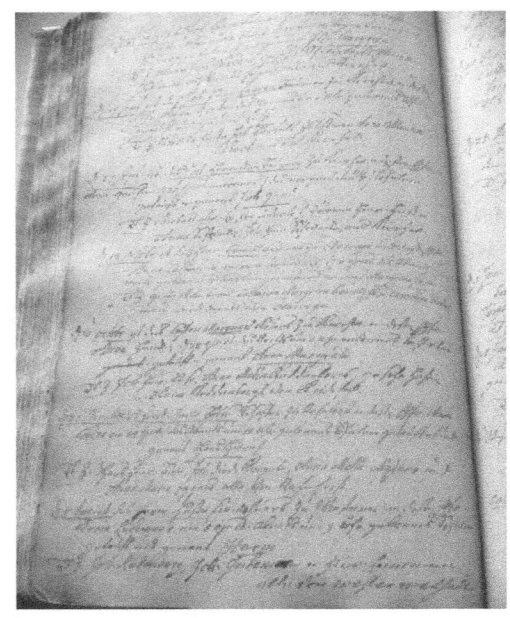

(Above) The Baptism Register of St. Bartholomäus Kirche, Kirchwalsede, Niedersachsen. The entry for Anna Margreta Marquardt on 30th October 1772 is the third from bottom.
(Below) St. Bartholomäus Kirche. Photograph taken in 2018.

(Above) Gravestone of John Pipe (1713-1797) at St Mary's Church, Horham, Suffolk. The year of birth is the earliest found to date of any member of the direct family line. Photograph taken in 2022.
(Below) Charles Tyler Wilson (c1838-1888) when aged about 20.

(Above) Patrick Kelly (1830-1893), Frances Kelly (1830-1902, née Davis) and their family. Helen English (1869-1949, née Kelly) is standing directly behind Jane. Photograph taken in around 1891.

(Below) An extract from the Army records of Joseph Stapleton (1859-1933), which lists his wife Josephine (Guiseppa) Stapleton (1863-1954, née Brincau) and their children (to 1898). Josephine's maiden name is given in a handwritten correction.

(Above) The household record of John Murray (c1839-?) and Margaret Murray (c1846-?, née Mullowney) in the 1901 Census of Ireland. The return illustrates the generational differences in those able to read and write and those able to speak Irish as well as English.

(Below) John Murray (1873-1952) and Honoria (Annie) Murray (1878-1967, née McManaman)

(Above) St Johannis Kirche, Visselhovede, Niedersachsen. The location of the baptism of Johann Friedrich Borstelmann (1811-1854). His great (x2) grandfather (Johann Bostelmann) was buried there in 1716. Photograph taken in 2018.
(Below left) Die Peter und Paul Kirche, Elze, Hannover. The location of the marriage of Charles James Niblett (1851-1927) and Anna Karoline Borstelmann (1853-1938) in 1872. Photograph taken in 2018.
(Below right) St John the Baptist Church, Peterborough. Location of the marriage of Daniel Whines (1827-1906) and Mary Whines (1831-1916, née Wadsworth) in 1851. Photograph taken in 2022.

(Above) John Rigg (1887-1959) in his First World War uniform of the Royal Garrison Artillery.
(Below) John Rigg (born 1954, the author) and William (Bill) Rigg (1921-2004) at the grave of Robert Rigg (1885-1918) in Montigny-sur-Hallue, France. Photograph taken in 1990.

(Above) Catherine Kerr Rigg (1893-1969, née McBride)
(Below) Marie Rosa Niblett (1890-1968, née Wilson) with John Rigg (born 1954, the author)

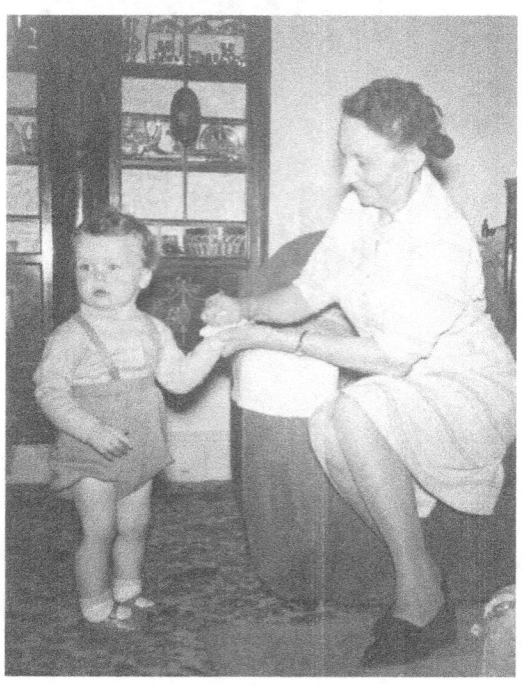

(Above) Alfred Edgar Niblett (1888-1973)
(Below) First World War Ruhleben camp magazine

(Above) Arthur Joseph English (1892-1970)
(Below) Mary Stella English (1899-1978, née Stapleton)

(Above) Certificate of Competency as Steamship Master in the Merchant Service of Arthur Joseph English (1892-1970)

(Below) Ph.D. dissertation of Alfred Edgar Niblett (1888-1973)

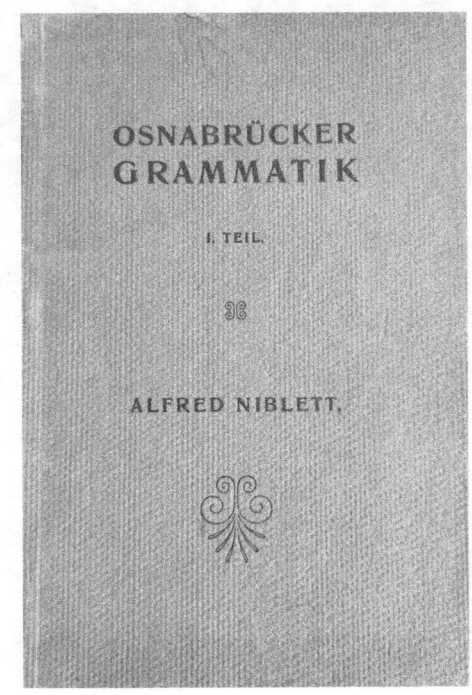

(Above) Denis Arthur Stapleton English (1921-2009) and Anne Catherine English (1919-1994, née Murray)
(Below) Bill Rigg (1921-2004) and Peggie Rigg (1922-2000, née Niblett). Ruby wedding photograph taken in 1989.

CHAPTER SIX

MALTA

LINE OF 16: 11. JOSEPH STAPLETON (c1859-1933)
and 12. GUISEPPA LUCARDA BRINCAU (1863-1954)

The Royal Artillery

I was indebted to an Ancestry contributor, Kevin Chivers, for the initial lead on **JOSEPH STAPLETON** (c1859-1933), the next in the Line of 16. This took the form of a series of documents on Joseph's military record as a member of the Royal Artillery, which were in the *UK, Royal Hospital Chelsea Pensioner Soldier Service Records, 1760-1920* database and which Mr Chivers submitted to the public pages of Ancestry. In the familiar way, however, it also produced a number of questions.

Joseph Stapleton enlisted in Liverpool on 28th November 1877. His Military History Sheet, compiled when he left the Army on 12th April 1899 after 21 years and 135 days service, shows that his periods overseas were a year and half in Malta from August 1882, a year in Egypt from February 1884 and over 9½ years back in Malta from September 1889. He had been awarded the "Long Service Good Conduct" medal (without gratuity) and his pension was "30 pence per diem for life". He had not taken part in any campaigns and there had been no wounds in action.

That is not to say that Joseph did not have an interesting medical history. In Malta in 1890, he suffered a "compound fracture tibia, lower third fragment protruding, and fractured fibula". This required side and back splints and plaster of Paris, which produced a "good union" according to his surgeon, albeit with a ¼ inch shortening of the leg. The cause of the injury was investigated in a Court of Enquiry held in February 1890, the opinion of which was that it was accidental; Joseph had not been on duty and he had been sober at the time.

Joseph's medical history contained two other entries whilst in Malta in 1882 – for colic and for an "itch". In Abbassinyah (sic) in 1884, he had suffered from a wound on the side and from sunstroke. Earlier, he had contracted gonorrhoea in Gosport in 1880, the treatment for which was "injections".

Joseph made some progress through the ranks. His attestation was as a gunner. Thereafter, he was promoted to bombardier in March 1880, corporal in September 1881 and sergeant in January 1883. He was made the Company Sergeant Major in August 1892. There appeared to have been virtually no formal training: Joseph's Military History Sheet referred only to a short course of gunnery in July 1880.

The Army's formal documentation provided some of Joseph's personal details. He was stated to have been born in Liverpool. On his enlistment, he was 67 7/8ths inches tall with a 35 inch chest and a weight of 127 lbs. He had a fresh complexion, grey eyes and brown hair with no distinguishing marks. His pulse was 78 beats, his respiration was 16 inspirations and his muscular development was "good". The last of these was probably related to his pre-enlistment occupation as a labourer. His religious denomination was given as "RC". Apart from an (unspecified) indiscretion in June 1891, for which he was tried and fined £1, Joseph's conduct was consistently marked as good and, on his discharge, his character was stated to be "very good". His intended place of residence on discharge was Sliema, Malta.

For family history purposes, the main military record of interest was the one showing Joseph Stapleton's marriage to Josephine Brincau and the births and baptisms of their children (up until September 1898). The marriage took place in the parish of St Dominco, Valletta, on 24th November 1883, by which time Joseph had reached the rank of sergeant. It was this document that linked Joseph into the family tree as, from my wife's side of the family, it confirmed (almost) the knowledge that there had been a marriage between a Stapleton and a Brincat (sic) on Malta.

The children listed on the document were: William Joseph (born in January 1886 and baptised in Gosport), Josephine (June 1887, Portsmouth), Bertha Florence (April 1889, Portland), Mary Caroline (September 1891, Malta), Mabel Florence (June 1893, Malta), Kate (April 1895, Malta) and Emily Maud (December 1896, Malta).

The other personal details of interest on Joseph's enlistment form were the name of Joseph's mother – Maria, who was listed as his next of kin and resident at 33 Gerrard Street, Liverpool – and the fact that he did not have any brothers. Maria's surname was not given. It was in attempting to follow this up that I started to run into problems. I could not find either Maria Stapleton or Joseph Stapleton in either the 1861 or 1871 Censuses of England and Wales.[1] Nor could I find any

---

[1] The name of the street in central Liverpool on which Joseph Stapleton stated that his mother lived in 1879 was actually Gerard (with one "r") Street. There is no record of anyone called Maria living at number 33 in either the 1871 or 1881 Censuses. Of course, Maria Stapleton could have been a temporary resident at this address in the year in question.

Gerard Street was a crowded location in 1881. There were about 100 properties housing around 1300 people. In 1871, 22 people lived in number 33 in five families. I looked through all the entries for Gerard Street in both

record of a birth of Joseph Stapleton in Liverpool in 1859 or 1860, either in the usual BMD registers or even in a separate database available on Ancestry called *Liverpool, England, Catholic Baptisms 1802-1906*. This uncertainty over the Joseph's year and place of birth was compounded by the two different ages given in separate records for Joseph's enlistment in the Royal Artillery in November 1877: in one he was 18 years and 1 month; in the other 17 years at the last birthday.[2]

Certain questions began to emerge. Was Stapleton the surname of Joseph's mother? Had he actually been born in Liverpool – or somewhere else (Ireland?) Had he been untruthful about his age when joining the Army? Or – a factor that can never been discounted – did the absences or inconsistencies of these records simply reflect transcription errors in the available databases, compared with the original sources? I return to this below.

Kevin Chivers's contribution on the public pages of Ancestry provided a number of details about Joseph Stapleton's family. According to this, his parents were Michael Stapleton (1837-before 1883) and Maria Roche, and his wife – the next in the Line of 16, of course – was **GUISEPPA LUCARDA BRINCAU** (1863-1954). Their children were: William Joseph (born in 1886), Josephine (1887-1979), Bertha Florence (1889), Carmela Maria Angelica (1891), Laurentia Aloysia Josepha (1893), Kate (1895), Emilia Maria Rosaria Elisabeth (1896), Anna Melita Maria Carmela (1899) and Maria Stella Antonia (also 1899). It can be seen that, of the 7 children born before 1898, there is some correspondence and some variation with the names given on Joseph Stapleton's military record (as well as the localised and original version of his wife's Christian names). The last two children were born after 1898 and the name of one of these – Stella – was recognised by my wife as that of her grandmother.

Useful contacts

Mr Chivers's family tree on Ancestry showed that his grandmother, Josephine Stapleton, had married Gordon Chivers (1884-1967) in Alexandria, Egypt, in

---

1871 and 1881, but could find no record for Maria Roche or Maria Stapleton. Several of the properties were boarding houses.

2 Initially, I was interested in the 60 year-old Mary Stapleton – born in Ireland and living in Marylebone Road, Liverpool, with her 24 year-old son, Michael P Stapleton – who was recorded in the 1881 Census. She was described as married and the head of the household; Michael was a general dock labourer. Neither appear to have been in the 1871 Census and nor can I find a record of a Michael Stapleton born in Liverpool between 1855 and 1859, although *Liverpool, England, Catholic Marriages 1754-1921* records that Michael Paul Stapleton married Marriam Jennings in Liverpool in 1885. However, I judged that this family was not relevant for my purposes, given that Joseph Stapleton stated on his Army enlistment form that he did not have any brothers. This view was later confirmed when I found the details of Mary Stapleton's second marriage (see below).

1911.[3] She had died in Hounslow in 1979 at the age of 92. The tree also revealed that Guiseppa Brincau's parents were Lorenzo Brincau (born 1828) and Antonia Gatt (born 1833) and that her two grandfathers were Giovanni Brincau and Salvatore Gatt.

I contacted Mr Chivers and we exchanged some useful information. He reported that he had also not found the records for Michael/Maria/Joseph Stapleton in the relevant Censuses or the record of Joseph's birth, but that the details of Joseph's parents had been derived from his marriage certificate.

Mr Chivers has placed both Joseph/Josephine's marriage certificate and Josephine's birth certificate on the Ancestry public pages. The former reveals that Michael Stapleton had been a policeman in Liverpool, though he was deceased by 1883. Lorenzo Brincau had been a *barcajuolo* (boatman) and *pilote*, though he had also died by the time of the marriage. Guiseppa Brincau had been a 20 year-old servant in Valletta in 1883, when her mother, Antonia, had been a dressmaker.

For my part, I referred to a useful online source that stated its aims were "to assist family researchers and contains information about British men and women who were born, married, died, served in the Royal Navy, Royal Air Force, Royal Marines, the British Army, were resident on the island, or in some manner are connected with Malta".[4] This contained a number of transcribed databases of interest, one of which was for the Santa Maria Addolorata Cemetery in Paola: "the main Roman Catholic cemetery in Malta, the faith followed by almost 100% of the population". The details for the cemetery included references to "Emily Maude Stapleton, died 17 April 1908 aged 6 years 4 months, the daughter of Joseph and Josephine Stapleton" and "Mabel Stapleton, died 23 September 1902 aged 7 years 5 months, the daughter of Joseph and Josephine Stapleton".

The immediate difficulty here was that neither of these ages/dates of death corresponded with the known dates of birth (from Joseph Stapleton's military record). My interpretation was that there may have been transcription errors, but that, unfortunately, these siblings of Josephine and Stella Stapleton did die as young children.

Three other references within this set of databases were of interest. One was of baptisms and included that of George Michael Stapleton in 1898; I thought this might be another sibling. Secondly, the database called "Maltese Brides" noted that Josepha Brincat (sic) married Joseph Stapleton. Finally, a database of deaths included that of William Stapleton in Sliema in May 1906 at the age of 20.

---

3 The *Daily Malta Chronicle and Garrison Gazette* of 21st August 1911 reported that the marriage took place in the British Consulate in Alexandria. Josephine (Jessy) Violet Stapleton was the "eldest daughter of Mr and Mrs Stapleton of "Llandrindod", Victoria Avenue, Sliema".

4 website.lineone.net/-stephaniebidmead/

There was no direct link made between William Stapleton and the family of Joseph and Josephine Stapleton, but I think it reasonable to assume that he was their first-born child. Following on from this, the archives of the *Daily Malta Chronicle and Garrison Gazette* provide several references to W Stapleton featuring in boys' cricket matches in Malta between 1897 (when he would have been aged 11) and 1903. (For example, as reported on 3rd July 1903, he opened the batting for the Boys Empire League in a two-innings match against Sliema Union Cricket Club scoring 14 and 16. He also took 12 wickets in the match as his side won by 63 runs). Fifteen months later, in October 1904, he was playing for the Essex Regiment against the Hampshire Regiment. I could not find any subsequent references to him in the newspaper, nor any reports of the cause of his death in 1906.

It is clear that there is conflicting evidence on whether Guiseppa's maiden name was Brincau or Brincat. In correspondence with Kevin Chivers, he confirmed that, although in different records he had also seen references to Brincat and Brincon, Brincau was the surname given on Guiseppa's baptism certificate. This is clearly a relevant point to consider, given that this was an official record. However, the certificate – which is neatly typed – also (twice) spells Guiseppa's name as "Giuseppa", suggesting that its 100% accuracy might not have been guaranteed.

On the other hand, Brincat was the name that my wife Angela had recalled from discussions with her father. Moreover, it appears to be much the more common of the two surnames.[5] In addition, it was the name used in the registration of the family plot at the cemetery at the Santa Maria Addolorata Cemetery (see below). However – for the present – I have taken as the decisive item of evidence the document cataloguing the details of Joseph and Josephine's marriage and family that was included in his military records. On this, the (handwritten) surname Bilncon has twice been crossed out and replaced (in a different hand) with Brincau. Accordingly, Brincau is the name used in Table 6.1.

---

5   A Google search (on www.forebears.co.uk/surnames/) for the present-day worldwide distribution of the Brincau name reveals a concentration in Malta, Spain and Australia (at around 49%, 30% and 20%, respectively). However, the total number given for the name in this source is relatively small: 169.

In contrast, for the Brincat name, the total is much larger at 3,148. The highest proportions are again in Malta and Australia – 52% and 17%, respectively – but not in Spain; the next highest proportions are in the USA and England at 10% each.

In *Surnames of the Maltese Islands: An Etymological Dictionary* (2003), Mario Cassar states that Brincat is an Italian personal name, being a form of Brancato, itself an arabicised form of Pancrazio (English: Pancras) meaning "omnipotent". Brincau is another form of Brincat: its ending of 'au' "suggests a Sardinian morphological influence". According to Cassar, the surname Brincau (as distinct from Brincat) did not feature in the *Status Animarum* (diocesan census) of Malta of 1687 and, hence, it must have been adopted at a later stage.

Table 6.1. The parents and family of Joseph and Guiseppa/Josephine Stapleton		
Joseph Stapleton c1860-1933 (probably born in Liverpool, though possibly as William Stapleton in County Kildare, Ireland) (son of Michael Stapleton 1837-before 1883 and Maria Roche ?-1903) (died in Malta aged 73)		
	married	
Guiseppa Lucarda Josepha (Josephine) Brincau 1863-1954 (born in Vittoriosa, Malta) (daughter of Lorenzo Brincau 1828-? and Antonia Gatt 1833-?) (died in Malta aged 90)		William Joseph Stapleton 1886-1906 (born in Gosport, Hampshire) (died in Sliema, Malta, aged 20)
		Josephine Stapleton 1887-1979 (born in Portsmouth) (died in Hounslow, London, aged 92) *married* Gordon Chivers 1884-1967 (born in Redruth, Cornwall) (died in Richmond-on-Thames district, London, aged 83)
		Bertha Florence (Beatrice) Stapleton 1889-1958 (born in Portland, Hampshire) (died in Newport, Wales, aged 69) *married* Robert Dilley 1881-1939 (born in Aldershot) (died aged 58)
		Mary Caroline Stapleton 1891-? (born in Malta)

	Florence Mabel Stapleton 1893-1971 (born in Malta) (died in Uckfield, Surrey, aged 78) *married* Frederick William Windebank 1879-1950 (died in Surbiton, Surrey, aged 71)
	Kate Stapleton 1895-1902 (born in Malta) (died in Malta aged 7)
	Emily Maude Stapleton 1896-1903 (born in Malta) (died in Malta aged 6)
	George Michael Stapleton 1898-1898 (born in Malta) (died in Malta aged 0)
	Anne Melita (Nita) Stapleton 1899-1966 (born in Sliema) (died in Twickenham, London, aged 67) *married* Stanley Acton Gammon 1893-1956 (born on the Isle of Wight) (died in Isleworth, London, aged 63)
	Mary Stella Stapleton 1899-1978 **(born in Sliema)** **(died in Wandsworth district aged 79)** *married* **Arthur Joseph English 1892-1970** **(born in North Shields)** **(died in Richmond-on-Thames district aged 78)**

In a separate exercise, I logged on to the *Catholic Parish Registers, 1655-1915* database which has been made available by the National Library of Ireland on Ancestry. It includes the marriage of Michael Stapleton and Maria Roche at St Peter's, Athlone, Roscommon, Ireland, on 21st September 1858. There is no direct link to the Stapleton family here, but given the names – and, especially, the date – I think it entirely reasonable to assume that these were Joseph Stapleton's parents. I also think that the record adds weight to the theory that Joseph was born in Ireland, not Liverpool, and that – like Arthur English elsewhere in the extended family tree at a later date (see Chapter 5 above) – he had judged it prudent to be economical with the truth about his country of birth.

I sought to confirm this by examining the original baptism register of St Peter's for this period, which has been made available on www.registers.nli.ie/registers. I looked at the records for 1859-1861 without finding an entry for the birth of Joseph Stapleton. However, the script was quite difficult to read in places and, whilst I studied the records with some care, it is possible that I missed something.

It was at this point – in October 2015 – that I was contacted by Lucy (surname unknown), who was a family friend of a daughter-in-law of, in turn, the daughter-in-law (!) of Beatrice Stapleton, one of the daughters of Joseph and Josephine Stapleton (and a sister of Stella Stapleton) and otherwise known as Bertha Florence Stapleton. Lucy and I exchanged several mutually helpful e-mails.

Lucy informed me that Beatrice Stapleton had married Robert Dilley in Malta in 1912 and that they had had 5 children.[6] In turn, I was able to tell her about Stella Stapleton's marriage to Arthur Joseph English (1892-1970) – see Chapter 10 below – and their subsequent family. I was also able to pass on some information about Stella's twin sister, Anne Stapleton (1899-1966), and her marriage to Stanley Acton Gammon (1893-1956).

Lucy and I compared notes on the anomalous records given for Emily Maude Stapleton and Mabel Stapleton in the transcription of the Santa Maria Addolorata Cemetery in Malta. I suggested that it was possible that Emily had died in 1903 (not 1908, as it might easily have been misread on a worn gravestone) as her age at death would then have corresponded exactly with her year of birth.

As for "Mabel", Lucy persuaded me that the death in 1902 was actually that of another of the Stapleton sisters – Kate – as, again, the age and date would then match with the known date of birth. Lucy knew that Florence Mabel Stapleton (who had been baptised Laurentia Aloysia Josepha Stapleton) had lived to the age of 78 (before dying in Uckfield, Sussex, in 1971) and that she had married Frederick William Windebank (1879-1950).[7] Frederick and Florence Windebank are recorded in the 1921 Census as being resident in Hackney, London.

Lucy and I had both come across the reference to the birth of George Michael Stapleton in 1898. Later, Lucy was also able to report a death record in

---

6   The *Daily Malta Chronicle and Garrison Gazette* of 12th August 1912 carried a detailed report of the "very pretty wedding". It was noted that:
> "[T]he attending Bridesmaids, Miss Stella [my wife Angela's grandmother] and Annie, twin sisters of the Bride, who carried bouquets of hydrangea, looked most attractive in very pretty white embroidered dresses, trimmed with pink ribbons with hats to match, and wearing silver wrist watches, the gift of the Bridegroom".

7   The announcement of this wedding was made in the *Daily Malta Chronicle and Garrison Gazette* on 9th September 1911, three weeks after Josephine Stapleton's wedding to Gordon Chivers. Three of Stella Stapleton's older sisters were married, therefore, within a 12-month period in 1911-12. (I have been unable to find out what became of Mary Caroline Stapleton, who was born in Malta in 1891).

the same year. It is reasonable, I think, to assume that this was another member of Joseph and Josephine's family.

We were able to make less progress with the date and place of birth of Joseph Stapleton or with the birth and death of his parents, Michael Stapleton and Maria Roche. Lucy had examined the police records at the National Archives and found that there had been 5 Michael Stapletons in the Royal Irish Constabulary, but only one had possibly consistent details and even this said that he had resigned in February 1857 in order to emigrate (whereas we know that "our" Michael Stapleton married Maria in Athlone in 1858). She added, intriguingly, that there were several criminal records for people with the name of Michael Stapleton from Tipperary, some of which matched the age range we were looking in.[8][9]

The British in Malta

At this point, there were three general issues to follow up – with a fourth presenting itself at a later stage. The first was to read into the background of the British involvement in Malta. For this, I drew on Brian Blouet's authoritative *The Story of Malta*, first published in 1967.

Britain took Malta from Napoleon's France in 1800 and during the 19th Century – including the period of Joseph Stapleton's postings there – administered the islands as a crown colony with a Governor heading a Council of Government and reporting to the Colonial Secretary in the British Government. Malta was of obvious strategic importance both militarily and on the Mediterranean trade routes, especially after the opening of the Suez Canal in 1869. Blouet describes it as a link in the great chain of imperial stations that stretched from the United Kingdom to Gibraltar, through the Mediterranean to the Red Sea, down to India, the Straits and Singapore and eventually reaching the China coast and the colonies of Australia and New Zealand. Malta was the headquarters of the Royal Navy's Mediterranean fleet.

Blouet makes some interesting observations about the presence of the British armed forces in Malta in the latter half of the 19th Century. On the one hand, there was a "sympathetic relationship between the Royal Navy and Malta". By contrast, "the Army commanders attempted to obstruct various [large-scale investment] works on the grounds that they might interfere with the defences". More generally,

---

8 The only other record I could find in which the names of Michael and Maria Stapleton appear together is in their role of parents (to someone with a different surname) in a marriage register for the parish of Croghan in 1874, when their residence was given as Hill Street. Croghan and Hill Street are in Roscommon, though both are some distance from Athlone. However, as before, the later discovery of Mary Stapleton's second marriage rendered this irrelevant.

9 The www.rootsireland.ie online database includes one record for the death of Michael Stapleton in Roscommon.

"there was a complete lack of appreciation for the feelings of the local inhabitants". Joseph Stapleton would have been caught in the middle of this, of course, given his professional responsibilities with the Army and (from 1883) his formal attachment to the locally based Brincau family.

The Santa Maria Addolorata Cemetery

The second issue to pursue further was the Santa Maria Addolorata Cemetery in Paola, which Angela and I visited in May 2016. Designed by Emmanuele Luigi Galizia in the Gothic Revival style and inaugurated in 1869, it is widely acknowledged as one of the great cemeteries of Europe with a "population" of about 300,000. (The current total – and living – population of Malta is about 400,000).

In order to track down a particular grave, one needs the surname and the date of death. We had this for Kate Stapleton (23 September 1902) and so the official at the administrative office at the cemetery's entrance was able to look in her ledgers and give us the reference in the Eastern Cemetery of O-E-14. She said that it was a family plot, purchased by Joseph Stapleton, whose wife's maiden name was Brincat (with a "t").

The grave was reached by a short walk along an ascending ramp and then up some stone steps to the "O" tier of that part of the cemetery. It was in a shady spot under a tall tree. A stone monument had two plaques which read:

IN LOVING MEMORY OF
MABEL
DAUGHTER OF JOSEPH AND JOSEPHINE STAPLETON
WHO DIED AFTER A
FEW HOURS ILLNESS
23 SEPT 1902
AGED 7 YEARS AND 5 MONTHS
SUDDEN A LOSS AND SHOCK SEVERE
TO PART WITH HER WE LOVED SO DEAR
BUT TRUST IN CHRIST TO MEET AGAIN

IN LOVING MEMORY OF
EMILY MAUDE
DAUGHTER OF JOSEPH AND JOSEPHINE STAPLETON
WHO DIED AFTER A PAINFUL ILLNESS
17 APRIL 1903 AGED 6 YEARS AND 4 MONTHS
SUFFER THE LITTLE CHILDREN TO COME TO ME

The stone was of a soft limestone and badly eroded; indeed, it looked as it might collapse before too long. However, there was no sign that any other inscriptions had been worn away. Hence, although this was a family plot, there was no sign that either Joseph or Josephine or any other members of the family were buried there. Nor were there any other Stapleton or Brincau/Brincat graves in the immediate vicinity.

We were able to make progress on a couple of mysteries. First, the year of death on Emily Maude's plaque was clearly 1903; there had indeed been a transcription error (to 1908) in the website database. Second, the name on the larger plaque was given as Mabel, even though the deceased child was Kate (and, moreover, the reference to Kate had been the means by which the grave had been located at the cemetery's offices). This suggests that either Mabel had been a second name given to Kate (as it also was to one of her sisters, Florence Mabel Stapleton) or there had been an error in the grave's inscription which had never been corrected.

It was sometime later, when I consulted the archive of the *Daily Malta Chronicle and Garrison Gazette* that I came across two short entries in the Local News section:

> **26th September 1902** [following the death of the 7 year-old Kate Stapleton].
> "Mr and Mrs Stapleton are much touched by the kind sympathy shewn in their time of trouble and thank all those who shewed their regard by sending wreaths"

> **21st April 1903** [following the death of the 6 year-old Emily Maude Stapleton].
> "Mr and Mrs Stapleton are much touched by the deep sympathy shewn in their recent bereavement and convey through us their grateful thanks to all those who have sent wreaths and condolences"

Whilst Angela and I were able to resolve the inscriptions on the plaques, another intriguing mystery presented itself at the time of our visit which, to date, remains unsolved. At the foot of the stone monument, there was a small photograph of the face of a woman of late middle age. The photograph had obviously been there for some time – many years, I would guess – as the front was cracked and part of the back had broken off. Angela thought that the woman bore something of a resemblance to her late aunt Anne, a granddaughter of Joseph and Josephine Stapleton. I can only speculate on who this might have been, but one possibility is Mary Caroline Stapleton, who was born in 1891 and who does not subsequently appear in any of the records that Kevin Chivers, Lucy and I have been able to compile.

A revealing footnote to our visit to the Santa Maria Addolorata Cemetery occurred in the form of a feature article in *The Sunday Times of Malta* a few days later ("Gravesite for sore eyes", Michela Spiteri, 15th May 2016). There was clearly some local concern about the lack of resources being expended on maintaining the location, compared with the "Heritage Malta" sites that attract the bulk of tourists.

> "The place is suffering from deep and serious neglect… The stone, which must have been originally of superb quality, is crumbling. Pinnacles and finials have dropped off and the gothic balustrades… are eroded and missing…
>
> The Addolorata really is a microcosm of Malta. Everything we battle over in our lives, all the national narratives and agendas, the slow crumbling of Malta's masterpieces, the litter, the neglect and the dust – they're all there… It's shockingly neglected".

It was some time after our return from Malta – in March 2017 – that I contacted the Public Registry of births, marriages and deaths (pubreg.civilstatus@gov.mt) to ask for advice about tracking the deaths of Joseph and Josephine Stapleton. I received an immediate reply from a clerical officer, Jacqueline Camilleri, who informed me that Joseph had died in April 1933 and Josephine had died in June 1954. (As with the responses from the public record offices in Leeds and Peterborough, I thought that this was impressively efficient).

I subsequently purchased Joseph and Josephine's death certificates, which stated that their ages at death had been 73 and 92,[10] respectively, and that the causes had been "cirrhosis of the liver" and "senility". Joseph and Josephine had both been resident in Sliema and both were buried in the Santa Maria Addolorata Cemetery. The witnesses to Joseph's death, which occurred at 48 Victoria Terrace, had been two police constables in their twenties; Josephine died at the St Vincent de Paul Hospital.

Other information (typed) on the death certificates was also revealing. Joseph Stapleton's occupation at the time of his death was "military pensioner" and his place of birth was again given as Liverpool. The names of his parents were Michael Stapleton (which I knew) and Mary Preston, both deceased. I return to the latter below.

Josephine Stapleton's place of birth was given on her death certificate as Cospicua, which is slightly inland from Vittoriosa, the birthplace given on her marriage certificate. However, the certificates do not clear up the mystery surrounding the definitive version of her maiden name. Joseph's death certificate

---

[10] Josephine Stapleton was actually aged 91 when she died. Her birth certificate gives a date of birth in April 1863.

states that he was the husband of Josephine Brincau; Josephine's certificate records that her father was the deceased Lawrence Brincat.

Given that I now had the dates of death of Joseph and Josephine Stapleton, I was able to ring the Santa Maria Addolorata Cemetery to enquire about the plot details of their grave(s). The helpful official there was able to tell me straightaway that Joseph was buried in plot O-E-14 in the Eastern Cemetery: the same location as his two children. This was not a surprise, of course, given that I had previously been informed that this was a family plot purchased by Joseph although, as also noted, there is no inscription or other indication that he was buried there.

Josephine was buried in a different plot – S-B-2 in the Western Cemetery – that was owned by the church. I discussed this briefly with the cemetery official and we agreed that, at the time of her death, there might not have been any other family members resident on Malta who knew about the family plot, given that Joseph had died over 20 years earlier. On the other hand, there were at least five of Josephine's daughters still alive, albeit all resident in Britain. It is difficult to believe that one or more of them did not know about the plot, especially as it contained two of their long-deceased young sisters. This suggests, perhaps, that the maintenance of the family contacts had not been particularly strong and I wonder if there are family stories here which will now always remain untold.

On a separate point, the question is prompted as to whether the old photograph that Angela and I found at the family plot when we visited it in May 2016 was actually that of Josephine herself.

Joseph Stapleton's origins

The third issue to follow up was, of course, the question of Joseph Stapleton's birth. The *Ireland, Catholic Parish Registers, 1655-1915* database – compiled by the National Library of Ireland and available on Ancestry – records that a Joseph Stapleton was baptised on 27th May 1861 at St Andrew's Roman Catholic Church in Westland Row, Dublin, having been born on the 3rd May with a residence ("habitantibus in") given as Kildare. Crucially – and unusually for this database – whilst the child's surname was obviously given, there were no details at all about the parents. An entry in the register's final column on the circumstances of the baptism might be "a child at home", though it is difficult to read. The other available online databases do not give any obvious corresponding entries to the Joseph Stapleton identified here.

Another source was the www.rootsireland.ie database of the Irish Family History Foundation (IFHF), to which I took out a temporary subscription in July 2020. This database records the birth of William (sic) Stapleton to Corporal Michael Stapleton of the 2nd Battalion 10th Regiment and Maria Roche at the Curragh Camp in County Kildare in September 1859 (one year after their marriage in County Roscommon).¹¹ The unanswered questions, therefore, are whether the Joseph Stapleton baptised in May 1861 belonged in this family and, if so, why the parents' names were not given in the Catholic register for the baptism of their second child.

Having reflected at length on the birth of Joseph Stapleton, I think that there are two possibilities. First: that he was indeed a second son of Mary Stapleton (née Roche), born in May 1861. Under this scenario, I think that his father might well have died by the time of his birth, which could account for the absence of the usual parental details in the baptism record, but still be consistent with Kildare being given as the place of residence.¹² In this case, William Stapleton would indeed have been a brother of Joseph, notwithstanding that Joseph stated that he did not have any brothers in his Army enlistment form. (Alternatively, It could be that William himself had also died by 1877). It is feasible that Joseph remained with his mother when she remarried in 1864 (see below), but left the household to join the Army – at the age of only 16½ – in November 1877.

The second possibility is rather startling: that the William Stapleton born in September 1859 and the Joseph Stapleton who joined the Army are the same person.

The 1861 Census of England and Wales does not record any one or two year-old infants named William Stapleton living in Liverpool. Interestingly, a 12 year-old of this name is registered as living there (and having been born in the city) in the 1871 Census – as one of over 1,100 scholars listed as being at the Liverpool Industrial Schools in Kirkdale¹³ – although the corresponding 22 year-old does not appear 10 years later (when "Joseph" Stapleton would have been in the Army, of course).¹⁴

---

11 The plain in County Kildare – approximately 35 miles from the centre of Dublin – had been a mustering site for armies since the earliest times. A formal camp was established there by the British Army in 1855 to meet the need for additional training areas following the outbreak of the Crimean War the previous year. The camp was handed over to the Irish Free State Army in 1922. It is now the home of the Defence Forces Training Centre of the Irish Defence Forces.

12 On the www.rootsireland.ie database, there are half a dozen deaths registered for the name of Michael Stapleton (of a roughly relevant age) in Ireland between 1858 and 1878, but, apart from a couple of labourers, none of the occupations listed – carpenter, mason, farmer – really stand out as logical progressions from an Army career.

13 The website www.workhouses.org.uk/liverpool includes a brief history of the Industrial School at Kirkdale. A report in the *Illustrated London News* in 1850 stated that it had been opened in May 1845 in order to give "young children thrown upon the parish… instruction not only in the elements of a plain education – reading, writing and arithmetic – and in their religious duties, but in the most common and useful trades". For boys, these included tailoring, shoemaking and carpentering. An 1866 report by the Poor Law Inspector found overcrowding and unsanitary conditions with the result that he was "unable to report that this school is in a satisfactory state". Additional buildings were operational from 1868 taking the school's capacity to 1,900.

14 A 47 year-old Mary Roche (note: not Mary Stapleton or Mary Preston) also appears in Liverpool in the 1871 Census as a widowed seamstress, born in Ireland, living as a lodger at 35 Vine Street. I am again minded to rule out this census entry as being relevant, however, given the evidence (below) of what appears to have been Mary's second marriage.

I have to concede that the evidence supporting the theory that William Stapleton transformed into Joseph Stapleton is, at best, circumstantial. In this respect, the fact that Joseph stated that he did not have any brothers in his Army enlistment form is an argument in its favour, as it would be technically correct. In addition, it is perhaps also significant that his own first child (born in 1886, the later teenage cricketer) was named William Joseph Stapleton.

The argument for a William-to-Joseph transformation would be undermined, of course, if a post-1877 reference could be found in any of the various online sources to a William Stapleton born in County Kildare in September 1859. However, none such appear in the available databases on the Ancestry and Findmypast sites.

These sources list births under the name of William Stapleton in Tipperary and Ballyregget (County Kilkenny) in March and July 1859, respectively. There are also records for corresponding births in Dublin in June 1858 and November 1860, the first of which adds to the complexity of the search as this William Stapleton is one of the 7 children of James Stapleton and his wife Julia (née Reilly) who were baptised in the same St Andrew's RC Church in Westland Row, Dublin, as "our" Joseph Stapleton in 1861.[15]

All these other William Stapletons do feature in the subsequent online records. The 1858 and 1860 births in Dublin carry through to the 1911 Census of Ireland in the same city, as does the 1859 birth in Ballyregget. More dramatically – if not bizarrely – the *Ireland, Prison Registers, 1790-1924* database reveals that, when aged 15, the William Stapleton born in Tipperary in 1859 was jointly sentenced in 1875 to one month's hard labour in Kilmainham Gaol with the 14 year-old James Stapleton (presumably a brother, as they were both living at the same address in Dublin and "without a father") for being "drunk and disorderly, fighting and assaulting each other". Nine years later, the 25 year-old William – by then a "manager in a spirit establishment" – graduated to a 5-year term of penal servitude in Mountjoy Prison from 1884 for "making of false entries in the stock book with intent to de-fraud".

This lack of evidence of a post-1877 William Stapleton in the available records who had been born in County Kildare in 1959 does not prove the transformation theory – only that the case against it has not been definitively made. I have recorded the argument here as an example of how a little conjecture by the family historian might suggest an unusual or unanticipated finding, which

---

15 The relevant births in this family are those of Anne Stapleton (19th February 1860) and James Stapleton (11th February 1962). It is difficult to see how the latter could be consistent with the birth of Joseph Stapleton on 3rd May 1861. There is also no explanation as to why the names of the parents of Joseph Stapleton (if they had been James Stapleton and Julia Reilly) would not have been entered in the baptism register. This leads to the conclusion that Joseph Stapleton was not part of this family.

it is appropriate to examine, but which must not be allowed to become "fact" in the absence of supporting evidence.

Joseph Stapleton is the name by which my wife Angela's great grandfather was generally known – certainly from 1877 onwards – and it is this one that I shall retain (with a birth in Liverpool in about 1859, given the absence of firm evidence to the contrary) in presenting his place in the Line of 16.

Mary Stapleton's second marriage

The reference to his mother's surname as Preston on Joseph Stapleton's death certificate generates the fourth of the main issues to follow up. It indicates, of course, that Maria Stapleton married again after the death (sometime between 1859 and 1883) of her husband, Michael. However, as with Maria Roche and Maria Stapleton, I was not able to place Mary Preston or Maria Preston definitively within the 1871 or later Censuses in England. In addition, as there is no record of a relevant Preston/Stapleton or Preston/Roche marriage in England and Wales in the long period from 1860 to 1920, I decided that any such marriage must have been in Ireland.[16]

Initially, I could not find any reference to the marriage in the online Irish databases www.rootsireland.ie or www.irishgenealogy.ie. However, a later examination of Family Search's *Ireland, Civil Registration Marriages, 1845-1958* database, compiled by the Mormon Church's researchers from the quarterly return of Ireland's General Register Office, led me to the marriage of Eugene Treston (sic) to Mary Roach (sic) in Claremorris, County Mayo, in January 1864.[17] (The Preston name on Joseph Stapleton's death certificate was typed; the original name could easily have been misread, especially given its rareness). Subsequently, I noted that the Family Search site *Ireland, Births and Baptisms, 1620-1881* gave references to the births of six children – all in Claremorris – between January 1867 and October 1880. In addition, several contributors to the public pages of Ancestry list up to eight children in total for the Treston/Roach (or Roache) family, albeit with none of them having identified Mary's earlier marriage to Michael Stapleton.

Owen (sic) Treston and his wife Mary are recorded in the 1901 Census of Ireland – aged 61 and 56 respectively – as still resident in Claremorris with three of their (grown up) children also in the household; Owen was a farmer. Owen was a 73 year-old widower in the following Census in 1911 as, according to the Family Search's *Ireland, Civil Registration Deaths Index, 1864-1958*, Mary had died in 1903 at the age of 58. He died in Drumneen, County Mayo, in 1916 at the age of 79.

---

16   There is also no-one with this surname in the Santa Maria Addolorata Cemetery.

17   The respective fathers were James Treston and Michael Roach.

There are some puzzles relating to the Treston/Roach(e) findings. For one thing, Owen Treston was born Eugene Michael Treston in Drumneen sometime between 1837 and 1840 (according to the much later Census records). He would have been in his mid-twenties at the time of his marriage to Mary at the beginning of 1864.

It is not clear why the change in name from Eugene Michael Treston to Owen Treston occurred. One explanation might be if he were attempting to distance himself from his past. The National Archives of Ireland's *Ireland, Prison Registers, 1790-1924* reveals that the 20 year-old Michael Treston – an uneducated marble-polisher[18] – was sentenced to 10 days hard labour in the Richmond bridewell (or jail) in Dublin in June 1862 for assaulting a police officer. However, the more likely explanation is a reversion to a long-established family name.

For her part, given her reported age at death, Mary Stapleton would have been aged 18 at the time of her marriage to Eugene Treston. However, this also means that she would have been barely 13 when she married Michael Stapleton in 1858 and only 14 when she gave birth to their son William a year later (see above). I think this can be easily explained, however. None of the official records – nor the various Ancestry contributors – provide a definitive year of birth for Mary; I suspect that, like so many others in this narrative, she was being somewhat economical with the truth when the 1901 Census of Ireland return was being compiled.

I cannot say for certain that the Mary Roche who had married Michael Stapleton in County Kildare in 1858 was the same Mary Roache who subsequently married Eugene/Owen Treston in County Mayo in 1864 and went on to have a large family. However, it seems highly probable; the similarity between the Treston name and the Preston reference given on Joseph Stapleton's death certificate is too close to ignore.

This being the case, it means, of course, that Joseph Stapleton – or the William who became "Joseph" – had a number of step-siblings in the Treston family. Three of these – Bridget, Catharine and James Edward Treston – migrated to the United States (the first two as teenagers), where they settled in Philadelphia, Pennsylvania, each marrying and raising large families of their own.

A productive source of information

We have seen that the *Daily Malta Chronicle and Garrison Gazette* has been a productive source of information about the marriages and deaths of (some of) the siblings of Stella Stapleton. (Its coverage of Stella's own wedding is described in Chapter 10 below). In addition to the cricketing exploits of William Stapleton,

---

18   This is consistent with Owen Treston being recorded as unable to read or write in the 1911 Census of Ireland. His latter occupation – farmer – is obviously different, however.

noted above, it recorded other aspects of their life in the Malta of the early 20th Century. Hence, for example, on 19th August 1910, Miss B Stapleton [Beatrice] was listed amongst those due to arrive on the P and O ss *Palawan* from London. The following month, at the "Aquatic Sports of the Army School, Malta Command", A Stapleton [Annie] came second in the race for girls aged under 14. (Two years later, in the same event, Annie's form appears to have slipped as she came third). Throughout 1916, there were several reports of the performance of Miss Stapleton [either Annie or Stella] at a series of Army Service Corps concert parties. The report of 23rd February, for example, noted that:

> "…Miss Stapleton quite enraptured her audience with her delightfully vivacious rendering of "Oh? For the sight of a girl" to which she added a graceful style of acting…"

However, it was the activities of Joseph Stapleton, shortly before and following his retirement from the Army in 1899, that were the most extensively reported in the newspaper. Some of these were related to his final post, such as that captured in the long article on 28th March 1899 on the Royal Artillery Annual Ball, "for which the working committee was necessarily a strong one" and included Company Sergt-Major [CS-M] Stapleton. The following January, in a "Report of a Supper and Smoking Concert in the Sergeant's Mess in Tigné for the Staff Sergeants and Sergeants of No 5 Company ED Royal Garrison Artillery previous to their departure for active service in South Africa", it was noted that, in one of the speeches given by Mr Stapleton, the retired CS-M of 5E stated that "he would carefully watch their career in the land to which they were journeying".[19]

It was inevitable that Josephine Stapleton, as the wife of the retired CS-M, would be drawn into the round of post-Army social engagements. Hence, for example, the same newspaper's reports that Mr and Mrs Stapleton attended "a Quadrille at the fort at Upper St Elmo" (12th January 1901) through to Mr and Mrs Stapleton being listed amongst those attending "the Farewell Ball held at the Valetta Gymnasium for the 1st Suffolk Regiment prior to their departure for Egypt" (20th December 1910).

The most intriguing of Joseph Stapleton's post-retirement roles was undoubtedly that of being a senior figure in the Royal Antediluvian Order of Buffaloes – Grand Lodge of England (RAOB-GLE). The first reference I saw of this was in the *Daily Malta Chronicle and Garrison Gazette* of 2nd January 1913:

---

19 The Second Boer War lasted from October 1899 to May 1902.

RAOB-GLE
UNITY LODGE NO. 1206

The annual dinner of the above lodge was held at the United Service Hotel on 23rd December 1913 when eighteen brethren of the Order sat down.

Mr J Stapleton was in the chair supported by Mr Storace and Mr J Muscat,

After the toast of "The King", Mr Stapleton in proposing the toast of "Success to Buffaloism" said it was a great pleasure to say that the Unity Lodge was now in a much more flourishing condition than it was six months ago. This was owing to the number of new brothers from the W Yorkshire Regt.

A musical programme was then gone through…

…A most enjoyable evening was brought to a close by the singing of "Auld Lang Syne" and the National Anthem.

My lack of knowledge of the RAOB meant that I was somewhat puzzled by this, as what I initially (and mistakenly) took to be a version of Masonry would surely have been incompatible with the Roman Catholicism that Joseph Stapleton had stated to be his religious denomination on his Army attestation forms. His wife, Josephine, would certainly have been Catholic and the marriage of his daughter Beatrice Stapleton to Robert Dilley had taken in St Patrick's Church in Don Bosco Street, Sliema.

In the event, the information available on Wikipedia clarified matters. The Order started in 1822 and spread throughout the British Empire (not least because of its prevalence within members of the Armed Services) and elsewhere. Men of any religious or political views are allowed to join and discussion of religion and politics is forbidden at meetings. The members of the lodges meet together for fellowship and conviviality and to raise funds to help sick or indigent members or their families.

Joseph Stapleton's role within the RAOB in Malta was clearly revealed in a notice placed with the *Daily Malta Chronicle and Garrison Gazette* of 23rd July 1915. It was repeated on several occasions over the following two years, with Joseph as the first-named Primo each time.[20]

RAOB-GLE

Will Any Brothers of the above Order amongst our wounded in any of the military Hospitals in Malta kindly communicate with the following Primos who will be pleased to greet them:

J Stapleton	St Andrews Hospital
A Storace	St Georges do
J Gracey	do do

---

20   The Primo is the second of four Degrees (or levels) within the RAOB.

By the Autumn of 1916, Joseph Stapleton had reached the third Degree – the Knight Order of Merit – which is granted to those who have been members of 10 years or more after being raised to the second Degree. The available references in the newspaper's archive continue to the end of 1917.

3rd October 1916
RAOB

"A large and well-attended meeting of the Unity Lodge RAOG-GLE was held at Valetta on Saturday last when the opportunity was availed of to raise Primo Gracey to the dignity of Knighthood. About sixty members of the Order were present. After the ordinary business was carried out, the Minor Lodge was turned into Grand Lodge and charge was assumed by Knight Sir Joseph Stapleton who in a most impressive manner went through the quaint ritual of raising the chosen Primo to the degree of Knight, preceding the ceremony with a few remarks eulogising Primo Gracey for the useful work he had done for the Order and the "Unity Lodge" in particular…".

29th December 1917
RAOB ANNUAL DINNER

"… [Knight Stapleton] remarked that the closing year had been a most prosperous one for the Order in Malta both financially and as regards initiations and in raising degrees. Special praise was given by Knight Stapleton to Knight J Gracey for his services as Grand Secretary; when he assumed that office the DPL was in a chaotic state but under his regime he had brought it as near to a state of perfection as could be wished for.

The success of the evening was due to the energetic working committee which comprised Kts Stapleton, Gracey and Ashby, Primo Aspinal and Bro. Carter…"

Obvious lessons

It is clear that Joseph and Josephine Stapleton had a large family in Malta after their marriage in 1883 (see Table 6.1). If one includes the infant George Michael Stapleton (1898-1898), this would extend to two sons and eight daughters. At least five of the daughters – including Josephine (also known as Jessie), who died aged 92 – married and lived to good ages. Each of these also returned (or migrated) to southern England or Wales for the latter part of their lives.

For family historians, the research into the Stapletons in Malta confirms two obvious points. First – as shown through the communications with Kevin Chivers and Lucy and through the internet access to the transcribed Maltese records – it is important to develop contacts in areas of mutual benefit. Where possible, of course, it is vital to check for oneself that the information received is correct, but, in the case of both Kevin and Lucy, the critical point is that we were all able to provide information of which the others were previously unaware. In the mathematician's jargon, it is a positive-sum game.

The information that these other researchers have provided (plus that also available from the BMD records and elsewhere) has enabled me to identify at least 8 grandchildren of the sisters of Mary Stella Stapleton, the daughter of the Line of 16's Joseph Stapleton and Guiseppa Brincau. These are more second cousins of my wife, Angela.

The second point is more specific to a Catholic family that crosses national boundaries and cultures. This concerns the complications that are introduced through the combination of the Anglicisation of birth names and the duplication of names between siblings. In many other branches of the Line of 16, there are examples of duplication occurring when one child has died and the later child is given the same name. In Malta, by contrast, the same Christian name was given to more than one living child – or adopted by that child in later life – for example, Florence, Mabel and Mary in the Stapleton family. This adds to the tangled thicket of information through which one is attempting to make progress.

CHAPTER SEVEN

COUNTY MAYO

LINE OF 16: 13. JOHN MURRAY (c1839-?)
and 14. MARGARET MULLOWNEY (c1846-?)

The parish of Burrishoole

The remaining four members of the Line of 16 lived in County Mayo, Ireland. They were the maternal great grandparents of my wife, Angela, and the critical documents that provided access to their details were the 1901 and 1911 Censuses of England and Wales, which gave information on her grandparents, John and Honoria (also known as Annie) Murray.

1901: 3 Lansdowne Place, Gosforth

					Occupation	Where born
John Murray	Head	Married	M	26	Bricklayer's labourer	Ireland
Annie	Wife	Married	F	23		"

1911: 35 Longley Street, Newcastle-on-Tyne

					Occupation	Where born
John Murray	Head	Married	M	37	Tramway Motor Man	Mayo, Burrishoole
Honoria	Wife	Married	F	33		"
Mary Agnes	Daughter		F	8		Northumberland, Gosforth
Thomas Patrick	Son		M	2		Newcastle-upon-Tyne

In 1911, John and Honoria were living with their young family in Newcastle-upon-Tyne. That year's Census record shows that, in both cases, their place of birth was Burrishoole in County Mayo. This means that the births would have been registered in the district of Newport and, sure enough, John Murray was born there on 7th June 1873 and Honor McManamon (the surname being known by Angela) was born on 21st January 1878.

The database for these births is *Ireland, Select Births and Baptisms, 1620-1911*, which, as noted in Chapter 5, has been compiled by the Church of the Latter Day Saints. Crucially, it gives the names of the parents. In the case of John Murray, these were **JOHN MURRAY** (probably 1839-?) and **MARGARET MULLOWNEY** (probably 1846-?). (For consistency, I have taken the younger John Murray's mother's name as that given here, rather than Margret Mullowny, as it appears in the database, as this is the one typically used in the records for John's siblings).

The Ulster Historical Foundation (UHF) researchers I commissioned in 2019 located the marriage between John Murray and Margaret Mullowney as having taken place at the Newport Roman Catholic Church in Srahmore in January 1870. The marriage record names John's father as Pat Murray, a deceased labourer; Margaret's father was Michael Mullowny. (The church records for the parish of Burrishoole only survive after 1870 and thus are not useful in searching for earlier Murray or Mullowney ancestors).

Under the name of Murray in the Burrishoole parish, the researchers found 19 entries in the tithe applotment books of 1832 – although none were in the Srahmore townland – and 13 entries in the Griffith's Valuation of 1857. In Srahmore, the latter dataset included separate entries for Patrick junior, Thomas and Dominick Murray; the researchers have suggested that these could have been family members of John Murray senior after whom some of his sons would later be named (see below).

The corresponding numbers in the Burrishoole parish applotment books of 1832 and the Griffith's Valuation of 1857 for the Mullowney name are 7 and 3, the former including a Michael Mullowney of Pulnashelmeda.

The household of John and Margaret Murray is shown in Table 7.1.

Table 7.1. The family of John and Margaret Murray		
John Murray c1839-? (born in County Mayo) (1911: aged c72 in Srahmore, County Mayo)		
married		
Margaret Mullown(e)y c1846-? (born in County Mayo) (1911: aged c65 in Srahmore)		Mary Murray 1871-1936 (born in Srahmore) (died in Srahmore aged 65)
		Bridget Murray 1872-1872 (born in Srahmore) (died in Srahmore aged 14 days)

	John Murray 1873-1952 (born in Burrishoole, County Mayo) (died in Newcastle-upon-Tyne aged 79) *married* **Honoria (Honor, Annie) McManamon 1878-1967** (born in Burrishoole) (died in Gosforth, Northumberland, aged 89)
	Patrick Murray 1875-1875 (born in Srahmore) (died in Srahmore aged 6 days)
	Thomas Murray 1877-1944 (born in Srahmore) (died in Newcastle-upon-Tyne aged 67) *married* Mary Mason Smith 1883-1938 (born in Alnwick, Northumberland) (died in Newcastle upon-Tyne aged 55)
	Domnick Murray 1879-? (born in Srahmore) (1927: aged 47 in Srahmore) *married* Mary Conway 1882-? (born in Srahmore (tbc)) (1927: aged 45 in Srahmore)
	Michael Murray 1881-1884 (born in Srahmore) (died in Srahmore aged 3)
	Margaret Murray 1884-1921 (born in Srahmore) (died in Srahmore aged 37)
	Patrick Murray 1887-? (born in Srahmore) (1901: aged 14 in Srahmore)

As shown below, the Murray household appeared in the Census of Ireland in both 1901 and 1911 as resident in the townland of Srahmore in the parish of Burrishoole.[1] The headings of the respective characteristics given here were: "name and surname", "relation to head of family", "religious profession", "education", "age and sex", "rank, profession or occupation", "and "Irish language", the last enquiring about whether the individual could speak Irish and/or English. There were also questions on "particulars as to marriage" (single in all cases for the sons and daughters in both years) and "where born" (County Mayo in all cases).

1901

John Murray	Head	Roman Catholic	Cannot read	60	Tenant farmer	Irish & English
Margaret	Wife	"	Cannot read	50	Farm servant	Irish & English
Mary	Daughter	"	Read	25	Farmer's daughter	Irish & English
Dom	Son	"	Read & write	21	Farmer's son	Irish & English
Margret	Daughter	"	Read & write	16		English
Patrick	Son	"	Read & write	14		English

1911

John Murray	Head	Roman Catholic	Cannot read	83	Farmer	Irish & English
Margaret	Wife	"	Cannot read	69		Irish & English
Mary	Daughter	"	Read & write	40		
Domnick	Son	"	Read & write	30	Farmer's son	
Margaret	Daughter	"	Read & write	24	Farmer's daughter	

The Censuses of Ireland in 1901 and 1911 had three questions that were not asked in England and Wales, relating to religion, literacy and the languages spoken. Neither John nor Margaret Murray could read and nor could John write his name; in 1911, he signed the Census form with a cross, witnessed by the enumerator, Patrick Meaney. However, John and Margaret could speak both Irish and English, as could their two oldest children included on the Census forms; for the youngest children, Margaret and Patrick, only English could be spoken.

The 1911 Census of Ireland also provided details about the houses and other buildings in which each household lived. The 5 members of John and Margaret's household lived in 2 rooms of a house that had one window at the front. It was designated as a "3rd class" house – based on the structure of the walls and the numbers of rooms and windows – which was also the standard of most of the other 26 residences in Srahmore. John and Margaret had one outbuilding: a cow house; most of the other households had 2 or more outbuildings and a couple of them had four. The total population of Srahmore was 160 – 80 males and 80 females

---

1 The Censuses are available online from the National Archives of Ireland at www.census.nationalarchives.ie.

– and, of these, the total number of Roman Catholics was 160. Four of the other households were headed by a Murray.

Other sources

One question that was asked in Ireland as well as England and Wales in 1911 concerned the total number of children born to the couple in the marriage and the number still alive. For John and Margaret, this figure was given as 6 in both cases (following the record that they had been married for 42 years). Four of the children were listed in 1901. Of the two absent children, one would be the younger John Murray, of course, who was already resident in England (in Gosforth) in 1901. However, the identification of the other presents something of a mystery as the *Ireland, Select Births and Baptisms, 1620-1911* database includes four other births to John Murray and Margaret Mullowney in Newport, Mayo: Bridget in 1872, Patrick in 1875, Thomas in 1877 and Michael in 1881.

I found a later record for Thomas Murray – a 23 year-old farm labourer born in Newport, Ireland – as resident in Leyland, Lancashire in the 1901 Census of England and Wales. I strongly suspect that this is the 33 year-old of the same name who, 10 years later, was living in Worley Street in the same Westgate district of Newcastle in which John and Honoria Murray were resident in Longley Street.

This suggested that Bridget, Patrick and Michael Murray had died at an early age and, indeed, according to the *Ireland Civil Registrations Deaths Index, 1864-1958*, Bridget Murray died in 1872 and Patrick Murray died in 1876, both aged 0 in Newport. (The UHF researchers confirmed that Bridget had died at the age of 14 days, Patrick at 6 days and Michael at the age of 3 in 1884).

This raised the question of whether John and Margaret Murray had forgotten about Bridget, Patrick and Michael by the time that the 1911 Census of Ireland form was completed. I suspect not. The assumption must be that the question in the Census about the number of children born alive had not been completed correctly by the enumerator (bearing in mind that neither John nor Margaret could read or write). The name Patrick was given to another son in 1887, who appeared in the 1901 Census of Ireland as a 14 year-old in Srahmore and – I think – in the 1911 Census of England and Wales as a 23 year-old general labourer in Salford, Lancashire.

The information on the births to John Murray and Margaret Mullowney is also given in the www.rootsireland.ie database made available by the Irish Family History Foundation. This enables the researcher to track the occupation of John Murray over time: from "landholder" in the years between the births of Mary (1871) and Michael (1881) to "farmer" at the time of the births of Margaret (1884) and Patrick (1887).

The comparison of the 1901 and 1911 Census of Ireland records shows a glaring inconsistency in terms of the ages of John and Margaret. Taken at face value, they appear to have aged by 23 years and 19 years, respectively, between 1901 and 1911 with John's implied year of birth shifting from 1841 to 1828 and Margaret's from 1851 to 1842. Interestingly, however, the marriage record (for January 1870) located by the UHF researchers gives their respective ages as 30 and 23 years, implying that their years of birth were 1839 and 1846 (if their births were post-January). I shall use these as having been the most likely.[2]

The civic registration of BMD in Ireland commenced on 1st January 1864 and a good source for interrogating these databases is the Irish Government's website www.irishgeneaology.ie. From this, it can be seen that Domnick Murray – one of the younger John Murray's brothers – married Mary Conway in 1927. By this time, whilst still bachelor and spinster, their respective ages were 47 and 45. It was Domnick who had taken over the running of the family farm, both his two older surviving brothers – John and Thomas – having migrated to Newcastle. Domnick is also named as the witness on the certificates recording the deaths of his two adult sisters in Srahmore: Margaret in 1921 of pulmonary tuberculosis at the age of 34 (though I think she was 36) and Mary, a 66 year-old servant, of "old age" in 1936.

The fact that John and Thomas Murray migrated to the same city is not surprising, of course. It fits the overall pattern of migration from Ireland (or migration in general) in which family groups established – or were drawn to – a network of contacts in the new location. These networks often extended to occupation as well as residence and would be sustained through the succeeding generations. In the 1911 Census, the occupation of both the 37 year-old John Murray and the 33 year-old Thomas Murray was recorded as "tramway motor man" with Newcastle Corporation. At the time of the 1939 Register, Thomas's son – Thomas Gerard Murray – was a 28 year-old train-driver in Newcastle.

It will be seen in Chapter 11 below that it is John Murray's line that leads directly to my wife, Angela, his granddaughter. One of Thomas Murray's grandchildren was Veronica Mary Rafferty (née Murray) – Angela's second cousin

---

2   One reason why people's ages were sometimes "stretched" between the 1901 and 1911 Censuses of Ireland relates to the introduction of the state pension (for those aged 70 and over with incomes below a certain threshold) which was implemented from January 1909. As noted in Chapter 5, the National Archives of Ireland hold records of searches of the 1841 and 1851 Censuses by applicants wishing to prove their years of birth. There are 25 records under the name of John Murray (though none for Margaret Murray), of which the most promising for our purposes appeared to be for an applicant resident in the townland of Cogaula in County Mayo. I ruled this out, however, given that the John Murray in whom we are interested was resident in Srahmore in both 1901 and 1911.

On a similar track, I also ruled out the death record for the 102 year-old John Murray in Srahmore in January 1924. Even allowing for the inaccuracies in the ages registered at death, this was six years more than that implied by the 83 year-old John Murray's entry in the 1911 Census. In addition, crucially, the witness on this death record was the son, Patrick Murray, who made his mark with a cross; we know from the 1901 Census that John Murray's son, Patrick, could read and write. The centurion was a different John Murray.

– with whom she kept in close contact until Veronica's death in 1999 at the age of 68.

In *Surnames of Ireland*, Edward Neafsay states that the anglicised surname Murray is ultimately derived from the old Irish *muireadhagh*, which had meanings of either seaman or lord. There were several distinct Murray families in different parts of Ireland with, after the Anglo-Norman invasion, the most important based in Counties Galway and Roscommon.

LINE OF 16: 15. FRANCIS McMANAMON (c1836-1882)
and 16. HONOR McMANAMON (c1838-1917)

The household in Srahrevagh

The final members of the Line of 16 are **FRANCIS McMANAMON** (probably 1836-1882) and **HONOR McMANAMON** (c1838-1917), the details of whose family are also to be found in the Census of Ireland records of 1901 and 1911 for the townland of Srahrevagh in the district of Srahmore, in I*reland, Select Births and Baptisms, 1620-1911* and in the www.rootsireland.ie database. The references in the last source to the births of their children include those for Mary (June 1864), Margaret (March 1867), John (April 1869), Francis (March 1871), Bridget (July 1873), Peter (July 1875), Honor (January 1878), Sarah (June 1880) and Francis (1882).[3] The household of Francis and Honor McManamon is shown in Table 7.2.

Table 7.2. The family of Francis and Honor McManamon		
Francis McManamon c1836-1882 (born in Newport, County Mayo) (died in Newport aged 46)		
married		

---

[3] The information provided on the www.rootsireland.ie database contains an intriguing mystery. The marriage record for Patrick McManamon (to Winifred Dyra in Burrishoole in December 1897) gives his parents as Francis and Honor McManamon. However, in Patrick McManamon's birth record (in Clogernah in February 1875), his parents are given as Francis McManamon (landholder) and Margaret Moran. (Honor McManamon was obviously not his mother, as she gave birth to her son – Peter – in July of that year).

Honor McManamon c1838-1917 **(born in County Mayo)** **(died in Srahrevagh, County Mayo, aged 78)**	Mary McManamon 1864-1941 (born in Srahrevagh) (died in Newport aged 76) *married* Patrick McFadian c1855-1930 (aka Patrick Faddin or Fadden) (died in Newport aged c75)
	Margaret McManamon 1867-1959 (born in Srahrevagh) (died in Srahmore aged 92) *married* Domnick Murray 1858-1933 (born in Newport) (died in Srahmore aged 74)
	John McManamon 1869-1945 (born in Srahrevagh) (died in Castlebar aged 76)
	Francis McManamon 1871-1872 (born in Newport) (died in Newport aged 1)
	Bridget McManamon 1873-1875 (tbc) (born in Srahrevagh) (died in Westport aged 2 (tbc))
	Peter McManamon 1875-1931 (born in Srahmore) (died in Srahrevagh aged 55) *married* Bridget (Bridgie) Chambers 1885-1965 (born in Srahmore) (died aged 80)

	Honoria (Honor, Annie) McManamon 1878-1967 (born in Burrishoole, County Mayo) (died in Gosforth, Northumberland, aged 89) *married* John Murray 1873-1952 (born in Burrishoole) (died in Newcastle-upon-Tyne aged 79)
	Sarah McManamon 1880-1959 (born in Srahrevagh) (died in Salamanca, New York, aged 79) *married* James M Nolan 1886-1947 (born in Ireland) (died in Salamanca aged 61)
	Francis McManamon 1882-? (born in Srahrevagh) (1917: aged 35 in Srahrevagh *married* Jane Cleary

The Census information includes the second Francis in the household as a 17 year-old in 1901 and a 29 year-old farmer in 1911. This suggests that the Francis McManamon who was born in Newport in 1871 died at some time before 1882 and, indeed, the death records provided on www.irishgenealogy.ie show that a 1 year-old of this name died in Srahmore in the Newport district in July 1872.

1901

Honor McManamon	Head	Roman Catholic	Can read	62	Farmer, Widow	Irish & English
John		"	Can read	30		Irish & English
Peter		"	Read & write	27		Irish & English
Sarah		"	Read & write	20		Irish & English
Francis		"	Read & write	17		English
Norah Murray		"	Cannot read	4	Visitor	English

1911

Honor McManamon	Head	Roman Catholic	Can read	73	Widow	Irish & English
Francis	Son	"	Read & write	29	Farmer, Single	Irish & English
Peter	Son	"	Read & write	36	Married	Irish & English
Bridget	D in law	"	Read & write	26	Married	Irish & English

Francis	Grandson	"	Cannot read	4	
Mary K	Granddaughter	"	Cannot read	2	
Patrick T	Grandson	"	Cannot read	7 mths	

The birth records for her children indicate that McManamon was Honor's maiden name as well as that of her husband. The 4 year-old Norah Murray listed as a visitor in the household in 1901 was Honor's niece, the daughter of Dominick Murray and Margaret McManamon, the latter being an older sister of Honor.[4] We return to Norah below.

In the 1911 Census, as with the Murray household, there was a generational difference in literacy and language. Honor McManamon could read, but not write, her mark on the Census form again being witnessed by the enumerator, Patrick Meaney. In general, the younger members of the household could speak English, but not Irish, although one of Honor's sons – Francis – did add Irish reading and writing in the period between the 1901 and 1911 Censuses.

At this time, the townland of Srahrevagh comprised two households, headed by Honor McManamon (with 7 people in 3 rooms) and Patrick J McManamon (with his wife and 4 children in 4 rooms). The former also had a cow-house, whilst the latter had a stable, cow-house and piggery. Both homes were designated as "2nd class", the principal difference with the Murray home in Srahmore being that the McManamon dwellings both had 3 windows at the front of the house.

I did wonder if there was a family relationship between Honor McManamon and Patrick J McManamon. At first, it seemed reasonable to assume that there was one, given their proximity in such an isolated location. One possibility was that they were sister and brother, though this was unlikely as they were aged 73 and 46, respectively, in 1911; an alternative explanation was aunt and nephew, either with Patrick being the son of a brother of Honor, or with him being the son of a brother of Honor's deceased husband, Francis. (The common McManamon surname meant that both these were possibilities).

A closer inspection of Patrick McManamon's census returns cleared this matter up completely, however. He and his family were members of the Irish Church – the Protestant denomination – whereas Honor's household was Roman Catholic.

As in the case of John Murray, the information available on www.rootsireland.ie on Francis McManamon at the time of his children's births enables us to track his occupation over time: from "clerk and steward" (1864) to "steward"

---

[4] I did wonder if Norah Murray's father (Domnick) was one of John Murray's brothers. However, this was not the case. As noted, John's brother (Domnick) was aged 30 and single at the time of the 1911 Census; he later married Mary Conway in 1927. The other Domnick Murray was listed in the same Census as a 53 year-old farmer living with his wife (Margaret) and 7 children (including the now 14 year-old Norah) in Srahmore.

(1867, 1869, 1873), "landholder" (1875, 1878) and "farmer" (1880, 1882).[5] Francis died in Srahmore in 1882 at the age of 46. His cause of death was "chronic disease of stomach and vomiting: 6 years certified" and Mary McManamon (probably his 18 year-old oldest daughter) was the informant.[6] This is obviously consistent with Honor's status as a widow in 1901, though much earlier evidence of Francis's death is provided in Mary's own marriage record (in 1884), which reported that her father was deceased. As noted, 1882 was the year of birth of the second of Francis and Honor McManamon's two sons called Francis, which would imply that the 44 year-old Honor was left as a widow with seven surviving children. Honor died in Srahrevagh in 1917 at the age of 78, her status at this time being recorded on the death certificate as "landholder".

Srahmore, England and Chicago

The records on the www.irishgenealogy.ie and www.rootsireland.ie databases allow a picture to be built up of the families of Francis and Honor McManamon's children. The 19 year-old Mary McManamon married Patrick McFadian, a 26 year-old farmer, in Burrishoole in 1884; the record shows that she could not write. It was a similar story when the 21 year-old Margaret McManamon married Domnick Murray, a 30 year-old farmer, in Newport Church in 1890; neither of the couple could write. From a modern perspective, it appears strange that both Mary and Margaret should have been illiterate, given that Francis himself – as a clerk and steward – had obviously been able to read and write; this can only reflect the low significance given to the education of young girls in the rural Ireland of the 1860s and 1870s.

Patrick and Mary are present in the 1901 and 1911 Censuses – initially with the surname of Faddin and then as Fadden – living in the same three-roomed house in Newport. In 1901, Patrick's occupation is given as farmer and shopkeeper, with the order reversed in 1911, by which time they had had eight children, all of whom were still alive. (They had five children and two servants in 1901). Again,

---

5   The hierarchy of estate management in 19th Century Ireland has been summarised by Terence Dooley in "Estate ownership and management in nineteenth and early twentieth century Ireland" in his *Sources for the History of Landed Estates in Ireland* (2000): "Agents were often local solicitors, retired army officers, or wealthy gentlemen. Other more routine administrative duties on an estate were carried out by bailiffs, stewards and agriculturalists. Larger estates sometimes employed surveyors and valuators although individual landlords and their agents often carried out these duties themselves. The day to day running of an estate office, where established, was the duty of an accountant. Large estates also employed a number of clerks".

6   The UHF researchers have suggested that this is the Frank McManmon (sic) of Srahmore who is listed in the Griffith's Valuation. This source also lists John McManmon in the same townland. Could John have been the father or brother of Frank, given that John and Francis are the names of Francis and Margaret McManamon's first two sons? I can only speculate: the McManamon surname and its variants are common in the Burrishoole parish in both the pre- and post-Famine eras.

it is interesting to note that both Patrick and Mary Fadden could speak both Irish and English, though their children spoke English only.

Patrick McFadden (his full name restored in the death register) died in the Newfield district of Newport in 1930 of "old age, probably" – he was about 75 – Mary registering the death with her mark. She died in the same district in 1941 of "senile decay" at the age of about 76.

Of the other children of Francis and Honor McManamon who survived into adulthood, Peter McManamon married Bridget Chambers in Burrishoole in 1905 and Francis McManamon married Jane Cleary in Newport in 1914. (In adulthood, three of Peter and Bridget's children migrated to Chicago in Illinois). As we will see, the marriage of Honoria McManamon to John Murray took place in England, not Ireland, and it is this branch of the family tree that will be picked up again in Chapter 11 below. John McManamon – the 30 year-old in his mother Honor's household in 1901 – did not marry and died in Castlebar in 1945 at the age of 76, the cause of death being "acute gastritis and myoenditis, 2 months certified".

The tree shown for the McManamon family in Table 7.2 (as with that for the Murray family in Table 7.1) is incomplete, most notably in terms of some of the dates of death. In these cases, I have shown the last entry available from the Censuses or other official records.[7]

For some entries, one can make some reasonable assumptions from the available records. For example, one case was that of Francis McManamon, who, as a 35 year-old, was the witness to his mother Honor's death in 1917; as far as I could see, the only appropriate death record in either England or Ireland for a Frank or Francis McManamon was that of a 36 year-old in Croydon in 1918. However, what appear to be authoritative sources on the public pages of Ancestry have reported that Frank died in Newport in 1977 at the age of 94 and his wife Jane (née Cleary) in Castlebar in 1948 at the age of 69.

The same sources note that Bridget McManamon (whom I have tentatively identified as having died as the two-year old daughter of Francis McManamon "landholder" in Westport in 1875) actually lived to the age of 88 and died in Boulder, Colorado, in 1962. All family researchers will be familiar with these types of tantalising – but unconfirmed – possibility for taking the narrative forward. But a certain discipline must be maintained. Whilst I have no reason to doubt the validity of this information, I must seek out further evidence before these details for Francis, Bridget and Jane McManamon can be definitively included in the family tree.

I can be more confident about the family of Margaret McManamon and her husband, Domnick Murray, whom we have seen were married in Newport

---

[7] There was no Census in Ireland in 1921. The first one held in the Irish Free State was in 1926.

in 1890, and this in turn leads to an important finding. In the 1911 Census, Domnick and Margaret are resident in Srahmore with 7 of their children aged between 3 and 17 years (two others having died in infancy and a tenth child born later in the year). Although the parents remained in the locality for the rest of their lives – Domnick dying in 1933 aged 74 and Margaret in 1959 aged 92 – no fewer than 5 of the 6 children who survived into adulthood migrated to Chicago, of whom four married and had families. (Of the adults who did not cross the Atlantic, Peter Murray (1903-1972) remained in Srahmore and Sarah Jane Murray (later Garvey, 1911-2000) migrated to England).

As with most migrations, the significant locational shift of this generation of the Murray family would have been brought about by a combination of "pull" and "push". The former might have been encouraged by the experience of Nora Mary Murray, who migrated in 1913 as a 17 year-old and married Edward Butler in Chicago four years later. (Nora – with an additional 'h' in her name – had been the 4 year-old niece in the household of Honor McManamon in Srahrevagh in 1901). However, given the dates of the other migrations – siblings John Francis Murray and Margaret Mary Murray in 1923 followed by Catherine Elizabeth Murray in 1925 and Bridget Ann Murray in 1927 – the stronger influence is likely to have been the economic and social conditions in County Mayo in the 1920s.

The historians Bernard O'Hara and Nollaig O'Muraile note that, following the War of Independence and the Anglo-Irish Treaty of December 1921:

> "The subsequent split in Republican ranks led to a tragic civil war (1922-23) with a number of so-called "incidents" in County Mayo, but nothing compared to the atrocities which took place elsewhere in Ireland.
>
> The rights and wrongs of the ""civil war" dominated Irish political life for a generation and relegated economic, social and cultural development to second place.... [W]ith a high birth rate and few opportunities for employment at home, numerous sons and daughters of the county became part of the great extended Irish family scattered throughout the globe. The population [of County Mayo] fell from 172,690 in 1926 and 161,349 in 1936..."[8]

It is a now familiar story. We have already identified (in Chapter 5) a network of English/Woods/Magee contacts on Tyneside following migration from Ulster and (above) a similar Murray network in Newcastle, albeit on a smaller scale. The relocation of a significant portion of Domnick and Margaret Murray's family to Chicago meant that – when combined with the three migrants from the family

---

8 The several references to the research of O'Hara and O'Muraile given in this chapter are taken from *History of County Mayo in the West of Ireland*, www.mayo-ireland.ie.

of Peter McManamon and Bridget Chambers (also noted above), there was a substantial network of Murray/McManamon relations on the shores of Lake Michigan from the 1930s onwards.[9][10]

Finally, there was the mystery of Sarah McManamon – the youngest sister of Honor McManamon – who was born in 1881 and a 20 year-old living in Srahrevagh in 1901, but whom I could not find in the English or Irish records after that. Intriguingly, a 26 year-old with this name (and a next of kin named as Mrs McManamon of Srahmore, mother) travelled from Queenstown (the name until 1920 of the port of Cobh) in County Cork to New York in August 1907 on the SS *Baltic* with a final destination given as Chicago.

A 28 year-old Sarah McManamon married James Nolan in Cook County, Illinois in 1915 (implying a birth year of around 1887).[11] The inconsistency of age suggested that this was not the same person, but James's wife then appeared as a 35 year-old when their first child was born in 1917 (implying a birth year of 1882) and a 37 year-old in the 1920 US Census (1883). She was a 40 year-old in the New York State Census of 1925 (1885), her implied year of birth then remaining consistent in the US Censuses of 1930 and 1940. In other words, there was a certain flexibility about the age of this particular Sarah Nolan (née McManamon) in the official US records which caused me to not entirely eliminate her from our enquiries.

This persistence was rewarded. The first-born child of James Nolan and Sarah McManamon was Susan Marion Nolan (1917-2005), who married Francis (Frank) Bruno Fortuna (1916-1997) in 1941. My wife Angela distinctly recalls that, when she was younger, her parents corresponded with the Fortuna family in the United States. (Susan Marion Nolan was a first cousin of Angela's mother, Anne Catherine English (née Murray). Sarah Nolan (née McManamon) was Angela's great aunt).

Frank Fortuna and his wife Susan Marion Nolan Fortuna are buried in the Allegany Cemetery in New York State. Their entry is in the *US Find a Grave Index*, which also reveals that Susan's parents – James M Nolan (1886-1947) and Sarah E McManamon Nolan – are buried in the Calvary Cemetery in Salamanca, New York. (I'm not sure where the 'E' came from). Sarah's dates are given as 1893-1959, implying that she died at the age of 66. However, it is not a surprise

---

9   There are a number of contributors to the Ancestry public pages on the Murray migrants in Chicago, including Jennifer Fulbrook, who has reported in particular on the family of Bridget Ann Murray (1908-79) and Robert E Nicholson (1907-1984).

10   I have not yet made the direct connection between the respective Murray strands – i.e. the Line of 16's John Murray (the father-in-law of Honor McManamon, Table 7.1) and Domnick Murray (the husband of Honor's sister, Margaret McManamon, Table 7.2).

11   James Nolan was also born in Ireland. In 1920, he and Sarah remained in Chicago, where he was a motorman with the Street Car Co; Sarah was the keeper of a boarding house (where they lived) with half a dozen lodgers. By 1925, James and Sarah had moved to Salamanca, New York, where he was a railroad labourer. In the 1930, his occupation is recorded as pipeline labourer.

to learn that she played fast and loose with her age right to the end (and beyond). The adventurous 26 year-old from Srahmore, who had sailed from Queenstown to begin her new life in Chicago over half a century earlier, was actually 79 when she died.

The Courts

There are several references to the Line of 16's Honor McManamon in the *Ireland, Petty Session Court Registers, 1818-1919* database released by the National Archive of Ireland and available on Ancestry. For the most part, these relate to disputes with neighbours – either as complainant or defendant – in alleged cases of trespass by livestock on fields. For example, on 13th August 1889, Honor was the complainant in a case against Peter Connolly that he "did on the 31st July 1889 at Shrarevagh in the County of Mayo unlawfully permit his horse to trespass in the complainant's growing crops of oats and meadow contrary to law". The complaint was upheld with the "portion of fine to be paid to complainant" totalling £18 5 shillings.[12]

The interesting thing about this case is that Peter Connolly's occupation is given as "landholder of Shramore in the Parish of Burrishoole". In other words, Honor McManamon, who by this time was the head of the household following her husband's death three years earlier, apparently had no alternative but to take a near neighbour to court. Likewise, Honor McManamon was also the complainant in the cases of trespass in July 1883 and August 1896 and the defendant in two cases brought in March 1883.

The local frictions are confirmed in the Court Register's records for 7th August 1883. On the same day that John McManamon (one of Honor's sons) was the defendant in a case pursued by Anthony Walsh (of Leamadartaum in Bunaveela) of "unlawfully impounding 7 head of his cattle" from a market pound, Honor McManamon took an action against Martin Walsh (also of Leamadartaum) alleging that he "did unlawfully set on a dog to attack and worry complainant". Both cases were referred for arbitration.

Honor McManamon's entry in the Court Register on 27th March 1888 had more serious consequences. She pleaded guilty to the charge that she did:

> "…unlawfully harbour keep or conceal or knowingly permitted to be harboured kept or concealed in her dwelling house of Srahrevagh aforesaid a quantity of illicit spirits unlawfully made or distilled the full duties whereon

---

12 The unfortunate Mr Connolly had a bad day. The next but one item on the Court's agenda was the charge that he on "the 1st day of August 1889 at Newport in the County of Mayo was found drunk and disorderly on the public streets of Newport aforesaid contrary to law". He was sentenced to 7 days hard labour in Castlebar Gaol in default of the payment of a fine of 6 shillings.

have not been paid contrary to the form of the statute in such case made and provided whereby. The defendant had forfeited the sum of £100".[13]

The sentence handed down was imprisonment of 3 calendar months without hard labour in Castlebar Gaol in the event of a default or distress on the payment of a fine of £6.[14] However, this was not the end of the matter, as there is a subsequent entry (on 28th April) on the same line of the Court Register that is a submission from a government official (whose signature is illegible) based in Dublin Castle:

"Gentlemen
I have the honour to acquaint you that the papers in the case of Honor McManamon having been laid before the Commissioners of Inland Revenue a communication has been received from that Board stating that they must decline to order any mitigation of the penalty of the case.
I have this honour to be gentlemen your obedient servant".

The episode can be followed up using the *Ireland, Prison Registers, 1790-1924* database – also released by the National Archive of Ireland – which records that on 22nd May 1888, Honor was in default in the payment of the fine. She was committed to 3 months imprisonment in Castlebar Gaol (with an expiry date of 21st August) for "having illicit spirits (revenue)". Thereafter, we must revert back to the original line in the Court Register which states that the warrant for imprisonment had been issued on the 6th May. However, below this, there is a series of insertions that suggest that the £6 was paid in two instalments on 31st May and 1st June. It is not clear whether Honor was released from Castlebar Gaol at that point or whether the Commissioners' view that there was no mitigation meant that the full sentence was served.[15] I return to this below.

---

13   A charge on the distillation of spirits in Ireland was introduced in 1661. Private distillation not licensed by the state was outlawed, including that undertaken by a household solely for its own consumption. The 19th Century amendments and consolidations of the laws were introduced in the Illicit Distillation (Ireland) Act of 1831 (which included the £100 forfeit to which Honor McManamon was subject), the Spirits (Ireland) Act of 1854, the Illicit Distillation (Ireland) Act of 1857 and the Spirits Act of 1880.

14   The successive steps in the hierarchy of Honor McManaman's sentence – payment of the fine, (if not) the "distress" and sale of the defendant's goods to pay the fine, (if not again) imprisonment – replicates that handed down to George Rigg in Baldersby, North Yorkshire, five years earlier for his contravention of the Local Authority Regulation concerning the movement of certain animals during a period of Foot and Mouth Disease. George Rigg's sentence was less severe, however: a fine of one pound plus a further 8s 6d to be paid to the informant, if not one month's imprisonment (see Chapter 2 above).

15   In "An insight into old Castlebar Gaol", published in the *Connacht Telegraph* on 23rd May 2020, Tom Gillespie noted that there had been a number of old prisons in Castlebar and that this one had been built between 1830 and 1835. There had been 4 prisoner buildings for males with a separate compound for women and children. Each cell measured 4 feet 6 inches wide and 14 feet long with a bed of bare planks, a small wooden table and chair. Gillespie presumed that there had been a barred window on the outer walls. The Gaol was demolished in 1932 to make way for the Mayo University Hospital.

The entry in the Prison Register did cause me some uncertainty that the Honor McManamon receiving the prison sentence was indeed my wife Angela's direct ancestor and, therefore, one of the Line of 16 due to two of its specific details: that she was aged 59 and that she was a "housekeeper". By contrast, her ages as given in the 1901 (62) and 1911 (73) Censuses and her death record in 1917 (78) consistently imply a year of birth of around 1838/39 and that she was therefore aged about 50.

On the other hand, the earlier Court Register gives her status as "widow and householder" and, critically, the Prison Registers record gives her places of birth and residence as Srahmore and Srahrevagh, respectively. It is the latter location which is significant, I think, given that it was a very small community. The record that she was Roman Catholic and also able to read (but not write) is consistent with Honor's entries in the two later Censuses, though these details are really no more than circumstantial information. Assuming. therefore, that this is indeed the Honor McManamon who was one of the Line of 16, the Prison Register is (ironically) useful in providing a detailed description of her: that is, she was 5 feet 3 inches tall and weighed 10 stones 7 lbs, her eyes and hair were brown and she had a sallow complexion.

I have been struck by the parallel in Honor's McManamon's life experiences with those of Jane Runcorn (née Twaddle), the accidental death of whose husband in 1874 made her a widow aged 44 with eight children (as reported in Chapter 2 above). Of course, there are some differences, not least that Jane lived in a rapidly industrialising urban environment (Warrington), whilst Honor was based in the secluded rural townland of Srahrevagh. But, as noted, Francis McManamon's death at the age of 46 in 1882 meant that Honor was the head of a household in which the eldest of the 7 surviving children was the 18 year-old Mary and the youngest (the second child called Francis) was born in the year of his father's death. It would have needed a strong and determined woman to head the household in these circumstances, but this is what Honor did for some 35 years until her own death in 1917.

For the family historian, there can be something unsettling in the discovery that an ancestor – particularly someone in the direct line – had aspects of their life that are blemished. On my side, as reported in the earlier chapters, there are the examples of the bigamist (Charles Tyler Wilson) and the alcoholic Jane Runcorn, who was a repeat inmate in jail, probably in the Warrington Bridewell. However, I make no judgements about these cases, but rather seek to understand the particular circumstances that led to these outcomes.

For my wife, the challenge is more difficult. Although Honor McManamon died over a century ago, Angela has an affectionate and respectful memory of Honor's daughter, Honoria – Angela's grandmother – who left County Mayo and married John Murray in Preston in 1901 (see Chapter 11 below). Honoria died in Gosforth, Northumberland, in 1967 at the age of 89 and is remembered as someone who lived an unequivocally honest and upstanding life. It has come as a shock to attempt to reconcile the values consistently demonstrated by Honoria with the fact that her mother was sentenced to the harshness of Castlebar Gaol, but – again – it is important for us to have some recognition of (and sympathy with) the specific conditions with which Honor McManamon was having to deal.

An additional point to note here is that there is some evidence – from an unlikely, if incidental, source – that Honor McMamanon's admitted guilt for "having illicit spirits" does not seem to represent a general disregard on her part for the law and its constraints. Although this particular use of the database is somewhat unconventional, it is perhaps relevant that *Ireland, Dog Licence Registrations, 1810-1926* (available on Ancestry and based on data from the National Archives of Ireland) has 17 individual entries for her registering a sheepdog by the end of March each year between 1888 and 1915. (The charges of two shillings for the licence and a sixpence fee were unchanged over the period. What did change were the colours of the dogs: variously, black, black and white, grey, red and yellow).

The issue that I had to resolve was whether Honor McManamon did serve the full 3 month sentence in Castlebar Gaol or whether the apparent payment of the £6 fine secured her release, notwithstanding the Board of Commissioners' dismissal of any mitigation. To advise on this, I consulted Dr Michael O'Connor, a Westport-based expert on illicit distilling and the penal system that applied to it as part of his general research on crime and punishment in 19th Century County Mayo. Having also consulted the Prison Register, Dr O'Connor confirmed that Honor was committed on 22 May 1888 and released on 26 May 1888 after paying the fine. Therefore, her confinement in Castlebar Gaol would only have been for a few days.[16]

The visit to County Mayo

My wife and I visited County Mayo in July 2014. For Angela, it was an opportunity to get a feel for the location of a historical novel she was writing, as well as to see if there was some sort of emotional attachment to the environs in which her mother's ancestors had been born and raised (which there was).

Our starting point was the impressive ruin of the Burrishoole Dominican Friary and the Burrishoole Cemetery, which are a couple of miles from Newport.

---

16 Interestingly, in his research on an earlier period (to 1823), Dr O'Connor found that few of those in Honor McManamon's position actually did pay the fine because they did not have the money. One consequence of this was that the courts and prisons were full of people who were prosecuted and imprisoned for illegal distilling. In the period from 1814 to 1823, no fewer than 413 of the 785 convictions for crime in Mayo – 52 per cent – were for illicit distilling (a revenue crime): as Dr O'Connor described it to me, "everyone was at it" either for domestic consumption or for sale. The data are taken from *County Mayo: A History of Imprisonment, Capital Punishment and Transportation: Anatomy of a County Gaol* (2020), Part 2 of which will cover the period 1835 to 1919.

The Monumental Inscription of the graves in the older section of the cemetery around the friary (www.bernieworld.net/Cemeteries/Burrishoole) lists 5 entries for Murray and 7 for McManamon (or their near spellings). One of the graves is for Peter McManamon – one of the brothers of Honor McManamon and, therefore, a great uncle of Angela – and his wife. The inscription reads: "Sacred Heart of Jesus have mercy on the soul of PETER MCMANAMON, Srahrevagh, Srahmore, died 5th July 1931 aged 55 years. And his wife BRIDGET died 24th May 1965".

The large public house at the end of the road bridge in Newport was licensed to a landlord named McManamon. We made some general enquiries of the middle-aged lady serving behind the bar, who – somewhat disinterestedly, I thought – referred us to someone living a few houses away up a nearby road. Unfortunately, there was no answer at that address and the line of enquiry drew a blank. That did not detract from a good day in Newport, however. The guide in the tourist information centre was very helpful and we had a delightful conversation with the man doing some general tidying up work in St Patrick's Church.

The former townships of Srahmore and Srahrevagh are situated along the minor road that runs to the north of Burrishoole Friary alongside Lough Feeagh. We came across a couple of ruined stone barns and there is a small Srahmore Roman Catholic Church, but otherwise there was not much to see or find. What we did get, however, was a sense of the craggy and undulating countryside. It did not need much imagination to envisage what a harshly difficult living environment this must have presented to the Murray and McManamon families of the 19th Century and earlier.[17]

As ever in this part of the country, the sense of its turbulent history is never far away. The tourist office in Newport is located only a few yards from the site at which Fr Manus Sweeney was hanged in 1799, following the suppression of the previous year's Rebellion.[18][19] Earlier, in Westport, I noted that one of the stained-

---

17   As noted in Chapter 5, *Griffith's Valuation Record, 1847-1864* lists all property holdings in each townland, the person from whom the property was leased and the size of the holding. There is an entry for a John Murray leasing property from his landlord, James Kelly, in Lower Skerdagh in the Burrishoole parish in 1855. The map provided with the index on www.mayolibrary.ie showed that this related to an area adjacent to what is now the minor road heading north from Newport on which we travelled in 2014. However, I cannot confirm that this property record is connected to our Murray family story.

18   In August 1798, the French landed an expeditionary force in County Mayo in support of an insurrection led by the Society of United Irishmen against the British Crown. It surrendered the following month and a second French force was defeated in a naval battle in October.

The abstract of the trial of Fr Sweeney given in the Appendix to "Father Manus Sweeney, 1763-1799" by Sheila Mulloy in the *Journal of the Westport Historical Society* (No. 14, 1994) states that he was found guilty of "levying money for the use of the French force that invaded this country and of being an active rebel leader".

A cross to the memory of Fr Sweeney was erected in the ruins of Burrishoole Friary in 1912. The inscription reads: "This cross has been erected by the parishioners of Burrishoole to the memory of Father Manus Sweeney, a Holy and Patriotic Priest who was hanged in Newport June 8th 1799 because he had bowed with his countrymen in the rebellion of 1798".

19   Dr Mulloy notes that the maiden name of Manus Sweeney's mother was Mulloy and that of his paternal grandmother was MacManamon.

glass windows in St Mary's Church was dedicated "To the memory of deceased members of the third battalion (Westport) IRA".[20] Just outside Westport, at Murrisk on the road to Louisburgh, stands the National Famine Monument. This is a haunting work by John Behan, erected in 1997 to mark the 150th anniversary of the Great Famine, depicting a "coffin ship" of the type that took its human cargo across the Atlantic as ballast, its sails represented as skeletons.

The continued presence in County Mayo

The challenge for the family historian is to place the individuals about whom some information has been found – most obviously, their dates of birth, marriage and death and their places of residence – in the context of the broader economic, social and political circumstances of their time. We have noted above that, for some of those within the post-Line of 16 generation of the extended Murray and McManamon families, this involved migration either to England or North America, and this theme will be explored further in later chapters. For the remainder of this chapter, I shall re-focus on the Murray/Mullowney/McManamon (x2) members of the Line of 16.

It can be seen that, whilst the evidence is not complete, all four were born in County Mayo between about 1820 and 1846. This being the case, the most significant event affecting the childhoods/adolescences/young adulthoods of these members of the Line of 16 would have been the Great Famine of 1845-1849 when, across Ireland as a whole, about a million people died and a further million went into exile. There is general agreement amongst historians that the effects were especially traumatic in County Mayo. Bernard O'Hara and Nollaig O'Muraile state:

> "[T]he catastrophe was particularly bad in County Mayo, where nearly ninety per cent of the population were dependent on the potato. By 1848, Mayo was a county of total misery and despair, with any attempts at alleviating measures in complete disarray. People were dying and emigrating in their thousands... It can safely be said that over 100,000 died in Mayo from the famine epidemic".

---

20 The Killeen Cemetery on the north shore of Newport Bay contains the grave of Michael McManamon, who died in December 1921 at the age of 25. The gravestone, which was erected by his mother Catherine McManamon, states that he was "tortured in prison by British soldiers for being a free and brave soldier of the Irish Republic". The *Ireland Military Service Pension Index, 1916-1923*, published by Defence Forces Ireland at www.mspcsearch.militsaryarchives.ie records that, as well as being a farmer, Michael McManamon was a captain in the West Mayo Brigade of the IRA and notes that the official cause of death was consumption/phthisis pulmonalis. Catherine McManamon was granted an annuity of £150. As far as I am aware, Catherine and Michael McManamon were not related to Francis and Honor McManamon.

Donald E Jordan Jr has summarised the findings of other researchers on why this should have been the case, for example those of Joel Mokyr – "…dependency on the potato for food, low incomes per capita, the lack of an urban population, high rates of illiteracy and a substantial portion of farms under twenty acres" – and SH Cousens – "… the highest Famine mortality occurred in County Mayo during 1847, when relief efforts were at their most inadequate".[21]

For the purposes of this narrative, perhaps the most relevant fact is that the members of the Line of 16 not only survived the Great Famine – recognising that there is an obvious self-selection in this statement, as they are the ones who feature in this family tree – but also remained in County Mayo during the decades that followed. John Murray and his wife Margaret (née Mullowney) were still resident in Srahmore in 1911; Honor McManamon lived until 1917 and died in the Westport district at the age of 78; and Francis McManamon, whilst the Census of Ireland reveals that he had died by 1901, had obviously been alive in the early 1880s, given the years of birth of his children.

In the two families combined, 18 children were born between 1864 and 1887, of whom 13 survived into adulthood. It is important, therefore, to reflect on the post-Famine economic and social circumstances that were faced by these rural families.

The Famine prompted a structural change in Ireland's agrarian economy. O'Hara and O'Muraile make a significant point in this regard:

> "Rather ironically, perhaps, the great reduction in Mayo's population, and especially the virtual annihilation of the formerly numerous class of landless cottiers who had been hardest hit by the Great Famine, enabled those who remained to considerably improve their standard of living in the following decades".

However, around this general observation, there are some important subtleties. Donald Jordan notes that:

> "Famine depopulation and post-Famine land clearances and emigration accelerated a trend, established before the Famine, of consolidation of holdings into larger, more productive ones…. Within the agrarian community, the class balance shifted markedly to the advantage of the larger farmers…
>
> [However], these changes occurred more slowly in Mayo than they did in the more prosperous counties of Ireland. There were proportionately fewer large farm families in Mayo to lead the way…

---

21 *Land and Popular Politics in Ireland: County Mayo from the Plantation to the Land War*, page 108.

> [There were] lines of division between large farmers, concentrated in central Mayo and the small farmers increasingly relegated to the peripheral regions.... Mayo developed more fully than previously into a county that contained two economies and two social systems".[22]

An obvious question to pose concerns which of the "two economies" the households headed by John Murray and Honor McManamon might have been placed in the closing decades of the 19th Century. By simply looking at the map, it might be argued that the townships of Srahmore and Srahrevagh are geographically fairly centrally located within County Mayo with a road heading south to the nearest town of Newport; they are not on the periphery of the county near to the coast that is a long way from the main centres of population.

However, the road to Newport would not have been a major and well-maintained thoroughfare and, significantly, the surrounding countryside largely comprises rough and hilly ground which would not have been conducive to large-scale agricultural development. It is in the central corridor of Mayo that the location of the prime agricultural land was – and is – to be found, as reflected in the land valuations of 1881 (based on that year's Census returns and reproduced by Donald Jordan);[23] in the parishes of the central corridor, the valuation was often in excess of 10 shillings per acre, compared with under 4 shillings in the western periphery of which, in this exercise, the parish of Burrishoole was part.[24]

Further evidence on the status of the two families is provided by the conditions of their respective dwellings at the time of their enumeration in the 1901 and 1911 Censuses. John and Margaret Murray's dwelling was designated as "3rd Class" on both occasions, which does not appear consistent which a huge increase in prosperity, and a single cow house was their only external building. Honor McManamon's Census return in 1911 also recorded a cow house, though not the piggery that had been noted ten years earlier. Nonetheless, her household's dwelling had been upgraded from 3rd Class to fall just within the category of 2nd Class on the basis on an extra window. Neither dwelling had a stable, coach house or harness room.

Of course, it is also of relevance that, notwithstanding the dispersal of some of the household members through marriage or migration, both households

---

22 ibid., pages 104-105.

23 ibid., page 133.

24 This is supported by the events in and following the agricultural crisis of 1879-81, when Ireland again suffered from bad weather and poor harvests. This led to food shortages and unemployment, with western Ireland being particularly affected. The relatively small value of rateable property falling within the Newport Union (which included the townships of Srahmore and Srahrevagh) made it increasingly difficult to raise sufficient funds for the Union's purposes. The Newport Union was officially dissolved by the Irish Local Government Board in September 1885 and amalgamated with the Westport Union (www.workhouses.org.uk/NewportMayo).

provided employment for three of their adult (and unmarried) sons or daughters. All this suggests that John Murray and Honor McManamon headed modest farming enterprises that were certainly not in the extreme periphery of the County Mayo rural economy, but were nonetheless in the second of Jordan's "two economies".

In addition to being years of economic and social change, the period of the Murray and McManamon families living and working in County Mayo was one of political turmoil, particularly from the mid-1870s onwards. O'Hara and O'Muraile have set out the background:

> "The new National Schools… succeeded in reducing the rate of illiteracy by almost half in the forty years between 1841 and 1881. The result was a population with rising expectations and with growing confidence in their own strength and in their ability to bring about a change in conditions".

Events in Mayo provided the springboard for the land agitation in the last two decades of the 19th Century, beginning with a meeting held in Irishtown in April 1879 led by Michael Davitt and James Daly and attended by several thousand people. The National Land League of Mayo was founded in Castlebar the following August, the precursor to the Irish National Land League, which was inaugurated in October with Charles Stewart Parnell as its President.[25]

O'Hara and O'Muraile note that, whilst the story of what became known as the "Land War" – the first and most intense period of which was between 1879-1882 – is part of Irish history, rather than of the Mayo story specifically, Mayo played a prominent role. These were times of frequent violence, including the maiming of cattle, the destruction of property and the wounding and killing of land agents and landlords.

Again, however, it is important to recognise the local variations that existed within Mayo in the aims of those conducting the Land War. The driving force came from the owners of the larger grazing farms and the urban merchants in the centre of the county for whom the War had an over-riding political context, rather than being simply about agrarian rents or evictions. Donald Jordan states that:

> "The large landholders and merchants wanted the full extension of capitalism in the countryside, through the abolition of the landlord monopoly on land ownership, and sought to seize political power from the landed gentry and, if necessary, from the clergy. In contrast, the smaller farmers, who had no

---

25 It was the campaign of ostracism against a landlord's Mayo agent – Captain Charles Boycott – that introduced the new word "boycott" into the English language.

objection to assaulting landlordism, hoped for a more equitable distribution of the land at the expense of both landlords and large tenant graziers".[26]

These differences in objective between those seeking fundamental political change at the national level – through the abolition of landlordism and/or the introduction of Home Rule (or independence) – and the smaller farmers focusing on the immediate challenges of rent payments and potential eviction were given a clearer definition in the agricultural depression of the late 1870s. Drawing on returns compiled by the Royal Irish Constabulary, Jordan estimates that the number of families evicted (and not re-instated) in County Mayo rose from 6 in 1876 and 27 in 1878 to 114 in 1881 and 559 in 1884. Against this background he notes that the small farmers of Mayo "lost faith in the small farm economy…. leading [them] to find their own solution to the land agitation: emigration"; the 1883 figure of over 7,800 emigrants from Mayo was the largest for a single year since the Famine.[27]

> "[It] was an acute economic crisis that crumbled the pillars of the small farm economy. A decline in demand for seasonal labour in Britain, the loss of easy credit, the potato failure, depressed cattle market and the decline of the chicken population combined to raise the spectre of famine".[28]

This was a period which, of course, the Murray and McManamon households experienced and endured (and in which there occurred the death of Francis McManamon in 1882).

Eventually, however, the agrarian issue reached a peaceful resolution, the process for which was begun by the second Land Act of 1881 of WE Gladstone's Liberal Government which

> "… corrected some of the most glaring abuses of landlord power, established land courts to arbitrate rent disputes, and laid the foundation for the transfer of land ownership from landlords to working farmers".[29]

In his *Ireland: A History*, Robert Kee notes that, in subsequent legislation:

> "…Parliament completed a great social revolution on the land… By a series of so-called Land Purchase Acts, the Irish tenant was enabled to become the owner of the land he farmed. 'Land Purchase' meant that the State bought

---

26 op. cit. page 196.
27 ibid., Table 4.1, page 115; page 312.
28 ibid., page 208.
29 ibid., page 1.

out the landlords, advancing mortgages to the former tenants over a long period to be paid off by annual instalments which with interest usually amounted to less than the previous rent. As a result of two further great Land Purchase Acts in 1903 and 1909, the latter of which introduced the principle of compulsory sale by landlords, 11 million acres had changed hands by 1920 and the sale of a further two million acres was being negotiated – by far the greater part of the land of Ireland".[30]

O'Hara and O'Muraile succinctly summarise the huge significance of these developments:

> "Tenant farmers became owner-occupiers within a generation and in the process created the foundations for the politically stable society we enjoy today".

I have summarised some of the academic research on the agrarian economy and society of the era because the Murray and McManamon families lived through these turbulent times. By 1901, the occupation of John Murray was given in the Census of Ireland as "tenant farmer", whilst that of Honor McManamon was "farmer". 10 years later, John Murray was also a "farmer".

It remained the case, however, that the country's progress in moving towards a more equitable distribution of land ownership did not prevent the migration of many of the most ambitious out of Ireland. As we have seen, by 1901, their respective son and daughter of the Line of 16's John Murray and Honor McManamon – the 26 year-old John Murray and his 23 year-old wife Annie (Honoria) – were living in Gosforth, Northumberland.

---

30 Pages 142-145.

PART TWO

Great Grandparents:
THE LINE OF EIGHT

We have already come across the Line of 8: Tom and Katie's great grandparents. In the order that they will be introduced in the following chapters, they are:

		Dates	Place of birth
*	John Rigg	1887-1959	Baldersby, North Yorkshire
*	Catherine Kerr McBride	1893-1969	Govan, Glasgow, Scotland
*	Alfred Edgar Niblett	1888-1973	Osnabrück, Germany
*	Marie Rosa Wilson	1890-1968	Wood Green, London
*	Arthur Joseph English	1892-1970	North Shields, Northumberland
*	Mary Stella (Eugenia) Stapleton	1899-1978	Sliema, Malta
*	John Murray	1873-1952	Burrishoole, County Mayo, Ireland
*	Honoria (Honor, Annie) McManamon	1878-1967	Burrishoole

Not surprisingly, the ranges in the years of birth and the years of death have narrowed compared with the Line of 16. These are 26 years in both cases. The list of the places of birth comprises 4 localities within the UK and 3 within other European countries.

Each member of the Line of 8 lived into old age. Notwithstanding the dramatic (and, at times, dangerous) circumstances through which they lived – including two world wars, of course – the youngest age at death was John Rigg at 72. Some caution is required here, however: the 4 family members of the next generation – Tom and Katie's grandparents – were all born after the First World War, so there is an obvious circularity in noting that each member of the Line of 8 survived that conflict.

CHAPTER EIGHT

RIGG/McBRIDE

The Royal Garrison Artillery

Our children's great grandfather – **JOHN RIGG** (1887-1959) – was the fourth of Henry and Jane Rigg's eight children. He died when I was four years old and, whilst I think I remember him, I cannot be sure. It is more likely that the dominant image of the tall, elderly white-haired man has come to me solely from the photographs of the time.

The earliest family document I have seen on John Rigg was passed on to me by my aunt May. It was a reference that he had received at the age of about 14 in 1901 or 1902, when seeking a job on the North Eastern Railway, given by A W Howard ("Trinity College, Cambridge") of Torquay. Rev. Howard had been the vicar in the parish of Pickhill and had "never had any fault to find with him… for he was a good steady lad". My father said that, when only a few years older, John (his dad) and his brother Robert had been big, strong farm boys, an impression confirmed by my uncle Jack, who recalled that he had been "a tough fellow… able to lift eighteen stones of grain".

The early photographs of John Rigg were to be found in Jack's album, including of his pre-First World War police career. One – labelled Hull Dock Strike 1911 and taken by A.C. Garton of Hull – would have dated from two years after he joined the force. About 50 policemen (and there seem to have been others just out of the picture) are standing or sitting in 6 rows; John is standing on the fourth row.[1]

---

[1] An online entry entitled "The Great Unrest 1910-11: Part 5: Hull", posted at www.rooksmoor.blogspot.com, draws on *The Hull Strikes of 1911* (1979) by Keith Brooker.
Local dock trade union leaders called a strike on 20th June 1911, following earlier dock strikes on the south coast and in neighbouring Goole and a series of other strikes in the city. Although a deal was reached with the union leaders, it was rejected by the workforce and the strike escalated into a riot involving the wrecking of shipping companies' offices and the looting of shops. A total of 1,300 police reinforcements were called from other constabularies, including London and Leeds. Two squadrons of cavalry were held on standby in York, but these were not needed as, on 4th July, most strikers accepted the original settlement and returned to work.

The photograph in Hull was taken two months after the 1911 Census of England and Wales, when John Rigg was resident in the household of Alfred Gale, a 47 year-old police inspector, and his wife Emma in Hunslet, Leeds. There were a total of 12 people in the household, including 5 other police constables aged between 22 and 29, so this represented his (temporary) extended family after his move from North Yorkshire.

John had been working as a porter on the railway when he joined the police force in September 1909. The *West Yorkshire, England, Police Records, 1833-1914* – made available by the West Yorkshire Archive Service (WYAS) on Ancestry – note that he was 5 feet 11 inches tall and a Wesleyan. Having been appointed as a "Second Class Constable", he was promoted to "First Class Constable" after a year. This particular set of records covers the period to the end of December 1919, during which time John's promotions continued to be based on years of service, including to the "10 Years Service Class" in September 1919.[2]

Another photograph in Jack's collection showed a tough-looking man in his First World War army uniform. The *British Army World War I Service Records, 1914-1920* summarise John Rigg's war record beginning with his Oath of Attestation of 22nd September 1915. Once again, the rudimentary personal details seem strangely poignant: age, 28 years 4 months; height, 5 feet 11¼ inches; girth when full expanded, 39 inches. Catherine Kerr Rigg was given as the next-of-kin.

John Rigg and Catherine McBride had married the previous year and their address in the Oath of Attestation was given as 54 Moor Crescent, Dewsbury Road, Leeds. We noted in Chapter 2 that this was also the address given for Catherine's parents – Peter and Agnes McBride (with 6 of their other children) – in the 1921 Census. It is clear, therefore, that for at least the first 18 months of their marriage, John and Catherine were living with the latter's parents and family.

My dad described to me his own father's wartime experience. John Rigg was with 225 Siege Battery of the Royal Garrison Artillery (RGA) in France when a gun battery blew up, burying him for some time and badly injuring his spleen. His casualty report of 26th August 1918 stated that he was "seriously ill" and that his next-of-kin were to be informed. The spleen was removed in Manchester General Hospital by Sir Berkeley Moynihan, one of the day's most distinguished surgeons and later the first Baron Moynihan of Leeds (1865-1936). According to dad, 300 police officers had offered to give blood.

John Rigg was discharged from the RGA on 23rd October 1918 judged "no longer physically fit for war service" in line with Para 392 (xvi) of the King's Regulations. His disability of "splenic anaemia agg 60%" entitled him to a weekly

---

2   Having volunteered for service, John Rigg joined the Army in September 1915. The period in Army service counted for "the purposes of pension or gratuity" in the police force "in accordance with [the] resolution of the Watch Committee of 13th November 1914 and Emergency Legislation".

pension of 16s 6d, which was to be reviewed after 52 weeks. The King's Certificate on his discharge was dated 18th November 1918 i.e. one week after Armistice Day. His address on discharge was 49 Pemberton Street, Dewsbury Road, Leeds.[3] With reference to medals, the records stated that John Rigg received the "SW & V" in September 1921.[4]

After the war, again according to the family anecdote, John Rigg was not initially issued with a new police uniform because it was thought he would not survive long enough. (The story was that he threw the second-hand one he had been given back at the supplying officer and demanded to be measured for a new one). In the event, he became the acting desk sergeant at Beeston police station in south Leeds, retiring in 1935 at the age of 48 (as noted in footnote 4, the year of his receipt of the King George V Silver Jubilee Medal). He returned to the police service when the Second World War broke out four years later.

My father was born in March 1921, 2½ years after John Rigg had sustained his life-threatening injuries. Such are the fragile circumstances on which all our existences depend.

The death of Robert Rigg

John Rigg's brother, Robert, was older by two years, having been born in Baldersby in 1885. As before, my uncle Jack's precious album included some photographs of him. He had a strong, penetrative eyes which, together with a thick moustache, gave character to his face. In one photograph, he is dressed in his best suit and sitting informally on the corner of a table. In another, he is standing to attention in his police uniform (number 344) in a country lane with the rim of his helmet shading his eyes.

The *1907-1911 Examination Book for the West Riding (of Yorkshire) Constabulary* has also been made available online by the WYAS. Robert's signature

---

3   The 1921 County Series of Ordnance Survey maps of Yorkshire shows that Moor Crescent (or Moor Crescent Road) and Pemberton Street were parallel roads within the complex of shops and back-to-back terraced housing on the opposite side of the main road from the Dewsbury Road police station, where John Rigg later worked as a desk sergeant. None of the street's original housing remains – it is now an open space overlooked by the two imposing blocks of Crescent Towers – although there is a short (and different) street called Moor Crescent. A nearby war memorial is situated within the garden of an old-peoples' home.

There are some evocative photographs of Moor Crescent Road (including number 54) and Pemberton Street, taken in 1958 and 1959, on the Leodis photographic archive of Leeds at www.leodis.org.

4   The Silver War Badge was awarded from September 1916 to officers and men who were discharged or retired from the military forces as a result of sickness or injury caused by their war service; 1.15 million were issued.

I do not know what became of John Rigg's Silver War Badge. However, three other of his medals were passed on to my father and, from him, to my sister Rosie. Two of these were very widely issued: there were 5.7 million recipients of the Victory Medal and 6.5 million recipients of the silver British War Medal 1914-1918, which was established in July 1919 (www.greatwar.co.uk). The third award was the King George V Silver Jubilee Medal, which was received in 1935. About 85,000 of these were issued, including to government officials and public servants.

is given to confirm his date of appointment as 20th July 1908, when he was aged 23. He had previously been with the railway police of the North Eastern Railway Company for 1¾ years. Robert is described as 5 ft 9½ inches tall with a fair complexion, blue eyes, dark brown hair and, under "particular marks", a cut mark on the back of the head. The police record shows that he advanced from 3rd to 2nd Class on 1st August 1909 and from 2nd to 1st Class on 16th October 1910.

My father and I visited Robert Rigg's grave in the Montigny Cemetery Extension of the Montigny-sur-Hallue cemetery in June 1990. I had been keen to locate the site ever since dad had mentioned Robert's death during our initial family history conversation in the Travellers' Rest in Harewood three years earlier. We were on a pilgrimage organised by the Pilgrimage Department of the Royal British Legion; I had first contacted the War Graves Commission Enquiry Department in Maidenhead in May 1989 and they had informed me that Robert had been in D Battery of the 232 Brigade of the Royal Field Artillery.[5]

As the crow flies, Montigny-sur--Hallue is about 6 miles from the north-eastern outskirts of Amiens. Robert Rigg died on the day before the start of the Battle of Amiens (also known as the Third Battle of Picardy) on 8th August 1918: the opening phase of the Allies "Hundred Days Offensive" that ultimately led to the end of the war. Allied forces advanced over 7 miles on the first day, one of the greatest advances of the conflict. The Battle of Amiens was notable for being one of the first to involve armoured warfare and for the large number of surrendering German troops.

Wikipedia's account of the preliminaries to the battle draws on Gregory Blaxland's *Amiens* (1981). It states that there was some concern among the Allies on 6th August when the German 27th Division actually attacked north of the Somme on part of the front on which the Allies planned to attack two days later. The German division (a specially selected and trained *Stosstruppen* formation) penetrated roughly 800 yards into the one-and-a-half mile front before moving back towards its original position on the morning of 7th August. For some time, I did wonder whether it was this particular German assault that brought about the death of Sergeant Robert Rigg.

However, I think that the *War Diary of 232 Army Field Artillery Brigade* – made available at The National Archives – enables me to work out what happened.

The entry for 4th August 1918, when the Brigade began the day in the village of Beauquesne – about 20 miles north/north-east of the city of Amiens – states "Brigade receives orders to march to Behencourt and leaves at 9pm". This was a distance of about 8 miles to the south east. The entry for 6th August then states "Brigade goes into action at Ribermont". This was a further 5 miles or so.

---

5   In the major re-organisation of January 1917, the artillery brigades were removed from Divisions and placed with the Army Corps. The 232 Brigade of the Royal Field Artillery became the 232 Army Field Artillery Brigade.

After that, the War Diary focuses on the Battle of Amiens which, as noted, began on 8th August. The entry for the 7th states "Position stocked with ammunition and everything prepared for attack tomorrow" and that of the 8th includes "Attack on Morlancourt. Partially successful".

Robert Rigg died on 7th August. Accordingly, my best guess is that he was killed or fatally injured at Ribermont on the previous day, having completed the march to Behencourt on the 4th. Had he been injured before the 4th, he would not have been taken from Beauquesne to Behencourt.[6]

The Montigny-sur-Hallue cemetery

The war cemetery at Montigny-sur--Hallue is about half a mile from Behencourt. It is a lovely place. Montigny-sur-Hallue is a small village north-east of Amiens on the D919 road between Bavelincourt and Frechencourt in the Departement of the Somme. On either side of the cemetery, which is itself small, are the two smaller extensions for the war graves. Robert Rigg lies in the West Extension, which we entered under an archway towards a cenotaph. He is one of about 15 graves in a single line, the fifth from the far end. As with all the cemeteries we visited on this trip, the plot was immaculately maintained with the short grass neatly trimmed and edged.

The white headstones had a uniform height and design. On Robert's was engraved:

L/27582 SERJEANT
R. RIGG
ROYAL FIELD ARTILLERY
7TH AUGUST 1918

Robert Rigg had been killed just over three months before Armistice Day – and just under three weeks before his brother John received his own life-threatening injuries.

I was told by Colin Nutt, the British Legion council member who accompanied the pilgrimage, that Robert was almost certainly buried in the cemetery, otherwise the inscription would have said "buried near this site". My father laid the two wreaths that we had been given by the British Legion and planted one of the two small crosses. Attached to one of the wreaths we added:

In memory of ROBERT RIGG
Of Pickhill, North Yorkshire
With Love and Thanks. Rest in Peace

---

6 Further information on Robert Rigg's death is given in footnote 20 below.

John Alexander Rigg	BOB RIGG
William A Rigg	JOHN K RIGG
	BILL RIGG
	MAY RIGG

June 29th 1990

Dad and I signed the note on the left hand side and, on the right, we listed the names of the children of John Rigg, Robert's brother, including my father (Bill). We agreed afterwards that we had both felt a lump in the throat on approaching the grave. Dad said that he had been keen to put the wreaths down on it in order to give himself something to do and help compose himself.[7][8]

In my diary of the trip, I remarked that, although each of the 17 cemeteries we visited had its own distinctive character – in size, shape and entrance – all were peaceful and quiet. On the Sunday, we attended a commemoration service at the Thiepval Memorial; it was 1st July 1990: the 74th anniversary of the first day of the Battle of the Somme. A strong wind and squally showers drove us under the trees for part of the service. The surrounding fields were of corn ripening in the breeze. Poppies grew at the roadside.

I also noted that, as might have been expected within a pilgrimage group such as ours, there was a mixture of characters: the First World War widow of 95 years of age doing her keep-fit exercises on the bus; the pleasant couples from Scarborough and Newcastle; the loud chap in the seat in front of us. Dad and I were impressed by the British Legion's organisation of the trip, which was managed by Stuart Campbell MC. It was not his fault that we waited for over 10 hours outside

---

7 In the 1911 Census, Robert Rigg was the sole boarder in the household of George and Ann Lee in Grassington, North Yorkshire. I had initially thought that he had been in the North Yorkshire Police Force and it was therefore something of a disappointment when his name was not to be found in *The ultimate sacrifice in the Great War: the twelve North Yorkshire Constabulary police officers who died as soldiers*, a booklet prepared by Jane Palmer, North Yorkshire Police's Chief Finance Officer, for the dedication of a new memorial garden in Northallerton in October 2017.

Closer inspection of the Census record reveals that Robert's employment in 1911 was with the West Riding Yorkshire Constabulary. However, Grassington is some way from the West Riding (and also from Robert's parents' household in Pickhill) and it is not obvious why he should have been living there at the time.

Some light on this might have been thrown by Keith Taylor in his *Swaledale & Wharfedale Remembered: Aspects of Dales' Life Through Peace and War*, which was published in 2006. He reports that Robert had indeed been a popular officer in Grassington for three years before moving on. He was serving in the Normanton area, between Wakefield and Castleford (in the West Riding), when he enlisted with the West Riding Regiment in August 1915, embarking to France in January 1916.

8 I noted in Chapter 1 that I had been frustrated by the prevalence of evident transcription errors when the 1911 Census of England and Wales was made available at the end of 2009. (My letter to the *Cleveland Family History Society Journal* on this, published in January 2010, is reproduced in Annex A2 below). One of the errors was in relation to Robert Rigg, whose surname was transcribed as "Rigy". As mentioned in the letter:

"The error relating to Robert Rigg was particularly galling. Robert was killed in action in France in August 1918 at the age of 33. The 1911 Census was, of course, the last in which he – and so many others – was recorded. The least we can do is show him due respect and get his details right".

Boulogne before being diverted to Calais by a French seaman's strike. (This was before the opening of the Channel Tunnel, of course). We spent part of the time listening to the commentary on the bus's radio of the England/Cameroon World Cup quarter-final.

Telegrams

Over the years, I learned that Robert Rigg was not the only casualty within the extended Rigg family in the First World War. I was first alerted to this in 1994 in correspondence with another Robert Rigg – the son of Douglas Rigg and a great nephew of my grandfather, John – who had referred to the family in Pickhill receiving telegrams (in the plural) during the war and how the recollection of this had distressed Douglas in his old age. Drawing on information provided in the Census records and on the website of the Commonwealth War Graves Commission (www.cwgc.org), I came across 4 other casualties:

* Harry Rigg (1893-1918) was a grandson of William Rigg, Henry Rigg's oldest brother. Harry was a gunner in the North Riding Heavy Battery of the Royal Garrison Artillery when he was killed in France aged 25. He is commemorated at the Soissons Memorial in Aisne. In the 1911 Census, Harry had been a 17 year-old clerk in an iron and steel works in Stockton, one of the first members of the extended family to find white-collar employment.

* William Rigg (1891-1917) was the grandson of another of Henry's brothers, George. He was a private in the 1/5th Battalion, Durham Light Infantry, when he was killed in France aged 25. He is commemorated at La Neuville Cummal Cemetery, Corbie.

* Tom Rigg (1889-1918) was another of George Rigg's grandsons. He was killed in Belgium at the age of 28, having been a private in the 13th Battalion, Princess of Wales's Own (Yorkshire Regiment). His body was not recovered and he is commemorated on the Ploegsteert Memorial, Hainaut. Tom was born in Baldersby and his name is also on the war memorial – "See what great things they have done for us" – inside the St James Church in the village. We noted in Chapter 1 that his brother Edward – born in 1891, younger by two years and the probable 16 year-old cricketer representing Baldersby

in 1907 – lived to the age of 91 and died in Harrogate in 1982. Such are the quirks of fate.[9]

* Thomas Hyland (1886-1918) was the husband of Gertrude Rigg (1891-1967), a granddaughter of Henry Rigg's brother, Robert. After marrying in 1915, Thomas and Gertrude had a son – Thomas Bertram Hyland – in 1916. Thomas senior, a native of County Offaly in Ireland and a private in the 884th Mechanical Transport Company of the Army Service Corps, was killed in Belgium two years later. He is buried in the Lijssenthoek Military Cemetery in Poperinge, West-Vlaanderen. Gertrude Hyland later married Stephen Campion (1891-1938). Thomas Bertram Hyland lived to the age of 87 and died in Stockton in 2004.[10]

Some supplementary information on these fatalities is provided by the *Army Registers of Soldiers' Effects, 1901-1929*, which is available on Ancestry, and draws on the "Soldiers Effects Records, 1901-60" files of the National Army Museum in Chelsea. The introductory paragraph states:

> "This database contains records detailing the money owed to soldiers of the British Army who died in service from 1901 to 1929. A small percentage of soldiers who were discharged as 'insane' are also listed here… Payments went first to widows or, if the soldier wasn't married, to a parent (often a mother) or siblings".

---

9   I learned from Steve Erskine – Researcher at the Green Howards' Museum in Richmond, North Yorkshire – that Tom Rigg had been a pre-war Territorial soldier. His death is recorded on the Roll of Honour in *The Green Howards' Gazette*, Volume XXVI, No. 309, p19, June 1918. Mr Erskine copied across to me the relevant section of the *War Diary of 13th Battalion, Yorkshire Regiment*, which describes in the usual precise detail the engagement in operations in the Bois Grenier area south of Armentieres between 9th-12th April 1918. Tom Rigg's Medal Index Card, which states that he was entitled to the British War Medal and the Victory Medal, includes a stark (and poignant) entry in its "Remarks" column: "dead".

10   Thomas Hyland's role in the MTC was appropriate. On 14th August 1914, he had placed an advertisement in the *Yorkshire Post and Leeds Intelligencer*:
> Wanted. Situation as CHAUFFEUR; 7 years' clean license; careful driver; all running repairs; age 27 – Thomas Hyland, High Street, Yarm.

Thomas's unblemished driving record had not been without incident, however, as reported – three years earlier, on 3rd August 1911 – in the *Daily Gazette for Middlesbrough*:
> CHAUFFEUR IN DILEMMA
> Thomas Hyland, chauffeur of Barton House, Thornaby, was charged under the Motor Car Act at Stockton today with driving a motor car to the danger of the public… Sergt Humphreys stated that… several people were about at the time and when the sudden turn was made [by Hyland] they had to run quickly to get out of danger.
> Thomas Hyland was (successfully) defended by Mr TW Malkin and the Bench dismissed the case on payment of costs.

I looked up the details for the 5 members of the extended Rigg family whom I knew to have been killed in the First World War. It made for sad reading; the sums involved were pitifully low. I assumed that the sums were for the outstanding pay at the time of death. In some cases, an additional War Gratuity had been given at a later date; in others, the War Gratuity was included in the original sum.

In the case of Robert Rigg, "£18 15s 2d was authorised for payment to Robert's father, Henry, on 6th November 1918. A further War Gratuity of £17 was authorised on 9th December 1919". The bureaucratic mindset of the times was confirmed by the payments to the widow of Thomas Hyland – Gertrude – of £8 10s 9d and £17 1s on 10th May 1919 and 22nd July 1920, respectively. Incredibly, 4d was deducted to pay for a stamp.

The First World War casualty list extended to the branches of other families linked to the Rigg family by marriage, of course. One of the names on the memorial at St Mary's Church in Thirsk is WH Boynton, who was a private in the Yorkshire Hussars (Alexandra, Princes of Wales' Own) when he died of his wounds in France in September 1917 at the age of 20. He was William Henry Boynton – one of the sons of Wilson and Jane Boynton – who was born in Middlesbrough in 1897 and resident in Thirsk as a 14 year-old at the time of the 1911 Census. He is buried in the Bucquoy Road Cemetery, Ficheux, Nord-Pas-de-Calais.

Wilson Boynton had been born in Sowerby in 1859, a son of Thomas and Ellen Boyanton (as spelt in the 1861 Census).[11] In turn, Thomas had been born in Thirkleby in 1834, the son of John Boynton (c1801-1878) and his wife Jane (née Holmes, 1798-1860).

We have already come across John Boynton. In Chapter 1, it was seen – based on the researches that Virginia Burrell posted on the public pages of Ancestry – that he was also the father of William Boynton (1822-1895) who, in turn, was the father of Jane Boynton (1859-1939), the wife of my great grandfather, Henry Rigg (1847-1920). In other words, Jane Boynton was a second cousin of Wilson Boynton, the father of the ill-fated William Henry Boynton commemorated at St Mary's Church in Thirsk.

Moving on to the next generation, William Henry Boynton was a third cousin of my grandfather John Rigg (1887-1959) and his brother Robert, the latter

---

11   Thomas Boynton (1834-1905) married Ellen Lofthouse (1833-1879) in 1858. After Ellen's death at the age of 46, Thomas married the 48 year-old spinster, Mary Lofthouse, four years later. She outlived him by 14 years, dying in the Thirsk district in 1919 at the age of 83.
    I did wonder if Ellen and Mary were sisters. However, this turned out not to be the case. Ellen was one of the children of John Lofthouse and his wife Jane (née Spears) of Sowerby. John and Jane died within two months of each other in 1876 at the ages of 76 and 83, respectively (see *North Yorkshire, England, Church of England Deaths and Burials, 1813-1995*). Mary's mother was another Jane Lofthouse, a spinster who gave birth illegitimately and later (in 1841) married George Turner, but who died in the Thirsk district in 1846. Mary Lofthouse is recorded as the daughter (though probably the step-daughter) of the widowed George Turner in the 1851 Census of England and Wales.

sharing with him the sad fate of not surviving the killing fields of France in the First World War.[12]

Other First World War action

Given the size of the family into which John Rigg's father – Henry – had been born in 1847 (as shown in Table 1.1 above), it is not surprising that a considerable number of John's distant cousins were also heavily involved in the First World War. The *British Army World War I Service Records, 1914-1920* show, for example, that two more of the grandsons of William Rigg (Henry's oldest brother) enlisted in November 1914: the 23 year-old Walter Rigg was posted with the Machine Gun Corps (MGC) and contracted malaria in Salonika, Greece;[13] his younger brother, Alfred, was with the British Expeditionary Force (BEF) when he was wounded in France in July 1917. Looking at the records, I was again touched by the personal details: Walter was 5 ft 6½ ins tall with "a fresh complexion, blue eyes, light brown hair and a 'good' physical development" (as one would expect of a farm labourer); on his discharge from the Army in March 1919, a certificate recorded that he was "in possession of a greatcoat". The two brothers survived the war: no small miracle in Walter's case, as he also contracted influenza.

Likewise, Stephen Rigg – another of William Rigg's grandsons – was stated in a medical report of March 1919 as having a "history of malaria" brought about by "active service and malarial climate" (in Salonika again, where the disease was rife). His catalogue of wartime misfortune also included a bullet wound received in April 1917, though this was not sufficient for him to qualify for any sort of disability award after the war: on an Award Sheet dated May 1919 is twice written "reject". Stephen Rigg married Catherine (or Katie) Coulton in Middlesbrough in 1920 and lived to the age of 71; through the Ancestry connection, I have had a nice e-mail correspondence with his great granddaughter, Nicola Burnham.

A post-war disability payment was made to William Kitching – the husband of Minnie Hare, who was a granddaughter of one of Henry Rigg's sisters (Elizabeth Rigg, 1837-1863) – who was "dangerously wounded" in France in June 1916, spending time in hospital in Rouen and Stourbridge before returning to France in February 1917. Injuries to his buttock and groin meant that he qualified for a weekly pension of 12s for himself and 5s 3d for his wife and child in July 1921; these sums were increased two months later before reverting back to their original amounts in March 1922 (until September of that year). Thankfully, the

---

12 Annex A4 – "The Roll of Honour" – lists all those described in this narrative as having died whilst in HM Forces, plus one American casualty.

13 Wikipedia notes that a total of 170,500 officers and men served in the MGC, of whom 62,049 were killed, wounded or missing.

injuries did not prevent William and Minnie having three more children after the war.

Like the ill-fated Tom Rigg, William Kitching had been a pre-war Territorial, prior to enlisting in the 1st Battalion of the West Yorkshire Regiment (Prince of Wales' Own), famously known as "The Leeds Pals" in March 1915, his "trade or calling" having been as an insurance agent. Steve Erskine of the Green Howards' Museum informed me that the battalion suffered badly at Serre on the Somme in 1916. It is fortuitously ironic, therefore, that the "dangerous" wounds that William Kitching incurred in the middle of June 1916 might well have saved his life, given that the major offensive in the Somme was to commence only two weeks later on 1st July.[14]

I could go on, but the underlying message from the published Army records of the First World War is clear. Virtually every family was affected in some way and, even when the protagonists survived, the poignancy of the everyday detail – the home address, the civilian occupation, the naming of next-of-kin, the locations of active service – becomes very powerful, not least because it is usually in handwritten form with the urgency of the immediate.

Some of the detail does raise questions about those involved. One member of the extended family tree (not mentioned above) was discharged as "no longer physically fit for active service" in October 1916, his medical history including a combination of dysentery and severe deafness (from Gallipoli) and rheumatism. It is clear, however, that this was against the advice of one of the Army doctors, who had written in the previous February that "[I]n my opinion he is much better and can walk much better than he says – I think a great deal is put on".

Yet other detail is ironically amusing. Alfred Kitson – a grandson of another of Henry's brothers (George Rigg, 1832-1893) – was a motor driver/chauffeur in civilian life when he entered the 700th Motor Transport Company of the Army Service Corps as a private in August 1916. As with the case of Thomas Hyland, noted earlier, this might have seemed to have been a neat fit. I wonder what his thoughts were, therefore, when he was only graded as "fair" – i.e. fourth highest on a six-point scale running from "skilled" to "bad" – when assessed for his Certificate of Trade Proficiency in February 1917. Alfred was another with medical problems – "subject to asthma and also to tremors after short exercise" according to a report of August 1918 – but he was also another to survive the war and to raise a family afterwards.

Finally, the Army records confirm that there was also death on the home front. Reginald Waller Midgley joined the Royal Field Artillery in 1902, initially

---

14 By the time of the 1921 Census of England and Wales, William Kitching had resumed his career as an insurance agent in Boroughbridge, North Yorkshire. However, in the 1939 Register, he is recorded as a builder in North Stainley, near Ripon. He died in the Claro district in 1971 at the age of 84.

for three years active service and nine years in reserve. The conclusion of the latter period coincided with the beginning of the war, of course, and he was mobilised to the BEF in France in August 1914. His Army record includes a reference to the granting of a two-week furlough from 19th October to 2nd November 1918; Reginald's wife – Hilda Fozzard, a granddaughter of George Rigg (and, therefore, a great niece of my great grandfather, Henry Rigg) – died of "acute influenza" and "acute pneumonia" in Wetherby on 29th October at the age of 26, so his leave of absence must obviously have been to see her in her last few days.

An earlier British Army casualty

The *UK, Army Register of Soldiers' Effects, 1901-1920* database provided information on an earlier member of the extended Rigg family of North Yorkshire who had died in the service of the British Army.

For some time, I had been puzzled by what happened to John William Rigg – yet another grandson of William Rigg, Henry oldest brother. We noted in Chapter 1 that he had been a 13 year-old at the South Bank Wesleyan School in Middlesbrough in 1899 and he was given as a 15 year-old hairdresser's apprentice in Normanby, North Yorkshire, in the Census two years later. I had also recorded that the Army database included his attestation into the East Yorkshire Regiment in January 1904, when his age was given as 18 years and 1 month. (He was actually born in the second quarter of 1886). In April of the same year – i.e. after 90 days – he was "discharged having claimed it on payment of £10 within 3 months of attestation". In November, £5 was refunded to his father, William Rigg.

Although his attestation form gave John William's occupation as "farm labourer", there is no doubt that this is the same person: his father's address was given as South Bank, which is where John William was born. (The only other birth of a John William Rigg in 1886 was in Todmorden, Lancashire). The attestation form gave a full physical description: 5ft 5 3/8ths ins tall; 119 pounds; 2 teeth missing, 3 decayed; fresh complexion; grey eyes; dark brown hair.

At that stage, from the limited amount of information I had about him, I concluded that John William Rigg had been something of a restless spirit: he did not remain an apprentice hairdresser; he apparently did not stay in the Army; and I could not find him in the official records after the age of 18. I wondered if the 1921 Census might eventually reveal something when it was published in 2022.

As it turned out, I did not have to wait that long. I looked again at David Pratt's extensive (and accurate) contribution to the public pages of Ancestry and noted that he had included a separate entry from *UK, Army Register of Soldiers' Effects, 1901-1920* for John William Rigg, a Private in the 1st Battalion of the Yorkshire Regiment, dying in Al Qahirah, Cairo. Egypt, in November 1909. (The cause of death is not given). The sum of £9 7s 11d was credited to his father,

William, the same month. (The £5 payment refunded to William in November 1904 had been made on John William's re-enlistment into the Army).

I obtained more information on John William Rigg from Steve Erskine of the Green Howards' Museum in Richmond. He had re-enlisted in the Yorkshire Regiment in October 1904. The circumstances of his death were included in a paragraph in "1st Battalion News" from Abbassia, Cairo, on 4th December 1909, as recorded in *The Green Howards' Gazette*, Volume XVII, No. 202, p151, January 1910:

> "I regret to have to report the sad death of No. 7879 Pte. J. W. Rigg of "D" company. He was one of his company team in the bayonet fighting competition. After his round was over he felt very ill, was taken to hospital, where he died on the 22nd inst. His death was caused by a rupture of the stomach. He was very popular, and his death is a sad loss to his comrades".

The "test pilot"

John Rigg's brothers and sisters were shown in the family tree in Table 1.3 above. For a considerable time in the early 1990s, the focus of the family research effort was on mapping out the respective families of Margaret, Mary, Annie Elizabeth and Thompson. Their children would have been cousins of my father; their grandchildren my second cousins. It was with Mary's family that I made the most fruitful contact.

From the early discussions of the family with my father, uncle Jack and aunt May, I learned that Mary Rigg had been a housekeeper at the "St Ives" mill in Yeadon.[15] When she had had an illegitimate son, Douglas, her father (Henry) had told her that the child would be brought up in the family as his son. According to the family legend, Douglas Rigg later drove racing cars at Brooklands[16] and was some sort of test pilot in the Second World War. May said that she had met Douglas with his wife and children some time before the war and that his wife had been called Winnie.

In the BMD records at St Catherine's House in London, I discovered that

---

15 James Ives & Sons was formed in 1848. The company manufactured woollen cloth in Manor Mill and Leafield Mill in Yeadon. Following the retirement of James Ives (1829-1904) in 1884, it was run by his descendants until the closure of Manor Mill in 1980. The first 100 years of the company were commemorated by Eric B Dobson in a book published in 1948: *A Century of Achievement: The History of James Ives and Company Limited 1848-1948, Woollen Manufacturers, Leafield Mill and Manor Mill, Yeadon, Yorkshire, England.*

16 The Wikipedia entry for what was the 2¾ mile Brooklands motor circuit near Weybridge in Surrey states that it opened in 1907 and was the world's first purpose-built "banked" racing circuit. It hosted the first British Grand Prix in 1926. Racing ceased with the outbreak of the Second World War in 1939, when the site was turned over to the war-time production of military aircraft.

I contacted the Brooklands Museum in 2024. Its records cover the drivers who raced there to 1939 and do not include Douglas's name; however, the staff indices are incomplete with regard to mechanics and other workers.

Douglas Rigg married Winifred Mary Hayward from Atcham, Shropshire, in 1927. The marriage certificate said that Douglas was a 21 year-old motor mechanic[17] and Winifred was an 18 year-old spinster. Douglas had been born in Pickhill in 1905, when his mother Mary was 22; Winifred had been born in either 1908 or 1909. A search through all the death registers that were available to that time (September 1992) did not yield any record of their deaths, so it looked as if both Douglas and Winnie might still be alive at the respective ages of 87 and 83/84.[18]

It was at this stage that I took advantage of a rather strange book called *The World Book of Riggs*, a publication by Halbert's Family Heritage which I purchased for £19·95p. Much of the book covered general genealogical topics such as heraldry and emigration, although there was also a discussion of the derivation of the Rigg name (which replicated information I had seen in other sources, namely "a dweller by a ridge") and a copy of what was claimed to be a "unique heraldic blazon granted to an early Rigg", about which I was slightly sceptical.

The bulk of the book comprised "The Rigg 1992 International Registry", which listed 2,834 Rigg households in 9 countries. Although I judged that this might not have been an exhaustive list – on the basis that, whilst dad and Jack were included, I was not – it did contain 4 entries for Douglas Rigg in Great Britain: in East Sussex, West Sussex, Shropshire and Wiltshire, all of which were plausible locations for Douglas and Winnie. Thus armed, in August 1994, I wrote to Douglas Rigg at each of the addresses, fully aware that my enquiries needed to be appropriately sensitive, given that I was contacting elderly people whom I had never met.

The search was successful. Within a short period of time, I had exchanged some delightful correspondence with Winifred Rigg, who lived in Condover near Shrewsbury, and her children, Jean Wheeler, Douglas Paul Rigg and Robert Rigg, who were resident in Stockport, Chichester and near Guildford, respectively. Winifred informed me that Douglas had recently celebrated his 89th birthday, but was now frail through illness. They had had 5 children, the details of whom were subsequently passed on to me by Jean. In turn, I relayed some information to Jean about my grandfather, John Rigg – her great uncle, making us second cousins – and the families of his 4 children.

Robert Rigg said that he had also visited his namesake Robert Rigg's grave in the Somme (eight months earlier than me, in October 1989). He said that he had talked to his father about it and the experiences of the family who were there and "those left behind in Pickhill receiving telegrams and the like". (I couldn't help but notice the plural reference – "telegrams" – and wondered at that stage who else

---

17 The entry for Douglas's father on the marriage certificate was "Henry Rigg (deceased), a railway platelayer", reflecting the commitment that Henry had made. There was no entry for the father on Douglas's birth certificate.

18 Mary Rigg lived to the age of 80; she died in Sowerby, near Thirsk, in 1964.

in the extended family had also received these dreadful communications. As noted above, it turned out that there had been at least 4 other members of the extended Rigg family killed in action in the First World War). Poignantly, Robert reported that it had distressed Douglas to recall those times, which he could remember very clearly; this was consistent with an earlier reference by Jean Wheeler that Douglas had adored his uncle Robert. (Douglas would have been aged 13 when Robert was killed).

I was touched to have been let in to the memories of this newly discovered part of the extended Rigg family and, hence, it was with some sadness that I received the letters from Jean in 1995 and 2005 informing me that Douglas and Winifred had passed away at the ages of 90 and 97, respectively.[19] It was a pleasure to exchange Christmas cards with Jean each year, when she proudly brought me up to date with the new arrivals of great grandchildren and great nieces/nephews, as well as the passing of other family members; she died in 2019 at the age of 91.[20]

Inter-War Leeds

John Rigg married **CATHERINE KERR McBRIDE** (1893-1969) in Leeds in 1914. Their family is summarised in Table 8.1.

Three of John and Catherine Rigg's four children had been born by the time of the 1921 Census, when my father – William Alexander (Bill) Rigg – was the youngest at 3 months. (The fourth child – Agnes May Rigg – was born in 1924). The family was still living at 49 Pemberton Street, which had been John Rigg's address on discharge from the Army in November 1918. He completed the Census form in his neat handwriting, recording that he was a 34 year-old police constable based at Armley police station.

Table 8.1. The family of John and Catherine Kerr Rigg	
John Rigg 1887-1959 (born in Baldersby, Yorkshire) (died in Leeds aged 72)	
married	

---

19 As noted in Chapter 1, Winifred Mary Rigg reached the greatest age of any member of the extended Rigg family born in the UK.

20 Following Jean Wheeler's death, I corresponded with her daughter, Christina MacEachran. In addition to updating me with some of the recent additions to the branches of the family tree spreading from Douglas and Winifred Rigg, Christina provided a short summary of some of the notes that Jean had recorded on the Rigg family. One line jumped off the page: "Robert Rigg died WW1 shot by sniper while grooming his horse. 7/8/1918".

Catherine Kerr McBride 1893-1969 **(born in Govan, Glasgow)** **(died in Leeds aged 76)**	Robert Henry Rigg 1914-1978 (born in Leeds) (died in Leeds aged 64) *married* Joan Wilkinson 1919-2016 (died in Cairns, Australia, aged 96)
	John Kerr Rigg 1916-1999 (born in Leeds) (died in Leeds aged 82) *married* Audrey Ellis 1923-1999 (born in Thirsk district) (died in Leeds aged 75)
	William Alexander Rigg 1921-2004 **(born in Leeds)** **(died in Leeds aged 83)** *married* **Enid Peggie Niblett 1922-2000** **(born in Palmer's Green, London)** **(died in Leeds aged 77)**
	Agnes May Rigg 1924-2009 (born in Leeds) (died in Oxford aged 85) *married* Victor Hough 1919-2006 (born in Birmingham) (died in Chandler's Ford, Hampshire, aged 87)

In Chapter 1, I referred to the family historian's familiar retrospective lament: "I wished I'd asked him/her that". In this chapter, I can report that I did actually ask him. Over a weekend in December 2000, I taped a series of conversations with my father about growing up in John and Catherine Rigg's household in south Leeds, from his birth in March 1921 to the outbreak of the Second World War in September 1939. I subsequently transcribed these conversations, which were arranged around four themes: family and home; school; friends and play; and work and war.[21] I draw on brief extracts here; they are more or less verbatim, with the syntax and detail of recollection left unaltered.

---

21 *Bill Rigg: Early Memories – In Conversation with John Rigg*, unpublished, August 2002.

My father began by relating the story of how his parents met:

"My mother was a manageress at a firm called Cahill's, which was a cake shop… This shop, where my mother was, it wasn't a little shop. It had 3 or 4 big windows and masses of groceries and God knows what. They did their own baking… She was walking down Dewsbury Road and she passed a pub – it was in Pemberton Street, I think – it was near where my granny lived. This chap come flying out of this pub door and finished up on the pavement. And then there was another one come and followed him. And then my father come out of the back and, with my father, was another policeman. They'd been called to the pub and they'd slung them out. My mother saw this. She saw him marching them off to Dewsbury Road police station. That's how she met my dad".

The central role of the policeman in the local community was clearly evident to the young Bill Rigg:

"I was very proud of my dad. People respected the police and they looked up to them and they thought the world of my father. Any bit of trouble, they'd go to him and he'd advise them and tell them, do this, do that. He was very strong, he was 6 foot, powerful build. He used to go to Oxford Place Chapel with my grandad [Peter McBride] on a Sunday when he wasn't working. Everybody looked up to him. John Rigg: Policeman".

My father's recollections about the Rigg household complemented the evidence provided in my uncle Jack's photograph album. This included a photograph of the house at 68 Cross Flatts Crescent, Beeston – a solid terraced dwelling – to which the family moved when John Rigg was posted to Beeston police station.

"It was a rented house. There were gardens at back and front, and quiet open spaces. It was a lovely area. There was a big field at the bottom, which belonged to the Roman Catholic church, and we used to go in there and play cricket and rugby.

There was an attic with two nice bedrooms. Then there was the first floor with two bedrooms and a bathroom. Downstairs was the hall, the kitchen and the front lounge. I shared a bedroom with Jack. We had little beds.

[It was] coal fired – a regular delivery, in sacks. We had a cellar and they used to lift the lid up and empty the sack down into the cellar.

There was a Co-op: the Leeds Co-operative Society. You made your order and they delivered it for you every week. A very good system. There was a chemist near hand, who we knew. They knew you by your first name.

There was a confectioners. Milk was delivered. You used to get [rag and bone men]".[22]

My father related many examples of local life. One was quite touching:

"What you did used to get was singers. He'd come at the top of the street. He'd start. Some of them had quite good voices and they sung popular songs. He'd slowly walk down the street, singing, and people would go out and give a penny, tuppence or sixpence or a shilling. Just singing on his own [with no musicians or microphones]. This was regular throughout the year. Not every week; you might go 3 or 4 weeks with no-one coming down. Some couldn't sing at all and they were terrible".

Another was more sinister:

"There was one occasion. We'd be 8 or 9, maybe 10 or 11. [Oswald] Mosley was holding a rally on Holbeck Moor. By that time, we'd moved to Beeston. I was with all my pals. 6 or 7 of us; all my age; all good pals. He was having this rally – massed bands – so we decided to go down. We went up Dewsbury Road; we had to go through the cemetery and across to Holbeck Moor, which wasn't far from where we used to live.

The moor was packed. There was thousands of people. There was a big stand. And he comes marching through with his band. And his Blackshirts. There was a big shout. And all of a sudden there was a big interruption and fighting broke out in the middle of this crowd. And I'll always remember. We were at the back. And all of a sudden, the whole crowd turned and run towards us to get away from it. Of course, we saw them all coming. And so we turned round and run like blazes. It was quite frightening actually, if you can imagine. There was thousands on that moor. And that was Mosley and the Blackshirts. It was a right do. The police were there, but not as many as maybe there should be... We did an about turn and a bunk... It was quite an experience".

Bill Rigg was actually aged 15 when the so-called "Battle of Holbeck Moor" occurred on 27th September 1936. Newspaper reports stated that a huge crowd – perhaps 30,000 – gathered to hear an address by Mosley after he had led a procession of 1,000 Blackshirts from Calverley Street in Leeds. A sizeable proportion were his political enemies, as the Communist Party had had some time to organise

---

22 Apart from the addition of a skylight, the exterior of the property did not seem to have changed much from my father's description, when I took a walk down the street in August 2019.

the opposition protests. Stones were thrown and the resulting violence caused the planned rally to disperse.

Some of my father's memories of school – Far Beeston Council School – were equally vivid:

> "Discipline was very strict. [It was meted out] with a cane by the head. Sometimes the odd teacher would give you a little bit of stick. Half hearted. But if you'd done anything that they thought was really bad, you'd to go stand at the headmaster's door, because he'd maybe be out somewhere. And you stood there until he came back. You went in and you told him what had happened. And he'd get his stick out and really give you one… You just held your hand out. A left handed bloke might hold his left hand out. I held my right hand out.
>
> I got the stick, yeah. By gum, it stung. It went off after a bit, but I know that when you went back to your classroom, you had trouble writing. You couldn't write for a bit. [You got it for] just bad work, clumsiness, carelessness, talking in class, anything like that. It was quite regular. Not that you were getting it every day, but somebody would go and get the stick…
>
> There was a local library at the school. It wasn't run by the school, but at night certain rooms were turned into a library. There was a special junior section, which I was in. I used to go and get a book out like you normally do. My favourite author was Percy F Westerman. It sticks in my mind does that. He wrote adventure books for boys and I always used to go for his books. Percy F Westerman.[23]
>
> The first things you did when you went in was you walked to this desk and there was a woman behind it. "Show me your hands". She'd have a good look at them. If you'd dirty hands, you didn't get in".

I have written more generally about south Leeds in the 1920s and 1930s, the years of Bill Rigg's youth and adolescence, in my memoir of half a century of sport spectating – *An Ordinary Spectator: 50 Years of Watching Sport* – which was published in 2012 and dedicated to him.

> "The sense of local identity within Hunslet… was a powerful one. It meant something to be part of a community in which people looked out for each other. Confirmation of this has been provided in the evocative recollections of some of my father's near contemporaries, who have made their names in wider fields.

---

23 Percy Francis Westerman (1876-1959) was a prolific English author of boys' military and adventure stories, who sold over a million and a half books during the course of his lifetime.

In *City Lights: A Street Life*, the writer Keith Waterhouse (born in Hunslet in 1929) vividly describes the bustling locality of his childhood with its "tram-rattling arteries" lined by shops, warehouses, offices, breweries, foundries, factories and workshops. The industrial base of Hunslet ranged from "nook and cranny businesses crammed into small yards and down narrow alleys" through to the major sources of employment in clothing, engineering and printing. Waterhouse remarks on the extensive scale of the area's amenities, ranging from swimming baths and wash-houses, churches, chapels and mission halls through to temperance hotels, billiard halls, cinemas, stables and dog racing tracks. It was "a neighbourhood of great liveliness".

Waterhouse does not romanticise about the hard and dirty environment of Hunslet at this time, referring to "the soot and grime of industrial Leeds" and the blackened terraces which stemmed off the main roads. His description of the area echoed that of the distinguished social commentator, Richard Hoggart (born in Hunslet in 1918), who has noted that, in the years before the Second World War, this was one of the poorest districts in northern England. Although there were heavy duty jobs for men in glassblowing, railway engineering and the mills, with employment for women in the ready-made clothing factories, the environmental conditions were bleak. Hoggart described "the smell of heavy industry, chemicals and human sweat, especially in crowded tram-cars" and noted that "there was muck enough to blacken your lace curtains in a week". In his seminal work on the culture of the locality – *The Use of Literacy*, published in 1957 – Hoggart referred evocatively to "the miles of smoking and huddled working class houses". He also used his sociologist's perspective to detect "the great number of differences, the subtle shades, the class distinctions, within the working class themselves. To the inhabitants there is a fine range of distinctions in prestige from street to street".

…Hoggart [also referred] to "a hugely rooted sense of place, of belonging". My father would not have disagreed. He enjoyed his childhood in Hunslet, with his loving family and his small group of friends – "my little pals", as he later described them – with whom he shared the experiences of school and play. Most significantly, the values he learned from his family and the locality never left him. He lived in Moortown [in north Leeds] for over 50 years, but he was always a Hunslet man".[24]

My uncle Jack's album contained several photographs of John and Catherine

---

24 *An Ordinary Spectator*, pp 6-8.

Rigg's family. Robert Henry Rigg and John Kerr Rigg – Bob and Jack – were the two older children and my dad said that it seemed as if he and (Agnes) May were children for a long time after Bob and Jack had reached the status of grown-ups. (There was a five year gap between Jack and my father; Bob was older by another two years).

One photograph was of John Rigg sitting in his police uniform (number 162) on the corner of a table with Bob standing next to him. Bob inherited his uncle Robert's strong eyes and face and he really looked the part in his own uniform and with his hair parted strictly down the middle. There was also an excellent photograph of John and Catherine, which must have been taken shortly after they were married in 1914. Their hands rested on each other's shoulders. Catherine had a sweet smile – which her daughter, May, undoubtedly inherited – and wore her hair bunched with a parting on the right. In an earlier, formal photograph – possibly taken before she married – she rested her hand on what seems to be the same table as that used over twenty years later by John and Bob when posing in their police uniforms.

Bill Rigg had a clear recollection of his oldest brother following in his father's footsteps:

> "Bob decided to join the police. [My dad] didn't discourage him [to go for the police]. They had a little talk, I think, and Bob said he'd like to go in. He was off like a shot. The funny thing was, Bob got in with a broken wrist… At that time, you wound the car up at the front with a handle – you know what I mean – and the handle swung round out of his hand and broke his wrist. That week, he going for the police medical and, of course, my dad knew the police doctor and he knew Bob was going… Bob went and passed his police medical with a broken wrist. Of course, he didn't go in until the wrist was better and then he joined the police. He'd be 19 or 20.
>
> He joined the motor patrol. He was in there for 2 or 3 years. In them days, the fire brigade were all policemen. It was the Leeds City Police Fire Brigade. Besides driving the motor patrol vehicles or cars, he drove the fire engines. They decided to split and break away from the police and have a separate unit – nothing to do with the police – and Bob got the alternative of staying in the police or staying in the fire brigade and he chose the fire brigade.
>
> He [became] second-in-command in Leeds, a divisional officer. He went right to the top.

When I joined the airforce, he tried to join and they wouldn't let him because of his job. He was transferred to Hull and spent the majority of the war fighting bomb damage in Hull, on the docks".[25]

Following his return to Leeds, one incident was reported in the *Yorkshire Post and Leeds Mercury* of October 11th 1943. It captures the routine dangers of the fireman's job – as well as the lack of protective clothing that was available of this occasion.

> FIREMAN RESCUED FROM BURNING STACK
>
> Considerable damage was done by a fire at the weekend which burned out 14 stacks of corn and hay on a farm at Shadwell and at one time threatened the Parish Church, some of the windows being cracked. The fire was on the farm of J Greenwood and Sons and broke out in an eight-bay Dutch barn. Firemen from Leeds used 1,000 gallon dam trucks to help the local water supply.
>
> When a smouldering stack collapsed, Leading Fireman Walker was carried down with it and Company Officer Robert Rigg rescued him by pulling aside the glowing straw with his bare hands The NFS prevented outbuildings near the stacks from catching fire.

Occasionally during family history research, the conventional sources of official records or family photographs can be fortuitously supplemented. In 1989, my father drew my attention to two such examples in the "Old Yorkshire Diary" section of the *Yorkshire Evening Post*. In the first, in August, there was a photograph from 1927-28 of pupils at Ingram Road School, Leeds, comprising about 50 boys, one teacher and one headteacher. Dad recognised a 13 year-old Bob on the back row. Without telling me which one he thought Bob was, he asked me; I chose the same boy without hesitation.[26]

For my father, Bob was always the adventurous and protective big brother. In his youth, he had been the one who had started smoking cigarettes and who had bought the family's first car. Later, he had ambitiously taken his own family – his wife and two daughters – on motoring holidays through France and Italy or to

---

25 Kingston-upon-Hull had 95 per cent of its houses damaged or destroyed during the Second World War. In terms of the number of damaged or destroyed buildings, it was the most severely hit British city or town, apart from London. 1,200 people were killed, including 400 in one week in May 1941. Another 3,000 were injured and 152,000 made homeless out of a total population of approximately 320,000. (See T Geraghty, *A North-East Coast Town: Ordeal and Triumph – The Story of Kingston-upon-Hull in the 1939-1945 Great War*, The Kingston-upon-Hull Corporation, 1951, and P Graystone, *The Blitz on Hull, 1940-1945*, Lampada Press, 1991).

26 Later that year, in October, the same newspaper carried a photograph of the Hunslet Swimming Club, which won the Leeds and District League between 1928 and 1930. Dad recognised the first swimmer on the left on the top row as his uncle, Charlie McBride, whom he said had died of a heart attack some time after the Second World War at the age of about 40. I later checked out the details; he was Charles Osborne McBride, who died in Leeds in 1954 at the age of 45.

Spain and Portugal. Afterwards, he would recount these exotic adventures through occasional and (by me) eagerly anticipated Sunday evening showings of his 8mm cinefilms when, after dinner, both families would settle down in and around the sofa and armchairs in the spacious living room of my uncle's house in north Leeds to watch the flickering images of the intrepid travellers on the temporarily erected white screen. As a young boy, I admired Bob for his drive and energy, as well as his toughness and his optimism; I sensed that he thought that anything was possible, if one had the courage to attempt it. The suddenness of Bob's final illness and death in 1978 was a huge shock to everyone and to my father in particular.

My father's other older brother had a different character:

> "Jack wasn't really the athletic type and didn't go in for any sports whatsoever. He was more studious, I should say. He was very clever. Nice quiet lad. He didn't really mix much".

The official record of John and Catherine Rigg's family on the outbreak of the Second World War is given in the *1939 England and Wales Register*. John Rigg was a 52 year-old "police constable, retired" and Catherine Kerr Rigg did "unpaid domestic duties" living at 27 Valley Terrace, Moortown, Leeds, with John Kerr Rigg (aged 23, "clerk, auto electrical") and William Alexander Rigg (aged 17, "joiner/shopfitter"). Robert Henry Rigg was a 25 year-old "police constable (fireman driver)" resident at 9 Park Street, Leeds.

It was Bob Rigg's wife – and then widow – Joan (née Wilkinson), who became the longest lived of all those in the cohort of my (and Angela's) parents and their spouses and siblings. After Bob's death, she emigrated to Australia to live with one of her daughters; she died in Cairns in July 2016 at the age of 96.

CHAPTER NINE

NIBLETT/WILSON

The Ruhleben internment camp

The next in the list of our children's great grandparents are **ALFRED EDGAR NIBLETT** (1888-1973) and **MARIE ROSA WILSON** (1890-1968).

I remember my maternal grandparents in their old age, when they lived in Nunroyd Road in north Leeds. My granddad was a small, alert man with a sharp mind and an obvious love of learning. In my primary school years, his weekly gift to me was the latest edition of the *Look and Learn* magazine, which I received with due gratitude, but which I have to confess ranked below the *Beano* and *Dandy* on my list of essential reading. At this time – on a Friday evening – he also gave me a weekly French lesson, drawing on his long years as a teacher of modern languages, although by then he was in retirement. Again, this was something that I probably did not fully appreciate, when the post-school alternative was kicking a football around with my friends.

My grandma was also formal and correct and held in huge respect by my mother. At the age of about 6, I can recall running with my mother to one of the bus-stops on the Harrogate Road, where we were meeting grandma to go into "town" – the centre of Leeds – for a shopping trip. The prospect of being even a minute late for the rendezvous was out of the question.

At that age, I did not know of the dramas of my granddad's early adulthood. He had been born in Osnabrück, Germany, one of the 10 children of Charles James Niblett (1851-1927) and Anna Karoline Borstelmann (1853-1938). After taking a first degree at the University of Birmingham, graduating in 1911, he had returned to Germany – to the Ludwig Maximilian University of Munich (LMU) – to read for his Ph.D, which he completed in 1913.

On 6th November 1914, the German military authorities ordered the arrest of around 4,000 British men of military age then living in Germany and their internment at the Ruhleben racecourse, near Spandau just outside Berlin. Alfred Niblett was one of them. He was interned for the war's duration.

There is some excellent material available on the Ruhleben camp. I would recommend, in particular, the website created by the researcher and genealogist Chris Paton (http://ruhleben.tripod.com) – to which I have contributed a couple of paragraphs on Alfred Niblett – and the authoritative *British civilian internees in Germany: the Ruhleben camp, 1914-18* (2008) by Matthew Stibbe of Sheffield Hallam University.

Stibbe points out that the conditions in Ruhleben, whilst not as tough as in other First World War camps for "enemy aliens" in Germany, were especially poor (notably in terms of the quality of food and the crampedness of living space) during the first months, although the internees were perhaps fortunate that the camp's siting near to Berlin meant that it was easily accessible by neutral observers, including (until 1917) diplomats from the US Embassy. It is also clear that the internees' difficulties could be psychological as well as physical and, moreover, that this continued after the war through their reaction to the perception by some in Britain that they had been lucky to avoid the carnage of the Western Front and other theatres of war.

Sport featured prominently at Ruhleben, as the internees looked for ways to pass the time and to let off steam. Stibbe reports that "football stood out in particular as a collective obsession, reflecting its dominance in pre- (and post-) war British popular culture", whilst boxing bouts "attracted big crowds, including German guards and officers who came to watch as spectators". One of the internees was the famous footballer, Steve Bloomer, who had scored 28 goals for England between 1895 and 1907, a record that was not beaten until 1956.[1]

My mother, who was born four years after the end of the First World War, said that Alfred did not speak at all about his experience in Ruhleben. What he did do, however, was retain two editions of the *Ruhleben Camp Magazine* – dated Christmas 1916 and June 1917 – which respectively run to 64 and 72 pages of neatly printed articles and sketches. They have been passed down to me and are amongst my most prized possessions.

Today, Ruhleben is the name of a small railway station at the end of the U2 line in the northwest suburbs of Berlin. It could be a commuter halt in one of a thousand towns or cities. Outside the entrance, on the other side of the main road, is the local branch of Lidl, which includes (as I can attest from a visit in April 2014) a rather good bakery section. The internment camp was situated a couple of miles down the road, bound by the main Hannover-Berlin railway line and the River

---

[1] Matthew Stibbe notes that those interned at Ruhleben also included Sir John Balfour (nephew of the Conservative statesman Arthur Balfour), Sir Timothy Eden (the elder brother of the future Prime Minister, Anthony Eden), Carl Fuchs (the celebrated cellist), George Merritt (actor on stage and screen) and the Oxford historian John Masterman (later head of MI5's counter-intelligence unit in Britain during the Second World War and Master of Worcester College).

Spree. The site later became a sewage processing centre and, as far as I know, there is nothing to mark its former use.[2 3]

One question I have been unable to answer concerns the location of Alfred Niblett's parents – Charles James Niblett and Anna Karoline Niblett (née Borstelmann) – during the First World War. There is a tantalising reference to his father in a file held at The National Archives entitled *Germany: Prisoners, including Prisoners at Ruhleben* which reads "Charles James Niblett: request to the Foreign Office from Harry Niblett for the return of the copy of his birth certificate previously remitted". However, the name of Charles James Niblett does not appear on the lengthy list of Ruhleben internees published on Chris Paton's website. (As noted in Chapter 3, Charles James and Anna Karoline Niblett's permanent address was given as England in a 1919 Passenger List and they are recorded in the 1921 Census as resident in Beckenham, Kent).

Businessman and teacher

Alfred Niblett completed his doctorate at LMU and it was published in 1913. I have a copy of the first part of it – *Grammatik der Osnabrückischen Mundart (The Grammar of the Osnabrück Dialect)* – which my mother passed down to me. Remarkably, there was an interest in this work almost a century later. In 2007, I was contacted by Joachim Kreimer-de-Fries of Berlin who explained that, in addition to working as a sociologist for the German trade union federation, he was researching the East-Westphalian Saxon dialect of the Osnabrück region and requesting permission to place Alfred's thesis on a website dedicated to the old Osnabrück language. It is available on http://gdz.sub.uni-goettingen.de.[4]

---

2   A slightly expanded version of this section – "Ruhleben" – was published at www.anordinaryspectator.com/news-blog on 4th November 2014, the 100th anniversary of Alfred Niblett's internment.

3   References to the Ruhleben internment camp occur in places that, at first sight, might seem most unlikely, though a moment's reflection suggests the logic for them. In *Losing Eden: Why Our Minds Need the Wild* (2020), Lucy Jones states that the internees "fought and begged to be allowed to bring nature into the camp". Their requests granted, they
> "...grew a vast range of flowers, from asters to dahlias, nasturtiums to petunias and begonias to sweet peas, with seeds, bulbs and instructions sent in from the Royal Horticultural Society in London. Flowers weren't, as one might imagine, a luxury for internees, they symbolised an act of psychological resistance and much-needed hope... they might have reminded the men of their gardening at home, their families and loved ones, as well as Britain and its green and pleasant land".

4   Further research on Google has revealed that Alfred Niblett's Ph.D. dissertation has been regularly referenced since its publication. It was noted in Wolfgang Stammler's *Deutsche Philologie in Aufriss (German Philology in Outline)*, published in Berlin in 1952, in *Germanic and Its Dialects: A Grammar of Proto-Germanic* by TL Markey, RL Kyes and Paul T Roberge, published in Amsterdam in 1977, and in *Gemination, Lenition and Vowel Lengthening: On the History of Quantity in Germanic* by Kurt Goblirsch of the University of South Carolina in 2018. It has also been digitised by the Niedersächsische Staats- und Universitätsbibliotek (SUB) at the University of Göttingen and is available through the extensive library of online publications made available by a network of universities across Europe.

After the First World War, Alfred Niblett spent some time as a businessman. We saw in Chapter 3 that he was the company secretary in the family business of Niblett Limited, with four of his brothers as directors. However, this aspect of his career was relatively short-lived: The National Archives include a record for Winding-Up Proceedings against Niblett Limited in 1922.

I was able to learn more about Niblett Limited in December 2021, when I made contact with Sally Dinham-Scott, a great grand-daughter of one of Alfred's older brothers, Adolf Niblett. Ms Dinham-Scott informed me that the Niblett brothers had been very successful cotton merchants in Liverpool and had invested in the new Cotton Exchange Building, which was completed in 1906. This was a state-of-the-art building with its telephone lines enabling the merchants to conduct their business much more efficiently than previously.[5]

In the early 1920s, the development of man-made fibres, combined with the import of cheap cotton goods from India, led to the demise of the Liverpool cotton trade and many merchants went bankrupt. Ms Dinham-Scott informed me that the Niblett brothers refused to declare themselves bankrupt and paid off all their creditors, leaving them with little wealth. She thought that this would have accounted for Alfred's change of career and, indeed, this does seem a likely scenario.

It is the information provided to me by Ms Dinham-Scott that has also caused me to re-interpret the newspaper report referring to a speculative loss of £30,000 on cotton trading incurred by Adolf Niblett's nephew – Charles Joseph Niblett – which was mentioned as background to his theft of a bicycle in Norwich in 1934 (see Chapter 3 above). It was also noted in the same chapter (drawing on the research undertaken by the family historian Mike Niblett) that it was Charles Joseph's father – Charles Julius Henry Niblett – who had been one of the directors of the cotton merchants Niblett Limited (along with Adolf, Harry and George Niblett and with my grandfather, Alfred Niblett, as company secretary) on its winding-up in 1922 (when Charles Joseph Niblett would have been aged 15). Given that their creditors were all paid off, my thoughts now are that the £30,000 refers to the amount made good by Charles Julius Henry Niblett, which was thereby lost to his branch of the family, including Charles Joseph Niblett.

Adolf Niblett and his wife Charlotte (née Patterson) moved to Taunton and then to Southampton. Both were accomplished musicians with Adolf also a highly skilled linguist; Sally Dinham-Scott thought that he could speak 7 languages fluently. As noted in Chapter 3, Adolf and Charlotte's son, Eric Harry Niblett, was in the Royal Army Service Corps when he was lost at sea in 1941 at the age of 34.

---

5 The old photographs on Wikipedia of the Liverpool Cotton Exchange show it to have been a beautiful building. Sadly, only part of the façade now exists, as most of the structure was demolished in 1967. The civil planners of the 1960s and 1970s have a lot to answer for.

At the time of the demise of Niblett Limited, Alfred was living at 69 Lakeside Road, Palmers Green. This was the address given in the 1921 Census for Alfred and Marie Niblett and their 8-month old daughter (Rosemary Joy Niblett) as well as a servant, the 25 year-old Gladys Simms. (My mother – Enid Peggie Niblett, Joy's younger sister – was born the following year). Alfred's occupation was "whole merchant (general produce)" with the business address given as 21 Mincing Lane, London EC3. (We saw in Chapter 3 that this was the address in 1921 for Niblett Limited, in which Alfred's father and brother (Charles James and Harry) were also employers and his sister, Elisabeth Miriam Niblett, was a private secretary).

Alfred Niblett is recorded at the Lakeside Road address in the *London Electoral Registers of 1921-23*, in the first two years by himself and then with Marie and also his oldest brother (Charles Julius Henry Niblett) and his wife (Maria Niblett).[6 7] The same group were then listed at an address in Old Park Ridings, Enfield, in 1924 and 1925.

The bulk of Alfred's working life was spent as a schoolteacher and, later, private tutor in modern languages (principally French and German). For part of this time, he taught at Roundhay School in Leeds (which I later attended, though he had retired long before my time there). In the 1939 Register, he is recorded as a "schoolmaster, languages specialist" in Leeds. Alfred is also mentioned in G Hinchliffe's *Roundhay School: The First Half Century* (1973) as being on the staff during the later stages of the Second World War, when the size of the pupil roll had doubled to almost exactly 1,000 due to the closure of other Leeds schools and the placing of evacuees.

I obtained a one-page summary of Alfred Niblett's teaching career from John Mattinson, the archivist of Roundhay School. His service there commenced on 4th November 1940 – his 52nd birthday – and lasted until his retirement at the age of 65 on New Year's Eve 1953. Prior to that, Alfred had been at the City of Leeds School between November 1923 and January 1940 and then West Leeds High School between January and November 1940. The "subjects for which [he was] specially qualified" were German and French. The summary page does throw up two particular mysteries, however, to which I return below.

A first-hand recollection of Alfred Niblett's teaching style at Roundhay School was provided – rather improbably – in 2021, when the 91 year-old David

---

6   Lakeside Road is not far from the former site of St George's Presbyterian Church, where Alfred and Marie Rosa were married in 1919 (see below), and St George's Road, where they lived at that time. When I visited the street in October 2019, number 69 was one of the few that had a sizeable hedge bordering the small front garden; most of the other gardens had been converted into parking bays. The street comprises solid and sizeable terraced houses and is close to Palmers Green railway station and Broomfield Park.

7   In 1923, the "abode" of Charles and Maria Niblett was an address in Oporto, Portugal.

Gabbitas posted a contribution to the school alumni's Facebook site.[8] Mr Gabbitas had been aged 12 when he had entered the school in 1942.

> "One major impact of the war on Roundhay School was on the teaching staff. They were mostly quite old and had perhaps been called out of retirement. The staff who taught me were superb teachers, if anything over qualified, which I didn't appreciate at the time. My form master and German teacher from the second year onwards was Dr. Niblett. Dr. Niblett's doctorate was in Low German dialects and he really brought his subject alive.
>
> I remember a couple of stories of his. One concerned a local train in Germany before the 1914-1918 War. He was travelling on what was called a *Bummelzug*. I think it meant slow train. This steam train included fourth class accommodation which consisted of benches along each side of the carriage. Farm animals would stand in the central aisle. Because of the depth of the snow the train ran out of fuel. The passengers had to descend, struggle across a field to a farm and obtain enough wood to continue.
>
> Another story he told us was about his shotguns which he left in the care of the local police station at the end of his holiday just before the war broke out in 1914. After the end of the war he went back on holiday again and recovered his shotguns which had been cared for, cleaned and oiled during the whole period of the war…
>
> …I remember him with affection although I think it was a great disappointment to him when he found me delivering his newspapers and working as an apprentice electrician after I left school".

Mr Gabbitas had an extraordinary recollection of Alfred Niblett's doctorate nearly 70 years after being told about it. However, I'm not sure about Alfred's "holidays" before and after the war, though it might well be that he did refer to a pre-war holiday, given his known reluctance to discuss his experience of internment. The post-war visit to recover the shotguns was certainly new information for me and obviously predates his later journeys to Osnabrück in the 1930s.[9]

Alfred's teaching career had begun before the First World War and it is during this period that the two mysteries are generated. A contributor to the public pages of Ancestry has placed a copy of a one-page staff report of Alfred's tenure at Kimbolton Grammar School in Cambridgeshire. The reports lists the schools and colleges at which he had been educated as: Real Gymnasium, Osnabrück, Prussia (1900), University of Birmingham (1908-11) and University of Munich (1911-13). His qualifications were "Matriculation" (Germany) (1907), Birmingham

---

8   See 4.4.44school.doc at www.facebook.com/groups/1415661402028531.

9   See below and also Chapter 3.

University Inter Arts (1908), Birmingham University MA (Honours, Foreign Languages) (1911) and University of Munich Ph.D. (1913).

The report also states that Alfred took a temporary post at Kimbolton Grammar School in the Autumn term of 1913 with the definitive appointment dating from 13th January 1914. At the school, his principal duties were stated to be: "Teaches German. Takes charge of the Department in his second term. Assists in teaching of French". His salary was £160 "rising according to Middlesex Scale". He left the school on 28th July 1914.

This chronology is not consistent with the career summary for Alfred Niblett presented to me by John Mattinson at Roundhay School. This states that Alfred was only at Kimbolton between October and December 1913 and that between January and July 1914 he taught at Southgate County School in London N13. (We will recall that, in the 1911 Census, Alfred's future wife – Marie Rosa Wilson – was recorded as a 21 year-old living with her parents and uncle in Reservoir Road, Southgate). This is the first mystery.

The second mystery concerns the date on which Alfred left his teaching post in England – irrespective of whether it was in Kimbolton or Southgate. 28th July 1914 was the very day on which the Austro-Hungarian Empire declared war on Serbia and the First World War began. In the Kimbolton school record, under "post, if any, taken up after leaving the School", there is written – frustratingly – "Has gone into..." and then a word which has faded on the page. It could be "Industry", but I cannot be certain.

The question then arises as to how Alfred, who was in either Kimbolton or Southgate as late as the end of July 1914, ended up being interned in Germany in November of that year. For some time I had wondered if Alfred had returned to the University in Munich, perhaps to teach. However, I now think that the answer is provided in Chris Paton's research on the Ruhleben Camp, in which he refers to Alfred, a resident of Hut 3, as having been an "assistant master in Osnabrück" when he was interned. This makes sense: I assume that Alfred's mother – Anna Karoline Borstelmann – was still in Germany (and in Osnabrück) at that point, along with at least some (and possibly all five) of Alfred's sisters (see Chapter 3 above).

With the benefit of a century's hindsight, it is easy to argue that Alfred should not have ventured back to Germany at the outbreak of the war or – at least – should have returned to Britain in its opening weeks. However, I suspect that he would have regarded both countries – Germany and Britain – as "home". In terms of the former, it was where he had been born and brought up, where he had conducted his postgraduate research and where a large part of his family still lived.

Photographs

The family – two daughters – of Alfred Edgar Niblett and Marie Rosa Wilson is shown in Table 9.1. The younger is my mother, known as Peggie as she strongly disliked her first given name of Enid. Her older sister was also known by her second name – Joy – notwithstanding that her first name was the one with the strong family tradition: Rosemary Joy Niblett was the daughter of Marie Rosa Wilson, the grand-daughter of Rosa Mary Whines and the great grand-daughter of Mary Wadsworth.

Table 9.1. The family of Alfred Edgar and Marie Rosa Niblett	
Alfred Edgar Niblett 1888-1973 (born in Osnabrück, Germany) (died in Leeds aged 84)	
married	
Marie Rosa Wilson 1890-1968 (born in Wood Green, London) (died in Leeds aged 78)	Rosemary Joy Niblett 1920-2009 (born in Edmonton, London) (died aged 88) *married* Hugh Drummond Gardiner 1925-2007 (born in Camberwell, London) (died in Dunfermline, Scotland, aged 82)
	Enid Peggie Niblett 1922-2000 (born in Palmer's Green, London) (died in Leeds aged 77) *married* William Alexander Rigg 1921-2004 (born in Leeds) (died in Leeds aged 83)

I mentioned in Chapter 3 that I have Alfred Niblett's passport for the years 1935 to 1940, which include the stamps marking the visits to his mother Anna Karoline Niblett (née Borstelmann) in Osnabrück in 1935 and 1937. His journey would have been by train; there is a separate stamp for the customs post *(die Zollzweigstelle)* at Aachen. Alfred's profession was given as "modern language master". He was 5 ft 4 ins tall and had penetrating blue eyes and fair hair. The photograph would have been taken when he was in his mid-40s. He also had a prominent nose: perhaps that explanation of the family name – as researched by Mike Niblett in Canada[10] – was correct after all.

The passport of Marie Rosa Niblett that I possess dates from an earlier period: 1921 to 1923. She was also 5 ft 4 ins with blue eyes, though her hair was dark brown. She would have been about 30 years old when the photograph was taken. Her eyes were round and inquisitive and her hair was neatly brushed to the right, but there was no smile: the pose was business-like. The passport was valid for Belgium, Holland and Germany, though not for the occupied German territory "except for one journey in transit only". There were stamps to mark her reporting on arrival to the Military Police in Cologne Main Station and for transit through the Netherlands, both from September 1921.

Assuming that Alfred was with her on this journey, the question does arise as to what the purpose of the visit to Germany actually was. We know that Anna Karoline Niblett was resident in England at that time (from the 1919 Passenger List and the 1921 Census referred to earlier), so it seems unlikely that the Alfred was making a special journey to visit his mother. My best guess – and it is only a guess – is that Alfred and his wife might have been visiting one of his married sisters. Cologne is about 100 miles from Osnabrück. (Perhaps it was on this 1921 journey that Alfred retrieved the shotguns that had been stored away in safekeeping for him during the First World War, as recounted by David Gabbitas).

In addition to the passports and the two magazines from the Ruhleben First World War internment camp, my mother passed on to me a copy of Alfred and Marie's marriage certificate from December 1919. They were aged 31 and 29 years, respectively, resident in St George's Road, Palmers Green. Both their fathers – Charles James Niblett and Charles Herbert Wilson – were described as merchants and the profession of Alfred himself was "general merchant". The wedding took place in the St George's Presbyterian Church "at the corner of Fox Lane and St George's Road".[11] My mother also kept Alfred and Marie's death certificates and the bill for the latter's funeral service – totalling £60 17s 3d – with the Leeds Industrial Co-operative Society Limited in December 1968.

My mother also passed on a handful of photographs, mainly of Alfred through the years: a full length shot (probably pre-First World War) of him wearing a jacket, cravat and cap and smoking his pipe (a habit he maintained through his life); a slightly later pose from the early 1920s with one of his daughters (probably Rosemary Joy) crouching on a garden lawn with two dogs seated on either side; some later poses (dated June 1958, after he had retired from teaching) outside the front door of his house in Leeds, again with a dog at his heel and accompanied by one of the students to whom he gave private tuition; in his old age (supported by

---

10 See Chapter 3 above.

11 The church was demolished in the 1980s. The site is now the Lady Shaw Court blocks of flats.

Hamish and Chrissie Mackenzie, whom I cannot place, according to a note on the back) in the garden of a cottage in Grasmere, the location of which I recognised from a separate family holiday in about 1970.

It is not much in the way of photographic evidence – supplemented by some film footage that my father took on his 8mm camera – but it is enough to trigger a sense of the passage of Alfred's post-First World War life. In all the photographs – apart from the first one with the cravat – even in the informal poses, he is wearing a jacket and tie with either a waistcoat or light jumper and his shoes are brightly polished. One can detect a great deal from what appears to be the simplest collection of photographs.

The album

Apart from Marie Rosa Niblett's passport of 1921-23, the only specific document of hers that has been passed down the generations is a hard-backed "album" that she compiled between 1906 and 1915 (when she was Marie Rosa Wilson and aged between 16-25). This consists of about 50 entries from family friends and work colleagues: short poems, aphorisms, drawings, water colours, and so on.

There are some entries from family members. One dated 29th March 1914 is from Rose Wilson, accompanied by some neat ink sketches of flowers:

> "I shall pass through this world but once, therefore any good thing that I may do, or any kindness that I may show, let me do it now: let me not neglect it as I shall not pass this way again".

At first, I thought this was Marie's mother. However, tellingly, the entry is signed by "Rose", rather than "Rosa". On reflection, I think it more likely to have been Marie's aunt – the Alabama-born Rose Mary Wilson (née Easby-Smith, 1876-1953) – who was married to Marie's father's brother (Leonard Kebbel Wilson, 1869-1946). This branch of the family was usually resident in the USA, but we know (from Chapter 4) that Leonard was a regular visitor to the UK to undertake his heraldry research.

There is a separate entry from Leonard Wilson in August 1908, when he labelled himself as "The Anglo American":

> "To Great Britain – on whose glorious possessions the sun never sets.
> And to the great United States – the only nation which ever succeeded in effectually twisting the British Lion's tail,
> We drink a toast:
> May these two nations – which together control the destiny of the world – ever be friends.
> Truly the Anglo-Saxon rules the earth!"

Harold Wilson of "Baltimore, USA" wrote to "My cousin Marie" on 19th September 1912:

> "She like the hazel twig,
> As straight and slender; not quite so brown in hue
> As hazel unto, but sweeter than their kernels".

As with Rose Wilson, I had to re-examine my initial assumption about Harold's place in the family. At first, I thought he must have been a son of Leonard and Rose Wilson, given the reference to Baltimore. However, the later US Federal Census record (for 1920) does not list anyone called Harold in Leonard and Rose's family when they were living in Washington DC, although the youngest of the eight children (William) was born in Maryland in about 1912 (the year in which Harold signed the album). On reflection, I think Harold is the son (born in about 1890) of another of Marie's uncles (George Herbert Wilson) and his wife (the former Retti Betsy Maud Maxon Skinner) and that he also emigrated to the USA.[12] (We saw in Chapter 4 that George and Maud had separated by 1901, when George, living in Chelsea, erroneously described himself as a widower in that year's Census). George Wilson has a separate entry in Marie's album on 22nd July 1908.

The first entry in the album is from Albert J Pearce on Christmas Day 1906 and there are others on the same day from Rhoda Pearce and E (or possibly G) Wilson.[13] I concluded from this that the album was a gift to Marie at that time. The subsequent pages do not follow any chronological order and, interestingly, there is nothing from Alfred Edgar Niblett.

Many of the contributors have names which make it impossible to distinguish the individuals from their namesakes alive in England at the same time. However, some members of the cast list can be confidently identified in the 1911 Census. Of these, several have years of birth close to Marie's in 1890 and, therefore, must have been friends or work colleagues. We know from the Census that Marie was a shorthand typist in 1911 and, in that record, it can be seen that this was also the occupation of the 20 year-olds Winifred Buggs and Hilda Blackley, who lived in New Southgate and Palmer's Green, respectively, and the 18

---

12 Mystery surrounds several of the official records relating to Harold Wilson. In the 1891 and 1901 Censuses, he is listed as a 1 year-old and then an 11 year-old in the family of George Wilson, having been born in Chatham, Kent. There is no record of such a birth in the Medway district between 1889 and 1891. (The Harry Gooding Skinner born in that district in 1889 was a member of a different family).

I cannot be certain about Harold's life in the USA, but there is a strong possibility that he is the Harold Wilson who appears in the World War I Draft records as having been born in London on 14th March 1890. A 30 year-old married railroad clerk with this name, born in England, is in the 1920 Federal Census as resident in Chicago, Illinois; ten years later, the 40 year-old is working on the railroad as an assistant general purchasing agent in Douglas, Nebraska. The 43 year-old Harold Wilson died in 1933 and is buried in Douglas County, Omaha.

13 Emma or George Wilson, perhaps – see Chapter 4.

year-old Ethel Cornell, who lived in Tottenham. Amy G(ertrude) Naylor was aged 20 and a student, whilst Alan M(elvern) Dawbarn was an 18 year-old commercial clerk in Enfield. Albert John Pearce was slightly older – aged 29 when he made the first entry in 1906 – and he was also a clerk in New Southgate. Poignantly, we also know the fates of some of this group: Alan Dawbarn died at the age of 48 in Market Harborough, Leicestershire in 1941; Orlando Victor Nieri, another contemporary of Marie's, who was later recorded as a schoolteacher in Leicestershire in 1939, died in Ealing in 1958; Hilda Mary Winifred Hynes (née Blackley) lived to the age of 99 and died in Bideford, Devon, in 1990.

One particular entry provides a clue about Marie's training as a shorthand typist. The delightfully named Percival Jasper Varley-Tipton wrote a couple of lines from Robert Burns's *A Man's A Man For A'That*:

"The rank is but the guinea stamp
The man's the gold…"[14]

and then, after his signature, he wrote "Clark's College, Wood Green, 31 viii '10".[15]

Clark's College in Wood Green, London, had been established in 1909, so Marie would have been amongst its earliest intake. It was the most recently formed establishment under the Clark's College name that dated from 1880, when a 20 year-old civil servant – George E Clark – opened the first premises in Chancery Lane, London, as a business educational institution with an emphasis on competitive examination courses for entry into civil service appointments. Clark's College was also one of the early pioneers in distance learning (correspondence courses) as well as the training of women. The Wood Green establishment closed in the 1960s.[16]

Another of Marie's contemporaries was Amy C(lara) Hildyard, who, in addition to an exquisite little watercolour, contributed the following short verse:

"In purity be as the Lily white
Be modest as the Violet low
In kindness as an evergreen be bright
So shall those as a Rose in beauty glow".

In the 1911 Census, Amy Hildyard is recorded as a 22 year-old typist resident

---

14 The Burns original is "gowd" – the Scots word for gold.

15 In 1901, the Census of England and Wales recorded Varley-Tipton as a 25 year-old "Jehovah's witness (priest)" in Ecclesall Bierlow, Sheffield, with the additional information that he was a graduate of the University of London. Ten years later, he was a Professor of Mathematics in Leeds. He died in Birmingham in 1957 at the age of 81.

16 See www.clarkscollege.co.uk and TDT Baker (ed), *A History of the County of Middlesex, Volume 5, Victoria County History*, London, 1976.

in Southgate and working for a firm of wallpaper manufacturers. All that was to change, however. Her name appears on two Passenger Lists to New York (from Southampton in 1922 and London in 1928), with her occupation given as "nurse" and then "nurse lecturer" and with the latter having a final destination of Cincinnati. She is also on the *UK, The Midwives Roll, 1904-59* for 1920 and 1931, having taken her CMB Examination in 1917.[17] Amy married Edward Clinton Loomis – a merchant – in 1932, but was widowed five years later. In the US Federal Censuses of 1940 and 1950, she is living alone in San Luis Obispo, Arroyo Grande County in California. When she died in California in 1972 at the age of 83, it had been 64 years since she carefully composed her neat entry in Marie's album.

The entries in the album dating from the First World War include one or two servicemen from overseas. Hence, Pte Francis Herman McLennan of E Company of the 37th Battalion of the Canadian Expeditionary Force wrote that he came from Owen Sound, Ontario, Canada.

> "In quiet remembrance of the pleasant Christmas spent at the home of Miss Wilson on Dec 25 1915".

Later records show that Francis McLennan married an English girl in Camberwell in 1919 and returned to Canada, where he died at the age of 51 in 1944.

The most curious entries in the album are those from Julius and Agnes Zancig on 7th August 1908. My follow-up of the couple in the 1911 Census record showed that they were a husband and wife resident in Balham, supposedly aged 45 and 54 respectively at that time, and both born in Copenhagen. All duly routine, until I noticed that Julius Zancig's occupation was "mind reader, psychic". Moreover, one of their visitors on the day of the Census record was a 27 year-old Londoner – Cyril Laston – who was a "date rememberer".[18]

The Wikipedia entry for Julius and Agnes Zancig – born Julius Jörgensen and Agnes Claussen – records that they "...were stage magicians and authors on occultism who perfomed a spectacularly successful two-person mentalism act during the late 19th and early 20th centuries... The Zancigs managed to fool many spiritualists into believing they had genuine psychic powers". The strapline on their promotional advertising was "Two minds with but a single thought". Julius had become a naturalised US citizen in 1900 and the occupations of both Julius

---

17 See Chapter 3, footnote 46.

18 From 1908, Edward (sic) Laston – Edward Cyril de Hault Laston – had a successful 15-year career touring UK music halls and overseas as "The Memory Mystic". He memorised the dates of 1,400 battles and an overall total of 40,000 other event dates.

and Agnes were again registered as "mindreader" in the 1910 US Federal Census when they were resident in Manhattan, New York.

Agnes and Julius made two full entries on consecutive pages of Marie's album, respectively:

> "I resolve to do the best I can today.
> That may not be much.
> But whatever I do I am
> going to be cheerful about it.
> That's a lot".

and

> "It's easy enough to be pleasant
> when life flows along like a song.
> But the woman worthwhile
> is the one whom [sic] can smile
> when everything's going dead wrong".

Agnes Zancig died in Washington in 1916 and Julius married Ada May Fawcett in New York two years later; he died in Los Angeles, California, in 1929. Towards the end of his life, he confessed that the mentalist act had been based on a complex code that he and Agnes had used. However, at the time of Julius and Agnes's entries in Marie's album – in 1908 – they were at the height of their fame, such that they would tour not only the UK and Europe, but as far afield as the USA, Australia and South Africa.

The obvious question relates to how Marie obtained the Zancigs' entries for her album. One possibility is that she went to see them perform and, effectively, used her album as an autograph book. *The Hanwell Gazette* (and presumably other newspapers) had reported on 1st August 1908 that the Zancigs were appearing at the Shepherd's Bush Empire "next week", so this would have been consistent with the date of the album entries. The argument against this, however, is that Marie did not obtain their rushed autographs, but carefully composed and neatly written contributions for the album. (Somewhat eerily, the couple's handwriting is almost – but not quite – identical).

An alternative explanation is that – like several other contributors to Marie's album – Julius and Agnes Zancig were visitors to the home of Charles Herbert Wilson and his family. In turn, this leads to other speculative possibilities. Was Charles Herbert himself a follower of spiritualism? Was he – or his wife, Rosa Mary Whines – seeking some way of contacting Marie's long-deceased siblings (Winifred Flora Wilson, who died aged 10 days in 1895 and/or Gladys Emma Wilson, who died aged 9 months in 1898)? These can only be tentative suppositions, however, which cannot now be resolved and they do seem rather unlikely. The Zancigs' entries in the album make no mention of any of the Wilson family or of a visit to their home.

The album of Marie Rosa Niblett (née Wilson) is a fascinating and valuable document because it gives a personal insight into the social milieu – that of lower middle-class North London – in which she moved in the years leading up to and extending into the First World War. Her circle of friends and acquaintances, the values of the extended family and the educated, literate circumstances in which she found herself are all fully revealed. The contribution to the album from Rose Wilson, noted above, is a quote from the early 19th Century French-American Quaker missionary Stephen Grillet, whilst Harold Wilson's reference is from a speech by Petruchio in William Shakespeare's *Taming of the Shrew*. Other references in the album draw on Robert Louis Stevenson, Rudyard Kipling and John Greenleaf Whittier.

Marie Rosa Niblett died in Leeds in December 1968 at the age of 78. Alfred Edgar Niblett outlived her by five years, dying in September 1973 at the age of 84.[19] Both were cremated at the Lawnswood Crematorium in north Leeds; on enquiry, I was informed in June 2010 whereabouts in the cemetery their ashes were strewn.

---

19 It has been a matter of personal regret that this quiet and studious man, who always took a considerable interest in my scholastic achievements, died only a few weeks before I learned that I had been offered a place to study at the University of Cambridge.

CHAPTER TEN

ENGLISH/STAPLETON

The Merchant Navy

When my father-in-law, Denis English, died in 2009, he left a small collection of personal papers to my wife, Angela – mainly documentation about his working life and letters and photos of family and friends.

Denis had had a distinguished career in the Merchant Navy, later as an executive with Shell International Marine, before taking early retirement to care for his wife, Anne, who had suffered a severe stroke in her mid-50s. I shall return to Denis and Anne in a later chapter but, for the present, I shall note that several items of these family papers concerned Denis's father. **ARTHUR JOSEPH ENGLISH** (1892-1970) was married to **MARY STELLA (EUGENIA) STAPLETON** (1899-1978) and they constitute the next in line of Tom and Katie's great grandparents.

Arthur was born in North Shields in 1892. We noted in Chapter 5 that he was the youngest of the three children of Arthur English (1869-1936) and Helen Kelly (1869-1949) and that the seafaring tradition was evident in both sides of his family via his own father and his mother's grandfather and great grandfather (the two drowned seaman called John Davis).

Denis English had carefully looked after the documentation of Arthur's early progress in his Merchant Navy career: his Ordinary Apprentice's Indenture at the age of 15 on 24 May 1907 (a date of some significance, as we shall see later); the certificates for attendance at St John Ambulance Association lectures (October 1911, repeated in September 1915); his Certificate of Competency as a Master for Foreign-Going Steamships in the Merchant Service (October 1915); his appointment as a Sub-Lieutenant in the Royal Naval Reserve (November 1915). To these can be added the Certificates of Competency published by Ancestry in *UK and Ireland, Masters and Mates Certificates, 1850-1927* as Second Mate (November 1911) and First Mate (July 1913).[1]

Other items held by Denis English set out Arthur's career over a longer period. The Continuous Certificate of Discharge lists his engagements from his first major voyage (from Tilbury to New York as third mate on the *Narragansett* in December 1911) through to his discharge from the *Knight of Malta* in Malta in June 1940. Together with his Royal Naval Reserve (RNR) Officer's Training Certificate Book, this provides a rich source of personal information: Arthur was 5 feet 7 inches tall with blue eyes, brown hair and a fair complexion. A British Seaman's Identity Card gives a complete set of finger- and thumb-prints, accompanied by a small photograph of a stern-looking – and possibly weary – middle-aged man. A much better photograph shows a head-and-shoulders of Arthur in his Master's uniform, his face softer and with the hint of a wry smile.

In Denis English's file, there was a series of "to whom it may concern" references relating to Arthur's conduct, expertise and experience. The earliest of these was from Prince Line Ltd in September 1911. Arthur had served his four years as an apprentice with the company from May 1907 and had stayed on for 4 months as an AB (able-bodied seaman). The testimonial stated: "He is reported by the Masters to have conducted himself during this period in a sober and satisfactory manner". The final sentence helpfully set out (for us) the context within which the reference was given: "This testimonial is given to comply with the rule of the Board of Trade requiring a certificate of conduct from the employers of the seaman presenting himself for examination".

Reading through these references, one quickly becomes used to a familiar form of words. The testimonial from C Harwood, Master, of the Anglo American Oil Company Ltd in February 1912 stated that Mr AJ English served with him on board the SS *Narragansett* as 3rd Mate (as noted above) and then transferred to the SS *Seneca*: "He always conducted himself in a strictly sober manner, and most attentive to his duties". In Arthur's handwriting is an annotation next to the name of the first vessel: "Sunk off the Scillies, March 1917. No survivors or wreckage".[2]

After his First World War service in the Royal Navy Reserve (see below), Arthur returned to the Merchant Navy with the Marine Staff of Cable and Wireless Ltd in May 1919 until his resignation in September 1930. His Continuous Certificate of Discharge catalogued the places of engagement over this period

---

1 The First Mate Certificate of Arthur J English of North Shields was reported in the *Sunderland Daily Echo and Shipping Gazette* of 16th August 1913. 25 years later – on 24th December 1938 – the same newspaper reported that Arthur English of South Shields had been successful in becoming a Master at Nellist's Nautical School in Newcastle-upon-Tyne.

2 The SS *Narragansett* was a British Steam Tanker on route from New York to London with a cargo of lubricating oil when she was sunk by a German torpedo on 16th March 1917. 46 lives were lost, including that of the Master – the 54 year-old Charles Edward Harwood – who had provided Arthur English with his reference four years earlier (see www.wrecksite.eu).

– Suez, Aden, Durban, Cape Town, Sierra Leone, Malta – with the consistent "very good" stamp marked for both "ability" and "general conduct" on every voyage. A short reference from the company (in 1946) stated that "whilst in our employ his conduct and ability were entirely satisfactory".

From 1935, Arthur served in the Mediterranean – on Cassar Coy Ltd's RMS *Knight of Malta* – as Chief Officer from December of that year until the vessel was requisitioned by the Admiralty for war service in June 1940. That company's reference (in 1948 from C Cassar Torreggiani, Managing Director) stated that "Mr English was always found to be very efficient in carrying out his duties, always sober, and conscientious".

The path not followed

Before moving on to describe Arthur Joseph English's experiences in the First World War, it is important to go back to 1912 and his period of service on SS *Seneca*. It was during this time that he made some preparations for a change of circumstances that would have had fundamental implications for his subsequent life and family story.

The *New York, US, State and Federal Naturalization Records, 1794-1943* – compiled by the US National Archives and Records Administration and made available on Ancestry – include a Declaration of Intention signed by Arthur on 24th September 1912. After providing details of his name, age, occupation, personal characteristics and place of birth, Arthur completed the document so that it read:

> I now reside at 194 Pearl Street, New York. I emigrated to the United States of America from London, England, on the vessel *Ocean Prince*; my last foreign residence was North Shields, England.
>
> It is my *bona fida* intention to renounce forever all allegiance and fidelity to any foreign prince, potentate, state or sovereignty, and particularly to George V, King of Britain and Ireland, of which I am now a subject. I arrived at the port of New York in the State of New York on or about the [blank] day of December, anno Domini 1907; I am not an anarchist; I am not a polygamist nor a believer in the practice of polygamy; and it is my intention in good faith to become a citizen of the United State of America and to permanently reside therein; SO HELP ME GOD.

It is clear that, in the event, Arthur did not follow up his intention to become a US citizen. It was to be less than two years until the start of the First World War, in which Arthur was to maintain his "allegiance and fidelity" to King George V (as described below) and which the United States did not enter until 1917. The

Declaration of Intention would have been deemed invalid after 7 years.[3]

What is interesting are the circumstances which might have prompted Arthur to sign the Declaration of Intention. He had made his first voyage to the US in 1907 when he had been aged 15. By 1912, he was a single 20-year old with the occupation of 3rd Mate. It is perhaps relevant that he was employed by the Anglo American Oil Company Ltd and thus might have been exposed to the opportunities that an American residence and citizenship could bestow.[4]

How different the English line through the subsequent generations would have been, had Arthur's initial intentions been carried through to completion. It would not have been the line described in this narrative, of course. Such are the potentially seismic impacts – albeit not delivered – of the paths not followed on any family tree.

The "K" Boats

In the family records passed on by Arthur Joseph English to his son and my father-in-law, Denis English, there was also something else to grab the attention. Among the papers were two lengthy articles from *The Sunday Times Weekly Review* in January 1963 by an author called Don Everitt, respectively entitled "The Astonishing History of the K Boats" and "Ordeal in K13". These were accompanied by a review of Everitt's book (*The K Boats* published by Harrap at 18 shillings) by David Holloway in the *Daily Telegraph* later the same month: "White Elephants at Sea".

Denis's file also included a short handwritten note from his father, dated 5 January 1970, which referred to another press cutting (which was not with the papers), though with a caveat – "[It] may be of interest to you, though [I] expect you're sick of the whole subject". The note was poignantly signed off with "Hope to see you soon. Cheerio Lad. Pop". (Arthur died in Twickenham in December of that year at the age of 78).

All sorts of questions arose. Why had Denis kept these particular press cuttings, which were nearly half a century old? What was "the whole subject"? And what was the family connection to it? As so often with family stories, the immediate reaction was one of regret that Denis was not around to ask in person. There was now a mystery to solve.

---

3   The Declaration of Intention (or "First Papers") requirement of immigrants to the United States ended in 1952, although there remains the option for current immigrants to file a Declaration.

4   The Anglo-American Oil Company Ltd was established in 1888 as the first foreign affiliate of John D Rockefeller's US company, the Standard Oil Trust. The Esso brand was introduced in the USA in 1926 and in the UK in 1934. (www.exxonmobil.co.uk).

The solution to the puzzle emerged from two separate strands of enquiry: the detailed career of "Pop" – Arthur Joseph English – and the truly "astonishing" story of the development of Britain's submarine capability in the First World War.

By November 1916, Arthur was a Lieutenant (Temporary) in the RNR serving on HMS H2. On his discharge from that vessel, in April 1918, his captain reported that he was "a most energetic and efficient navigating officer of his submarine". Following a period of service on HMS Maidstone, it was what came next for Arthur that draws the two strands of our story together.

Don Everitt's 1963 book described how, in 1915, the Admiralty secretly laid down a class of submarines of revolutionary design. In response to the German U-boats successes in the early stages of the war – three cruisers were sunk in the English Channel in one particular attack – Britain's new submersible destroyers were to be the largest, heaviest and fastest submarines in the world. Between August 1916 and May 1918, 17 of these steam-powered vessels were commissioned, designated as the K class.

It is difficult to summarise the full extent of the K class's deficiencies, though, in his contemporary review of Everitt's book, Holloway made a good attempt: "K boats had a habit of sinking of their own accord, diving out of control or merely failing to go down when required".

Modern analysts offer no kinder judgement. In the Winter 2013 edition of *Undersea Warfare*, the official magazine of the US submarine force, Edward C Whitman stated that "the K boats compiled an almost unbroken record of disaster and death, unredeemed by even a single instance of combat effectiveness". Among the technical deficiencies, in 1917, were "fuel leaks, explosions, fires, boiler flashbacks, hydraulic failures and groundings". The article also noted that "loss of depth control was common and nosing into the bottom was a regular occurrence".[5]

Everitt drew on Admiralty papers and interviews with the (then) surviving participants to catalogue the series of tragedies, disasters and ill-luck that befell the K class of submarines. These included the so-called Battle of May Island in January 1918 (so-called because it took place on the way to fleet exercises, rather than being an actual battle), when two submarines were sunk, three others badly damaged and 105 lives lost.

Back to Arthur English's wartime records and it is the next entry in his RNR Training Certificate Book that jumps off the page. From October 1918 until May 1919, he was the "navigating officer of a K class submarine (K11)".

We cannot be sure how much Arthur was aware of the K class's characteristics as an underwater death-trap when he joined K11. It is reasonable to assume, however, that, among the officers and crew, there would have been some

---

5 ""K" for Katastrophe: K Class Submarines in the Royal Navy", *Undersea Warfare*, No. 49, pp 28-33, Winter 2013.

well-informed speculation and insider knowledge about the severe difficulties that the K class had experienced by that stage of the war. Indeed, *Undersea Warfare* magazine states that "[the] wretched living conditions, coupled with a growing reputation for crew lethality, made the K class unpopular boats to serve in, and morale was a recurring problem".

The Great War had only a month or so to run when Arthur was first exposed to the dangers of K11. He was not to know that, of course. Moreover, the remaining duration of combat was only partly relevant to Arthur's survival prospects. The six sinkings within the K class were all due to accidents of various types; only one of the K class ever engaged an enemy vessel (when its torpedo failed to explode on hitting a U-boat) and none of the class's death toll was attributable to enemy action. As late as 1921, K5 was lost with all hands during fleet exercises and K15 sank at Portsmouth.

When the war started, Arthur Joseph English was 22 years old. In 1918, having survived four years at sea, he was given a position of huge responsibility in a type of vessel that was almost certainly known to have had an appalling track record. What must he have thought? What must his expectations have been? How had he reconciled himself to the increased possibility of death by drowning or fire or asphyxiation?

Of course, there was no question of Arthur turning his back on what was required. He did his duty and (as noted in Chapter 5) this was recognised, in October 1919, with the award of the Mercantile Marine Medal. Nonetheless, one can only wonder at a bravery which – as with that of countless others across the different theatres of the Great War – evokes strong emotions of pride and gratitude, even a century on.

Marriage in Malta

Many years ago, my wife Angela was informed by one of her uncles that Arthur Joseph English had married Mary Stella Stapleton in Brindisi, Italy, just after the end of the First World War and this was duly incorporated as an incidental detail within the accepted family history. In fact, as revealed in the marriage certificate that I purchased from the Public Registry in Malta, Arthur and Stella were married in the Church of St Patrick, attached to the Salesian Institute, Sliema, in August 1918.

The 26 year-old Arthur's occupation was "naval officer on active service" and his residence given as "on board warship". Stella was aged 19 and her occupation was simply "home duties". The maiden name of her mother (Giuseppa, sic) was given as Brincau. By the time of the marriage, Stella's father (Joseph Stapleton) was in his late fifties, his occupation being "retired military officer non-commissioned, barrack accountant". The witnesses to the marriage were Douglas Munro and

Robert Dilley. The former, born in Glasgow, was a 25 year-old Assistant Paymaster with the Royal Australian Navy whose residence was given as HMS *Swan*; the latter – a 38 year-old businessman from Aldershot – we have already met (in Chapter 6 above) as the husband of one of Stella's older sisters: Bertha Florence (Beatrice) Dilley, née Stapleton.

A report of the "interesting" wedding was given in the *Daily Malta Chronicle and Garrison Gazette* of 29th August 1918:

> NAVAL WEDDING
>
> An interesting wedding took place on the 17th inst at St Patrick's Church, Sliema, the contracting parties being Lieut AJ English RNR and Miss Stella Eugenie Stapleton, twin daughter of Mr and Mrs J Stapleton, 48 Victoria Terrace, Sliema. The ceremony was performed by the Very Rev. PJ O'Grady OS. Shortly before 5pm the bridegroom arrived accompanied by Asst. Paymaster D Munro, Royal Australian Navy, as best man, and a few minutes later the bride, charmingly attired in white satin entered the church accompanied by her father, who gave her away, and attended by her bridesmaids Miss Annie Stapleton (sister) and Miss Beatrice Dilley (niece) with Master Robert Dilley as page attired in naval uniform, the choir singing an appropriate hymn. The ceremony ended and the register signed, the happy couple left the church while the organ peeled forth a wedding march, and passed under an archway of drawn swords held by a party of the bridegroom's brother officers.
>
> A largely attended reception was held at the residents of the bride's parents where the impromptu wedding cake was cut by the bride with her husband's sword. The presents were numerous and useful. After the customary congratulations the happy couple left for Berzebbugia for the honeymoon.

The newspaper report probably explains where the English family reference to Brindisi came from. The honeymoon destination of Birżebbuġa is a seaside town in the south of Malta, approximately 8 miles from the capital, Valletta.

Arthur and Stella visited England for a short time before returning to Malta, where their first two children were born: Anthony (Tony) Terence English in 1920 and Denis Arthur Stapleton English (Angela's father) in 1921.

There is a poignant reference to this visit in a letter – dated June 1982 – to Denis English from one of his cousins that he retained in the possessions later passed on to Angela:

> "…I remember her [Stella] coming to England as a young bride. She was good to look at, full of high spirits and I imagined her excitement at coming

to join her husband's people. You can imagine her disappointment. I'm sure she must have had some very sad times".

It would appear that some strain was put on the marriage, initially by the relatively cool welcome that Stella had received when first meeting the English family and, later, when Arthur Joseph English was absent for long periods from the home, being away at sea.

There was clearly some movement by the family between Britain and Malta in the early years of the marriage. The *UK and Ireland Outward Passenger List, 1890-1960* on Ancestry includes an entry for 2nd January 1925 for the 25 year-old Stella (with her sons, 4 year-old Anthony Stapleton and 3 year-old Denis Arthur) on the *Morvada*, which was calling at Malta, Port Said and Bombay on its way to Karachi. Tony and Denis's sister – Helen Josephine Anne English – would be born in Bridport, Dorset, in 1930.

Prisoner of War

Arthur's wartime experiences were not over. The next item in Denis English's file was a handwritten note by Arthur describing an exchange of prisoners-of-war that the Swiss Red Cross had arranged in Turkey in March 1943. Arthur had been captured when the port of Tobruk in Libya fell to the Axis forces on 21st June 1942.[6]

The Battle of Gazala had been fought during the Western Desert Campaign of the Second World War around Tobruk between 26th May and 21st June 1942. The Allied Eighth Army lost 50,000 men killed, wounded or captured, including about 35,000 prisoners at Tobruk. The Axis casualties were 3,360 Germans and a smaller number of Italians.

To begin with, the news of Arthur was that he was simply missing. The *Shields Daily News* of 9th July 1942 reported:

> FORMER NORTH SHIELDS NAVAL OFFICER MISSING
> Lieut-Comndr Arthur Joseph English RNR, a former North Shields resident, is reported missing in the Middle East after two years of active service there. This information was cabled to his wife, who lives in Sliema, Malta.

---

6   In his excellent *Cricketing Lives*, Richard H Thomas notes that two England cricketers – Freddie Brown (a future captain) and Bill Bowes, both veterans of the famous "Bodyline Tour" of Australia in 1932-33 – were amongst those captured at Tobruk. Inevitably, alongside the horror and trauma of capture and internment, there were poignant examples of the British stiff upper-lip:
> "The two arranged cricket matches in front of bewildered Italian and German guards who thought the batsman's blockhole might be the start of an escape tunnel. When the Americans rescued him [Brown] in 1945, he'd shed over four stone".

Lieut-Comndr English is the son of Mrs English and the late Mr Arthur English, who was well known in North Shields as a chief engineer.

Fifty years of age, Lieut-Comndr English was educated at St Cuthbert's RC School and Tynemouth Municipal High School. On leaving school at the age of 16 he became an apprentice with the Prince Line and has been going to sea ever since.

During the last war, he served in HM submarines. Later he was captain of the Eastern Telegraph Company's cable ship.

Lieut-Comndr English married an English girl in Malta and has two sons and a daughter. One of his sons is serving with the Merchant Navy and the other is in the paratroops.

His mother is now living at 5 Chollerford Avenue, Whitley Bay.

The news report was understandably vague about Arthur's field of operations: Tobruk was simply "the Middle East". It was also inaccurate about the nationality of his wife, Stella. Two weeks later, on 24th July, under the heading "North Shields Officer a Prisoner", the same newspaper reported that Arthur was a prisoner-of-war and that Stella, in Sliema, had again been informed. The remainder of the second article was virtually identical to the first, including the (totally irrelevant) details of the full address of Arthur's widowed mother.

Arthur was held in a POW camp in Padula in southern Italy – "a disused Cistercian monastery where four of us slept in a monk's cell". One morning, a total of about 20 of them were woken up at 2 o'clock and told to pack; all their gear was searched and anything written – books and letters – was taken away. They were taken by truck to the station where they were loaded on a train to Bari. A Red Cross officer told them that they would be embarking for Turkey where they would be exchanged for an equal number of Italian naval POWs.

In total, about 400 naval POWs and 50 merchant seaman were freed; Arthur noted that he did not know how the British exchanges were picked out. On reaching Mersina, they saw that their "opposite numbers" had arrived just before them. "When the Swiss and Turkish Red Cross officials boarded, the exchange began… Rank for rank, head for head, as the enemy repartee came up the port accommodation, each one of us was checked off and went down the starboard… [We were] given quite a reception and escorted to the bar, where the first question was 'what are you going to have?' It seemed like a dream". The exchange completed, the freed prisoners sailed for Port Said and then were sent by train to Alexandria.

Intriguingly, Arthur's notes included a list of senior naval personnel with various times and actions given under each name. I assumed that this was a shorthand version of the immediate events on the day of his capture. One of the names (Lieut AR Gilmore RNVR, HMT *Alisia*) had a later comment added "now a vicar C of E"; another (Lieut Chesney RNR) had an asterisk against it and a cryptic remark: "That Bad Man".[7]

Arthur concluded his note by stating that after about two weeks in Egypt, "most of us were embarked on the *Ile de France* and I got off at Durban and travelled by train to Cape Town".

This South African connection is interesting because an accompanying paper in Denis English's file was a "Prisoner-of-War Map of Italy" ("*Krygsgevangenekaart van Italie*") – written in English and Afrikaans – and issued by the South African Association of Relatives and Friends of Prisoners-of-War with an address in Cape Town.[8] The map included Padula, located about 20 miles to the north east of Salerno, as Camp 35; it was described as 2,000 feet up in the Apennines with "pretty but inaccessible scenery".

The map included guidance on "How to Send Letters to our Men in Italy" based on information published by the Red Cross. The guidance was succinct and clear: one sheet of ordinary notepaper only, though both sides could be used; the letter to bear the prisoner's name, number and address; dealing with purely personal matters; and so on. There was also guidance on personal clothing parcels: no food or sweets; no medicinal items; no cigarettes, tobacco, playing cards, games or books; no printed matter, not even "with love from…"

In addition to the personal notes, Arthur had passed on to his son, Denis, about a dozen small black and white photographs taken in Tobruk. Most were dated on the back as having been taken in 1941, though a couple were of the war cemetery at Acroma and dated 1 May 1952. These were clearly as personal to Arthur as his written notes had been. In addition to the photographs of the rows of uniform headstones, there was a close-up of the one belonging to Captain FM Smith CBE, DSO, RD of the Royal Naval Reserve, who died on 21 June 1942 aged 48. (This was Frank Montem Smith, who had been killed on the day that Tobruk fell). Amongst the earlier photographs was one taken from off-shore of the bombed-out Navy House, which had been the Italian Governor's Palazzo. The note on the back stated: "I was in the building (in the shelter mark you!) when that stick landed".

---

7 A Google search led me to the online publication of *Soldier, Sailor, Beggarman, Thief: Crime and the British Armed Services since 1914* (2013) by Clive Elmsley. Ronald John Chesney – previously known as John Donald Merrett – is described as "a singularly nasty individual". After joining the Royal Navy in 1940, he commanded a schooner supplying Tobruk with official supplies and black market merchandise. Later in the war, in northern Germany, he ran a black market operation supplying chocolate, cigarettes, arms and penicillin. He committed suicide in Germany whilst being sought by the British police for the murders of his wife and mother-in-law in Ealing. As a teenager, he had benefited from a "not proven" verdict in Scotland at his trial for the murder of his mother.

8 Both the 1st South African Division and 2nd South African Division fought at the Battle of Gazala. The entire Natal Field Artillery Regiment was killed or captured in June 1942 and the regiment was not re-formed until after the war.

Arthur English's Order of Release from Naval Service was sent in September 1946 and applied from 22 December of that year; it was sent to his home address in Whitley Bay, Northumberland. This appears to have been something of a relief. From his RNR Officer's Training Certificate Book, we know that, from March, Arthur was on duty with the SO Reserve Fleet – based at Sheerness – with HMS *Wildfire*. Apart from taking two corvettes (one in tow) to Hong Kong, there was little activity with "most officers and ratings filling in time awaiting demobilisation". Discipline was very poor and the CO "just a sick headache". All in all, it was "not a pleasant six months".

Meanwhile... in Malta

Arthur Joseph English's wife and daughter – Mary Stella and Helen Josephine Anne – were resident in Malta for a substantial part of the Second World War. They would have been aged 41 and 8, respectively, when Italy entered the war on 11th June 1940; on the same day, Malta suffered its first air attack when Italian aircraft bombed the naval dockyard and one of the airfields.

There is a considerable literature on the Maltese experience during the war; I have drawn on the chapter in Brian Blouet's *The Story of Malta* and Max Hastings's *Operation Pedestal: The Fleet That Battled to Malta 1942*.

Blouet notes the inadequate preparations that had been made in Malta at the time of the war's commencement in September 1939.

> "The island's anti-aircraft defences were still inadequate, fighter cover was completely lacking, there were no air-raid shelters and aircraft servicing facilities were limited. There was a lack of reconnaissance aircraft and bombers. It was extremely doubtful if the coastal defences were strong enough to resist a seaborne assault and stocks of food and other supplies were miserable".

Blouet reports that total civilian war deaths in Malta were 1,490, not including Maltese serving with the British forces. His description of this figure as "not particularly high" might seem to reflect a historian's professional indifference, but the comment is made with reference to the fact that Maltese houses were built principally of stone with the result that, unlike elsewhere in Europe, there was no burning out of large sections of towns brought about by incendiary bombs.

Blouet refers to Malta's war being "short and fiery" with the islanders subjected to the tension of bombing raids for long periods, the discomfort of evacuation and acute food shortage. The laws of economics applied:

> "Wealth tended to congregate in the hands of those with goods to sell, particularly farmers, many of whom made considerable sums during the war. There were powerful regulations to prevent the development of a black market, but one certainly existed, and in the period of excessive scarcity eggs were fetching twelve new pence each".

By the late summer of 1942, Malta was within weeks of surrender to the Axis because its 300,000 population could no longer be fed:

> "…the greatest part of Malta's population, both civil and military, was slowly starving. A soldier on active service was supposed to be fed 4,000 calories a day – in Malta he got 2,000. An adult Maltese male worker got 1,609 calories and an adult woman 1,500".

In Operation Pedestal, the Royal Navy committed the largest fleet assembled in the western theatre of the Second World War to escort 14 merchant ships on the thousand mile journey from Britain through the Straits of Gibraltar and across the Mediterranean to Malta. Hastings describes in terrifying detail the battles that ensued between 11th-14th August as the convoy came under attack from Axis aircraft, surface ships and submarines. Five merchant ships succeeded in reaching the Grand Harbour in Valetta – to a rapturous welcome – at the cost of over 450 Royal Navy and merchant seaman deaths plus other casualties in the RAF and Fleet Air Arm. An aircraft carrier, two cruisers and one destroyer were lost and three other RN vessels badly damaged.

The shortages of food and other essential supplies continued even after the arrival of the Operation Pedestal convoy and the subsequent Allied air victories in the summer of 1942 allowed more convoys to reach Malta; it was not until the beginning of 1943 that food supplies really became adequate and it was possible to increase rations. It was in the latter year that Stella English and her daughter, Anne, were evacuated from Malta to Cairo and then to South Africa.

The older of Arthur Joseph and Mary Stella English's two sons – my wife Angela's uncle – was Anthony Terence Stapleton (Tony) English, who was born in 1920. In the *1939 England and Wales Register*, he is listed as an "architectural assistant" resident in East Barnet. (He qualified as an architect after the War).

In Angela's inherited papers, there is a typed version of an airmail letter sent by Tony English to his sister Anne in May 1945. He was on leave from the Army in Whitley Bay, Northumberland, and she was in South Africa. It is a poignant example of the many – probably millions – of such communications sent between family members and loved ones across the world at that time.

"We are certainly living in historic days – and now today, VE Day, is a day I shall always remember. Listened to Churchill this afternoon at 3 o'clock – and have just heard the King's speech, which was really splendid, a simply perfect collection of words. I have not, as I previously imagined, been wildly excited but can only think of thousands of thoughts – of the grim time mummy and you had in Malta, of our Daddy and all he has done for king and country, and of old Denis, who is still in danger, and say a prayer for all our deliverances…

Hope to be getting leave soon – shall probably be seeing Aunty Nita and John[9] – can I give them any messages? I have told them how little time you get for writing.

Tomorrow we have a pukka church parade and will have the pipe band out… My fellas will have to look their best…

God Bless

XX Tony XX"

The Suez Campaign

The date of Arthur English's Order of Release from Naval Service (September 1946) accounts for the timing of his request for a reference from Cable and Wireless Ltd (in October) – noted earlier – for whom he had stopped working over 16 years earlier. Thereafter, notwithstanding his status as a Master in his mid-50s, Arthur was obliged to apply for individual commands by presenting his latest testimonials. These included those from Wheelock Marden & Co Limited of London (May 1948) and RS Dalgliesh Limited of Newcastle-upon-Tyne (September 1948). There was also a (short) letter from the former (GE Marden, Director) in June 1948 – clearly in response to an enquiry about employment from Arthur – stating that "I… shall certainly put you very high up the list if ever we should require a Master".

Arthur English's RNR Officer's Training Certificate Book had two further entries in his precise and neat handwriting for periods of active service. Between June and November 1951, he was involved in the transport of troops and equipment to the Persian Gulf during the Abadan Crisis.[10] There were frequent exercises in Kuwait "but nothing happened" and he eventually returned to the Canal Zone.

---

9   Anne Melita (Nita) Gammon, (née Stapleton, 1899-1966) was Tony's mother's twin sister. Her son, John Gammon, was born in 1932.

10   The Abadan Crisis began in March 1951, when the Iranian Parliament nationalised the Anglo-Iranian Oil Company (AIOC) and expelled Western companies from oil refining in the city of Abadan. The government of Iran was overthrown in August 1953; a year later, the AIOC was set under the control of an international consortium.

It was a different story at Suez in 1956. As he had also been five years earlier, Arthur had been given command of the WD LST *Humfrey Gale*.[11] Between July – when President Nasser seized the Canal – and October, Arthur was on the routes between Cyprus, Malta, Tripoli and Benghazi "carrying vehicles, tanks and military personnel building up for the invasion". Then, he "sailed with troops and vehicles of the Parachute Regiment and arrived off Port Said whilst the attack was going on… [There was a] "fair amount of sniping" before "hostilities stopped at 18.00" on 6 November.

Arthur's personal experience of the Suez campaign is described in a handwritten note entitled "Impressions" and dated 11 November 1956. He begins – and ends – with the weather: "Oh, how it has rained, thundered, lightened since 8 o'clock this morning… Don't remember ever striking such a long continuous spell of rain – real heavy stuff too in the Med". The heavy swell made the transfer off one ship and on to another – HMS *Tyne* for a meeting of the Masters – particularly hazardous: "…never more pleased to feel the deck of the Humf under my two feet".

Arthur was clearly familiar with Port Said and some of its inhabitants from his previous experience in the Merchant Navy: "[I]t all looked so different. The harbour, usually so busy, was blocked with sunken ships, many of them Canal Company's dredgers and tugs and old acquaintances of mine". Most poignantly, on landing, Arthur "nipped across the road a few yards [to the Casino Palace Hotel, which was being used as a casualty station] to see if I could see the head porter – Hafeez by name – just to find out his reactions. But he (Hafeez) had been killed".

Arthur did not excessively dramatise the dangers around him, although they were described clearly enough: "Fires burning all over the place, ammunition dumps going up with terrific explosions, much intense sniping and shooting from pockets of resistance… Boys of 13 upwards with pistols or guns to shoot the 'invaders'". There was also something of a dark humour: "Went up on the top bridge about 2.0am to have a 'look see', but came down quicker than that when a spate of machine gun bullets whistled close by".

These actions took place almost 40 years after Arthur's exposure to the huge risks posed by the K-class of submarines in the First World War. By the time of Suez, he was 64 years old. The eventual sense of relief jumps off the page of his note: "We went out to anchor. In weather rapidly getting worse, [I] was damned glad when the guard ship signalled us to say 'Proceed to Malta forthwith'".

---

11   LST – Landing Ship (Tank) – was the designation given to a category of ships built in the Second World War to support amphibious operations. They carried tanks, vehicles, cargo and troops directly on to the shore without the need for docks or piers.

The family of Arthur Joseph English and Mary Stella Stapleton

The family of Arthur Joseph English and Mary Stella Stapleton is summarised in Table 10.1. After the Second World War, Arthur and Stella lived at various addresses in Twickenham, Middlesex: Rosslyn Road, Cambridge Road and Hampton Road. Arthur died in the Richmond-on-Thames district in 1970 at the age of 78. His wife outlived him by eight years, dying at the age of 79 in the Wandsworth district in 1978. My wife, Angela, recalls that Stella remained fit and active in her later years and died suddenly one day in church.

The other members of the family also made their homes in the suburbs of London. Tony English – the uncle of Angela – married Daphne May Wicks (1927-1996) in 1952; he died in Enfield in 2000 at the age of 80. Angela's auntie Anne married Patrick Collins (1922-2012), with whom she had four sons, in 1960; she was 76 when she died in Sunbury in 2008.

Table 10.1. The family of Arthur Joseph and Mary Stella English	
Arthur Joseph English 1892-1970 (born in North Shields) (died in Richmond-on-Thames district, London, aged 78)	
married	
Mary Stella Stapleton 1899-1978 (born in Sliema, Malta) (died in Wandsworth district, London, aged 79)	Anthony (Tony) Terence Stapleton English 1920-2000 (born in Malta) (died in Enfield, Middlesex, aged 80) *married* Daphne May Wicks 1927-1996 (born in Barnet, Middlesex) (died in Hendon, Middlesex, aged 68)
	Denis Arthur Stapleton English 1921-2009 (born in Sliema, Malta) (died in Ealing, London, aged 87) *married* **Anne Catherine Murray 1919-1997** (born in Gosforth, Northumberland) (died in Ealing aged 77)

	Helen Josephine Anne English 1932-2008 (born in Bridport, Dorset) (died in Sunbury, Middlesex, aged 76) *married* Joseph Patrick Collins 1922-2012 (born in Richmond, Yorkshire) (died in Sunbury aged 90)

CHAPTER ELEVEN

MURRAY/McMANAMON

Roman Catholicism

According to my wife, Angela, the family story concerning **JOHN MURRAY** (1873-1952) and **HONORIA (ANNIE) McMANAMON** (1878-1967) – the last in the line of our children Tom and Katie's great grandparents – is that Honoria's parents disapproved of the match and that the couple ran away to England. The family's preferred option would have been for Honoria to have married one of their neighbours in Srahrevagh, Mayo – thereby consolidating the respective households' adjacent landholdings – rather than an unskilled labourer.

The identity of the neighbour is something of a mystery. Other things equal, the obvious candidate would appear to have been Honaria's namesake in Srahrevagh – Patrick J McManamon – as, in 1901, he was the head of the only other household in the township. However, as noted in Chapter 7, the difficulty with this explanation – and it is a significant hurdle – is that Patrick and his family were members of the Irish Church, not Roman Catholic. Moreover, the 1911 Census of Ireland shows that, by then, Patrick and his wife Jane had been married for 17 years i.e. since 1894, when Honoria would have been aged only 16.

At this point, I should note that Honoria Murray (née McManamon) is one of the characters in this family chronicle, whose given name varies over time. As noted at the beginning of Chapter 7, in the 1901 Census of England and Wales, she was Annie Murray, aged 23, married to John Murray and sharing a house with another family at 1 Lansdowne Place, Gosforth; John's occupation was "bricklayer's labourer". In the following Census, in 1911, John Murray was by then aged 37 and a "tramway motor man" with Newcastle-upon-Tyne Corporation.[1] His wife was named as Honoria Murray and they were living with their two children (a third child having previously died) at 35 Longley Street in Newcastle-upon-Tyne. Ten

---

[1] We noted in Chapter 7 that John's brother – the 33 year-old Thomas – was also recorded as having that occupation in Newcastle in 1911. He held the same post ten years later.

years later, John was still working for Newcastle Corporation – as a "tramway inspector" – and he and his wife were living at the same address, though she had reverted back to being Annie Murray. (For the purposes of this narrative, I shall refer to her as Annie).

The couple had had two more children – including Angela's mother, Anne Catherine Murray, who was then aged 18 months – by the time of the 1921 Census. In the 1939 Register, John and Annie are recorded as still living in Longley Street, although the house number is 37.[2] A separate (later) source of information on John Murray's occupation was the marriage certificate of Anne Catherine Murray to Denis English in 1945; on that, it was given as "hotel manager".

John Murray and Annie McManamon were married in St Walburge's Roman Catholic Church in the Maudlands district of Preston, Lancashire, in February 1901.[3] At the time, John was resident in Preston – at 32 Allen Street – though, interestingly, Annie's place of residence was given on the marriage certificate as Malvern Wells in Shropshire. John Murray's occupation was "labourer", whilst that of both of their respective fathers – John Murray and Francis McManamon – was given as "farmer". The surname of one of the witnesses was Murray and, though the initial is hard to read on the certificate, it could be "T", which would be consistent with John's brother, Thomas, at that time being a farm labourer in Leyland, which is only a few miles to the south of Preston.

John and Annie Murray's family is shown in Table 11.1.

Table 11.1. The family of John and Honoria (Annie) Murray	
John Murray 1873-1952 (born in Burrishoole, County Mayo) (died in Newcastle-upon-Tyne aged 79)	
married	
Honoria/Honor/Annie McManamon 1878-1967 (born in Burrishoole) (died in Gosforth, Northumberland, aged 89)	Mary Agnes Murray 1902-1934 (born in Gosforth) (died in Newcastle-upon-Tyne aged 31)

---

2 The area around Longley Street has been considerably redeveloped since the Second World War; numbers 35 and 37 no longer exist.

3 The Wikipedia reference to St Walburge's Church notes that it was designed by Joseph Hansom, who also designed the hansom cab. The church was founded in 1847 and consecrated in 1854. It has the tallest spire of any parish church in England.

	John Francis Murray 1906-1907 (born in Newcastle-upon-Tyne) (died in Newcastle-upon-Tyne aged 0)
	Thomas Patrick Murray 1909-1977 (born in Newcastle-upon-Tyne) (died in Newcastle-upon-Tyne aged 68)
	Margaret Honoria Murray 1915-1991 (born in Gosforth) (died in Gateshead, Northumberland, aged 75) *married* Daniel Gerard Sweeney 1914-1977 (born in Donegal, Ireland) (died in Gateshead aged 63)
	Anne Catherine Murray 1919-1997 **(born in Gosforth)** **(died in Ealing, London, aged 77)** *married* **Denis Arthur Stapleton English 1921-2009** **(born in Sliema, Malta)** **(died in Ealing aged 87)**

The deceased child noted in the 1911 Census was John Francis Murray, who was born in Newcastle in the second quarter of 1906 and died at the beginning of the following year. The first-born child was Mary Agnes Murray, who was a 19 year-old Post Office clerk in Newcastle at the time of the 1921 Census. She died of cancer at the age of 31.

The next son – Thomas Patrick Murray – was ordained as a priest in 1935 and he is recorded in the *1939 England and Wales Register* as one of three Roman Catholic priests at St Mary's Grammar School in Darlington; he lived to the age of 68 and died in Newcastle in 1977.

The report of the death of Thomas Murray was carried in the *Newcastle Journal* of 9th April 1977:

CATHEDRAL PRIEST DIES

Canon Thomas Murray, parish priest of St Mary's Roman Catholic Cathedral, Newcastle, died yesterday.

Canon Murray, who was 68, had been the cathedral's parish priest for 13 years. He was formerly parish priest of Holy Rosary in Gateshead and at one time parish chaplain of La Sagesse Convent in Jesmond, Newcastle.

Canon Murray, who was born in Newcastle, will be buried on Thursday at Ashburton Cemetery, Wolsingham, Gosforth at 11am.

Next Wednesday, his body will be taken into the cathedral.

It is clear from other newspaper coverage, particularly in the *Newcastle Evening Chronicle*, that Thomas Murray was an active member of the church, especially on ecumenical affairs and Christian Unity. A January 1968 report referred to his role as Chairman of the local Diocesan Ecumenical Commission and, five years later, the same newspaper noted that he was Chairman of the Newcastle Council of Churches. In January 1970, he contributed an article to the newspaper's "Churches in the 70s" series. In his role as Administrator of St Mary's Cathedral, Thomas gave the sermon at the Requiem Mass following the death of the Bishop of Hexham and Newcastle in July 1974 and, in February 1975, the Address of Welcome at the installation of his successor.

The opening paragraphs of the January 1968 piece, referring to a meeting that been arranged between Thomas and a French au pair in Newcastle, noted his training (at the Douai Seminary) in France.

> THE CANON AND THE AU PAIR SHARE A COMMON LANGUAGE
> The entente couldn't have been more cordial if De Gaulle had devalued the franc. Through many cups of coffee the talk flowed like vin ordinaire… Canon Thomas Murray and Chantel Girard were in their element, relaxing in the language they love.
>
> Chantel, 20, is an au pair with a family in Elmfield Road, Gosforth. Canon Murray is the Administrator of St Mary's Roman Catholic Cathedral in Newcastle.
>
> At the moment they share a lack of chances to speak in French. Chantel is over here to perfect her English, from a college in Rouen, where she is studying journalism, while Canon Murray, who speaks fluent French, doesn't meet many French around the streets of the city.
>
> "I trained at a seminary in France… but these days I don't often get the opportunity to speak French. I read a lot, but it's not the same".

St Mary's Cathedral was opened to a design by Augustus Welby Pugin in 1844, having been paid for by the halfpenny subscriptions of the impoverished local community. Angela and I visited it between services one Sunday morning in April 2023. She had some memories of the cathedral from her youth, as she had been a regular visitor to her uncle Tom and it was where her older brother, Michael, had married Hilary Jones in 1970. However, not surprisingly, much had changed since that time. The interior – brightly lit during our short stay – has been extensively renovated in recent years, a new organ installed and a café and bookshop now occupy part of the precincts. Happily, during our visit, we met an elderly lady – and a member of the extended family – who had acted as Canon Murray's sacristan during his time in office, although that had ended 46 years earlier. Her face lit up with a gentle smile as she recalled "Tommy Murray".

The Murray family's deep commitment to the Roman Catholic faith was clearly evident in some of the papers passed on to my wife by her late father, Denis English. These included a handwritten copy of the homily used at the Requiem Mass following the death of Margaret Sweeney – one of Anne and Thomas Murray's sisters – in Low Fell, Gateshead in 1991: "It was the simple life of a devout Catholic woman… a life of deep faith lived in the service of Our Blessed Lord".

Two items of poignant correspondence from 1977 reveal that this strong devotion to Catholicism was complemented by a respectful admiration of other faiths. The first, dated 19th January, was from Thomas Murray to Denis and Anne English, which concluded with a reference to him being about to prepare a sermon for the Protestant Cathedral. This was accompanied by a sad letter, also to Denis and Anne, from Margaret Sweeney which was undated but obviously followed shortly afterwards. It lamented Thomas's sudden death:

> "A month or so ago, he preached at the YMA and we begged him pass it up, as his blood pressure had risen under the strain. He said, as the Protestants had very kindly asked him, he would not let them down…
>
> Two weeks ago, at the Legion of Mary meeting, he [Thomas] had spoken of charity and told how his mother had been watched over and enabled to have a wonderful old age due to the kindness of a neighbouring Methodist".

This was a reference to Annie Murray (née McManamon), who had died in Gosforth in 1967 at the age of 89. Her husband, John Murray, had long pre-deceased her, dying in The Royal Victoria Infirmary in Newcastle in July 1952 at the age of 79. The occupation given on John's death certificate was "corporation transport inspector (retired)" and the informant was his son, TP Murray, of St Clare's Abbey, Carmel Road, Washington.

For my wife Angela's aunt, Margaret, 1977 was a devastating year. Her brother Thomas Murray's death was followed a few months later by that of her husband, Daniel Gerard Sweeney, in Gateshead at the age of 62. Daniel, who had been born in Glenties, Donegal, was a General Practitioner in Low Fell, having previously been in practice in Darlington.

Angela held her aunt Margaret in great affection, not least for her keen sense of humour. Notwithstanding the despair of the 1977 letter noted above, she ended it with the hope that "our Brenda Foster" would have a lovely Easter: a reference to Angela's prowess as a runner. An earlier letter to Denis was signed off by "Sweeney

Todd". My fondest memory is of her guiding the pushchair containing our young son, Tom, through the shoppers at the Metro Centre in Gateshead in the year she died. (Perhaps "guiding" does not quite do the action justice: it was done at a speed that would have pleased Brendan Foster himself).

Patterns of Irish migration to England

It was seen in the Introduction to Part One above that (at least) five members of the Line of 16 – Arthur English, John Murray, Margaret Mullowney, Francis McManamon and Honor McManamon – were born in Ireland: four in County Mayo and one in County Down. Another member of the Line – Joseph Stapleton – might well have been born near Dublin, though his Army records give his place of birth as Liverpool. Yet another – Helen Kelly – had a father who was born in Roscommon in Connacht.

Apart from (possibly) Joseph, the only one of the Line of 16 to undertake the migration from Ireland to England was the infant Arthur English (born in 1869) with his parents John and Catherine and his siblings. In the case of the family of his wife, Helen Kelly, the journey had been made a generation earlier by the 17 year-old Patrick (with his father, James) in 1847. John Murray (born in 1873) and Annie McManamon (born in 1878) were in the next generation from the Line of 16's John/Margaret Murray and Francis/Honor McManamon when they followed this well-worn path in about 1901.

A good summary of the academic research on the migration of the Irish to England is given in Donald M MacRaild's *The Irish in Britain, 1800-1914*. This notes that, whilst there were well-known connections between places of departure and initial settlement – for example, Ulster to Scotland and Connacht (via Dublin) to Liverpool – there were also clear patterns in the subsequent secondary migrations within the country during the second half of the 19th Century. These "were not characterised by aimless wandering… [as there were] established routes for Irish migrants within Britain". Of particular interest for our purposes:

> "[T]he mixing of Irish populations meant that, while a quarter of Newcastle's population derived from Ulster, nearly half came from western Connacht, particularly Sligo and Mayo. The same patterns were noticeable in the wider Northumberland population, where the Ulster proportion virtually duplicated that of Newcastle, while Sligo and Mayo were also prominent".

Both the Kelly and Murray families form part of this significant migration from the west of Ireland to the north-east of England. The Kelly connections were described in Chapter 5, where it was seen (in Table 5.2) that 12 of the 14 children of Patrick Kelly (1830-1893) and his wife Frances Kelly (née Davis, 1830-1902) were born in North Shields. (The other two children were born in New York).

In the case of the Murrays, not only is there the example of John and Annie Murray, but also (from Table 7.1) that of John's brother – Thomas Murray (1877-1944) – who married Mary Mason Smith (1883-1938) in Castle Ward, Northumberland, in 1904. Thomas is recorded in the 1939 Register as a 62 year-old widowed (and invalided) train-driver in Newcastle – when John was a retired trams inspector – and his branch of the Murray family continued with 3 children and 5 grandchildren born in the region.

The historian Donald MacRaild also states that, whilst many migrants were trapped in poverty or the lowest occupational groups, there were also indications of upward mobility:

> "Contemporary investigators offered evidence concerning the improving socio-economic status of the Irish. Hugh Heinrick, "special correspondent" for the *Nation* of Dublin, toured England in 1872… In Newcastle-upon-Tyne he found signs of economic advancement through the creation of an Irish middle-class which comprised some 400 businessmen – a figure surpassed only by the larger Irish communities of London, Liverpool, Glasgow and Manchester".

In addition:

> "The Irish found both skilled and semi-skilled work as blacksmiths, fitters, turners, riveters and drillers in shipbuilding towns such as Birkenhead, Barrow, Sunderland, Jarrow, Wallsend and Greenock… Hugh Heinrick reckoned that a total of one-sixth of the entire Irish community had pulled itself up from 'the severest drudgery to a condition of comparative prosperity'".

MacRaild makes another relevant observation in his discussion of the religious backgrounds (Protestant and Catholic) of the Irish migrants to Britain and their relative impacts on the Irish sense of "community":

> "Even after overt Irishness faded, Catholicism remained as its lasting marker – a marker which did not wane until the 1950s, when new processes of secularisation and suburbanisation undermined religious communities still further".

Finally, I note one of MacRaild's overall conclusions:

> "[T]he Irish in Britain suffered from an overspill of many of the prejudices and much of the bitterness which affected Anglo-Irish relations more

generally in this period [of the Act of Union (1801-1922)]. The migrants provided a human connection between the two countries and their reception attested to the political and cultural tensions which influenced life in the United Kingdom during the period".

From the evidence of this chapter (and also Chapters 5 and 7 above), it can be seen that many of the general themes identified by MacRaild – the significance of the North East of England as a final destination for migrants from Connacht and Ulster, the incidence of drudgery in unskilled work, the acquisition by some migrants and their descendants of skilled trades, the importance of Roman Catholicism – find strong echoes in the experiences of those family branches within the Line of 16 that were associated with migration from Ireland to England: Kelly, Murray, McManamon and English.

PART THREE

Grandparents and Parents

All four of Tom and Katie's grandparents were post-First World War births – in the 3 years from 1919. Their ages at death ranged from 77 to 87 years.

		Dates	Place of birth
*	William Alexander Rigg	1921-2004	Hunslet, Leeds, Yorkshire
*	Enid Peggie Niblett	1922-2000	Palmer's Green, London
*	Denis Arthur Stapleton English	1921-2009	Sliema, Malta
*	Anne Catherine Murray	1919-1997	Gosforth, Northumberland

Finally, Tom and Katie's parents:

		Dates	Place of birth
*	John Alexander Rigg	1954-	Leeds
*	Angela Mary English	1957-	Gosforth

CHAPTER TWELVE

RIGG/NIBLETT

The apprentice joiner

Tom and Katie's paternal grandparents – **WILLIAM ALEXANDER (BILL) RIGG** (1921-2004) and **ENID PEGGIE NIBLETT** (1922-2000) – were married at St John's Church, Moortown, Leeds in 1949. Their family is shown in Table 12.1.

Table 12.1. The family of William Alexander and Enid Peggie Rigg	
William Alexander Rigg 1921-2004 (born in Leeds) (died in Leeds aged 83)	
married	
Enid Peggie Niblett 1922-2000 (born in Palmer's Green, London) (died in Leeds aged 77)	John Alexander Rigg (born 1954) (born in Leeds) *married* Angela Mary English (born 1957) (born in Gosforth, Northumberland)
	Rosemary Jill Rigg

Bill Rigg was a joiner and foreman in the construction industry. His pathway into this trade became clear at a very early stage, as he informed me in the long conversation that I recorded with him in December 2000.

> "I must tell you this. When I was about 8, we went to woodwork classes for one afternoon a week and, later on, you went all day. A day a week. The

class was at Cross Flatts School joinery department [in south Leeds]. There were two woodwork teachers and the one I got was very peppery – a small, aggressive type of a teacher, who everybody was a bit frightened of. I think [his name] was Nesbit, but I wouldn't swear to it. He told me how to handle the tools – started right at the beginning – how to sharpen, how to lay them down so you didn't cut yourself.

The first thing you'd to make was called the oblong prism. It was a piece of timber. Rough. About a foot long and two inches square. To get this, you'd to hold the plane right and you'd to make it smooth, straight and square. So you had a square and you'd put it on the prism and square it… and you'd to turn it round and square the other way until all the four sides were dead square. Well I was a disaster. And I was frightened. He said, "Right. Stop. All gather round my desk". And we gathered round his desk and you'd to take your prism up and he had his square. I remember this as if it was yesterday. And he'd get mine. At the wall at the end, there was a big basket, full of timber. And he used to throw it, like that [throws vigorously]. "Go, get another one", he said, "and start again". And I'd to get another piece of wood and start again.

Some of the lads were passing, but he must have thrown about 6 or 7 of mine in that basket. I thought, I'm never going to do it. And all of a sudden, I clicked. I did it. And, do you know, his face lit up and there was a smile. So I went on to the next objects: coatrails, coathooks, and all like that. I passed everybody and went right up until, at the finish, I made a beautiful little tender with a drawer at the bottom and a parallel door, and he thought it was marvellous. I took it home and gave it to my mother. After that, I loved joinery, I loved it. That started me off on it. And I'd such a bad start. I can remember him throwing it into this bin.

I left school at 14. I went to John Curtis's, which was the biggest shopfitting firm in the country. It was up East Street [in Leeds].

I went to Leeds College of Technology evening classes. You had to pay your fee. It wasn't a lot, but my dad had to pay for the first year. I won the exam for the first year, so all my fees were paid for the next 4 years.

I had theory and practice. I did everything: drawing, geometry, building construction and the practical work. You got everything in the building trade. Three or four evenings a week. I went to evening class from 14 to 17 and I went during the day once or twice. I did a mock City and Guilds and I passed it. The teacher said I could go in for it proper next year. The next year, war broke out. I went to the evening class and I told him I won't be going any more, because I was joining up. He just said, "You're a silly boy. You should stay until you've been in for your City and Guilds". But I didn't: that were another story.

> When I first started at Curtis's, I got ten shilling a week. You worked Saturday morning and 8 till 5 [during the week]. When you first went, you were in what they called the "boy's room" and there were all lads – 14, maybe to 16 – and you were under the tuition of an experienced craftsman.
>
> For every little job you got, there was a drawing. No matter how small, there was a drawing. And that drawing was on your bench. Now you worked for 6 months in this shop and then they decided "Well, this lad's going to be ok", so they booked you next to a joiner. And you had a bench and he had a bench, and you worked next to him. Your jobs got bigger, and sometimes you got a big job, and you helped the joiner and he was watching you all the time. And that's how they brought you up, you see. You couldn't help but be good.
>
> It was all for Woolworth's: counters – some of the counters were 20 foot long; wall fixtures; ceiling fixtures; cabinets; office furniture. And it was all mahogany timber. Polished mahogany. Beautiful timber. And everything was polished. Everything was examined and anything you did you'd to write your name on and it went in the polish shop and if they found a flaw, they'd look up who's done this and you were called in to rectify what you'd done. They were very strict and very good".[1]

My sister, Rosie, is the custodian of two small boxes of some of our father's memorabilia and possessions: certificates, papers and other items. These include his report card for the term ending 19th December 1935 (when he would have been aged 14) at the Jack Lane Evening Institute in Leeds: Science 81%, English 80%, arithmetic 50% and drawing 15½ out of 25, with general progress marked as "very satisfactory". There are also the Sessional Record Cards for 1938-39 and 1939-40 issued by the College of Technology in Cookridge Street. However, pride of place would have gone to the letter of 22nd November 1940 from the latter's Principal (JH Everett BSc), announcing that he had been awarded the "Wynne" Prize to the value of 10 shillings for Session 1939-40. By then he had joined the Royal Air Force.

Flight rigger airframe

Bill Rigg was 18 years old when the Second World War began.

> "I got in with a good set of pals [at Curtis's]… We used to go to the window in our dinnertime and aeroplanes were going across. So we were all going to

---

1   John William Curtis, a cabinetmaker, established a shopfitting business – John Curtis & Sons Ltd – in Bond Street, Leeds, in 1852. In 1925, the company moved to York Road, where it remained until 2013, when it relocated to larger premises in south Leeds. The company was relaunched as Curtis Shopfitters Ltd in 1998 and renamed Curtis Furniture Ltd in 2004. (Source: www.curtisfurniture.co.uk).

join the airforce and my best pal, Bill Verity, he said, "Well, let's join up". About 6 of us. One of the others was the son of a policeman. We all decided that, the next dinnertime, we were going to go down to Leeds and join up. Well, when it come to the next dinnertime, there were only two of us left, and that was me and Bill Verity. The policeman's son told us, "My mother won't let me go". I hadn't told my dad and Bill Verity hadn't told his dad, so we were the only two left.

We were walking down to town and he says, "We won't join airforce. Let's join navy". So we went to the navy recruiting office, which was near City Square, and we go in there. And [the recruiting officer] said, "Age? What do you want to join navy for? And what do you do?" "We're apprentice joiners at John Curtis's". "Can't take you", he says, "I'm not allowed to take any apprentices. You've to wait until you're called up". This meant waiting until we were 21 and had finished our apprenticeship. "I'm sorry, but I can't take you".

So we come out and walk down City Square. And [Verity] said, "Well, let's join airforce then. The recruiting office is in Vicar Lane, near the bus stop down that little street going towards the Quarry Hill flats". So we went there, and he goes in first. He's in for about 20 minutes, half an hour, and I followed him in. We were in a queue, you know. I come out and he's sat on the steps. He said, "When do you go in then?" I says, "I'm not going". He said, "Why?" I says, "They don't take apprentices". "Well", he said, "you didn't tell him you were apprentice, did you?" I said, yes… He said, "I told them I was a labourer. They've taken me". So I went back in, saw the very same bloke, perfectly true. He said, "What are you?" I said, "A labourer". He says, "I asked your pal when he wanted to go and he says as soon as possible. Do you want to do the same?" I says, "Yes". So that was it, that's how I joined.

We did us square-bashing and then they sent us to Kirkham, which is between Preston and Blackpool.[2] At Kirkham, I did 18 weeks with Bill Verity on a flight rigger's course. That was repairs to the aircraft. All repairs, except the engines. There was flight rigger airframe, which was me. And there was flight rigger mechanic, which was for the engines. So we did everything: main frames, undercarriage, wings, fuselage. There was a mixture of metal, wood, fabric. We did the hydraulics, which was all metal piping. The same class went right through and did their square-bashing together and their

---

2   RAF Kirkham opened in 1940 as a training camp for RAF tradesmen. Up to 1945, it trained 72,000 British and allied service men and women. In November 1941, Kirkham became the main armament training centre for the RAF, with 21 different trades and 86 different courses on equipment and weapons. Pupils came from the Commonwealth, USA, Netherlands, Poland, France, Norway, Czechoslovakia and Belgium. The camp closed in December 1957. (Source: www.forces-war-records-co.uk/units/806/raf-kirkham). In the early 1960s, part of the facility was taken over by the Home Office with HMP Kirkham opening in 1962 as an open prison.

flight rigger training together. Then they sent us on leave and that's when I got the letter. And I met him [Verity] coming to meet me and he'd been posted to South Wales and I'd been posted to Scotland… He finished up in Burma somewhere, or India… He got back ok.

…My other pal – the policeman's son – about two years after, he jiggered off like us and joined the Merchant Navy. His first voyage he was sunk and killed. He was a big lad. I was tall, but he was bigger than me. Big, strong lad. Verity was a big strong lad as well".[3]

In April 2017, I obtained my father's Service Record (at a cost of £30) from the RAF Disclosures Department at RAF Cranwell in Sleaford. It provided a limited amount of information – "a purely administrative record of movements, promotions, etc and… no day-to-day information" – to confirm what I already knew. William Alexander Rigg – a "labourer" – enlisted on 5th June 1940 at the age of 19 as an AC2 (Aircraftman Second Class) and was promoted to AC1 in June 1941 and LAC (Leading Aircraftman) four months later. (The RAF documentation included a useful 11-page glossary of common abbreviations). His effective date of release was 18th December 1945.

Bill Rigg was attached to 408 Squadron, initially at Syerston in Nottinghamshire and later at other bases in Rutland and Yorkshire. This was the "Goose" Squadron of the Royal Canadian Air Force (RCAF) that operated as part of RAF Bomber Command from its formation in June 1941 until the end of the war. It began operations with the Handley Page Hampden before switching to the Merlin-powered Halifax and then the Avro Lancaster II and then the Hercules-powered Halifax III and IV. The Squadron flew 4,610 sorties, beginning with a raid on Rotterdam docks in August 1941, and gained more than 210 awards, including 160 DFCs and 30 DFMs. It was disbanded after the surrender of Japan in August 1945 removed the need for Tiger Force, the bombing campaign which was scheduled to accompany the planned invasion of that country.[4]

One of the boxes of my father's memorabilia contains two ties: one of Hunslet RLFC and one of the RAF. There is also his RAF cap, his dog-tags and his Service and Release Book in which the Squadron Leader (whose name is illegible, unfortunately) stated that he was a "[V]ery good worker and tradesman. Is recommended for re-employment as joiner upon his return to civilian life". The box also contains Bill Rigg's Defence Medal and War Medal 1939-45, though I

---

3   My father's friend – Dennis Albert Tordoff – was one of 379 seamen killed in March 1943 when an explosion on HMS *Dasher* caused the vessel to sink in the Firth of Clyde. He was a 21 year-old carpenter's mate. He is commemorated on the Naval Memorial on the waterfront in Liverpool. Francis William Verity died in Leeds in 2001 at the age of 80.

4   See www.historyofwar.org/air/units/RCAF/408_wwII.html and www.raf.mod.uk/history/bombercommandno408squadron.cfm.

am not sure that he regarded these as being of any great significance: "Everybody got those", I recall him telling me once. He was much prouder of his general RAF experience and, in later life, would read various short histories of aspects of the Service during the Second World War.[5]

My father also told me that John Curtis and Son Ltd had reneged on their offer of keeping a place open for him on his return from the War. The documentary evidence on this is not clear, although I can hazard a guess at the sequence of events. An official paper headed "Ministry of Labour and National Service: Interrupted Apprenticeships" states that he renewed his apprenticeship with the firm from the period 19th December 1945 to 27th December 1946. However, there are also three letters of reference – from September 1946 – from Dr JW Silversides (a General Practitioner, whom I remember from my childhood 20 years later as a kindly elderly doctor), Norman Pullan (a director of John Sproston & Son Ltd, a firm of printers and stationers) and W Hirst (the owner of Hirst's Stores, whose wide-ranging interests included drapery, jewellery and house furnishing). These related to Bill Rigg's application to join the Leeds City Police Force.

Given the dates of the letters, I can assume that Curtis's had informed my father that they would not be retaining him after his apprenticeship had been completed and, accordingly, that he had considered an alternative line of employment. In the event, he remained as a joiner and foreman – though not with Curtis's – for the remainder of his working life.

Family roles

I have written about my early years with my parents in *An Ordinary Spectator*:

> "Within the family arrangements, the division of responsibilities between my parents [Bill and Peggie Rigg] had been established and agreed, though probably also unspoken. My father provided the physical lead. He earned the family wage through his sheer hard work and long hours. He was the one who re-landscaped the lower part of the back garden or painted the window frames or, using tradesman's skills that I never came anywhere near to replicating, constructed a new coffee table for the living room. He also ran the family transport: a small green van to start with, later to be followed by the luxury of a Singer Chamois (which Dad always made sure was not mistaken for its near neighbour, the Hillman Imp).
>
> ... [The car's] major annual expedition would be for our summer holiday at the seaside, almost always for the week before the new school term started

---

5   The box contains *Glasgow's Spitfire* (2003), edited by Alex Robertson, Dugald Cameron and Susan Pacitti, *Airfield Focus, 43: Upper Heyford* (2001) by Peter Davis and *Airfield Focus, 52: Donibristle* (2002) by Malcolm Fife. I am not aware that Bill Rigg was ever posted to either Upper Heyford or Donibristle.

in September – Filey or Bridlington on the Yorkshire coast, Morecambe or St Annes on the west – in the preparation for which Dad would spend long hours on the previous Friday evening. The car would be washed and polished, the tyres and oil checked, the petrol topped up, as if we were about to engage in a long-haul endurance operation. Which we were, of course: the tortuous pre-motorway route through York and Malton in one direction or Clitheroe and Preston in the other was not to be undertaken lightly".[6]

The reference to the family transport leads to the final item in the box of Bill Rigg's papers which Rosie keeps. This is an invoice from Tate of Leeds Limited of New York Road for the first (I think) vehicle that my father ever bought – a "linden green" Thames 7 cwt. van – for a total cost of £404 8s 6d in September 1960.[7]

At face value, the invoice covers a routine transaction of 60 years ago and should really be of no interest. However, for me, I think it is of much greater significance. Not only is it a revealing social document, suggesting what was affordable for the hard-working family head of almost 40 years of age – the "extras" included a passenger seat, a heater, a sun visor and "flasher indicators" – but it strikes a personal chord that brings back the memories of over half a century ago.

> "When he first started taking me to watch Hunslet [play rugby league, in 1961]… the van was the means by which we travelled from Moortown through the centre of the city, across the river, and up the Dewsbury Road into south Leeds. As the crow flies, it is not a long journey: perhaps seven or eight miles. However, for the young boy, excited with nerves at venturing into a strange land, and struggling for breath against the van's heady aroma of petrol fumes and the dankness of old bits of timber, it was an epic undertaking. We parked in the open spaces of the car park outside the ground, an apparently boundless expanse of loosely bound asphalt, ash and gravel, my father being careful to avoid the large potholes that lay in wait to test the van's suspension".[8]

My mother's role in the family is also described in *An Ordinary Spectator*:

> "In the meantime, my mother ran the household. She handled the family finances and made sure the pantry was adequately stocked and, when the need arose and a home visit was not possible, shepherded us over the two bus

---

6   *An Ordinary Spectator,* page 18.

7   Equivalent to approximately £9,400 in 2021 prices.

8   *An Ordinary Spectator,* pp8-9

journeys that were necessary to reach the practice of our family doctor, Dr Silversides. In common with millions of her counterparts before and since, my mother saw to it that the rest of the family set off fully prepared for the events of the day. She was the one who rose in the cold darkness of a winter's morning to light the coal fire in the living room before preparing my dad's sandwiches and arranging my school uniform and sending me on my way with a bowl of cereal or porridge and a final run through of that day's spelling test".[9]

Final illnesses

Although she had been christened Enid Peggie Niblett, my mother detested her first name and used her middle name throughout her life. The first signs of Peggie Rigg's final illness – though we did not realise it at the time – came in the mid-1990s, when she adopted the curious habit of surreptitiously turning off the immersion heater in her house whenever someone else had put it on to heat the water. Then, on one occasion, after I had asked her where the red three-volumed *The Reader's Digest Great Encyclopaedic Dictionary* was, my mother claimed that we did not possess a set. The reason for my disquiet was that completing the general knowledge crossword in the *Sunday Express* had been a weekly exercise that she had attempted for as long as I could remember using the same reference book. Sometime afterwards, my sister informed me that my father had later found some of the smaller Christmas presents – wrapped up and unopened – squirreled away behind the living room sofa. Peggie Rigg's battle with the effects of multi-infarc dementia ended in April 2000 at the age of 77.

Bill Rigg was diagnosed with a malignant mesothelioma – the growth in the lining between the lung and the chest brought about by exposure to asbestos dust – in the autumn of 2002. He died in June 2004 at the age of 83. I described the outcome of the inquest into his death in *An Ordinary Spectator*.

> "At the time, we thought that his condition had been brought about by the close proximity in Armley (in south Leeds) of the building firm for which he had been employed for most of his working life to the notorious JW Roberts Ltd company, as the two businesses had been near neighbours in Canal Road. Although the Roberts asbestos factory had closed down in 1959, the time lag between exposure to the dust and evidence of the mesothelioma can be substantial and, indeed, can run into decades. My father had begun working in the area at the end of the 1940s. He had said that he had often

---

9   op cit, page 19.

walked through the Roberts factory as a short cut on his way to work and he could remember the dust lying thick on the ground.

The West Yorkshire Coroner was to take a different view, however. On the basis of the advice of a cancer expert, he concluded that dad's exposure to asbestos dust had occurred because of the nature of many of the jobs at which he had been present in his routine work as a joiner and foreman, where these had involved the removal of asbestos from old buildings prior to their destruction or renovation. In my father's case, therefore, the mesothelioma had most probably been brought about, not by the specific proximity to JW Roberts Ltd, but through an aspect of his job that constituted a routine part of his everyday work. It is a salutary thought to consider the implications of the Coroner's conclusion for those thousands of others in the building industry who, whilst working for similar small building companies throughout the country, have also undertaken this type of activity.

My sister and I attended the inquest in November 2004. It was the day of my fiftieth birthday".[10]

Bill and Peggie Rigg were buried in the Lawnswood Cemetery in north Leeds.

---

10 *op. cit*, pp 339-340

CHAPTER THIRTEEN

ENGLISH/MURRAY

Two sets of Indentures

Tom and Katie's maternal grandparents – **DENIS ARTHUR STAPLETON ENGLISH** (1921-2009) and **ANNE CATHERINE MURRAY** (1919-1997) – were married at the St Charles Catholic Church in Gosforth, Northumberland, in November 1945. Their family is shown in Table 13.1.

Table 13.1. The family of Denis Arthur Stapleton and Anne Catherine English	
Denis Arthur Stapleton English 1921-2009 (born in Sliema, Malta) (died in Ealing, London, aged 87)	
married	
Anne Catherine Murray 1919-1997 (born in Gosforth, Northumberland) (died in Ealing aged 77)	Michael John Murray English *married* Hilary Jones
	Angela Mary English (born 1957) (born in Gosforth) *married* John Alexander Rigg (born 1954) (born in Leeds)
	Adrian Thomas English *married* Emma Jane Whitewood

A good starting point from which to present Denis English's life is an obituary prepared for a newsletter for the West Middlesex Circle of the Catenians[1] by his daughter Angela, following his death in January 2009.

> "Denis Arthur Stapleton English was born in Sliema, Malta, on 24th August 1921. He followed his father into the Merchant Navy and was apprenticed 30 years to the day after him. Denis was happy to make the sea and ships his life's work.
>
> He was 18 when war broke out and served in both Atlantic and Pacific convoys. He faced dive-bombers and mines and learnt how to operate his ship's anti-submarine and anti-aircraft guns. His worst moment came when he had to witness the torpedoing of the *City of Benares*,[2] which was carrying several hundred children being evacuated to North America. Family life was difficult during the war: he didn't see his father for five years; his mother and sister were in Malta during the heavy bombing; and his older brother was serving in the Army.
>
> After nearly eighteen years at sea, Denis finished his sea-going career as a tanker captain and Master Mariner. He spent the rest of his forty-year career with Shell in a variety of shore jobs. He travelled in South America scouting for new oil ports and was finally made responsible for dealing with tanker casualties, notably the *Metula*, which was stranded in the Magellan Straits in 1974. Through his expertise, the pollution was minimised, 75% of the cargo saved and the boat itself was salvaged. He also acted as an expert witness in cases of oil pollution.
>
> Denis took early retirement from Shell in 1976. His wife, Anne, had suffered a major stroke in 1975 and he felt that he alone could give her the care she needed. They began a new life together punctuated by the rituals of ironing and the daily crossword and by entertaining friends. Denis joined the Catenians at this point and he and Anne made many good friends in the West Middlesex Circle. He looked after Anne devotedly, but also found time to serve his parish of St Benedict's as a Eucharistic Minister.
>
> Anne died in 1997, leaving Denis bereft. He continued to care for the housebound as a Eucharistic Minister until his own health deteriorated and he became a resident at St David's Home for Ex-Servicemen (and latterly Servicewomen). Even there, he still took the Eucharist to others and looked after "his old ladies" for as long as he was able.

---

1 The Catenian Association is a Roman Catholic lay society with approximately 10,000 members in a number of English-speaking countries. It was founded in Manchester in 1908.

2 The SS *City of Benares* was torpedoed in 1940 by a German submarine with heavy loss of life, including 77 children being evacuated to Canada.

Denis was a devoted husband, father and grandfather. He was also a generous and loyal friend, renowned for his hospitality. His faith was deep and hard-won, providing great comfort in his later years. He was very successful in his career, but broke that mould to take on the very demanding role of principal carer. In his own inimitable way, he lived a life full of love, faith and gratitude. He is greatly missed by his family and friends".

As noted in Chapter 10, Denis English left a small collection of personal papers to Angela. As with the information that this material provided about his father – Arthur Joseph English – the documents are a source of fascinating detail with which to complement the content of the obituary.

One envelope in the collection probably represented one of Denis's most treasured possessions. It is labelled "My father's and my Indentures – His dated 24 May 1907 – Mine 24 May 1937".

Interestingly, the latter certificate gives Denis's name as Denis Arthur Robert English, including in his 15 year-old's signature and in a separate initialling in one of the margins. (The certificate was also signed for surety by Denis's father). This name also appeared in Denis's Certificate of Service as an apprentice with The Anglo-Saxon Petroleum Company Ltd[3] on m.v. *Adula* from May 1937 to February 1938 and on m.v. *Opalia* from May 1938 to February 1941. (During the intervening period – from February to May 1938 – Denis was on "special leave", which, Angela has informed me, was when he was recovering from severe burns to his feet and legs resulting from the spill of a corrosive liquid. The marks remained with him for life).

There is no obvious explanation as to why Robert – rather than Stapleton – appeared as a middle name in this documentation. It might simply have been a mistake, which all the parties – including Denis and his father – chose to ignore, if there was an urgent need to obtain the certificate. On the other hand, the Indenture would have been a highly significant item for Denis to have had and one presumes that there would have been a desire to ensure that all its details were correct. To add to the mystery, the name of Denis Arthur Stapleton English is given on the copy of the birth certificate registered with the Public Registry Office in Valletta, Malta. The copy was made in March 1937, two months before the date of the Indenture, so this does not suggest that Robert was an original given name that was subsequently changed to Stapleton.

The witness to Arthur Joseph English's signature of surety on Denis English's Indenture was SA Gammon, a Master Mariner with Cable and Wireless, based at Victoria Embankment in London. This was Denis's uncle – Stanley Acton

---

3   The Anglo-Saxon Petroleum Company Ltd was founded in 1907. It ceased to function as a separate company in 1955, when its assets were taken over by The Shell Petroleum Company Ltd.

Gammon (1893-1956) – who was married to his mother's twin sister, Anne Melita (Nita) Stapleton (1899-1966).

Career progression

A separate record of Denis's first ship is to be found in *California Passenger and Crew Lists, 1882-1959*, which is available on Ancestry and based on original data held in the National Archives in Washington, DC. The m.v. *Adula* sailed from Curacao in Venezuela to San Francisco – arriving on 25th August 1937 – Denis having initially joined the ship in Hull. This was one day after his 16th birthday. What a thrilling adventure this must have been for the young – sturdy – man: the record states that he was 5 ft 11 ins tall and weighed 205 lbs.

Denis's collection of papers provided details of his career progression. The key document here was his Continuous Certificate of Discharge which, after reporting Denis's personal details – height, 6 feet 1 inch; eyes, grey; hair, brown; complexion, fresh – listed his various engagements between August 1941 (6 weeks as 3rd Mate on the *Mytilus* from Harwich) to December 1951 (4 months as 1st Officer on the 6476 gross ton m.s. *Limatula* from Heysham). The list of destinations in between these dates included some that were slightly more colourful and exotic: Sydney, Hong Kong, Singapore, Suez.

There was an impressive collection of certificates – for the rendering of first aid to the injured by The St John Ambulance Association (in Sydney in June 1944), the operation of Gyro Compass Equipment (October 1945), Efficiency as Lifeboatman (June 1947), Radar Observer on Merchant Ships (February 1952), amongst others – as well as the Certificate of Competency as a Master: Steamship (July 1947). The last of these was complemented by a faded press cutting from the *Journal of Commerce* of 28th July 1947 headed "The Merchant Navy: New Ships' Officers", which listed English DAS (C) as having passed examinations under the provisions of the Merchant Shipping Acts. (The "C" denoted a Master).

As with the papers that covered his father's life in the Merchant Navy, there were a series of "to whom it may concern" references – dating from June 1940 to April 1947 – relating to Denis's conduct, expertise and experience in his various postings. As before, the general consistencies in the form of words – "strictly sober and attentive to his duties" – are apparent, though the Master of SS *Fragum* also added (after Denis's 8 month engagement as 2nd Mate to Hong Kong in December 1946) that "Mr English has conducted himself in a thorough gentlemanly manner, being courteous at all times, strictly sober, and an efficient and conscientious navigator".

However, perhaps the most dramatic testimonial of this period was the letter written from The Anglo-Saxon Petroleum Company Ltd to Captain R Ranson of m.v. *Opalia* in September 1940. This named 6 members of the crew – including

"D English, Apprentice" – who "during an air raid over Birkenhead on the 31st July last… showed much promptitude in dealing with an incendiary bomb which dropped through the skylight into the engine room". The letter noted specifically that "Apprentice English sustained some damage to a pair of flannel trousers and shirt, and in this connection we shall be pleased to receive his application for the replacement of the clothing concerned".

Denis's collection of papers included a small number of passport-sized or slightly larger photographs showing his development from sturdy youth into a good-looking young man; his eyes penetrate the camera in each one. Usefully for the family historian, he had the habit of dating the photographs on the back: aged 16 for his first passport in 1938; a full-length shot standing on the gangway of a ship aged 17 or 18; as an 18 year-old in his uniform with "Granny English" – Helen Kelly, see Chapter 5 – in 1940; in a suit and tie in 1946. To these could be added items of formal identification: a British Seaman's Identity Card (as a 26 year-old in 1947); a Colony of Singapore Identity Card (as a full-faced 32 year-old in 1954). Denis had also kept the page from his wife Anne's 1951-1955 passport on which the firm stare of a handsome woman looked straight at the viewer; assuming the photograph had been taken just before the passport application, she would have been aged 31 at the time.

The first command

Denis English's first command letter from the Anglo-Saxon Petroleum Company Ltd was dated 6th February 1952: "[W]e have pleasure in confirming our intention to appoint you to the command of the m.s. *Ta-U-Shan* trading in the Hong Kong area". He kept this in his file together with the subsequent correspondence that followed up on the mechanics of his appointment: the confirmation of his cholera inoculation in his International Booklet of Inoculation and Vaccination; the arrangements for receiving "final instructions" in London; and the settling of "all matters appertaining to the ship… to our mutual satisfaction" with its previous Master, Captain GA Blackwood.

From the historical perspective, there is a particular interest in the detail of Denis's appointment: his salary was to be £100 per month plus a Master's monthly allowance of £6; there was a strict instruction that the luggage allowance for his flight to Singapore (from where he would connect to Hong Kong) could not exceed 100 pounds above which "the cost would be very heavy and for your own account"; and there was a reminder that "in accordance with existing currency regulations you are permitted to take out of the country only £10 sterling".

Angela's obituary of her father mentioned his involvement in dealing with the grounding of the Shell VLCC [Very Large Crude Carrier] *Metula* in August 1974. The tanker had been carrying a cargo of over 190,000 tons of crude oil when, due to a navigational error, it ran aground at the western end of the First Narrows of the Magellan Straits. Initially holed in her forward bunker and cargo tanks, the ship was swung round by the exceptionally strong currents with the result that her stern struck the sea bed. Further hull deterioration meant that 8 of the 13 cargo tanks leaked.

Denis's papers included several documents of interest, including those from a seminar for an invited audience on the grounding and salvage of the VLCC *Metula*, which was held at Shell Centre on 20th February 1975 and reported in *Lloyd's List* two days later. The description of the salvaging of the vessel in a remote and inhospitable part of the world and the recovery of 140,000 tons of its cargo made for fascinating – indeed, thrilling – reading. The *Metula* was re-floated in September 1974 and taken to Santander in Spain to be scrapped in June 1976.

As a senior member of Operational Services at Shell International Marine Ltd, Denis's role at the seminar had been the presentation of a paper entitled "Lessons learned": 7 pages of closely typed text, complete with last minute annotations. It was a comprehensive and well-written piece, covering a range of issues: navigational, commercial, men, materials, pollution, certification and communications. The paper was obviously prepared by someone on top of his brief and, knowing Denis as I did, I could envisage him standing up to deliver it with a calm authority.

It is clear from this – and other – papers in Denis's collection that he not only took a pride in his role as a Master Mariner, but that he had a considerable knowledge about the history of the merchant marine industry and a keen interest in its (then) current and future development. The script of his talk on "Problems of Manning in Tankers", given at the City of London College in October 1960, did not provide a dry discussion of a specialised but dull subject (as its title might suggest), but a fascinating summary of the industry's history – including a reference to the 30,000 Merchant Seaman who perished in the Second World War (roughly a 1-in-6 fatality rate) – and a cogent analysis of the main issues affecting the manning of all merchant ships. At the time, these related to the (only recently changed) history of casual labour attaching to merchant seafaring as a mode of life and "the drift from the sea" of men in the 25-30 age group, who were reaching their peak professional value after long years of training. As Angela mentioned in his obituary, Denis's expertise was called upon in later years as an expert witness in several important court cases dealing with maritime matters. He retained some correspondence on this, dating from 1979 to 1983, in an envelope poignantly labelled ""Kept to boost my ego when feeling low!!".

Mementoes

At the more personal level, Denis's collection of papers contained mementoes of times spent with family, friends and colleagues: a superb cartoon, dating from his time in the Far East, entitled "Mr English buys a uniform" with the line "I'm afraid it will be two thousand coupons, Mr English" (and stamped on the back "Passed by Naval Censor"); a photograph of Denis and Anne at the dinner table with the Reverend Dom Michael Hopley, Monk of Ealing, a close family friend, probably taken in the 1990s; some correspondence, also from the 1990s, from a longstanding friend in Australia, Captain Bob Allen of Glen Iris, Victoria; a touching airmail letter of July 1957 from his father in Cyprus, in which Arthur Joseph English appeared to be attempting to heal some family quarrel: "How I would have loved to have seen Nancy [the family name for Anne] and to have held your beautiful baby daughter [Angela]. [I] can almost picture what she is like. Lovable, and adorable. Bless her – God bless her".

It is the eclectic nature of this apparently random collection of items that adds to its poignancy, I think. And, of course, they were far from random: they were selected and stored by Denis as sources of memories of times past.

The final item in the collection was the Order of Service dated 10th November 1995 for a Mass in Thanksgiving held in Ealing Abbey for the 50 years of marriage between Anne and Denis English. Father Hopley was the priest.

Anne English died in 1997 at the age of 77, 22 years after the serious stroke that had critically debilitated her. Her husband, who had cared for her so unstintingly, lived to the age of 87, dying in 2009. Father Hopley died on a pilgrimage to Lourdes in 2001 at the age of 72.[4] They were kind, loving people, in whose company it was always a pleasure to be.

---

4   Father Michael Hopley's longstanding contribution to the community of Ealing was recognised in 1985, when Cardinal Basil Hume opened Hopley House in Bayham Road. This is a sheltered home for pensioners built by the Ealing Family Housing Association, of which Father Hopley was a member. The opening was reported, with photographs, in the *Hammersmith and Shepherd's Bush Gazette* on 8th March.

CHAPTER FOURTEEN

RIGG/ENGLISH

I shall – rather awkwardly – address this brief chapter in the third person.

JOHN ALEXANDER RIGG (born 1954) married **ANGELA MARY ENGLISH** (born 1957) in Ealing Abbey in 1988.

John Rigg was educated at Roundhay School in Leeds and Trinity College, Cambridge. He obtained a First Class degree in Economics and later completed a Ph.D. in the same subject. (A copy of "*The Decision-making Processes of Young Males in an Urban Labour Market*" is held in Cambridge University Library).

After working for a year as a Research Assistant at the (then) Queen Mary College at the University of London, John joined a firm of economic consultants in London, where he remained for 10 years. In 1992, he and Angela moved to Scotland, when he took up a post as an Economic Adviser in the pre-devolution Scottish Office. Three years later, he was promoted to Senior Economic Adviser and became a member of the Senior Civil Service. In the Scottish Executive/Government, he subsequently headed Divisions with administrative responsibility for student and other learner support and European Structural Funds.

Following his retirement in 2011, John published three books on his long experience of being a sports spectator, particular of rugby (league and union), football and cricket: *An Ordinary Spectator: 50 Years of Watching Sport* (2012), *Still An Ordinary Spectator: Five More Years of Watching Sport* (2017) and *An Ordinary Spectator Returns: Watching Sport Again* (2023). The first of these was drawn upon to provide some context to William Rigg's childhood and adolescence in Chapter 12. He has also contributed articles for the *Rugby League Journal* and *Forty-20* as well as the football magazine *Backpass* and the cricket magazines *Backspin* and *The Nightwatchman*.

Angela English was born in Gosforth, Northumberland. She went to the Convent of the Sacred Heart GS in Hammersmith and entered Girton College, Cambridge, in 1975, taking an Honours Degree in History and Education. After graduation, she worked as a teacher in Hertfordshire and then in Human Relations for a large power company in London.

John and Angela Rigg have lived in Milngavie, near Glasgow, since 1993. Their family is shown in Table 14.1

Table 14.1. The family of John Alexander and Angela Mary Rigg	
John Alexander Rigg (born 1954) (born in Leeds)	
married	
Angela Mary English (born 1957) (born in Gosforth, Northumberland)	Thomas Alexander Rigg
	Katherine Anne Rigg *married* Marcus Joseph Bazley

PART FOUR

Reflections and Chronology

CHAPTER FIFTEEN

REFLECTIONS

The first column of the family tree shown in Table 15.1 reproduces the list of the Line of 16 – Tom and Katie's great, great grandparents – that was first presented at the beginning of Part 1 of this volume. As noted in Part 1, in going back only four generations, the ranges of the dates of birth and death stretch to over 30 years and over 70 years, respectively. There is a relatively short period – the thirteen years from 1869 to 1882 – in which all the Line of 16 are living.

This narrative has described the "journeys" of the four generations from the Line of 16 down to Tom and Katie – reading from left to right in the table – as well as the genealogical backgrounds of the Line of 16 themselves.

Table 15.1. The family tree of the Line of 16				
Line of 16	Line of 8	Grandparents	Parents	
Henry Rigg 1847-1920 *married* Jane Boynton 1859-1939				
	John Rigg 1887-1959 *married* Catherine Kerr McBride 1893-1969			

345

Peter McBride 1861-1949 *married* Agnes Charlotte Runcorn 1862-1942				
		William Alexander Rigg 1921-2004 *married* Enid Peggie Niblett 1922-2000		
Charles James Niblett 1851-1927 *married* Anna Karoline Borstelmann 1853-1938				
	Alfred Edgar Niblett 1888-1973 *married* Marie Rosa Wilson 1890-1968			
Charles Herbert Wilson 1862-1946 *married* Rosa Mary Whines 1863-1937				**Thomas Alexander Rigg**
			John Alexander Rigg (born 1954) *married* Angela Mary English (born 1957)	

Arthur English 1869-1936 *married* Helen (Ellan/Hellen/Nellie) Kelly 1869-1949				**Katherine Anne Rigg** *married* **Marcus Joseph Bazley**
	Arthur Joseph English 1892-1970 *married* Mary Stella Stapleton 1899-1978			
Joseph Stapleton c1859-1933 *married* Guiseppa Lucarda Josepha (Josephine) Brincau 1863-1954				
		Denis Arthur Stapleton English 1921-2009 *married* Anne Catherine Murray 1919-1997		
John Murray c1839-? *married* Margaret Mullown(e)y c1846-?				
	John Murray 1873-1952 *married* Honoria (Honor/Annie) McManamon 1878-1967			
Francis McManamon 1836-1882 *married* Honor McManamon 1838-1917				

I suspect that any researcher into their family history would confirm that an overwhelming conclusion – quickly reached – concerns the infinitesimally small chance that he or she would actually exist. In their different ways, the generations given in Table 15.1 somehow survived the perils of life over the best part of two centuries so that the story could feed through into present times. And that is only the last 200 years or so. The fragile seeds go back through the countless generations before that, of course.

The "perils of life" do not only include the major events that have been featured in this story: the Irish Famine, the trenches of the First World War, the U-Boat threat to merchant shipping, and so on. They cover the myriad of other factors that might have brought about an early death.

Thus it is that, in the branches of the family tree shown in the previous chapters, there are 13 cases of death before the age of 1 (the last being John Francis Murray in Newcastle in 1907) and 11 other deaths before the age of 3. In addition, as noted in Chapter 1, seven cases of maternal mortality have been identified across the extended family as a whole although, again, the most recent is over a century ago (Louisa Mary Whines, née Durant, in 1915).

The branches of the family tree also list a dozen cases of siblings (or their spouses) of the Line of 16 who died between the ages of 20 and 35 (excluding those killed in action or in/following childbirth). The feeling here with all these examples of truncated existences is one of sadness of lives started – but not fulfilled – in terms of achievements, careers or family trees of their own.

In addition to the range of factors that prevented the branches of so many other family trees from extending through to modern times, one must also recognise the critical role – replayed a hundred times and more – of sheer happenchance. Even allowing for their survival into the family-formation years of adulthood, what were the particular circumstances in which a Rigg was introduced to a Boynton, or a Murray to a Mullowney, or an English to a Kelly? Even more improbably, what remote chance had there been of the contact being made across countries or cultures – a Niblett to a Borstelmann, or a Stapleton to a Brincau? Every one of the matchings in the direct family tree shown in Table 15.1 – 15 in all – falls into this category, the total rising exponentially as we go back into the previous generations.

By definition, each of the members of the Line of 16 has a direct – and, of course, essential – link in a line that leads through to Tom and Katie. Our children's fourth generational ancestors include two men born a quarter of the century apart in County Mayo and Cambridge (Frances McManamon and Charles Herbert Wilson) and two women born in the same year in London and Malta (Rosa Marie Whines and Josephine Brincau).

Indeed, extending this exercise further back through another four generations, the eighth generational ancestors of Tom and Katie include John Stirk (born in Ilkley, Yorkshire, in 1731), Theodosia Gould (born in Hadleigh, Suffolk, in 1736) and Johann Hinrich Bostelmann (born in Heelsen, Niedersachsen, in 1683). Four generations before that would include the twelfth generational ancestors Thomas Welles (born in North Yorkshire in 1529), Sarah Neal (born in Brandish, Suffolk, in 1620) and Harm Hencke (born in Kirkwalsede, Niedersachsen, in 1582).[1] Again – the key point – all are in one of the direct lines to the current generation and all are essential for our story.

I wonder if it is the implicit – and almost certainly subconscious – recognition of the fragility of existence that accounts for a common theme to be found amongst many of the branches of the family tree described in this volume: namely, resilience. Of course, there is an element of self-definition here: for a branch of any family tree to have survived through to modern times implies a high degree of steadfastness in times gone by. But I have been struck by the repeated examples of dogged determination by successive generations who remained in a locality and worked hard and raised their families and carried the story forward. This theme was initially encountered in the book's first chapter (in North Yorkshire) and has been repeated thereafter – in Suffolk and Gloucestershire and County Mayo and Roscommon and Niedersachsen…

One aspect of the variations of the starting points is therefore obviously locational. However, there are also other differences within the Line of 16, not least the respective economic roles – and, by definition, the places within the social class structure – of the (male) breadwinners: John Murray and Francis McManamon farming the land of County Mayo, the working-class occupations of Henry Rigg (a semi-skilled railway platelayer) and Peter McBride (a skilled engineer's patternmaker), the entrepreneurial Charles James Niblett in Germany, the security of Charles Herbert Wilson's clerical employment as a member of the lower middle-class in north London.

I mention the theme of resilience. Of course, this does not necessarily imply immobility. It is also consistent with the examples of migration which, as we have seen, have been undertaken for a variety of (overlapping) reasons: the search for better employment or income prospects, the desire to link up with earlier family or village connections, the seeking of adventure or the flight from death, the last of these most obviously from the west of Ireland in the 1840s. The examples are intriguing and, each in their individual ways, heroic: the walk of Patrick and James Kelly from Glasgow to North Shields, Charles James Niblett establishing his business (and large family) in Osnabrück, Joseph Stapleton and Arthur English pursuing their respective careers in the Army and Merchant Navy, Peter McBride leaving his native Scotland with his family to search for work across the north of England.

---

1 For completeness, these would be part of the Line of 256 and the Line of 4096, respectively – a family history research exercise too far, I suspect.

By contrast, other members of the Line of 16 spent their whole lives very close to where they had been born: John and Margaret Murray and Francis and Honor McManamon in County Mayo, Guiseppa Stapleton (née Brincau) in Malta, Helen English (née Kelly) on Tyneside, Henry and Jane Rigg in North Yorkshire. They were longstanding members of their respective local communities and, in each case no doubt, became established as representatives of those communities and custodians of local mores and traditions.

It is also the case that resilience implies durability. For many of the members of the branches of the family tree presented in the previous chapters, it was a question of keeping going from one year to the next… and one decade to the next. Thus, having reflected on the cases of death in infancy and early adulthood, it is only appropriate that I note the many examples of longevity. There are 253 individuals (including spouses) listed within the branches of the tree for whom the years of both birth and death are known and, of these, no fewer than 130 – that is, over one-half, lived to the age of at least 70. (The breakdown by century was 48% of those born in the 19th Century and, amongst a much smaller sample, 72% of those born in the 20th Century). Of the total number, no fewer than almost one-quarter – 24 per cent – lived until at least their 80th year.[2]

Within the narrower scope of the Line of 16 and their direct descendants (to Tom and Katie) for whom the years of birth and death are known (26 in total in Table 15.1), the numbers living to the ages of at least 70 and 80 are 24 and 11, respectively.

****

The family history researches described here have not yielded any connections to the rich and famous. I do take some pride from the (somewhat distant) link to William Yield – a distinguished England rugby player of the 1890s – but there is no royalty here and there are no connections to generals or admirals or politicians or revolutionaries. Perhaps these members of the extended family remain to be discovered.

Does this matter? Not in the slightest. I have read that some editions of the excellent television programme *Who Do You Think You Are?* have been researched and then scrapped because the subject matter has been deemed not to be sufficiently "interesting". This strikes me as a limited way of proceeding with family history research and, if it is not the approach adopted by the programme's producers, I apologise for doing them a disservice. I am firmly of the view that all family histories are interesting.

In the case of the Line of 16, it certainly does add up to a rich tapestry. Of which – I suspect – there is more to discover.

---

2   These figures are consistent with those given in one of the bull-points in Chapter 1, which covered those who were born between 1829-1900 and lived in North Yorkshire and/or South Durham.

CHAPTER SIXTEEN

CHRONOLOGY

Many history books focus on the "big" events – those concerning kings and queens, presidents and prime ministers, wars and revolutions… – and, in these, I share the general interest. But history is also about the "journey" of families – from one generation to the next, from one century to the next, sometimes from one country to the next.

In this chapter, I present a chronology for the last two hundred-plus years in which two strands are juxtaposed: the events that have reached the standard history textbooks (with one or two more idiosyncratic entries) and the journey through the direct family lines to the present day.

Hence, it can be seen in Table 16.1 that James Kelly – later to "tramp" with his son Patrick from Glasgow to North Shields after migrating from County Mayo due to the Irish Famine – was born in the same year (1803) as the Louisiana Purchase, when the US Government bought 530 million acres of the North American landmass from France for $15 million. Or that the year of the assassination of Abraham Lincoln (1865) also saw the death of George Rigg – an agricultural labourer in North Yorkshire – who had been unable to write his name on his teenage daughter's death certificate. Or that, in 1938, the year of the ill-fated Munich Agreement signed by Neville Chamberlain and Adolf Hitler – Anna Karoline Niblett died in Osnabrück at the age of 84.

And so on. The momentous and the familial – on the same page.

	Table 16.1. A chronology of events	
1800	Thomas Jefferson elected President of the United States	

1801	Act of Union with Ireland establishes the United Kingdom; William Pitt (the Younger) resigns after 11 years as Prime Minister	Birth of Alexander Ker(r) in South Sannox on the Isle of Arran; Birth of James Goodchild in Horham, Suffolk
1802		Birth of George Rigg in Baldersby, Yorkshire; Birth of Mahala Holmes in Laxfield, Suffolk
1803	Louisiana Purchase	Birth of James Kelly in Ireland; John Davis (the older) drowns in Cork Harbour
1804	Napoleon Bonaparte crowns himself Emperor of France; Death of Alexander Hamilton after being shot in a duel	(Probable) birth of Lucy Purvis in Sussex
1805	Battle of Trafalgar	
1806	Dissolution of the Holy Roman Empire	
1807	Abolition of the slave trade in the British Empire	Birth of Jane Wells in Helperby, Yorkshire
1808	Peninsular War begins	Marriage of Peter Christop Borstelmann and Anna Margreta Marquardt in Visselhoevede, Germany
1809		Marriage of Archibald Shaw and Catherine McBride on the Isle of Arran
1810		Birth of Jane Shaw on the Isle of Arran
1811		Birth of Johann Friedrich Borstelmann in Visselhovede, Germany
1812	Anglo-American War begins; Napoleon retreats from Moscow; Assassination of Prime Minister Spencer Perceval	
1813	Jane Austin's *Pride and Prejudice* published	Marriage of Daniel Niblett and Maria Wood in Painswick, Gloucestershire
1814		
1815	Battle of Waterloo	
1816		

1817		(Probable) birth of Charles Niblett in Painswick; Marriage of John Whines and Rebecca Rycraft in Peterborough
1818		
1819	Peterloo massacre	
1820	Accession of George IV	Marriage of Peter McBride and Williamina Walker in Port Glasgow
1821		
1822		
1823		Birth of Joseph Runcorn in Runcorn; (Probable) birth of William Boynton in Thirkleby, Yorkshire; (Probable) birth of Harriet Stirk in Kilburn, Yorkshire
1824	First performance of Beethoven's Ninth Symphony	
1825	George Stephenson's first steam locomotive	
1826		Birth of Selina Hunt in Stroud
1827		Birth of Anna Perlasky in Bad Münder am Diester, Germany; Birth of Daniel Whines in Peterborough
1828		(Probable) birth of John Murray in County Mayo; Birth of Lorenzo Brincau in Malta; Marriage of George Rigg and Jane Wells in Topcliffe, Yorkshire
1829	Catholic Emancipation Act	Birth of Peter McBride in Glasgow; Marriage of Robert Twaddle and Elizabeth Irwin in Liverpool
1830	Accession of William IV; Opening of Liverpool to Manchester railway	Birth of Jane Twaddle in Liverpool; Birth of Patrick Kelly in Strokeston, Roscommon; Marriage of John Davis and Lucy Purvis in Eyemouth, Scotland

Year	Historical Event	Family Event
1831		(Probable) birth of Mary Wadsworth in Peterborough; Birth of Frances Davis in North Shields; Marriage of Alexander Kerr and Janet Shaw on the Isle of Arran
1832	Great Reform Act	Birth of Catherine Kerr on the Isle of Arran
1833	Abolition of slavery in the British Empire	Birth of Antonia Gatt in Malta
1834	Poor Law Amendment Act; Prosecution of Tolpuddle Martyrs	
1835		
1836	Siege of the Alamo in San Antonio, Texas	Birth of John English in Ireland; (Probable) birth of Francis McManamon in Newport, County Mayo
1837	Accession of Queen Victoria	Birth of Michael Stapleton in Ireland
1838	People's Charter published; Morse Code invented	(Probable) birth of Honor McManamon in County Mayo; Birth of Charles Tyler Wilson in Overseal, (then) Leicestershire; Birth of Emma Goodchild in Norwich
1839	First Opium War begins	(Probable) birth of John Murray in County Mayo
1840	Penny Post introduced	
1841		Birth of Catherine Woods in Clonallon, County Down
1842		
1843	*The Economist* first published	
1844	Rochdale Equitable Pioneers establish Cooperative Movement	
1845	Irish Famine begins	Marriage of William Boynton and Harriet Stirk in Thirsk, Yorkshire John Davis (the younger) drowns in Moray Firth; Death of Mary Rigg in Baldersby aged 85
1846	Repeal of Corn Laws	(Probable) birth of Margaret Mullowney in County Mayo
1847		James Kelly and Patrick Kelly "tramp" from Roscommon to North Shields; Birth of Henry Rigg in Baldersby

1848	Publication of Karl Marx's *Communist Manifesto*; Revolutions in France, Austro-Hungary and States within Germany and Italy; California Gold Rush	
1849		Marriage of Charles Niblett and Selina Hunt in Bristol
1850		Marriage of Patrick Kelly and Frances Davis in North Shields
1851	Great Exhibition in Hyde Park	Birth of Charles James Niblett in Cheltenham; Marriage of Daniel Whines and Mary Wadsworth in Peterborough; Marriage of Johann Borstelmann and Anna Perlasky in Hannover, Germany
1852		Patrick and Frances Kelly live in New York (until 1855)
1853	Crimean War begins	Birth of Anna Karoline Borstelman in Elze, Germany
1854		Death of Joseph Friedrich Borstelmann in Hannover, Germany, aged 54
1855		Marriage of Joseph Runcorn and Jane Twaddle in Warrington
1856		
1857	Indian Mutiny	
1858		
1859	Publication of Charles Darwin's *Origin of the Species*	Birth of Jane Boynton in Thirkleby
1860	Great Eastern lays Atlantic cable	(Possible) birth of Joseph Stapleton in Liverpool; Marriage of Peter McBride and Catherine Kerr in Rutherglen; Marriage of Charles Tyler Wilson and Emma Goodchild in Hellesdon, Norfolk
1861	American Civil War begins; Emancipation of serfs in Russia; Kingdom of Italy proclaimed	Birth of Peter McBride in Rutherglen; Marriage of John English and Catherine Woods in Clonallon

Year	World Events	Family Events
1862		Birth of Agnes Runcorn in Warrington; Birth of Charles Herbert Wilson in Cambridge; Death of Alexander Kerr in South Kiscadale on the Isle of Arran aged 61
1863	Formation of Yorkshire CCC; Gettysburg Address	Birth of Rosa Whines in London; Birth of Guiseppa/Josephine Brincau in Vittoriosa, Malta
1864		Death of Peter McBride in Rutherglen aged 65
1865	Assassination of President Abraham Lincoln	Death of George Rigg in Baldersby aged 63
1866		
1867	Second Reform Act	
1868	WE Gladstone becomes Prime Minister for the first time	
1869	Suez Canal opens; US transcontinental railroad opens	Birth of Arthur English in Clonallon; Birth of Helen Kelly in North Shields
1870	Franco-Prussian War; Elementary Education Act	Marriage of John Murray and Margaret Mullowney in Srahmore, County Mayo
1871	Proclamation of German Empire; Trades Union Congress formed; First rugby international between Scotland and England	
1872	First soccer international between Scotland and England; Wanderers win first FA Cup final	
1873		Birth of John Murray in Burrishoole, County Mayo; Marriage of Charles James Niblett and Anna Karoline Borstelmann in Elze, Germany
1874	First Impressionist Exhibition held in Paris	Death of Joseph Runcorn in Warrington aged 54
1875		
1876	Alexander Graham Bell patents the telephone; Battle of the Little Bighorn	

1877	First cricket test match between Australia and England; First Wimbledon tennis championship; Queen Victoria becomes Empress of India		Joseph Stapleton enlists in the Army
1878	Thomas Edison patents the phonograph		Birth of Honoria/Annie McManamon in Burrishoole, County Mayo
1879	Thomas Edison patents the incandescent light bulb; Battles of Isandhlwana and Rorke's Drift; Establishment of Irish National Land League		
1880			Marriage of Henry Rigg and Jane Boynton in Baldersby; Bigamous marriage of Charles Tyler Wilson and Charlotte Hambling in Poplar, London
1881	Assassination of Tsar Alexander II; Gunfight at OK Corral; Second Land Act improves rights of tenant farmers in Ireland		Death of Charles Niblett in Cheltenham aged 64
1882			Death of Lucy Davis (née Purvis) in Tynemouth aged 78; Death of Francis McManamon in Srahrevagh, County Mayo, aged 46
1883			Marriage of Joseph Stapleton and Josephine Brincau in Valletta, Malta; Death of Mahala Goodchild in Norwich aged 80
1884			
1885	General Gordon killed at Khartoun		Death of Williamina McBride in Glasgow aged 84; Death of John English in South Shields aged 48
1886			Death of Jane Rigg in Baldersby aged 79
1887			Birth of John Rigg in Baldersby

1888		Birth of Alfred Niblett in Osnabrück, Germany; Marriage of Charles Herbert Wilson and Rosa Whines in Edmonton, London; Marriage of Arthur English and Helen Kelly in Tynemouth; Death of Charles Tyler Wilson in London aged 50
1889	Eiffel Tower opens	William Yiend wins the first of 6 rugby caps for England
1890		Birth of Marie Wilson in Palmer's Green, London; Marriage of Peter McBride and Agnes Runcorn in West Derby, Merseyside; Death of Selina Niblett in Cheltenham aged 64
1891		
1892	Sir Arthur Conan Doyle submits first Sherlock Holmes stories to *Strand Magazine*	Birth of Arthur Joseph English in North Shields
1893		Birth of Catherine McBride in Glasgow; Death of Jane Runcorn in Warrington aged 63; Death of Patrick Kelly in Tynemouth aged 63
1894		
1895	Formation of Northern Rugby Union (later Northern Rugby League)	
1896	First modern Olympic Games	
1897	First Boston Marathon	
1898	Pierre and Marie Curie discover radium	
1899	Second Boer War begins; Felix Hoffman creates Aspirin	Joseph Stapleton discharged from the Army after 21 years service; Birth of Mary Stella Stapleton in Sliema, Malta; Death of Janet Kerr in South Kiskadale aged 88
1900	Boxer Rising in China	

1901	Commonwealth of Australia established; Accession of Edward VII; Guglielmo Marconi sends first wireless transmission across the Atlantic Ocean; First Nobel Prizes awarded; Assassination of President William McKinley	Marriage of John Murray and Honoria McManamon in Preston, Lancashire
1902		Death of Frances Kelly in Tynemouth aged 70
1903	Orville Wright makes first flight in powered aircraft; First Baseball World Series	
1904	Russo-Japanese War begins	
1905		
1906		Death of Daniel Whines in London aged 79
1907		Indenture of Arthur English as Apprentice with the Prince Line Ltd
1908	Hunslet RLFC win All Four Cups; SOS adopted as international distress signal; The "People's Budget" introduces Old Age Pensions; Introduction of Model T Ford	
1909	Louis Blériot flies the English Channel;	John Rigg joins the Leeds City Police Force as a constable
1910	Accession of George V	
1911	First performance of Giacomo Puccini's *Madame Butterfly*; South Pole first reached by Roald Amundsen	Alfred Niblett graduates from the University of Birmingham and matriculates at the University of Munich; (Probable) death of Catherine Campbell (née Woods, formerly English) in Sunderland aged 69
1912	*Titanic* disaster	Death of Emma Goodchild in Stoke Mandeville aged 74
1913		
1914	First World War begins	Alfred Niblett interned in Ruhleben; Marriage of John Rigg and Catherine McBride in Leeds;

Year	Events	Family events
1915	*Lusitania* sunk	
1916	Easter Rising in Dublin; Battle of Jutland; Battle of the Somme	Death of Mary Whines in Peterborough aged 83
1917	Russian Revolution	Arthur English torpedoed off the south coast of Ireland; Death of Honor McManamon in Srahrevagh aged 78
1918	Influenza pandemic; British women aged 30 gain the right to vote	Arthur Joseph English in K-class of submarines; John Rigg severely injured on Western Front; Robert Rigg killed near Montigny-sur-Hallue in France aged 33
1919	Treaty of Versailles	Birth of Anne Murray in Gosforth; Marriage of Alfred Niblett and Marie Wilson in Tottenham
1920	League of Nations created; Government of Ireland Act provides for an Irish Free State	Death of Henry Rigg in Pickhill aged 72
1921		Birth of Denis English in Sliema; Birth of William Rigg in Leeds
1922	Tutankhamun's tomb discovered; Creation of USSR; Establishment of BBC	Birth of Peggie Niblett in London
1923		
1924	Ramsey MacDonald becomes Labour's first Prime Minister	
1925		
1926	General Strike	
1927	Charles Lindbergh flies solo across the Atlantic; The first full-length talking picture – *The Jazz Singer* – is released	Death of Charles James Niblett in London aged 76
1928	Alexander Fleming discovers penicillin; First appearance of Walt Disney's Mickey Mouse	

Year	Event	Family Event
1929	Wall Street Crash; First "Oscar" awards	Arthur English retires from Eagle Oil Transport Co. Ltd.
1930	Uruguay win the first FIFA World Cup final	
1931		
1932	First splitting of the atom	
1933	New Deal introduced in the USA	Death of Joseph Stapleton in Malta aged c73
1934		
1935		Thomas Murray ordained as priest; John Rigg retires from the Leeds City Police Force
1936	Accession and abdication of Edward VIII and Accession of George VI; Spanish Civil War begins; Jarrow Crusade; First public television broadcasts; Jesse Owens wins 4 gold medals at the Berlin Olympics	Death of Arthur English in Whitley Bay aged 67
1937	The first full-length animated film – *Snow White and the Seven Dwarfs* – is released; Hindenburg airship crashes in New Jersey	Indenture of Denis English as Apprentice with the Anglo-Saxon Petroleum Company Ltd; Death of Rosa Wilson in Leeds aged 74
1938	Munich Agreement	Death of Anna Karoline Niblett in Osnabrück aged 84
1939	Second World War begins	Death of Jane Rigg in Pickhill aged 80
1940	Winston Churchill becomes Prime Minister; Battle of Britain	William Rigg joins the RAF as a flight rigger; Mary Stella English and Helen Josephine English in Malta during sustained bombing
1941	Germany declares war on Soviet Union; Pearl Harbour attacked by Japan: USA enters war	
1942	Beveridge Report	Arthur Joseph English taken prisoner at Tobruk; Death of Agnes McBride in Leeds aged 80
1943		
1944	D-Day landings in Normandy	

1945	VE and VJ Days end the Second World War; Atomic bombs dropped on Hiroshima and Nagasaki; United Nations established; Publication of George Orwell's *Animal Farm*	Marriage of Denis English and Anne Murray in Gosforth
1946		Death of Charles Herbert Wilson in Leeds aged 84
1947	Independence of India and Pakistan; Chuck Yeager first to exceed the speed of sound	"Kelly Centenary" celebrated in North Shields
1948	National Health Service founded; State of Israel established	
1949	NATO established; Mao Zedong proclaims People's Republic of China	Marriage of William Rigg and Peggie Niblett in Leeds; Death of Peter McBride in Leeds aged 87; Death of Helen English in Whitley Bay aged 80
1950	Korean War begins	
1951	Festival of Britain on South Bank of Thames	
1952	Accession of Elizabeth II; Great Smog of London	Death of John Murray in Newcastle aged 79
1953	Mount Everest scaled for first time; Death of Joseph Stalin	
1954	Roger Bannister runs the first sub-four minute mile; Great Britain win the first Rugby League World Cup; Publication of JRR Tolkien's *The Fellowship of the Ring*	Birth of John Rigg in Leeds; Death of Guiseppa/Josephine Stapleton in Malta aged 91
1955		
1956	Suez crisis; Elvis Presley has his first hit record, *Heartbreak Hotel*	Arthur Joseph English commands WD LST *Humfrey Gale* in the Mediterranean
1957	Treaty of Rome establishes European Economic Community; Sputnik 1 launched	Birth of Angela English in Gosforth

Year	Event	Family Event
1958	Campaign for Nuclear Disarmament formed	
1959		Death of John Rigg in Leeds aged 72
1960	First episode of *Coronation Street*	
1961	Yuri Gagarin is the first man in space; Berlin Wall built	
1962	Cuban Missile Crisis; Telstar transmits first live television programme; The Beatles release their first single, *Love Me Do*	
1963	Assassination of President John F Kennedy	
1964	The pirate station Radio Caroline begins broadcasting	
1965	First US troops arrive in Vietnam	
1966	England win the World Cup	
1967	Six Day War; The Green Bay Packers win the first Superbowl	Death of Annie Murray in Gosforth aged 89
1968	Anti-Vietnam War protests escalate in USA and Europe; Soviet troops enter Czechoslovakia; First successful heart transplant	Death of Marie Niblett in Leeds aged 78
1969	Neil Armstrong is the first man to walk on the moon; Start of "The Troubles" in Northern Ireland; Death penalty abolished in the UK	Death of Catherine Rigg in Leeds aged 76
1970		Death of Arthur Joseph English in Richmond-upon-Thames aged 78
1971	Decimal Currency introduced in Britain	
1972	Watergate	
1973	Britain joins European Economic Community	Death of Alfred Niblett in Leeds aged 84
1974	Resignation of President Richard M Nixon	John Rigg matriculates at the University of Cambridge

1975	North Sea oil first piped ashore; Steven Spielberg's *Jaws* released; Microsoft founded by Bill Gates and Paul Allen	Angela English matriculates at the University of Cambridge
1976	Britain obtains bail-out from IMF; Steve Jobs and Steve Wozniak create the Apple Computer Company	
1977		
1978	First test tube baby	Death of Mary Stella English in London aged 79
1979	Margaret Thatcher becomes Prime Minister; Soviet Union invades Afghanistan	
1980		
1981	Wedding of Prince of Wales and Lady Diana Spencer; AIDS virus identified in USA	
1982	Falklands War	
1983	Release of Microsoft Word	
1984	First Eurostar train	
1985	Live Aid	
1986	City of London "Big Bang" admits foreign firms into merchant banking; Chernobyl nuclear reactor explodes; Space Shuttle *Challenger* explodes shortly after launch	
1987		A casual conversation in the Traveller's Rest, Harewood, prompts 30+ years of research into the family history of the extended Rigg and English families
1988	Soviet Union withdraws troops from Afghanistan	Marriage of John Rigg and Angela English in Ealing, London
1989	Fall of Berlin Wall; Tiananmen Square protests and massacre; Exxon Valdez oil spillage in Alaska	John Rigg obtains Ph.D. from the University of Cambridge

Year	Event	Family
1990	Re-unification of Germany; Britain joins Exchange Rate Mechanism (ERM); Nelson Mandela released from prison; Tim Berners-Lee begins work on the WorldWideWeb browser	
1991	First Gulf War	
1992	Britain withdraws from ERM	
1993	European Single Market established	
1994	Channel Tunnel opens	
1995		
1996		
1997	Tony Blair becomes Prime Minister; JK Rowling's *Harry Potter* series launched	Death of Anne English in London aged 77
1998	Good Friday Agreement in Northern Ireland	
1999	Euro launched	
2000	First stage of the Human Genome Project completed	Death of Peggie Rigg in Leeds aged 77
2001	9/11 attacks in USA	
2002		
2003	Iraq War; England win Rugby World Cup	
2004		Death of William Rigg in Leeds aged 83
2005	7/7 attacks in London	
2006	British Army leads NATO expedition in Helmand province, Afghanistan	
2007		
2008	Global financial crisis	
2009	British Army withdraws from Iraq	Death of Denis English in London aged 87
2010	Conservative-Liberal Democrat coalition	

ANNEX A1

THE RIGGS IN NORTH AMERICA

Two of the sons of William Rigg – my great grandfather Henry Rigg's oldest brother – emigrated to Vermont, USA, in the 1890s, where they lived eventful lives and raised large families. I described my researches into them – Stephen Rigg (later Riggs, 1868-1951) and Henry Rigg (later Riggs, 1863-1924) – in three articles for the Cleveland Family History Society Journal *in January 2015, April 2015 and April 2020.*

A NORTH YORKSHIRE COUPLE IN VERMONT, USA:
Part 1 (January 2015)

The starting point: Baldersby, North Yorkshire

For many years I have been mapping the descendants of George Rigg (1802-1865) and his wife Jane Rigg (née Wells, 1807-1886). George was born in Baldersby, North Yorkshire, and Jane in nearby Helperby. The youngest of their 8 children – Henry Rigg (1847-1920) – was my great grandfather.

Henry's oldest brother – William Rigg (1829-1905) – had 6 sons of whom 5 survived into adulthood. In the course of my researches I was puzzled for a long time by the disappearance of two of them, both also born in Baldersby – Henry Rigg in 1863 and Stephen Rigg in 1868 – after the 1891 Census, when they were living together in Stockton-on-Tees and working as railway porters. Neither were recorded in either the 1901 or 1911 Censuses; nor were there any records of possible deaths.

I later discovered (via a contributor to the Ancestry web pages) that Stephen Rigg had emigrated to the United States, married Rose Burnett from Dishforth and lived in Vermont until his death at the age of 82 in 1951. Rose died at the age of 81 the following year. A photograph of their neat gravestone in the Waterbury Center Cemetery can be seen on the excellent "Vermont, Find a Grave" website.

Why have I subsequently spent some considerable time mapping the descendants of Stephen Riggs (with the additional "s", acquired soon after his arrival in the US) and Rose Burnett? I think there are three main reasons.

First, there is the thrill of the chase familiar to most compilers of their family tree: unearthing a promising source; discovering a new name; fitting the pieces into the ever-expanding jigsaw. We like a good detective story.

In addition, there was the realisation that – however distant – those in the direct family line from Stephen and Rose were my relatives. Their grandchildren would be my third cousins, albeit that the distortion of the generations means that the years of birth of those grandchildren stretch from 1917 through to 1962. My year of birth falls towards the end of this period; the grandchildren of Henry Rigg have years of birth ranging from 1945 to 1964.

Perhaps most important, however, was something of which I became increasingly aware as I made progress with my researches into the extended family tree of Stephen Riggs and Rose Burnett. The individual stories – considered as a whole – seemed to capture the sweeping history of America in the twentieth century. Time and again it seemed that many of the vast changes occurring there between Stephen's migration in 1892 (and naturalisation in 1898) and the turn of the millennium – economic, social and cultural – were reflected in the lives of those jigsaw pieces.

American sources

For those CFHS members who might be unfamiliar with the main American sources, I should report that I was fortunate in three respects. First the US Federal Census material is available up to 1940. Unlike its UK counterpart, therefore, the latest US Census includes some people who are alive today. Moreover, its content is imaginative as well as functional. Not only is there the usual information on family composition, ages, places of birth, occupations and so on, but also, in its last year, the Census specifies the rental (or purchase) value of the property being lived in, the level of schooling reached, the number of weeks worked in the previous year and the annual wage.

This enables one to get a real feel for the lives being led. Thus, in 1940, the 38 year-old Jennie Burnett Riggs (1901-1981) – a daughter of Stephen and Rose – was the school bus driver in Waterbury, who had worked 20 hours the previous week and had earned $270 the previous year. Her nephew, 16 year-old Foster Riggs Smith (1923-1995), having left formal education after the 8th grade of elementary school, was an attendant at a gasoline filling station in Richmond and had worked 64 hours in the previous week.

Second, I certainly benefited from having Vermont as the principal State in which I was interested. Of course, many of the extended Riggs family subsequently migrated to other parts of the US, but, for those who remained in Vermont, the local birth/marriage/death (BMD) records are very informative. For example, the marriage records include the names of the parents of the bride and groom (including maiden names), which means that the inter-generational tracking of families is usually relatively straightforward. Judging on what is available through my Ancestry subscription, the BMD data for many other States are much thinner or not available. Some caution is required, however: as the Vermont BMD records are available up to 2008, the reporting of family lines has to be done with some sensitivity so as not to invade the privacy of the current generations.

Third, I would advise family history researchers to look out for obituaries, particularly in the local US newspapers, many of which are available on-line. These can be not only touching and poignant, but often take us beyond the simple cataloguing of the names of relatives and the dates of births, marriages and deaths. In other words, the obituaries can be also very revealing about the real lives of those whom they are describing, particularly when, as is often the case, they are presented with the neighbourliness and affection of small-town America.

Hence, the *Stowe Reporter* noted that Virginia Maynard DeCelle (1935-2012) was known as "the horse show mom" as she travelled with her daughters on the show circuit; she also "loved participating in church functions and believed in a higher power"; touchingly, after serious illness from 2001, "she made it back home from Florida… before peacefully passing on". The obituary for her husband Paul DeCelle (1929-2012) later in the year referred to his love of animals and his habit of "driving down to Cotton Brook where he would release all the gray squirrels he had humanely trapped… the family joke was that the squirrels always followed him back home". I also liked the way that the obituary of Martha Agnes Riggs DeCelle – another daughter of Stephen and Rose and the mother of Paul DeCelle – after noting her death at the age of 89 in 1999 and that she was "a homemaker", casually reported that she "also owned and operated Colbyville TV Co".

The American Dream

Stephen Rigg's family background in North Yorkshire had been in hard manual work. His grandfather, George, had died aged 63 in 1865 unable to write – he had marked his name with a cross on his daughter Jane's death certificate – having spent most of his life as an agricultural labourer; a year before his death, at the age of 62, he was working as a road repairer. Stephen's grandmother, Jane, is also consistently recorded as an agricultural labourer in successive Censuses. His father, William, was an agricultural labourer and, later, a railway platelayer.

It is reasonable to assume that, having tried out the life of a railway porter in Stockton, Stephen came to the conclusion that the risks associated with the alternative of starting over again in Vermont were worth taking. Those risks were probably mitigated by the fact that his future wife – Rose Burnett, whom he married in Williston, Vermont, in 1893 – already seems to have had family members in the State.

The US Census information suggests that Stephen and Rose's economic progress was, at best, uncertain. In 1900, they lived in Richmond, Vermont, and Stephen's occupation is given as farmer. Also in the household were the then 6 year-old Gladys Mabel Riggs (1893-1949) and a servant and farm labourer, Henry Kenyon. Ten years later, Stephen is still a farmer on a "general farm", which is owned with a mortgage, this time in Huntingdon, Vermont. However, in 1920, Stephen and Rose are back in Richmond, where his occupation is "labor" with a milk company. In 1940, he is near-retired and living in Waterbury, Vermont, in a property with a rental value of $10 per month, though he and Rose are stated as also having income from "other sources".

The impact of the Depression is not hard to find. The husbands of two of Stephen and Rose's granddaughters were on public emergency works programs in 1940 – one had been a laborer in a woollen mill who had been out of work for 12 weeks, the other a wholesale shoe salesman who had been unemployed for 36 weeks – living with their families in the same rented property in Richmond as Gladys Mabel Riggs and her husband Sidney Smith (1883-probably 1963). In this instance, where there were wages coming in, it was mainly from the employment of the household's women.

In addition to Gladys Mabel Riggs and Jennie Burnett Riggs, Rose Burnett gave birth to two other (twin) daughters: Martha Agnes Riggs (1909-1999) and Mary Edna Riggs (1909-2001). Stephen and Rose also adopted a girl called Leona Abbiati, who appears in the 1930 Census as a 4 year-old "boarder" and in the 1940 Census as a 14 year-old daughter. She becomes Leona Emma Riggs. As, between them, these 5 daughters had 8 husbands and at least 21 children, it is not surprising that the family tree headed by Stephen Rigg(s) and Rose Burnett becomes very extensive. However, with the significant exception of Leona, the Riggs name does not survive after the next generation in the form of Foster Riggs Smith, the son of Gladys Mabel Riggs and Sidney Smith.

Let's stay with Leona for a moment. Her husband, Daniel Tarasevich, was born in Berisso, Argentina, in 1921. In the US City Directories, there are several records of Daniel and Leona living in Groton, Connecticut, in the 1950s and 1960s, including a couple of references to Dan's Trailer Park. I made a mental note of these references and drew the appropriate assumptions about Leona and Daniel's living conditions – or so I thought.

Daniel Tarasevich died at the age of 91 in 2013. His obituary in *The Day* newspaper, New London, set out the fuller picture. He had emigrated to the US with his family when he was aged 3, arriving at the Ellis Island Immigration Center; he had married Leona in 1944 and enlisted in the US Army three days later; he had fought on the German front and been decorated; after the Second World War, he had worked as a signal maintenance man on the railroads; he and Leona had had 4 children, 8 grandchildren and 2 great grandchildren; and, not least, he and his wife had developed their 10 acre homestead in Groton, constructed a number of trailer lots and cottages, and *owned* Dan's Trailer Park. The obituary stated that the business "continues today, managed by Mrs Tarasevich". That is: by the 87 year-old Leona.

Leona's husband of 69 years was an ethnic Russian who migrated to a strange country, fought for and was decorated by it, worked hard, raised his family and used his skills to improve their standard of living. The epitome of the American Dream, I'd say.

To be continued. In Part 2 – migration, marriage and murder.

A NORTH YORKSHIRE COUPLE IN VERMONT, USA: Part 2 (April 2015)

The story so far. Stephen Rigg, born in Baldersby, North Yorkshire, in 1868 disappears – along with his brother Henry – from the UK records after the 1891 Census, when they were railway porters in Stockton-on-Tees. He becomes Stephen Riggs (with a "s"), who marries Rose Burnett from Dishforth in Williston, Vermont, in 1893. They have 5 daughters who, between them, have 8 husbands and (at least) 21 children. Stephen and Rose live to their 80s and are buried in the Waterbury Center Cemetery, Vermont.

Vermont

It is not surprising that, over the course of the years, many of Stephen and Rose's extended family migrated from Vermont to other parts of the US. There are references in the birth/marriage/death (BMD) and other records to members of the family in South and West of the US – Florida (often for retirement), North Carolina, Georgia and California – as well as States closer to Vermont such as Pennsylvania, New York State, Connecticut and Rhode Island.

It is clear, however, that many branches of the family have chosen to stay in Vermont. One has to be slightly careful here, as there is bound to have been an element of self-selection in my research to the extent that it has focused on the Vermont records because they are so informative. But there are at least three branches of the family tree currently in Burlington containing people born in the 1990s or the 2000s, who are 5 generations on from Stephen and Rose (via their daughter Gladys Mabel Riggs). There are also at least two separate branches currently in Berlin that are 4 generations on (via two of the other daughters, Mary Edna Riggs and Jennie Burnett Riggs).

It is interesting that, within the Vermont records, the names of some places recur regularly throughout the century, notably Burlington, Waterbury and Montpelier. However, there is also evidence of migration within the State, for example to Milton and St Albans further north up Interstate 89. Nonetheless, the extended Riggs/Burnett family has tended to remain geographically focused in the middle of the State in towns on or near to the Winooski river, which flows into Lake Champlain.

The significance of farming to the Vermont economy – dairy products in particular – is reflected in many of the occupations registered to the Riggs/Burnett family in the US Censuses or on the Vermont BMD forms over the years: laborer in a creamery, milk deliverer, shipping clerk in milk plant, dairy farmer. The post-Second World War period has seen a significant rationalisation in the industry, however – according to Wikipedia, from over 11,000 dairy farms in 1947 to just over 1,000 in 2007.

As the century progressed, other jobs opened up for the family in retailing and distribution (baker, truck driver for oil and gas, postmaster, store clerk) or in skilled occupations (electrician, plumber). I noted one married couple who, in 1940, were attendants at the Vermont State Hospital for the Insane. There were also jobs taken at the large IBM plant at Essex Junction, which opened in 1958. In later years, some skilled white collar occupations start to register (physician, design artist). This is largely through marriage, though again I am aware of the risks of selection bias, as I will have lost track of some of those who moved outside the State to study at college or university.

The reference to Lake Champlain reminded me of some of my (distantly recalled) history lessons at school and the eighteenth century colonial wars fought out between the British and French in Canada and its border States. The French and French-Canadian legacy is obvious today, of course, not only in the actual name of the Green Mountain State and those of some of its principal towns, but in the surnames of many families long resident in that part of the US. These include various spouses within the Riggs/Burnett family tree: LaPointe, Brousseau, Lacaillade, DesLauriers.

Death, marriage and relationships

As is inevitably the case with this type of family history research, there are the dramatic incidents of everyday life, including infant mortality and/or the early deaths of adults. The Riggs/Burnett extended family is no different: a child dying 30 minutes after his birth; a boy dying on his fourth birthday; a 23 year-old drowning in a boating accident; a 39 year-old man dying of AIDS; another 39 year-old collapsing with a coronary thrombosis. This unfortunate roll-call includes – perhaps most shockingly – a murder-suicide in Texas.

By contrast, there appears to have been an absence of death in wartime within the family tree. There are several examples of enlistment in the Second World War, Korean War and/or Vietnam War, but, to date, my research suggests that all the participants seem to have survived the conflicts. It might be noted that the period of interest starts too late for there to be any impact from the First World War. There is an obvious contrast here with the corresponding research into the Rigg family tree in North Yorkshire, where 5 members of the extended family were killed in action between 1914-1918, including my great uncle (Robert Rigg, 1885-1918).

A significant characteristic of American society is revealed in the marriage data of the extended Rigg/Burnett family. There are several instances of teenage marriage and parenthood, sometimes to be followed by divorce and re-marriage, particularly in the latter half of the century. For the females across the family tree as a whole, one-third of first marriages took place before the age of 20 and the median age at the time of the first marriage was 21. (It was 23 for the men). And, of course, there are individual examples of domestic arrangements that were – to say the least – somewhat turbulent: one member of the family tree has a first child at the age of 17 and a third divorce aged 34.

However, lest it be thought that I am suggesting the marriage patterns of the extended Riggs/Burnett family exhibited a chronic instability, I should report that there is also good evidence to suggest the opposite. One example is that of the squirrel-loving Paul DeCelle and his wife Virginia (the "horse show mom") – whom we met in Part 1 – whose marriage of 56 years was only brought to an end with the latter's death in 2012.

The development of the theme of marriage and relationships provides an excellent illustration of how the extended Riggs/Burnett family has been caught up in – and contributed to – the profound social changes affecting modern America. On 1st July 2000, Vermont became the first state to introduce civil unions for same-sex couples encompassing the same legal rights and responsibilities as marriage. The Wikipedia reference to this states that "the debate on civil unions [in Vermont] was acrimonious and deeply polarising". It is perhaps no surprise that a member of the extended family was in the vanguard. Within a week of the change in the law, she had been joined in civil union with her partner in Stowe, Vermont.

Taking stock and next steps

By the time I paused for breath in compiling the extended Riggs/Burnett family tree, I had found no fewer than 115 members in the direct family line from Stephen Riggs and Rose Burnett distributed across America with an additional 77 members attached as spouses. It was at this point that I came across an entry on Family Tree Maker submitted by Rose Ann Barnes Farkas, then of Gaithersburg, Maryland. This confirmed most of what I had unearthed, omitted some names and, tantalisingly, added a few more.

The additions included marriages by three members of the extended family to wives born outside the US – in the Philippines, Mexico (probably) and what was then North Vietnam. Further evidence – if any were needed – of the family's contribution to the social development of America, in this case via the country's cultural melting pot.

Finally, what of Henry Rigg, Stephen's older brother and the second lost cause to railway portering in Stockton? He emigrated to the US six years after Stephen – in 1898. I am now about to embark on researching his family's story. If it is half as interesting as that of Stephen Rigg(s) and Rose Burnett, I shall have much to look forward to.

FROM BALDERSBY TO VERMONT – VIA STOCKTON-ON-TEES (April 2020)

North Yorkshire origins

In the 1891 Census of England and Wales, brothers Stephen and Henry Rigg were recorded as railway porters in Stockton-on-Tees. They had been born in Baldersby, North Yorkshire – the two youngest of the six children of William Rigg (my great grandfather's oldest brother) and his wife, Ann Jefferson – and, at this time, were both single and in their twenties, Henry the older at 27. They lived in Sydney Street with another brother and his wife (John and Mary Rigg), their 5 nephews and nieces aged under 10 and a lodger.

By the end of the decade, Stephen and Henry were permanently resident over 3,000 miles away – in the US State of Vermont – with wives and young children of their own. The story of the descendants of these two men is the story of America through the 20th Century.

I have reported previously in the *CFHS Journal* on the descendants of Stephen Riggs (both brothers took on the extra 's' in the USA) and his wife Rose Burnett (from Dishforth) in the two-part *"A North Yorkshire Couple in Vermont, USA"* (January and April 2015). Stephen lived to the age of 82 and is buried in the Waterbury Center Cemetery in Washington County, Vermont. In this article, I shall follow the path taken by Henry Riggs and his wife Amelia Heath (from Littlethorpe), who were married in Middlesbrough in 1893.

It had been Stephen who had been the first to migrate, in 1892. Henry and Amelia followed six years later, together with 4 children aged under 10 (a fifth child, also Stephen, having died in infancy) and Amelia's recently widowed mother, the 61 year-old Hannah Heath. They were to have 4 more children in Vermont, though two of these also died in infancy and a third at the age of 12.

The spreading family tree

By 1900, Stephen and Henry had settled in the small town of Richmond, where they were both working in dairy farming, a significant industry within the Vermont economy.

Researchers into family history in the USA have the advantage over their British counterparts in that the US Federal Census material has been published to 1940 (under the 72-year rule) and includes a range of information that does not feature in the UK, for example wage levels and housing costs. I was additionally fortunate in that, whilst the availability of birth/marriage/death records varies by State on databases such as Ancestry, the Vermont data are very comprehensive. I would also recommend seeking out the on-line obituary sections of local newspapers via www.legacy.com and other sources.

Five of Henry and Amelia Riggs's 9 children lived into adulthood to marry and raise families of their own. To date, I have identified a total of 26 grandchildren and 53 great-grandchildren. The spread of the family tree is now such that it has extended to another two generations beyond that.

Four main themes

What are the main themes to emerge? I think there are four that stand out.

The first will be familiar to all family history researchers: that of hard work and progress through the generations. It is clear that Henry and Amelia had demanding lives. Henry was a farm labourer in 1900 and still a general farm labourer in 1920 (when he was aged 57); he died in Richmond four years later of "chronic cholecystisis". His wife, who moved to the neighbouring town of Hinesburg after Henry's death, outlived him by over 30 years but, even as a 70 year-old in the 1940 Census, Amelia was recorded as working 66 hours per week in a hardware store (and 52 weeks in the year) for an annual wage of $260. (The store belonged to her son, the 43 year-old Herbert J Riggs, who owned it on his own account and had worked 52 weeks the previous year for an income of $1300). Amelia died in 1958 at the age of 88 and is buried in the Riverview Cemetery in Richmond.

Henry and Amelia's three adult sons (Robert Heath, John William and Herbert J) worked in demanding manual jobs – respectively, dairy farmer and later factory machinist, general labourer in a milk company and cereal mill, and plumber and later hardware storekeeper – though they all lived until at least their 70s. However, in the next generation is to be found Heath Kenyon

Riggs (1918-2011), who graduated from the University of Vermont (UVM) in Burlington, received a Doctorate from the University of Chicago and then had a long and distinguished career in the maths faculty of the UVM, where he was involved with the introduction of computers at the beginning of the 1960s.

The occupations of Heath Riggs's brothers, male cousins and in-laws reflect the opportunities that were available in the expanding – though also cyclical – Vermont economy: from "labourer in needle shop" to "rural mail carrier with the US Postal Service" through to architect and general manager on the railways. One of Heath's sisters – Claire Aleen Riggs Moran (1926-2013) – became the head nurse in obstetrics at the Mary Fletcher Hospital in Burlington.

In turn, the later generations were able to take advantage of the further development of the Vermont (and American) economies, as their respective service sectors consolidated in depth and/or took on new shapes. The recent or current occupations listed in the family tree include a ski race center manager and an orthopaedic specialist in Vermont, a lawyer in Florida and a micro brewer in Connecticut.

This leads to my second theme. For many members within the family as a whole – though by no means all – a corollary of career progression was the willingness to migrate. This did not happen straightaway. Of Henry and Amelia's 5 adult children, only Edith Annie Falby (née Riggs) was to die in another State (in her case, neighbouring Massachusetts). However, the lifespan of the next generation – in most cases through to the latter part of the last Century or into this one – was such as to produce a host of different States on the death certificates: these ranged from New York and Connecticut in the east to Florida in the south and the distant California and Idaho.

Other branches of the family remained in Vermont. As a result, today – five generations on from Henry and Amelia – there are descendants in a cluster of towns and counties flanked by Route 89 as it approaches Burlington from the east and then heads north, including Colchester, Fletcher, Essex Junction and Bakersfield.

It was predominantly Henry and Amelia's grandchildren's generation that saw action in the Second World War and the impact of military service is another recurrent theme in the Riggs family tree. The various newspaper obituary notices refer proudly to the service records in that conflict of, for example, Kenneth Frank Riggs (1920-2005) in the US Air Corps, Murray Lincoln Riggs (1921-2005) in the US Army and Charles Edward Dunn (1916-1977) in the US Navy. Earlier, two of Henry and Amelia's sons – Robert Heath Rigg and Herbert J Riggs – had been veterans of the First World War. (They had both been born in Middlesbrough but, by then, were naturalised US citizens). Later, Richard Derwent Bird (1930-2010) served in the Korean War.

However, the most poignant reference is to Walter Ripley "Rip" Tyrrell (1947-1969), who was a petty officer (2nd class) when he was killed in a helicopter crash at Tam Ky, Vietnam, at the age of 22. He was a great grandson of Henry and Amelia Riggs and his mother – Helena Elizabeth Tyrrell (née Riggs, 1917-1997) – was, therefore, my third cousin.

Finally – again in keeping with all our family stories – there are the events and occurrences of everyday life: not only marriage and divorce (in some cases more than once), but cases of infant mortality and early deaths in young adulthood, the incidence of Alzheimer's, the establishment of civil partnerships, ownership of "Dick's barbers shop", 4 years in the UVM women's soccer team, ordination as a deacon and priest… And so on. All human life is here.

The obituaries in US local newspapers are a rich source of information on the characters who populate the family grid. Who could not be intrigued by the exotically named Norma Theresa Falby Lorre Goodrich (1917-2006) – a granddaughter of Henry and Amelia – who, as the author of *"The Ancient Myths"*, revealed definitively (perhaps) that King Arthur was a Scottish king. However, for my part, I am more interested in Christine Moffat Riggs (1925-2016) – a native of Nova Scotia and the wife of one of Henry and Amelia's grandsons – who, after graduating from high school, attended an airplane mechanics school in Maine and then worked in engineering. Her obituary in the *Burlington Free Press* noted that she "was very proud of her plaque that commemorated her contributions to the Manhattan Project, which helped end World War II".

The flourishing Riggs surname

There will be other facets of the family trees of the two brothers from Baldersby to be uncovered, of course. I have only skimmed the surface here. So far, the descendants (and their spouses) of Stephen and Henry Rigg(s) whom I have identified number well over 500, and counting.

There is one difference between the two lines. Stephen and Rose Riggs had 5 daughters, so, on their side, the surname did not survive beyond one of their grandsons – Foster Riggs Smith – who died in Florida in 1995 at the age of 72. However, as we have seen, Henry and Amelia had 3 adult sons (who, in turn, had a total of 8 adult sons of their own). It is not surprising, therefore, that the Riggs surname has been carried forward into the Vermont births of the 21st Century.

It is a far cry from the two unskilled labourers working on the railway in the Stockton-on-Tees of 1891. And it is a vibrant American tale.

ANNEX A2

THE 1911 CENSUS OF ENGLAND AND WALES: TRANSCRIPTION ERRORS

> *The excitement at being able to access the 1911 Census of England and Wales towards the end of 2009 was tempered by the frustration caused by the prevalence of transcription errors. I set out my views in a letter to the* Cleveland Family History Society Journal, *which was published in January 2010. It prompted a number of supportive responses.*

Dear Editor

1911 CENSUS TRANSCRIPTS

Members of the Society might be interested in my initial experience of viewing the transcripts of the 1911 Census for England and Wales. I have been looking at the household records of my great grandparents, Henry and Jane RIGG of Pickhill, Thirsk, and Peter and Agnes McBRIDE of Hunslet, Leeds. I also looked at the other households in North Yorkshire in which 6 of Henry and Jane's 7 surviving children were living.

    I discovered that:

*　　Henry's age was given as 68. (He was 63).

*　　One of Henry and Jane's daughters – also JANE Rigg, living in the same household – was listed as JUNE.

*　　Another daughter, Mary RIGG, living in Ilkley, had her surname listed as KIGG.

*　　A son, Robert RIGG, living in Grassington, had his surname listed as RIGY.

* The birthplace of Peter was given as RESTHERGLERE, ANARKSHIRE (sic). He was actually born in RUTHERGLEN, LANARKSHIRE.

* The birthplace of Agnes was given as WARWICKSHIRE, LANSHIRE (sic). She was actually born in WARRINGTON, LANCASHIRE.

The error relating to Robert Rigg was particularly galling. Robert was killed in action in France in August 1918 at the age of 33. The 1911 Census was, of course, the last in which he – and so many others – was recorded. The least we can do is to show him due respect and get his details right.

I appreciate that, in general, the transcribers of the 1911 Census might have had a difficult job reading from the original records. However, it does not augur well that, of the initial sample of 11 individuals whose details I examined, no fewer than 6 had major errors, including 3 incorrect names. Moreover, this is not simply a case of difficulty with ineligible handwriting in a single household: the errors given here were in 4 separate households out of the 8 viewed. In addition, the errors of birthplace do not give confidence that the transcriptions have been done by someone with any feel for the geography of Britain, as the WARRINGTON reference is very clear in the original record and the transcription is obviously nonsense.

To its credit, the on-line system for the 1911 Census has a "report error" facility, which allows family researchers to suggest corrections that might be made and which gives a prompt response to those suggestions. I am pleased to report that, in this case, all the errors are being corrected.

An important lesson for researchers is, perhaps, to call up copies of the original records, rather than the transcripts, if there are any doubts when studying a particular household. This is more expensive, of course, costing 30 credits per view to the transcript's 10, although the annotations and corrections made on the original record can yield additional information. However, this assumes that one can find the household – or the individual – in the first place, as it is the transcripts that provide the raw material on which the Census's search facility is based.

I wonder if other Members of the Society are encountering similar problems.

In the meantime, I will try to come to terms with the fact that my great grandmother was a lassie from Lancashire.

Yours sincerely

JOHN RIGG

ANNEX A3

"HERE I STAND"

My sister, Rosie, and I spent a week in Niedersachen (Lower Saxony) in September 2018 visiting some of the places associated with the German side of the family history. The visit had a profound impact of how I consider the results of my genealogical research and the insights that it can give on our ancestors' journeys through the centuries.

I provided some reflections on this in an article for the Cleveland Family History Society Journal *in April 2019. The article was slightly trimmed by the editor, though it still read well. The full version is given here.*

I have spent many years examining the extended Rigg family tree in North Yorkshire. The direct paternal line goes back to George Rigg, who was born in 1802 to Mary Rigg of Baldersby and an unknown father. That particular trail ends there, as the North Yorkshire County Record Office does not hold the Bastardy Papers for that year. However, George (and his wife, Jane Wells) had 8 children and 33 grandchildren, so there has been no shortage of distant cousins to trace.

Of course, it goes without saying that our genealogical interests are not only concerned with the male lineage. Other branches are equally direct and it was when I was examining the ancestors on my mother's side that some profound truths were registered with me.

Last Autumn, my sister, Rosie, and I spent several days in the Niedersachsen (Lower Saxony) *Land* of Germany visiting some of the places associated with our family history. Our maternal grandfather, Alfred Edgar Niblett, was born in Osnabrück in 1888 to an English father, Charles James Niblett, and a German mother, whose maiden name was Anna Karoline Borstelmann.

It was a highly successful trip. I knew that Anna Karoline Borstelmann died in her residence in Ludwig Strasse in Osnabrück in 1938 at the age of 84. The city's cemetery authority had previously informed me that the street no longer exists, but, in a local bookshop, I came across a map of the Osnabrück tram system of 1906 on which the location was marked. It is now called Ludwig Baete Strasse (after a 20th Century writer and historian) and is a pleasant tree-lined street of post-Second World War housing.

In the small town of Elze, to the south of Hannover, we visited *die Peter und Paul-Kirche*, in which Charles and Anna had married in 1873. It was curiously empty for a Sunday lunchtime, apart from two middle-aged women – the organist and a singer – who held a long practice session, perhaps 40 minutes or so, for the time we were there. The melodic sounds resonated down from the balcony and around the clean white walls of the church's interior.

Outside, I found the statue of Martin Luther, erected in 1883 on the 400th anniversary of his birth, to be both powerful and moving. The inscription read: *Hier stehe ich. Ich kann nicht anders. Gott helfe mir. Amen!* "Here I stand. I can do no other. God help me. Amen!" This is reputed to have been Luther's statement to the Holy Roman Emperor, Charles V, at the formal hearing in Worms in 1521. (In his monumental *A History of Christianity*, published in 2009, Diarmid MacCulloch notes that the phrase was only attributed to Luther after his death by the editor of his collected works).

For the following day, we had hired an excellent local guide to show us around the village of Kirchwalsede and the town of Visselhoevede, including the two beautiful parish churches. At the former, we were able to see some of the original church records. We started by finding the baptism record of Anna Margreta Marquardt – the mother of Anna Karoline Borstelmann's father, Johann Friedrich Borstelmann, (and my great (x3) grandmother) – in 1772. I felt the lump in my throat as I saw her name on the page: I just about held it together.

I have previously spent some time examining the comprehensive online database of Lutheran church records in Niedersachsen (www.genpluswin-database.de) and was familiar with the long direct family line that goes back through the Marquardt, Lange, Dieckhof and Henke families to the baptism of Harm Henke in 1582. We looked up some of the other original records: the burial of Gert Dieckhof in 1713, the burial of Casten Henke in 1691, and so on.

An unexpected bonus was that the written records contained additional information. Even in the Lutheran church, the type of service was, to some extent, dependent on the amount spent by the worshippers. Hence, the burial of Anna Marie Henke in 1711 was accompanied by "a sermon from the pulpit". Elsewhere, the causes of death were given: the unfortunate Johann Lange died at the age of 56 three weeks before the Christmas of 1686 when a stone fell on him as he was digging a hole (presumably in the graveyard).

The baptism of Harm Henke in 1582 was, of course, relatively early in the history of the Protestant Church; it had been only two generations earlier that Luther had nailed his 95 Theses to the door of the Castle Church in Wittenberg. Or, to put it another way, it was six years before Philip of Spain sent his Armada into the English Channel. As I looked around the church in Kirchwalsede, its interior neatly decorated with flowers from a recent wedding, I was aware that, even though it had been modified and repaired many times over the centuries, this was still the space in which my great (x9) grandfather had lived and breathed. And it was now, in a different context to Luther, that here I stood.

On the Tuesday, our family researches completed for the time being, Rosie and I did the tourist run in Hannover. The bus tour took us past the Eriebnis Zoo and out to the Royal Gardens of Herrenhausen. Towards the end of the route we passed the HDI Arena – the home of the *Bundesliga 1* side, Hannover 96 – the street in front of which is called Robert Enke Strasse.

Robert Enke was a goalkeeper who played for Hannover 96 for five years from 2004. He also played for Benfica and Borussia Muenchengladbach, amongst other clubs, and won eight caps for Germany. He took his own life in 2009 at the age of 32. (The excellent *A Life Too Short: the Tragedy of Robert Enke* by Ronald Reng, published in 2011, is a detailed and poignant biography).

After the bus tour, Rosie and I briefly went our separate ways and I paid my three euros to take the escalator to the top of the dome of the *Neues Rathaus* (the New Town Hall) for the views across the city and the surrounding plains. Then, in the late afternoon, I walked back to the football stadium, even though I knew that the gates were closed and access was not possible. (This was an obvious flaw in the schedule I had planned: Hannover 96 were at home to Hoffenheim on the following Tuesday). As I returned to the hotel, I attempted to marshal the conflicting themes that the overall visit had generated in the back of my mind.

There is an obvious point about continuity and longevity, even amongst the turmoil and destruction that the centuries have brought to this part of the world. The *Rathaus* in Osnabrück, heavily damaged in the Second World War, has been repaired to the Late Gothic design of the 1512 original; it was where one of the treaties of the Peace of Westphalia was signed in 1648 to bring an end to the Thirty Years' War. In Bad Münder am Deister (where my great (x2) grandmother, Anna Perlasky, was born in 1827), the door of the imposing *Steinhof* is dated 1721 and names the family who owned the property at that time. Even in the *Marktkirche* in Hannover, also destroyed in the War and impressively rebuilt in red brick subsequently, the striking triptych at the altar dates from 1480.

The theme of continuity is also evident in the robustness of the family line in Niedersachsen, irrespective of whichever of the various armies – Swedish or Napoleonic or Hannoverian or Prussian – have marched through the territory to claim the land. The local inhabitants – farmers, shepherds, builders, *et al* – got on with their lives and raised their families and prayed to God and kept going from one generation to the next.

At the same time, I am conscious that there is also transience and fragility. In this respect, I think my researches re-emphasised something which has also been evident in the strong connection with Yorkshire on the other side of the family tree. This concerns the powerful significance of connections and relationships and how, against the deep background of the long centuries, there is an inevitable impermanence to our being – whether 32 years for Robert Enke or 56 years for Johann Lange or 84 years for Anna Karoline Borstelmann.

We all dip our hand in the flowing stream – some just a finger, others up to the wrist – and, in the rippling of the water, we leave the memories and traces for those that are left behind.

ANNEX A4

ROLL OF HONOUR

It was noted in the Preface that one of the significant prompts that encouraged me – as long ago as 1987 – to research the family histories set out in this book was my father's reference one evening to the death of his uncle, Robert Rigg, in the First World War.

During the course of the narrative, there have been several references to other deaths of individuals serving in the Armed Services during the two World Wars. These have not been as close as Robert Rigg to one of the direct family lines, but most can be placed within the dense network of the extended family tree and are listed in the Roll of Honour presented below.

The Roll of Honour includes Walter Ripley Tyrrell (1947-1969) – a great (x3) grandson of George Rigg of Baldersby (1802-1865) – who was in the US Navy when he was killed in Vietnam.

Four of the individuals listed are not in the family tree, but their deaths were recorded in the text. They are denoted with a double asterisk. In the cases of John Davis of the Royal Navy and John William Rigg (1st Battalion of the Yorkshire Regiment), the deaths were recorded during periods of active service though not in action.

<u>Ireland</u>
John Davis   died 1803 (probable)

<u>Egypt</u>
John William Rigg   1886-1909

<u>First World War</u>
Christopher Boynton   1893-1918
William Henry Boynton   1897-1917
Charles Edward Harwood **   1862-1917
Thomas Hyland   1886-1918

Thomas Chalmers McBride	1899-1918
Thomas Rennie McLeod McBride **	1887-1916
Harry Rigg	1893-1918
Robert Rigg	1885-1918
Thomas Rigg	1889-1918
William Rigg	1891-1917
Albert Rogers	1893-1917
Neil Shaw	1886-1917

<u>Second World War</u>

Thomas Chalmers Glen McBride	1918-1945
Charles Joseph Niblett	1907-1944
Eric Harry Niblett	1907-1941
Frank Montem Smith **	1894-1942
Dennis Albert Tordoff **	1922-1943

<u>USA-Vietnam War</u>

Walter Ripley Tyrrell	1947-1969

ANNEX A5

SOURCES

Initial researches

The discussion of the sources that I have used in this family history research must allow for the fact that the work has been undertaken for nearly 40 years – i.e. in both the pre-Internet and Internet eras. It will be inevitable that some of the sources I quote here will have become obsolete.

The Censuses for England and Wales are managed by The National Archives (TNA, formerly the Public Record Office). At the time of my initial researches (in 1987), the Censuses for 1841 to 1881 were open to the public on microfilm in the Public Record Office in London and in local record offices. I began by consulting the relevant returns in the North Yorkshire County Record Office (NYCRO) in Northallerton. Later, in 1992, I was able to consult the 1891 Census in the public library in Harrogate. By the time of the release of the 1901 Census (in 2002), the material was available on-line at www.census.pro.gov.uk via vouchers purchased from the Census Helpdesk. Since the release of the 1911 Census (in 2011), I have taken out a subscription to www.ancestry.co.uk. In 2021, I took out a subscription to Findmypast.co.uk (FMP), partly in anticipation of FMP's release of the 1921 Census of England and Wales in 2022.

When commencing my examination of the Census records, I noted the advice given in Stella Colwell's *Tracing Your Family Tree* (1985) and Don Steel's *Discovering Your Family History* (1986). These sources were especially useful on the use of census material to get a sense of community life at the time and on the possible inaccuracies that might be present in the records.

My early researches on parish records drew on Cecil Humphrey-Smith's *The Phillimore Atlas and Index of Parish Registers* (1984), which listed the availability of the parish records of England and Wales at the Society of Genealogists, the International Genealogical Index (IGI) of the Genealogical Society of the Church of the Latter Day Saints and individual county record offices. Colwell's book was also useful in setting out the value of the parish registers to the genealogist.

Indexes of the Registrations of Births, Marriages and Deaths (BMD) in England and Wales were available by quarter-year on open shelves at what was then the Office of Population, Censuses and Surveys in St Catherine's House in Kingsway in London. During the 1990s, these were transferred to the Family Research Centre in Myddleton Street, London. Since 2008, they have been available at The National Archives in Kew. For my researches, useful early guidance on using these indices was found in Patrick Belgrave-Moore's *Tracing Ancestors: A Beginner's Guide* (1986) and the comprehensive *Tracing Your Ancestors in the Public Record Office* (4th edition, 1990) by Amanda Bevan and Andrea Duncan.

My general introduction to family history sources benefited greatly from David Hey's excellent *Oxford Guide to Family History* (1993), particularly Chapter 5 "A Guide to the Records".

A publication by Halbert's Family Heritage called *The World Book of Riggs* (1992) provided possible addresses when I was seeking to contact Douglas Rigg (1905-1995), the son of Mary Rigg and grandson of Henry Rigg, in 1994. As noted in Chapter 10, this search was successful and I have acknowledged the other members of this family with whom I subsequently made contact in Annex A8 below.

Whilst not part of the direct family line, my interest in the Rigge family of Westmorland and Yorkshire – particularly Fletcher Rigge (1743-1829) – was noted in Chapter 1; the family's papers for the period 1581 to 1880 have reference number DDHJ/3 in the Cumbrian Archive Service Catalogue (CASCAT).

I have had longstanding memberships of the Society of Genealogists (from 1988) and the Cleveland Family History Society (from 1993). Their respective journals – *Genealogists' Magazine* and the *CHFS Journal* – provide excellent reading and useful ideas each quarter. The coronavirus crisis of 2020-22 obliged the Society of Genealogists to present its extensive lecture series online and this has continued post-lockdown. I took advantage of this for "My Ancestor was from Yorkshire" and "My Ancestor was an Agricultural Labourer" in 2020, "Ancestry vs Findmypast" in 2021, "The 1921 Census of England and Wales" in 2022, "Merchant Navy Ancestors" in 2023 and "Researching Your Ancestors in Today's Austria and Germany" in 2024.

The Federation of Family History Societies has published a number of occupational guides for family historians. I purchased *Was Your Grandfather a Railwayman?* (1995) by Tom Richards.

Online sources

It is the case, of course, that the access to material on the Internet has revolutionised the nature of family history research compared with the distant days of the 1980s. Some of this material remains free of charge – for example, the FreeBMD database of births, marriages and deaths in England and Wales from 1837 to 1984 (www.Freebmd.co.uk) and the databases of the IGI (via www.familysearch.org) – of both of which I have made very considerable use.

There are a number of sites cataloguing graves and their inscriptions. Amongst others, I have drawn on www.billiongraves.com, www.findagrave.com and www.deceasedonline.com (the last of these via subscription).

It was inevitable that I would delve into a miscellany of other online sources. These have included: www.rcog.org.uk, which provided access to *The Midwives Roll, 1904-59*; www.workhouses.org.uk on the workhouses 19th Century Britain; www.localhistories.org on 19th Century Warrington; the photographic archive of Leeds at www.leodis.org; www.peterborofhs.org.uk for the database of the Peterborough and District Family History Society; www.rooksmoor.blogspot.com on the Hull Dock Strikes of 1911; www.closedpubs.co.uk on the former Prince of Wales public house in Cheltenham; www.winsongreentobrookfields.co.uk on the former Railway Inn public house in Winson Green, Birmingham; www.churchdb.gukutils.org.uk for the Places of Worship Database references to the Bridge Street Chapel, Bristol and the Highbury Congregational Chapel, Cheltenham; www.clarkscollege.co.uk on the history of the Clark's College establishments in England and Wales; www.greatwar.co.uk on the war medals of the First World War; www.cwgc.org, the website of the Commonwealth War Graves Commission; www.1915crewlists.rmg.co.uk for the National Maritime Museum's Crew Lists of the British Merchant Navy in 1915; www.wrecksite.eu for the details of the sinking of SS *Narragansett* in 1917; www.historyofwar.org/air/units/RCAF/408_wwII.html and www.raf.mod.uk/history/bombercommandno408squadron.cfm on the Second World War 408 Squadron of the Royal Canadian Air Force; www.forces-war-records.co.uk/units/806/raf-kirkham on the Second World War training camp at RAF Kirkham; www.sciencemuseumgroup.org.uk on the history of Joshua Buckton and Company Ltd; www.curtisfurniture.co.uk on the history of Curtis Furniture Ltd; http://ruhleben.tripod.com, Chris Paton's website on the First World War Ruhleben Internment Camp in Berlin; and www.exxonmobil.co.uk on the origins of the Anglo-American Oil Company Ltd.

The University of London records are available at www.senatehouselibrary.ac.uk. I drew on the *List of Nineteenth Century University of London Examinees* and *Part I of the University of London General Register* (which includes those who were undergraduates up to 31st March 1883, but had not passed an examination before 31st December 1890) as well as the *University of London Historical Record, 1836-1926*.

The Project Gutenberg e-book project released FR Melville's *Melville and Co's Directory and Gazetteer, 1856* (on Norwich and the surrounding villages) in 2020.

An online source of local newspaper obituaries is www.legacy.com.

I accessed the database of Holocaust victims compiled by the World Holocaust Remembrance Center in Jerusalem – www.yadvashem.org – though this did not contain any direct links to the narrative presented in this volume.

Other online material is only available by subscription. The text of this volume makes frequent reference to the sources I have accessed via www.ancestry.co.uk, particularly the national censuses for England and Wales (1841 to 1911), Ireland (1901 and 1911, also at www.census.nationalarchives.ie), Canada (1921) and the United States (1900 to 1950). As noted, I have subscribed to Ancestry since 2011.[1]

For England and Wales and/or the UK, a number of national databases were accessed on Ancestry having been made available by – or based on information held by – the TNA: *UK, Royal Hospital Chelsea Pensioner Soldier Service Records, 1760-1920*; *1939 England and Wales Register*; *British Army World War I Service Records, 1914-1920*; *England and Wales Civil Divorce Records, 1858-1916*; *England and Wales Criminal Records, 1791-1892*; *England and Wales Nonconformist and Non-parochial Registers, 1567-1970*; *UK Incoming Passenger Lists, 1878-1960*; *UK Outward Passenger Lists, 1890-1960*; *UK Registers of Birth, Marriages and Deaths at Sea, 1844-1890*. TNA's own website was the source for *Royal Navy Officers Service Records, 1756-1931*, *Registry of Shipping and Seamen: Index of First World War Mercantile Marine Medals and the British War Medal* and the (1914-1918) *War Diary of the 232 Army Field Artillery Brigade*. Separately, I obtained an important extract of the *War Diary of the 13th Battalion, Yorkshire Regiment* directly from Steve Erskine, Researcher at the Green Howards' Museum in Richmond, North Yorkshire.

A range of other national databases (with the original sources noted here in parentheses) have been accessed on Ancestry: *Army Registers of Soldiers' Effects, 1901-1929* and *Soldiers Effects Records, 1901-1960* (National Army Museum, Chelsea); *England and Wales, National Probate Calendar (Index of Wills and Administrations), 1858-1995* (Principal Probate Registry, London); *England and Scotland Select Cemeteries Register, 1800-2016*; *UK and Ireland, Masters and Mates Certificates, 1850-1927* (National Maritime Museum, London).

At the local level, I have drawn on Ancestry for: *All Gloucestershire, England, Church of England Baptisms, Marriages and Burials, 1538-1813*; *All Gloucestershire, England, Church of England Burials, 1813-1988*; *Gloucestershire, England, Marriages and Banns, 1754-1938*; *Lancashire Church of England Marriage and Banns, 1813-1921*; *Liverpool Church of England Baptisms, 1813-1919*; *Liverpool, England, Church of England Marriages and Banns, 1754-1932*; *Liverpool, England, Catholic Baptisms, 1802-1906*; *Liverpool, England, Catholic*

---

1   Ancestry continually revises the scope of its individual databases. The references given here are those that applied at the time of my use of them. Some will subsequently have had their periods of coverage changed (usually extended). Others may have been merged with complementary databases.

Marriages, 1754-1921; All London Church of England Births and Baptisms, 1813-1906; London, England, Church of England Marriages and Banns, 1754-1921; London, England, Electoral Rolls, 1832-1965; London Electoral Registers of 1923-25; London, England, Workhouse Admission and Discharging Records, 1764-1930; Northamptonshire, England, Church of England Baptisms, Marriages and Burials, 1754-1912; Northamptonshire, England, Church of England Marriages, 1754-1912; Northamptonshire, England, Church of England Burials, 1813-1912; Northamptonshire Baptisms, 1813-1912; Surrey, England, Electoral Roll, 1832-1962; North Yorkshire, Church of England Births and Baptisms, 1813-1921; West Yorkshire, England, Police Records, 1833-1914; 1907-1911 Examination Book for the West Riding (of Yorkshire) Constabulary. These databases were originally compiled by Gloucestershire Archives, Lancashire Archives, Liverpool Record Office, London Metropolitan Archives, National Army Museum, Chelsea, Northamptonshire Record Office, Surrey History Centre, North Yorkshire County Record Office and West Yorkshire Archive Service. *Oxford Men and Their Colleges, 1880-1892* was published in two volumes by Joseph Foster in 1893.

It should be noted that many of the UK records listed above can be accessed online directly from the IGI or TNA, in the latter case with specific entries available for purchase.

The IGI was the original source for *England, Select Births and Christenings, 1538-1975*. It has also been the source of many of the non-UK sources accessed on Ancestry. These have included: *Argentina National Census, 1895; Belgium, Antwerp Police Immigration Index 1840-1930; Germany, Select Births and Baptisms, 1558-1898; Germany, Select Deaths and Burials, 1582-1958; Ireland, Selected Births and Baptisms, 1620-1911; India Marriages, 1792-1948; New York Marriages, 1686-1980* and *US, City Directories, 1822-1995*.

The other non-UK databases accessed on Ancestry have extensively covered Europe and North America. The former (with the sources again in parentheses) have been: *Adressbucher der Stadt und des Landkreises Osnabrück [Osnabrück and Surrounding Areas Address Books], 1815-1974* and *Hamburger Adressbuch, 1925* (Deutsche National Bibliothek, Leipzig); *Bremen, Germany, and Hannover, Prussia, Germany, Lutheran Baptisms, Marriages and Burials 1574-1945, Hannover, Germany, Lutheran Baptisms, Marriages and Burials, 1643-1887* and *Handels- und Gewerke- Adressbuch der Provinz Hannover [Trade and Trades Address Book for the Province of Hannover]* (Niedersächsisches Landesarchiv, Hannover); *Ireland, Catholic Parish Register, 1655-1915* (National Library of Ireland, Dublin); *Ireland, Select Catholic Birth and Baptism Registers, 1763-1917* (E-Celtic Limited, Dublin); *Ireland, Civil Registrations of Births Index, 1864-1958* and *Ireland Civil Registrations Deaths Index, 1864-1958* (General Register Office, Dublin, and PRONI, Belfast); *Ireland, Griffith's Valuation, 1847-1864* (National Archives of Ireland, Dublin, and PRONI); *Ireland, Dog Licence Registrations,*

1810-1926, Ireland, Petty Session Court Registers, 1818-1919 and *Ireland, Prison Registers, 1790-1924* (National Archives of Ireland).

The other North American databases accessed on Ancestry have been: *British Colombia Death Index, 1872-1990* (British Colombia Vital Statistics Agency); *Canada, Ocean Arrivals (Form 30A), 1919-1974* (Library and Archives Canada); *Canada, Immigration and Settlement Correspondence and Lists, 1817-1896* (The National Archives); *US Social Security Applications and Claims Index* (US Social Security Administration, Washington DC); *New York, US, State and Federal Naturalization Records, 1794-1943, California Passenger and Crew Lists, 1882-1959* and *US World War I Draft Registration Cards, 1917-18* (US National Archives and Records Administration, Washington DC); *California, US, State Census, 1852* (California State Library, Sacramento); *California Death Index, 1940-1997* (California Department of Health Services); *New York, New York City Municipal Deaths, 1795-1949* and *New York, New York Death Index, 1862-1948* (New York Department of Health, Albany); *New York State Census, 1875* (New York State Archives, Albany); *Oregon Death Index, 1898-2008* (Oregon State Archives and Record Center); *San Francisco Area Funeral Home, 1895-1985* (Researchity, San Francisco).

As noted above, my subscription to Findmypast.co.uk (FMP) commenced in 2021, partly in order to access the 1921 Census of England and Wales on its release the following year. Of course, FMP provides access to many of the databases held by Ancestry and it is a subject of debate amongst family history researchers as to whether one really needs to subscribe to both.

In addition to accessing the 1921 Census, I used FMP specifically to consult the databases of: *Gloucestershire, Bigland's Monumental Inscriptions* (compiled by the Bristol and Gloucester Archaeological Society from Ralph Bigland's *Historical Monumental and Genealogical Collections Relative to the County of Gloucester, 1791-94); Britain Trade Union Membership Registers* (the Modern Records Centre, University of Warwick); *British Army Service Records* (The National Archives); *National School Admission Registers and Log-Books, 1870-1914* (Teesside Archives); *New South Wales and Tasmania: Settlers and Convicts, 1787-1859; United States Marriages.*

Scotland

The centralisation of BMD records in Scotland dates from 1855. Details of births/baptisms, banns/marriages and burials are available from the Old Parish Registers, which date from 1553. My interrogation of these sources began in 2007 with the purchase of credits to access the databases via the www.scotlandspeople.gov.uk website. I also made use of the hard copies available in the Mitchell Library, Glasgow.

In my unsuccessful search to track down Neil McBride's work as a "King's Searcher (Customs)" in Port Glasgow, I consulted two sets of files in West Register

House in Edinburgh: *Officers of His Majesty's Customs in North Britain – Their Salaries for the Quarter Ended* (ref: CE3/14-21) and *Officers of His Majesty's Salt Duties in North Britain – Their Salaries for the Quarter Ended* (ref: CE/12/4). The former ran from January 1783 to October 1822 and the latter from April 1782 to July 1798.

Ancestry has a limited amount of Scottish material available via subscription. I made use of *Scotland, Select Marriages, 1561-1910*. As noted above, I also consulted *England and Scotland Select Cemeteries Register, 1800-2016*.

Ireland

My wife, Angela, and I attended the excellent 3-day family history course provided by the Ulster Historical Foundation (UHF) in Belfast in June 2017. This gave me a temporary access to the UHF database at www.ancestryireland.com and the files of the Public Record Office of Northern Ireland (PRONI) in Belfast. I later commissioned follow-up research from the UHF on the 19th Century records of the English and Woods families in County Down and the Murray, Mullowney and McManamon families in County Mayo. The additional sources on which the researchers drew included the Valuation Office Books of 1824-1854 as well as 19th Century freeholder records and Tithe Applotment records.

In addition to the many online Irish databases that I have accessed via Ancestry (noted above with the original sources), I made use of the genealogical databases at www.rootsireland.ie (maintained by the Irish Family History Foundation) and the Irish Government's site www.irishgenealogy.ie. The latter is free-to-access, as is www.nli.ie, which provides online microfilm images of the National Library of Ireland's church registers of baptisms and marriages.

Defence Force Ireland's *Ireland Military Service Pension Index, 1916-1923* is available at www.mspcsearch.militaryarchives.ie.

The Monumental Inscriptions of the graves in the ruin of Burrishoole Abbey, near Newport in County Mayo, are given in www.bernieworld.net/Cemeteries/Burrishoole. The DVD *Old Port to Newport: An Historical Journey*, produced by Purple Foxglove Films in 2013, covers this area; the same production company's *The West Mayo Flying Column in the War of Independence* (2021) is available on YouTube. A useful general history of County Mayo can also be found at www.mayo-ireland.ie.

Germany

As with the online Irish databases, I have noted earlier those for Germany that were accessed via Ancestry, together with the original sources.

In addition, I registered with a Hannover-based genealogical network – hannover-l@genealogy.net – in 2014. It was through that link that I became aware of the www.genpluswin-database.de/nofb website, which was a comprehensive source of Lutheran baptism, marriage and death records dating back to the 16th Century. The English language versions of the network and website were closed in 2021.

Another useful source was the set of databases published online at www.compgen.de by Compgen, a German genealogical association. These gave me access to *Germany and Surrounding Areas, Address Books, 1815-1974, Adressbuch Kreis Grafschaft Bentheim, 1927* [Address Book for the Bentheim district], *Adressbuch Oldenburg* (for 1940 and 1955) and *Verlustlisten 1 Weltkreig* [Loss List for the First World War].

The www.kartezumnamen.eu site revealed the geographical distribution of the Borstelmann surname in present-day Germany.

Malta

The Public Registry of Malta (pubreg.civilstatus@gov.mt) holds records on that country's births, marriages and deaths. A more specific source on the BMD of the families of British armed services families in Malta was www.lineone.net/-stephaniebidmead. The www.forebears.co.uk/surnames site provided information on the distribution of the Brincau and Brincat surnames in Malta and elsewhere.

Local Area researches

It was inevitable that, as the scope of my family history research expanded, it would take me to a number of locations in the UK and overseas. Thus, in addition to the NYCRO and the Harrogate Public Library, noted above, the public sources on which I have drawn – either by personal visit or in correspondence – are: Northallerton Public Library; The Mitchell Library, Glasgow; The Isle of Arran Heritage Museum; Peterborough City Council; Leeds City Council; West Yorkshire Archive Service, Morley; Lancashire County Council; The Senate House Library of the University of London; the RAF Disclosures Department at RAF Cranwell in Sleaford; Public Record Office of Northern Ireland, Belfast; The Santa Maria Addolorata Cemetery in Paola, Malta; Public Registry of Malta.

The Acknowledgements in Annex A8 record the individuals who dealt with my various requests and enquiries.

Individual family records

The information provided by individuals to the public forum pages of the family history companies can be very useful, when used in the correct way. I have acknowledged the contributions made on several branches of the family tree in North Yorkshire and elsewhere in Annex A8 below.

A strong word of caution is required here, however. Put simply, some of the information made available on the public pages is simply wrong. My detailed knowledge of the extended Rigg family in North Yorkshire gave me a good insight into the types and extent of errors that are to be found. Moreover, because some Ancestry contributors simply replicate the work of others without any scrutiny, those errors are repeated and magnified. Where appropriate, I have contacted those responsible to suggest corrections. In some cases, I received a friendly reply; in others, no response at all. The most effective use of the public forum pages, therefore, should be as prompts and generators of ideas and linkages, which should always be checked with the official records.

Newspapers

The text presented in this volume draws on a number of newspaper and directory reports from the 19th and 20th Centuries. The online versions of the newspapers were available from the British Newspaper Archive, which is available on Findmypast. (I also accessed the database from my local library in Milngavie, near Glasgow). The individual newspapers and directories are listed in the Bibliography given in Annex A6.

ANNEX A6

BIBLIOGRAPHY

Books and Booklets

TFT Baker (Ed.), *A History of the County of Middlesex: Volume 5*, Victoria County History, 1976.
Patrick Belgrave-Moore, *Tracing Ancestors: A Beginner's Guide*, Elvery Dowers Publications, 1986.
Ralph Bigland, *Historical, Monumental and Genealogical Connections relative to the County of Gloucester (1786-1794)*, Bristol and Gloucester Archaeological Society, 1989-1995.
Gregory Blaxland, *Amiens*, WH Allen & Co., 1981.
Brian Blouet, *The Story of Malta*, 3rd edition, Progress Press Co. Ltd, Malta, 1987
Julia Boyd, *Travellers in the Third Reich: The Rise of Fascism Through the Eyes of Everyday People*, Elliott and Thompson Limited, 2017.
Keith Brooker, *The Hull Strikes of 1911*, East Yorkshire Local History Society, 1979.
Helen Bynum, *Spitting Blood: The History of Tuberculosis*, Oxford University Press, 2012.
Thorbjorn Campbell, *Arran: A History*, Birlinn Limited, 2007.
Lucille H Campey, *Les Ecossais: The Pioneer Scots of Lower Canada, 1763-1855*, Natural Heritage Books, 2006.
Stella Colwell, *Tracing Your Family Tree*, Faber and Faber, 1985.
Patricia EC Croot (Ed.), *A History of the County of Middlesex: Volume 12, Chelsea*, Victoria County History, 2004.
Peter Davis, *Airfield Focus, 43: Upper Heyford*, GMS Enterprises, 2001.
Angelique Day and Patrick McWilliams (Eds.), *Ordnance Survey Memoirs of Ireland* (40 volumes), Institute of Irish Studies, 1993.
T.M. Devine, *The Scottish Nation, 1700-2000*, Allen Lane, The Penguin Press, 1999.

Eric B Dobson, *A Century of Achievement: The History of James Ives and Company Limited 1848-1948, Woollen Manufacturers, Leafield Mill and Manor Mill, Yeadon, Yorkshire, England*, William Sessions, 1948.
Terence A.M. Dooley "Estate ownership and management in nineteenth- and early twentieth century Ireland" in *Sources for the History of Landed Estates in Ireland*, Dublin Irish Academic Press, 2000.
Clive Elmsley, *Soldier, Sailor, Beggarman, Thief: Crime and the British Armed Services since 1914*, Oxford University Press, 2013.
Eric Eunson, *Old Govanhill*, Stenlake Publishing Ltd, 1994.
Don Everitt, *The K Boats*, Harrap, 1963.
R Faulkner, *Chapel Allerton: from village to suburb*, Chapel Allerton Residents Association, 1986.
Malcolm Fife, *Airfield Focus, 52: Donibristle*, GMS Enterprises, 2002.
Peter Fleming and Michael Wood, *Gloucestershire's Forgotten Battle: Nibley Green, 1470*, The History Press Ltd, 2003.
Joseph Foster, *Oxford Men and their Colleges, 1880-1892*, James Parker & Co, 1893.
T Geraghty, *A North-East Coast Town: Ordeal and Triumph – The Story of Kingston-upon-Hull in the 1939-1945 Great War*, The Kingston-upon-Hull Corporation, 1951.
Kurt Goblirsch, *Gemination, Lenition and Vowel Lengthening: On the History of Quantity in Germanic*, Cambridge University Press, 2018.
P Graystone, *The Blitz on Hull, 1940-1945*, Lampada Press, 1991.
Ralph Glasser, *Growing Up in the Gorbals*, Chatto and Windus Ltd, 1986.
JFC Harrison, *Early Victorian Britain, 1832-1851*, Fontana, 1979.
Max Hastings, *Operation Pedestal: The Fleet That Battled to Malta 1942*, William Collins, 2021.
James Henderson, *Arran to Canada – One Way*, Voice for Arran, 2012.
David Hey, *The Oxford Guide to Family History*, Oxford University Press, 1993.
G Hinchliffe, *Roundhay School: The First Half Century*, Fredk Duffield & Sons, 1973.
Richard Hoggart, *The Uses of Literacy: aspects of working class life with special references to publications and entertainment*, Chatto and Windus Ltd, 1957.
Lucy Jones, *Losing Eden: Why Our Minds Need the Wild*, Allen Lane, 2020.
Donald E Jordan Jr, *Land and Popular Politics in Ireland: County Mayo from the Plantation to the Land War*, Cambridge University Press, 1994.
Robert Kee, *Ireland: A History*, Wiedenfeld & Nicholson Ltd, 1980.
George E Kirk, *The Church in Chapel Allerton, Leeds*, Yorkshire Archaeological Society, 1949.
Stephen Lally, *The Leaving of Loughrea*, AuthorHouse, 2013.
Diarmid MacCulloch, *A History of Christianity*, Allen Lane, 2009.

WM Mackenzie, *The Book of Arran Vol ii: History and Folklore*, The Arran Society of Glasgow/Hugh Hopkins, 1910.
Dugald McKenzie McKillop, *Annals of Megantic County, Quebec*, D. McKillop, 1902.
Edward MacLysaght, *More Irish Families*, O'Gorman Ltd, Galway & Dublin, 1960.
Janet McLeman, *Peathill: The Auld Kirk and Kirkyard*, Lulu.com, 2012.
Andrew McMahon, *The Diocese of Dromore: Past and Present. Parish of St. Peter's, Clonallon*, Dromore Diocesan Historical Society, 2004.
Donald M MacRaild, *The Irish in Britain, 1800-1914*, Dundalgan Press (W Tempest) Ltd, 2006.
TL Markey, RL Kyes and Paul T Roberge, *Germanic and its Dialects: A Grammar of Proto-Germanic*, John Benjamins Publishing, Amsterdam, 1977.
Peter Matthias, *The First Industrial Nation: An Economic History of Britain, 1700-1914*, Methuen & Co., 1969.
Jim Melton, *Ships' Deserters 1852-1900: Including Stragglers, Strays and Absentees from HM Ships*, Library of Australian History, 1986.
Alison Mitchell (Ed.), *Pre-1855 Gravestone Inscriptions in Bute and Arran*, Scottish Genealogical Society, 1987.
Joy Montieth, *Old Port Glasgow*, Stenlake Publishing, 2003.
Michael M O'Connor, *County Mayo: A History of Imprisonment, Capital Punishment and Transportation: Anatomy of a County Gaol*, Dr M. M. O'Connor, 2020.
Jane Palmer, *The ultimate sacrifice in the Great War: the twelve North Yorkshire Constabulary police officers who died as soldiers.* Booklet prepared for the Chief Constable of North Yorkshire Police, 2017.
Roy Porter, *Enlightenment: Britain and the Creation of the Modern World*, Penguin Books, 2001.
PH Reaney, *The Origin of English Surnames*, Routledge and Kegan Paul, 1967.
Ronald Reng, *A Life Too Short: the Tragedy of Robert Enke*, Yellow Jersey Press, 2011.
Tom Richards, *Was Your Grandfather a Railwayman?* Federation of Family History Societies, 1995.
John Rigg, *An Ordinary Spectator: 50 Years of Watching Sport*, SilverWood Books, 2012.
John Rigg, *Still An Ordinary Spectator: Five More Years of Watching Sport*, SilverWood Books, 2017.
John Rigg, *An Ordinary Spectator Returns: Watching Sport Again*, SilverWood Books, 2023.
Alex Robertson, Dugald Cameron and Susan Pacitti (Eds.), *Glasgow's Spitfire*, Glasgow Museums, 2003.

Judith Rowbotham and Kim Stevenson (Eds.), *Behaving Badly: Social Panic and Moral Outrage – Victorian and Modern Parallels*, Routledge, 2017.
Don Steel, *Discovering Your Family History*, BBC Books, 1986.
Matthew Stibbe, *British civilian internees in Germany: The Ruhleben camp, 1914-18*, Manchester University Press, 2008.
Keith Taylor, *Swaledale & Wharfedale Remembered: Aspects of Dales' Life Through Peace and War*, Ashridge Press, 2006.
Richard H Thomas, *Cricketing Lives: A Characterful History from Pitch to Page*, Reaktion Books, 2011.
Ian H Waller, *My Ancestor was an Agricultural Labourer*, Society of Genealogists, 2019.
Keith Waterhouse, *City Lights: A Street Life*, Hodder and Stoughton, 1994.
A Wemyss (Ed.), *Barbarian Football Club*, Playfair Books Ltd, 1955.
Rhona Wilson, *Old Rutherglen*, Richard Stenlake Publishing, 1996.

Dictionaries and Reference

Mario Cassar, *Surnames of the Maltese Islands: An Etymological Dictionary*, Book Distributors Ltd, Malta, 2003.
Halbert's Family Heritage, *The World Book of Riggs*, USA, 1992
Jane Hewitt and Paul Jack Hewitt, *Dictionary of Old Occupations*, Kindle Edition, 2001.
Cecil Humphrey-Smith, *The Phillimore Atlas and Index of Parish Registers*, Phillimore & Co Ltd, 1984.
London A-Z, Geographers' A-Z Map Company Limited, Edition 11, 2015.
AM MacDonald (Ed.), *Chambers Twentieth Century Dictionary*, Chambers, 1972.
Edward Neafsay, *Surnames of Ireland: Origins, Numbers and Distribution of Selected Irish Surnames*, Irish Genealogical Foundation, 2002.
PH Reaney, *A Dictionary of British Surnames*, Oxford University Press, 1968.
George Redmonds, *A Dictionary of Yorkshire Surnames*, Shaun Tyas, 2015.

First World War Diaries

War Diary of 232 Army Field Artillery Brigade.
War Diary of 13th Battalion, Yorkshire Regiment.

Government Publications

Amanda Bevan and Andrea Duncan, *Tracing Your Ancestors in the Public Record Office*, 4th edition, HMSO, 1990.

Joe Hicks and Grahame Allen, *A Century of Change: Trends in UK Statistics Since 1900*, House of Commons Research Paper 99/111, December 1999.
Office for National Statistics, *Child and Infant Mortality in England and Wales: 2019*, February 2021.
Elizabeth Rough and Carl Baker, *Infant Mortality and Health Inequalities*, House of Commons Library Research Briefing No. 9904, November 2023.
Royal Commission of Inquiry into the Condition of the Hand-Loom Weavers in England and Wales (1837-41), Gloucestershire Section by WA Miles, The Sessional Papers of the House of Lords, Vol. XXXVIII, 1840.
The Statistical Account of Scotland, Sir John Sinclair (Ed.), W Creech publisher, Edinburgh, 1791-1799.

Journals, Journal Articles, Magazines and Monographs

Geoffrey Chamberlain, "British maternal mortality in the 19th and early 20th centuries", *Journal of the Royal Society of Medicine*, Vol. 99, No. 11, November 2006.
Cleveland Family History Society, *Cleveland Family History Society Journal*, quarterly.
The Green Howards Gazette, esp. Volume XVII, 1910, and Volume XXVI, 1918.
Carol McLee, "Know Your Parish – Thirkleby", *Cleveland Family History Society Journal*, April 2024.
FJW Miller and Mary D Thompson, "Decline and fall of the tubercle bacillus: the Newcastle story, 1882-1988", *Archives of Disease in Childhood*, 1992, Vol. 67, pp 251-255.
Sheila Mulloy, "Father Manus Sweeney, 1763-1799", *Journal of the Westport Historical Society*, No. 14, 1994.
John Rigg, "A North Yorkshire Couple in Vermont, USA – Part 1", *Cleveland Family History Society Journal*, January 2015.
John Rigg, "A North Yorkshire Couple in Vermont, USA – Part 2", *Cleveland Family History Society Journal*, April 2015.
John Rigg, "The 1911 Census – and a Century-old Message", *Cleveland Family History Society Journal*, April 2016.
John Rigg, "Here I Stand", *Cleveland Family History Society Journal*, April 2019.
John Rigg, "From Baldersby to Vermont – via Stockton-on-Tees", *Cleveland Family History Society Journal*, April 2020.
Society of Genealogists, *Genealogists' Magazine: Journal of the Society of Genealogists*, quarterly.
Southern Necropolis Newsletter, December 1988 [reproduced on the website of the South Glasgow Heritage Educational Trust, 2021].

Edward C Whitman, ""K" for Katastrophe: K Class Submarines in the Royal Navy", *Undersea Warfare*, No.49, pp 28-33, US Government Publishing Office, Winter 2013.

Foreign Language Publications

Klaus Heinze (Ed.), *Visselhövede: Chronik einer Stadt [Visselhövede: Chronicle of a City]*, Geiger-Verlag, 1999, especially Chapter 2: "Visselhövede im Spätmittelalter und in der frühen Neuzeit" ["Visselhövede in the late Middle Ages and early modern times"] by Dieter Brosius.

Rolf Spilker and Birte Tost (Eds.), *Lichtenberg – Bilder einer Stadt II: Fotografische Ansichten Osnabrück, 1900-1930 [Scenes of a City II: Photographic sights of Osnabrück, 1900-1930]*, Rasch, 2007.

Alfred Spuhr and Claude Jeanmarie, *Die Geschichte der elektrischen Strassenbahn, deren Voraenger und Nachfolger [The History of Electric Tramway and its Predecessor and Successor]*, Verlag Eisenbahn, Switzerland, 1980.

Wolfgang Stammler, *Deutsche Philologie im Aufriss [German Philology in Outline]*, Erich Schmidt Verlag, Berlin, 1952.

Newspapers and Directories

United Kingdom: 19th Century

Aberdeen Press and Journal
Army & Navy Gazette
Cambridge Independent Press
Cheltenham Chronicle
Cheltenham Examiner
Cheltenham Mercury
Devizes Advertiser
Gloucester Journal
Gloucestershire Echo
Hartlepool Northern Daily Mail
Jarrow Express
Kelly's Directory of Durham and Northumberland, 1890
Kelly's Directory of Gloucestershire, 1889.
Kelly's Directory of Newcastle and Suburbs, 2nd edition, 1887
Leominster News
London Daily News
Melville & Co's Directory & Gazetteer, 1856 [of Norfolk and surrounding areas]
Newcastle Evening Chronicle
Newry Telegraph

Norfolk Chronicle
Norfolk News
North Eastern Daily Gazette
Peterborough Advertiser
Richmond and Ripon Chronicle
Ripon Chronicle
Slater's Warrington Directory, 1895
Shields Daily News
Stamford Mercury
Warrington Evening Post
Warrington Examiner
York Herald

United Kingdom: 20th/21st Centuries
Barrow Herald and Furnace Advertiser
Birmingham Daily Gazette
Cheltenham Chronicle
Daily Gazette for Middlesbrough
Daily Telegraph
Darlington and Stockton Times
Gloucestershire Echo
Hammersmith and Shepherd's Bush Gazette
Hanwell Gazette
The Herald [Glasgow]
Jarrow Express
Kelly's Directory of Leeds, 1908
Leeds Mercury
Lloyd's List
Newcastle Evening Chronicle
Newcastle Journal
Newry Reporter
Peterborough Standard
Ripon Chronicle
The Scotsman
Shields Daily News
South West Suffolk Echo
Sunday Times
Sunderland Daily Echo and Shipping Gazette
Yorkshire Evening Post
Yorkshire Post
Yorkshire Post and Leeds Intelligencer

Yorkshire Post and Leeds Mercury

Overseas
Burlington Free Press [Vermont]
Connacht Telegraph
Daily Malta Chronicle and Garrison Gazette
The Day [Vermont]
Imperial Gazetteer of India, 1908
New York Herald
Osnabrücker Zeitung
The Province [British Colombia]
San Jose News
Stowe Reporter [Vermont]
The Sunday Times of Malta
The Washington Post

University Theses
Alfred Niblett, *Grammatik der Osnabrückischen Mundart [The Grammar of the Osnabrück Dialect]*, Ph.D. thesis, University of Munich, 1913 (available at http://gdz.sub.uni-goettingen.de).
John Rigg, *The Decision-Making Processes of Young Males in an Urban Labour Market*, University of Cambridge, 1989.

Unpublished papers
Denis English, *Problems of Manning in Tankers*, paper given at the City of London College, October 1960.
Henry Kelly, *The Kelly Centenary*, 1947.
John Rigg, *Bill Rigg: Early Memories – In Conversation with John Rigg*, August 2002.

DVD
Old Port to Newport: An Historical Journey, Purple Foxglove Films, 2013.

Facebook
David Gabbitas, *4.4.44school.doc* at www.facebook..com/groups/1415661402028531. [Memories of Roundhay School, Leeds, in the 1940s].

YouTube
The West Mayo Flying Column in the War of Independence, Purple Foxglove Films, 2021.

ANNEX A7

GLOSSARY

BEF	British Expeditionary Force
BMD	Births, marriages and deaths
CASCAT	Cumbrian Archive Service Catalogue
CFHS	Cleveland Family History Society
CMB	Central Midwives Board
CS-M	Company Sergeant-Major
FAC	Friends of Anfield Cemetery
FMP	Findmypast
GRO	General Registry Office
HMP	Her Majesty's Prison
IGI	International Genealogical Index (compiled by the Genealogical Society of The Church of Jesus Christ of Latter Day Saints)
IFHF	Irish Family History Foundation
LMU	Ludwig Maximilian University of Munich
LNER	London and North Eastern Railway
LNR	Leeds Northern Railway
MGC	Machine Gun Corps
MI	Monumental Inscription
MMR	Maternal Mortality Ratio
MTC	Mechanical Transport Company
m.v.	Motor Vehicle [ship]
NER	North Eastern Railway
NYCRO	North Yorkshire County Record Office
PRONI	Public Record Office of Northern Ireland
RAOB-GLE	Royal Antidiluvian Order of Buffaloes – Grand Lodge of England
RGA	Royal Garrison Artillery
RNR	Royal Naval Reserve
SGHET	South Glasgow Heritage Educational Trust
SGS	Scottish Genealogical Society

SUB	*Niedersächsische Staats- und Universitätsbibliotek* (Lower Saxony, Statistics and University Library, Gottingen)
TNA	The National Archives
UHF	Ulster Historical Foundation
UVM	University of Vermont
VLCC	Very Large Crude Carrier
WYAS	West Yorkshire Archive Service
YMI	Yorkshire Monumental Inscriptions

ANNEX A8

ACKNOWLEDGEMENTS

As with my three publications in the *An Ordinary Spectator* series on sports watching, I am grateful to the team at SilverWood Books – under the leadership of the Publishing Director, Helen Hart – for the professional way in which this book has been produced. The technical requirements of the page layouts have again been met with considerable care and skill.

The text of this volume records those occasions in which – either through meetings or via correspondence – a number of individuals have provided me with helpful responses to my various requests. Although some of these contacts were made many years in the past – with those concerned no doubt having now moved on to other things – it is certainly appropriate for me to acknowledge here with gratitude the assistance that I received.

I begin with the Public Record Offices. I am pleased to refer, in particular, to: MY Ashcroft, Judith A Smeaton, Daniel Sudron and Kimberley Starkie of the North Yorkshire County Record Office in Northallerton; David Wright and Shelbie Foster at Leeds City Council; Teena Wright at Peterborough City Council; Harriet Harmer of the West Yorkshire Archive Service; John Rogan, Searchroom Manager and his colleague Bern of Lancashire County Council; Kathy Scott, Cemetery Assistant at idverde (the company that maintains the Bandon Hill Cemetery in Sutton); Padej Kumlertsakul, Records Adviser (Overseas and Defence) at The National Archives in Kew, Surrey; Jacqueline Camilleri, Clerical Officer in the Public Registry, Valletta, Malta.

My researches in both the UK and overseas have necessitated the inputs of experts in their respective local or institutional domains. Accordingly, I have been grateful for the assistance given by: Colin Dews of the Yorkshire branch of the Wesley Historical Society; Grace Small, Margaret Wright and Charles Currie of The Isle of Arran Heritage Museum; Tom Bradburn and Ray Beeton of the Friends of Anfield Cemetery; Richard Temple and Charles Harrowell at the Senate House Library of the University of London; William Roulston, Gillian Hunt and Heather Graham of the Ulster Historical Foundation in Belfast; Maria

A Robbins of the RAF Disclosures Department at RAF Cranwell, Sleaford; Ann Hubble, Colin Nutt and Stuart Campbell MC of the Royal British Legion; Steve Erskine of the Green Howards' Museum in Richmond, North Yorkshire; June Bull, archivist of St John the Baptist Church, Peterborough; Beatrice Meecham of the Brooklands Museum in Weybridge, Surrey. Bronach Joyce and James Kelly responded separately to the queries I made of the Clew Bay Heritage Centre in Westport, County Mayo, about illicit distillation in 19th Century Ireland and the penal system that was applied to it; I was put in touch with Dr Michael M O'Connor of Westport, to whom I am grateful for his analysis of the specific case in which I was interested and the background context of crime and punishment in Mayo.

For any family history researcher, the membership of any local society means that there is no shortage of willing respondents to particular queries. At the Cleveland Family History Society, I have benefitted from advice given by Rosemary Allen. I have also drawn on the detailed historical knowledge (of Alnwick) of Mary George of the Northumberland and Durham Family History Society.

Likewise, at the Hannover-based genealogical network (hannover-l@genealogy.net), I was grateful for the assistance given by Heinz Promann, Uschi Boes and Christiane Feder.

When preparing for the visit to Niedersachsen that my sister, Rosie, and I made in 2018, I commissioned a genealogist – Monika Mohring – to undertake some research on the extended Niblett family in the Lower Saxony State Archives in Osnabruck. Her detailed work was most gratefully received.

In Germany, Rosie and I enjoyed a day in the company of our guide – Almtuh Quehl – who showed (and transported) us around Visselhoevede and Kirchwalsede. She arranged for the small museum in Scheesel to open its doors for us (on a Monday) and for us to see the original church records in Kirchwalsede courtesy of the church's curator and Public Relations Officer, Ursula Hoppe. Ms Quehl's expertise was recommended to us by Verena Henke of the *Touristverband Landreis* in Rotenburg, Niedersachsen. Christian Henke confirmed our joint presence in the branch of the Henke family tree dating back to the 16th Century.

A later contact in Germany was Andreas Fahrmeir, Professor of Modern History at the Johann Wolfgang Goethe University in Frankfurt-am-Main, who is an expert on 19th Century citizenship in the states and countries of Europe. Professor Fahrmeir provided an immediate and detailed response to my query about the status of Anna Karoline Borstelmann, following her marriage to Charles James Niblett in Elze in 1873, and the daughters of this marriage who subsequently married German men. This is summarised in Chapter 3. One of these daughters was Annetta Frömbling (née Niblett), about whose extended family I was very grateful to receive information from Simone Frömbling-Fülbier and her husband Günther Fülbier.

As noted in the Sources given in Annex A5, the information provided by individuals to the public forum pages of the family history companies can be very useful. From the Ancestry site, I have noted the contributions made on several branches of the family tree in North Yorkshire: Nicola Burnham, Lesley Hamilton-Moore and David Pratt (the Rigg family); Virginia Burrell (the Boynton family); Janet McNeilly (the Fairweather and Holmes families); Ron Smith (the Dade, Raistrick and Stirk families); Vicky Rogers and Edward Thornton (the Stirk family); Judith Wilde (the Rigge family of the 17th and 18th Centuries); Roselyn Kirton (the Wells family). I have also noted the contributions of: Judy Hitchcock/Sue Stenning and Mariner Tonge (the Runcorn family); Caroline Webber (the Wilson family); Terry Wilkins (the Whines family); Sally Dinham-Scott and Hazel Hill (on different branches of the Niblett family); Kevin Chivers and "Lucy" (the Stapleton family); Patricia Goodman (the Rosenberg/Goodman family); and Jennifer Fulbrook on the Murray family migrants from County Mayo to Chicago. In addition, although not constituents of the main family tree, I have drawn on the contributions in the USA of Heather Shepard (the Walter/Kracke family) and Rose Ann Barnes Farkas (the extended Riggs families in Vermont). In several cases, I have enjoyed productive e-mail correspondence with the contributors, as described in the relevant sections of the narrative. On the Isle of Arran, my wife and I enjoyed the kind hospitality of John and Lynne O'Hare, when Lynne outlined to us the detailed knowledge she has accumulated of the McKillop clan.

Other individual researchers warrant particular acknowledgement. In Chapter 5, I referred to the detailed Kelly family trees compiled by Adrian McMullen, Joseph Scarr and Kathleen Johnson in the early 1980s. Similarly, in Chapter 4, I noted the huge body of research undertaken on the Niblett family by Mike Niblett of Canada (which was initially made available at www.telbin.dreamstation.com) and the extensive (pre-Internet) work undertaken on that family's European connections by John S Eckersley of New Hudson, Michigan. Likewise, I was impressed with the research undertaken by David Pratt (and reported in Chapter 2) on the several generations of the Wells family in North Yorkshire, which took one branch of the family tree back to the time of Henry the Eighth. On www.otterson.org, Michael Otterson has reported on the detailed research on his direct family line, including the Pipe, Pype and Dowsing branches; we share William Dowsing (1526-1614) as our great (x12) grandfather.

I noted in Chapter 8 that, in 1994, I was hugely rewarded in attempting to track down Douglas Rigg (1905-1995), a nephew of my grandfather (John Rigg). His wife Winifred Rigg (née Hayward) kindly responded to my speculative enquiry and I was subsequently in correspondence over many years with their daughter, Jean Wheeler. From that (extended) family, I have also corresponded with Douglas Rigg, Robert Rigg, Christina MacEachran and Margaret Gillingwater.

In Chapter 9, I referred to David Gabbitas's recollections – posted on the Roundhay School, Leeds, alumni Facebook site – of being a pupil at the school in the 1940s. I have reproduced his kind references to my grandfather, Alfred Niblett, who was his form-master and German teacher. I am also grateful to John Mattinson, the Roundhay School archivist and teacher, for providing me with a summary record of Alfred Niblett's teaching career.

Any errors in the content of this book are entirely my responsibility.

The photographs of Harriet Boynton (née Stirk) and Charles Tyler Wilson were posted on their respective Ancestry public pages by Edward Thornton and Caroline Webber and I am grateful for their kind permission to reproduce them in this volume. Likewise, I am grateful to The National Archives for the permission to include the extract from the Army Record of Joseph Stapleton, of which it holds the Crown Copyright; Paul Johnson, Image Library Manager at the TNA, did a great job in lightening the image from its original very dull state. The reproduction of the household record of John and Margaret Murray from the Census of Ireland, 1901 – the official citation of which is "Census1901, Mayo, 149/8, Srahmore, Co. Mayo" – is by kind permission of the Director of the National Archives of Ireland; Linda Tobin, Collection Care and Public Services, arranged for it to be lightened by the reprographics team. The photographs of St Bartholomäus-Kirche, Kirkwalsede and its Baptism Register were taken by Rosie Rigg; I am grateful to Ursula Hoppe and the Church Council for agreeing to the use of the photographs in this volume.

The photographs of Patrick and Frances Kelly and their family, John and Honoria (Annie) Murray, Arthur Joseph English, Mary Stella English and Denis and Anne English are from the English family records as is the image of Arthur Joseph English's Certificate of Competency as Steamship Master in the Merchant Service. The images of the First World War Ruhleben camp magazine and the Ph.D. Dissertation of Alfred Niblett are from the Rigg family records as are the individual photographs of John Rigg in the First World War, Catherine Kerr Rigg and Alfred Niblett as well as the photographs of William (Bill) and Peggie Rigg, Marie Rosa Niblett with her grandson (the author) and the author with his father (William Rigg) at the grave of Robert Rigg in Montignuy-sur-Hallue in France. The author took the photographs of *die Peter and Paul-Kirche*, Elze, St John the Baptist Church, Peterborough, and the gravestones of William Boynton in Thirkleby, Yorkshire, and John Pipe in Horham, Suffolk. Rosie Rigg took the photograph of *St Johannis-Kirche*, Visselhovede.

Helen Dawkins of Black and White Revival in Bedford (helen@blackandwhiterevival.co.uk) oversaw the reproduction of all the photographs. Some of them, dating from the 19th and early 20th Centuries, required careful cleaning and restoration, which Helen undertook with great skill using traditional techniques.

All reasonable efforts have been made to contact copyright holders. If anyone feels that their copyright has been breached, I should be happy to address that in any future reprint.

I complete this list of acknowledgements by giving grateful thanks to my wife Angela, son and daughter Tom and Katie, and sister Rosie. They have provided the essential love and support – with ideas, suggestions and feedback – as I have followed the trails of family history described in this volume. When, one evening at my suggestion, one of those trails led us (with my now son-in-law Marcus) through a near-pitch black and overgrown graveyard in Leeds – guided by only the lights from our mobile phones – they really must have thought me either obsessive or mad. Or both.

ANNEX A9

INDEX OF SURNAMES

The surnames listed in this Annex relate only to the direct lines of family ancestry leading down to Tom and Katie Rigg.

The first group contains members of the Line of 16 i.e. Tom and Katie Rigg's great, great grandparents. 15 surnames are listed because one of them – McManamon – appears twice. In some cases, the narrative presented in this book has also covered earlier generations of these direct lines.

The second group contains surnames that appear in (some of) the direct lines of generations before the Line of 16, but which – due to the marriage of a female to a husband with a different surname – are not continued beyond the (pre-Line of 16) date of that marriage.

Surnames of other members of the extended family tree are not included.

Line of 16 (and earlier)

Borstelmann   3, 102, 104, 106, 112-121, 124, 126-127, 130, 135, 137, 140, 281, 283, 287-8, 346, 348-9, 352, 355-6, 379-80, 382, 405

Boynton/Bointon   3, 19, 22, 25-31, 33-34, 36-37, 45, 92, 112, 203, 266, 345, 348, 353-5, 357, 406-7

Brincau/Brincat   3, 209-214, 221, 229, 347-8, 353, 356-7

English   3, 174-175, 177-186, 189, 200, 202, 205-208, 215-216, 257, 296-310, 313-4, 316, 319, 323, 325, 334-42, 346-50, 354-65, 391, 407

Kelly   3, 187, 189-195, 197-198, 202, 204-206, 208, 296, 317, 319, 338, 348-9, 351-9, 406-7

McBride   3, 45, 47-60, 62, 64, 72-73, 85-92, 163, 169, 257-9, 272-4, 345-6, 349, 352-3, 355-9, 361-2, 377, 390

McManamon   3, 153, 230, 232, 236-247, 250-254, 257, 312-3, 316-7, 319, 347, 349-50, 354, 357, 359-60

Mullowney   3, 230-231, 234, 250, 317, 347-8, 354, 356, 391

Murray   3, 230-235, 238-239, 241, 243, 246, 250-254, 257, 310, 312-4, 316-9, 323, 334, 347-50, 353-4, 356, 359-63, 391, 407

Niblett   3, 93-108, 111-114, 117, 121, 124-127, 129-132, 135, 137-140, 165-167, 172, 273, 281-91, 295, 323, 325, 332, 346, 348-9, 351-3, 355-63, 379, 405-7

Rigg xii-xiii, xvi-xvii, 3, 5-7, 9-14, 16-25, 28, 61, 87, 91-92, 140, 170, 257-60, 263, 266-7, 270-6, 278-80, 323, 325-34, 341-2, 345-54, 356-7, 359-67, 377, 379, 383, 386, 406-7

Runcorn 3, 52, 72-73, 75-83, 85-88, 246, 346, 353, 355-6, 358, 406

Stapleton 3, 206, 209-229, 257, 296, 301-2, 310, 317, 347-50, 354-5, 357-8, 361-2, 406-7

Whines 3, 141, 146-147, 155-166, 168-169, , 294, 346, 348, 353, 355-6, 358-60, 406

Wilson 3, 129, 135, 141-143, 145-150, 154-156, 160, 163-170, 172, 257, 281, 287-9, 293-5, 346, 348-9, 354, 356-8, 360-2, 406-7

Pre-Line of 16

Apps 113-114
Bentley 27, 30
Bilton 20
Brown 63
Browning 30, 96, 106, 112-113
Cordy 112-113
Cox 112
Croft 20
Crum/Crumb 53
Dade 30-31, 406
Davis 187-188, 195-199, 206-207, 296, 317, 352-5, 357, 383
Dear 156, 158
Dieckhoff/Dieckhof 114, 380
Dowsing 170-173, 406
Fairweather 29
Gatt 212, 214, 354
Gevers/Gefers 114
Goodchild 143-145, 147-148, 153, 169-170, 172, 352, 354-5, 357, 359
Gorstage 75
Gould 348
Hardwick 29
Henke 114, 116, 349, 380
Herwig 113, 117
Holmes (born in Suffolk) 147, 352
Holmes (born in Yorkshire) 27, 29
Howe 194, 206
Hunt 95-97, 99, 105-106, 112, 353, 355
Hunter 64
Irwin 73, 83-84, 353
Kennedy 64

Kerr 50, 52, 62-68, 71-72, 352, 354-6, 358
Koopmann 114
Lange 114, 380, 382
Lindsay 53-54
Luck 97
McGuire 199, 206
McKillop 63, 70-71
Marquardt 113-114, 117, 122, 352, 380
Neal 349
Paul 29
Perlasky 113, 116-121, 127, 353, 355, 381
Pipe/Pype 144, 170-173, 406-7
Purvis 197, 352-3, 357
Raistrick 30, 406
Rebacker 170
Roche 211, 214-215, 217, 222, 224-225
Rycraft 156-158, 353
Seed 73, 76
Sharrow 30
Shaw 62, 64, 67, 71, 352, 354
Stirk 27, 30, 112, 203, 348, 353-4, 406-7
Tarbet 53
Thymblethorpe 170
Twaddle 72-73, 76, 82-85, 246, 353, 355
Tyler 147
Wadsworth 155, 157-158, 163-164, 354-5
Walker 51, 53, 55-6, 353
Wells/Welles 9, 12, 18, 20-21, 170-171, 349, 352-3, 366, 379, 406
Wielding/von Wiehen 114
Wood 95-96, 105, 352
Woods 175-180, 184, 354-5, 359, 391

ANNEX A10

INDEX OF LOCATIONS

This Annex adopts the same principles as those outlined for Annex A9. The locations given relate only to the places of birth, marriage, residence and/or death of those in the direct lines of family ancestry leading down to Tom and Katie Rigg. Locations relating to other members of the extended family tree are not included; nor are those places which were only temporarily visited.

ENGLAND

<u>East Anglia</u>
Brundish   170-171, 173, 349
Cambridge   3, 141-142, 145, 148, 156, 166, 341, 348, 356, 363-4
Hadleigh   348
Hellesdon   355
Horham   143, 153, 171, 352
Hoxne   170-171
Kimbolton   286-7
Laxfield   143, 170-172, 352
Norwich   142-145, 147, 149-150, 354, 357
Wenhaston   160

<u>Greater London</u>
Beckenham   137, 283
Camberwell   159
Charing Cross   95
Chelsea   141, 147-150, 157, 159-160, 165
Croydon   117, 127
Ealing   310, 314, 334, 364
Edmonton   358
Enfield   285
Hammersmith   341
Islington   142, 158
Mitcham   137
Palmers Green   166, 273, 285, 288-9, 323, 325, 358
Pimlico   3, 142, 148, 156, 159, 166
Poplar   145, 150, 160, 357
Richmond-on-Thames   215, 310, 363
St Pancras   157, 159
Southgate   141, 150, 287
Sutton   137-138, 165
Tottenham   146, 161, 360
Twickenham   310
Wallington   117, 127
Wandsworth   206, 215, 310
Westminster   3, 148, 156, 166
Wood Green   129, 142, 165-166, 169, 257, 288

<u>Rest of South East</u>
Gravesend   207
Stoke Mandeville   359
Uckfield   163

Midlands
Birmingham   286-7, 359
Desford   142
Leicester   145, 150, 155, 160
Malvern Wells   313
Overseal   142, 145, 147, 354
Peterborough   141, 156-159, 161, 169, 353-5, 360
Syerston   329

North East
Alnwick   157, 159
Gosforth   230, 232, 238, 254, 310, 312-4, 316, 323, 325, 334, 341-2, 360, 362-3
Jarrow   174-175, 179-180, 182, 184, 200
Newcastle   230, 232, 234-235, 238, 242, 312-3, 316, 362
North Shields   3, 175, 180, 185-190, 192-195, 197, 199, 207, 215, 257, 296-7, 303-4, 310, 318, 349, 351, 354-6, 358, 362
South Shields   297, 357
Sunderland   180, 184, 359
Tynemouth   187, 357-9
Whitley Bay   180, 189, 194, 205-206, 208, 304, 306, 361-2

North West
Cheetham   145-146
Kirkham   328
Knutsford   86
Latchford   78, 86
Liverpool   3, 72-73, 83-85, 209-210, 212, 214, 284, 353, 355, 358
   Everton   84-85
   West Derby   72, 85-86, 358
Manchester   163
Preston   246, 313, 359
Prestwich   49
Runcorn   52, 73, 75
Warrington   3, 73, 75-76, 78-80, 86-87, 92, 246, 355-6, 358, 378

South West
Berkeley   112-113
Bisley   96
Bristol   96-97, 355
Cam   112-113
Charlton Kings   99-104, 125
Cheltenham   3, 95, 98-102, 104-1-8, 117, 127, 355, 357-8
Painswick   95-99, 105, 352-3
Stonehouse   112
Stroud   95-96, 99, 106, 353
Woodchester   112

Yorkshire
Azerley   21
Baldersby   3, 7, 9-12, 14, 18-19, 22-23, 25-26, 28, 44-45, 87, 116, 257, 259, 272, 352, 354, 356-7, 366, 379, 383
Galphay   20-21, 171
Hawnby   29
Helperby   18, 20, 352
Hull   259
Ilkley   348
Kilburn   26-27, 112, 353
Kirkby Malzead   21
Leeds   6, 45, 48-50, 52, 73, 86-87, 89, 91-92, 129, 148, 156, 163, 165-167, 259, 272-7, 280-1, 285-9, 295, 323, 325-7, 330-4, 341-2, 359-63, 365, 377, 407
   Armley   332
   Beeston   274-5
   Holbeck   275
   Hunslet   48, 165, 259, 276-7, 323, 377
   Moortown   277, 280, 331
   Roundhay   285-7, 407
Northallerton   38
Otley   30
Pickhill   xii, xvi-xvii 6, 13, 17, 19, 23, 25-26, 28, 38, 43-45, 258, 360-1, 377
Ripon   20, 171
Snape   29
Thirkleby   3, 26-31, 45, 353, 355

Thirsk   27, 30, 38, 354
Topcliffe   6, 10-13, 353

NORTHERN IRELAND

County Down   3, 175-180, 189, 206, 354-6, 391
   Clonallon   3, 175-180, 189, 206, 354-6
   Warrenpoint   178-179

IRELAND

Cork   195, 197-198, 352
County Kildare   214, 221
County Mayo   3, 230-234, 236-240, 242, 244-251, 252-253, 257, 312-3, 348-51, 353-4, 356-7, 360, 391
   Burrishoole   230-233, 238, 247, 257, 313, 356-7
   Castlebar   245, 247
   Newport   3, 231, 234, 236, 247-248, 251, 354
   Shrarevagh   236-237, 239-240, 242, 244, 246, 248, 251, 312, 357, 360
   Srahmore   231, 233, 236, 246, 248, 250-251, 356
   Westport   250
County Roscommon   187, 190, 215, 222, 353-4
   Athlone   215
   Strokeston   187, 190, 353

SCOTLAND

Edinburgh   85
Eyemouth   197
Glasgow   45, 47, 48, 51, 56-58, 87, 91-92, 163, 257, 273, 342, 349, 351, 357-8
   Govan   57, 91, 257, 273
   Govanhill   48
Isle of Arran   52, 55, 62-65, 70-72, 92, 352, 354, 356, 358
   Lamlash   64-65
   Sannox/North Sannox/South Sannox   55, 62-63, 70-72
   South Kiscadale   62-63, 65, 71-72, 358
   Largybeg   52
   Whiting Bay   62-63, 65, 71
Port Glasgow   52-56, 353, 390
Rosehearty   195-196
Rutherglen   3, 47, 49, 51-52, 58-59, 64, 73, 86-87, 355-6, 378
Stewarton   64

GERMANY

Bad Münder am Deister   117-118, 122, 353, 381
Elze   3, 102, 106, 117, 122, 124, 126-127, 355-6, 380, 405
Hannover   117-119, 122, 355
Kirchwalsede   114-115, 122, 349, 380-1
Munich   286-7, 359
Osnabrück   103, 106, 117, 119, 121-122, 125-127, 129, 137, 166, 257, 281, 286-9, 349, 351, 358, 361, 379
Ruhleben (Berlin)   281-3, 287, 359
Visselhövede   113-116, 122, 352, 380

MALTA

Cospicua   218
Paola   212, 218
Sliema   206, 210, 215, 218, 257, 301-3, 314, 323, 334-5, 358, 360
Valetta   210, 212, 226-228, 336, 357
Vittoriosa   3, 214, 218, 356

USA

New York   193, 355

www.ingramcontent.com/pod-product-compliance
Lightning Source LLC
Chambersburg PA
CBHW080404300426
44113CB00015B/2404